CAVENDISH

PRIMARY SCHOOL

Year 6 Leavers, 2015

gem

Collins

School

Dictionary

HarperCollins Publishers
Westerhill Road
Bishopbriggs
Glasgow
G64 2QT

Fourth Edition 2012

Reprint 10 9 8 7 6 5 4 3 2 1

© HarperCollins Publishers 2005,
2006, 2008, 2012

ISBN 978-0-00-745625-3

Collins® and Collins Gem®
are registered trademarks of
HarperCollins Publishers Limited

www.collinslanguage.com

A catalogue record for this book is
available from the British Library

Typeset by Aptara in India

Printed and bound in Italy by LEGO
SpA, Lavis (Trento)

Acknowledgements
We would like to thank those
authors and publishers who kindly
gave permission for copyright
material to be used in the Collins
Word Web. We would also like to
thank Times Newspapers Ltd for
providing valuable data.

Contents

Editorial Staff

Editors

Gerry Breslin

Jamie Flockhart

Robert Groves

Cordelia Lilly

Elspeth Summers

For the publisher

Lucy Cooper

Kerry Ferguson

Elaine Higgleton

Susanne Reichert

Foreword

Being able to read, understand and write good English are vital and fundamental skills that underpin success in exams and, ultimately, success in the world beyond school. A dictionary is an essential tool for all students who want to do well in exams, because if you know how to use a dictionary effectively you can improve your performance in all subjects, not just English. This is why literacy strategies all over the world set ambitious targets for students to acquire dictionary skills at every stage of their education.

Collins Gem School Dictionary has been carefully researched with teachers and students to ensure that it includes the information on language that students need, to allow them to improve their performance in all school subjects, and to achieve exam success.

The dictionary provides essential information on what words mean, how they are used, spelling, grammar and punctuation, so that students can use language well, communicate with others and express their ideas effectively. It also provides comprehensive coverage of core vocabulary from a wide range of curriculum subjects, such as Science, Information and Communications Technology, History, Geography and Religious Education, to help with success in *all* subjects.

Collins Gem School Dictionary is very straightforward, with an accessible layout that's easy on the eye, guiding students quickly to what they want. It is relevant to school work in all subjects, accessible and student-friendly, and offers essential help on the route to success.

Using this Dictionary

Main entry words are printed in large bold type:

> **abbey**

All main entry words, including abbreviations, prefixes and suffixes are listed in alphabetical order:

> **abbot**
> **abbreviate**

Variant spellings are shown in full:

> **adrenalin** or **adrenaline**

Parts of speech are shown in italics:

> **athlete** *noun*

When a word can be used as more than one part of speech, the change of part of speech is shown after a triangle:

> **blight** *noun* **1** something that damages or spoils other things …
> ▷ *verb* **3** to harm

Parts of speech may be combined for some words:

> **alone** *adjective, adverb* without anyone or anything else; on your own

Cross references are shown in bold type:

> **am** *verb* see **be**

Irregular Parts or confusing forms of verbs, nouns, adjectives, and adverbs shown in blue type after the main entry word:

> **go** goes, going, went, gone
> **mushy** mushier, mushiest

Meanings are shown in separate categories:

> **electric** *adjective* **1** powered or
> produced by electricity **2** exciting
> or tense

Related Words are shown in the same paragraph as the main entry word. Where the meaning of a related word is not given, it may be understood from the main entry word, or from an example:

> **abduct** *verb* to take (someone)
> away by force > **abduction** *noun*:
> *the abduction of a boy* > **abductor**
> *noun*

Subject label boxes show when a main entry word is core vocabulary for a curriculum subject:

> **addition** *noun* **1** MATHS process
> of adding numbers together

Abbreviations

AD	anno Domini
Aust	Australia(n)
BC	before Christ
Brit	British
C of E	Church of England
Canad	Canada/Canadian
D&T	Design and Technology
E	East
e.g.	for example
esp.	especially
etc	et cetera
ICT	Information and Communications Technology
N	North
NZ	New Zealand
orig	originally
PE	Physical Education
PSHE	Personal, Social, Health and Economic Education
®	trademark
RC	Roman Catholic
RE	Religious Education
S	South
S Afr	South Africa(n)
Scot	Scottish
US	United States
usu.	usually
W	West

a

a an *indefinite article* (before a vowel sound *an*) used before a noun being mentioned for the first time: *a tractor; an apple*

a- *prefix* **1** (before a vowel *an-*) not, without or opposite to: *amoral* **2** towards or in the state of: *aback; asleep*

aardvark *noun* S African anteater with long ears and snout

aback *adverb* **taken aback** startled or very surprised

abacus abacuses *noun* beads on a wire frame, used for doing calculations

abalone [ab-a-**lone**-ee] *noun* edible sea creature with a shell lined with mother of pearl

abandon *verb* **1** to desert or leave (someone or something) **2** to give up (something) completely ▷ *noun* **3** lack of inhibition: *He began to laugh with abandon* > **abandoned** *adjective* **1** deserted **2** uninhibited > **abandonment** *noun*

abate *verb* to make or become less strong

abattoir [ab-a-**twahr**] *noun* place where animals are killed for meat

abbey *noun* church with buildings attached to it in which monks or nuns live or lived

abbot *noun* head of an abbey of monks

abbreviate *verb* to shorten (a word) by leaving out some letters

abbreviation *noun* shortened form of a word or words

abdicate *verb* to give up (the throne or a responsibility) > **abdication** *noun*

abdomen *noun* part of the body containing the stomach and intestines > **abdominal** *adjective* relating to the stomach and intestines

abduct *verb* to take (someone) away by force > **abduction** *noun*: *the abduction of a boy* > **abductor** *noun*

aberration *noun* **1** sudden change from what is normal, accurate or correct **2** brief lapse in control of your thoughts or feelings

abet abets, abetting, abetted *verb* to help (someone) do something criminal or wrong

abhor abhors, abhorring, abhorred *verb* (*formal*) to hate (something) > **abhorrence** *noun*: *their abhorrence of racism* > **abhorrent** *adjective* hateful, loathsome

abide abides, abiding, abided *verb* **1** to bear or stand: *I can't abide that song* **2 abide by** to act in accordance with (a rule or decision) > **abiding** *adjective* lasting

ability abilities *noun* PSHE intelligence or skill needed to do something

abject *adjective* **1** very bad: *abject failure* **2** lacking all self-respect > **abjectly** *adverb*

ablaze *adjective* burning fiercely

able abler, ablest *adjective* PSHE capable or competent

a
b
c
d
e
f
g
h
i
j
k
l
m
n
o
p
q
r
s
t
u
v
w
x
y
z

-able *suffix* (forming adjectives) **1** capable of or susceptible to (an action): *enjoyable; breakable* **2** causing (something): *comfortable*

ably [**ay**-blee] *adverb* skilfully and successfully

abnormal *adjective* not normal or usual > **abnormality** *noun* something that is not normal or usual > **abnormally** *adverb*

aboard *adverb, preposition* on, in, onto or into (a ship, train or plane)

abode *noun* (old-fashioned) home

abolish *verb* to do away with > **abolition** *noun*: *the abolition of slavery*

abominable *adjective* detestable or very bad > **abominably** *adverb*

abominable snowman *noun* mythical apelike creature

Aborigine [ab-or-**rij**-in-ee] *noun* someone descended from the people who lived in Australia before Europeans arrived > **Aboriginal** *adjective*

abort *verb* **1** to cause (a foetus) to be deliberately expelled from the womb ending the pregnancy prematurely so that the baby does not survive **2** to end (a plan or process) before completion

abortion *noun* operation or medical procedure to end a pregnancy

abortive *adjective* unsuccessful

abound *verb* to exist in large numbers

about *preposition* **1** concerning or on the subject of **2** in or near (a place) > *adverb* **3** nearly, approximately **4** nearby **5** about to shortly going to **6** not about to determined not to

above *adverb, preposition* **1** over or higher (than) **2** greater (than) **3** superior (to)

above board *adjective* completely open and legal

abrasion *noun* scraped area on the skin

abrasive *adjective* **1** unpleasant and rude **2** rough and able to be used to clean or polish hard surfaces

abreast *adjective* **1** alongside and facing in the same direction **2** abreast of up to date with: *He will be keeping abreast of the news*

abroad *adverb* GEOGRAPHY to or in a foreign country

abrupt *adjective* **1** sudden and unexpected **2** not friendly or polite > **abruptly** *adverb* > **abruptness** *noun*

abscess [**ab**-sess] *noun* painful swelling containing pus

abseiling *noun* sport of going down a cliff or a tall building by sliding down ropes

absent *adjective* **1** not present **2** lacking **3** inattentive > *verb* **4** absent yourself (formal) to stay away > **absence** *noun*

absentee *noun* person who should be present but is not

absent-minded *adjective* inattentive or forgetful > **absent-mindedly** *adverb* > **absent-mindedness** *noun* forgetfulness

absolute *adjective* **1** complete or perfect: *absolute honesty* **2** not limited, unconditional: *the absolute ruler* **3** pure: *absolute alcohol* > **absolutely** *adverb* **1** completely **2** certainly, yes

absolve *verb* to declare (someone) to be free from blame or sin

absorb verb **1** SCIENCE to soak up (a liquid) **2** to deal with or cope with (a shock, change or effect)

absorbent adjective able to absorb liquid

absorption noun **1** soaking up of a liquid **2** great interest in something

abstain verb **1** to choose not to do or have (something) **2** to choose not to vote > **abstainer** noun **1** person who does not drink alcohol **2** person who chooses not to vote > **abstention** noun abstaining, especially from voting

abstinence noun state or practice of choosing not to take or do something, especially not to drink alcohol

abstract [ab-strakt] adjective **1** existing as a quality or idea rather than objects or events **2** (Art) using patterns of shapes and colours rather than realistic likenesses **3** ENGLISH (of nouns) referring to qualities or ideas rather than to physical objects, e.g. *happiness; a question* > noun **4** summary **5** abstract work of art > verb [ab-strakt] **6** to summarize **7** to remove or extract

absurd adjective **1** ridiculous and stupid **2** obviously senseless and illogical > **absurdity** noun: *the absurdity of the situation* > **absurdly** adverb

abundance noun **1** great amount or large number > **abundant** adjective present in great amounts or large numbers > **abundantly** adverb

abuse [ab-yooze] verb **1** to use (something) wrongly **2** to ill-treat (someone) violently **3** to speak harshly and rudely to (someone) > [ab-yoose] **4** prolonged ill-treatment **5** harsh and vulgar comments **6** wrong use of something > **abuser** noun: *a convicted child abuser*

abusive adjective **1** cruel and violent **2** (of language) very rude and insulting > **abusively** adverb

abysmal [ab-biz-ml] adjective very bad indeed > **abysmally** adverb

abyss noun very deep hole or chasm

acacia [a-kay-sha] noun type of thorny shrub with small yellow or white flowers

academic adjective **1** of an academy or university **2** of theoretical interest only > noun **3** lecturer or researcher at a university > **academically** adverb

academy academies noun **1** organization of scientists, artists, writers or musicians **2** institution for training in a particular skill: *a military academy* **3** (Scot) secondary school

accelerate verb to move or cause to move more quickly

acceleration noun rate at which the speed of something is increasing

accelerator noun pedal in a motor vehicle, which is pressed to increase speed

accent noun **1** distinctive style of pronunciation of a local, national or social group: *She had an Australian accent* **2** mark over a letter to show how it is pronounced **3** an emphasis on something: *The accent is on action and special effects*

accentuate verb to stress or emphasize (something)

A

accept *verb* **1** to receive (something) willingly **2** to tolerate (a situation) **3** to consider (something) to be true **4** to receive (someone) into a community or group > **acceptable** *adjective* **1** tolerable **2** satisfactory > **acceptably** *adverb* > **acceptance** *noun* **1** act of accepting something **2** favourable reception **3** belief or agreement

access *noun* **1** right or opportunity to enter a place or to use something ▷ *verb* **2** to obtain (data) from a computer

accessible *adjective* **1** easy to reach **2** easily understood or used > **accessibility** *noun*

accession *noun* taking up of an office or position: *her accession to the throne*

accessory *accessories* *noun* **1** an extra part **2** person involved in a crime although not present when it is committed

accident *noun* **1** mishap, often causing injury or death **2** event that happens by chance

accidental *adjective* happening by chance or unintentionally > **accidentally** *adverb*

accolade *noun* (*formal*) great praise or an award given to someone

accommodate *verb* **1** to provide (someone) with lodgings **2** to have room for **3** to oblige or do a favour for

accommodating *adjective* willing to help and to adjust to new situations

accommodation *noun* house or room for living in

accompaniment *noun* **1** something that accompanies: *Melon is a good accompaniment to cold meats* **2** (*Music*) supporting part that goes with a solo

accompany *accompanies, accompanying, accompanied* *verb* **1** to go with **2** to occur at the same time as or as a result of **3** to provide a musical accompaniment for

accomplice *noun* person who helps another to commit a crime

accomplish *verb* to succeed in doing (something)

accomplished *adjective* very talented at something

accomplishment *noun* **1** completion of something **2** personal ability or skill

accord *noun* **1** agreement or harmony **2** of your own accord willingly ▷ *verb* **3** to grant (something to someone) **4** accord with (*formal*) to fit in with or be consistent with

accordance *noun* in accordance with conforming to or according to

according to *preposition* **1** as stated by **2** in conformity with > **accordingly** *adverb* **1** in an appropriate manner **2** consequently

accordion *noun* portable musical instrument played by moving the two sides apart and together and pressing a keyboard or buttons to produce the notes

accost *verb* to approach, stop and speak to (someone)

account *noun* **1** report or description **2** business arrangement making credit available **3** record of money received and paid out with the resulting balance **4** person's money held in a bank **5** on account of because of **6** of no account of no importance or value ▷ **account** for verb **1** to give reasons for; explain **2** to be a particular amount or proportion of (something): The brain accounts for 3% of body weight

accountable adjective responsible to someone or for something: The committee is accountable to Parliament ▷ **accountability** noun: In a democracy there is accountability for error ▷ **accountably** adverb

accountancy noun job of keeping or inspecting financial accounts

accountant noun person whose job is to keep or inspect financial accounts

accounting noun keeping and checking of financial accounts

accrue accrues, accruing, accrued verb (of money or interest) to increase gradually

accumulate verb to gather together in increasing quantity ▷ **accumulation** noun something that has been collected

accurate adjective completely correct or precise ▷ **accurately** adverb

accuse verb to charge (someone) with wrongdoing ▷ **accused** noun defendant appearing on a criminal charge ▷ **accuser** noun

accustom verb accustom yourself to to become familiar with or used to (something) from habit or experience ▷ **accustomed** adjective **1** usual

2 **accustomed to a** used to (something) **b** in the habit of (doing something)

ace noun **1** playing card with one symbol on it **2** (informal) expert ▷ adjective **3** (informal) good or skilful

acerbic [as-**ser**-bik] adjective (formal) harsh or bitter

ache noun **1** dull continuous pain ▷ verb **2** to be in or cause continuous dull pain

achieve verb (PSHE) to gain by hard work or ability

achievement noun (PSHE) something accomplished

acid noun **1** (Chemistry) one of a class of compounds, corrosive and sour when dissolved in water, that combine with a base to form a salt **2** (informal) the drug LSD ▷ adjective **3** containing acid **4** sour-tasting ▷ **acidic** adjective ▷ **acidity** noun

acid rain noun rain polluted by acid in the atmosphere which come from factories

acknowledge verb **1** to recognize or admit the truth or reality of **2** to show recognition of a person by a greeting or glance **3** to let someone know that you have received (their letter or message) ▷ **acknowledgment** or **acknowledgement** noun **1** act of acknowledging something or someone **2** something done or given as an expression of gratitude

acne [**ak**-nee] noun lumpy spots that cover someone's face

acorn noun fruit of the oak tree, consisting of a pale oval nut in a cup-shaped base

A
B
C
D
E
F
G
H
I
J
K
L
M
N
O
P
Q
R
S
T
U
V
W
X
Y
Z

acoustic [a-**koo**-stik] *adjective* **1** relating to sound and hearing **2** (of a musical instrument) not electronically amplified

acoustics *noun* **1** science of sounds ▷ *plural noun* **2** features of a room or building determining how sound is heard within it

acquaintance *noun* person known slightly but not well

acquire *verb* to obtain (something), usually permanently

acquisition *noun* **1** thing acquired **2** act of getting

acquit acquits, acquitting, acquitted *verb* **1** to pronounce (someone) innocent **2 acquit yourself** to behave or perform in a particular way: *The French team acquitted themselves well*

acre *noun* unit for measuring areas of land. One acre equals 4840 square yards (4046.86 square metres)

acrid [**ak**-rid] *adjective* sharp and bitter: *the acrid smell of burning*

acrimony [**ak**-rim-on-ee] *noun* (*formal*) bitterness and anger > **acrimonious** *adjective* (of a dispute or argument) bitter and angry

acrobat *noun* person skilled in gymnastic feats requiring agility and balance > **acrobatic** *adjective* involving agility and balance > **acrobatics** *plural noun* acrobatic feats

acronym *noun* word formed from the initial letters of other words, such as 'NASA' and 'NATO'

across *adverb, preposition* **1** from side to side (of) **2** on or to the other side (of)

acrylic [a-**kril**-lik] *noun* **1** type of man-made cloth **2** kind of artists' paint which can be used like oil paint or thinned down with water

act *noun* **1** single thing done: *It was an act of disloyalty to the King* **2** law or decree **3** section of a play or opera **4** one of several short performances in a show **5** pretended attitude ▷ *verb* **6** to do something: *It would be irresponsible not to act swiftly* **7** to behave in a particular way **8** to perform in a play, film, etc

acting *noun* **1** art of an actor ▷ *adjective* **2** temporarily performing the duties of: *the acting manager*

action *noun* **1** process of doing something **2** thing done **3** legal proceeding: *a libel action* **4** operating mechanism **5** fighting in a war or battle: *255 men killed in action*

activate *verb* to make active or capable of working > **activation** *noun*: *A computer controls the activation of the air bag*

active *adjective* **1** moving or working **2** PE busy and energetic **3** (*Grammar*) (of a verb) in a form indicating that the subject is performing the action, e.g. *threw* in *Kim threw the ball* > **actively** *adverb*

activist *noun* person who works energetically to achieve political or social goals

activity activities *noun* **1** situation in which a lot of things are happening or being done **2** PE something you spend time doing

actor *noun* person who acts in a play, film, etc

actress *noun* woman who acts in a play, film, etc

actual *adjective* real, rather than imaginary or guessed at > **actually** *adverb* really, indeed

acumen [ak-yew-men] *noun* ability to make good judgments: *business acumen*

acupuncture *noun* treatment of illness or pain involving the insertion of needles at various points on the body

acute *adjective* 1 severe or intense: *an acute shortage of beds* 2 very intelligent 3 sensitive or keen 4 (of an angle) less than 90° ⊳ *noun* 5 accent (´) over a letter to indicate the quality or length of its sound, as in *café* > **acutely** *adverb*

ad *noun* (*informal*) advertisement

AD *abbreviation* anno Domini: used in dates to indicate the number of years after the birth of Jesus Christ: *70 AD*

ad- *prefix* near or next to: *adjoining*

adage [ad-dij] *noun* wise saying

adamant *adjective* unshakable in determination or purpose > **adamantly** *adverb*

Adam's apple *noun* a lump at the front of the neck which is more obvious in men than in women or young boys

adapt *verb* 1 to adjust (something or yourself) to new conditions 2 to change (something) to suit a new purpose > **adaptability** *noun: adaptability to a changing environment* > **adaptable** *adjective* able to adjust to new conditions

adaptor or **adapter** *noun* device for connecting several electrical appliances to a single socket

add *verb* 1 to combine (numbers or quantities) 2 to join (something to something else) 3 to say or write (something more)

adder *noun* small poisonous snake

addict *noun* 1 [PSHE] person who is unable to stop taking drugs 2 (*informal*) person devoted to something > **addicted** *adjective* 1 dependent on a drug 2 devoted to something > **addiction** *noun*

addictive *adjective* causing addiction

addition *noun* 1 [MATHS] process of adding numbers together 2 thing added 3 in addition besides, as well

additional *adjective* extra or more: *the decision to take on additional staff* > **additionally** *adverb*

additive *noun* something added, especially to a foodstuff, to improve it or prevent deterioration

address addresses, addressing, addressed *noun* 1 place where a person lives 2 destination or sender's location written on a letter, etc 3 location 4 formal public speech ⊳ *verb* 5 to mark the destination on (an envelope, parcel, etc) 6 to attend to (a problem, task, etc) 7 to talk to (someone)

adept *adjective* very skilful at doing something: *adept at motivating others*

adequate *adjective* enough in amount or good enough for a purpose > **adequately** *adverb*

adhere *verb* 1 to stick (to) 2 to act according (to a rule or agreement) 3 to continue to support or hold (an opinion or

a b c d e f g h i j k l m n o p q r s t u v w x y z

belief) > **adherence** noun: strict adherence to the rules > **adherent** noun devotee, follower

adhesive noun **1** substance used to stick things together ▷ adjective **2** able to stick to things

adjacent [ad-**jay**-sent] adjective **1** near or next (to): a hotel adjacent to the beach **2** (Maths) (of angles) sharing one side and having the same point opposite their bases

adjective noun word that adds information about a noun or pronoun > **adjectival** adjective of or relating to an adjective

adjoining adjective next to and joined onto: adjoining rooms

adjourn verb **1** to stop (a trial or meeting) temporarily; suspend **2** (of a court, parliament or meeting) to come to a stop with a temporary suspension of activities **3** to go (to another place): We adjourned to the lounge

adjust verb **1** to adapt to new conditions **2** to alter (something) slightly to improve its suitability or effectiveness > **adjustable** adjective able to be adapted or altered: adjustable seats > **adjustment** noun slight alteration

ad-lib ad-libs, ad-libbing, ad-libbed verb **1** to improvise a speech etc without preparation: I ad-lib on radio but use a script on TV ▷ noun **2** comment that has not been prepared beforehand

administer verb **1** to manage (business affairs) **2** to organize and put into practice **3** to give (medicine or treatment)

administration noun **1** management of an organization **2** people who manage an organization **3** government: the Bush administration

admirable adjective very good and deserving to be admired > **admirably** adverb

admiral noun highest naval rank

admire verb to respect and approve of (a person or thing) > **admiration** noun respect and approval > **admirer** noun > **admiring** adjective: an admiring glance > **admiringly** adverb

admission noun **1** permission to enter **2** entrance fee **3** confession: an admission of guilt

admit admits, admitting, admitted verb **1** to confess or acknowledge (a crime or mistake) **2** to concede (the truth of something) **3** to allow (someone) to enter **4** to make (someone) an in-patient in a hospital: He was admitted to hospital with chest pains

admittedly adverb it must be said

adolescent noun person between puberty and adulthood > **adolescence** noun period between puberty and adulthood

adopt verb **1** to take (someone else's child) as your own **2** to take up (a plan or principle) > **adoption** noun **1** taking up of a plan or principle **2** process of adopting a child

adorable adjective sweet and attractive

adore verb **1** to love intensely or deeply **2** (informal) to like very much: I adore being in the countryside

adorn verb to decorate or embellish > **adornment** noun decoration

adrenalin or **adrenaline** [a-**dren**-al-in] noun hormone produced by the body when a person is angry, nervous or excited, making the heart beat faster and giving the body more energy

adrift *adjective, adverb* **1** drifting **2** without a clear purpose

adulation [ad-yoo-**lay**-shn] *noun* uncritical admiration > **adulatory** *adjective*: adulatory reviews

adult *adjective* **1** fully grown; mature ▷ *noun* **2** adult person or animal

adultery adulteries *noun* sexual intercourse between a married person and someone he or she is not married to > **adulterer** *noun* person who commits adultery > **adulterous** *adjective* of or relating to adultery

adulthood *noun* time when a person is an adult

advance *verb* **1** to go or bring forward **2** to further (a cause) **3** to propose (an idea) **4** to lend (a sum of money) ▷ *noun* **5** forward movement **6** improvement: scientific advance **7** loan **8** in advance ahead ▷ *adjective* **9** done or happening before an event

advantage *noun* **1** more favourable position or state **2** benefit or profit **3** (Tennis) point scored after deuce **4** take advantage of **a** to use (a person) unfairly **b** to use (an opportunity) > **advantageous** *adjective* likely to bring benefits > **advantageously** *adverb*

advent *noun* **1** arrival or coming into existence **2 Advent** season of four weeks before Christmas in the Christian calendar

adventure *noun* exciting and risky undertaking or exploit

adventurer *noun* **1** person who enjoys doing dangerous and exciting things **2** person who unscrupulously seeks money or power

adventurous *adjective* willing to take risks and do new and exciting things > **adventurously** *adverb*

adverb *noun* word that adds information about a verb, adjective or other adverb > **adverbial** *adjective*

adversary adversaries [**ad**-ver-sar-ee] *noun* opponent or enemy

adverse *adjective* unfavourable to your interests > **adversely** *adverb*

adversity adversities *noun* time of danger or difficulty

advert *noun* (informal) advertisement

advertise *verb* **1** to present or praise (goods or services) to the public in order to encourage sales **2** to make (a vacancy, event, etc) known publicly > **advertiser** *noun* person or company that pays for something to be advertised > **advertising** *noun*: He works in advertising

advertisement [ad-**ver**-tiss-ment] *noun* (ENGLISH) public announcement to sell goods or publicize an event

advice *noun* recommendation as to what to do

> **WORD TIP**
> The noun *advice* is spelt with a *c* and the verb *advise* with an *s*

advisable *adjective* prudent, sensible > **advisability** *noun*: doubts about the advisability of surgery

A
B
C
D
E
F
G
H
I
J
K
L
M
N
O
P
Q
R
S
T
U
V
W
X
Y
Z

advise verb 1 to offer advice to 2 (formal) to inform or notify: We advised them of our decision

> **WORD TIP**
> The verb advise is spelt with an s and the noun advice is spelt with a c

adviser or **advisor** noun person who offers advice, for example on careers

advocate verb 1 to propose or recommend ▷ noun 2 person who publicly supports a cause 3 (Scot, SAfr) barrister > **advocacy** noun public support of a cause

aerial [**air**-ee-al] adjective 1 in, from or operating in the air: aerial combat ▷ noun 2 metal pole, wire, etc, for receiving or transmitting radio or TV signals

aerial top dressing noun spreading of fertilizer from an aeroplane onto remote areas

aero- prefix involving the air, the atmosphere or aircraft: aerobatics

aerobics noun exercises designed to increase the amount of oxygen in the blood > **aerobic** adjective designed for or relating to aerobics

aerodynamic adjective having a streamlined shape that moves easily through the air

aeroplane noun powered flying vehicle with fixed wings

aerosol noun pressurized can from which a substance can be dispensed as a fine spray

aerospace noun 1 earth's atmosphere and space beyond ▷ adjective 2 involved in making and designing aeroplanes and spacecraft

aesthetic [iss-**thet**-ik] adjective (D & T) (formal) relating to

the appreciation of art and beauty > **aesthetically** adverb

afar adverb (literary) **from afar** from or at a great distance

affable adjective friendly and easy to talk to > **affably** adverb

affair noun 1 event or happening 2 sexual relationship outside marriage 3 thing to be done or attended to: My wife's career is her own affair 4 **affairs** a personal or business interests b matters of public interest

affect verb 1 to influence (someone or something): The difficult conditions continued to affect our performance 2 to move (someone) emotionally 3 to put on a show of: He affects ignorance

> **WORD TIP**
> Do not confuse the spelling of the verb affect with the noun effect. Something that affects you has an effect on you

affectation noun attitude or manner put on to impress

affection noun 1 fondness or love 2 **affections** feelings of love for someone

affectionate adjective full of fondness for someone; loving > **affectionately** adverb

affiliate verb 1 (of a group) to link up with a larger group ▷ noun 2 organization which has a close link with another, larger group > **affiliation** noun: The group has no affiliation to any political party

affinity noun affinities noun close similarity or understanding between two things or people

affirm verb 1 to declare to be true 2 to indicate support or confirmation of (an idea or belief)

> **affirmation** noun: His work is an affirmation of life

affirmative adjective meaning or indicating yes

afflict verb to cause someone unhappiness or suffering > **affliction** noun **1** something that causes unhappiness or suffering **2** condition of great distress or suffering

affluent adjective having plenty of money > **affluence** noun wealth

afford verb **1** to have enough money to buy **2** to be able to spare (the time etc) **3** to give or supply > **affordable** adjective: an affordable small car

affray noun (Brit, Aust, NZ law) noisy fight; brawl

affront verb **1** to offend the pride or dignity of > noun **2** insult: Our prisons are an affront to civilized society

afield adverb **far afield** far away

afloat adverb, adjective **1** floating on water **2** at sea or aboard ship **3** successful and making enough money: Companies are struggling hard to stay afloat

afoot adverb, adjective happening; in operation: Plans are afoot to build a new museum

afraid adjective **1** frightened **2** regretful: I'm afraid I lost my temper

afresh adverb again and in a new way

Africa noun second largest continent, which is surrounded by sea, with the Atlantic on its west side, the Mediterranean to the north and the Indian Ocean and the Red Sea to the east

African adjective **1** belonging or relating to Africa > noun

2 someone, especially a Black person, from Africa

African-American noun American whose ancestors came from Africa

Afrikaans [af-rik-**ahns**] noun language used in S Africa, descended from Dutch

Afrikaner noun White South African whose mother tongue is Afrikaans

aft adverb at or towards the rear of a ship or aircraft

after preposition **1** following in time or place **2** in pursuit of: He was after my mother's jewellery **3** concerning: He asked after Laura **4** considering: You seem all right after what happened last night **5** next in excellence or importance to **6** with the same name as: The building is named after the architect > conjunction **7** at a later time than the time when: She arrived after the reading had begun > adverb **8** at a later time

afterlife noun life after death

aftermath noun results of an event considered together

afternoon noun time between noon and evening

aftershave noun pleasant-smelling liquid men put on their faces after shaving

afterthought noun **1** idea occurring later **2** something added later

afterwards or **afterward** adverb later

again adverb **1** happening one more time: He looked forward to becoming a father again **2** returning to the same state or place as before: there and back again **3** in

a
b
c
d
e
f
g
h
i
j
k
l
m
n
o
p
q
r
s
t
u
v
w
x
y
z

addition to an amount that has already been mentioned: I could eat twice as much again

against preposition **1** in opposition or contrast to: the Test match against England **2** touching and leaning on: He leaned against the wall **3** as a protection from: precautions against fire **4** in comparison with: The euro is now at its highest rate against the dollar

age ages, ageing or aging, aged noun **1** length of time a person or thing has existed: What age was he when he died? **2** time of life: He should know better at his age **3** state of being old or the process of becoming older: The fabric was showing signs of age **4** period of history: the Iron Age **5** ages (informal) long time: He's been talking for ages **6** come of age to become legally responsible for your actions (usually at 18) ▷ verb **7** to make or grow old

aged adjective **1** [ay-jid] old: an aged invalid **2** [rhymes with raged] being at the age of: people aged 16 to 24

agency agencies noun organization providing a particular service

agenda noun list of things to be dealt with, especially at a meeting

agent noun **1** person acting on behalf of another **2** person who works for a country's secret service **3** person or thing producing an effect: bleaching agents

aggravate verb **1** to make (a disease, situation or problem) worse **2** (informal) to annoy > **aggravating** adjective > **aggravation** noun

WORD TIP
Some people think that using aggravate to mean 'annoy' is wrong

aggregate noun **1** total made up of several smaller amounts **2** rock consisting of a mixture of minerals **3** sand or gravel used to make concrete ▷ adjective **4** gathered into a mass **5** total or final

aggression noun violent and hostile behaviour

aggressive adjective **1** full of hostility and violence **2** determined and eager to succeed: aggressive sales techniques > **aggressively** adverb > **aggressiveness** noun: a breed of dog with a reputation for aggressiveness

aggressor noun person or country that starts a fight or a war

aggrieved adjective upset and angry

aghast [a-gast] adjective overcome with amazement or horror

agile adjective **1** [PE] able to move quickly and easily **2** mentally quick > **agilely** adverb > **agility** noun ability to move or think quickly

agitate verb **1** to disturb or excite **2** to stir or shake (a liquid) **3** to stir up public opinion for or against something > **agitation** noun **1** state of disturbance or excitement **2** act of stirring or shaking something **3** stirring up of public opinion for or against something > **agitator** noun: a political agitator

agnostic noun **1** person who believes that it is impossible to know whether God exists or not ▷ adjective **2** of agnostics **> agnosticism** noun belief that it is impossible to know whether God exists or not

ago adverb in the past

agog adjective excited and eager to know more about something

agonizing or **agonising** adjective extremely painful, either physically or mentally

agony agonies noun extreme physical or mental pain

agoraphobia [a-gor-a-**foe**-bee-a] noun fear of open spaces **> agoraphobic** adjective suffering from agoraphobia

agrarian [ag-**rare**-ee-an] adjective (formal) of land or agriculture: agrarian economies

agree agrees, agreeing, agreed verb **1** to be of the same opinion **2** to consent: She agreed to go **3** to reach a joint decision **4** to be similar or consistent **5 agree with** to be good for (someone): I don't think milk agrees with me

agreeable adjective **1** pleasant and enjoyable **2** prepared to consent to something **> agreeably** adverb

agreement noun **1** decision that has been reached by two or more people **2** legal contract

agriculture noun raising of crops and livestock **> agricultural** adjective of or relating to agriculture

aground adverb onto the bottom of shallow water

ahead adverb **1** in front: He looked ahead **2** more advanced

than someone or something else: We are five years ahead of the competition **3** in the future

aid noun **1** money, equipment or services provided for people in need **2** help or support **3** something that makes a task easier ▷ verb **4** to help or assist

aide noun assistant to an important person, especially in the government or the army

AIDS abbreviation acquired immunodeficiency syndrome: a viral disease that destroys the body's ability to fight infection

ailing adjective **1** sick or ill, and not getting better **2** getting into difficulties, especially with money: an ailing company

ailment noun minor illness

aim verb **1** to point (a weapon or missile) or direct (a blow or remark) at someone or something **2** to propose or intend ▷ noun **3** intention or purpose; goal **4** aiming

aimless adjective having no purpose **> aimlessly** adverb

air noun **1** mixture of gases forming the earth's atmosphere **2** space above the ground or sky **3** breeze **4** quality or manner: an air of defiance **5** simple tune **6 on the air** in the act of broadcasting on radio or television **7 airs** manners put on to impress people: We never put on airs ▷ verb **8** to make known publicly **9** to expose to air to dry or ventilate

airborne adjective **1** carried by air **2** (of aircraft) flying

air-conditioning noun system that controls the temperature and humidity of the air in a

building > **air-conditioned**
adjective: *an air-conditioned hotel*

aircraft noun any machine that
flies, such as an aeroplane

> **WORD TIP**
The plural of *aircraft* is *aircraft*

airfield noun place where aircraft
can land and take off

air force noun branch of the armed
forces responsible for air warfare

air gun noun gun fired by
compressed air

air hostess noun female flight
attendant

airless adjective stuffy

airlift noun **1** transport of troops
or cargo by aircraft when other
routes are blocked ▷ verb **2** to
transport by airlift

airline noun company which
provides air travel

airliner noun large passenger
aircraft

airmail noun **1** system of sending
mail by aircraft **2** mail sent in
this way

airman airmen noun man who
serves in his country's air force

airport noun airfield for civilian
aircraft, with facilities for aircraft
maintenance and passengers

air raid noun attack by aircraft, in
which bombs are dropped

airship noun large aircraft,
consisting of a rigid balloon
filled with gas and powered by
an engine, with a passenger
compartment underneath

airstrip noun cleared area where
aircraft can take off and land

airtight adjective sealed so that air
cannot enter

airy airier, airiest adjective **1** full of
fresh air and light **2** light-hearted

and casual: *an airy wave of his hand*
> **airily** adverb

aisle [rhymes with **mile**] noun
passageway separating the
seating areas in a church, theatre,
etc, or the rows of shelves in a
supermarket

ajar adjective, adverb (of a door)
partly open

akin adjective **akin to** similar,
related: *The taste is akin to veal*

alabaster noun type of smooth
white stone used for making
ornaments

alacrity noun **with alacrity**
quickly and eagerly

alarm noun **1** sudden fear
caused by awareness of danger
2 warning sound **3** device that
gives this **4** alarm clock ▷ verb
5 to fill with fear ▷ **alarming**
adjective: *The disease has spread at
an alarming rate*

alas adverb unfortunately,
regrettably

albatross noun **1** large white sea
bird with very long wings **2** a
commitment that causes a great
deal of difficulty

albeit [awl-**bee**-it] conjunction
(formal) even though: *He was
making progress, albeit slowly*

albino albinos noun person or
animal with white skin and hair
and pink eyes

album noun **1** CD, cassette or
record with a number of songs
on it **2** book with blank pages
for keeping photographs or
stamps in

alchemy [**al**-kem-ee] noun
medieval form of chemistry
concerned with trying to turn
base metals into gold and to find

the elixir of life > **alchemist** noun medieval scientist who tried to turn base metals into gold

alcheringa [al-cher-**ring**-ga] noun same as **Dreamtime**

alcohol noun **1** colourless flammable liquid present in intoxicating drinks **2** intoxicating drinks generally

alcoholic adjective **1** of alcohol: alcoholic drinks > noun **2** person addicted to alcohol > **alcoholism** noun addiction to alcohol

alcopop noun (Brit, Aust, S Afr informal) alcoholic drink that tastes like a soft drink

alcove noun recess in the wall of a room

ale noun kind of beer

alert adjective **1** paying full attention to what is happening: The criminal was spotted by an alert member of the public > noun **2** warning of danger **3 on the alert** watchful > verb **4** to warn of danger > **alertness** noun: mental alertness

A level noun an advanced exam taken by students in many British schools and colleges, usually following GCSEs

algae [al-jee] plural noun plants which live in or near water and have no true stems, leaves or roots

algebra noun branch of mathematics in which symbols and letters are used instead of numbers to express relationships between quantities > **algebraic** adjective: algebraic equations

Algerian adjective **1** belonging or relating to Algeria > noun **2** someone from Algeria

alias aliases [**ay**-lee-ass] adverb **1** also known as > noun **2** false name

alibi alibis [**al**-li-bye] noun **1** plea of being somewhere else when a crime was committed **2** (informal) excuse

alien [**ay**-lee-an] adjective **1** foreign **2** strange and outside your normal experience; different **3** from another world > noun **4** foreigner **5** being from another world

alienate verb to cause (someone) to become hostile

alight verb **1** (formal) to step out (of a vehicle): We alighted at Lenzie station **2** to land: thirty finches alighting on a ledge > adjective **3** on fire

align [a-**line**] verb **1** to bring (a person or group) into agreement with the policy of another **2** to place (two objects) in a straight line > **alignment** noun

alike adjective **1** like or similar > adverb **2** in the same way

alimony [**al**-li-mon-ee] noun allowance paid under a court order to a separated or divorced spouse

alive adjective **1** living; not dead **2** lively and active

alkali [**alk**-a-lie] noun [SCIENCE] substance with a pH value of more than 7 > **alkaline** adjective: Some soils are too alkaline for certain plant life

all adjective, pronoun **1** whole quantity or number (of): 90% of all households; all our belongings; That was all I had **2 give your all** to make the greatest possible effort > adverb **3** wholly, entirely **4** (in the score of games) each: The final score was six points all

a b c d e f g h i j k l m n o p q r s t u v w x y z

A

Allah noun name of God in Islam

allay verb to reduce (someone's fears or doubts)

allege [a-**lej**] verb to state without proof: *It is alleged that she was poisoned* > **alleged** adjective: *an alleged beating* > **allegedly** adverb

allegiance [al-**lee**-jenss] noun loyalty to a person, country or cause

allegory allegories [**al**-li-gor-ee] noun story with an underlying meaning as well as the literal one. For example, George Orwell's novel *Animal Farm* is an allegory in that the animals who revolt in the farmyard are symbols of the political leaders in the Russian Revolution > **allegorical** adjective: *an allegorical novel*

allergy allergies noun extreme sensitivity to a substance, which causes the body to react to it > **allergic** adjective having or caused by an allergy

alleviate verb to lessen (pain or suffering): *measures to alleviate poverty* > **alleviation** noun: *the alleviation of pain*

alley noun **1** narrow street or path **2** long narrow enclosure in which tenpin bowling or skittles is played

alliance noun **1** state of being allied **2** formal relationship between countries or groups for a shared purpose

alligator noun reptile of the crocodile family, found in the southern US and China

alliteration noun ENGLISH (literary) use of the same sound at the start of words occurring together, e.g. *moody music*

> **alliterative** adjective relating to or connected with alliteration

allocate verb to assign (something) to someone or for a particular purpose > **allocation** noun: *the allocation of funding*

allot allots, allotting, allotted verb to assign as a share or for a particular purpose: *Space was allotted for visitors' cars*

allotment noun **1** (Brit) small piece of public land rented to grow vegetables on **2** share of something

allow verb **1** to permit (someone to do something) **2** to set aside **3 allow for** to take into account > **allowable** adjective able to be accepted or admitted

allowance noun **1** amount of money given at regular intervals **2** amount permitted **3 make allowances for a** to treat or judge (someone) less severely because he or she has special problems **b** to take (something) into account

alloy noun mixture of two or more metals

all right adjective **1** adequate or satisfactory **2** unharmed ▷ interjection **3** expression of approval or agreement

allude verb **allude to** to refer indirectly to

> **WORD TIP**
> You *allude to* something. Do not confuse *allude* with *elude*

allure noun attractiveness: *the allure of foreign travel* > **alluring** adjective: *the most alluring city in South-East Asia*

allusion noun indirect reference: *English literature is full of classical allusions*

ally allies, allying, allied *noun*
1 country, person or group with
an agreement to support another
▷ *verb* **2 ally yourself with** to join
as an ally

almanac *noun* **1** yearly calendar
with detailed information on
anniversaries, phases of the
moon, etc **2** book published every
year giving information about a
particular subject

almighty *adjective* **1** having
absolute power **2** (*informal*) very
great ▷ *noun* **3 the Almighty** God

almond *noun* edible brown
oval-shaped nut which grows on
a small tree

almost *adverb* very nearly

alms [ahmz] *plural noun* (*old-
fashioned*) gifts of money, food or
clothing to poor people

aloft *adverb* up in the air or in a
high position

alone *adjective, adverb* without
anyone or anything else; on
your own

along *preposition* **1** over part or all
the length of ▷ *adverb* **2** moving
forward: *We marched along, singing
as we went* **3** in company with
others: *Why not take her along?*
4 all along from the beginning of
a period of time right up to now:
You've known that all along

alongside *preposition, adverb*
beside (something)

aloof *adjective* distant or haughty
in manner

aloud *adverb* spoken in a voice that
can be heard

alphabet *noun* LIBRARY set of
letters used in writing a language
▷ **alphabetical** *adjective* in the
conventional order of the letters
of an alphabet ▷ **alphabetically**
adverb

alpine *adjective* existing in or
relating to high mountains

already *adverb* **1** before the
present time **2** sooner than
expected

alright *adjective, interjection* all
right

> **WORD TIP**
> Some people think that *all right*
> is the only correct spelling and
> that *alright* is wrong

Alsatian [al-**say**-shn] *noun* large
wolflike dog

also *adverb* in addition, too

altar *noun* **1** table used for
Communion in Christian churches
2 raised structure on which
sacrifices are offered and religious
rites are performed

alter *verb* to make or become
different ▷ **alteration** *noun*:
simple alterations to your diet

> **WORD TIP**
> Do not confuse the spellings of
> *alter* and *altar*

altercation *noun* (*formal*) heated
argument

alternate *verb* **1** to occur or to
cause (something) to occur by
turns ▷ *adjective* **2** occurring
by turns **3** every second (one)
of a series **4** MATHS (of two
angles) on opposite sides
of a line that crosses two
other lines ▷ **alternately**
adverb ▷ **alternation** *noun*:
*The alternation of sun and snow
continued all week*

alternating current *noun*
electric current that reverses
direction at frequent regular
intervals

A

alternative noun **1** something you can do or have instead of something else: *alternatives to prison such as community service* ▷ *adjective* **2** able to be done or used instead of something else **3** (of medicine, lifestyle, etc) not conventional > **alternatively** *adverb*

although *conjunction* despite the fact that

altitude *noun* height above sea level: *an altitude of 1330 metres*

altogether *adverb* **1** entirely **2** on the whole **3** in total

aluminium *noun* light silvery-white metal that does not rust

always *adverb* **1** at all times **2** for ever

am *verb* see **be**

a.m. *abbreviation* (*Latin*) *ante meridiem*: before noon: *We got up at 6 a.m.*

amalgamate *verb* to combine or unite > **amalgamation** *noun*: *an amalgamation of two organizations*

amandla [ah-**mand**-lah] *noun* (*S Afr*) political slogan calling for power to the Black population

amass *verb* to collect or accumulate: *He amassed a huge fortune*

amateur *noun* **1** person who engages in a sport or activity as a pastime rather than as a profession **2** person unskilled in something ▷ *adjective* **3** not professional

amateurish *adjective* lacking skill > **amateurishly** *adverb*

amaze *verb* to surprise greatly; astound > **amazed** *adjective*: *You'd be amazed at the mess people leave* > **amazement** *noun*: *I stared at her*

in amazement > **amazing** *adjective* very surprising or remarkable > **amazingly** *adverb*

ambassador *noun* senior diplomat who represents his or her country in another country

amber *noun* **1** clear yellowish fossil resin ▷ *adjective* **2** brownish-yellow

ambi- *prefix* both: *ambidextrous*

ambidextrous *adjective* able to use both hands with equal ease

ambience *noun* (*formal*) atmosphere of a place

ambient *adjective* surrounding: *low ambient temperatures*

ambiguous *adjective* having more than one possible meaning > **ambiguity** *noun*: *considerable ambiguity about the meaning of the agreement* > **ambiguously** *adverb*

ambition *noun* **1** desire for success: *He's talented and full of ambition* **2** something desired; goal: *His ambition is to be an actor*

ambitious *adjective* **1** having a strong desire for success **2** requiring great effort or ability: *an ambitious rebuilding schedule* > **ambitiously** *adverb*

ambivalent *adjective* having or showing two conflicting attitudes or emotions > **ambivalence** *noun*: *her ambivalence about getting married again*

amble *verb* to walk at a leisurely pace ▷ *noun* **2** leisurely walk or pace

ambulance *noun* motor vehicle designed to carry sick or injured people

ambush *noun* **1** act of waiting in a concealed position to make a surprise attack **2** attack from a concealed position ▷ verb **3** to attack suddenly from a concealed position

amen *interjection* so be it: used at the end of a prayer

amenable [am-**mee**-na-bl] *adjective* likely or willing to cooperate: *Both brothers were amenable to the arrangement*

amend *verb* to make small changes to correct or improve (something) ▷ **amendment** *noun* improvement or correction

amenity amenities [am-**mee**-nit-ee] *noun* GEOGRAPHY useful or enjoyable feature available for the public to use

America *noun* **1** the whole of North, South and Central America **2** the United States

American *adjective* **1** of the United States of America or the American continent ▷ *noun* **2** someone from America or the American continent

amethyst [am-myth-ist] *noun* bluish-violet variety of quartz used as a gemstone

amiable *adjective* friendly, pleasant-natured: *The hotel staff were very amiable* ▷ **amiability** *noun*: *I found his amiability charming* ▷ **amiably** *adverb*

amicable *adjective* fairly friendly: *an amicable divorce* ▷ **amicably** *adverb*

amid or **amidst** *preposition* (formal) in the middle of; among

amiss *adverb* **1** wrongly, badly **2 take something amiss** to be offended by something ▷ *adjective* **3** wrong or faulty

ammonia *noun* strong-smelling alkaline gas containing hydrogen

and nitrogen, used in household cleaning materials, explosives and fertilizers

ammunition *noun* **1** bullets, bombs and shells that can be fired from or as a weapon **2** facts that can be used in an argument

amnesia *noun* loss of memory

amnesty amnesties *noun* general pardon for offences against a government

amoeba amoebae or amoebas [am-**mee**-ba] *noun* smallest kind of living creature, consisting of one cell. Amoebas reproduce by dividing into two

amok [a-**muck**, a-**mock**] *adverb* **run amok** to run about in a violent frenzy

among or **amongst** *preposition* **1** surrounded by **2** in the company of **3** to each of: *divide it among yourselves*

WORD TIP
If there are more than two things, you should use *among*. If there are only two things you should use *between*

amoral [aim-**mor**-ral] *adjective* without moral standards

WORD TIP
Do not confuse *amoral* and *immoral*. You use *amoral* to talk about people with no moral standards, but *immoral* for people who are aware of moral standards but go against them

amorous *adjective* feeling, showing or relating to sexual love: *an amorous relationship* ▷ **amorously** *adverb*

amount *noun* **1** extent or quantity ▷ *verb* **2 amount to** to be equal or add up to

amp noun **1** ampere **2** (informal) amplifier

ampere [**am**-pair] noun basic unit of electric current

ampersand noun the character (&), meaning and

amphetamine [am-**fet**-am-meen] noun drug used as a stimulant

amphibian noun [SCIENCE] animal that lives on land but breeds in water

amphibious adjective **1** (of an animal) living partly on land and partly in the water **2** (of a military operation) using boats to land soldiers on an enemy shore **3** (of a vehicle) able to move on both land and water

amphitheatre noun large, semicircular open area with sloping sides covered with rows of seats

ample adjective **1** more than sufficient **2** large > **amply** adverb

amplifier noun piece of equipment in a radio or stereo system which causes sounds or signals to become louder

amplify amplifies, amplifying, amplified verb **1** to increase the strength of (a current or sound signal) **2** to explain in more detail **3** to increase the size or effect of > **amplification** noun: a voice that needed no amplification

amplitude noun (Physics) the amplitude of a wave is how far its curve moves away from its normal position

amputate verb to cut off (a limb or part of a limb) for medical reasons > **amputation** noun: the amputation of his left leg

Amrit noun **1** mixture of sugar and water used in rituals of the Sikh religion **2** ceremony during which someone is accepted as a full member of the Sikh community

amuse verb **1** to cause to laugh or smile **2** to entertain or keep interested > **amused** adjective: an amused look on her face > **amusing** adjective funny or entertaining

amusement noun **1** state of being amused **2** something that amuses or entertains someone

an adjective form of a used before vowel sounds

-an suffix -an comes at the end of nouns and adjectives which show where or what someone or something comes from or belongs to: American; Victorian; Christian

anachronism [an-**nak**-kron-iz-zum] noun person or thing placed in the wrong historical period or seeming to belong to another time: The President regarded the Church as an anachronism > **anachronistic** adjective: Many of its practices seem anachronistic

anaemia [an-**neem**-ee-a] noun deficiency in the number of red blood cells, resulting in tiredness and a pale complexion > **anaemic** adjective

anaesthetic [an-niss-**thet**-ik] noun **1** substance causing loss of bodily feeling > adjective **2** causing loss of bodily feeling

anaesthetist [an-**neess**-thet-ist] noun doctor trained to administer anaesthetics

anaesthetize or **anaesthetise** verb to cause to feel no pain by administering an anaesthetic

anagram noun word or phrase made by rearranging the letters of another word or phrase

anal [**ain**-al] adjective relating to the anus

analgesic [an-al-**jee**-sik] adjective 1 pain-relieving ▷ noun 2 substance that relieves pain

analogy analogies [an-**al**-o-jee] noun comparison made to show a similarity > **analogous** adjective similar in some respects

analyse verb 1 to examine (something) in detail in order to discover its meaning or essential features 2 to break (something) down into its components 3 to psychoanalyse (someone)

analysis analyses noun 1 separation of a whole into its parts for study and interpretation 2 short for **psychoanalysis**

analyst noun person skilled in analysis

analytical or **analytic** adjective using logical reasoning > **analytically** adverb

anarchy [an-ark-ee] noun lawlessness and disorder > **anarchic** adjective: anarchic attitudes and complete disrespect for authority

anatomy anatomies noun 1 science of the structure of the body 2 physical structure 3 person's body > **anatomical** adjective: anatomical details > **anatomically** adverb

ANC abbreviation African National Congress

ancestor noun 1 person from whom you are descended 2 forerunner > **ancestral** adjective: the family's ancestral home

ancestry ancestries noun 1 family descent: of Japanese ancestry 2 origin or roots

anchor noun 1 heavy hooked device attached to a boat by a cable and dropped overboard to fasten the ship to the sea bottom ▷ verb 2 to fasten with or as if with an anchor

anchorage noun place where boats can be anchored

anchovy anchovies [**an**-chov-ee] noun small strong-tasting fish

ancient [**ayn**-shent] adjective 1 dating from very long ago: ancient Greece 2 very old or having a long history

ancillary [an-**sil**-lar-ee] adjective 1 supporting the main work of an organization: hospital ancillary workers 2 used as an extra or supplement

and conjunction 1 in addition to 2 as a consequence 3 then or afterwards

androgynous [an-**droj**-in-uss] adjective (formal) having both male and female characteristics

android noun robot resembling a human

anecdote noun short amusing account of an incident > **anecdotal** adjective based on individual accounts rather than on reliable research and statistics: anecdotal evidence

anemone [an-**nem**-on-ee] noun plant with white, purple or red flowers

anew adverb 1 once more 2 in a different way

angel noun 1 spiritual being believed to be an attendant or messenger of God 2 person who is

A

kind, pure or beautiful > **angelic** adjective **1** of or relating to angels **2** very kind, pure or beautiful > **angelically** adverb

anger noun **1** fierce displeasure or extreme annoyance ▷ verb **2** to make (someone) angry

angina [an-**jine**-a] noun (also **angina pectoris**) heart disorder causing sudden severe chest pains

angle noun **1** space between or shape formed by two lines or surfaces that meet **2** distance between two lines or surfaces at the point where they meet, measured in degrees **3** corner **4** point of view: the same story from a German angle ▷ verb **5** to bend or place (something) at an angle **6** to fish with a hook and line ▶ **angle for** verb to try to get (something) by hinting

angler noun person who fishes with a hook and line ▶ **angling** noun sport of fishing with a hook and line

Anglican noun **1** member of the Church of England ▷ adjective **2** of the Church of England

Anglo-Saxon noun **1** member of any of the West Germanic tribes that settled in England from the fifth century AD **2** language of the Anglo-Saxons ▷ adjective **3** of the Anglo-Saxons or their language

Angolan [ang-**goh**-ln] adjective **1** belonging or relating to Angola ▷ noun **2** someone from Angola

angora noun **1** variety of goat, cat or rabbit with long silky hair **2** hair of the angora goat or rabbit **3** cloth made from this hair

angry angrier, angriest adjective **1** full of anger **2** inflamed > **angrily** adverb

anguish noun great mental pain > **anguished** adjective: an anguished cry

angular adjective **1** (of a person) lean and bony **2** having straight lines and sharp points

animal noun **1** any living being except a plant or any mammal except a human being ▷ adjective **2** of animals **3** of physical needs or desires

animate verb **1** to give life to **2** to make lively **3** to produce (a story) as an animated cartoon ▷ adjective **4** having life

animated adjective **1** lively and interesting: an animated conversation **2** (of a film) made using animation: an animated cartoon > **animatedly** adverb

animation noun **1** technique of making cartoon films **2** liveliness and enthusiasm: The crowd showed no sign of animation > **animator** noun person who makes animated cartoons

animosity animosities noun feeling of strong dislike and anger towards someone

aniseed noun liquorice-flavoured seeds of the anise plant

ankle noun joint between the foot and leg

anklet noun ornamental chain worn round the ankle

annex verb **1** to seize (territory) **2** to take (something) without permission **3** to join or add (something) to something larger > **annexation** noun: Indonesia's annexation of East Timor

annihilate [an-**nye**-ill-ate] verb to destroy (a place or a

group of people) completely
> **annihilation** noun

anniversary anniversaries noun
1 date on which something
occurred in a previous year
2 celebration of this

announce verb to make known
publicly > **announcement** noun
public statement

announcer noun person who
introduces radio or television
programmes

annoy verb to irritate or displease
> **annoyance** noun: a long list
of annoyances; To her annoyance
the stranger did not go away
> **annoyed** adjective displeased
by something or someone
> **annoying** adjective irritating

annual adjective **1** happening
once a year: their annual conference
2 lasting for a year: the United States'
annual budget for national defence
▷ noun **3** plant that completes its
life cycle in a year **4** book published
once every year > **annually** adverb

annuity annuities noun fixed sum
paid every year

annul annuls, annulling, annulled
verb to declare (something,
especially a marriage) officially
invalid > **annulment** noun official
declaration that something is
invalid

anoint verb to smear with
oil as a sign of consecration
> **anointment** noun act of
anointing someone

anomaly anomalies [an-**nom**-a-
lee] noun something that deviates
from the normal: a statistical
anomaly > **anomalous** adjective:
This anomalous behaviour has baffled
scientists

anon. abbreviation anonymous

anonymous adjective by someone
whose name is unknown or
withheld > **anonymity** noun:
the anonymity of the voting booth
> **anonymously** adverb

anorak noun light waterproof
hooded jacket

anorexia noun (also **anorexia
nervosa**) psychological disorder
characterized by fear of becoming
fat and refusal to eat > **anorexic**
adjective **1** suffering from anorexia
▷ noun **2** person suffering from
anorexia

another adjective, pronoun **1** one
more **2** different (one)

answer noun **1** reply to a question,
request, letter, etc **2** solution to
a problem **3** reaction or response
▷ verb **4** to give an answer (to)
5 to be responsible for (a person)
6 to respond or react: a dog that
answers to the name of Pugg

answerable adjective
answerable for or to responsible
for or accountable to

answering machine noun
device for answering a telephone
automatically and recording
messages

ant noun small insect living in large
colonies

-ant suffix used to form adjectives
and nouns: important; deodorant

antagonism noun open
opposition or hostility

antagonist noun opponent or
adversary

antagonistic adjective in active
opposition > **antagonistically**
adverb

antagonize or **antagonise** verb
to arouse hostility in

Antarctic noun **1 the Antarctic** area around the South Pole ▷ *adjective* **2** of this region

Antarctic Circle noun imaginary circle around the southernmost part of the earth

ante- *prefix* before in time or position: *antedate; antechamber*

antecedent [an-tis-**see**-dent] noun **1** event or circumstance happening or existing before another ▷ *adjective* **2** preceding, prior

antelope noun deerlike mammal with long legs and horns

antenatal *adjective* concerned with the care of pregnant women and their unborn children

antenna antennae, antennas noun **1** long thin feeler, of which there are two, attached to an insect's head **2** (*Aust, NZ, US*) radio or television aerial

> **WORD TIP**
> Note that the plural of sense 1 is
> *antennae* and the plural of sense
> 2 is *antennas*

anthem noun **1** song of loyalty, especially to a country **2** piece of choral music, usually set to words from the Bible

anther noun part of a flower's stamen containing pollen

anthology anthologies noun [LIBRARY] collection of poems or other literary pieces by various authors

anthropo- *prefix* involving or to do with human beings: *anthropology*

anthropology noun study of human origins, institutions and beliefs ▷ **anthropological** *adjective*: *anthropological theories* ▷ **anthropologist** noun person

who studies or is an expert in anthropology

anti- *prefix* **1** against or opposed to: *anti-war* **2** opposite to: *anticlimax* **3** counteracting: *antifreeze*

antibiotic noun **1** chemical substance capable of destroying bacteria ▷ *adjective* **2** of antibiotics

antibody antibodies noun protein produced in the blood, which destroys bacteria

anticipate *verb* to foresee and act in advance of > **anticipation** noun: *smiling in happy anticipation*

anticlimax noun something that does not live up to expectations or is disappointing, especially in contrast to what has gone before

anticlockwise adverb, adjective in the opposite direction to the rotation of the hands of a clock

antics *plural noun* funny or silly ways of behaving

antidote noun substance that acts against the effect of a poison

antihistamine noun drug used to treat allergies

antipathy [an-**tip**-a-thee] noun strong feeling of dislike or hostility towards something or someone

antiperspirant noun substance used to reduce or prevent sweating

antipodes [an-**tip**-pod-deez] *plural noun* **1** any two places diametrically opposite one another on the earth's surface **2 the Antipodes** (*Brit*) Australia and New Zealand ▷ **antipodean** *adjective*: *our antipodean visitors*

antiquarian *adjective* of or relating to antiquities or rare books: *antiquarian books*

antiquated *adjective* out-of-date

antique [an-**teek**] noun **1** object of an earlier period, valued for its beauty, workmanship or age ▷ adjective **2** from or concerning the past **3** old-fashioned

antiquity antiquities noun **1** great age **2** distant past, especially the time of the ancient Egyptians, Greeks and Romans **3** antiquities objects dating from ancient times

anti-Semitism noun hatred of or discrimination against Jews > **anti-Semite** noun person who hates or discriminates against Jews > **anti-Semitic** adjective: anti-Semitic literature

antiseptic adjective **1** preventing infection by killing germs ▷ noun **2** antiseptic substance

antisocial adjective **1** avoiding the company of other people **2** (of behaviour) harmful to society

antithesis antitheses [an-**tith**-iss-iss] noun (formal) **1** exact opposite: Work is the antithesis of leisure **2** (literary) placing together of contrasting ideas or words to produce an effect of balance

antivenene noun substance which reduces the effect of a venom, especially a snake venom

antivirus adjective (usually of computer software) protecting computers from viruses

antler noun branched horn of male deer

antonym noun word that means the opposite of another

anus [**ain**-uss] noun hole between the buttocks through which bodily wastes are excreted

anvil noun heavy iron block on which metals are hammered into particular shapes

anxiety anxieties noun nervousness or worry

anxious adjective **1** worried and tense **2** intensely desiring: She was anxious to have children > **anxiously** adverb

any adjective, pronoun **1** one, some or no matter which ▷ adverb **2** at all: It isn't any worse

anybody pronoun any person

anyhow adverb **1** in any case **2** in a careless way

anyone pronoun **1** any person **2** person of any importance

anything pronoun any object, event, situation or action

anyway adverb **1** at any rate, nevertheless **2** in any manner

anywhere adverb in, at or to any place

Anzac noun **1** (in World War 1) a soldier serving with the Australian and New Zealand Army Corps **2** Australian or New Zealand soldier

aorta [eh-**or**-ta] noun main artery of the body, carrying oxygen-rich blood from the heart

apart adverb **1** to or in pieces **2** to or at a distance **3** individual, distinct

apartheid [ap-**par**-tide] noun (in South Africa until its abolition in 1994) former official government policy of keeping people of different races apart

apartment noun **1** room in a building **2** flat

apathetic adjective not interested in anything

apathy [**ap**-path-ee] noun lack of interest or enthusiasm

ape noun **1** tailless monkey such as the chimpanzee or gorilla

a b c d e f g h i j k l m n o p q r s t u v w x y z

A

2 stupid, clumsy or ugly man ▷ *verb* **3** to imitate

aphid [**eh**-fid] *noun* small insect which sucks the sap from plants

aphrodisiac [af-roh-**diz**-zee-ak] *noun* **1** substance that arouses sexual desire ▷ *adjective* **2** arousing sexual desire

apiece *adverb* each

aplomb [uh-**plom**] *noun* relaxed confidence

apocalypse [uh-**pok**-ka-lips] *noun* **1** end of the world **2** event of great destruction **3 the Apocalypse** book of Revelation, the last book of the New Testament ▷ **apocalyptic** *adjective: an apocalyptic vision*

apocryphal [ap-**pok**-rif-al] *adjective* (of a story) generally believed not to have really happened

apolitical [ay-poll-**it**-i-kl] *adjective* not interested in politics

apologetic *adjective* showing or expressing regret ▷ **apologetically** *adverb*

apologize or **apologise** *verb* to make an apology

apology apologies *noun* **1** expression of regret for wrongdoing **2 apology for** poor example (of)

apostle *noun* **1** ardent supporter of a cause or movement **2 Apostle** one of the twelve disciples chosen by Christ to preach his gospel

apostrophe [ap-**poss**-trof-ee] *noun* ENGLISH punctuation mark (') showing the omission of a letter or letters in a word, e.g. *don't* or forming the possessive, e.g. *Jill's car*

appal appals, appalling, appalled *verb* to fill with horror

appalling *adjective* so bad as to be shocking

apparatus *noun* SCIENCE equipment for a particular purpose

apparent *adjective* **1** readily seen; obvious **2** seeming as opposed to real > **apparently** *adverb*

apparition *noun* figure, especially a ghostlike one

appeal *verb* **1** to make an earnest request **2** to attract, please or interest **3** (*Law*) to apply to a higher court to review (a case or issue decided by a lower court) ▷ *noun* **4** earnest request: *an appeal for peace* **5** attractiveness **6** (*Law*) request for a review of a lower court's decision by a higher court > **appealing** *adjective: It was a very appealing idea*

appear *verb* **1** to become visible or present **2** to seem: *He appeared to be searching for something* **3** to be seen in public

appearance *noun* **1** sudden or unexpected arrival of someone or something at a place **2** an act or instance of appearing **3** introduction or invention of something **4** way a person or thing looks

appease *verb* **1** to pacify (a person) by yielding to his or her demands **2** to satisfy or relieve (a feeling) > **appeasement** *noun* pacification of a person by yielding to his or her demands

appendage *noun* less important part attached to a main part

appendicitis [app-end-i-**site**-uss] *noun* painful illness in which a person's appendix becomes infected

appendix appendices or appendixes noun 1 separate additional material at the end of a book 2 (Anatomy) short closed tube attached to the large intestine

WORD TIP

The plural of the extra section in a book is *appendices*. The plural of the body part is *appendixes*

appetite noun 1 desire for food or drink 2 liking or willingness

appetizing or **appetising** adjective (of food) looking and smelling delicious and stimulating the appetite

applaud verb 1 to show approval of (something) by clapping your hands 2 to approve strongly of

applause noun (DRAMA) approval shown by clapping your hands

apple noun round firm fleshy fruit that grows on trees

appliance noun device with a specific function: kitchen appliances

applicable adjective relevant or appropriate

applicant noun person who applies for something

application noun 1 formal request 2 act of applying something to a particular use 3 diligent effort 4 act of putting something, such as a lotion or paint, onto a surface

appliqué [ap-**plee**-kay] noun 1 (ART) Appliqué is the art of decorating material by sewing other pieces of material on top of it

apply applies, applying, applied verb 1 to make a formal request

2 to put to practical use: He applied his mind to the problem 3 to put onto a surface: She applied lipstick to her mouth 4 to be relevant or appropriate: The legislation applies only to people living in England and Wales 5 **apply yourself** to concentrate on doing something or thinking about it

appoint verb 1 to assign (someone) to a job or position 2 to fix or decide (a time or place for something)

appointment noun
1 arrangement to meet a person 2 act of placing someone in a job 3 the job itself; position 4 **appointments** fixtures or fittings

apposite [**app**-o-zit] adjective appropriate and relevant: This year her theme was particularly apposite

appraise verb to estimate the value or quality of

appreciable [a-**pree**-shuh-bl] adjective large enough to be noticed: an appreciable difference
> **appreciably** adverb

appreciate verb 1 to value highly 2 to be aware of and understand 3 to be grateful for 4 to rise in value

appreciative adjective
1 understanding and enthusiastic 2 thankful and grateful
> **appreciatively** adverb

apprehend verb (formal) 1 to arrest and take into custody 2 to understand (something) fully

apprehensive adjective fearful or anxious about a future event
> **apprehension** noun 1 dread, anxiety 2 arrest 3 understanding
> **apprehensively** adverb

a b c d e f g h i j k l m n o p q r s t u v w x y z

A

apprentice noun **1** someone working for a skilled person for a fixed period in order to learn his or her trade ▷ verb **2** to take or place (someone) as an apprentice > **apprenticeship** noun period of learning a trade from a skilled worker

approach verb **1** to come near or nearer (to): As autumn approached, the trees began to change colour **2** to make a proposal or suggestion to **3** to begin to deal with (a matter) ▷ noun **4** act of coming close or closer: the approach of spring **5** suggestion or proposal made to someone **6** road or path that leads to a place **7** approximation

appropriate adjective **1** suitable or fitting: He didn't think jeans were appropriate for a vice-president ▷ verb **2** (formal) to take (something) for yourself **3** (formal) to put (money) aside for a particular purpose: The cash has already been appropriated for the youth club > **appropriately** adverb > **appropriation** noun

approval noun **1** agreement given to a plan or request **2** favourable opinion **3** on approval (of goods) with an option to be returned without payment if unsatisfactory

approve verb **1** to consider good or right **2** to authorize; agree to > **approved** adjective: an approved method > **approving** adjective: an approving look

approximate adjective **1** almost but not quite exact ▷ verb **approximate to 2** to come close to **3** to be almost the same as > **approximately** adverb

apricot noun **1** yellowish-orange juicy fruit like a small peach ▷ adjective **2** yellowish-orange

April noun **1** fourth month of the year **2** April fool victim of a practical joke played on April 1 (April Fools' Day)

apron noun **1** garment worn over the front of the body to protect the clothes **2** area at an airport or hangar for manoeuvring and loading aircraft **3** part of a stage in front of the curtain

apse noun arched or domed recess, especially in a church

apt adjective **1** having a specified tendency: They are apt to jump to the wrong conclusions **2** suitable: a very apt description **3** quick to learn: an apt pupil > **aptly** adverb

aptitude noun natural ability

aqua- prefix of or relating to water: aquatic

aquarium aquariums or aquaria noun **1** tank in which fish and other underwater creatures are kept **2** building containing such tanks

Aquarius noun eleventh sign of the zodiac, represented by a person carrying water

aquatic adjective **1** living in or near water **2** done in or on water: aquatic sports

aqueduct noun long bridge with many arches carrying a water supply over a valley

Arab noun **1** member of a group of people who used to live in Arabia but who now live throughout the Middle East and North Africa ▷ adjective **2** of the Arabs

Arabic noun **1** language of the Arabs ▷ adjective **2** of Arabic, Arabs or Arabia

arable *adjective* suitable for growing crops on

arbiter *noun* person empowered to judge in a dispute

arbitrary *adjective* based on personal choice or chance, rather than reason > **arbitrarily** *adverb*

arbitrate *verb* to settle a dispute by acting as an impartial referee

arc *noun* 1 part of a circle or other curve ▷ *verb* 2 to form an arc

> **WORD TIP**
> Do not confuse the spellings of *arc* and *ark*

arcade *noun* 1 covered passageway lined with shops 2 set of arches and their supporting columns

arcane *adjective* mysterious and secret

arch *noun* 1 curved structure supporting a bridge or roof 2 something curved 3 curved lower part of the foot ▷ *verb* 4 to (cause to) form an arch ▷ *adjective* 5 superior or knowing 6 coyly playful: *an arch smile*

arch- *prefix* chief, principal: *archenemy*

archaeology or **archeology** [ark-kee-**ol**-loj-ee] *noun* study of ancient cultures from their physical remains > **archaeological** *adjective*: *an archaeological dig* > **archaeologist** *noun* person who studies the physical remains of ancient cultures

archaic [ark-**kay**-ik] *adjective* 1 ancient 2 out-of-date

archangel [ark-ain-jell] *noun* chief angel

archbishop *noun* chief bishop

archdeacon *noun* Anglican priest ranking just below a bishop

archer *noun* person who shoots with a bow and arrow

archery *noun* sport in which people shoot at a target with a bow and arrow

archipelago archipelagos [ark-ee-**pel**-a-go] *noun* group of islands

architect [**ar**-kit-tekt] *noun* person qualified to design and supervise the construction of buildings

architecture *noun* 1 style in which a building is designed and built 2 designing and construction of buildings > **architectural** *adjective*: *a unique architectural style*

archive [**ark**-ive] *noun* (often plural) 1 collection of records or documents 2 place where these are kept ▷ *verb* 3 to store (something) in an archive

Arctic *noun* 1 the Arctic area around the North Pole ▷ *adjective* 2 of this region 3 **arctic** (*informal*) very cold

Arctic Circle *noun* imaginary circle around the northernmost part of the world

ardent *adjective* full of enthusiasm and passion > **ardently** *adverb*

ardour *noun* strong and passionate feeling of love or enthusiasm

arduous [**ard**-yoo-uss] *adjective* hard to accomplish and requiring much effort

are *verb* see **be**

area *noun* 1 particular part of a place, country or the world 2 size of a two-dimensional surface 3 subject field

arena *noun* 1 seated enclosure for sports events 2 area of a Roman

a
b
c
d
e
f
g
h
i
j
k
l
m
n
o
p
q
r
s
t
u
v
w
x
y
z

amphitheatre where gladiators fought **3** sphere of activity: *the political arena*

Argentinian [ar-jen-**tin**-ee-an] *adjective* **1** belonging to or relating to Argentina ▷ *noun* **2** someone from Argentina

arguable *adjective* (of an idea or point) not necessarily true or correct and therefore worth questioning > **arguably** *adverb*

argue argues, arguing, argued *verb* **1** to try to prove by giving reasons: *She argued that her client had been wrongly accused* **2** to debate **3** to quarrel

argument *noun* **1** quarrel **2** discussion **3** point presented for or against something

argumentative *adjective* always disagreeing with other people

aria [**ah**-ree-a] *noun* elaborate song for solo voice, especially one from an opera

arid *adjective* **1** parched, dry **2** uninteresting

Aries [**air**-reez] *noun* first sign of the zodiac, represented by a ram

arise arises, arising, arose, arisen *verb* **1** to come about **2** to come into notice **3** (*formal*) to get up from a sitting, kneeling or lying position

aristocracy aristocracies *noun* highest social class

aristocrat *noun* member of the aristocracy > **aristocratic** *adjective: a wealthy, aristocratic family*

arithmetic *noun* **1** calculation by or of numbers ▷ *adjective* **2** of arithmetic > **arithmetical** *adjective* of arithmetic > **arithmetically** *adverb*

ark *noun* (*Old Testament*) boat built by Noah, which survived the Flood

WORD TIP
Do not confuse the spellings of *arc* and *ark*

arm *noun* **1** either of the upper limbs from the shoulder to the wrist **2** sleeve of a garment **3** side of a chair **4** section of an organization: *the political arm of the armed forces* **5** arms **a** weapons used in a war **b** heraldic symbols of a family or country ▷ *verb* **6** to supply with weapons **7** to prepare (a bomb etc) for use

armada [ar-**mah**-da] *noun* large number of warships

armadillo armadillos *noun* small South American mammal covered in strong bony plates

Armageddon *noun* **1** (*New Testament*) final battle between good and evil at the end of the world **2** catastrophic conflict

armament *noun* **1** military weapons **2** preparation for war

armchair *noun* upholstered chair with side supports for the arms

armed *adjective* **1** carrying a weapon or weapons **2** (of an explosive device) prepared for use

armistice [**arm**-miss-stiss] *noun* agreed suspension of fighting

armour *noun* **1** metal clothing formerly worn to protect the body in battle **2** metal plating of tanks, warships, etc

armoured *adjective* covered with thick steel for protection from gunfire and other missiles: *an armoured car*

armoury armouries *noun* place where weapons are stored

armpit *noun* hollow under the arm at the shoulder

army armies *noun* military land forces of a nation

aroma *noun* pleasant smell > **aromatic** *adjective* having a distinctive pleasant smell

aromatherapy *noun* massage with fragrant oils to relieve tension

around *preposition, adverb* **1** on all sides (of) **2** from place to place (in) **3** somewhere in or near **4** (at) approximately

arouse *verb* **1** to stimulate; stir up **2** to awaken > **arousal** *noun: Thinking angry thoughts can provoke strong physical arousal*

arrange *verb* **1** to plan **2** to agree **3** to put in order: *He started to arrange the books in piles* **4** to adapt (music) for performance in a certain way > **arrangement** *noun: travel arrangements; flower arrangement*

array *noun* **1** impressive display or collection ▷ *verb* **2** to arrange in order

arrears *plural noun* **1** money owed: *mortgage arrears* **2 in arrears** late in paying a debt

arrest *verb* **1** to take (a person) into custody **2** to stop the movement or development of **3** to catch and hold (the attention) ▷ *noun* **4** act of taking a person into custody **5** slowing or stopping > **arresting** *adjective* attracting attention, striking

arrival *noun* **1** the act or time of arriving **2** person or thing that has just arrived

arrive *verb* **1** to reach a place or destination **2** to happen or come **3** (*informal*) to attain success

arrogant *adjective* proud and overbearing > **arrogance** *noun: the arrogance of those in power* > **arrogantly** *adverb*

arrow *noun* **1** pointed shaft shot from a bow **2** arrow-shaped sign or symbol used to show direction

arsenal *noun* place where arms and ammunition are made or stored

arsenic *noun* highly poisonous substance

arson *noun* crime of intentionally setting property on fire > **arsonist** *noun* person who sets property on fire intentionally

art *noun* **1** creation of works of beauty, especially paintings or sculpture **2** works of art collectively **3** skill **4 arts** literature, music, painting and sculpture, considered together

artefact [**ar**-tif-fact] *noun* something made by human beings

artery arteries *noun* **1** one of the tubes carrying blood from the heart **2** major road or means of communication

artful *adjective* cunning, wily > **artfully** *adverb*

arthritis *noun* painful inflammation of a joint or joints > **arthritic** *adjective* affected by arthritis

artichoke *noun* flower head of a thistle-like plant, cooked as a vegetable

article *noun* **1** LIBRARY written piece in a magazine or newspaper **2** item or object: *an article of clothing* **3** clause in a document **4** (*Grammar*) any of the words the, a or an

articulate adjective **1** able to express yourself clearly and coherently ▷ verb **2** to speak or express (something) clearly and coherently > **articulately** adverb > **articulation** noun **1** expressing of an idea in words **2** process of articulating a speech sound

artificial adjective **1** not occurring naturally; man-made: artificial colouring **2** made in imitation of something natural **3** not sincere: an artificial smile > **artificially** adverb

artillery noun **1** large, powerful guns **2** branch of the army who use these

artist noun **1** person who produces works of art, especially paintings or sculpture **2** person skilled at something

artiste [ar-**teest**] noun professional entertainer such as a singer or dancer

artistic adjective **1** able to create good paintings, sculpture or other works of art **2** concerning or involving art or artists > **artistically** adverb

artistry noun artistic skill: his artistry as a cellist

arty artier, artiest adjective (informal) interest in painting, sculpture and other works of art

as conjunction **1** while or when **2** in the way that **3** that which: do as you are told **4** since or seeing that **5** for instance ▷ adverb, conjunction **6** used to indicate amount or extent in comparisons: He is as tall as you (are) ▷ preposition **7** in the role of; being: As a mother, I am concerned

asbestos noun fibrous mineral which does not burn

ascend [ass-**end**] verb (formal) to go or move up

ascendancy noun (formal) condition of being dominant

ascendant adjective **1** dominant or influential ▷ noun **2 in the ascendant** increasing in power or influence

ascent noun upward journey

ascertain [ass-er-**tain**] verb (formal) to find (something) out definitely

ascribe verb **1** to attribute or put (something) down (to): His stomach pains were ascribed to his intake of pork **2** to attribute (a particular quality to someone or something)

ash noun **1** powdery substance left when something is burnt **2** tree with grey bark **3 ashes** remains after burning, especially of a human body after cremation

ashamed adjective feeling shame

ashen adjective grey or pale

ashore adverb towards or on land

ashtray noun receptacle for tobacco ash and cigarette butts

Asia noun largest continent, with Europe on its western side, the Arctic to the north, the Pacific to the east, and the Indian Ocean to the south. Asia includes several island groups, including Japan, Indonesia and the Philippines

Asian adjective **1** of the continent of Asia or any of its peoples or languages ▷ noun **2** someone from Asia or a descendant of one

aside adverb **1** to one side **2** out of other people's hearing ▷ noun **3** remark not meant to be heard by everyone present

ask verb **1** to say or write (something) in a form that requires an answer **2** to make a request or demand **3** to invite **4 asking for trouble** doing something that will cause problems

askew adverb, adjective to one side; crooked

asleep adjective **1** not awake; sleeping **2** (of limbs) numb

asparagus noun plant whose shoots are cooked as a vegetable

aspect noun **1** feature or element **2** position facing a particular direction: *The southern aspect of the cottage faces over fields* **3** appearance or look

asphalt noun black hard tarlike substance used for road surfaces etc

aspiration noun strong desire or aim

aspire verb **aspire to** to yearn for: *He aspires to public office* > **aspiring** adjective: *an aspiring actor*

aspirin noun **1** drug used to relieve pain and fever **2** tablet of this

ass noun **1** donkey **2** (informal) stupid person

assailant noun someone who attacks another person

assassin noun person who murders a prominent person

assassinate verb to murder (a political or religious leader) > **assassination** noun: *the assassination of Martin Luther King*

assault noun **1** violent attack ▷ verb **2** to attack violently

assegai [ass-a-guy] noun slender spear used in S Africa

assemble verb **1** to collect or congregate **2** to put together the parts of (a machine)

assembly assemblies noun **1** assembled group **2** assembling

assent [as-sent] noun **1** agreement or consent ▷ verb **2** to agree

assert verb **1** to declare forcefully **2** to insist upon (your rights etc) **3 assert yourself** to put yourself forward forcefully

assertion noun firm statement, usually made without evidence

assertive adjective confident and direct in dealing with others > **assertively** adverb > **assertiveness** noun: *his lack of assertiveness*

assess verb **1** to judge the worth or importance of **2** to estimate the value of (income or property) for taxation purposes > **assessment** noun evaluation of someone or something

assessor noun person whose job is to assess the value of something

asset noun **1** valuable or useful person or thing **2 assets** property that a person or firm can sell, especially to pay debts

assign verb **1** to appoint (someone) to a job or task **2** to give a task or duty (to someone) **3** to set apart (a place or time) for a particular event

assignation [ass-ig-**nay**-shn] noun (literary) secret meeting with someone, especially a lover

assignment noun **1** job someone is given to do **2** act of assigning

assimilate verb **1** to learn and understand (information) **2** to absorb or be absorbed > **assimilation** noun: *assimilation of knowledge; assimilation of minority ethnic groups*

assist verb to give help or support
> **assistance** noun help or support

assistant noun **1** helper ▷ adjective
2 junior or deputy: an assistant
teacher

associate verb **1** to connect in
the mind **2** to mix socially ▷ noun
3 partner in business **4** friend or
companion ▷ adjective **5** having
partial rights or subordinate
status: associate member

association noun **1** society or club
2 act of associating **3** friendship:
Their association had to remain a
secret **4** mental connection of
ideas or feelings

assonance noun rhyming of vowel
sounds but not consonants, as in
time and light

assorted adjective consisting of
various types mixed together:
assorted swimsuits

assortment noun group of similar
things that are different sizes and
colours

assume verb **1** to take to be
true without proof: I assumed
that he would turn up **2** to take
(something) upon yourself: He
assumed command **3** to pretend: I
assumed indifference

assumption noun **1** belief that
something is true, without
thinking about it **2** taking of
power or responsibility: their
assumption of power in 1997

assurance noun **1** something
said which is intended to make
people less worried **2** confidence
3 insurance that provides for
events that are certain to happen,
such as death

assure verb **1** to promise or
guarantee **2** to convince **3** to
make (something) certain **4** to
insure against loss of life

asterisk noun **1** star-shaped
symbol (*) used in printing or
writing to indicate a footnote etc
▷ verb **2** to mark with an asterisk

astern adverb **1** at or towards the
stern of a ship **2** backwards

asteroid noun any of the small
planets that orbit the sun
between Mars and Jupiter

asthma [**ass**-ma] noun illness
causing difficulty in breathing
> **asthmatic** adjective suffering
from asthma

astonish verb to surprise greatly
> **astonished** adjective greatly
surprised > **astonishing** adjective:
an astonishing display of physical
strength > **astonishingly** adverb
> **astonishment** noun: We won,
much to our astonishment

astound verb to overwhelm
with amazement > **astounded**
adjective: I was astounded by its
beauty > **astounding** adjective:
The results are quite astounding

astray adverb off the right path

astride adjective **1** with a leg on
either side **2** with legs far apart
▷ preposition **3** with a leg on either
side of

astringent [ass-**trin**-jent]
adjective **1** causing contraction of
body tissue **2** checking the flow of
blood from a cut **3** severe or harsh
▷ noun **4** astringent substance

astro- prefix involving the stars
and planets: astronomy; astronaut

astrology noun study of the
alleged influence of the stars,
planets and moon on human
affairs > **astrologer** noun
person who studies astrology

> astrological *adjective:* *astrological predictions*

astronaut *noun* person trained for travelling in space

astronomical *adjective* **1** involved with or relating to astronomy **2** extremely large in amount **> astronomically** *adverb*

astronomy *noun* scientific study of stars and planets

Astroturf ® *noun* artificial grass

astute *adjective* perceptive or shrewd: *an astute diplomat* **> astutely** *adverb* **> astuteness** *noun: the astuteness of his observations*

asunder *adverb* (*literary*) into parts or pieces

asylum [ass-**eye**-lum] *noun* **1** refuge or sanctuary **2** (*old-fashioned*) mental hospital

asymmetrical [ay-sim-**met**-ri-kl] or **asymmetric** *adjective* unbalanced or with one half not exactly the same as the other half **> asymmetry** *noun* lack of symmetry

at *preposition* **1** indicating location or position: *She met us at the airport* **2** towards or in the direction of: *She was staring at the wall behind him* **3** indicating position in time: *We arrived at 2.30* **4** engaged in: *children at play* **5** during the passing of: *She works at night as a nurse's aide* **6** for or in exchange for: *Crude oil is selling at its highest price for 14 years* **7** indicating the object of an emotion: *I'm angry at you because you were rude to me*

atheist [**ayth**-ee-ist] *noun* someone who believes there is no God **> atheism** *noun* belief

that there is no God **> atheistic** *adjective:* *atheistic philosophers*

athlete *noun* PE person trained in or good at athletics

athletic *adjective* PE **1** physically fit or strong **2** relating to an athlete or athletics **> athletically** *adverb*

athletics *plural noun* track-and-field sports such as running, jumping, throwing, etc

Atlantic *noun* ocean separating North and South America from Europe and Africa

atlas atlases *noun* GEOGRAPHY book of maps

atmosphere *noun* **1** mass of gases surrounding a heavenly body, especially the earth **2** air in a particular place: *a musty atmosphere* **3** prevailing tone or mood (of a place etc): *a relaxed atmosphere* **4** ENGLISH mood created by the writer of a novel or play **> atmospheric** *adjective* **1** relating to the atmosphere of a planet **2** (of a place or a piece of music) having a quality which is interesting or exciting and which evokes an emotion

atom *noun* **1** smallest unit of matter which can take part in a chemical reaction **2** very small amount

atomic *adjective* **1** relating to or using atomic bombs or atomic energy **2** relating to atoms

atomic bomb *noun* bomb in which the energy is provided by nuclear fission

atone *verb* (*formal*) to make amends (for sin or wrongdoing) **> atonement** *noun: a gesture of atonement*

atrocious adjective **1** extremely cruel or wicked **2** horrifying or shocking **3** (informal) very bad > **atrociously** adverb

atrocity atrocities noun act of cruelty

attach verb **1** to join, fasten or connect **2** to attribute or ascribe: He attaches particular importance to the proposed sale

attaché [at-**tash**-shay] noun specialist attached to a diplomatic mission: the Russian Cultural Attaché

attached adjective **1** married, engaged or in an exclusive sexual relationship **2 attached to** fond of

attachment noun **1** affection or regard for **2** piece of equipment attached to a tool or machine to do a particular job **3** (Computing) file attached to an e-mail message

attack verb **1** to launch a physical assault (against) **2** to criticize: He attacked the government's economic policies **3** to set about (a job or problem) with vigour **4** to affect adversely: fungal diseases that attack crops **5** to take the initiative in a game or sport > noun **6** act of attacking **7** sudden bout of illness > **attacker** noun person who attacks someone

attain verb (formal) to achieve, accomplish or reach: He eventually attained the rank of major > **attainable** adjective: an attainable goal > **attainment** noun accomplishment

attempt verb **1** to try; make an effort: They attempted to escape > noun **2** effort or endeavour: He made no attempt to go for the ball

attend verb **1** to be present at **2** to go regularly to a school, college, etc **3** to look after: They were attended by numerous servants **4 attend to** to apply yourself to (something) > **attendance** noun **1** attending **2** number attending

attendant noun **1** person who assists, guides or provides a service ▷ adjective **2** accompanying: increasing road traffic and its attendant pollution

attention noun **1** concentrated direction of the mind **2** consideration **3** care **4** alert position in military drill

attentive adjective **1** giving attention: an attentive audience **2** considerately helpful > **attentively** adverb > **attentiveness** noun **1** alertness **2** thoughtfulness

attest verb (often followed by to) to affirm or prove the truth of

attic noun space or room within the roof of a house

attire noun (formal) clothing

attitude noun **1** way of thinking and behaving **2** way of sitting, standing or lying

attorney [at-**turn**-ee] noun **1** person legally appointed to act for another **2** (US, SAfr) lawyer

attract verb **1** to arouse the interest or admiration of **2** (of a magnet) to draw (something) closer by exerting a force on it

attraction noun **1** act or quality of attracting **2** object or place people visit for interest or pleasure **3** quality that attracts someone or something

attractive adjective **1** pleasant to look at or be with:

2 interesting and possibly advantageous: *an attractive proposition* > **attractively** *adverb* > **attractiveness** *noun*: *his attractiveness to women*

attribute *verb* **1** attribute something to something to regard something as belonging to or produced by: *a play attributed to Shakespeare* ▷ *noun* **2** quality or feature representative of a person or thing > **attributable** *adjective*: *deaths attributable to smoking* > **attribution** *noun* act of attributing

attrition *noun* constant wearing down to weaken or destroy

attuned *adjective* accustomed or well adjusted (to something)

aubergine [oh-bur-zheen] *noun* (Brit) dark purple tropical fruit, cooked and eaten as a vegetable. It is also called an *eggplant*

auburn *adjective* (of hair) reddish-brown

auction *noun* **1** public sale in which articles are sold to the highest bidder ▷ *verb* **2** to sell (something) by auction

auctioneer *noun* person who conducts an auction

audacious *adjective* recklessly bold or daring: *an audacious escape from jail* > **audaciously** *adverb* > **audacity** *noun* audacious behaviour

audi- *prefix* involving hearing or sound: *audible; auditorium*

audible *adjective* loud enough to be heard: *She spoke in a barely audible whisper* > **audibly** *adverb*

audience *noun* **1** group of spectators or listeners **2** private or formal meeting with an important person: *an audience with the Queen*

audio *adjective* **1** of sound or hearing **2** of or for the transmission or reproduction of sound

audit *noun* **1** official examination of business accounts ▷ *verb* **2** to examine (business accounts) officially > **auditor** *noun* person qualified to audit accounts

audition *noun* **1** test of a performer's ability for a particular role or job ▷ *verb* **2** to test (someone) or be tested in an audition

auditorium *noun* auditoriums or auditoria *noun* area of a concert hall or theatre where the audience sits

augment *verb* (formal) to increase or enlarge

August *noun* eighth month of the year

aunt *noun* **1** father's or mother's sister **2** uncle's wife

au pair [oh **pair**] *noun* young foreign person who does housework in return for board and lodging

aura *noun* distinctive air or quality of a person or thing

aural [rhymes with **floral**] *adjective* relating to or done through the sense of hearing

auspices [**aw**-spiss-siz] *plural noun* (formal) **under the auspices of** with the support and approval of

auspicious *adjective* (formal) showing signs of future success: *It was an auspicious start to the month* > **auspiciously** *adverb*

austere *adjective* **1** stern or severe **2** without luxuries **3** severely simple or plain > **austerely** *adverb*

A

Australasia [ost-ral-**lay**-sha] noun Australia, New Zealand and neighbouring islands in the Pacific > **Australasian** adjective

Australia noun smallest continent and the largest island in the world, situated between the Indian Ocean and the Pacific

Austrian adjective **1** belonging or relating to Austria ▷ noun **2** someone from Austria

authentic adjective known to be real; genuine > **authentically** adverb > **authenticity** noun: doubts cast on the painting's authenticity

author noun **1** ENGLISH writer of a book etc **2** originator or creator

> **WORD TIP**
> Use author to talk about both men and women writers, as authoress is now felt to be insulting

authoritarian adjective insisting on strict obedience to authority: thirty years of authoritarian government > **authoritarianism** noun **1** state of being authoritarian **2** belief that the state has a right to control its citizens' lives

authoritative adjective **1** recognized as being reliable **2** possessing authority > **authoritatively** adverb

authority authorities noun **1** power to command or control others: the authority of the state **2** GEOGRAPHY (Brit) local government department: local health authorities **3** expert in a particular field: the world's leading authority on fashion **4** the **authorities** people with the power to make decisions: A third escapee turned himself in to the authorities

authorize or **authorise** verb **1** to give authority to **2** to give permission for > **authorization** noun: authorization to use military force

auto- prefix self-: autobiography

autobiography autobiographies noun account of a person's life written by that person > **autobiographical** adjective (of a piece of writing) relating to events in the life of the author

autograph noun **1** handwritten signature of a (famous) person ▷ verb **2** to write your signature on or in

automatic adjective **1** (of a device) operating mechanically by itself **2** (of a process) performed by automatic equipment **3** done without conscious thought **4** (of a firearm) self-loading **5** occurring as a necessary consequence: The penalty for murder is an automatic life sentence ▷ noun **6** self-loading firearm **7** vehicle in which the gears change automatically as the vehicle's speed changes > **automatically** adverb

automobile noun (US) motor car

autonomous [aw-**ton**-nom-uss] adjective **1** having self-government **2** independent of others > **autonomy** noun self-government

autopsy autopsies noun examination of a corpse to determine the cause of death

autumn noun season between summer and winter > **autumnal** adjective: the autumnal colour of the trees

auxiliary auxiliaries adjective **1** secondary or supplementary: auxiliary fuel tanks **2** supporting ▷ noun **3** person or thing that supplements or supports: nursing auxiliaries

auxiliary verb noun verb used to form the tense, voice or mood of another, such as will in I will go

avail verb **1** to be of use or advantage (to) **2** avail yourself of to make use of ▷ noun **3** use or advantage: to no avail

available adjective **1** obtainable or accessible **2** ready for work or free for people to talk to ▷ **availability** noun: the easy availability of guns

avalanche [av-a-lahnsh] noun **1** mass of snow or ice falling down a mountain **2** sudden overwhelming quantity of anything

avant-garde [av-ong-**gard**] noun **1** group of innovators, especially in the arts ▷ adjective **2** innovative and progressive

avarice [av-a-riss] noun (formal) greed for wealth and possessions ▷ **avaricious** adjective greedy for wealth and possessions

avenge verb to take revenge in retaliation for (harm done) or on behalf of (a person harmed) ▷ **avenger** noun

avenue noun **1** wide street **2** road between two rows of trees **3** means of doing something: We are exploring a number of avenues

average noun **1** typical or normal amount or quality **2** result obtained by adding quantities together and dividing the total by the number of quantities **3** on

average usually or typically: Men are, on average, taller than women ▷ adjective **4** usual or typical: the average American teenager **5** calculated as an average ▷ verb **6** to calculate the average of **7** to amount to as an average: Monthly sales averaged more than 110,000

averse adjective averse to disinclined or unwilling: He's not averse to publicity

aversion noun **1** strong dislike **2** person or thing disliked

avert verb **1** to turn away: He had to avert his eyes **2** to ward off: a final attempt to avert war

avian adjective relating to birds

aviary aviaries noun large cage or enclosure for birds

aviation noun art or science of flying aircraft

aviator noun (old-fashioned) pilot of an aircraft

avid adjective **1** keen or enthusiastic **2** greedy (for) ▷ **avidly** adverb

avocado avocados noun pear-shaped tropical fruit with a leathery green skin and yellowish-green flesh

avoid verb **1** to prevent from happening **2** to refrain from doing **3** to keep away from ▷ **avoidable** adjective: This accident was avoidable ▷ **avoidance** noun: the avoidance of stress

avowed adjective (formal) **1** openly declared: an avowed supporter of vegetarianism **2** (of a belief or aim) strongly held: the council's avowed intention to stamp out racism ▷ **avowedly** adverb

avuncular adjective friendly and helpful in manner towards younger people, rather like an uncle

await verb **1** to wait for **2** to be in store for

awake awakes, awaking, awoke, awoken verb **1** to emerge or rouse from sleep **2** to become or cause to become alert ▷ adjective **3** not sleeping **4** alert

awaken verb **1** to awake **2** to cause (someone) to be aware of

award verb **1** to give (something, such as a prize) formally ▷ noun **2** something awarded, such as a prize

aware adjective having knowledge, informed > **awareness** noun: an awareness of green issues

awash adverb, adjective washed over by water

away adverb **1** from a place: go away **2** to another place: put that gun away **3** out of existence: fade away **4** continuously: laughing away ▷ adjective **5** not present **6** distant: two miles away **7** (Sport) played on an opponent's ground

awe (formal) noun wonder and respect mixed with dread

awesome adjective **1** inspiring awe **2** (informal) excellent or outstanding

awful adjective **1** very bad or unpleasant **2** (informal) very great: It took an awful lot of courage > **awfully** adverb **1** in an unpleasant way **2** (informal) very

awkward adjective **1** clumsy or ungainly **2** embarrassed **3** difficult **4** inconvenient > **awkwardly** adverb > **awkwardness** noun **1** shyness **2** clumsiness

awning noun canvas roof supported by a frame to give protection against the weather

awry [a-**rye**] adverb, adjective **1** with a twist to one side; askew **2** wrong or not as planned: Why had their plans gone so badly awry?

axe axes, axing, axed noun **1** tool with a sharp blade for felling trees or chopping wood **2** (informal) dismissal from employment etc ▷ verb **3** (informal) to dismiss (employees), restrict (expenditure) or terminate (a project)

axiom noun **1** generally accepted principle **2** self-evident statement > **axiomatic** adjective self-evident

axis axes noun MATHS **1** (imaginary) line round which a body can rotate or about which an object or geometrical figure is symmetrical **2** one of two fixed lines on a graph, against which quantities or positions are measured

axle noun shaft on which a wheel or pair of wheels turns

ayatollah noun Islamic religious leader in Iran

azure [az-**yoor**] (literary) noun **1** deep blue colour of a clear sky ▷ adjective **2** deep blue

b

babble verb **1** to talk excitedly or foolishly

baboon noun large monkey with a pointed face and a long tail

baby babies noun **1** very young child; infant **2** (informal) sweetheart ▷ adjective **3** comparatively small of its type > **babyhood** noun period of being a baby > **babyish** adjective immature

baby-sit baby-sits, baby-sitting, baby-sat verb to take care of a child while the parents are out > **baby-sitter** noun person who baby-sits > **baby-sitting** noun taking care of a child while the parents are out

baccalaureate noun internationally recognized course of study made up of several different subjects, offered by some schools as an alternative to A levels

bach [batch] (NZ) noun **1** small holiday cottage ▷ verb **2** to look after oneself when one's spouse is away

bachelor noun unmarried man

back noun **1** rear part of the human body, from the neck to the pelvis; also the corresponding part of an animal's body **2** part or side of an object opposite the front **3** (Ball games) defensive player or position ▷ verb **4** to move (a car) backwards **5** to provide money for (a person or organization) **6** to bet on the success of (a competitor) **7 back onto** to have the back facing forwards (something) ▷ adjective **8** at, to or towards the rear ▷ adverb **9** at, to or towards the rear **10** to or towards the original starting point or condition > **back up** verb to support (someone)

backbone noun **1** spinal column **2** strength of character

backdate verb to make (a document or arrangement) valid from an earlier date than the one on which it is completed

backdrop noun **1** the background to a situation or event

backer noun person who gives (someone or something) financial support

backfire verb **1** (of a plan) to have the opposite result to the one intended; fail **2** (of an engine) to make a loud noise like an explosion

background noun **1** events or circumstances that help to explain something **2** a person's social circumstances, education and experience **3** part of a scene or picture furthest from the viewer

backing noun **1** support or help **2** music that accompanies a pop song

backlash noun sudden and hostile reaction

backlog noun accumulation of things still to be done

backpack noun large bag carried on the back

backside noun (informal) buttocks

backward adjective **1** directed towards the back **2** (of a country or society) not having modern industries or technology **3** (of a child) unable to learn as quickly as other children ▷ adverb **4** the same as **backwards** ▷ **backwardness** noun being backward

backwards adverb **1** in reverse **2** in the reverse direction **3** behind

bacon noun salted or smoked pig meat

bacteria plural noun very tiny organisms which can cause disease ▷ **bacterial** adjective: a bacterial infection

> **WORD TIP**
> The word bacteria is plural. The singular form is bacterium

bad worse, worst adjective **1** of poor quality **2** lacking skill or talent **3** harmful **4** immoral or evil **5** rotten or decayed **6** unpleasant ▷ **badly** adverb: They have behaved badly ▷ **badness** noun being bad

bade verb a past tense of **bid**

badge noun piece of metal, plastic or cloth worn to show membership of an organization, support for a cause, etc

badger noun **1** burrowing animal of Europe, Asia and North America with a black and white stripe ▷ verb **2** to pester or harass

badminton noun game played with rackets and a shuttlecock, which is hit back and forth over a high net

Bafana bafana [bah-**fan**-na] plural noun (SAfr) South African national soccer team

baffle verb to perplex or puzzle ▷ **baffled** adjective: The police

are baffled ▷ **baffling** adjective perplexing or puzzling

bag noun container for carrying things in

baggage noun suitcases packed for a journey

baggy baggier, baggiest adjective (of clothes) hanging loosely

bagpipes plural noun musical wind instrument with reed pipes and an inflatable bag

bail noun **1** (Law) money deposited with a court as security for a person's reappearance in court **2** (Cricket) either of two wooden bars across the tops of the stumps ▷ **bail out** verb **1** to remove (water) from a boat **2** to make an emergency parachute jump from an aircraft

bailiff noun **1** law officer who makes sure that the decisions of a court are obeyed **2** landlord's agent

Baisakhi noun Sikh festival celebrated every April

bait noun **1** piece of food put on a hook or in a trap in order to catch fish or animals ▷ verb **2** to put a piece of food on or in (a hook or trap) **3** to persecute or tease

baize noun woollen fabric, usually green, used to cover billiard and card tables

bake verb **1** to cook (food) by dry heat, as in an oven **2** to heat (earth or clay) until it hardens

baker noun person whose business is to make or sell bread, cakes, etc ▷ **bakery** noun place where bread, cakes, etc are baked or sold

bakkie [**buck**-ee] noun (SAfr) small truck

balance noun 1 state in which a weight or amount is evenly distributed 2 amount that remains: *the balance of what you owe* 3 difference between the credits and debits of an account ▷ verb 4 to remain steady 5 to equalize the money going into and coming out of (an account) > **balanced** adjective 1 having weight evenly distributed 2 (of a report, etc.) presenting information in a fair and objective way 3 (PSHE) (of a diet) having all the nutrients essential to maintain health

balcony balconies noun 1 platform on the outside of a building with a rail along the outer edge 2 area of upstairs seats in a theatre or cinema

bald adjective 1 having little or no hair on the scalp 2 plain or blunt > **baldly** adverb plainly or bluntly > **baldness** noun being bald

bale noun large bundle of hay or paper tightly bound together > **bale out** verb same as **bail out**

balk or **baulk** verb (followed by at) to object to and refuse to do (something)

ball noun 1 round or nearly round object, especially one used in games 2 large formal social event at which people dance

ballad noun 1 long song or poem that tells a story 2 slow romantic pop song

ballast noun substance, such as sand, used to stabilize a ship when it is not carrying cargo

ballerina noun female ballet dancer

ballet [**bal**-lay] noun 1 classical style of expressive dancing based on conventional steps 2 theatrical performance of this

balloon noun 1 inflatable rubber bag used as a plaything or decoration 2 large bag inflated with air or gas, that travels through the air with passengers in a basket underneath

ballot noun 1 method of voting in which other people do not see how you vote 2 actual vote or paper indicating a person's choice ▷ verb 3 to ask for a vote from (people)

ballpoint or **ballpoint pen** noun pen with a tiny ball bearing as a writing point

ballroom noun very large room used for dancing or formal balls

balm [**bahm**] noun sweet-smelling soothing ointment

balmy balmier, balmiest adjective (of weather) mild and pleasant

balsa [**bawl**-sa] noun very light wood from a tropical American tree

balustrade noun railing or wall on a balcony or staircase

bamboo noun tall tropical plant with hard hollow stems used for making furniture

ban bans, banning, banned verb 1 to prohibit or forbid (something) officially ▷ noun 2 official prohibition

banal [ban-**nahl**] adjective ordinary and unoriginal > **banality** noun being ordinary and unoriginal

banana noun long curved fruit with a yellow skin

band noun 1 group of musicians playing together 2 group of

a b c d e f g h i j k l m n o p q r s t u v w x y z

people with a common purpose **3** strip of some material, used to hold objects **4** (*Physics*) range of frequencies or wavelengths between two limits > **band together** *verb* to unite

bandage *noun* **1** piece of material used to cover a wound or wrap an injured limb > *verb* **2** to cover (a wound) with a bandage

bandit *noun* robber, especially a member of an armed gang

bandstand *noun* roofed outdoor platform for a band

bandwagon *noun* **jump on the bandwagon** to become involved in something that seems assured of success

bandy bandies, bandying, bandied *verb* **1** to exchange (words) in a heated manner **2** to use (a name, term, etc) frequently

bane *noun* person or thing that causes misery or distress

bang *noun* **1** short loud explosive noise **2** hard blow or loud knock > *verb* **3** to hit or knock (something), especially with a loud noise **4** to close (a door) noisily

Bangladeshi [bang-glad-**desh**-ee] *adjective* **1** belonging or relating to Bangladesh > *noun* **2** person from Bangladesh

bangle *noun* decorative ring worn round the arm or the ankle

banish *verb* **1** to send (someone) into exile **2** to get rid of (something) > **banishment** *noun* being banished

banisters *plural noun* railing supported by posts on a staircase

banjo banjos or banjoes *noun* guitar-like musical instrument with a circular body

bank *noun* **1** business that looks after people's money **2** any supply, store or reserve **3** sloping side of an area of raised ground **4** sloping ground at the side of a river **5** long row or mass of something > *verb* **6** to deposit (cash or cheques) in a bank **7** (of an aircraft) to tip to one side on turning > **banker** *noun* manager or owner of a bank > **banking** *noun* business activity of banks > **bank on** *verb* to rely on (something happening)

bank holiday *noun* public holiday, when banks are officially closed

banknote *noun* piece of paper money

bankrupt *noun* **1** person declared by a court to be unable to pay his or her debts > *adjective* **2** financially ruined > *verb* **3** to make (someone) bankrupt > **bankruptcy** *noun* bankrupt state

banksia *noun* (*Aust*) Australian evergreen tree or shrub

banner *noun* **1** long strip of cloth with a message or slogan on it **2** placard carried in a demonstration or procession **3** advertisement that extends across the top of a web page

banquet *noun* grand formal dinner

banter *noun* teasing or joking conversation

baobab [**bay**-oh-bab] *noun* small fruit tree that grows in Africa and northern Australia

baptism noun RE ceremony in which someone is baptized ▷ **baptismal** adjective

Baptist noun member of a Protestant church that believes in adult baptism by immersion

baptize or **baptise** verb to sprinkle water on (someone) or immerse (someone) in water, as a sign that he or she has become a Christian

bar bars, barring, barred noun **1** counter or room where alcoholic drinks are served **2** long straight piece of metal, wood, etc **3** solid, usually rectangular block, of any material: a bar of soap **4** (Music) one of the many very short sections into which any piece of music is divided. Each bar in a piece usually contains the same set number of beats **5** unit of atmospheric pressure **6 the Bar** profession of a barrister ▷ verb **7** to secure (a door) with a bar **8** to obstruct (the way) **9** to ban or forbid (someone or something) ▷ preposition **10** except for

barb noun point facing in the opposite direction to the main point of a fish-hook etc

barbarian noun member of a wild or uncivilized people

barbaric adjective cruel or brutal ▷ **barbarity** noun state of being barbaric

barbecue barbecues, barbecuing, barbecued noun **1** grill on which food is cooked over hot charcoal, usually outdoors **2** outdoor party at which barbecued food is served ▷ verb **3** to cook (food) on a barbecue

barbed adjective unkind or spiteful remark that appears innocent

barbed wire noun strong wire with protruding sharp points

barber noun person who cuts men's hair and shaves beards

barbiturate noun drug that is used to help people sleep

bar code noun arrangement of numbers and lines on a package, which can be electronically scanned at a checkout to give the price of the goods

bard noun (literary) poet

bare adjective **1** unclothed or naked **2** without the natural or usual covering **3** empty **4** plain, simple and unadorned **5** just sufficient ▷ verb **6** to uncover (something)

barefoot adjective, adverb not wearing anything on the feet

barely adverb only just

bargain noun **1** agreement establishing what each party will give, receive or perform in a matter that involves them both **2** something bought or offered at a low price ▷ verb **3** to negotiate the terms of an agreement ▷ **bargain for** verb to anticipate (something) or take (something) into account

barge noun **1** flat-bottomed boat used to transport freight ▷ verb **2** (informal) to push violently

bark noun **1** loud harsh cry of a dog **2** tough outer layer of a tree ▷ verb **3** (of a dog) to make its typical cry **4** to shout (something) in an angry tone

barley noun tall grasslike plant grown for grain

bar mitzvah noun ceremony that takes place on a Jewish boy's

A
B
C
D
E
F
G
H
I
J
K
L
M
N
O
P
Q
R
S
T
U
V
W
X
Y
Z

13th birthday, after which he is regarded as an adult

barmy barmier, barmiest *adjective* (*informal*) insane

barn *noun* large building on a farm used for storing grain

barnacle *noun* shellfish that lives attached to rocks, ship bottoms, etc

barometer *noun* instrument that measures air pressure and shows when the weather is changing

baron *noun* member of the lowest rank of nobility > **baronial** *adjective* of or relating to a baron

baroness *noun* woman who has the rank of baron or who is the wife of a baron

barracks *plural noun* building where soldiers live

barracuda *noun* large tropical sea fish with sharp teeth

barrage [bar-rahzh] *noun* 1 continuous delivery of questions, complaints, etc 2 continuous artillery fire 3 artificial barrier across a river to control the water level

barrel *noun* 1 cylindrical container with rounded sides and flat ends 2 tube-shaped part of a gun through which bullets are fired

barren *adjective* 1 (of a woman or female animal) incapable of having babies or young; infertile 2 (of land) unable to support the growth of crops, fruit, etc > **barrenness** *noun* being barren

barricade *noun* 1 barrier, especially one put up hastily for defence > *verb* 2 to put up a barricade across (an entrance)

barrier *noun* anything that prevents access, progress or agreement

barrister *noun* (Brit, Aust, NZ) lawyer qualified to plead in a higher court

barrow *noun* 1 wheelbarrow 2 movable stall used by street traders

barter *verb* 1 to trade (goods) in exchange for other goods > *noun* 2 trade by the exchange of goods

base *noun* 1 bottom or supporting part of anything 2 centre of operations, organization or supply 3 (*Chemistry*) compound that reacts with an acid to form a salt > *verb* 4 (followed by *at, in*) to position or place (someone) somewhere 5 **base something on** or **upon** to make up the basic elements of something using > *adjective* 6 dishonourable or immoral 7 of inferior quality or value

baseball *noun* team game in which runs are scored by hitting a ball with a bat then running round four bases

basement *noun* partly or wholly underground storey of a building

bases *noun* [bay-seez] the plural of **basis**

bash (*informal*) *verb* 1 to hit (someone) violently or forcefully > *noun* 2 heavy blow

bashful *adjective* shy or modest

basic *adjective* 1 of or forming a base or basis 2 elementary or simple > **basically** *adverb*: It's *basically a vegan diet* > **basics** *plural noun* essential main principles, facts, etc

basilica noun rectangular church with a rounded end and two aisles

basin noun 1 round open container 2 sink for washing the hands and face 3 bowl of land from which water runs into a river

basis bases noun essential main principle from which something is started or developed

bask verb to lie in or be exposed to something, especially pleasant warmth

basket noun container made of thin strips of cane woven together

basketball noun team game in which points are scored by throwing the ball through a high horizontal hoop

bass[1] [rhymes with **lace**] noun 1 man with a very deep singing voice 2 musical instrument that provides the rhythm and lowest part in the harmonies

bass[2] basses [rhymes with **gas**] noun edible sea fish

basset hound noun smooth-haired dog with short legs and long ears

bassoon noun low-pitched woodwind instrument

bastard noun 1 (offensive) despicable person 2 (old-fashioned) person whose parents were not married when he or she was born

baste verb to moisten (meat) during cooking with hot fat

bastion noun something that protects a system or way of life

bat bats, batting, batted noun 1 any of various types of club used to hit the ball in certain sports 2 mouselike flying animal, active at night ▷ verb 3 to strike (a ball) with or as if with a bat

batch noun group of people or things dealt with at the same time

bated adjective **with bated breath** in suspense or fear

bath noun 1 large container in which to wash the body 2 act of washing in such a container 3 baths public swimming pool ▷ verb 4 to wash in a bath

bathe verb 1 to swim in open water for pleasure 2 to apply liquid to (the skin or a wound) in order to cleanse or soothe 3 (followed by in) to fill (a place) with something: bathed in sunlight > **bather** noun person who swims > **bathing** noun swimming or washing

bathroom noun room with a bath or shower, washbasin and, usually, a toilet

baton noun 1 thin stick used by the conductor of an orchestra 2 short stick passed from one runner to another in a relay race 3 police officer's truncheon

batsman batsmen noun (Cricket) person who bats or specializes in batting

battalion noun army unit consisting of three or more companies

batten noun strip of wood fixed to something, especially to hold it in place > **batten down** verb to secure (something) with battens

batter verb 1 to hit (someone) repeatedly ▷ noun 2 mixture of flour, eggs and milk, used

in cooking > **battering** noun
beating or defeat

battery batteries noun **1** device
that produces electricity in a
torch, radio, etc **2** group of heavy
guns operating as a single unit
▷ adjective **3** (of hens) kept in small
cages for the mass production
of eggs

battle noun **1** fight between
large armed forces **2** conflict or
struggle ▷ verb **3** to struggle

battlefield noun place where a
battle is fought

battlement noun wall with gaps
along the top for firing guns or
arrows through

battleship noun large heavily
armoured warship

batty battier, battiest adjective
(informal) eccentric or crazy

bauble noun trinket of little value

bawdy bawdier, bawdiest adjective
(of writing etc) containing
humorous references to sex

bawl verb to shout or weep noisily

bay noun **1** stretch of coastline
that curves inwards; inlet **2** area
set aside for a particular purpose:
loading bay **3** Mediterranean
laurel tree **4** reddish-brown horse
▷ adjective **5** (of a horse) reddish-
brown ▷ verb **6** to make a deep
howling noise

bayonet noun **1** sharp blade that
can be fixed to the end of a rifle

bazaar noun **1** sale in aid of charity
2 market area, especially in
Eastern countries

BC abbreviation before Christ

be verb **1** to exist or live **2** used to
link the subject of a sentence and
its complement: John is a musician
3 used to form continuous tenses:

The man is running **4** used to form
the passive voice: He was brought
up by his grandparents

be- prefix (forming verbs from
nouns) to treat as: to befriend

beach noun area of sand or pebbles
on a shore

beacon noun fire or light on a hill
or tower, used as a warning

bead noun **1** small piece of plastic,
wood, etc, pierced for threading
on a string to form a necklace etc
2 small drop of moisture

beady adjective (of eyes) small,
round and glittering

beagle noun small hound with
short legs and drooping ears

beak noun **1** projecting horny jaws
of a bird **2** (informal) nose

beaker noun **1** large drinking cup
2 glass container with a lip that is
used in laboratories

beam noun **1** broad smile **2** ray of
light **3** long thick piece of wood,
metal, etc, used in building ▷ verb
4 to smile broadly

bean noun seed or pod of various
plants, eaten as a vegetable or
used to make coffee etc

bear bears, bearing, bore, borne
verb **1** to support (something)
or hold (something) up
2 (passive born) to give birth to
(a baby) **3** to tolerate or endure
(someone or something) **4** to
hold (something) in the mind
▷ noun **5** large strong wild
animal with a shaggy coat
> **bearable** adjective able to
be tolerated > **bearer** noun
person who carries or presents
something > **bear out** verb to
show (what someone says) to
be truthful

beard noun hair growing on the lower parts of a man's face > **bearded** adjective having a beard

bearing noun **1** relevance **2** way in which a person moves or stands

beast noun **1** large wild animal **2** brutal or uncivilized person

beastly beastlier, beastliest adjective unpleasant or disagreeable

beat beats, beating, beat, beaten verb **1** to hit (someone or something) hard and repeatedly **2** to move (wings) up and down **3** (of a heart) to pump blood with a regular rhythm **4** to stir or mix (eggs, cream or butter) vigorously **5** to overcome or defeat ▷ noun **6** regular pumping action of the heart **7** area patrolled by a particular police officer **8** main rhythm of a piece of music > **beater** noun tool for beating eggs, cream or butter > **beating** noun hitting someone hard and repeatedly > **beat up** verb to injure (someone) by repeated blows or kicks

beaut noun (Aust, NZ informal) **1** outstanding person or thing ▷ adjective **2** good, excellent

beautiful adjective very attractive or pleasant > **beautifully** adverb

beauty beauties noun **1** combination of all the qualities of a person or thing that delight the senses and mind **2** very attractive woman **3** (informal) something outstanding of its kind

beaver noun animal with a big flat tail and webbed hind feet

because conjunction **1** on account of the fact that **2** because of on account of

beck noun **at someone's beck and call** having to be constantly available to do as someone asks

beckon verb (followed by to) to summon (someone) with a gesture

become becomes, becoming, became, become verb **1** to come to be (something) **2** to suit (someone) **3** become of to happen to (someone or something)

bed beds, bedding, bedded noun **1** piece of furniture for sleeping on **2** area of ground in which plants are grown **3** bottom of a river, lake or sea **4** layer of rock > **bed down** verb to sleep somewhere for the night

bedclothes plural noun sheets and covers that are used on a bed

bedding noun sheets and covers that are used on a bed

bedlam noun noisy confused situation

bedpan noun container used as a toilet by people too ill to get out of bed

bedraggled adjective untidy, wet or dirty

bedridden adjective confined to bed because of illness or old age

bedrock noun **1** solid rock beneath the surface soil **2** basic facts or principles

bedroom noun room used for sleeping in

bedspread noun cover put over a bed, on top of the sheets and blankets

bedstead *noun* metal or wooden frame of an old-fashioned bed

bee *noun* winged insect that makes wax and honey

beech *noun* tree with a smooth greyish bark

beef *noun* flesh of a cow, bull or ox

beefy beefier, beefiest *adjective* **1** like beef **2** (*informal*) strong and muscular

beehive *noun* structure in which bees live

beeline *noun* **make a beeline for** (*informal*) to go to (a place) as quickly and directly as possible

been *verb* past participle of **be**

beer *noun* alcoholic drink brewed from malt and hops

beetle *noun* insect with a hard wing cover on its back

beetroot *noun* type of plant with a dark red root

befall befalls, befalling, befell, befallen *verb* (*old-fashioned*) to happen to (someone)

before *conjunction, preposition, adverb* **1** earlier than or prior to: *before I go; before the war* **2** previously: *I'd never been there before* **3** in front of: *They stopped before a large white castle* **4** in preference to or rather than: *Death before dishonour*

beforehand *adverb* in advance

befriend *verb* to become friends with (someone)

beg begs, begging, begged *verb* **1** to ask for money or food, especially in the street **2** to ask (someone) anxiously to do something

beggar *noun* person who lives by begging

begin begins, beginning, began, begun *verb* to start or commence ▷ **beginner** *noun* person who has just started learning to do something ▷ **beginning** *noun* first part of something or the time when something starts

begonia [be-**go**-nya] *noun* tropical plant with brightly coloured flowers

begrudge *verb* to be envious of (someone) for something that he or she possesses

behalf *noun* **on behalf of** in the interest of or for the benefit of

behave *verb* **1** to act in a particular way **2** to conduct (oneself) properly

behaviour *noun* manner of behaving

behead *verb* to cut off the head of

beheld *verb* past of **behold**

behind *preposition* **1** at the back of: *behind the wall* **2** not as far advanced as: *behind schedule* **3** responsible for or causing: *the reasons behind her departure* **4** supporting: *The whole country was behind him* ▷ *adverb* **5** remaining after other people have gone: *He stayed behind to clear up* **6** not up to date: *He's behind with his rent* ▷ *noun* **7** (*informal*) buttocks

behold beholds, beholding, beheld *verb* (*old-fashioned*) to look at

beige [bayj] *adjective* pale creamy-brown

being *noun* **1** state or fact of existing **2** something that exists or is thought to exist **3** human being ▷ *verb* **4** present participle of **be**

belated *adjective* late or too late ▷ **belatedly** *adverb*

belch verb 1 to expel wind from the stomach noisily through the mouth 2 (of smoke or fire) to come out in large amounts: Smoke belched from the factory ▷ noun 3 act of belching

beleaguered adjective 1 struggling against difficulties or criticism 2 besieged by an enemy

belfry belfries noun part of a tower where bells are hung

Belgian adjective 1 belonging or relating to Belgium ▷ noun 2 person from Belgium

belief noun 1 faith or confidence 2 opinion 3 principle accepted as true, often without proof

believe verb 1 to accept (something) as true or real 2 to think, assume or suppose (something) > **believable** adjective: The book is full of believable characters > **believe in** verb to be convinced of the truth or existence of (something or someone) > **believer** noun: a great believer in herbal medicines

belittle verb to treat (someone) as having little value or importance

bell noun 1 hollow, usually metal, cup-shaped or round instrument with a swinging piece inside that causes a ringing sound when it strikes against the sides as the bell is moved 2 device that rings or buzzes as a signal

bellbird noun (Aust, NZ) Australian or New Zealand bird that makes a sound like a bell

belligerent adjective aggressive and keen to start a fight or an argument > **belligerence** noun

aggressiveness > **belligerently** adverb

bellow verb 1 to make a low deep cry like that of a bull 2 to shout (something) in anger ▷ noun 3 loud deep roar

belly bellies noun 1 part of the body that contains the intestines 2 stomach 3 front, lower or inner part of something

belong verb 1 (followed by to) to be the property (of someone) 2 (usually followed by to) to be a part or member of (something) 3 to have a rightful place; go: It belongs in the kitchen > **belongings** plural noun personal possessions

beloved [bil-**luv**-id] adjective dearly loved

below preposition, adverb at or to a position lower (than); underneath

belt noun 1 band of cloth, leather, etc, usually worn round the waist 2 long narrow area: a belt of trees 3 circular strip of rubber that drives moving parts in a machine ▷ verb 4 (informal) to hit (someone) very hard 5 (informal) to move very fast

bemused adjective puzzled or confused

bench noun 1 long seat 2 long narrow work table 3 **the bench** judge or magistrate sitting in court, or judges and magistrates collectively

bend bends, bending, bent verb 1 to form a curve or cause (something) to form a curve 2 (often followed by down, forward etc) to move the head and shoulders forwards and downwards ▷ noun 3 curved part

bene- *prefix* good or well: *beneficial*

beneath *adverb* **1** below
▷ *preposition* **2** below **3** not
worthy of

benefactor *noun* person who
supports a person or institution
by giving money

beneficial *adjective* helpful or
advantageous ▷ **beneficially**
adverb helpfully or
advantageously

beneficiary beneficiaries *noun*
person who gains or benefits from
something

benefit *noun* **1** something
that improves or promotes
2 advantage or sake: *I'm doing
this for your benefit* **3** money
given by the government to
people who are unemployed or
ill ▷ *verb* **4** (followed by *from*) to
gain an advantage or help from
(something)

> **WORD TIP**
> *Benefit* is spelt with two es,
> not two is

benevolence *noun* kindness
and helpfulness ▷ **benevolent**
adjective kind and helpful
▷ **benevolently** *adverb*: smiling
benevolently

benign [bin-**nine**] *adjective*
1 showing kindliness **2** (of a
tumour) not threatening to life
▷ **benignly** *adverb* kindly

bent *verb* **1** past of **bend** ▷ *adjective*
2 curved **3** (*informal*) dishonest or
corrupt **4** bent on determined to
do (something)

bequeath *verb* to leave (money or
property) to someone in a will

bequest *noun* legal gift of money
or property by someone who
has died

berate *verb* to scold (someone)
harshly

bereaved *adjective* having recently
lost a close friend or relative
through death ▷ **bereavement**
noun: those who have suffered a
bereavement

bereft *adjective* (followed by *of*)
deprived (of something): *bereft
of ideas*

beret [**ber**-ray] *noun* round flat
close-fitting brimless cap

berm *noun* (NZ) narrow grass
strip between the road and the
footpath in a residential area

berry berries *noun* small soft
stoneless fruit

berserk *adjective* go berserk to
become violent or destructive

berth *noun* **1** bunk in a ship or
train **2** space in a harbour where
a ship stays when being loaded or
unloaded

beseech beseeches, beseeching,
beseeched or besought *verb*
to ask (someone) earnestly
for something ▷ **beseeching**
adjective: She gave him a beseeching
look

beset besets, besetting, beset *verb*
to trouble or harass (someone)
constantly

beside *preposition* **1** at, by or to
the side of **2** as compared with
3 beside yourself overwhelmed
or overwrought

besiege *verb* **1** to surround (a
place) with military forces **2** to
overwhelm (someone), as with
requests

besought *verb* a past of **beseech**

best *adjective* **1** most excellent of a
particular group etc ▷ *adverb* **2** in
a manner that is better than all

others ▷ *noun* **3** most outstanding or excellent person, thing or group in a category

best man *noun* groom's attendant at a wedding

bestow *verb* (followed by *on*) to give (something) to someone

bet bets, betting, bet *noun* **1** the act of staking a sum of money on the outcome of an event **2** sum of money risked on the outcome of an event ▷ *verb* **3** to make or place a bet **4** (*informal*) to predict (something) > **betting** *noun*: *a fine for illegal betting*

betray *verb* **1** to do something that harms (someone who trusts you), such as helping his or her enemies **2** to reveal (your feelings or thoughts) unintentionally > **betrayal** *noun* act of betraying someone or something > **betrayer** *noun* person who betrays someone

betrothed *adjective* (*old-fashioned*) engaged to be married > **betrothal** *noun* engagement to be married

better *adjective* **1** more excellent than others; superior **2** improved or fully recovered in health ▷ *adverb* **3** in a more excellent manner **4** in or to a greater degree

between *preposition, adverb* indicating position in the middle, alternatives, etc

WORD TIP
If there are two things, you should use *between*. If there are more than two things you should use *among*.

beverage *noun* drink

bevy bevies *noun* flock or group

beware *verb* (usually followed by *of*) to be on your guard (against)

bewilder *verb* to confuse (someone) utterly > **bewildered** *adjective* greatly confused > **bewildering** *adjective* very confusing > **bewilderment** *noun* great confusion

bewitch *verb* **1** to attract and fascinate (someone) **2** to cast a spell over (someone) > **bewitched** *adjective* > **bewitching** *adjective*: *bewitching brown eyes*

beyond *preposition* **1** at or to a point on the other side of **2** outside the limits or scope of ▷ *adverb* **3** at or to the far side of something

bi- *prefix* two or twice: *bifocal; biweekly*

bias biases or biasses, biasing or biassing, biased or biassed *noun* **1** mental tendency, especially prejudice ▷ *verb* **2** to cause (someone) to have a bias > **biased** or **biassed** *adjective* prejudiced

bib *noun* **1** piece of cloth or plastic worn to protect a very young child's clothes when eating **2** upper front part of dungarees etc

Bible *noun* [RE] sacred writings of the Christian religion > **biblical** *adjective* of or relating to the Bible

bicentenary bicentenaries *noun* 200th anniversary

biceps *noun* [PE] large muscle in the upper part of your arm

WORD TIP
The plural of *biceps* is *biceps*

bicker *verb* to argue over petty matters

bicycle noun vehicle with two wheels, one behind the other, pedalled by the rider

bid bids, bidding, bade or bid, bidden verb **1** (past bid) to offer (a sum) in an attempt to buy something **2** (old-fashioned) to give (a greeting) (to someone) ▷ noun **3** offer to buy something for a specified amount **4** attempt to do something > **bidding** noun command

WORD TIP

When bid means 'offer a certain sum' (sense 1), the past tense and past participle are bid. When bid means 'give a greeting' (sense 2), the past tense is bade and the past participle is bidden

biddy-bid or **biddy-biddy** noun (NZ) prickly low-growing plant found in New Zealand

bide bides, biding, bided verb **bide your time** to wait patiently for an opportunity

bidet [bee-day] noun low basin for washing the genital area

big bigger, biggest adjective large or important > **biggish** adjective fairly big > **bigness** noun largeness

bigamy noun crime of marrying a person while still legally married to someone else > **bigamist** noun person who commits bigamy

bigot noun person with strong, unreasonable prejudices, especially regarding religion or race > **bigoted** adjective extremely prejudiced in an unreasonable way, especially regarding religion or race > **bigotry** noun: religious bigotry

bike noun (informal) bicycle or motorcycle

bikini bikinis noun woman's brief two-piece swimming costume

bilateral adjective (of an agreement) made between two groups or countries

bile noun bitter yellow fluid produced by the liver

bilge noun the lowest part of a ship, where dirty water collects

bilingual adjective involving or using two languages

bill noun **1** statement of money owed for goods or services supplied **2** formal statement of a proposed new law **3** poster **4** (Chiefly US & Canadian) piece of paper money **5** list of events, such as a theatre programme **6** bird's beak

billabong noun (Aust) lagoon or pool formed from part of a river

billboard noun large board on which advertisements are displayed

billet verb **1** to assign a lodging to (a soldier) ▷ noun **2** building for housing soldiers

billiards noun game played on a table with balls and a cue

billion adjective, noun **1** one thousand million (1,000,000,000) **2** formerly, one million million (1,000,000,000,000) **3** billions large but unspecified number; lots > **billionth** adjective, noun

WORD TIP

As the meaning of billion has changed from one million million to one thousand million, a writer may mean either of these things when using it, depending on when the book or article was written

billow noun **1** large sea wave ▷ verb **2** to rise up or swell out

billy billies noun (Aust) metal pot for boiling water over a camp fire

bin noun container, especially one for rubbish

binary [by-nar-ee] adjective **1** composed of two parts **2** ICT (Maths, computers) of or in a counting system with only two digits, 0 and 1

bind binds, binding, bound verb **1** to make (something) secure with or as if with a rope **2** to place (someone) under an obligation **3** to enclose and fasten (the pages of a book) between covers ▷ noun **4** (informal) annoying situation

bindi-eye noun (Aust) small Australian plant with prickly fruits

binding noun **1** anything that binds or fastens **2** book cover

binge noun (informal) wild bout of drinking or eating too much

bingo noun gambling game in which numbers are called out and covered by the players on their individual cards

binoculars plural noun instrument with lenses for each eye through which you look in order to see distant objects or people

bio- prefix life or living things: biology

bioactive adjective having an effect on living tissue

biochemistry noun study of the chemistry of living things > **biochemical** adjective relating to chemical processes that happen in living things > **biochemist** noun

biodegradable adjective capable of being decomposed by natural means

biodiversity noun existence of a wide variety of species in their natural environment

biofuel noun any biological substance used as fuel

biography biographies noun account of a person's life by another person

biology noun study of living things > **biological** adjective of or relating to biology > **biologically** adverb: Much of our behaviour is biologically determined > **biologist** noun

biometric adjective (of any automated system) using physiological or behavioural traits as a means of identification: biometric fingerprinting

bionic adjective having a part of the body that is operated electronically

biopsy biopsies noun examination of tissue from a living body

birch noun tree with thin peeling bark

bird noun creature with feathers and wings, most types of which can fly

birth noun **1** process of bearing young; childbirth **2** act of being born **3** beginning of something **4** give birth to to bear (a baby)

birthday noun anniversary of the day of your birth

birthmark noun mark on the skin formed before birth

biscuit noun small flat dry sweet or plain cake

bisect verb to divide (a line or area) into two equal parts

bisexual adjective sexually attracted to both men and women

bishop noun 1 high-ranking clergyman in some Christian Churches 2 chessman which is moved diagonally

bison noun large hairy animal of the cattle family, native to North America and Europe

bistro bistros [**bee**-stroh] noun small restaurant

bit noun 1 small piece, portion or quantity 2 metal mouthpiece on a horse's bridle 3 cutting or drilling part of a tool 4 (Computers) smallest unit of information held in a computer's memory, either 0 or 1 5 **a bit** rather, somewhat 6 **bit by bit** gradually ▷ verb 7 past tense of **bite**

bitch noun 1 female dog, fox or wolf 2 (offensive) spiteful woman > **bitchy** adjective spiteful

bite bites, biting, bit, bitten verb 1 to cut into (something or someone) with your teeth ▷ noun 2 act of biting 3 wound or sting inflicted by biting 4 snack

bitter adjective 1 having a sharp unpleasant taste; sour 2 showing or caused by hostility or resentment 3 extremely cold > **bitterly** adverb: They bitterly resented their loss of power > **bitterness** noun: the bitterness of the dispute

bivouac [**biv**-oo-ak] noun temporary camp in the open air

bizarre [biz-**zahr**] adjective odd or unusual

blab blabs, blabbing, blabbed verb to reveal (secrets) indiscreetly

black adjective 1 of the darkest colour, like coal 2 (of a situation) without hope 3 angry or resentful: black looks 4 involving jokes about death or suffering: black comedy 5 **Black** dark-skinned ▷ noun 6 darkest colour 7 complete darkness 8 **Black** member of a dark-skinned race > **blackness** noun being very dark ▷ **black out** verb to lose consciousness

> **WORD TIP**
> When you are writing about a person or people, Black should start with a capital letter

blackberry blackberries noun small blackish edible fruit

BlackBerry ® noun hand-held wireless device incorporating e-mail, browser and mobile-phone functions

blackbird noun common European bird, the male of which has black feathers

blackboard noun hard black surface used by teachers for writing on with chalk

black box noun an electronic device in an aircraft which collects and stores information during flights

blackcurrant noun very small blackish edible fruit that grows in bunches

blacken verb 1 to make (something) black 2 **blacken someone's name** to say bad things about someone

blackhead noun very small black spot on the skin caused by a pore being blocked with dirt

blacklist noun 1 list of people or organizations considered untrustworthy etc ▷ verb 2 to put (someone) on a blacklist

blackmail noun 1 act of attempting to obtain money from someone by threatening to reveal information ▷ verb 2 to attempt to obtain money from (someone) by blackmail ▷ **blackmailer** noun person who blackmails someone

black market noun illegal trade in goods or currencies

blackout noun temporary loss of consciousness

blacksmith noun person who makes things out of iron, such as horseshoes

bladder noun part of the body where urine is held until it leaves the body

blade noun 1 cutting edge of a weapon or tool 2 thin flattish part of a propeller, oar, etc 3 leaf of grass

blame verb 1 to consider (someone) responsible for something that is wrong ▷ noun 2 responsibility for something that is wrong

blameless adjective not responsible for something that is wrong

blanch verb 1 to become white or pale 2 to prepare (vegetables etc) by plunging them in boiling water

bland adjective dull and uninteresting > **blandly** adverb: She smiled blandly

blank adjective 1 not written on 2 showing no interest or expression

blanket noun 1 large thick cloth used as covering for a bed 2 thick covering of something, such as snow

blare verb 1 to make a loud harsh noise ▷ noun 2 loud harsh noise

blaspheme verb to speak disrespectfully of God or religion > **blasphemer** noun person who blasphemes > **blasphemous** adjective speaking disrespectfully of God or religion > **blasphemy** noun speech that shows disrespect for God or religion

blast noun 1 explosion 2 sudden strong gust of air or wind 3 sudden loud sound, as of a trumpet ▷ verb 4 to blow up (a rock etc) with explosives

blatant adjective extremely obvious

blaze noun 1 strong fire or flame 2 very bright light ▷ verb 3 to burn or shine brightly

blazer noun lightweight jacket, often in the colours of a school etc

bleach verb 1 to make (material or hair) white or pale ▷ noun 2 chemical used to make material or hair white or to disinfect

bleak adjective 1 exposed and barren 2 offering little hope

bleary blearier, bleariest adjective (of eyes) red and watery, through tiredness

bleat verb 1 (of a sheep or goat) to utter its characteristic high-pitched cry ▷ noun 2 cry of sheep and goats

bleed bleeds, bleeding, bled verb to lose blood from a wound

bleep noun short high-pitched sound made by an electrical device

blemish noun 1 mark that spoils the appearance of something ▷ verb 2 to spoil (someone's reputation)

a b c d e f g h i j k l m n o p q r s t u v w x y z

blend verb **1** to mix (parts or ingredients) **2** to look good together ▷ noun **3** mixture

blender noun machine for mixing liquids and foods at high speed

bless blesses, blessing, blessed or blest verb to ask God to protect (someone or something) > **blessed** adjective (followed by with) having (a particular quality or talent) > **blessing** noun **1** something good that you are thankful for **2 with someone's blessing** with someone's approval

blew verb past tense of **blow**

blight noun **1** something that damages or spoils other things **2** disease that makes plants wither ▷ verb **3** to harm (something) seriously

blind adjective **1** unable to see **2** (followed by to) unable or unwilling to understand (something) **3** not determined by reason: blind hatred ▷ verb **4** to deprive (someone) of sight **5** to deprive (someone) of good sense, reason or judgment ▷ noun **6** covering for a window > **blindly** adverb: She groped blindly for the glass > **blindness** noun inability to see

blindfold verb **1** to prevent (someone) from seeing by covering the eyes ▷ noun **2** piece of cloth used to cover the eyes

blinding adjective (of a light) so bright that it hurts your eyes > **blindingly** adverb **blindingly obvious** (informal) very obvious indeed

bling or **bling-bling** (informal) noun **1** jewellery that looks expensive in a vulgar way ▷ adjective **2** expensive-looking in a vulgar way; flashy

blink verb to close and immediately reopen (the eyes)

blinkers plural noun leather flaps on a horse's bridle to prevent sideways vision

bliss noun perfect happiness > **blissful** adjective: We spent a blissful week together > **blissfully** adverb: blissfully happy

blister noun **1** small bubble on the skin containing watery liquid, caused by a burn or rubbing ▷ verb **2** (of the skin) to develop a blister > **blistering** adjective **1** (of weather) very hot **2** (of criticism) extremely harsh

blithe adjective casual and indifferent > **blithely** adverb casually and indifferently

blitz noun **1** bombing attack by enemy aircraft on a city ▷ verb **2** to make a bombing attack on (a city)

blizzard noun heavy snowstorm with strong winds

bloated verb larger than normal, often because of the liquid or gas inside

blob noun **1** soft mass or drop **2** indistinct or shapeless form

bloc noun people or countries combined by a common interest

block noun **1** large solid piece of wood, stone, etc **2** large building of offices, flats, etc **3** area of land in a town that has streets on all its sides **4** obstruction or hindrance **5** (informal) person's head ▷ verb **6** to obstruct (something) by introducing an obstacle

blockade noun **1** action that prevents goods from reaching a place ▷ verb **2** to prevent supplies from reaching (a place)

blockage noun something that blocks a pipe or tunnel

blog noun person's online journal (also **weblog**)

blogger noun person who keeps a blog

blogosphere noun (informal) blogs on the internet as a whole

bloke noun (informal) man

blonde or **blond** adjective, noun fair-haired (person)

blood noun **1** red fluid that flows around the body **2** race or ancestors **3 in cold blood** deliberately

bloodless adjective **1** (of face, skin) very pale **2** (of coup, revolution) without casualties

blood pressure noun measure of how forcefully your blood is being pumped round your body

bloodshed noun slaughter or killing

bloodshot adjective (of an eye) inflamed

bloodstream noun flow of blood round the body

bloodthirsty adjective taking pleasure in violence

blood transfusion noun process in which blood is injected into the body of someone who has lost a lot of blood

blood vessel noun narrow tube in the body through which the blood flows

bloody bloodier, bloodiest adjective **1** covered with blood **2** marked by much killing

bloom noun **1** blossom on a flowering plant **2** youthful or

healthy glow ▷ verb **3** to bear flowers **4** to be in a healthy glowing condition

blossom noun **1** growth of flowers that appears on a tree before the fruit ▷ verb **2** (of a tree) to produce blossom

blot blots, blotting, blotted noun **1** drop of ink spilled on a surface **2** something that spoils something, such as someone's reputation ▷ **blot out** verb to be in front of (something) and hide (it) completely

blotch noun discoloured area or stain > **blotchy** adjective having discoloured areas or stains

blouse noun woman's shirtlike item of clothing

blow blows, blowing, blew, blown verb **1** (of air, the wind, etc) to move **2** to move or be carried as if by the wind **3** to expel (air etc) through the mouth or nose **4** to cause (a musical instrument) to sound by forcing air into it **5** (informal) to spend (money) freely ▷ noun **6** hard hit **7** sudden setback > **blow up** verb **1** to destroy (something) with an explosion **2** to fill (a balloon or tyre) with air **3** (informal) to enlarge (a photograph)

blubber noun fat of whales, seals, etc

bludge (Aust, NZ informal) verb **1** to avoid work **2** to scrounge ▷ noun **3** easy task

bludgeon noun **1** short thick club ▷ verb **2** to hit (someone) with a bludgeon **3** to force or bully (someone) into doing something

blue bluer, bluest; blues noun **1** colour of a clear unclouded sky

2 out of the blue unexpectedly ▷ *adjective* **3** of the colour blue > **bluish** or **blueish** *adjective* slightly blue

bluebell *noun* flower with blue bell-shaped flowers

bluebottle *noun* **1** large fly with a dark-blue body **2** (*Aust, NZ*) small stinging jellyfish

blue-collar *adjective* denoting manual industrial workers

blueprint *noun* description of how a plan is expected to work

blues *plural noun* **the blues** **1** feeling of depression **2** type of folk music of Black American origin

Bluetooth ® *noun* technology allowing short-range wireless communication

bluff *verb* **1** to pretend to be confident in order to influence (someone) ▷ *noun* **2** act of bluffing **3** steep cliff or bank ▷ *adjective* **4** good-naturedly frank and hearty

blunder *noun* **1** clumsy mistake ▷ *verb* **2** to make a blunder **3** to act clumsily

blunt *adjective* **1** not having a sharp edge or point **2** (of people, speech, etc) straightforward or uncomplicated

blur blurs, blurring, blurred *verb* **1** to become vague or less distinct or to make (something) vague or less distinct ▷ *noun* **2** something vague, hazy or indistinct > **blurred** *adjective: blurred vision*

blurt out *verb* to say (something) suddenly after trying to keep it a secret

blush *verb* **1** to become red in the face, especially from embarrassment or shame ▷ *noun* **2** reddening of the face

bluster *verb* **1** to speak loudly or in a bullying way ▷ *noun* **2** empty threats or protests > **blustery** *adjective* (of weather) rough and windy

boa *noun* **1** any of various large snakes that kill by crushing **2** long scarf of fur or feathers

boar *noun* **1** male pig used for breeding **2** wild pig

board *noun* **1** long flat piece of sawn timber **2** smaller flat piece of rigid material for a specific purpose: *ironing board; chess board* **3** group of people who run a company, trust, etc **4** meals provided for money **5 on board** on or in a ship, aeroplane, etc ▷ *verb* **6** to go aboard (a train, aeroplane, etc) **7** to cover (something) with boards **8** to receive meals and lodgings in return for money

boarder *noun* (*Brit*) pupil who lives at school during the school term

boarding school *noun* school where the pupils live during the term

boardroom *noun* room where the board of a company meets

boast *verb* **1** to speak too proudly about your talents etc; brag **2** to possess (something to be proud of) ▷ *noun* **3** bragging statement > **boastful** *adjective* speaking too proudly about your talents etc

boat *noun* small vehicle for travelling across water

bob bobs, bobbing, bobbed *verb* **1** to move up and down repeatedly **2** to cut (the hair) in a bob ▷ *noun* **3** short abrupt movement

4 hairstyle in which the hair is cut short evenly all round the head

bobbin noun reel on which thread is wound

bode verb to be an omen of (good or ill)

bodice noun upper part of a dress

bodily adjective **1** relating to the body ▷ adverb **2** by taking hold of the body

body bodies noun **1** entire physical structure of an animal or human **2** trunk or torso **3** corpse **4** organized group of people **5** main part of anything **6** woman's one-piece undergarment

bodyguard noun person or group of people employed to protect someone

bodywork noun outer shell of a motor vehicle

boer [boh-er] noun (in South Africa) a farmer, especially one of Dutch descent

boerewors [boo-rih-vorse] noun (SAfr) spiced sausage

bog noun **1** wet spongy ground **2** (informal) toilet

boggle verb to be surprised, confused or alarmed

bogus adjective not genuine

bohemian [boh-hee-mee-an] adjective leading an unconventional life

boil verb **1** to change from a liquid to a vapour or cause (a liquid) to change to a vapour so quickly that bubbles are formed **2** to cook (food) by the process of boiling ▷ noun **3** state or action of boiling **4** painful red swelling on the skin

boiler noun piece of equipment that provides hot water

boiling adjective (informal) very hot

boisterous adjective noisy and lively

bold adjective **1** confident and fearless **2** immodest or impudent **3** clear and noticeable: bold colours ▷ **boldly** adverb in a bold manner ▷ **boldness** noun being bold

bollard noun short thick post used to prevent the passage of motor vehicles

bolster verb to support or strengthen (something)

bolt noun **1** sliding metal bar for fastening a door etc **2** metal pin that screws into a nut **3** flash (of lightning) ▷ adverb **4 bolt upright** stiff and rigid ▷ verb **5** to run away suddenly **6** to fasten (a door) with a bolt **7** to eat (food) hurriedly

bomb noun **1** container fitted with explosive material **2** (informal) large amount of money **3 the bomb** nuclear bomb ▷ verb **4** to attack (a place) with bombs **5** to move very quickly > **bomber** noun **1** aircraft that drops bombs **2** person who throws or puts a bomb in a particular place

bombard verb **1** to attack (a place) with heavy gunfire or bombs **2** to attack (someone) verbally, especially with questions > **bombardment** noun: The capital is under constant bombardment

bombshell noun shocking or unwelcome surprise

bona fide [bone-a fide-ee] adjective genuine

bond noun **1** something that binds, fastens or holds things together **2** something that unites people; link **3** written or spoken agreement **4** (*Finance*) certificate of debt issued to raise funds

5 bonds chains or ropes used to restrain or imprison ▷ *verb* **6** to link or attach (things)

bondage *noun* slavery

bone *noun* **1** any of the hard parts in the body that form the skeleton ▷ *verb* **2** to remove the bones from (meat for cooking etc) > **boneless** *adjective* without bones

bonfire *noun* large outdoor fire

bonnet *noun* **1** metal cover over a vehicle's engine **2** hat that ties under the chin

bonny bonnier, bonniest *adjective* (*Scot*) beautiful

bonus *noun* something given, paid or received above what is due or expected

bony bonier, boniest *adjective* very thin

boo *interjection* **1** shout of disapproval ▷ *verb* **2** to shout 'boo' to show disapproval of (someone or something)

book *noun* **1** number of pages bound together between covers **2** long written work **3** number of tickets, stamps, etc fastened together ▷ *verb* **4** to reserve (a hotel room, travel, etc) in advance **5** to record the name of (a person who has committed an offence)

bookcase *noun* piece of furniture with shelves for books

booking *noun* arrangement to book something such as a hotel room

book-keeping *noun* recording of the money spent and received by a business

booklet *noun* small book with a paper cover

bookmaker *noun* person whose occupation is taking bets

bookmark *noun* piece of card put between the pages of a book to mark your place

boom *verb* **1** to make a loud deep echoing sound **2** to increase rapidly ▷ *noun* **3** loud deep echoing sound **4** rapid increase in something

boomerang *noun* curved wooden missile that can be made to return to the thrower

boon *noun* something helpful or beneficial

boost *noun* **1** encouragement or help **2** increase ▷ *verb* **3** to cause (something) to improve or increase

boot *noun* **1** outer covering for the foot that extends above the ankle **2** space in a car for luggage **3 to boot** in addition ▷ *verb* **4** (*informal*) to kick (someone or something) **5** to start up (a computer)

booth *noun* **1** small partly enclosed cubicle **2** stall at a fair or market

booty *noun* valuable articles obtained as plunder

booze *verb, noun* (*informal*) (to consume) alcoholic drink > **boozer** *noun* (*informal*) **1** person who is fond of drinking alcohol **2** (*Brit, Aust, NZ*) pub > **boozy** *adjective* fond of drinking alcohol

border *noun* **1** dividing line between political or geographical regions **2** band around or along the edge of something ▷ *verb* **3** to provide (something) with a border **4** (followed by *on*) to be nearly the same as (something): *resentment that borders on hatred*

borderline *adjective* only just acceptable as a member of a class or group: *a borderline case*

bore *verb* **1** to make (a hole) with a drill etc **2** to make (someone) weary by being dull and uninteresting **3** past tense of **bear** ▷ *noun* **4** dull or repetitive person or thing ▷ **bored***adjective* tired and impatient; fed up ▷ **boredom***noun* being bored ▷ **boring***adjective* dull and uninteresting

> **WORD TIP**
> You can say that you are *bored with* or *bored by* someone or something, but you should not say *bored of*

born *verb* **1** be born to come out of your mother's womb at birth ▷ *adjective* **2** possessing certain qualities from birth: *a born musician*

borne *verb* a past participle of **bear**

borough [bur-uh] *noun* (Chiefly Brit) town or district with its own council

borrow *verb* **1** to obtain (something) temporarily **2** to adopt (ideas etc) from another source ▷ **borrower***noun* person who borrows something

> **WORD TIP**
> You *borrow* something *from* a person, not *off* them. Do not confuse *borrow* and *lend*. If you *borrow* something, you get it from another person for a while; if you *lend* something, someone gets it from you for a while

Bosnian *adjective* **1** belonging to or relating to Bosnia ▷ *noun* **2** person from Bosnia

bosom *noun* **1** chest of a person, especially the female breasts ▷ *adjective* **2** very dear: *a bosom friend*

boss bosses, bossing, bossed *noun* person in charge of or employing others ▷ **boss around***verb* to keep telling (someone) what to do

bossy bossier, bossiest *adjective* enjoying telling other people what to do ▷ **bossiness***noun*: *They resent what they see as bossiness*

botany *noun* study of plants ▷ **botanic** or **botanical***adjective*: *an area of great botanical interest* ▷ **botanist***noun*

botch *verb* to spoil (something) through clumsiness

both *adjective, pronoun* two considered together

> **WORD TIP**
> You can use *of* after *both*, but it is not essential. *Both the boys* means the same as *both of the boys*

bother *verb* **1** to take the time or trouble (to do something) **2** to give annoyance or trouble to (someone) **3** to pester (someone) ▷ *noun* **4** trouble, fuss or difficulty ▷ **bothersome***adjective* causing annoyance or trouble

bottle *noun* **1** container for holding liquids **2** (Brit informal) courage ▷ *verb* **3** to put (something) in a bottle ▷ **bottle up***verb* to restrain (strong feelings)

bottleneck *noun* narrow stretch of road where traffic is held up

bottle store *noun* (S Afr) shop licensed to sell alcohol for drinking elsewhere

bottom noun **1** lowest, deepest or farthest removed part of a thing **2** buttocks ▷ adjective **3** lowest or last > **bottomless** adjective having no bottom or seeming to have no bottom

bough [rhymes with **now**] noun large branch of a tree

bought verb past of **buy**

> **WORD TIP**
>
> Do not confuse bought and brought. Bought comes from buy and brought comes from bring

boulder noun large rounded rock

boulevard [boo-le-vard] noun wide, usually tree-lined, street

bounce verb **1** (of a ball etc) to rebound from an impact **2** (informal) (of a cheque) to be returned uncashed owing to a lack of funds in the account ▷ noun **3** act of rebounding **4** springiness **5** (informal) vitality or vigour

bouncy bouncier, bounciest adjective **1** lively and enthusiastic **2** capable of bouncing

bound verb **1** past of **bind 2** to move forwards by jumps **3** to form a boundary of (something) ▷ noun **4** jump upwards or forwards **5** **bounds** limits ▷ adjective **6** destined or certain (to do something) **7** compelled or obliged (to do something) **8** going or intending to go towards: homeward bound

boundary boundaries noun dividing line that indicates the farthest limit

boundless adjective without end or limit

bountiful adjective freely available in large amounts

bounty bounties noun **1** generosity **2** generous gift or reward

bouquet [boo-**kay**] noun **1** bunch of flowers **2** aroma of wine

bourgeois [**boor**-zhwah] adjective (used expressing disapproval) typical of fairly rich middle-class people > **bourgeoisie** [boor-jhwah-**zee**] noun fairly rich middle-class people in a society

bout noun **1** period of activity or illness **2** boxing or wrestling match

boutique [boo-**teek**] noun small clothes shop

bovine adjective **1** relating to cattle **2** rather slow and stupid

bow[1] [rhymes with **now**] verb **1** to lower (one's head) or bend (one's knee or body) as a sign of respect or shame **2** (followed by to) to comply with or accept (something) ▷ noun **3** movement made when bowing **4** front end of a ship

bow[2] [rhymes with **low**] noun **1** knot with two loops and loose ends **2** weapon for shooting arrows **3** long stick stretched with horsehair for playing stringed instruments

bowel [rhymes with **towel**] noun **1** intestine, especially the large intestine **2** **bowels** innermost part

bowerbird noun (Aust) bird found in Australia, the male of which builds a shelter during courtship

bowl [rhymes with **mole**] noun **1** round container with an open top **2** hollow part of an object **3** large heavy ball ▷ verb **4** (Cricket) to send (a ball) towards the batsman > **bowling** noun game in which bowls are rolled at a group of pins

bowls noun game played on smooth grass with wooden bowls

bow tie [rhymes with **low**] noun man's tie in the form of a bow, often worn at formal occasions

box noun **1** container with a firm flat base and sides **2** separate compartment in a theatre, stable, etc **3** evergreen tree with shiny leaves **4 the box** (informal) television ▷ verb **5** to put (something) into a box **6** to fight (an opponent) in a boxing match

boxer noun **1** person who participates in the sport of boxing **2** medium-sized dog with smooth hair and a short nose

boxing noun sport of fighting with the fists, wearing padded gloves

box office noun place where tickets are sold in a theatre or cinema

boy noun male child > **boyhood** noun period of being a boy > **boyish** adjective: a boyish grin

boycott verb **1** to refuse to deal with (an organization or country) ▷ noun **2** instance of boycotting

boyfriend noun male friend with whom a person is romantically involved

bra noun woman's undergarment for supporting the breasts

braaivleis or **braai** [**brye**-flayss] (SAfr) noun **1** grill on which food is cooked over hot charcoal, usually outdoors **2** outdoor party at which food is cooked in this way

brace noun **1** object fastened to something to straighten or support it **2** pair, especially of

game birds ▷ verb **3** to steady or prepare (yourself) for something unpleasant **4** to strengthen or fit (something) with a brace

bracelet noun ornamental chain or band for the wrist

bracing adjective refreshing and invigorating

bracken noun large fern

bracket noun **1** pair of characters used to enclose a section of writing **2** group that falls within certain defined limits **3** support fixed to a wall ▷ verb **4** to put (words or letters) in brackets **5** to class (people or things) together

brag brags, bragging, bragged verb to speak arrogantly and boastfully > **braggart** noun person who brags

Brahma [**brah**-ma] noun Hindu god, one of the Trimurti

Brahman [**brah**-men] noun in the Hindu religion, the ultimate and impersonal divine reality of the universe

brahmin [**brah**-min] noun member of the highest caste in Hindu society

braid verb **1** to plait (hair, thread, etc) > noun **2** length of hair etc that has been plaited **3** narrow ornamental tape of woven silk etc

braille noun system of writing for the blind, consisting of raised dots interpreted by touch

brain noun **1** soft mass of nervous tissue in the head that controls the body and enables thinking and feeling **2** intellectual ability

brainchild noun idea produced by creative thought

brainwash verb to cause (a person) to alter his or her beliefs, especially by methods based on isolation, sleeplessness, etc ▷ **brainwashing** noun

brainwave noun sudden clever idea

brainy brainier, brainiest adjective (informal) clever

braise verb to cook (food) slowly in a covered pan with a little liquid

brake noun **1** device for slowing or stopping a vehicle ▷ verb **2** to slow down or stop a vehicle by using a brake

> **WORD TIP**
> Do not confuse the spellings of brake and break, or braking and breaking

bramble noun prickly shrub that produces blackberries

bran noun husks of cereal grain

branch noun **1** part of a tree that grows out from its trunk **2** one of the offices or shops that are part of an organization **3** one of the areas of study or activity that are part of a subject ▷ verb **4** (of stems, roots, etc) to divide, then develop in different directions > **branch out** verb to try something different

brand noun **1** particular product **2** particular kind or variety **3** identifying mark burnt onto the skin of an animal ▷ verb **4** to mark (an animal) with a brand **5** to give (someone) a reputation for being as specified: I was branded as a rebel

brandish verb to wave (a weapon etc) in a threatening way

brand-new adjective absolutely new

brandy noun alcoholic spirit distilled from wine

brash adjective offensively loud, showy or self-confident > **brashness** noun being brash

brass noun **1** alloy of copper and zinc **2** family of wind instruments made of brass **3** (N English dialect) money

brassiere noun bra

brat noun unruly child

bravado [bra-**vah**-doh] noun showy display of self-confidence

brave adjective **1** having or showing courage and daring ▷ noun **2** Native American warrior ▷ verb **3** to confront (an unpleasant or dangerous situation) with courage > **bravely** adverb > **bravery** noun brave behaviour

bravo interjection well done!

brawl noun **1** noisy fight ▷ verb **2** to fight noisily

brawn noun **1** physical strength > **brawny** adjective strong and muscular

bray verb **1** (of a donkey) to utter its loud harsh sound ▷ noun **2** donkey's loud harsh sound

brazen adjective shameless and bold > **brazenly** adverb in a shameless and bold manner

brazier [**bray**-zee-er] noun portable container for burning charcoal or coal

Brazilian adjective **1** belonging or relating to Brazil ▷ noun **2** person from Brazil

breach noun **1** breaking of a promise, obligation, etc **2** gap or break ▷ verb **3** to break (a promise, law, etc) **4** to make a gap in (a barrier)

bread noun **1** food made by baking a mixture of flour and water or milk **2** (informal) money

breadth noun extent of something from side to side

breadwinner noun person whose earnings support a family

break breaks, breaking, broke, broken verb 1 to separate (something) into two or more pieces or become separated into two or more pieces 2 to damage (something) or become damaged so as to be unusable 3 to fail to observe (an agreement etc) 4 to end: *The good weather broke at last* 5 to weaken or be weakened, as in spirit 6 (of a boy's voice) to become permanently deeper 7 **break even** to make neither a profit nor a loss ▷ noun 8 act or result of breaking 9 gap or interruption in continuity ▷ **breakable** adjective ▷ **break down** verb 1 to stop working 2 to start crying ▷ **break up** verb 1 to come to an end 2 (of a school) to close for the holidays

> **WORD TIP**
>
> Do not confuse the spellings of *break* and *brake*, or *breaking* and *braking*.

breakage noun act of breaking something or a thing that has been broken

breakaway adjective (of a group) separated from a larger group

breakdown noun 1 act or instance of breaking down 2 nervous breakdown 3 details relating to the separate elements of something

breaker noun large wave

breakfast noun first meal of the day

break-in noun illegal entering of a building, especially by a burglar

breakneck adjective fast and dangerous

breakthrough noun important development or discovery

breakwater noun wall that extends into the sea to protect a coast from the force of the waves

bream noun 1 freshwater fish with silvery scales 2 food fish of European seas

breast noun 1 either of the two soft fleshy milk-secreting glands on a woman's chest 2 chest

breath noun 1 taking in and letting out of air during breathing 2 air taken in and let out during breathing

breathe verb to take air into the lungs and let it out again

breathless adjective breathing fast or with difficulty ▷ **breathlessly** adverb in a breathless manner ▷ **breathlessness** noun

breathtaking adjective very beautiful or exciting

bred verb past of **breed**

breeches [brit-chiz] plural noun trousers reaching to just below the knee

breed breeds, breeding, bred verb 1 to keep (animals or plants) in order to produce more animals or plants with particular qualities 2 to mate and produce offspring; reproduce ▷ noun 3 group of animals or plants within a species that have particular qualities

breeze noun gentle wind

breve noun MUSIC rarely used note twice the length of a semibreve. In the United States

a
b
c
d
e
f
g
h
i
j
k
l
m
n
o
p
q
r
s
t
u
v
w
x
y
z

and Canada, a breve is known as a double whole note

brevity noun shortness

brew verb 1 to make (beer) by boiling and fermenting malt 2 to make (tea or coffee) in a pot by pouring hot water over it 3 to be about to happen ▷ noun 4 beverage produced by brewing > **brewer** noun person or company that brews beer

brewery breweries noun place where beer is brewed

briar noun same as **brier**

bribe verb 1 to offer or give something to (someone) to gain favour, influence, etc ▷ noun 2 something given or offered as a bribe > **bribery** noun practice of bribing

bric-a-brac noun small ornaments or pieces of furniture of no great value

brick noun rectangular block of baked clay used in building

bricklayer noun person who builds with bricks

bride noun woman who has just been or is about to be married > **bridal** adjective: a bridal gown

bridegroom noun man who has just been or is about to be married

bridesmaid noun girl or woman who attends a bride at her wedding

bridge noun 1 structure for crossing a river etc 2 platform from which a ship is steered or controlled 3 upper part of the nose 4 piece of wood supporting the strings of a violin etc 5 card game based on whist, played between two pairs

bridle noun headgear for controlling a horse

brief adjective 1 lasting a short time ▷ noun 2 set of instructions ▷ verb 3 D&T to give information and instructions to > **briefly** adverb

briefcase noun small flat case for carrying papers, books, etc

briefing noun meeting at which information and instructions are given

brier or **briar** noun wild rose with long thorny stems

brigade noun army unit smaller than a division

brigadier [brig-ad-**ear**] noun high-ranking army officer

brigalow noun (Aust) type of acacia tree

bright adjective 1 giving out or reflecting a lot of light; brilliant 2 (of colours) intense or vivid 3 clever > **brightly** adverb > **brightness** noun

brighten verb 1 to become brighter 2 to look suddenly happier > **brighten up** verb to make (something) more attractive and cheerful

brilliant adjective 1 shining with light 2 splendid 3 extremely clever > **brilliance** noun > **brilliantly** adverb

brim noun 1 upper rim of a cup etc 2 wide part of a hat that sticks outwards at the bottom

brine noun salt water

bring brings, bringing, brought verb 1 to carry, convey or take (something or someone) to a particular place or person 2 to cause (something) to happen > **bring about** verb to cause (something) to happen > **bring off** verb to succeed in achieving (something) > **bring out** verb to produce (a new product) and offer it for sale > **bring up** verb **1** to rear (a child) **2** to mention (a subject) **3** to vomit (food)

brinjal noun (S Afr) dark purple tropical fruit, cooked and eaten as a vegetable

brink noun edge of a steep place

brisk adjective lively and quick > **briskly** adverb > **briskness** noun

bristle noun **1** short stiff hair ▷ verb **2** (of hair on an animal's body) to stand up like bristles > **bristly** adjective (of hair) thick and rough

British adjective belonging or relating to the United Kingdom of Great Britain and Northern Ireland

Briton noun person from the United Kingdom of Great Britain and Northern Ireland

brittle adjective hard but easily broken

broach verb to introduce (a topic) for discussion

broad adjective **1** having great breadth or width **2** not detailed **3** having many different aspects or concerning many different people: *a broad American accent* **4** strongly marked: *a broad American accent* > **broadly** adverb to a large extent in most cases

broadband noun telecommunication transmission technique using a wide range of frequencies

broad bean noun thick flat edible bean

broadcast broadcasts, broadcasting, broadcast noun **1** programme or announcement on radio or television ▷ verb

2 to transmit (a programme or announcement) on radio or television **3** to make (information) widely known > **broadcaster** noun person who broadcasts radio or television programmes > **broadcasting** noun transmission of radio or television programmes

broaden verb **1** to become wider **2** to cause (something) to involve more things or concern more people

broad-minded adjective tolerant or open-minded

broadsheet noun newspaper with large pages and long news stories

brocade noun rich fabric woven with a raised design

broccoli noun green vegetable, similar to cauliflower

brochure [broh-sher] noun booklet that contains information about a product or service

brogue [broag] noun **1** sturdy walking shoe **2** strong accent, especially Irish

broke verb **1** past tense of **break** ▷ adjective **2** (informal) having no money

broker noun person whose job is to buy and sell shares for other people

brolga noun (also **native companion**) large grey Australian crane with a trumpeting call

brolly brollies noun (informal) umbrella

bronchitis [bronk-**eye**-tiss] noun inflammation of the bronchi

brontosaurus noun very large plant-eating four-footed dinosaur

A
B
C
D
E
F
G
H
I
J
K
L
M
N
O
P
Q
R
S
T
U
V
W
X
Y
Z

bronze noun **1** alloy of copper and tin **2** statue, medal, etc made of bronze ▷ adjective **3** made of, or coloured like, bronze

brooch [rhymes with **coach**] noun ornament with a pin, worn fastened to clothes

brood noun **1** number of birds produced at one hatching ▷ verb **2** to think long and unhappily

brook noun small stream

broom noun **1** long-handled sweeping brush **2** yellow-flowered shrub

broth noun soup, usually containing vegetables

brother noun **1** boy or man with the same parents as another person **2** member of a male religious order ▷ **brotherly** adjective : a brotherly kiss

brotherhood noun **1** affection and loyalty between brothers or close male friends **2** association, such as a trade union

brother-in-law brothers-in-law noun **1** brother of your husband or wife **2** husband of your sister

brought verb past of **bring**

> **WORD TIP**
> Do not confuse brought and bought. Brought comes from bring and bought comes from buy

brow noun **1** part of the face from the eyes to the hairline **2** eyebrow **3** top of a hill

brown noun **1** colour of earth or wood ▷ adjective **2** of the colour brown

Brownie Guide or **Brownie** noun junior Guide

browse verb **1** to look through (a book or articles for sale) in a casual manner **2** (Computers) to look for information on the internet **3** to nibble on young shoots or leaves ▷ noun **4** instance of browsing

browser (Computers) software package that enables a user to read hypertext on the internet

bruise noun **1** discoloured area on the skin caused by an injury ▷ verb **2** to cause a bruise on (a part of the body)

brumby brumbies noun (Aust) wild horse

brunette noun girl or woman with dark brown hair

brunt noun main force or shock of a blow, attack, etc

brush noun **1** device made of bristles, wires, etc used for cleaning, painting, etc ▷ verb **2** to clean or scrub (something) with a brush **3** to touch (something) lightly and briefly ▷ **brush off** verb (informal) to dismiss or ignore (someone) ▷ **brush up** verb to refresh your knowledge of (a subject)

brusque [**broosk**] adjective blunt or curt in manner or speech ▷ **brusquely** adverb ▷ **brusqueness** noun

Brussels sprout noun vegetable like a tiny cabbage

brutal adjective cruel and violent ▷ **brutality** noun ▷ **brutally** adverb

brute noun **1** brutal person **2** large animal ▷ adjective **3** wholly instinctive or physical, like an animal **4** without reason ▷ **brutish** adjective of or like an animal

bubble noun **1** ball of air in a liquid or solid ▷ verb **2** to form bubbles **3** to move or flow with a gurgling sound ▷ **bubble over** verb to express an emotion freely ▷ **bubbly** adjective **1** excited and lively **2** full of bubbles

bucket noun deep open-topped container with a handle; pail

buckle noun **1** clasp for fastening a belt or strap ▷ verb **2** to fasten (a belt or strap) with a buckle **3** to bend out of shape through pressure or heat

bud buds, budding, budded noun **1** swelling on a tree or plant that develops into a leaf or flower ▷ verb **2** to produce buds ▷ **budding** adjective just beginning to develop

Buddha noun Indian religious teacher and founder of Buddhism

Buddhism noun [RE] eastern religion founded by Buddha ▷ **Buddhist** noun **1** person who believes in Buddhism ▷ adjective **2** of or relating to Buddhism

budge verb to move slightly

budgerigar noun small cage bird bred in many different-coloured varieties

budget noun **1** financial plan for a period of time **2** money allocated for a specific purpose ▷ verb **3** to plan the spending of money or time ▷ adjective **4** cheap ▷ **budgetary** adjective of or relating to a financial plan

budgie noun (informal) short for **budgerigar**

buff adjective dull yellowish-brown

buffalo buffaloes noun **1** wild animal like a large cow with long curved horns **2** (US) bison

buffer noun something that lessens shock or protects from damaging impact, circumstances, etc

buffet[1] [boof-ay] noun **1** café at a station **2** meal at which people serve themselves

buffet[2] [buff-it] verb (of wind or sea) to strike (a place or person) violently and repeatedly

bug bugs, bugging, bugged noun **1** small insect **2** (informal) minor illness **3** small mistake in a computer program **4** concealed microphone ▷ verb **5** (informal) to irritate (someone) **6** to conceal a microphone in a room or telephone)

bugle noun instrument like a small trumpet ▷ **bugler** noun person who plays a bugle

build builds, building, built verb **1** to make, construct or form (something) by joining parts or materials ▷ noun **2** shape of the body

building noun structure with walls and a roof

building society noun organization where money can be borrowed or invested

bulb noun **1** same as **light bulb** **2** onion-shaped root which grows into a flower or plant

Bulgarian adjective **1** belonging or relating to Bulgaria ▷ noun **2** person from Bulgaria **3** language spoken in Bulgaria

bulge noun **1** swelling on an otherwise flat or smooth surface ▷ verb **2** to swell outwards

bulk noun **1** size or volume, especially when great **2** main part **3 in bulk** in large quantities

bulky bulkier, bulkiest *adjective* large and heavy

bull *noun* male of some animals, such as cattle, elephants and whales

bulldog *noun* squat dog with a broad head and a muscular body

bulldozer *noun* powerful tractor for moving earth

bullet *noun* small piece of metal fired from a gun

bulletin *noun* short official report or announcement

bullion *noun* gold or silver in the form of bars

bullock *noun* young castrated bull

bullroarer *noun* (*Aust*) wooden slat attached to a string that is whirled round to make a roaring noise, used by Australian Aborigines in religious ceremonies

bully bullies, bullying, bullied *noun* **1** person who uses strength or power to hurt or frighten other people ▷ *verb* **2** to make (someone) do something by using force or threats

bump *verb* **1** (often followed by *into*) to knock or strike (something or someone) with a jolt ▷ *noun* **2** soft or dull noise made by something knocking into something else **3** raised uneven part; lump > **bump off** *verb* (*informal*) to murder > **bumpy** *adjective*

bumper *noun* **1** bar on the front or back of a vehicle to protect against damage **2** unusually large or abundant

bun *noun* **1** small sweet bread roll or cake **2** hair gathered into a ball shape at the back of the head

bunch *noun* **1** number of things growing, fastened or grouped together ▷ *verb* **2** to group (things) together or be grouped together in a bunch

bundle *noun* **1** number of things gathered loosely together ▷ *verb* **2** to push (someone or something) somewhere quickly and roughly

bung *noun* **1** stopper for a cask etc ▷ *verb* **2** (*Brit informal*) to throw (something) somewhere in a careless manner > **bung up** *verb* (*informal*) to block (a hole)

bungalow *noun* one-storey house

bungle *verb* to spoil (something) through incompetence

bunion *noun* painful lump on the big toe

bunk *noun* **1** narrow shelflike bed **2 do a bunk** (*Brit informal*) to leave a place without telling anyone

bunker *noun* **1** sand-filled hollow forming an obstacle on a golf course **2** underground shelter **3** large storage container for coal etc

bunting *noun* decorative flags

bunyip *noun* (*Aust*) legendary monster said to live in swamps and lakes

buoy [**boy**] *noun* floating object anchored in the sea to warn of danger

buoyant *adjective* **1** able to float **2** lively and cheerful > **buoyancy** *noun*

bureau bureaux [**byoo-roh**] *noun* **1** office that provides a service

2 writing desk with shelves and drawers

bureaucracy noun complex system of rules and procedures that operates in government departments > **bureaucratic** adjective involving complicated rules and procedures

bureaucrat noun person who works in a government department, especially one who follows rules and procedures strictly

burgeoning adjective growing or developing rapidly

burglar noun thief who breaks into a building > **burglary** noun: arrested for burglary

burgle verb to break into (someone's house) and steal things

burial noun RE burying of a dead body

burly burlier, burliest adjective (of a person) broad and strong

burn¹ burns, burning, burned or burnt verb **1** to be on fire or set (something) on fire **2** to destroy (something) by fire or be destroyed by fire **3** to damage, injure or mark (someone or something) by heat **4** to feel strong emotion **5** to record data on (a compact disc) > noun **6** injury or mark caused by fire or exposure to heat

> **WORD TIP**
> You can write either burned or burnt as the past form of burn

burn² noun (Scot) small stream

burp (informal) verb **1** to belch > noun **2** belch

burrow noun **1** hole dug in the ground by a rabbit etc > verb **2** to dig holes in the ground

bursary bursaries noun sum of money given to someone to help fund their education

burst bursts, bursting, burst verb **1** to break open or apart noisily and suddenly **2** to come or go somewhere suddenly and forcibly **3** to be full to the point of breaking open > noun **4** instance of breaking open suddenly **5** sudden outbreak or occurrence > **burst into** verb to be overcome by (tears or an emotion) suddenly

bury buries, burying, buried verb **1** to place (a dead body) in a grave **2** to place (something) in the earth and cover it with soil **3** to conceal or hide (something)

bus noun large motor vehicle for carrying passengers

bush noun **1** dense woody plant, smaller than a tree **2** wild uncultivated part of a country

bushman bushmen noun **1** (Aust, NZ) person who lives or travels in the bush **2** (NZ) person whose job is to clear the bush for farming

Bushman Bushmen noun (SAfr) member of a group of people in southern Africa who live by hunting and gathering food

bushranger noun (Aust, NZ) in the past, an outlaw living in the bush

bushy bushier, bushiest adjective (of hair) thick and shaggy

business noun **1** purchase and sale of goods and services **2** commercial establishment; company **3** trade or profession **4** proper concern or responsibility **5** affair: it's a dreadful business

businesslike adjective efficient and methodical

busker noun street entertainer

bust busts, busting, bust or busted *noun* **1** woman's bosom **2** sculpture of the head and shoulders ▷ *verb* (*informal*) **3** to burst or break **4** (of the police) to raid (a place) or arrest (someone) ▷ *adjective* (*informal*) **5** broken **6 go bust** to become bankrupt

bustle *verb* **1** to hurry with a show of activity or energy ▷ *noun* **2** energetic and noisy activity

busy busier, busiest; busies, busying, busied *adjective* **1** occupied doing something **2** crowded or full of activity ▷ *verb* **3** to keep (yourself) busy > **busily** *adverb* very actively

but *conjunction* **1** contrary to expectation **2** in contrast **3** other than **4** without it happening ▷ *preposition* **5** except ▷ *adverb* **6** only **7 but for** if it had not been for

butcher *noun* shopkeeper who sells meat

butler *noun* chief male servant

butt *noun* **1** thicker end of something **2** unused end of a cigar or cigarette **3** person or thing that is the target of ridicule **4** large barrel ▷ *verb* **5** to strike (something or someone) with the head or horns > **butt in** *verb* to interrupt a conversation

butter *noun* **1** soft fatty food made from cream, often eaten spread on bread or used in cooking ▷ *verb* **2** to put butter on (bread etc)

buttercup *noun* small yellow wild flower

butterfly butterflies *noun* insect with brightly coloured wings

buttock *noun* either half of the human bottom

button *noun* **1** small disc or knob sewn onto clothing, which can be passed through a slit in another piece of fabric to fasten it **2** knob that operates a piece of equipment when pressed ▷ *verb* **3** to fasten (a garment) with buttons

buttonhole *noun* **1** slit in a garment through which a button is passed **2** flower worn on a lapel

buxom *adjective* (of a woman) large, healthy and attractive

buy buys, buying, bought *verb* **1** to acquire (something) by paying money for it ▷ *noun* **2** thing acquired through payment > **buyer** *noun* **1** customer **2** person employed to buy merchandise

buzz *noun* **1** rapidly vibrating humming sound **2** (*informal*) sense of excitement ▷ *verb* **3** to make a humming sound **4** to be filled with an air of excitement > **buzz around** *verb* to move around quickly and busily

buzzard *noun* bird of prey of the hawk family

buzzer *noun* device that makes a buzzing sound

by *preposition* **1** indicating the doer of an action: *bitten by a dog* **2** indicating the manner or means of something: *travelling by train; He frightened her by hiding in the bushes* **3** beside or next to: *down by the river* **4** past: *driving by the school* **5** at or before: *in bed by midnight* ▷ *adverb* **6** past **7 by and by** eventually **8 by and large** in general

by-election *noun* election held to choose a new member of

parliament after the previous
member has resigned or died

bygone *adjective* past or former

bypass *noun* main road built to
avoid a city

bystander *noun* person present
but not involved

byte *noun* [ICT] (*Computers*) group
of bits processed as one unit
of data

C

cab *noun* **1** taxi **2** enclosed driver's
compartment on a train, truck, etc

cabaret [kab-a-ray] *noun* dancing
and singing show in a nightclub

cabbage *noun* vegetable with a
large head of green leaves

cabbage tree *noun* (*NZ*) a palm-
like tree found in New Zealand
with a tall bare trunk and big
bunches of spiky leaves; also
a similar tree found in eastern
Australia

cabin *noun* **1** room in a ship or boat
where a passenger sleeps **2** area
where the passengers or the crew
sit in a plane **3** small wooden hut,
usually in the country

cabinet *noun* **1** piece of furniture
with drawers or shelves
2 Cabinet committee of senior
government ministers

cable *noun* **1** strong thick rope
2 bundle of wires that carries
electricity or electronic signals
3 telegram sent abroad ▷ *verb*
4 to send (someone) a message
by cable

cable car *noun* vehicle pulled up a
steep slope by a moving cable

cable television *noun* television
service people can subscribe
to and which is received from
underground wires which carry
the signals

cacao [kak-**kah**-oh] *noun* tropical tree with seed pods from which chocolate and cocoa are made

cache [kash] *noun* hidden store of weapons or treasure: *a cache of guns*

cachet [kash-shay] *noun* (*formal*) status and respect something has

cackle *verb* **1** to laugh harshly ▷ *noun* **2** harsh laugh

cacophony [kak-**koff**-on-ee] *noun* (*formal*) harsh discordant sound

cactus *noun*, *pl* **cacti** or **cactuses** fleshy desert plant with spines but no leaves

cad *noun* (*old-fashioned*) man who behaves dishonourably

caddie or **caddy** *noun* **1** person who carries a golfer's clubs ▷ *verb* **2** to act as a golf caddie

cadence [kade-enss] *noun* rise and fall in the pitch of the voice

cadet *noun* young person training for the armed forces or police

cadge *verb* (*informal*) to get (something) by taking advantage of someone's generosity: *I cadged a lift*

Caesarean or **Caesarian** [siz-air-ee-an] *noun* (also **Caesarean section**) surgical operation in which a pregnant woman's baby is delivered through a cut in its mother's abdomen

café [kaf-fay] *noun* **1** small or inexpensive restaurant serving light refreshments **2** (*S Afr*) corner shop or grocer

cafeteria [kaf-fit-**ee**-ree-ya] *noun* self-service restaurant

caffeine [kaf-feen] *noun* stimulant found in tea and coffee

cage *noun* **1** enclosure of bars or wires, for keeping animals or birds **2** enclosed platform of a lift in a mine ▷ **caged** *adjective* kept in a cage

cagey *adjective* cagier, cagiest [kay-jee] *adjective* (*informal*) reluctant to go into details

cagoule [ka-**gool**] *noun* (*Brit*) lightweight hooded waterproof jacket

cahoots *plural noun* **in cahoots** (*informal*) conspiring together

cairn *noun* mound of stones erected as a memorial or marker

cajole *verb* to persuade by flattery: *He allowed himself to be cajoled into staying on*

cake *noun* **1** sweet food baked from a mixture of flour, eggs, etc **2** flat compact mass of something, such as soap ▷ *verb* **3** to form into a hardened mass or crust

calamity *noun*, *pl* **calamities** event that causes disaster or distress > **calamitous** *adjective* resulting in or from disaster

calcium *noun* [**kal**-see-um] (*Chemistry*) silvery-white metallic element found in bones, teeth, limestone and chalk

calculate *verb* **1** to work out by a mathematical procedure or by reasoning **2** to plan deliberately; intend

calculating *adjective* selfishly scheming: *a calculating man*

calculator *noun* small electronic device for making calculations

calculus *noun* branch of mathematics dealing with infinitesimal changes to a variable number or quantity

calendar *noun* **1** chart showing a year divided up into months, weeks and days **2** system for determining the beginning, length and division of years: *the Jewish calendar* **3** schedule of events or appointments

calf calves *noun* **1** young cow, bull, elephant, whale or seal **2** leather made from calf skin **3** back of the leg between the ankle and knee

calibre [kal-lib-ber] *noun* **1** person's ability or worth: *a player of her calibre* **2** diameter of the bore of a gun or of a shell or bullet

call *verb* **1** to name **2** to shout to attract attention **3** to telephone **4** to summon **5** (often followed by *on*) to visit **6** to arrange (a meeting, strike, etc) *▷ noun* **7** cry or shout **8** animal's or bird's cry **9** telephone communication **10** short visit **11** summons or invitation **12** need or demand *▷* **call for** *verb* **1** to require **2** to come and fetch *▷* **call off** *verb* to cancel *▷* **call up** *verb* **1** to summon to serve in the armed forces **2** to cause you to remember (something)

call box *noun* kiosk for a public telephone

call centre *noun* office where staff deal with customers' orders or questions over the telephone

calling *noun* **1** profession or career, especially a caring one **2** strong urge to follow a particular career or profession, especially a caring one

callous *adjective* showing no concern for other people's feelings *▷* **callously** *adverb ▷* **callousness** *noun: the callousness of his attacker*

calm *adjective* **1** not agitated or excited **2** (of sea or weather) not affected by the wind *▷ noun* **3** peaceful state *▷ verb* **4** to calm

down *▷* **calm down** *verb* to make (someone) calm or become calm *▷* **calmly** *adverb ▷* **calmness** *noun*

calorie *noun* **1** unit of measurement for the energy value of food **2** unit of heat equal to about 4.187 joules *▷* **calorific** *adjective* of calories or heat

calves the plural of **calf**

calypso calypsos [kal-**lip**-soh] *noun* West Indian song with improvised topical lyrics

calyx calyxes or calyces [**kay**-lix] *noun* (*Botany*) outer leaves that protect a flower bud

camaraderie [kam-mer-**rah**-der-ree] *noun* feeling of trust and friendship between a group of people

camber *noun* slight upward curve towards the centre of a road

camel *noun* humped mammal that can survive long periods without food or water in desert regions

cameo cameos *noun* **1** small part in a film or play performed by a well-known actor or actress **2** brooch or ring with a carving on it, typically of a head in profile, in a different coloured stone from the background

camera *noun* **1** apparatus used for taking photographs or pictures for television or cinema *▷* **in camera** in private session

camomile or **chamomile** *noun* plant with a strong smell and daisy-like flowers which are used to make herbal tea

camouflage [kam-mof-flahj] *noun* **1** use of natural surroundings or artificial aids to conceal or disguise something *▷ verb* **2** to conceal by camouflage

camp noun 1 (place for) temporary lodgings consisting of tents, huts or cabins 2 group supporting a particular idea or belief: *the pro-government camp* ▷ verb 3 to stay in a camp ▷ adjective 4 (*informal*) effeminate or homosexual 5 (*informal*) consciously artificial or affected > **camper** noun person who stays temporarily in a tent, hut or cabin > **camping** noun activity of staying in tents, huts or cabins by holidaymakers, travellers, etc

campaign [kam-**pane**] noun 1 series of coordinated activities designed to achieve a goal ▷ verb 2 to take part in a campaign > **campaigner** noun person who campaigns to achieve a goal

camp-drafting noun (*Aust*) competition in which men on horseback select cattle or sheep from a herd or flock

campus campuses noun area of land and the buildings that make up a university or college

can¹ could verb 1 to be able to: *I can speak Italian* 2 to be allowed to: *You can go to the cinema*

can² cans, canning, canned noun 1 metal container for food or liquids ▷ verb 2 to put (something) into a can

Canadian adjective 1 belonging to or relating to Canada ▷ noun 2 someone from Canada

canal noun 1 artificial waterway 2 passage in the body

canary canaries noun small yellow songbird often kept as a pet

can-can noun lively high-kicking dance performed by a female group

cancel cancels, cancelling, cancelled verb 1 to stop (something that has been arranged) from taking place 2 to mark (a cheque or stamp) with an official stamp to prevent further use > **cancel out** to make ineffective by having the opposite effect: *Their opening goal was cancelled out just before half-time* > **cancellation** noun

cancer noun 1 serious disease resulting from a malignant growth or tumour 2 malignant growth or tumour > **cancerous** adjective resulting from cancer

candelabra or **candelabrum** noun large branched candle holder

candid adjective honest and straightforward > **candidly** adverb

candidate noun 1 person seeking a job or position 2 person taking an examination > **candidacy** or **candidature** noun position of being a candidate in an election

candied adjective covered or cooked in sugar

candle noun stick of wax enclosing a wick, which is burned to produce light

candlestick noun holder for a candle

candy candies noun (*US*) sweet or sweets

cane noun 1 stem of the bamboo or similar plant 2 flexible rod used to beat someone 3 slender walking stick ▷ verb 4 to beat with a cane

canine [**kay**-nine] adjective 1 of or like a dog ▷ noun 2 sharp pointed tooth between the incisors and the molars

canister noun metal container

cannabis *noun* drug obtained from the dried leaves and flowers of the hemp plant

canned *adjective* **1** preserved in a can **2** (of music or laughter on a television or radio show) recorded beforehand

cannibal *noun* **1** person who eats human flesh **2** animal that eats others of its own kind > **cannibalism** *noun* practice of eating the flesh of one's own kind

cannon *noun* large wheeled gun formerly used in battles to fire heavy metal balls

cannot *verb* can not: *She cannot come home yet*

canny cannier, canniest *adjective* clever and cautious > **cannily** *adverb*

canoe [ka-**noo**] *noun* light narrow open boat propelled by a paddle or paddles > **canoeing** *noun* sport of rowing in a canoe > **canoeist** *noun* person who rows a canoe

canon *noun* **1** priest serving in a cathedral **2** Church decree regulating morals or religious practices **3** general rule or standard: *the first canon of nursing*

canopy canopies *noun* **1** covering above a bed, door, etc **2** any large or wide covering: *the thick forest canopy*

cantankerous *adjective* quarrelsome or bad-tempered

canteen *noun* **1** restaurant attached to a workplace or school **2** box containing a set of cutlery

canter *noun* **1** movement of a horse at a speed between a trot and a gallop ▷ *verb* **2** to move at a canter

cantilever *noun* beam or girder fixed at one end only

canton *noun* political and administrative region of a country, especially Switzerland

canvas *noun* **1** heavy coarse cloth used for sails and tents **2** piece of canvas or similar material on which you can paint with oils **3** oil painting on canvas

canvass *verb* **1** to try to get votes or support for a particular person or political party: *a woman who canvassed for the Conservatives* **2** to find out the opinions of (people) by conducting a survey ▷ *noun* **3** activity of canvassing

canyon *noun* deep narrow valley

cap caps, capping, capped *noun* **1** soft, flat hat, often with a peak at the front **2** small lid **3** small explosive device used in a toy gun **4** upper financial limit ▷ *verb* **5** to cover or top with something **6** to select (a player) for a national team **7** to impose an upper limit on (a tax) **8** to outdo or excel: *capping anecdote with anecdote*

capable *adjective* **1** skilful or talented **2 capable of** able to do something: *a man capable of extreme violence* > **capably** *adverb*

capacitor *noun* D&T device for storing electrical charge

capacity capacities [kap-**pas**-sit-tee] *noun* **1** ability to contain, absorb or hold **2** maximum amount or number that can be contained or produced: *a seating capacity of eleven thousand* **3** physical or mental ability: *people's creative capacities* **4** position or role: *in his capacity as councillor*

cape *noun* **1** short cloak with no sleeves **2** large piece of land that juts out into the sea

caper noun **1** a light-hearted practical joke ▷ verb **2** to skip about playfully

capillary capillaries [kap-**pill**-lar-ree] noun very fine blood vessel

capital noun **1** chief city of a country **2** amount of money or property owned or used by a business **3** sum of money saved or invested in order to gain interest **4** large letter, as used at the beginning of a name or sentence **5** top part of a stone column, often decorated ▷ adjective **6** (Law) involving or punishable by death: a capital offence

capitalism noun economic system based on the private ownership of industry > **capitalist** adjective **1** of capitalists or capitalism **2** supporting capitalism ▷ noun **3** supporter of capitalism **4** person who owns a business

capitalize or **capitalise** verb **1** to write or print (words) in capitals **2** to convert into or provide with capital **3** capitalize on to take advantage of (a situation)

capital punishment noun legal killing used as a punishment for certain crimes

capitulate verb to surrender on agreed terms > **capitulation** noun surrender under agreed conditions

cappuccino cappuccinos [kap-poo-**cheen**-oh] noun coffee with steamed milk, sprinkled with powdered chocolate

capricious [kap-**prish**-uss] adjective often changing unexpectedly

Capricorn noun tenth sign of the zodiac, represented by a goat

capsize verb (of a boat) to overturn accidentally

capsule noun **1** soluble gelatine case containing a dose of medicine **2** plant's seed case **3** detachable crew compartment of a spacecraft

captain noun **1** commander of a ship or civil aircraft **2** middle-ranking naval officer **3** junior officer in the army **4** leader of a team or group ▷ verb **5** to be captain of > **captaincy** noun position of being captain

caption noun **1** title or explanation accompanying an illustration ▷ verb **2** to provide with a caption

captivate verb to attract and hold the attention of: I was captivated by her > **captivating** adjective: her captivating smile

captive noun **1** person kept in confinement ▷ adjective **2** kept in confinement: a captive bird **3** (of an audience) unable to leave > **captivity** noun state of being kept in confinement

captor noun person who captures a person or animal

capture verb **1** to take by force **2** to succeed in representing (a quality or emotion): Today's newspapers capture the mood of the nation ▷ noun **3** capturing: the fifth anniversary of his capture

car noun **1** motor vehicle designed to carry a small number of people **2** passenger compartment of a cable car, lift, etc **3** (US) railway carriage

carafe [kar-**raff**] noun glass bottle for serving water or wine

caramel noun **1** chewy sweet made from sugar and milk **2** burnt sugar, used for colouring and flavouring food

carat noun **1** unit of weight of precious stones **2** measure of the purity of gold in an alloy

caravan noun **1** large enclosed vehicle for living in, designed to be towed by a car **2** group travelling together in Eastern countries

carb noun short for **carbohydrate, carburettor**

carbohydrate noun D&T any of a large group of energy-producing compounds in food, such as sugars and starches

carbon noun non-metallic element occurring as charcoal, graphite and diamond, found in all organic matter

carbonated adjective (of a drink) containing carbon dioxide

carbon dioxide noun colourless gas breathed out by people and animals, and used in fire extinguishers and in making fizzy drinks

carbon footprint noun measure of the carbon dioxide produced by an individual or company

carbon offset noun act which compensates for carbon emissions of an individual or company

carburettor [**kahr**-bur-ret-ter] noun device which mixes petrol and air in an internal-combustion engine

carcass noun dead body of an animal

card noun **1** piece of thick stiff paper or cardboard used for identification, reference or sending greetings or messages: a birthday card **2** one of a set of cards with a printed pattern, used for playing games **3** small rectangle of stiff plastic with identifying numbers for use as a credit card, cheque card or charge card **4 cards** any card game, or card games in general **5 on the cards** very likely to happen

cardboard noun thin stiff board made from paper pulp

cardiac adjective relating to the heart

cardigan noun knitted jacket that fastens up the front

cardinal noun **1** any of the high-ranking clergymen of the RC Church who elect the Pope and act as his counsellors ▷ adjective **2** fundamentally important

care verb **1** to be concerned **2** to like (to do something) ▷ noun **3** careful attention or caution: Treat with extreme care **4** protection or charge: The children are now in the care of an orphanage **5** trouble or worry: money cares **6 care of** at the address of **7 in care** (of a child) cared for by the state > **care for** verb **1** to like or be fond of **2** to look after

career noun **1** series of jobs in a profession or occupation that a person has through their life **2** part of a person's life spent in a particular occupation ▷ verb **3** to rush in an uncontrolled way

carefree adjective having no worries or responsibilities

careful adjective **1** acting sensibly and with care: Be careful what you say to him **2** complete and well done: It needs very careful planning > **carefully** adverb

careless adjective **1** done badly without enough attention:

careless driving **2** relaxed and unconcerned: *careless laughter* ▷ **carelessly** *adverb* ▷ **carelessness** *noun*: *drivers who kill through carelessness*

caress *noun* **1** gentle affectionate touch or embrace ▷ *verb* **2** to touch gently and affectionately

caretaker *noun* **1** person employed to look after a place ▷ *adjective* **2** temporarily in charge until a new leader or government is appointed; acting: *O'Leary was named caretaker manager*

cargo *cargoes* *noun* goods carried by a ship, aircraft, etc

caricature *noun* **1** drawing or description of a person that exaggerates features for comic effect ▷ *verb* **2** to make a caricature of

carjack *carjacks, carjacking, carjacked* *verb* to attack (a driver in a car) in order to rob the driver or to steal the car for another crime

carnage [kahr-nij] *noun* violent killing of large numbers of people

carnal *adjective (formal)* of a sexual or sensual nature

carnation *noun* cultivated plant with fragrant white, pink or red flowers

carnival *noun* festive period with processions, music and dancing in the street

carnivore *noun* meat-eating animal ▷ **carnivorous** *adjective* meat-eating

carol *noun* joyful religious song sung at Christmas time

carousel [kar-roo-**sell**] *noun* **1** revolving conveyor belt for luggage or photographic slides **2** (*US*) merry-go-round

carp *noun* **1** large freshwater fish ▷ *verb* **2** to complain or find fault

carpel *noun* seed-bearing female part of a flowering plant

carpenter *noun* person who makes or repairs wooden structures ▷ **carpentry** *noun* skill or work of a carpenter

carpet *noun* **1** heavy fabric for covering floors ▷ *verb* **2** to cover with a carpet

carriage *noun* **1** one of the sections of a train for passengers **2** four-wheeled horse-drawn vehicle **3** moving part of a machine that supports and shifts another part: *a typewriter carriage* **4** charge made for conveying goods **5** way a person holds their head and body when they move

carriageway *noun* **1** (*Brit*) part of a road along which traffic passes in one direction **2** (*NZ*) part of a road used by vehicles

carrier *noun* **1** person or thing that carries something: *a troop carrier* **2** person or animal that does not suffer from a disease but can transmit it to others

carrier bag *noun* bag made of plastic or paper, used for carrying shopping

carrion *noun* dead and rotting flesh

carrot *noun* **1** long tapering orange root vegetable **2** something offered as an incentive

carry *carries, carrying, carried* *verb* **1** to take (something) from one place to another **2** to have (something) with you habitually, in your pocket etc **3** to be capable of transmitting (a disease) **4** to have as a factor or result: *The*

A
B
C
D
E
F
G
H
I
J
K
L
M
N
O
P
Q
R
S
T
U
V
W
X
Y
Z

charge carries a maximum penalty of twenty years **5** to secure the adoption of (a bill or motion) **6** (of sound) to travel a certain distance > **carry away** *verb* **be carried away, get carried away** to behave hastily or foolishly through excitement > **carry on** *verb* **1** to continue **2** (*informal*) to cause a fuss > **carry out** *verb* **1** to follow (an order or instruction) **2** to accomplish (a task)

cart *noun* **1** vehicle with wheels, used to secure goods and often pulled by horses, donkeys or oxen > *verb* **2** to carry, usually with some effort

cartilage *noun* strong flexible tissue forming part of the skeleton

carton *noun* container made of cardboard or waxed paper

cartoon *noun* **1** humorous or satirical drawing **2** sequence of these telling a story **3** film made by photographing a series of drawings which give the illusion of movement when projected > **cartoonist** *noun* person who draws cartoons

cartridge *noun* **1** casing containing an explosive charge and bullet for a gun **2** part of the pick-up of a record player that converts the movements of the stylus into electrical signals **3** sealed container of film, tape, etc

cartwheel *noun* acrobatic movement in which you turn over sideways in a wheel-like motion with your weight supported in turns by your hands and feet

carve *verb* **1** to cut (something) to form an object **2** to form (an object or design) by cutting **3** to slice (cooked) meat

carving *noun* carved object

cascade *noun* **1** waterfall or group of waterfalls **2** something flowing or falling like a waterfall > *verb* **3** to flow or fall in a cascade

case *noun* **1** particular situation, event or example: *a clear case of mistaken identity* **2** condition or state of affairs **3** set of arguments supporting an action or cause **4** person or problem dealt with by a doctor, social worker, solicitor or police officer **5** container or protective covering **6** trial or lawsuit **7** (*Grammar*) form of a noun, pronoun or adjective showing its relation to other words in the sentence: *the accusative case* **8 in case** allowing for the possibility that: *I didn't want to shout in case I startled you*

casement *noun* window that is hinged on one side

cash *cashes, cashing, cashed noun* **1** banknotes and coins > *verb* **2** to obtain cash for **3 cash in on** (*informal*) to gain profit or advantage from

cashew [**kash**-oo] *noun* edible kidney-shaped nut

cash flow *noun* money that a business makes and spends

cashier *noun* **1** person responsible for handling cash in a bank, shop, etc > *verb* **2** to dismiss (someone) with dishonour from the armed forces

cashmere *noun* fine soft wool obtained from goats

cash register *noun* till that displays and adds the prices of the goods sold

casing noun protective case, covering

casino casinos [kass-**ee**-noh] noun public building or room where gambling games are played

cask noun 1 barrel used to hold alcoholic drink 2 (Aust) cubic carton containing wine, with a tap for dispensing

casket noun 1 small box for valuables 2 (US) coffin

casserole noun 1 covered dish in which food is cooked slowly, usually in an oven 2 dish cooked in this way ▷ verb 3 to cook in a casserole

cassette noun plastic case containing a reel of film or magnetic tape

cassette recorder noun machine used for recording and playing cassettes

cassock noun long tunic, usually black, worn by priests

cassowary cassowaries noun large flightless bird of Australia and New Guinea

cast casts, casting, cast noun 1 actors in a play or film collectively 2 object shaped by a mould while molten 3 mould used to shape such an object 4 rigid plaster-of-Paris casing for immobilizing broken bones while they heal ▷ verb 5 to select (an actor) to play a part in a play or film 6 to give or deposit (a vote) 7 to throw (a fishing line) into the water 8 to shape (an object) by pouring molten material into a mould: An image of him has been cast in bronze 9 to throw with force 10 to direct (a glance)

castanets plural noun musical instrument, used by Spanish dancers, consisting of curved pieces of wood clicked together in the hand

castaway noun shipwrecked person

caste noun 1 any of the four hereditary classes into which Hindu society is divided 2 system of social classes decided according to family, wealth and position

caster sugar or **castor sugar** noun finely ground white sugar

castigate verb (formal) to reprimand (a person) harshly

cast-iron adjective 1 made of a hard but brittle type of iron 2 definite or unchallengeable

castle noun 1 large fortified building, often built as a ruler's residence 2 rook in chess

cast-off noun discarded person or thing

castor or **caster** noun small swivelling wheel fixed to the bottom of a piece of furniture for easy moving

castor oil noun oil obtained from an Indian plant, used as a lubricant and laxative

castrate verb to remove the testicles of > **castration** noun removal of the testicles from a male animal

casual adjective 1 careless or without interest: a casual glance over his shoulder 2 (of work or workers) occasional or not permanent: casual labour in the farm industry 3 for informal wear 4 happening by chance: a casual remark > **casually** adverb

casualty casualties noun 1 person killed or injured in an accident or war 2 person or thing that has suffered as the result of something

casuarina [kass-yew-a-**reen**-a] *noun* Australian tree with jointed green branches

cat *noun* **1** small domesticated furry mammal **2** related wild mammal, such as the lion or tiger **3 let the cat out of the bag** to reveal a secret

catacombs [**kat**-a-koomz] *plural noun* underground burial place consisting of tunnels with recesses for tombs

catalogue catalogues, cataloguing, catalogued *noun* **1** book containing details of items for sale **2** systematic list of items ▷ *verb* **3** to make a systematic list of

catalyst [**kat**-a-list] *noun* **1** substance that speeds up a chemical reaction without itself changing **2** something that causes a change to happen: *the catalyst which provoked civil war*

catamaran *noun* boat with two parallel hulls connected to each other

catapult *noun* **1** Y-shaped device with a loop of elastic, used by children for firing stones ▷ *verb* **2** to shoot forwards or upwards violently **3** to cause (someone) suddenly to be in a particular situation: *catapulted to stardom*

cataract *noun* **1** area of the lens of someone's eye that has become opaque instead of clear, preventing them from seeing properly **2** large waterfall

catarrh [kat-**tar**] *noun* condition in which you get a lot of mucus in your nose and throat

catastrophe [kat-**ass**-trof-fee] *noun* great and sudden disaster ▷ **catastrophic** *adjective* disastrous

catch catches, catching, caught *verb* **1** to seize and hold **2** to capture (a person or animal): *I caught ten fish* **3** to surprise in an act: *Two boys were caught stealing* **4** to hit unexpectedly: *His shoe caught me in the belly* **5** to be in time for (a bus, train, etc) **6** to see or hear **7** to become infected with (an illness) **8** to entangle or become entangled: *The white fibres caught on the mesh* **9** to understand or make out: *I didn't quite catch his meaning* **10 catch it** (*informal*) to be punished ▷ *noun* **11** device for fastening a door, window, etc **12** (*informal*) concealed or unforeseen drawback ▷ **catch on** *verb* (*informal*) **1** to become popular **2** to understand ▷ **catch out** *verb* (*informal*) to trap (someone) in an error or lie ▷ **catch up** *verb* **1** (often followed by with) to reach the same place or level (as someone): *She ran to catch up with him* **2** (often followed by on, with) to do something in order to get up to date (with something): *He had a lot of paperwork to catch up on* **3 be caught up in** to be unwillingly or accidentally involved in

catching *adjective* infectious

catchy catchier, catchiest *adjective* (of a tune) pleasant and easily remembered

catechism [kat-ti-kiz-zum] *noun* instruction on the doctrine of a Christian Church in a series of questions and answers

categorical *adjective* absolutely clear and certainly: *a categorical denial* > **categorically** *adverb*

categorize or **categorise** *verb* to put in a category

category categories *noun* set of things with a particular characteristic in common: *Occupations can be divided into four categories*

cater *verb* to provide what is needed or wanted, especially food or services

caterer *noun* person or business that provides food for parties and groups

caterpillar *noun* wormlike larva of a moth or butterfly

catharsis catharses [kath-**thar**-siss] *noun* (*formal*) relief of strong suppressed emotions, for example through drama or psychoanalysis > **cathartic** *adjective* causing catharsis: *His laughter was cathartic*

cathedral *noun* important church with a bishop in charge of it

cattle *plural noun* domesticated cows and bulls

catty cattier, cattiest *adjective* (*informal*) unpleasant and spiteful > **cattiness** *noun*

catwalk *noun* narrow pathway or platform that people walk along, for example over a stage

Caucasian [kaw-**kayz**-yn] *adjective* **1** of the race of people with light-coloured skin > *noun* **2** person belonging to this race

caught *verb* past of **catch**

cauldron *noun* large pot used for boiling

cauliflower *noun* vegetable with a large head of white flower buds surrounded by green leaves

cause *noun* **1** something that produces a particular effect **2** aim or principle supported by a person or group: *dedication to the cause of peace* **3** **cause for** reason or motive > *verb* **4** to be the cause of

causeway *noun* raised path or road across water or marshland

caustic *adjective* **1** capable of burning by chemical action **2** bitter and sarcastic

caution *noun* **1** care, especially in the face of danger **2** warning > *verb* **3** to warn or advise: *He cautioned against an abrupt turnaround* > **cautionary** *adjective* warning

cautious *adjective* acting with or involving great care in order to avoid danger or risk > **cautiously** *adverb*

cavalcade *noun* procession of people on horseback or in cars

cavalier [kav-val-**eer**] *adjective* **1** arrogant and behaving without sensitivity > *noun* **2** **Cavalier** supporter of Charles I in the English Civil War

cavalry cavalries *noun* part of the army originally on horseback, but now using fast armoured vehicles

cave *noun* hollow in the side of a hill or cliff > **cave in** *verb* **1** to collapse inwards > **2** (*informal*) to give way under pressure

caveman cavemen *noun* prehistoric cave dweller

cavern *noun* large cave

cavernous *adjective* large, deep and hollow

caviar or **caviare** [**kav**-ee-ar] *noun* tiny salted eggs of the sturgeon, regarded as a delicacy

cavity cavities *noun* **1** hollow space **2** decayed area on a tooth

cavort verb to jump around excitedly

caw noun 1 cry of a crow, rook or raven ▷ verb 2 to make this cry

cc abbreviation 1 cubic centimetre 2 carbon copy

CD abbreviation compact disc

CD-ROM abbreviation compact disc read-only memory

cease verb to bring or come to an end

ceaseless adjective going on without stopping > **ceaselessly** adverb

cedar noun 1 evergreen coniferous tree 2 its wood

cede [seed] verb to surrender (territory or legal rights): Haiti was ceded to France in 1697

ceiling noun 1 inner upper surface of a room 2 upper limit set on something: a ceiling on prices

celebrate verb 1 to hold festivities to mark (a happy event, anniversary, etc): a party to celebrate the end of the exams 2 [RE] to perform (a religious ceremony) > **celebration** noun: a celebration of his life > **celebratory** adjective: a celebratory meal

celebrated adjective well known

celebrity celebrities noun 1 famous person 2 state of being famous

celery noun vegetable with long green crisp edible stalks

celestial [sil-**lest**-yal] adjective (formal) 1 heavenly or divine 2 of the sky: stars, planets and other celestial objects

celibate [**sel**-lib-bit] adjective 1 unmarried and abstaining from sex ▷ noun 2 celibate person > **celibacy** noun state of being celibate

cell noun 1 smallest unit of an organism that is able to function independently 2 small room for a prisoner, monk or nun 3 small compartment of a honeycomb etc 4 small group operating as the core of a larger organization 5 device that produces electrical energy by chemical reaction

cellar noun 1 underground room for storage 2 stock of wine

cello cellos [**chell**-oh] noun large low-pitched instrument of the violin family > **cellist** noun person who plays the cello

Cellophane ® noun thin transparent cellulose sheeting used as wrapping

cellphone noun a small portable telephone

cellular adjective relating to the cells of animals or plants

cellular phone noun same as cellphone

celluloid [**sel**-yul-loyd] noun kind of plastic used to make toys and, formerly, photographic film

Celsius [**sel**-see-yuss] noun temperature scale in which water freezes at 0° and boils at 100°

Celtic [**kel**-tik] noun 1 group of languages including Gaelic and Welsh ▷ adjective 2 of the Celts or the Celtic languages

cement noun 1 fine grey powder mixed with water and sand to make mortar or concrete 2 something that unites, binds or joins 3 material used to fill teeth ▷ verb 4 to join, bind or cover with cement 5 to make (a relationship) stronger

cemetery cemeteries noun place where dead people are buried

cenotaph [sen-not-ahf] *noun* monument honouring soldiers who died in a war

censor *noun* **1** person authorized to examine films, books, etc, to ban or cut anything considered obscene or objectionable ▷ *verb* **2** to ban or cut parts of (a film, book, etc) > **censorship** *noun* practice or policy of censoring films, publications, etc

censure [sen-sher] *noun* **1** severe disapproval ▷ *verb* **2** to criticize (someone or something) severely

census censuses *noun* official count of a population

cent *noun* hundredth part of a monetary unit such as the dollar or euro

centaur [sen-tawr] *noun* Greek mythological creature with the head, arms and torso of a man, and the lower body and legs of a horse

centenary centenaries [sen-teen-a-ree] *noun* (Chiefly Brit) 100th anniversary or its celebration

centi- *prefix* one hundredth: *centimetre*

centigrade *adjective* same as **Celsius**

> **WORD TIP**
> Scientists say and write *Celsius* rather than *centigrade*

centilitre *noun* one hundredth of a litre

centime [sonn-team] *noun* unit of currency used in Switzerland and some other countries, and formerly used in Belgium

centimetre *noun* (MATHS) one hundredth of a metre

centipede *noun* small wormlike creature with many legs

central *adjective* **1** of, at or forming the centre **2** main or most important > **centrally** *adverb*

Central America *noun* another name for the Isthmus of Panama, the area of land joining North America to South America

central heating *noun* system of heating a building in which water or air is heated in a tank and travels through pipes and radiators round the building

centralize or **centralise** *verb* to bring (a country or an organization) under central control > **centralization** *noun* process of bringing under central control

centre *noun* **1** middle point or part **2** place for a specified activity: *a health centre* **3** political party or group favouring moderation **4** (Sport) player who plays in the middle of the field ▷ *verb* **5** to put in the centre of something **6** centre on to have as a centre or main theme

centrifugal [sen-trif-**yoo**-gl] *adjective* moving away from a centre

centripetal [sen-**trip**-pe-tl] *adjective* moving towards a centre

centurion *noun* (in ancient Rome) officer commanding 100 men

century centuries *noun* **1** period of 100 years **2** cricket score of 100 runs by a batsman

ceramic [sir-**ram**-mik] *noun* **1** hard brittle material made by heating clay to a very high temperature **2** object made of this **3** ceramics art of producing ceramic objects ▷ *adjective* **4** made of ceramic

cereal *noun* **1** grass plant with edible grain, such as oat or wheat

2 this grain **3** breakfast food made from this grain, eaten mixed with milk

cerebral [**ser**-rib-ral, ser-**reeb**-ral] *adjective* (*formal*) **1** of or relating to the brain **2** involving intelligence rather than emotions or instinct

cerebral palsy *noun* illness caused by damage to a baby's brain, which makes its muscles and limbs very weak

ceremonial *adjective* of or relating to ceremony or ritual: *ceremonial dress* > **ceremonially** *adverb*

ceremony ceremonies *noun* **1** set of formal actions performed at a special occasion or important public event: *his recent coronation ceremony* **2** very formal and polite behaviour: *He hung up the phone without ceremony* **3** **stand on ceremony** to insist on or act with excessive formality

certain *adjective* **1** sure: *He was certain we'd agree* **2** definite: *It's not certain it exists* **3** some but not much: *a certain resemblance*

certainly *adverb* **1** without doubt **2** of course

certainty certainties *noun* **1** state of being sure **2** something that is inevitable: *There are no certainties*

certificate *noun* official document stating the details of a birth, academic course, etc

certify certifies, certifying, certified *verb* **1** to confirm or attest to **2** to guarantee (that certain required standards have been met) **3** to declare legally insane

cervix cervixes or cervices *noun* (*technical*) entrance to the womb at the top of the vagina > **cervical** *adjective* relating to the cervix

cessation *noun* (*formal*) ending or pause: *a swift cessation of hostilities*

cf *abbreviation* compare

CFC *abbreviation* chlorofluorocarbon

chaff *noun* outer parts of grain separated from the seeds by beating

chaffinch *noun* small European songbird with black and white wings

chagrin [**shag**-grin] *noun* (*formal*) feeling of annoyance or disappointment

chain *noun* **1** flexible length of connected metal links **2** series of connected facts or events **3** group of shops, hotels, etc owned by one firm > *verb* **4** to restrict or fasten with or as if with a chain: *They had chained themselves to railings*

chain saw *noun* large saw with teeth fixed in a chain that is driven round by a motor

chain-smoke *verb* to smoke (cigarettes) continuously

chair *noun* **1** seat with a back, for one person **2** official position of authority **3** person holding this **4** professorship > *verb* **5** to preside over (a meeting)

chair lift *noun* series of chairs suspended from a moving cable for carrying people up a slope

chairman chairmen *noun* person in charge of a company's board of directors or a meeting > **chairmanship** *noun*: *during his chairmanship* > **chairperson** *noun* > **chairwoman** *noun*

> **WORD TIP**
> Some people don't like to use *chairman* when talking about a woman. You can use *chair* or

chairperson to talk about a man or a woman

chalet [**shall**-lay] noun 1 kind of Swiss wooden house with a steeply sloping roof 2 similar house, used as a holiday home

chalice [**chal**-liss] noun gold or silver cup used in churches to hold the Communion wine

chalk noun 1 soft white rock consisting of calcium carbonate 2 piece of chalk, often coloured, used for drawing and writing on blackboards ▷ verb 3 to draw or mark with chalk > **chalk up** verb to score or register (something): *He chalked up his first win* > **chalky** adjective containing or covered with chalk

challenge noun 1 testing situation: *a new challenge at the right time in my career* 2 call to take part in a contest or fight 3 questioning of the rightness or value of something: *a challenge to authority* 4 demand by a sentry for identification or a password ▷ verb 5 to invite or call (someone) to take part in a contest, fight or argument: *She challenged me to a game* 6 to call (a decision or action) into question 7 to order (a person) to stop and be identified > **challenger** noun competitor who takes on a champion or leader > **challenging** adjective requiring great effort and determination

chamber noun 1 hall used for formal meetings 2 legislative or judicial assembly 3 (*old-fashioned*) bedroom 4 hollow place or compartment inside something, especially inside an animal's body or inside a gun 5 **chambers** judge's room for hearing private cases not taken in open court

chambermaid noun woman employed to clean bedrooms in a hotel

chameleon [kam-**meal**-yon] noun small lizard that changes colour to blend in with its surroundings

chamois leather [**sham**-mee] noun soft leather cloth used for polishing

champagne [sham-**pain**] noun sparkling white French wine

champion noun 1 overall winner of a competition 2 someone who defends a person or cause ▷ verb 3 to support

championship noun competition to find the champion of a sport

chance noun 1 likelihood or probability 2 opportunity to do something 3 risk or gamble 4 unpredictable element that causes things to happen one way rather than another: *I found out by chance* ▷ verb 5 to try (something) in spite of the risk

chancellor noun 1 head of government in some European countries 2 honorary head of a university

Chancellor of the Exchequer noun (*Brit*) cabinet minister responsible for finance and taxes

chandelier [shan-dill-**eer**] noun ornamental light with branches and holders for several candles or bulbs

change noun 1 difference or alteration 2 variety or novelty 3 replacement of something by something else: *a change of clothes* 4 money returned to you if you pay for something with a larger sum than needed **5** coins of low value ▷ *verb* **6** to make or become different **7** to exchange (something for something else) **8** to exchange (money) for smaller coins of the same total value or for a foreign currency **9** to put on other clothes **10** to leave one train, bus, etc and board another

changeable *adjective* changing often

changeover *noun* change from one system or activity to another

channel channels, channelling, channelled *noun* **1** wavelength used to receive programmes broadcast by a television or radio station; also the station itself **2** means of access or communication **3** broad strait connecting two areas of sea **4** bed or course of a river, stream or canal **5** groove ▷ *verb* **6** to direct or convey through a channel or channels: *a system set up to channel funds to poorer countries*

chant *verb* **1** to repeat (a slogan, name, etc) over and over **2** to sing or recite (a psalm) ▷ *noun* **3** group of words repeated over and over again **4** psalm that has a short simple melody with several words sung on one note

Chanukah *noun* another spelling of Hanukkah

chaos [**kay**-oss] *noun* complete disorder or confusion > **chaotic** *adjective* in a state of disorder or confusion > **chaotically** *adverb*

chap *noun* (*informal*) man or boy

chapel *noun* **1** section of a church or cathedral with its own altar **2** type of small church

chaperone [**shap**-per-rone] *noun* **1** older person who accompanies and supervises a young person or young people on a social occasion ▷ *verb* **2** to act as a chaperone to

chaplain *noun* member of the Christian clergy who regularly works in a hospital, school or prison

chapter *noun* **1** division of a book **2** period in a life or history **3** branch of a society or club **4** group of Christian clergy who work in a cathedral

char chars, charring, charred *verb* to blacken by partial burning > **charred** *adjective* burnt

character *noun* **1** combination of qualities distinguishing a person, group or place **2** reputation, especially good reputation **3** unusual or interesting quality: *a building of great character* **4** person represented in a play, film or story **5** unusual or amusing person **6** letter, numeral or symbol used in writing or printing

characteristic *noun* **1** distinguishing feature or quality ▷ *adjective* **2** typical > **characteristically** *adverb*

characterize or **characterise** *verb* **1** to be a characteristic of **2** characterize as to describe as

characterless *adjective* dull and uninteresting

charade [shar-**rahd**] *noun* ridiculous and unnecessary activity or pretence > **charades** *noun* game in which one team acts out a word or phrase, which the other team has to guess

charcoal *noun* black form of carbon made by burning wood

a
b
c
d
e
f
g
h
i
j
k
l
m
n
o
p
q
r
s
t
u
v
w
x
y
z

without air, used as a fuel and also for drawing

charge *verb* **1** to ask (an amount of money) as a price **2** to enter a debit against a person's account for (a purchase) **3** (of the police) to accuse (someone) formally of a crime **4** to rush forward, often to attack **5** to fill (a battery) with electricity **6** (*formal*) to command or assign: *The president has charged his foreign minister with trying to open talks* ▷ *noun* **7** price charged for something **8** formal accusation of a crime in a court of law **9** onrush or attack **10** custody or guardianship: *in the charge of the police* **11** person or thing entrusted to someone's care **12** explosive put in a gun or other weapon **13** amount of electricity stored in a battery **14 in charge of** in control of

charger *noun* **1** device for charging or recharging batteries **2** (in the Middle Ages) horse ridden into battle by a knight

chariot *noun* two-wheeled horse-drawn vehicle used in ancient times in wars and races

charisma [kar-**rizz**-ma] *noun* person's power to attract or influence people > **charismatic** [kar-rizz-**mat**-ik] *adjective* having charisma

charity charities *noun* **1** organization that gives help, such as money or food, to those in need **2** giving of help to those in need **3** help given to those in need **4** kindly attitude towards people > **charitable** *adjective* **1** kind or lenient in your attitude towards others **2** of or for

charity: *charitable organizations* > **charitably** *adverb*

charlatan [**shar**-lat-tan] *noun* person who claims expertise that he or she does not have

charm *noun* **1** quality of attracting, fascinating or delighting people **2** trinket worn on a bracelet **3** magic spell ▷ *verb* **4** to attract, fascinate or delight **5** to influence by personal charm **6** to protect or influence as if by magic: *a charmed life*

charmer *noun* person who uses their charm to influence people

charming *adjective* very pleasant and attractive > **charmingly** *adverb*

chart *noun* **1** graph, table or diagram showing information **2** map of the sea or stars **3** **the charts** (*informal*) weekly lists of the best-selling pop records ▷ *verb* **4** to plot the course of **5** to make a chart of

charter *noun* **1** document granting or demanding certain rights **2** fundamental principles of an organization **3** hire of transport for private use ▷ *verb* **4** to hire by charter **5** to grant a charter to > **chartered** *adjective* officially qualified to practise a profession

chase *verb* **1** to pursue (a person or animal) persistently or quickly ▷ *noun* **2** act or an instance of chasing a person or animal

chasm [**kaz**-zum] *noun* **1** deep crack in the earth **2** very large difference between two things or groups of people; gulf: *the chasm between rich and poor*

chassis [**shass**-ee] *noun* frame, wheels and mechanical parts of a vehicle

> **WORD TIP**
> The plural of *chassis* is also *chassis*

chaste [**chayst**] *adjective* (old-fashioned) not having sex outside marriage or at all > **chastity** *noun* state of not having sex outside marriage or at all

chastise *verb* (formal) to scold severely

chat chats, chatting, chatted *noun* **1** informal conversation ▷ *verb* **2** to have an informal conversation > **chat up** *verb* (*informal*) to talk flirtatiously to (someone) with a view to starting a romantic or sexual relationship

chateau chateaux [**shat**-toe] *noun* large country house or castle in France

chatroom *noun* site on the internet where users have group discussions by email

chatter *verb* **1** to speak quickly and continuously about unimportant things **2** (of the teeth) to rattle with cold or fear ▷ *noun* **3** unimportant talk

chatty chattier, chattiest *adjective* talkative and friendly

chauffeur [**show**-fur] *noun* person employed to drive a car for someone

chauvinist [**show**-vin-ist] *noun* person who believes that their own country, race, group or sex is superior > **chauvinistic** *adjective* characterized by chauvinism

cheap *adjective* **1** costing relatively little **2** of poor quality **3** not valued highly: *cheap promises*

4 mean or despicable > **cheaply** *adverb*

cheat *verb* **1** to act dishonestly to gain profit or advantage ▷ *noun* **2** person who cheats

check *verb* **1** to examine or investigate **2** to slow the growth or progress of ▷ *noun* **3** test to ensure accuracy or progress **4** break in progress **5** (US) cheque **6** pattern of squares or crossed lines **7** (Chess) position of a king under attack > **check in** *verb* **1** to register your arrival at a hotel or airport **2** to register the arrival of (guests or passengers) at a hotel or airport > **check out** *verb* **1** to pay the bill and leave a hotel **2** to examine or investigate (something) **3** (*informal*) to have a look at

checkmate *noun* (Chess) winning position in which an opponent's king is under attack and unable to escape

checkout *noun* counter in a supermarket, where customers pay

checkpoint *noun* place where traffic has to stop in order to be checked

checkup *noun* thorough medical examination

cheek *noun* **1** either side of the face below the eye **2** (*informal*) impudence, boldness or lack of respect ▷ *verb* **3** (Brit, Aust, NZ *informal*) to speak impudently to

cheeky cheekier, cheekiest *adjective* rather rude and disrespectful > **cheekily** *adverb*

cheer *verb* **1** to applaud or encourage with shouts ▷ *noun* **2** shout of applause or encouragement > **cheer up** verb to become or make (someone) happy or hopeful

cheerful adjective **1** happy and in good spirits **2** bright and pleasant-looking > **cheerfully** adverb > **cheerfulness** noun happiness

cheerio interjection (informal) goodbye

cheery cheerier, cheeriest adjective happy and cheerful

cheese noun hard or creamy food made from milk

cheesecake noun dessert with a biscuit-crumb base covered with a sweet cream-cheese mixture

cheetah noun large fast-running spotted African wild cat

chef noun cook in a restaurant

chemical noun **1** substance used in or resulting from a reaction involving changes to atoms or molecules > adjective **2** involved in chemistry or using chemicals > **chemically** adverb

chemist noun **1** shop selling medicines and cosmetics **2** person who is qualified to make up prescription medicines; pharmacist **3** scientist who does research in chemistry

chemistry noun science of the composition, properties and reactions of substances

chemotherapy [keem-oh-**ther**-a-pee] noun treatment of disease, often cancer, using chemicals

cheque noun written order asking your bank to pay money out of your account to a person, shop or organization

chequered [**chek**-kerd] adjective **1** marked by varied fortunes: a

chequered career **2** having a pattern of squares

cherish verb **1** to care deeply about (something) and look after it lovingly **2** to care for

cherry cherries noun **1** small red or black fruit with a stone **2** tree on which it grows > adjective **3** deep red

cherub cherubs or cherubim noun angel, often represented as a winged child > **cherubic** [cher-**rew**-bik] adjective (of a baby or child) attractive

chess noun game for two players with 16 pieces each, played on a chequered board of 64 squares

chessboard noun board divided into 64 squares of two alternating colours on which chess is played

chest noun **1** front of the body, from neck to waist **2** large strong box with a hinged lid

chestnut noun **1** reddish-brown edible nut **2** tree on which it grows **3** reddish-brown horse **4** (informal) old joke > adjective **5** (of hair or a horse) reddish-brown

chest of drawers noun piece of furniture consisting of drawers in a frame

chew verb to grind (food) between the teeth > **chewy** adjective requiring a lot of chewing

chewing gum noun flavoured gum to be chewed but not swallowed

chic [sheek] adjective **1** stylish or elegant > noun **2** stylishness or elegance

chick noun baby bird

chicken noun **1** domestic fowl **2** its flesh, eaten as food: roast chicken

3 (*informal*) coward ▷ *adjective* **4** (*informal*) cowardly ▷ **chicken out** *verb* (*informal*) (often followed by *of*) to fail to do something through cowardice

chickenpox *noun* infectious disease with an itchy rash

chicory *noun* **1** plant whose bitter leaves are used in salads **2** root of this plant, used as a coffee substitute

chide chides, chiding, chided *verb* (*old-fashioned*) to rebuke or scold

chief *noun* **1** head of a group of people ▷ *adjective* **2** most important: *the chief source of oil* ▷ **chiefly** *adverb* **1** especially **2** mainly

chieftain *noun* leader of a tribe or clan

chiffon [**shif**-fon] *noun* very thin lightweight cloth made of silk or nylon

chihuahua [chee-**wah**-wah] *noun* breed of very small dog with pointed ears

chilblain *noun* inflammation of the fingers or toes, caused by exposure to cold

child children *noun* **1** young human being, boy or girl **2** son or daughter

childbirth *noun* act of giving birth to a child

childhood *noun* time when a person is a child

childish *adjective* immature and foolish > **childishly** *adverb* > **childishness** *noun* immature and foolish behaviour

> **WORD TIP**
> If you call someone *childish*, you think they are immature or foolish. If you call them *childlike*,

you think they are innocent like a young child

childless *adjective* having no children

childlike *adjective* like a child in appearance or behaviour

childminder *noun* person who is qualified and paid to look after other people's children while they are at work

Chilean *adjective* **1** belonging or relating to Chile ▷ *noun* **2** someone from Chile

chill *noun* **1** feverish cold **2** moderate coldness ▷ *verb* **3** to make (something) cool or cold **4** to cause (someone) to feel cold or frightened **5** (*informal*) to relax ▷ *adjective* **6** unpleasantly cold

chilli chillies *noun* **1** small red or green hot-tasting pepper, used in cooking **2** chilli con carne hot-tasting Mexican dish of meat, onions, beans and chilli powder

chilly chillier, chilliest *adjective* **1** rather cold **2** unfriendly and without enthusiasm

chilly-bin *noun* (*NZ informal*) portable container for keeping food and drink cool

chime *noun* **1** musical ringing sound of a bell or clock **2 chimes** set of bells or other objects which make ringing sounds ▷ *verb* **3** to make a musical ringing sound **4** to indicate (the time) by chiming

chimney *noun* hollow vertical structure for carrying away smoke from a fire

chimpanzee *noun* small ape with dark fur that lives in forests in Africa

chin *noun* part of the face below the mouth

a
b
c
d
e
f
g
h
i
j
k
l
m
n
o
p
q
r
s
t
u
v
w
x
y
z

china noun **1** fine earthenware or porcelain **2** dishes or ornaments made of this **3** (Brit, Aust, NZ, S Afr informal) friend

Chinese adjective **1** of China ▷ noun **2** person from China **3** any of the languages of China

> **WORD TIP**
> The plural of Chinese is also Chinese

chink noun **1** small narrow opening **2** short, light ringing sound, like one made by glasses touching each other

chintz noun glazed cotton fabric usually decorated with flowery patterns

chip chips, chipping, chipped noun **1** strip of potato, fried in deep fat **2** tiny wafer of semiconductor material forming an integrated circuit **3** counter used to represent money in gambling games **4** small piece removed by chopping, breaking, etc **5** mark left where a small piece has been broken off something ▷ verb **6** to break small pieces from > **chip in** verb (informal) **1** to contribute (money) **2** to interrupt with a remark

chipboard noun thin board made of compressed wood particles

chipmunk noun small squirrel-like North American rodent with a striped back

chiropodist [kir-**rop**-pod-ist] noun person who treats minor foot complaints > **chiropody** noun medical treatment of the feet

chirp verb **1** (of a bird or insect) to make a short high-pitched sound ▷ noun **2** chirping sound

chisel chisels, chiselling, chiselled noun **1** metal tool with a sharp end for shaping wood or stone ▷ verb **2** to carve or form with a chisel

chivalry [**shiv**-val-ree] noun **1** polite and helpful behaviour, especially by men towards women **2** medieval system and principles of knighthood > **chivalrous** adjective gallant or courteous

chives plural noun herb with a mild onion flavour

chlorine [**klaw**-reen] noun strong-smelling greenish-yellow gaseous element, used to disinfect water and to make bleach

chloroform [klor-rof-form] noun strong-smelling liquid formerly used as an anaesthetic

chlorophyll [klor-rof-fil] noun green colouring matter of plants, which enables them to convert sunlight into energy

chock-a-block or **chock-full** adjective completely full

chocolate noun **1** sweet food made from cacao seeds **2** sweet or drink made from this ▷ adjective **3** dark brown

choice noun **1** act of choosing or selecting **2** opportunity for choice or power of choosing: parental choice **3** person or thing chosen or that may be chosen: You've made a good choice **4** alternative action or possibility ▷ adjective **5** of high quality: choice food and drink

choir [**kwire**] noun MUSIC **1** organized group of singers, especially in church **2** part of a church occupied by the choir

choke verb **1** to hinder or stop the breathing of (a person) by strangling or smothering **2** to have trouble in breathing **3** to block or clog up

choko chokos noun fruit that is shaped like a pear and used as a vegetable in Australia and New Zealand

cholera [kol-ler-a] noun serious infectious disease causing severe vomiting and diarrhoea

cholesterol [kol-**lest**-er-oll] noun fatty substance found in animal tissue, an excess of which can cause heart disease

chook noun (Aust, NZ informal) hen or chicken

choose chooses, choosing, chose, chosen verb **1** to select from a number of alternatives **2** to decide (to do something) because you want to

choosy choosier, choosiest adjective fussy and difficult to satisfy

chop chops, chopping, chopped verb **1** to cut (something) with a blow from an axe or knife **2** to cut into pieces **3** (Boxing, Karate) to hit (an opponent) with a short sharp blow **4** chop and change to change your mind repeatedly ▷ noun **5** cutting or sharp blow **6** slice of lamb or pork, usually with a rib

chopper noun **1** (informal) helicopter **2** small axe

choppy choppier, choppiest adjective (of the sea) fairly rough

chopsticks plural noun pair of thin sticks used to eat Chinese or other East Asian food

choral adjective relating to singing by a choir: choral music

chore noun uninteresting job that has to be done

choreography [kor-ree-**og**-raf-fee] noun art of composing dance steps and movements ▷ **choreographer** noun person who composes dance steps and movements

chortle verb **1** to chuckle in amusement ▷ noun **2** amused chuckle

Christ noun Jesus of Nazareth, regarded by Christians as the Messiah

christen verb **1** to give a Christian name to in baptism **2** to give a name to (a person or thing) ▷ **christening** noun Christian ceremony in which a child is given a name and made a member of a church

Christian noun RE **1** person who believes in and follows Christ ▷ adjective **2** of Christ or Christianity **3** kind, good and considerate ▷ **Christianity** noun religion based on the life and teachings of Christ

Christian name noun personal name given to Christians at baptism: loosely used to mean a person's first name

Christmas noun **1** annual festival on Dec. 25 commemorating the birth of Christ **2** period around this time

chromatic [kro-**ma**-tik] adjective **1** of colour or colours **2** (Music) (of a scale) proceeding by semitones

chrome [krome] noun grey metallic element used in steel alloys and for electroplating

chromosome noun microscopic gene-carrying body in the nucleus of a cell

a b c d e f g h i j k l m n o p q r s t u v w x y z

chronic [kron-nik] *adjective*
1 (of an illness) lasting a long
time **2** habitual **3** (Brit, Aust,
NZ informal) of poor quality
> **chronically** *adverb*

chronicle *noun* **1** record of events
in order of occurrence ▷ *verb* **2** to
record in or as if in a chronicle

chronological [kron-nol-**loj**-i-kl]
adjective HISTORY arranged in the
order in which things happened
> **chronologically** *adverb*

chronology chronologies [kron-
nol-loj-jee] *noun* arrangement
or list of events in order of
occurrence

chrysalis chrysalises [**kriss**-a-liss]
noun insect in the stage between
larva and adult, when it is in a
cocoon

chrysanthemum [kriss-**an**-
thim-mum] *noun* garden flower
with a large head made up of
thin petals

chubby chubbier, chubbiest
adjective plump and round: *his
chubby cheeks*

chuck *verb* (informal) **1** to throw
2 to give up or reject

chuckle *verb* **1** to laugh softly
▷ *noun* **2** soft laugh

chug chugs, chugging, chugged
noun **1** short dull sound like the
noise of an engine ▷ *verb* **2** to
operate or move with this sound

chum *noun* (informal) close friend

chunk *noun* **1** thick solid piece
2 considerable amount

chunky chunkier, chunkiest
adjective **1** (of a person) broad
and heavy **2** (of an object) large
and thick

church *noun* **1** building for public
Christian worship **2** particular

Christian denomination:
the Catholic Church **3** Church
institutional religion as a political
or social force: *conflict between
Church and State*

Church of England *noun*
Anglican church in England,
where it is the state church, with
the King or Queen as its head

churchyard *noun* grounds round
a church, used as a graveyard

churn *noun* **1** machine in which
cream is shaken to make butter
▷ *verb* **2** to stir (cream) vigorously
to make butter **3 churn out**
(informal) to produce (things)
rapidly in large numbers

chute [shoot] *noun* steep slope
down which things may be slid

chutney *noun* pickle made from
fruit, vinegar, spices and sugar

cider *noun* alcoholic drink made
from fermented apple juice

cigar *noun* roll of cured tobacco
leaves for smoking

cigarette *noun* thin roll of
shredded tobacco in thin paper,
for smoking

cinder *noun* piece of material that
will not burn, left after burning
coal

cinema *noun* **1** place for showing
films **2** business of making films

cinnamon *noun* spice obtained
from the bark of an Asian tree

cipher or **cypher** [**sy**-fer] *noun*
1 system of secret writing
2 unimportant person

circa [**sir**-ka] *preposition* (formal)
about or approximately; used
especially before dates

circle *noun* **1** perfectly round
geometric figure, line or shape
2 group of people sharing an

interest or activity **3** (*Theatre*) section of seats above the main level of the auditorium ▷ *verb* **4** to move in a circle (round)

circuit [sir-kit] *noun* **1** complete route or course, especially a circular one, for example a motor-racing track **2** complete path through which an electric current can flow

circuit diagram *noun* [D & T] sketch showing the complete path through which an electric current can flow

circular *adjective* **1** in the shape of a circle **2** moving in a circle ▷ *noun* **3** letter or advert sent to a lot of people at the same time

circulate *verb* to send, go or pass from place to place or person to person

circulation *noun* **1** [SCIENCE] flow of blood around the body **2** number of copies of a newspaper or magazine sold **3** sending or moving round: *traffic circulation* > **circulatory** *adjective* of or relating to circulation: *the human circulatory system*

circumcise *verb* to remove the foreskin of (a male) > **circumcision** *noun*

circumference *noun* [MATHS] **1** outer line or edge of a circle **2** length of this line

circumstance *noun* **1** condition, situation or event affecting or influencing a person or event **2** unplanned events and situations which cannot be controlled: *a victim of circumstance* **3** **circumstances** person's position and conditions in life

circus circuses *noun* (performance given by) a travelling company

of acrobats, clowns, performing animals, etc

cistern *noun* water tank, especially one that holds water for flushing a toilet

citadel *noun* fortress in or near a city

cite *verb* (*formal*) **1** to quote or refer to **2** to bring forward as proof **3** to summon to appear before a court of law

citizen *noun* **1** native or naturalized member of a state or nation **2** inhabitant of a city or town > **citizenship** *noun* **1** condition or status of a citizen, with its rights and duties **2** person's conduct as a citizen

citrus fruit *noun* juicy sharp-tasting fruit such as an orange or lemon

city cities *noun* **1** large or important town **2** **the City** (*Brit*) part of London which contains the main British financial institutions such as the Stock Exchange

civic *adjective* of or relating to a city or citizens

civil *adjective* **1** relating to the citizens of a country **2** relating to people or things that are not connected with the armed forces: *civil aviation* **3** polite or courteous > **civility** *noun* polite or courteous behaviour > **civilly** *adverb*

civil engineering *noun* design and construction of roads, bridges and public buildings

civilian *noun* **1** person not belonging to the armed forces ▷ *adjective* **2** not relating to the armed forces or police

civilization or **civilisation** *noun* [HISTORY] **1** high level

a
b
c
d
e
f
g
h
i
j
k
l
m
n
o
p
q
r
s
t
u
v
w
x
y
z

of human cultural and social development **2** particular society which has reached this level: *the tale of a lost civilization*

civilized or **civilised** *adjective* **1** (of a society) having a developed social organization and way of life **2** (of a person) polite and reasonable

civil servant *noun* member of the civil service

civil service *noun* government departments responsible for the administration of a country

civil war *noun* war between people of the same country

cl *symbol* centilitre

clad *adjective* (literary) (often followed by *in*) dressed or clothed (in)

claim *verb* **1** to assert as a fact **2** to demand (something) as a right ▷ *noun* **3** assertion that something is true **4** assertion of a right **5** something claimed as a right

claimant *noun* person who is making a claim, especially for money

clairvoyant *adjective* **1** able to know about things that will happen in the future ▷ *noun* **2** person who is, or claims to be, clairvoyant

clam clams, clamming, clammed *noun* edible shellfish with a hinged shell ▷ **clam up** *verb* (informal) to stop talking, especially through nervousness

clamber *verb* to climb awkwardly, using hands and feet

clammy clammier, clammiest *adjective* unpleasantly damp and sticky

clamour *noun* **1** loud protest **2** loud persistent noise or outcry ▷ *verb* **3** **clamour for** to demand noisily

clamp *noun* **1** tool with movable jaws for holding things together tightly ▷ *verb* **2** to fasten with a clamp ▷ **clamp down** *verb* (often followed by *on*) to become stricter (about something) in order to stop or control it

clan *noun* **1** group of families with a common ancestor, especially among Scottish Highlanders **2** close group

clandestine *adjective* secret and hidden

clang *verb* **1** to make a loud ringing metallic sound ▷ *noun* **2** ringing metallic sound

clank *noun* **1** harsh metallic sound ▷ *verb* **2** to make such a sound

clap claps, clapping, clapped *verb* **1** to applaud by hitting the palms of your hands sharply together **2** to place or put quickly or forcibly: *He should be clapped in irons* ▷ *noun* **3** act or sound of clapping **4** sudden loud noise: *a clap of thunder*

clapper *noun* piece of metal inside a bell, which causes it to sound when struck against the side

claret [klar-rit] *noun* dry red wine from the Bordeaux region of France

clarify clarifies, clarifying, clarified *verb* (EXAM TERM) to make (something) clear and easy to understand ▷ **clarification** *noun* explanation that makes something easier to understand

clarinet *noun* woodwind instrument with a single reed

clarity noun clearness

clash verb 1 to come into conflict 2 (of events) to happen at the same time 3 (of colours) to look unattractive together 4 (of objects) to make a loud harsh sound by being hit together ▷ noun 5 a fight or argument 6 fact of two events happening at the same time

clasp noun 1 device for fastening things 2 firm grasp or embrace ▷ verb 3 to grasp or embrace firmly

class noun 1 group of people sharing a similar social position 2 system of dividing society into such groups 3 group of people or things sharing a common characteristic 4 group of pupils or students taught together 5 standard of quality 6 (informal) elegance or excellence: *a touch of class* ▷ adjective 7 (informal) excellent, skilful or stylish: *a class act* ▷ verb 8 to place in a class; classify or categorize: *They are officially classed as visitors*

classic adjective 1 being a typical example of something: *a classic symptom of iron deficiency* 2 of lasting interest because of excellence: *a classic film* 3 attractive because of simplicity of form: *the classic dinner suit* ▷ noun 4 something of the highest quality 5 **classics** study of ancient Greek and Roman literature and culture

classical adjective 1 of or in a restrained conservative style 2 denoting serious art or music 3 of or influenced by ancient Greek and Roman culture ▷ **classically** adverb

classified adjective officially declared secret by the government

classify classifies, classifying, classified verb to arrange into groups with similar characteristics ▷ **classification** noun LIBRARY 1 placing things systematically in categories 2 division or category in a classifying system

classroom noun a room in a school where pupils have lessons

classy classier, classiest adjective (informal) stylish and elegant

clatter verb 1 to make a loud rattling noise, as when hard objects hit each other ▷ noun 2 loud rattling noise

clause noun 1 section of a legal document 2 ENGLISH group of words with a subject and a verb, which may be a complete sentence or one of the parts of a sentence

claustrophobia [klos-trof-**foe**-bee-ya] noun abnormal fear of confined spaces ▷ **claustrophobic** adjective 1 (of a person) uncomfortable in a confined space 2 (of a place) enclosed, overcrowded or restricting movement

claw noun 1 sharp hooked nail of a bird or beast 2 similar part, such as a crab's pincer ▷ verb 3 to tear with claws or nails

clay noun fine-grained earth, soft when moist and hardening when baked, used to make bricks and pottery

clean adjective 1 free from dirt or impurities 2 without anything in it or on it: *a clean sheet of* *paper* **3** morally acceptable or inoffensive: *good clean fun* **4** (of a reputation or record) free from corruption or dishonesty **5** complete: *a clean break* **6** simple and streamlined in design: *the clean lines of the new model* **7 come clean** (*informal*) to reveal or admit something ▷ *verb* **8** to make (something) free from dirt > **cleaner** *noun* person, device or substance that removes dirt > **cleanly** *adverb*

cleanliness [klen-lin-ness] *noun* state or degree of being clean

cleanse [klenz] *verb* to remove dirt from > **cleanser** *noun*

clear *adjective* **1** free from doubt or confusion: *It was clear that he did not want to talk* **2** easy to see or hear **3** able to be seen through; transparent **4** free of obstruction **5** (of sky) free from clouds **6** (of skin) without blemish ▷ *adverb* **7** out of the way ▷ *verb* **8** to make or become clear **9** to pass by or over (something) without contact **10** to prove (someone) innocent of a crime or mistake **11** to make as profit > **clearly** *adverb* > **clear out** *verb* **1** to remove and sort the contents of (a room or container) **2** (*Brit, Aust, NZ informal*) to go away > **clear up** *verb* **1** to put (a place or thing that is disordered) in order **2** to explain or solve (a problem or misunderstanding) **3** (of the weather) to become brighter **4** (of an illness) to become better

clearance *noun* **1** act of clearing: *slum clearance* **2** official permission

clearing *noun* area of bare ground in a forest

cleavage *noun* **1** division between a woman's breasts, as revealed by a low-cut dress **2** division or split

cleaver *noun* butcher's heavy knife with a square blade

clef *noun* (MUSIC) symbol at the beginning of each line of a piece of written music which indicates the pitch of the notes

cleft *noun* narrow opening or crack

clementine *noun* small orange citrus fruit

clench *verb* **1** to close or squeeze (your teeth or fist) tightly **2** to grasp firmly

clergy *plural noun* priests and ministers as a group

clergyman *clergymen noun* male member of the clergy

clerical *adjective* **1** of or relating to clerks or office work **2** of the clergy

clerk [klahrk] *noun* employee in an office, bank or court who keeps records, files and accounts

clever *adjective* **1** intelligent and quick to understand **2** very effective or skilful > **cleverly** *adverb* > **cleverness** *noun*

clianthus [klee-**an**-thuss] *noun* plant with clusters of scarlet flowers, found in Australia and New Zealand

cliché [klee-shay] *noun* (ENGLISH) expression or idea that is no longer effective because of overuse > **clichéd** *adjective*: *The dialogue is clichéd and corny*

click *noun* **1** short sharp sound ▷ *verb* **2** to make this sound **3** (*informal*) (of two people) to get on well together **4** (*informal*) to become suddenly clear **5** (*Computers*) to press and release a button on a mouse in order, for example, to select an option on the screen or highlight something **6** (*informal*) to be a success

client *noun* person who uses the services of a professional person or company

clientele [klee-on-**tell**] *noun* customers or clients collectively

cliff *noun* steep rock face, especially along the sea shore

climate *noun* **1** typical weather conditions of an area **2** general attitude and opinion of people at a particular time: *the American political climate* **> climatic** *adjective: climatic changes*

climax *noun* **1** most intense point of an experience, series of events or story **2** same as **orgasm > climactic** *adjective: the film's climactic scene*

climb *verb* **1** to go up or ascend (stairs, a mountain, etc) **2** to move or go with difficulty **3** to rise to a higher point or intensity **> noun 4** act or an instance of climbing **5** place or thing to be climbed, especially a route in mountaineering **> climber** *noun*

clinch *verb* to settle (an argument or agreement) decisively: *Peter clinched the deal*

cling clings, clinging, clung *verb* **1** (*usually followed by to, onto*) to hold (onto) tightly or stay closely attached (to) **2** (*followed by to*) to continue to do or believe in: *still clinging to old-fashioned values*

clingfilm ® *noun* thin polythene material for wrapping food

clinic *noun* **1** building where outpatients receive medical treatment or advice **2** private or specialized hospital

clinical *adjective* **1** of or relating to the medical treatment of patients: *clinical tests* **2** logical and unemotional: *the cold, clinical attitudes of his colleagues* **> clinically** *adverb*

clip clips, clipping, clipped *verb* **1** to cut with shears or scissors **2** to attach or hold together with a clip **> noun 3** short extract of a film **4** (*informal*) sharp blow **5** device for attaching or holding things together

clippers *plural noun* tool for clipping

clipping *noun* something cut out, especially an article from a newspaper

clique [kleek] *noun* small group of people who stick together and do not mix with other people

clitoris [**klit**-or-iss] *noun* small, highly sensitive organ near the opening of a woman's vagina

cloak *noun* **1** loose sleeveless outer garment **> verb 2** to cover or conceal

cloakroom *noun* room for coats or a room with toilets and washbasins in a public building

clock *noun* **1** instrument for showing the time **2** device with a dial for recording or measuring **> verb 3** to record (time) with a stopwatch, especially in the calculation of a speed

clockwise *adverb, adjective* in the direction in which the hands of a clock rotate

clockwork *noun* **1** mechanism similar to that of a clock, used in wind-up toys **2** like clockwork with complete regularity and precision

clog clogs, clogging, clogged verb **1** to block or obstruct ▷ noun **2** wooden or wooden-soled shoe

cloister noun covered pillared arcade, usually in a monastery

clone noun **1** animal or plant produced artificially from the cells of another animal or plant, and identical to the original **2** (informal) person who closely resembles another ▷ verb **3** to produce as a clone

close[1] [rhymes with *nose*] verb **1** to shut **2** to prevent access to **3** to finish business or stop operating **4** to end **5** to bring or come nearer together ▷ noun **6** end or conclusion > **closed** adjective • **close down** verb to stop operating or working: *The factory closed down many years ago*

close[2] [rhymes with *dose*] adjective **1** near: *a restaurant close to their home* **2** intimate: *close friends* **3** careful or thorough: *close scrutiny* **4** (of weather) oppressive or stifling ▷ adverb **5** near: *He walked close behind her* **6** closely or tightly: *She held him close* > **closely** adverb • **closeness** noun

closed shop noun place of work in which all workers must belong to a particular trade union

closet noun **1** (US) cupboard **2** small private room ▷ adjective **3** private or secret ▷ verb **4** to shut (oneself away) in private

close-up noun detailed close view of something, especially a photograph taken close to the subject

closure [klohz-yur] noun closing

clot clots, clotting, clotted noun **1** soft thick lump formed from liquid **2** (*Brit, Aust, NZ informal*) stupid person ▷ verb **3** to form soft thick lumps

cloth noun **1** woven fabric **2** piece of woven fabric

clothe clothes, clothing, clothed verb **1** to put clothes on **2** to provide with clothes

clothes plural noun things people wear to cover them and keep them warm

clothing noun clothes collectively

cloud noun **1** mass of condensed water vapour floating in the sky **2** floating mass of smoke, dust, etc ▷ verb **3** to confuse: *His judgment was clouded by alcohol* **4** cloud over to become cloudy

cloudy cloudier, cloudiest adjective **1** having a lot of clouds **2** (of liquid) not clear

clout (informal) noun **1** hard blow **2** power or influence: *I don't have much clout round here* ▷ verb **3** to hit hard

clove noun **1** dried closed flower bud of a tropical tree, used as a spice **2** segment of a bulb of garlic

clover noun **1** plant with three-lobed leaves • **in clover** (informal) in ease or luxury

clown noun **1** comic entertainer in a circus **2** amusing person **3** stupid person ▷ verb **4** to behave foolishly **5** to perform as a clown

cloying adjective unpleasantly sickly, sweet or sentimental

club clubs, clubbing, clubbed noun **1** association of people with common interests **2** building used by such a group **3** thick stick used as a weapon **4** stick with a curved end used to hit the ball in golf **5** playing card with black three-leaved symbols ▷ *verb* **6** to hit with a club **7 club together** to combine resources for a common purpose

cluck *noun* **1** low clicking noise made by a hen ▷ *verb* **2** to make this noise

clue *noun* **1** something that helps to solve a mystery or puzzle **2 not have a clue** to be completely baffled

clump *noun* **1** small group of things or people **2** dull heavy tread ▷ *verb* **3 clump about** to walk or tread with heavy footsteps

clumsy clumsier, clumsiest *adjective* **1** lacking skill or physical coordination **2** said or done without thought or tact > **clumsily** *adverb* > **clumsiness** *noun*

cluster *noun* **1** small close group ▷ *verb* **2** to gather or be gathered in clusters

clutch *verb* **1** to grasp tightly **2 clutch at** to try to get hold of ▷ *noun* **3** foot pedal that the driver of a motor vehicle presses when changing gear **4 in someone's clutches** in someone's power or at the mercy of someone

clutter *verb* **1** to fill (a room, desk, etc) with objects that take up space and cause mess ▷ *noun* **2** untidy mess

cm *symbol* centimetre

co- *prefix* together, joint or jointly: *coproduction*

coach *noun* **1** long-distance bus **2** railway carriage **3** large four-wheeled horse-drawn carriage **4** person who coaches a sport or a subject ▷ *verb* **5** to train or teach

coal *noun* **1** black rock consisting mainly of carbon, used as fuel **2** burning piece of coal

coalition [koh-a-**lish**-un] *noun* temporary alliance, especially between political parties forming a government

coarse *adjective* **1** rough in texture **2** rude or offensive > **coarsely** *adverb* > **coarseness** *noun*

coast *noun* **1** place where the land meets the sea ▷ *verb* **2** to move by momentum, without the use of power > **coastal** *adjective* in or near the coast

coastguard *noun* **1** organization that aids ships and swimmers in trouble and prevents smuggling **2** member of this organization

coastline *noun* outline of a coast: *a rugged coastline*

coat *noun* **1** outer garment with long sleeves **2** animal's fur or hair **3** covering layer: *a coat of paint* ▷ *verb* **4** to cover (something) with a layer > **coating** *noun* covering layer

coax *verb* **1** to persuade (someone) gently **2** to obtain (something) by persistent coaxing

cobalt *noun* (*Chemistry*) brittle silvery-white metallic element which is used for producing a blue dye

cobble *noun* **1** rounded stone used for paving ▷ *verb* **2 cobble together** to put together clumsily

cobbler *noun* shoe mender

cobra [**koh**-bra] *noun* venomous hooded snake of Asia and Africa

cobweb *noun* very thin net that a spider spins for catching insects

cocaine *noun* addictive drug used as a narcotic and as an anaesthetic

cock noun **1** male bird, especially of domestic fowl **2** stopcock ▷ verb **3** to draw back (the hammer of a gun) to firing position **4** to lift and turn (part of the body)

cockatoo cockatoos noun crested parrot of Australia or the East Indies

cockerel noun young domestic cock

Cockney noun **1** native of the East End of London **2** London dialect

cockpit noun **1** pilot's compartment in an aircraft **2** driver's compartment in a racing car

cockroach noun large dark-coloured insect often found in dirty rooms

cocktail noun alcoholic drink made from several ingredients

cocky cockier, cockiest; cockies (informal) adjective **1** cheeky or too self-confident ▷ noun **2** (Aust) cockatoo **3** (Aust, NZ) farmer > **cockiness** noun

cocoa noun **1** powder made from the seed of the cacao tree **2** drink made from this powder

coconut noun **1** very large nut with white flesh, milky juice and a hard hairy shell **2** edible flesh of this fruit

cocoon noun **1** silky protective covering of a silkworm or other insect larva, in which the pupa develops **2** protective covering ▷ verb **3** to wrap up tightly for protection

cod noun large food fish of the North Atlantic

▌ **WORD TIP**
The plural of *cod* is also cod

code noun **1** system of letters, symbols or prearranged signals

by which messages can be communicated secretly or briefly **2** group of numbers or letters which is used to identify something **3** set of principles or rules: *a code of practice* ▷ verb **4** to put into code > **coded** adjective: *coded messages*

coffee noun **1** drink made from the roasted and ground seeds of a tropical shrub **2** beanlike seeds of this shrub ▷ adjective **3** medium-brown

coffin noun box in which a dead body is buried or cremated

cog noun **1** one of the teeth on the rim of a gearwheel **2** unimportant person in a big organization

cognac [kon-yak] noun French brandy

coherent adjective **1** logical and consistent **2** capable of intelligible speech > **coherence** noun logical or natural connection or consistency

cohesive adjective sticking together to form a whole

coil verb **1** to wind in loops or to move in a winding course ▷ noun **3** something coiled **4** single loop of this

coin noun **1** piece of metal money **2** metal currency collectively ▷ verb **3** to invent (a word or phrase) **4** coin it in (informal) to earn money quickly

coinage noun **1** coins collectively **2** currency of a country **3** newly invented word or phrase **4** act of coining

coincide verb **1** to happen at the same time **2** to agree or correspond exactly

coincidence noun **1** chance occurrence of simultaneous or apparently connected events: *I had moved to London, and by coincidence, Helen had too* **2** coinciding ▷ **coincidental** *adjective* resulting from coincidence ▷ **coincidentally** *adverb*

coke *noun* solid fuel left after gas has been distilled from coal

colander[kol-an-der] *noun* bowl-shaped container with holes in it for straining or rinsing food

cold *adjective* **1** lacking heat **2** lacking affection or enthusiasm **3** (of a colour) giving an impression of coldness ▷ *noun* **4** lack of heat **5** mild illness causing a runny nose, sneezing and coughing ▷ **coldly** *adverb* ▷ **coldness** *noun* lack of affection or enthusiasm

cold-blooded *adjective* **1** showing no pity **2** having a body temperature that varies according to the surrounding temperature

cold war *noun* political hostility between countries without actual warfare

coleslaw *noun* salad dish of shredded raw cabbage in a dressing

colic *noun* severe pains in the stomach and bowels

collaborate *verb* **1** to work with another on a project **2** to cooperate with an enemy invader ▷ **collaboration** *noun* **1** act of working with others on a joint project **2** something created by working with others **3** act of helping the enemy occupiers of one's country ▷ **collaborator** *noun*

collage [kol-**lahzh**] *noun* ART **1** art form in which various materials or objects are glued onto a surface **2** picture made in this way

collapse *verb* **1** to fall down suddenly **2** to fail completely **3** to fold compactly, especially for storage ▷ *noun* **4** collapsing **5** sudden failure or breakdown

collapsible *adjective* able to be folded up for storage

collar *noun* **1** part of a garment round the neck **2** band put round an animal's neck **3** cut of meat from an animal's neck ▷ *verb* **4** (Brit, Aust, NZ *informal*) to seize or arrest **5** (*informal*) to catch in order to speak to

collateral *noun* money or property which is used as a guarantee that someone will repay a loan, and which the lender can take if the loan is not repaid

colleague *noun* fellow worker, especially in a profession

collect *verb* **1** to gather together: *collecting money for charity* **2** to accumulate (stamps, coins, etc) as a hobby **3** to go to a place to fetch (a person or thing); pick up

collected *adjective* calm and self-controlled

collection *noun* **1** things collected: *a collection of paintings* **2** collecting: *tax collection* **3** sum of money collected: *a collection for charity*

collective *adjective* **1** of or done by a group: *a collective decision* ▷ *noun* **2** group of people working together on an enterprise and sharing the benefits from it ▷ **collectively** *adverb*

collective noun noun noun that refers to a single unit made up of a number of things, e.g. flock; swarm

college noun 1 place where students study after they have left school 2 name given to some secondary schools 3 one of the institutions into which some universities are divided 4 (NZ) teacher training college

collide verb to crash together violently

collie noun silky-haired dog used for rounding up sheep

colliery collieries noun coal mine

collision noun violent crash between moving objects

colloquial [kol-**loh**-kwee-al] adjective suitable for informal speech or writing > **colloquialism** noun colloquial word or phrase > **colloquially** adverb

cologne [kol-**lone**] noun mild perfume

colon noun 1 punctuation mark (:) 2 part of the large intestine connected to the rectum

colonel [**kur**-nl] noun senior commissioned army or air-force officer

colonial noun 1 inhabitant of a colony 2 adjective relating to a colony 3 (Aust) of the period of Australian history before the Federation in 1901 > **colonialism** noun policy of acquiring and maintaining colonies

colonize or **colonise** verb 1 to establish a colony in (an area) 2 (of plants and animals) to become established in (a new environment) > **colonization** noun: plans for the colonization of Mars

colony colonies noun [HISTORY] 1 group of people who settle in a new country but remain under the rule of their homeland 2 territory occupied by a colony 3 group of people or animals of the same kind living together

colossal adjective very large

colour noun 1 appearance of things as a result of reflecting light 2 substance that gives colour 3 skin complexion of a person 4 quality that makes something interesting or exciting: bringing more culture and colour to the city > verb 5 to apply colour to 6 to influence (someone's judgment) > **colouring** noun

colour-blind adjective unable to distinguish between certain colours

colourful adjective 1 with bright or varied colours 2 vivid or distinctive in character: a colourful personality > **colourfully** adverb

colt noun young male horse

column noun 1 pillar 2 vertical division of a newspaper page 3 regular feature in a newspaper 4 vertical arrangement of numbers 5 narrow formation of troops

columnist noun journalist who writes a regular feature in a newspaper

coma noun state of deep unconsciousness

comb noun 1 toothed implement for arranging the hair > verb 2 to use a comb on 3 to search (a place) with great care

combat noun 1 fight or struggle: his first experience of combat > verb 2 to fight or struggle against

combination noun 1 mixture 2 act of combining or state of being combined 3 set of numbers that opens a special lock

combine verb 1 to bring or mix (different things) together 2 to come together ▷ noun 3 association of people or firms for a common purpose 4 machine that reaps and threshes grain in one process

combustion noun [SCIENCE] process of burning

come comes, coming, came, come verb 1 to move towards a place or arrive there 2 to occur 3 to reach a specified point or condition: *The sea water came up to his waist* 4 to be produced or be available: *It also comes in other colours* 5 to become: *a dream come true* 6 **come from** to be or have been a native or resident of: *My mother comes from Norway* > **come about** verb to happen: *The discussion came about because of the proposed changes* > **come across** verb 1 to meet or find by accident 2 **come across as** to give the impression of being > **come off** verb 1 to emerge from a situation in a certain position: *The people who have come off worst are the poor* 2 (informal) to have the intended effect: *It was a gamble that didn't come off* > **come on** verb 1 to make progress 2 (of power or water) to start running or functioning 3 to begin: *I think I've got a cold coming on* > **come round** verb 1 to recover consciousness 2 to change your opinion > **come to** verb 1 to recover consciousness 2 to amount to (a total figure) > **come up** verb 1 to be mentioned

2 to be about to happen 3 **come up against** to come into conflict with 4 **come up with** to produce or propose: *a knack for coming up with great ideas*

comeback noun (informal) return to a former position or status: *The sixties singing star is making a comeback*

comedian noun 1 entertainer who tells jokes 2 person who performs in comedy

comedienne [kom-mee-dee-**en**] noun a female comedian

comedy comedies noun 1 humorous play, film or programme 2 such works as a genre

comet noun object that travels around the sun leaving a bright trail behind it

comfort noun 1 physical ease or wellbeing 2 something or someone that brings relief from worries or unhappiness 3 **comforts** things that make life easier or more pleasant ▷ verb 4 to soothe or console

comfortable adjective 1 providing comfort 2 physically relaxed 3 (informal) well-off financially > **comfortably** adverb

comic adjective 1 funny 2 of or relating to comedy ▷ noun 3 comedian 4 magazine containing strip cartoons

comical adjective amusing

comma noun [ENGLISH] punctuation mark (,)

command verb 1 to order 2 to have authority over 3 to deserve and get: *a public figure who commands respect* 4 to have (a view over something) ▷ noun 5 authoritative instruction that something must be done **6** authority to command **7** knowledge (of language) **8** military or naval unit with a specific function

commandant noun army officer in charge of a place or group of people

commander noun **1** military officer in command of a group or operation **2** middle-ranking naval officer

commandment noun RE one of ten rules of behaviour that, according to the Old Testament, people should obey

commando commandos or commandoes noun member of a military unit trained for swift raids in enemy territory

commemorate verb to honour or keep alive the memory of > **commemoration** noun: a commemoration of the battle of Stalingrad > **commemorative** adjective: a commemorative plaque

commence verb (formal) to begin > **commencement** noun beginning of something

commend verb **1** to praise **2** to recommend > **commendable** adjective: a commendable achievement > **commendation** noun: a commendation from the judges

comment noun **1** remark or gossip **2** explanatory note ▷ verb **4** to make a comment

commentary commentaries noun **1** spoken accompaniment to a broadcast or film **2** explanatory notes

commentator noun someone who gives a radio or television commentary

commerce noun buying and selling of goods and services

commercial adjective **1** of commerce **2** (of television or radio) paid for by advertisers **3** having profit as the main aim ▷ noun **4** television or radio advertisement > **commercially** adverb

commission noun **1** piece of work that an artist is asked to do **2** duty or task **3** percentage paid to a salesperson for each sale made **4** group of people appointed to perform certain duties **5** committing of a crime **6** (Military) rank or authority officially given to an officer **7** out of commission not in working order ▷ verb **8** to place an order for **9** (Military) to give a commission to **10** to grant authority to

commit commits, committing, committed verb **1** to perform (a crime or error) **2** to pledge (yourself) to a course of action **3** to send (someone) to prison or hospital > **committal** noun sending someone to prison or hospital

commitment noun **1** dedication to a cause **2** engagement or obligation: business commitments

committed adjective having strong beliefs; devout: a committed feminist

committee noun group of people appointed to perform a specified service or function

commodity commodities noun (formal) something that can be bought or sold

common adjective **1** occurring often **2** belonging to two or more people; shared **3** belonging to the whole community: *common property* **4** lacking in taste or manners ▷ *noun* **5** area of grassy land belonging to a community > **commonly** *adverb*

commoner *noun* person who does not belong to the nobility

commonplace *adjective* happening often

common sense *noun* ability to act or react sensibly, using good judgment

commotion *noun* noisy disturbance

communal *adjective* shared

commune *noun* **1** [**kom**-yoon] group of people who live together and share everything ▷ *verb* **2** [kom-**yoon**] **commune with** to feel very close to: *communing with nature*

communicate *verb* to make known or share (information, thoughts or feelings)

communication *noun* [PSHE] **1** process by which people or animals exchange information **2** thing communicated **3** (*formal*) letter or telephone call **4 communications** means of travelling or sending messages

communicative *adjective* talking freely

communion *noun* **1** sharing of thoughts or feelings **2 Communion** Christian ritual of sharing consecrated bread and wine **3** religious group with shared beliefs and practices

communism *noun* belief that all property and means of production should be shared by the community > **communist** *noun, adjective*

community communities *noun* **1** all the people living in one district **2** group with shared origins or interests

commute *verb* to travel daily to and from work

compact *adjective* **1** closely packed **2** taking up very little space **3** concise or brief ▷ *verb* **4** to pack closely together

compact disc *noun* plastic disc on which sound, images and data are or can be stored for use in CD players and computers

companion *noun* person who associates with or accompanies someone: *a travelling companion* > **companionship** *noun* relationship of friends or companions

company companies *noun* **1** business organization; firm **2** group of actors **3** having someone with you: *I enjoyed her company* **4** person or people with you

comparable [**kom**-pra-bl] *adjective* similar in size or quality: *The skill is comparable to playing the violin* > **comparably** *adverb*

comparative *adjective* **1** relative **2** involving comparison: *He studied comparative religion* **3** (*Grammar*) denoting the form of an adjective or adverb indicating *more* ▷ *noun* **4** (*Grammar*) comparative form of a word, such as *colder*, *faster*, *better* > **comparatively** *adverb*

compare *verb* **1** [EXAM TERM] to examine (things) and point out the resemblances or differences **2** (often followed by *with*) to be worth in comparison: *How do they compare?* **3 compare to** to liken (something) to

a b **c** d e f g h i j k l m n o p q r s t u v w x y z

comparison noun **1** analysis of the similarities and differences between things **2** comparing

compartment noun **1** section of a railway carriage **2** separate section

compass noun **1** instrument for showing direction, with a needle that points north **2 compasses** hinged instrument for drawing circles (also **pair of compasses**)

compassion noun pity or sympathy > **compassionate** adjective showing or having compassion

compatible adjective able to exist, work or be used together > **compatibility** noun

compatriot noun fellow countryman or countrywoman

compel compels, compelling, compelled verb to force (someone to be or do something)

compelling adjective **1** extremely interesting: a compelling novel **2** convincing: compelling new evidence

compensate verb **1** to make amends to (someone), especially for injury or loss **2 compensate for** to cancel out the effects of (something): The trip more than compensated for the hardship > **compensation** noun payment to make up for loss or injury > **compensatory** adjective: compensatory payments

compere [kom-pare] noun **1** person who presents a stage, radio or television show ▷ verb **2** to be the compere of

compete verb **1** to try to be more successful or popular than other similar people or organizations **2** to take part in a competition

competent adjective able to carry out tasks satisfactorily > **competently** adverb

competition noun **1** act of competing **2** event in which people compete **3** people against whom you compete

competitive adjective **1** involving rivalry **2** showing the urge to compete **3** cheap enough to be successful when compared with similar commercial rivals > **competitively** adverb

competitor noun person, team or firm that competes

compile verb to collect and arrange (information), especially to make a book > **compilation** noun: a compilation of his jazz works > **compiler** noun

complacent adjective self-satisfied and unconcerned, and therefore not taking necessary action > **complacency** noun: complacency about the risks of flooding > **complacently** adverb

complain verb **1** to express resentment or displeasure **2 complain of** to say that you are suffering from (an illness) > **complaint** noun **1** complaining **2** mild illness

complement noun **1** thing that completes something **2** complete amount or number **3** (Grammar) word or words added to a verb to complete the meaning ▷ verb **4** to make complete > **complementary** adjective: Two complementary strategies are necessary

WORD TIP

Do not confuse complement and compliment. The e spelling

complete adjective 1 thorough or absolute 2 finished 3 having all the necessary parts ▷ verb 4 to finish 5 to make whole or perfect > **completely** adverb > **completion** noun finishing is for senses that involve completion

complex adjective 1 made up of parts 2 complicated ▷ noun 3 whole made up of parts 4 group of unconscious feelings that influences behaviour > **complexity** noun: the complexity of modern weapons systems

complexion noun 1 skin of the face 2 character or nature

complicate verb to make or become complex or difficult to deal with

complicated adjective so complex as to be difficult to understand or deal with

complication noun something that makes a situation more difficult to deal with

compliment noun 1 expression of praise 2 **compliments** formal greetings ▷ verb 3 to praise

WORD TIP
Do not confuse compliment and complement

complimentary adjective 1 expressing praise 2 free of charge

comply complies, complying, complied verb (followed by with) to act in accordance (with)

component noun, adjective (being) part of a whole

compose verb 1 to put together 2 to be the component parts of 3 to create (a piece of music or writing) 4 to calm (yourself) 5 to arrange artistically

composed adjective calm and in control of your feelings

composer noun person who writes music

composition noun 1 way that something is put together or arranged 2 work of art, especially a musical one 3 essay 4 composing

compost noun decayed plants used as a fertilizer

composure noun ability to stay calm

compound noun 1 thing, especially a chemical, made up of two or more combined parts or elements 2 fenced enclosure containing buildings ▷ adjective 3 made up of two or more combined parts or elements ▷ verb 4 to combine or make by combining 5 to intensify or make worse

comprehend verb (formal) to understand > **comprehension** noun: This was beyond her comprehension

comprehensible adjective able to be understood

comprehensive adjective 1 including everything necessary or relevant ▷ noun 2 (Brit) comprehensive school > **comprehensively** adverb

compress verb [kum-**press**] 1 to squeeze together 2 to make shorter ▷ noun [**kom**-press] 3 pad applied to stop bleeding or cool inflammation > **compression** noun

comprise verb (formal) to be made up of or to make up

compromise [**kom**-prom-mize] noun 1 settlement reached by concessions on each side ▷ **verb 2** to settle a dispute by making concessions **3** to put (oneself or another person) in a dishonourable position > **compromising** *adjective* revealing an embarrassing or guilty secret about someone: *compromising photographs*

compulsion *noun* **1** irresistible urge **2** forcing by threats or violence

compulsive *adjective* **1** resulting from or acting from a compulsion **2** irresistible or absorbing: *compulsive viewing*

compulsory *adjective* required by rules or laws

computer *noun* electronic machine that stores and processes data

computer-aided design *noun* use of computers and computer graphics to help design things

computerize or **computerise** *verb* to adapt (a system or process) so that it can be handled by computer

computing *noun* use of computers and the writing of programs for them

comrade *noun* **1** fellow member of a union or socialist political party **2** fellow soldier > **comradeship** *noun* friendship between a number of people doing the same job or sharing the same difficulties

con cons, conning, conned (*informal*) *noun* **1** short for **confidence trick 2** pros and cons see pro ▷ **verb 3** to deceive or swindle

concave *adjective* curving inwards

conceal *verb* **1** to cover and hide **2** to keep secret > **concealment** *noun*: *concealment of weapons*

concede [kon-**seed**] *verb* **1** to admit (something) as true or correct **2** to acknowledge defeat in (a contest or argument)

conceit *noun* **1** too high an opinion of yourself **2** far-fetched or clever comparison

conceited *adjective* having an excessively high opinion of yourself

conceivable *adjective* imaginable or possible > **conceivably** *adverb*

conceive *verb* **1** to imagine or think **2** to form in the mind **3** to become pregnant

concentrate *verb* **1** to fix your attention or efforts on something **2** to bring or come together in large numbers in one place **3** to make (a liquid) stronger by removing water from it ▷ *noun* **4** concentrated liquid > **concentration** *noun* **1** concentrating **2** proportion of a substance in a mixture or solution

concentrated *adjective* (of a liquid) made stronger by having water removed

concentration camp *noun* prison camp for civilian prisoners, especially in Nazi Germany

concept *noun* abstract or general idea > **conceptual** *adjective* of or based on concepts > **conceptually** *adverb*

conception *noun* **1** notion, idea or plan **2** process by which a woman becomes pregnant

concern *noun* **1** anxiety or worry **2** something that is of importance to someone **3** business or firm

▷ *verb* **4** to worry (someone) **5** to involve (yourself) **6** to be relevant or important to

concerning *preposition* about or regarding

concert *noun* **1** musical entertainment **2 in concert a** working together **b** (of musicians) performing live

concerted *adjective* done together

concerto concertos or concerti [kon-**cher**-toe] *noun* large-scale composition for a solo instrument and orchestra

concession *noun* **1** grant of rights, land or property **2** reduction in price for a specified category of people **3** conceding **4** thing conceded

conch conches *noun* **1** shellfish with a large spiral shell **2** its shell

concise *adjective* brief and to the point ▷ **concisely** *adverb*

conclude *verb* **1** to decide by reasoning **2** to come or bring to an end **3** to arrange or settle finally ▷ **concluding** *adjective*

conclusion *noun* **1** decision based on reasoning **2** ending **3** final arrangement or settlement

conclusive *adjective* ending doubt, convincing ▷ **conclusively** *adverb*

concoct *verb* **1** to make up (a story or plan) **2** to make by combining ingredients ▷ **concoction** *noun*: *a concoction of honey, yogurt and fruit*

concourse *noun* **1** large open public place where people can gather **2** large crowd

concrete *noun* **1** mixture of cement, sand, stone and water, used in building ▷ *adjective*

2 made of concrete **3** definite, rather than general or vague **4** real or solid, not abstract

concubine [**kon**-kew-bine] *noun* (History) woman living in a man's house but not married to him and kept for his sexual pleasure

concur concurs, concurring, concurred *verb* (formal) to agree

concurrent *adjective* happening at the same time or place ▷ **concurrently** *adverb* at the same time

concussion *noun* sickness or loss of consciousness caused by a blow to the head ▷ **concussed** *adjective* having concussion

condemn *verb* **1** to express disapproval of **2** to sentence: *He was condemned to death* **3** to force into an unpleasant situation **4** to declare (something) unfit for use ▷ **condemnation** *noun*: *widespread condemnation of Saturday's killings*

condensation *noun* [SCIENCE] coating of tiny drops formed on a surface by steam or vapour

condense *verb* **1** to make shorter **2** to turn from gas into liquid

condescending *adjective* behaving in a way that suggests you feel superior to someone; patronizing

condition *noun* **1** particular state of being **2** necessary requirement for something else to happen **3** restriction or qualification **4** state of health or physical fitness **5** medical problem **6 conditions** circumstances **7 on condition that** only if ▷ *verb* **8** to train or influence to behave in a particular way

conditional adjective depending on circumstances

condolence noun 1 sympathy 2 **condolences** expression of sympathy

condom noun rubber sheath worn on the penis in the vagina during sexual intercourse to prevent conception or infection

condominium noun (Aust, US, Canadian) block of flats in which each flat is owned by the occupant

condone verb to overlook or forgive (wrongdoing)

conducive [kon-**joo**-siv] adjective **conducive to** likely to lead to

conduct noun 1 management of an activity 2 behaviour ▷ verb 3 to carry out (a task) 4 (formal) to behave (oneself) 5 to direct (musicians) by moving your hands or a baton 6 to lead or guide 7 to transmit (heat or electricity)

conductor noun 1 [MUSIC] person who conducts musicians 2 official on a bus who collects fares 3 something that conducts heat or electricity

cone noun 1 object with a circular base, tapering to a point 2 cone-shaped ice-cream wafer 3 (Brit, Aust, NZ) plastic cone used as a traffic marker on the roads 4 scaly fruit of a conifer tree

confectionery noun sweets

confederation noun organization formed for business or political purposes

confer confers, conferring, conferred verb 1 to discuss together 2 to grant or give

conference noun meeting for discussion

confess verb 1 to admit (a fault or crime) 2 to admit to be true 3 to declare (your sins) to God or a priest, in the hope of forgiveness

confession noun 1 something confessed 2 confessing

confessional noun small stall in which a priest hears confessions

confetti noun small pieces of coloured paper thrown at weddings

confidant [**kon**-fid-dant] noun (formal) person confided in ▷ **confidante** noun woman or girl confided in

confide verb 1 to tell someone (a secret) 2 to entrust

confidence noun 1 trust 2 self-assurance 3 something confided 4 **in confidence** as a secret

confidence trick noun swindle involving gaining a person's trust in order to cheat him or her

confident adjective sure, especially of yourself ▷ **confidently** adverb

confidential adjective 1 private or secret 2 entrusted with someone's secret affairs ▷ **confidentially** adverb ▷ **confidentiality** noun: the confidentiality of the client-doctor relationship

confine verb 1 to keep within bounds 2 to restrict the free movement of ▷ noun 3 **confines** boundaries or limits ▷ **confinement** noun 1 being confined 2 period of childbirth

confined adjective (of a space) small and enclosed

confirm verb 1 to prove to be true 2 to reaffirm or strengthen 3 (Christianity) to administer the rite of confirmation to

confirmation noun **1** confirming **2** RE rite that admits a baptized person to full church membership

confirmed adjective firmly established in a habit or condition

confiscate verb to seize (property) by authority

conflict noun **1** disagreement **2** struggle or fight ▷ verb **3** to be incompatible

conform verb **1** to comply with accepted standards or customs **2** conform to, conform with to be like or in accordance with > **conformist** noun, adjective (person) complying with accepted standards or customs > **conformity** noun compliance with accepted standards or customs

confront verb **1** to face **2** to come face to face with **3** (often followed by about, with) to tackle (someone) about something or present something as evidence

confrontation noun serious argument

confuse verb **1** to mix up **2** to perplex or disconcert **3** to make unclear > **confused** adjective: confused thinking > **confusing** adjective: The statement is highly confusing > **confusion** noun: confusion about the number of casualties

congeal [kon-jeel] verb (of a liquid) to become thick and sticky

congenial [kon-jeen-yal] adjective **1** pleasant or agreeable **2** having similar interests and attitudes

congenital adjective (Medicine) (of a condition) existing from birth

congested adjective crowded to excess > **congestion** noun: traffic congestion

conglomerate noun **1** large corporation made up of many companies **2** thing made up of several different elements

congratulate verb to express pleasure to (someone) at his or her good fortune or success > **congratulatory** adjective: a congratulatory telegram

congregate verb to gather together in a crowd

congregation noun people who attend a church

congress noun **1** formal meeting for discussion **2** Congress federal parliament of the US

conical adjective cone-shaped

conifer noun cone-bearing tree, such as the fir or pine > **coniferous** adjective

conjecture noun guesswork about something

conjugate [kon-joo-gate] verb to give the inflections of (a verb)

conjunction noun **1** combination **2** simultaneous occurrence of events **3** ENGLISH part of speech joining words, phrases or clauses, such as and, but or because **4** in conjunction done or used together

conjuror or **conjuror** noun someone who entertains people by doing magic tricks

conker noun (informal) nut of the horse chestnut

connect verb **1** to join together **2** to associate in the mind

connection or **connexion** noun **1** relationship or association **2** link or bond **3** opportunity to transfer from one public vehicle to another **4** influential acquaintance

a
b
c
d
e
f
g
h
i
j
k
l
m
n
o
p
q
r
s
t
u
v
w
x
y
z

connective noun word or short phrase that connects clauses, phrases or words

connoisseur [kon-noss-**sir**] noun person with special knowledge of the arts, food or drink

connotation noun associated idea conveyed by a word

conquer verb **1** to defeat **2** to overcome (a difficulty) **3** to take (a place) by force > **conqueror** noun

conquest noun **1** conquering of a country or group of people **2** lands captured by conquest

conscience noun sense of right or wrong as regards thoughts and actions

conscientious [kon-shee-en-shus] adjective painstaking > **conscientiously** adverb

conscious adjective **1** alert and awake **2** aware **3** deliberate or intentional > **consciously** adverb > **consciousness** noun: She hit her head and lost consciousness

consecrated adjective (of a building or place) officially declared to be holy

consecutive adjective in unbroken succession

consensus noun general agreement

consent noun **1** agreement or permission ▷ verb **2** (followed by to) to agree (to something)

consequence noun **1** result or effect **2** (formal) importance: We said little of consequence

consequent adjective resulting > **consequently** adverb as a result; therefore

conservation noun **1** protection of natural resources and the environment **2** conserving > **conservationist** noun

conservative adjective **1** opposing change **2** moderate or cautious **3** conventional in style **4** **Conservative** of the Conservative Party, the British right-wing political party which believes in private enterprise and capitalism ▷ noun **5** conservative person **6** **Conservative** supporter or member of the Conservative Party > **conservatism** noun > **conservatively** adverb

conservatory conservatories noun room with glass walls and a glass roof, attached to a house

conserve verb **1** to protect from harm, decay or loss **2** to preserve (fruit) with sugar ▷ noun **3** jam containing large pieces of fruit

consider verb **1** to regard as **2** to think about **3** to be considerate of **4** to discuss **5** to look at

considerable adjective large in amount or degree > **considerably** adverb

considerate adjective thoughtful towards others

consideration noun **1** careful thought **2** fact that should be considered **3** thoughtfulness **4** payment for a service

considered adjective presented or thought out with care

considering preposition taking (a specified fact) into account

consign verb **1** to put somewhere **2** to send (goods)

consignment noun shipment of goods

consist verb **1** consist in to have as its main or only feature **2** consist of to be made up of

consistency consistencies noun 1 being consistent 2 degree of thickness or smoothness

consistent adjective 1 unchanging or constant 2 consistent within agreement with or tallying with > **consistently** adverb

console verb [con-**sole**] 1 to comfort (someone) in distress ▷ noun [**con**-sole] 2 panel of controls for electronic equipment

consolidate verb 1 to make or become stronger or more stable 2 to combine into a whole > **consolidation** noun: the consolidation of power

consonant noun 1 speech sound made by partially or completely blocking the breath stream, such as b or f 2 letter representing this

consort verb [con-**sort**] 1 consort with to keep company (with) ▷ noun [**con**-sort] 2 husband or wife of a monarch

consortium consortia or consortiums noun association of business firms

conspicuous adjective 1 clearly visible 2 noteworthy or striking > **conspicuously** adverb

conspiracy conspiracies noun 1 conspiring 2 plan made by conspiring

conspirator noun someone involved in a conspiracy

conspire verb 1 to plan a crime together in secret 2 (literary) to act together as if by design

constable noun police officer of the lowest rank

constabulary constabularies noun police force of an area

constant adjective 1 continuous 2 unchanging 3 faithful ▷ noun

4 unvarying quantity 5 something that stays the same > **constancy** noun > **constantly** adverb

constellation noun group of stars

consternation noun anxiety or dismay

constipated adjective unable to empty your bowels > **constipation** noun difficulty in emptying your bowels

constituency constituencies noun 1 area represented by a Member of Parliament 2 voters in such an area

constituent noun 1 member of a constituency 2 component part ▷ adjective 3 forming part of a whole

constitute verb to form or make up

constitution noun 1 principles on which a state is governed 2 physical condition 3 structure > **constitutional** adjective 1 of a constitution 2 in accordance with a political constitution > **constitutionally** adverb

constrained adjective compelled or forced (to do something)

constraint noun something that limits someone's freedom of action

constrict verb to make narrower by squeezing > **constriction** noun: severe constriction of the arteries

construct verb to build or put together

construction noun 1 constructing 2 thing constructed 3 interpretation 4 (Grammar) way in which words are arranged in a sentence, clause or phrase

constructive adjective (of advice, criticism, etc) useful and helpful > **constructively** adverb

consul noun official representing a state in a foreign country > **consular** adjective: consular officials

consulate noun workplace or position of a consul

consult verb to ask advice from or discuss matters with (someone)

consultancy noun 1 organization whose members give expert advice on a subject 2 work or position of a consultant

consultant noun 1 specialist doctor with a senior position in a hospital 2 specialist who gives professional advice

consultation noun 1 act of consulting 2 meeting for discussion or the seeking of advice > **consultative** adjective giving advice

consume verb 1 to eat or drink 2 to use up 3 to destroy 4 to obsess

consumer noun person who buys goods or uses services

consumerism noun belief that a country will have a strong economy if its people buy a lot of goods and spend a lot of money

consuming adjective (of passion, interest, etc) most important and very engrossing

consummate [kon-sum-mate] verb 1 to make (a marriage) legal by sexual intercourse 2 to complete or fulfil ▷ adjective [kon-sum-mit] 3 supremely skilled: a consummate politician 4 complete or extreme: consummate skill > **consummation** noun: the consummation of marriage

consumption noun 1 amount consumed 2 consuming 3 (old-fashioned) tuberculosis

contact noun 1 communicating 2 touching 3 useful acquaintance 4 connection between two electrical conductors in a circuit ▷ verb 5 to get in touch with

contact lens noun lens placed on the eyeball to correct defective vision

contagious adjective spreading by contact

contain verb 1 to hold or be capable of holding 2 to consist of 3 to control or restrain > **containment** noun prevention of the spread of something harmful

container noun 1 object used to hold or store things in 2 large standard-sized box for transporting cargo by truck or ship

contaminate verb 1 to make impure or pollute 2 to make radioactive > **contamination** noun: the contamination of the sea

contemplate verb 1 to think deeply about 2 to consider as a possibility 3 to gaze at > **contemplation** noun: He was deep in contemplation > **contemplative** adjective: a quiet, contemplative person

contemporary contemporaries adjective 1 present-day or modern 2 living or occurring at the same time ▷ noun 3 person or thing living or occurring at the same time as another

contempt noun 1 dislike and disregard 2 open disrespect for the authority of a court

contemptible *adjective* not worthy of any respect

contemptuous *adjective* showing contempt ▷ **contemptuously** *adverb*

contend *verb* 1 (*formal*) to state or assert 2 to compete 3 **contend with** to deal with

contented *adjective* happy and satisfied with your life ▷ **contentedly** *adverb* ▷ **contentment** *noun*: *a strong feeling of contentment*

contention *noun* (*formal*) 1 disagreement or dispute 2 point asserted in argument

contest *noun* [**con**-test] 1 competition or struggle ▷ *verb* [con-**test**] 2 to dispute or object to 3 to fight or compete for

contestant *noun* person who takes part in a contest

context *noun* 1 circumstances of an event or fact 2 words before and after a word or sentence that help make its meaning clear

continent *noun* 1 one of the earth's large masses of land 2 **the Continent** mainland of Europe ▷ **continental** *adjective*: *the continental crust*

contingency contingencies [kon-**tin**-jen-see] *noun* something that may happen

contingent *noun* 1 group of people that represents or is part of a larger group ▷ *adjective* 2 **contingent on** dependent on (something uncertain)

continual *adjective* 1 constant 2 recurring frequently ▷ **continually** *adverb*

continuation *noun* 1 continuing 2 part added

continue continues, continuing, continued *verb* 1 to (cause to) remain in a condition or place 2 to carry on (doing something) 3 to resume after an interruption

continuous *adjective* continuing uninterrupted ▷ **continuously** *adverb*

contort *verb* to twist out of shape ▷ **contorted** *adjective*: *faces contorted with hatred*

contour *noun* 1 outline 2 GEOGRAPHY line on a map joining places of the same height

contra- *prefix* against or contrasting: *contraflow*

contraception *noun* prevention of pregnancy by artificial means

contraceptive *noun* device used or pill taken to prevent pregnancy ▷ *adjective* preventing pregnancy

contract *noun* [**con**-trakt] 1 (document setting out) a formal agreement ▷ *verb* [con-**trakt**] 2 to make a formal agreement (to do something) 3 to make or become smaller or shorter 4 to catch (an illness) ▷ **contractual** *adjective*: *contractual obligations*

contractor *noun* firm that supplies materials or labour

contradict *verb* 1 to declare the opposite of (a statement) to be true 2 to be at variance with ▷ **contradiction** *noun*: *a contradiction of all that the Olympics is supposed to be* ▷ **contradictory** *adjective*: *contradictory statements*

contraption *noun* strange-looking device

contrary *noun* 1 complete opposite ▷ *adjective* 2 opposed or completely different 3 perverse or obstinate ▷ *adverb* 4 in opposition

contrast noun 1 obvious difference 2 person or thing very different from another ▷ verb 3 to compare in order to show differences 4 **contrast with** to be very different from

contravene verb (formal) to break (a rule or law)

contribute verb 1 to give for a common purpose or fund 2 **contribute to** to be partly responsible (for) > **contribution** noun: charitable contributions > **contributor** noun: Old buses are major contributors to pollution > **contributory** adjective: contributory factors

contrive verb (formal) 1 to make happen 2 to devise or construct > **contrived** adjective planned or artificial

control controls, controlling, controlled noun 1 power to direct something 2 curb or check 3 controls instruments used to operate a machine ▷ verb 4 to have power over 5 to limit or restrain 6 to regulate or operate > **controller** noun

controversial adjective causing controversy

controversy controversies [**kon**-triv-ver-see or kon-**trov**-ver-see] noun fierce argument or debate

conundrum noun (formal) puzzling problem

convalesce verb to recover after an illness or operation

convection noun transmission of heat in liquids or gases by the circulation of currents

convene verb (formal) 1 to arrange or call (a meeting) 2 to gather for a formal meeting

convenience noun 1 quality of being convenient 2 useful object 3 (Brit formal) public toilet

convenient adjective 1 suitable or opportune 2 easy to use 3 nearby > **conveniently** adverb

convent noun 1 building where nuns live or lived 2 school run by nuns

convention noun 1 widely accepted view of proper behaviour 2 assembly or meeting 3 formal agreement

conventional adjective 1 (unthinkingly) following the accepted customs 2 customary 3 (of weapons or warfare) not nuclear, biological or chemical > **conventionally** adverb

converge verb to meet or join

conversation noun informal talk > **conversational** adjective: conversational German > **conversationalist** noun: a witty conversationalist

converse verb [con-**verse**] 1 (formal) to have a conversation ▷ noun [**con**-verse] 2 statement or idea that is the opposite of another ▷ adjective [**con**-verse] 3 reversed or opposite > **conversely** adverb

convert verb [con-**vert**] 1 to change in form, character or function 2 to cause to change in opinion or belief ▷ noun [**con**-vert] 3 person who has converted to a different belief or religion

convex adjective curving outwards

convey verb 1 to communicate (information) 2 to carry or transport

conveyor belt noun continuous moving belt for transporting things, especially in a factory

convict verb 1 to declare guilty ▷ noun 2 person serving a prison sentence

conviction noun 1 firm belief 2 instance of being convicted

convince verb to persuade by argument or evidence

convincing adjective believable > **convincingly** adverb

convoluted adjective 1 coiled or twisted 2 (of an argument or sentence) complex and hard to understand

convoy noun group of vehicles or ships travelling together

convulsion noun 1 violent muscular spasm 2 **convulsions** uncontrollable laughter

coo coos, cooing, cooed verb (of a dove or pigeon) to make a soft murmuring sound

cook verb 1 to prepare (food) by heating 2 (of food) to be cooked 3 **cook up** (informal) to devise (a story or scheme) ▷ noun 4 person who cooks food

cooker noun (Chiefly Brit) apparatus for cooking heated by gas or electricity

cookery noun art of cooking

cookie noun 1 (US) biscuit 2 ICT file on a computer with information about the user's preferences, used on future visits to a website

cool adjective 1 moderately cold 2 calm and unemotional 3 indifferent or unfriendly 4 (informal) sophisticated or excellent ▷ verb 5 to make or become cool ▷ noun 6 coolness 7 (informal) calmness or composure > **coolly** adverb > **coolness** noun

coolabah noun Australian eucalypt that grows along rivers

cooldown noun PE gentle stretching exercises done after more strenuous exercise

coop[1] noun cage or pen for poultry

coop[2] [koh-op] noun (Brit, US, Aust) (shop run by) a cooperative society

cooperate verb to work or act together > **cooperation** noun: cooperation between police and the public

cooperative adjective [koh-op-er-ut-tiv] 1 willing to cooperate 2 (of an enterprise) owned and managed collectively ▷ noun 3 cooperative organization

cop cops, copping, copped (informal) noun 1 policeman ▷ verb 2 to take or seize

cope verb (often followed by with) to deal successfully (with something); manage

copious [kope-ee-uss] adjective (formal) abundant or plentiful

copper noun 1 soft reddish-brown metal 2 copper or bronze coin 3 (Brit informal) policeman

copse noun small group of trees growing close together

copulate verb to have sexual intercourse > **copulation** noun

copy copies, copying, copied noun 1 thing made to look exactly like another 2 single specimen of a book etc 3 material for printing ▷ verb 4 to make a copy of 5 to act or try to be like > **copier** noun

copyright noun 1 exclusive legal right to reproduce and control a book, work of art, etc ▷ verb 2 to take out a copyright on ▷ adjective 3 protected by copyright

coral noun **1** hard substance formed from the skeletons of very small sea animals ▷ adjective **2** orange-pink

cord noun **1** thin rope or thick string **2** cordlike structure in the body **3** corduroy

cordial adjective **1** warm and friendly ▷ noun **2** drink with a fruit base

cordon noun **1** chain of police, soldiers, etc, guarding an area ▷ verb **2 cordon off** to form a cordon round

corduroy noun cotton fabric with a velvety ribbed surface

core noun **1** central part of certain fruits, containing the seeds **2** central or essential part ▷ verb **3** to remove the core from

cork noun **1** thick light bark of a Mediterranean oak **2** piece of this used as a stopper ▷ verb **3** to seal with a cork

corkscrew noun spiral metal tool for pulling corks from bottles

cormorant noun large dark-coloured long-necked sea bird

corn noun **1** cereal plant such as wheat or oats **2** grain of such plants **3** (US, Canadian, Aust, NZ) maize **4** painful hard skin on the toe

cornea [kor-nee-a] noun transparent membrane covering the eyeball

corner noun **1** area or angle where two converging lines or surfaces meet **2** place where two streets meet **3** remote place **4** (Sport) free kick or shot from the corner of the field ▷ verb **5** to force into a difficult or inescapable position **6** (of a vehicle) to turn a corner **7** to obtain a monopoly of

cornet noun **1** brass instrument similar to the trumpet **2** cone-shaped ice-cream wafer

cornflour noun **1** (Chiefly Brit) fine maize flour **2** (NZ) fine wheat flour

cornflower noun plant with blue flowers

cornice noun decorative moulding round the top of a wall

corny cornier, corniest adjective (informal) very obvious or sentimental and not at all original: corny old love songs

coronary coronaries [kor-ron-a-ree] noun condition in which the flow of blood to the heart is blocked by a blood clot

coronation noun ceremony of crowning a monarch

coroner noun (Brit, Aust, NZ) official responsible for the investigation of violent, sudden or suspicious deaths

coronet noun small crown

corporal noun noncommissioned officer in an army ▷ adjective **2** of the body

corporal punishment noun physical punishment, such as caning

corporate adjective **1** of business corporations **2** shared by a group

corporation noun **1** large business or company **2** city or town council

corps [kore] noun **1** military unit with a specific function **2** organized body of people

> **WORD TIP**
> The plural of corps is also corps

corpse noun dead body

corpuscle noun red or white blood cell

correa noun Australian shrub with large green and white flowers

correct adjective **1** true or free from error **2** in accordance with accepted standards ▷ verb **3** to put right **4** to indicate the errors in **5** to rebuke or punish > **correctly** adverb > **correction** noun **1** correcting **2** alteration correcting something > **corrective** adjective intended to put right something wrong

correlate verb to be closely connected or to have a mutually influential relationship: *Obesity correlates with increased risk of stroke and diabetes* > **correlation** noun: *the correlation between smoking and disease*

correspond verb **1** to be consistent or compatible (with) **2** to be the same or similar **3** to communicate by letter

correspondence noun **1** communication by letters **2** letters so exchanged **3** relationship or similarity

correspondent noun **1** person employed by a newspaper etc to report on a special subject or from a foreign country **2** letter writer

corresponding adjective resulting from a change to something else: *the rise in interest rates and corresponding fall in house values* > **correspondingly** adverb

corridor noun **1** passage in a building or train **2** strip of land or airspace providing access through foreign territory

corroboree noun (Aust) Aboriginal gathering or dance

corrode verb to eat or be eaten away by chemical action or rust

> **corrosion** noun: *metal corrosion*
> **corrosive** adjective: *Sodium is highly corrosive*

corrugated adjective folded into alternate grooves and ridges

corrupt adjective **1** open to or involving bribery **2** morally depraved **3** (of a text or data) unreliable through errors or alterations ▷ verb **4** to make corrupt > **corruptible** adjective

corruption noun dishonesty and illegal behaviour by people in positions of power

corset noun women's close-fitting undergarment worn to provide support or make the wearer look slimmer

cosmetic noun **1** preparation used to improve the appearance of a person's skin ▷ adjective **2** improving the appearance only

cosmic adjective of the whole universe

cosmopolitan adjective **1** composed of people or elements from many countries **2** having lived and travelled in many countries

cosmos noun the universe

cosset verb to pamper

cost costs, costing, cost noun **1** amount of money, time, labour, etc required for something **2** costs expenses of a lawsuit ▷ verb **3** to have as its cost **4** to involve the loss or sacrifice of **5** (past costed) to estimate the cost of

costly costlier, costliest adjective **1** expensive **2** involving great loss or sacrifice

costume noun **1** style of dress of a particular place or time, or for a particular activity **2** clothes worn by an actor or performer

cosy cosier, cosiest; cosies adjective **1** warm and snug **2** intimate or friendly ▷ noun **3** cover for keeping things warm: a tea cosy ▷ **cosily** adverb ▷ **cosiness** noun

cot noun **1** baby's bed with high sides **2** small portable bed

cottage noun small house in the country

cottage cheese noun soft mild white cheese

cotton noun **1** white downy fibre covering the seeds of a tropical plant **2** cloth or thread made from this ▷ **cotton on (to)** (informal) to understand

cotton wool noun fluffy cotton used for surgical dressings etc

couch noun **1** piece of upholstered furniture for seating more than one person ▷ verb **2** to express in a particular way

cough verb **1** to expel air from the lungs abruptly and noisily ▷ noun **2** act or sound of coughing **3** illness which causes coughing

could verb past tense of **can¹**

coulomb [koo-lom] noun SI unit of electric charge

council noun **1** group meeting for discussion or consultation **2** local governing body of a town or region ▷ adjective **3** of or by a council

councillor noun member of a council

counsel counsels, counselling, counselled noun **1** advice or guidance **2** barrister or barristers ▷ verb **3** to give guidance to **4** to urge or recommend ▷ **counselling** noun: Victims were

offered counselling ▷ **counsellor** noun: a marriage guidance counsellor

count verb **1** to say numbers in order **2** to find the total of **3** to be important **4** to regard as **5** to take into account ▷ noun **6** counting **7** number reached by counting **8** (Law) one of a number of charges **9** European nobleman ▷ **counting** preposition including: nearly 4000 of us, not counting women and children ▷ **count on** verb to rely or depend on

countdown noun counting backwards to zero of the seconds before an event

countenance noun (literary) face or facial expression

counter verb **1** to oppose or retaliate against ▷ adverb **2** in the opposite direction **3** in direct contrast ▷ noun **4** opposing or retaliatory action **5** long flat surface in a bank or shop, on which business is transacted **6** small flat disc used in board games

counteract verb to act against or neutralize

counterfeit [kown-ter-fit] adjective **1** fake or forged ▷ noun **2** fake or forgery ▷ verb **3** to fake or forge

counterpart noun person or thing complementary to or corresponding to another

countess noun **1** woman holding the rank of count or earl **2** wife or widow of a count or earl

countless adjective too many to count

country countries noun GEOGRAPHY **1** nation **2** nation's territory **3** nation's people **4** part of the land away from cities

countryman countrymen noun **1** person from your native land **2** (Brit, Aust, NZ) person who lives in the country > **countrywoman** noun

countryside noun land away from cities

county counties noun (GEOGRAPHY) (in some countries) division of a country

coup [koo] noun **1** successful action **2** sudden violent overthrow of a government

couple noun **1** two people who are married or romantically involved **2** two partners in a dance or game **3** a couple of a pair of > verb **4** to connect or associate

couplet noun two consecutive lines of verse, usually rhyming and of the same metre

coupon noun **1** piece of paper entitling the holder to a discount or gift **2** detachable order form **3** football pools entry form

courage noun ability to face danger or pain without fear > **courageous** adjective: a courageous decision > **courageously** adverb

courgette [koor-jet] noun type of small vegetable marrow

courier [koo-ree-er] noun **1** person employed to look after holiday-makers **2** person employed to deliver urgent messages

course noun **1** series of lessons or medical treatment **2** route or direction taken **3** area where golf is played or a race is run **4** any of the successive parts of a meal **5** mode of conduct or action **6** natural development of events **7** of course a (adverb) as expected, naturally **b** (interjection) certainly, definitely > verb **8** (of liquid) to run swiftly

court noun **1** body which decides legal cases **2** place where it meets **3** marked area for playing a racket game **4** courtyard **5** residence, household or retinue of a sovereign > verb **6** (old-fashioned) to try to gain the love of **7** to try to win the favour of **8** to invite: to court disaster

courteous [kur-tee-yuss] adjective polite

courtesy courtesies noun **1** politeness or good manners **2** courteous act **3** (by) courtesy of with the consent of

courtier noun attendant at a royal court

courtship noun (formal) courting of an intended spouse or mate

courtyard noun paved space enclosed by buildings or walls

cousin noun child of your uncle or aunt

cove noun small bay or inlet

covenant [kuv-ven-ant] noun **1** contract **2** (Chiefly Brit) formal agreement to make an annual (charitable) payment

cover verb **1** to place something over (something) to protect or conceal it **2** to extend over or lie on the surface of **3** to travel over **4** to insure against loss or risk **5** to include **6** to report (an event) for a newspaper **7** to be enough to pay for **8** now noun **8** anything that covers **9** outside of a book or magazine **10** insurance **11** shelter or protection > **cover up** verb **1** to cover completely **2** to conceal (a mistake or crime)

coverage noun amount or extent covered

covering noun layer of something which protects or conceals something else: *A morning blizzard left a covering of snow*

covert [**kuv**-vert] adjective concealed or secret > **covertly** adverb

covet [**kuv**-vit] verb to long to possess (what belongs to someone else)

cow noun mature female of cattle and of certain other mammals, such as the elephant or seal

coward noun person who lacks courage > **cowardly** adjective

cowboy noun (in the US) ranch worker who herds and tends cattle, usually on horseback

cower verb to cringe in fear

cox noun **1** person who steers a boat ▷ verb **2** to act as cox of (a boat)

coy adjective affectedly shy or modest > **coyly** adverb

coyote [koy-**ote**-ee] noun prairie wolf of N America

crab noun edible shellfish with ten legs, the first pair modified into pincers

crack verb **1** to split partially so that damage lines appear on the surface **2** to tell (a joke) **3** to solve (a code or problem) **4** to (cause to) make a sharp noise **5** to break down or yield under strain ▷ noun **6** line that appears on a surface caused by damage **7** narrow gap **8** sudden sharp noise **9** (informal) highly addictive form of cocaine

▷ adjective **10** (informal) first-rate; excellent: *a crack shot*

cracker noun **1** thin dry biscuit **2** decorated cardboard tube, pulled apart with a bang, containing a paper hat and a joke or toy **3** small explosive firework **4** (informal) outstanding thing or person

crackle verb **1** to make small sharp popping noises ▷ noun **2** crackling sound

cradle noun **1** baby's bed on rockers **2** supporting structure ▷ verb **3** to hold gently as if in a cradle

craft noun **1** activity such as weaving, carving or pottery that requires skill with one's hands **2** skilful occupation **3** boat, plane or spacecraft

WORD TIP
When *craft* means 'a boat, plane or spacecraft' (sense 3), the plural is *craft* rather than *crafts*

craftsman craftsmen noun skilled worker > **craftsmanship** noun: *the fine craftsmanship of his furniture* > **craftswoman** noun

crafty craftier, craftiest adjective skilled in deception

crag noun steep rugged rock

craggy craggier, craggiest adjective (of a mountain or cliff) steep and rocky

cram crams, cramming, crammed verb **1** to force into too small a space **2** to fill too full **3** to study hard just before an examination

cramp noun **1** painful muscular contraction **2** clamp for holding masonry or timber together ▷ verb **3** to confine or restrict

cramped *adjective* (of a room or building) not large enough for the people or things in it

cranberry cranberries *noun* sour edible red berry

crane *noun* 1 machine for lifting and moving heavy weights 2 large wading bird with a long neck and legs ▷ *verb* 3 to stretch (your neck) to see something

crank *noun* 1 arm projecting at right angles from a shaft, for transmitting or converting motion 2 (*informal*) eccentric person ▷ *verb* 3 to start (an engine) with a crank

cranny crannies *noun* narrow opening

crash *noun* 1 collision involving a vehicle or vehicles 2 sudden loud smashing noise 3 financial collapse ▷ *verb* 4 to (cause to) collide violently with a vehicle, a stationary object or the ground 5 to (cause to) make a loud smashing noise 6 to (cause to) fall with a crash 7 to collapse or fail financially

crash helmet *noun* protective helmet worn by a motorcyclist

crate *noun* large wooden container for packing goods

crater *noun* very large hole in the ground or in the surface of a planet or moon

cravat *noun* man's scarf worn like a tie

crave *verb* 1 to desire intensely 2 to beg or plead for ▷ **craving** *noun*: *a craving for chocolate*

crawl *verb* 1 to move on your hands and knees 2 to move very slowly 3 (*informal*) to act in a servile manner ▷ *noun* 4 crawling

motion or pace 5 overarm swimming stroke

crayfish crayfish or crayfishes *noun* edible shellfish like a lobster

crayon *noun* stick or pencil of coloured wax or clay

craze *noun* short-lived fashion or enthusiasm

crazy crazier, craziest *adjective* 1 ridiculous 2 insane 3 **crazy about** very fond of ▷ **crazily** *adverb* ▷ **craziness** *noun*: *the craziness of their last decision*

creak *verb* 1 to make a harsh squeaking sound ▷ *noun* 2 harsh squeaking sound ▷ **creaky** *adjective*: *a creaky door*

cream *noun* 1 fatty part of milk 2 food or cosmetic resembling cream in consistency 3 best part (of something) ▷ *adjective* 4 yellowish-white ▷ *verb* 5 to beat to a creamy consistency ▷ **creamy** *adjective*: *a creamy chocolate bar*

crease *noun* 1 line made by folding or pressing 2 (*Cricket*) line marking the bowler's and batsman's positions ▷ *verb* 3 to make or become wrinkled or furrowed ▷ **creased** *adjective*: *creased trousers*

create *verb* 1 to make or cause to exist 2 to appoint to a new rank or position

creative *adjective* imaginative or inventive ▷ **creatively** *adverb* ▷ **creativity** *noun*

creature *noun* animal, person or other being

crèche [kresh] *noun* place where small children are looked after while their parents are working, shopping, etc

credence noun belief in the truth or accuracy of a statement

credentials plural noun document giving evidence of a person's identity or qualifications

credible adjective 1 believable 2 trustworthy > **credibility** noun: The Minister has lost his credibility > **credibly** adverb

credit noun 1 system of allowing customers to receive goods and pay later 2 reputation for trustworthiness in paying debts 3 money at your disposal in a bank account 4 side of an account book on which such sums are entered 5 (source or cause of) praise or approval 6 **credits** list of people responsible for the production of a film, programme or record ▷ verb 7 to enter as a credit in an account 8 (followed by with) to attribute (to) 9 to believe

creditable adjective praiseworthy

credit card noun card allowing a person to buy on credit

creditor noun person to whom money is owed

creed noun statement or system of (Christian) beliefs or principles

creek noun 1 narrow inlet or bay 2 (Aust, NZ, US, Canadian) small stream

creep creeps, creeping, crept verb 1 to move quietly and cautiously 2 to crawl with the body near to the ground 3 (of a plant) to grow along the ground or over rocks ▷ noun 4 (informal) obnoxious or servile person 5 **give someone the creeps** (informal) to give someone a feeling of fear or disgust

creepy creepier, creepiest adjective (informal) causing a feeling of fear or disgust

cremate verb to burn (a corpse) to ash > **cremation** noun

crematorium crematoriums or crematoria noun building where corpses are cremated

crepe [krayp] noun 1 fabric or rubber with a crinkled texture 2 very thin pancake

crescendo crescendos [krish-end-oh] noun gradual increase in loudness, especially in music

crescent noun 1 (curved shape of) the moon as seen in its first or last quarter 2 crescent-shaped street

cress noun plant with strong-tasting leaves, used in salads

crest noun 1 top of a mountain, hill or wave 2 tuft or growth on a bird's or animal's head 3 heraldic design used on a coat of arms and elsewhere > **crested** adjective

crevice noun narrow crack or gap in rock

crew noun 1 people who work on a ship or aircraft 2 group of people working together 3 (informal) any group of people ▷ verb 4 to serve as a crew member (on)

crib cribs, cribbing, cribbed noun 1 baby's cradle ▷ verb 2 to copy (someone's work) dishonestly

crib-wall noun (NZ) retaining wall built against an earth bank

crick noun 1 muscle spasm or cramp in the back or neck ▷ verb 2 to cause a crick in

cricket noun 1 outdoor game played with bats, a ball and wickets by two teams of eleven 2 chirping insect like a grasshopper

crime noun **1** unlawful act **2** unlawful acts collectively

criminal noun **1** person guilty of a crime ▷ adjective **2** of crime > **criminally** adverb

criminology noun study of crime > **criminologist** noun

crimson adjective deep purplish-red

cringe verb to flinch or back away in fear or embarrassment

crinkle verb **1** to wrinkle, crease or fold ▷ noun **2** wrinkle, crease or fold

cripple noun **1** person who is lame or disabled ▷ verb **2** to make lame or disabled **3** to damage (something) > **crippled** adjective > **crippling** adjective

crisis crises [**kry**-seez in the plural] noun **1** crucial stage, turning point **2** time of extreme trouble

crisp adjective **1** fresh and firm **2** dry and brittle **3** clean and neat **4** (of weather) cold but invigorating **5** lively or brisk ▷ noun **(**Brit**)** very thin slice of potato fried till crunchy

crispy crispier, crispiest adjective hard and crunchy

criterion criteria noun standard of judgment

critic noun **1** professional judge of any of the arts **2** person who finds fault

critical adjective **1** very important or dangerous **2** fault-finding **3** able to examine and judge carefully **4** of or relating to a critic or criticism > **critically** adverb

criticism noun **1** fault-finding **2** analysis of a book, work of art, etc

criticize or **criticise** verb to find fault with

croak verb **1** (of a frog or crow) to give a low hoarse cry **2** to utter or speak with a croak ▷ noun **3** low hoarse sound

Croatian adjective **1** belonging to or relating to Croatia ▷ noun **2** person from Croatia **3** form of Serbo-Croat spoken in Croatia

crochet [**kroh**-shay] verb **1** to make by looping and intertwining yarn with a hooked needle ▷ noun **2** work made in this way

crockery noun dishes

crocodile noun **1** large amphibious tropical reptile **2** (Brit, Aust, NZ) line of people, especially schoolchildren, walking two by two

crocus crocuses noun small plant with yellow, white or purple flowers in spring

croft noun small farm worked by one family in Scotland > **crofter** noun

croissant [**krwah**-son] noun rich flaky crescent-shaped roll

crony cronies noun (old-fashioned) close friend

crook noun **1** (informal) criminal **2** bent or curved part **3** hooked pole ▷ adjective **4** (Aust, NZ informal) unwell, injured **5** **go crook** (Aust, NZ informal) to become angry

crooked [**kroo**-kid] adjective **1** bent or twisted **2** set at an angle **3** (informal) dishonest

croon verb to sing, hum or speak in a soft low tone

crop crops, cropping, cropped noun **1** cultivated plant **2** season's total yield of produce **3** group of things appearing at one time **4** (handle of) a whip ▷ verb **5** to cut very

a
b
c
d
e
f
g
h
i
j
k
l
m
n
o
p
q
r
s
t
u
v
w
x
y
z

short **6** to produce or harvest as a crop **7** (of animals) to feed on (grass) > **crop up** verb (informal) to happen unexpectedly

croquet [kroh-kay] noun game played on a lawn in which balls are hit through hoops

cross verb **1** to move or go across (something) **2** to meet and pass **3** to place (one's arms or legs) crosswise ▷ noun **4** structure, symbol or mark of two intersecting lines **5** such a structure of wood as a means of execution **6** representation of the Cross as an emblem of Christianity **7** mixture of two things ▷ adjective **8** angry or annoyed > **crossly** adverb > **cross out** verb to delete with a cross or lines

crossbow noun weapon consisting of a bow fixed at the end of a piece of wood

cross-country adjective, adverb **1** by way of open country or fields ▷ noun **2** long race run over open ground

cross-eyed adjective with eyes looking towards each other

crossfire noun gunfire crossing another line of fire

crosshatching noun ART drawing an area of shade in a picture using two or more sets of parallel lines

crossing noun **1** place where a street may be crossed safely **2** place where one thing crosses another **3** journey across water

cross-legged adjective sitting with your knees pointing outwards and your feet tucked under them

cross section noun **1** (diagram of) a surface made by cutting across something **2** representative sample: a cross section of society

crossword noun (also **crossword puzzle**) puzzle in which you work out clues and write the answers letter by letter in the numbered blank squares that go across or down on a grid of black and white squares

crotch noun part of the body between the tops of the legs

crotchet noun MUSIC musical note half the length of a minim and a quarter the length of a semibreve. In the United States and Canada, a crotchet is known as a quarter note

crouch verb **1** to bend low with the legs and body close ▷ noun **2** this position

crow noun **1** large black bird with a harsh call **2 as the crow flies** in a straight line ▷ verb **3** (of a cock) to make a shrill squawking sound **4** to boast or gloat

crowbar noun iron bar used as a lever

crowd noun **1** large group of people or things **2** particular group of people ▷ verb **3** to gather together in large numbers **4** to press together in a confined space **5** to fill or occupy fully

crowded adjective full of people

crown noun **1** monarch's headdress of gold and jewels **2** wreath for the head, given as an honour **3** top of the head or of a hill **4** artificial cover for a broken or decayed tooth ▷ verb **5** to put a crown on the head of (someone) to proclaim him or her monarch

6 to form or cause to form the top of **7** to put the finishing touch to (a series of events)

crucial [kroo-shl] *adjective* very important > **crucially** *adverb*

crucifix *noun* model of Christ on the Cross

crucify crucifies, crucifying, crucified *verb* to put to death by fastening to a cross

crude *adjective* **1** rough and simple **2** tasteless or vulgar **3** in a natural or unrefined state: *crude oil* > **crudely** *adverb* > **crudity** *noun*

cruel *adjective* **1** delighting in others' pain **2** causing pain or suffering > **cruelly** *adverb* > **cruelty** *noun*: *laws against cruelty to animals*

cruise *noun* **1** sail for pleasure > *verb* **2** to sail from place to place for pleasure **3** (of a vehicle) to travel at a moderate and economical speed

cruiser *noun* **1** large, fast warship **2** motorboat with a cabin

crumb *noun* **1** small fragment of bread or other dry food **2** small amount

crumble *verb* **1** to break into fragments **2** to fall apart or decay > *noun* **3** pudding of stewed fruit with a crumbly topping

crumbly crumblier, crumbliest *adjective* easily breaking into small pieces

crumpet *noun* round soft yeast cake, eaten buttered

crumple *verb* **1** to crush or crease **2** to collapse, especially from shock

crunch *verb* **1** to bite or chew with a noisy crushing sound **2** to make a crisp or brittle sound > *noun*

3 crunching sound **4** (*informal*) critical moment

crunchy crunchier, crunchiest *adjective* (of food) pleasantly hard or crisp and making a noise when eaten

crusade *noun* **1** vigorous campaign in favour of a cause > *verb* **2** to take part in a crusade

crush *verb* **1** to compress so as to injure, break or crumple **2** to break into small pieces **3** to defeat or humiliate utterly > *noun* **4** dense crowd **5** (*informal*) infatuation: *a teenage crush* **6** drink made by crushing fruit

crust *noun* **1** hard outer part of something, especially bread > *verb* **2** to cover with or form a crust

crusty crustier, crustiest *adjective* **1** having a crust **2** impatient and irritable

crutch *noun* long sticklike support with a rest for the armpit, used by a lame person

crux cruxes *noun* crucial or decisive point

cry cries, crying, cried *verb* **1** to shed tears **2** to call or utter loudly > *noun* **3** fit of weeping **4** loud utterance **5** urgent appeal: *a cry for help* > **cry off** *verb* (*informal*) to withdraw from an arrangement > **cry out for** *verb* to need urgently

crypt *noun* vault under a church, especially one used as a burial place

cryptic *adjective* obscure in meaning, secret

crystal *noun* **1** (single grain of) a symmetrically shaped solid formed naturally by some substances **2** very clear and brilliant glass,

a
b
c
d
e
f
g
h
i
j
k
l
m
n
o
p
q
r
s
t
u
v
w
x
y
z

usually with the surface cut in many planes 3 tumblers, vases, etc made of crystal ▷ *adjective* 4 bright and clear

crystallize or **crystallise** *verb* 1 to make or become definite 2 to form into crystals

cub *noun* young wild animal such as a bear or fox

Cuban [**kyoo**-ban] *adjective* 1 belonging or relating to Cuba ▷ *noun* 2 person from Cuba

cube *noun* 1 object with six equal square sides 2 number resulting from multiplying a number by itself twice ▷ *verb* 3 to cut into cubes 4 to find the cube of (a number)

cubic *adjective* 1 having three dimensions 2 cube-shaped

cubicle *noun* enclosed part of a large room, screened for privacy

cuckoo cuckoos *noun* migratory bird with a characteristic two-note call, which lays its eggs in the nests of other birds

cucumber *noun* long green-skinned fleshy fruit used in salads

cuddle *verb* 1 to hug ▷ *noun* 2 hug

cuddly cuddlier, cuddliest *adjective* (of people, animals or toys) soft and pleasing

cue cues, cueing, cued *noun* 1 signal to an actor or musician to begin speaking or playing 2 signal or reminder 3 long tapering stick used in billiards, snooker or pool ▷ *verb* 4 to give a cue to 5 to hit (a ball) with a cue

cuff *noun* 1 end of a sleeve 2 **off the cuff** (*informal*) without preparation

cuff link *noun* one of a pair of decorative fastenings for shirt cuffs

cuisine [quiz-**zeen**] *noun* style of cooking

cul-de-sac *noun* road with one end blocked off

culinary *adjective* of kitchens or cookery

cull *verb* 1 to choose or gather 2 to remove or kill (inferior or surplus animals) from a herd ▷ *noun* 3 culling

culminate *verb* to reach the highest point or climax > **culmination** *noun: the culmination of four years of training*

culprit *noun* person guilty of an offence or misdeed

cult *noun* 1 specific system of worship 2 devotion to a person, idea or activity 3 popular fashion

cultivate *verb* 1 to prepare (land) to grow crops 2 to grow (plants) 3 to develop or improve (something) 4 to try to develop a friendship with (someone) > **cultivation** *noun: the cultivation of fruit*

culture *noun* 1 ideas, customs and art of a particular society 2 particular society 3 developed understanding of the arts 4 cultivation of plants or rearing of animals 5 growth of bacteria for study > **cultural** *adjective: our cultural heritage*

cumulative *adjective* increasing steadily

cunjevoi [kun-jiv-voi] *noun* very small Australian sea creature that lives on rocks

cunning *adjective* 1 clever at deceiving 2 ingenious ▷ *noun* 3 cleverness at deceiving 4 ingenuity > **cunningly** *adverb*

cup cups, cupping, cupped *noun* 1 small bowl-shaped drinking

container with a handle
2 contents of a cup **3** (competition with) a cup-shaped trophy given as a prize ▷ *verb* **4** to put (your hands) together to form a shape like a cup **5** to hold in cupped hands

cupboard *noun* piece of furniture or alcove with a door, for storage

curable *adjective* (of disease) able to be cured

curate *noun* clergyman who assists a parish priest

curator *noun* person in charge of a museum or art gallery

curb *noun* **1** something that restrains ▷ *verb* **2** to control or restrain

curd *noun* coagulated milk, a thick white substance used to make cheese

curdle *verb* to turn into curd

cure *verb* **1** to get rid of (an illness or problem) **2** to make (someone) well again **3** to preserve (food) by salting, smoking or drying ▷ *noun* **4** (treatment causing) curing of an illness or person **5** remedy or solution

curfew *noun* **1** law ordering people to stay inside their homes after a specific time at night **2** time set as a deadline by such a law

curiosity *curiosities noun* **1** eagerness to know or find out **2** rare or unusual object

curious *adjective* **1** eager to learn or know **2** eager to find out private details **3** unusual or peculiar: *a curious discovery* > **curiously** *adverb*

curl *noun* **1** curved piece of hair **2** curved spiral shape ▷ *verb* **3** to make (hair) into curls or (of hair)

grow in curls **4** to make into a curved spiral shape > **curly** *adjective: naturally curly hair*

curler *noun* small tube for curling hair

curlew *noun* long-billed wading bird

currant *noun* **1** small dried grape **2** small round berry, such as a redcurrant

currawong *noun* Australian songbird

currency *currencies noun* **1** money in use in a particular country **2** general acceptance or use

current *adjective* **1** of the immediate present **2** most recent, up-to-date **3** commonly accepted ▷ *noun* **4** flow of water or air in one direction **5** flow of electricity **6** general trend > **currently** *adverb*

current affairs *plural noun* political and social events discussed in newspapers and on television and radio

curriculum *curriculums or curricula noun* all the courses of study offered by a school or college

curriculum vitae [vee-tie] *noun* outline of someone's educational and professional history, prepared for job applications. Often abbreviated to CV

curry *curries, currying, curried noun* **1** Indian dish of meat or vegetables in a hot spicy sauce ▷ *verb* **2** to prepare (food) with curry powder **3 curry favour** to ingratiate yourself with an important person > **curried** *adjective* flavoured with hot spices

curse curses, cursing, cursed *verb* 1 to swear (at) 2 to ask a supernatural power to cause harm to ▷ *noun* 3 a swearword 4 (result of) a call to a supernatural power to cause harm to someone 5 something causing trouble or harm > **cursed** *adjective*: *The whole family seemed cursed*

cursor *noun* arrow or box on a computer monitor which indicates where the next letter or symbol is

cursory *adjective* quick and superficial

curt *adjective* brief and rather rude > **curtly** *adverb*

curtail *verb* (*formal*) 1 to cut short 2 to restrict

curtain *noun* 1 piece of cloth hung at a window or used to form a screen 2 hanging cloth separating the audience and the stage in a theatre 3 opening or closing of the curtain at the theatre

curtsy curtsies, curtsying, curtsied *noun* 1 woman's gesture of respect made by bending the knees and bowing the head ▷ *verb* 2 to make a curtsy

curve *noun* 1 continuously bending line with no straight parts ▷ *verb* 2 to form or move in a curve > **curved** *adjective* > **curvy** *adjective*

cushion *noun* 1 bag filled with soft material, to make a seat more comfortable 2 something that provides comfort or absorbs shock ▷ *verb* 3 to lessen the effects of 4 to protect from injury or shock

custard *noun* sweet yellow sauce made from milk and eggs

custodian *noun* person in charge of a public building

custody *noun* 1 protective care 2 imprisonment prior to being tried > **custodial** *adjective*: *a custodial sentence*

custom *noun* 1 long-established activity or action 2 usual habit 3 (*formal*) regular use of a shop or business

customary *adjective* 1 usual 2 established by custom > **customarily** *adverb*

custom-built or **custom-made** *adjective* made to the specifications of an individual customer

customer *noun* 1 person who buys goods or services 2 (*informal*) person with whom you have to deal: *a tough customer*

cut cuts, cutting, cut *verb* 1 to open up, penetrate, wound or divide with a sharp instrument 2 to divide 3 to trim or shape by cutting 4 to shorten or reduce 5 to suppress 6 to pretend not to recognize ▷ *noun* 7 stroke or incision made by cutting 8 piece cut off 9 reduction 10 deletion in a text, film or play 11 (*informal*) share, especially of profits 12 style in which hair or a garment is cut > **cut back** *verb* 1 to shorten by cutting 2 to make a reduction > **cut down** *verb* 1 to fell 2 to make a reduction > **cut off** *verb* 1 to remove or separate by cutting 2 to stop the supply of 3 to interrupt (a person who is speaking), especially during a telephone conversation > **cut**

out verb **1** to shape by cutting **2** to delete or remove **3** (informal) to stop doing something **4** (of an engine) to cease to operate suddenly

cute adjective **1** appealing or attractive **2** (informal) clever or shrewd

cuticle noun skin at the base of a fingernail or toenail

cutlass noun curved one-edged sword formerly used by sailors

cutlery noun knives, forks and spoons

cutlet noun **1** small piece of meat like a chop **2** flat croquette of chopped meat or fish

cutting noun **1** article cut from a newspaper or magazine **2** piece cut from a plant from which to grow a new plant **3** passage cut through high ground for a road or railway ▷ adjective **4** (of a remark) hurtful

CV abbreviation curriculum vitae

cyanide noun extremely poisonous chemical compound

cyber- prefix computers: cyberspace

cyberpet noun electronic toy that imitates the activities of a pet, and needs to be fed and entertained

cyberspace noun place said to contain all the data stored in computers

cycle verb **1** to ride a bicycle ▷ noun **2** (Brit, Aust, NZ) bicycle **3** (US) motorcycle **4** complete series of recurring events **5** time taken for one such series

cyclical or **cyclic** adjective occurring in cycles

cyclist noun person who rides a bicycle

cyclone noun violent wind moving round a central area

cygnet [**sig**-net] noun young swan

cylinder noun **1** solid or hollow body with straight sides and circular ends **2** chamber within which the piston moves in an internal-combustion engine ▷ **cylindrical** adjective: a cylindrical container

cymbal noun percussion instrument consisting of a brass plate which is struck against another or hit with a stick

cynic [**sin**-ik] noun person who believes that people always act selfishly

cynical adjective believing that people always act selfishly ▷ **cynically** adverb ▷ **cynicism** noun: He viewed politicians with cynicism

cypher noun same as **cipher**

cypress noun evergreen tree with dark green leaves

cyst [**sist**] noun (abnormal) sac in the body containing fluid or soft matter

czar [**zahr**] noun same as **tsar** ▷ **czarina** same as **tsarina**

Czech [**chek**] adjective **1** belonging or relating to the Czech Republic ▷ noun **2** person from the Czech Republic **3** language spoken in the Czech Republic

Czechoslovak [chek-oh-**slow**-vak] adjective **1** belonging to or relating to the country that used to be Czechoslovakia ▷ noun **2** someone who came from the country that used to be Czechoslovakia

d

dab dabs, dabbing, dabbed verb
1 to pat lightly **2** to apply with
short tapping strokes ▷ noun
3 small amount of something
soft or moist **4** light stroke or tap
5 dab hand (informal) person who
is particularly good at something

dabble verb **1** to be involved in
something superficially **2** to
splash about

dachshund noun dog with a long
body and short legs

dad noun (informal) father

daddy-long-legs noun **1** (Brit)
crane fly **2** (US, Canadian) small
web-spinning spider with long legs

> **WORD TIP**
> The plural of daddy-long-legs is
> daddy-long-legs

daffodil noun yellow trumpet-
shaped flower that blooms in
spring

daft adjective (informal) foolish
or crazy

dagga noun (S Afr informal)
cannabis

dagger noun **1** short knifelike
weapon with a pointed blade **2 at
daggers drawn** in a state of open
hostility

dahlia [**day**-lya] noun brightly
coloured garden flower

daily dailies adjective **1** occurring
every day or every weekday

▷ adverb **2** every day ▷ noun **3** daily
newspaper **4** (Brit informal) person
who cleans other people's houses

dainty daintier, daintiest adjective
delicate or elegant > **daintily**
adverb

dairy dairies noun **1** place for the
processing or sale of milk and its
products **2** (NZ) small shop selling
groceries and milk often outside
normal trading hours **3** food
containing milk or its products:
She can't eat dairy ▷ adjective **4** of
milk or its products

dais [**day**-iss, **dayss**] noun raised
platform in a hall, used by a
speaker

daisy daisies noun small wild
flower with a yellow centre and
white petals

dale noun (esp. in N England) valley

dalmatian noun large dog with a
white coat and black spots

dam dams, damming, dammed
noun **1** barrier built across a river
to create a lake ⚫ lake created by
this ▷ verb **3** to build a dam across
(a river)

damage verb **1** to harm or spoil
▷ noun **2** harm to a person or thing
3 damages money awarded as
compensation for injury or loss
> **damaging** adjective

dame noun **1** (Chiefly US & Canadian
informal) woman **2 Dame** title of
a woman who has been awarded
the OBE or another order of
chivalry

damn verb **1** to condemn as bad or
worthless **2** (of God) to condemn
to hell **3** interjection **3** (informal)
exclamation of annoyance
▷ adverb, adjective **4** (informal)
extreme(ly)

damnation noun eternal punishment in Hell after death

damp adjective **1** slightly wet ▷ noun **2** slight wetness; moisture ▷ verb **3** to make damp > **damp down** verb to reduce the intensity of (feelings or actions) > **damply** adverb > **dampness** noun: The smell of dampness was overpowering

dampen verb **1** to reduce the intensity of **2** to make damp

damper noun **1** movable plate to regulate the draught in a fire **2** pad in a piano that deadens the vibration of each string **3** put a damper on to have a depressing or inhibiting effect on

damson noun small blue-black plumlike fruit

dance verb **1** to move the feet and body rhythmically in time to music **2** to perform (a particular dance) **3** to skip or leap **4** to move rhythmically ▷ noun **5** series of steps and movements in time to music **6** social meeting arranged for dancing > **dancer** noun: a ballroom dancer > **dancing** noun: a meal followed by music and dancing

dandelion noun yellow-flowered wild plant

dandruff noun loose scales of dry dead skin shed from the scalp

D and T abbreviation design and technology

dandy dandies; dandier, dandiest noun **1** (old-fashioned) man who is too concerned with the elegance of his appearance ▷ adjective **2** (informal) very good

Dane noun someone from Denmark

danger noun **1** possibility of being injured or killed **2** person or thing that may cause injury or harm **3** likelihood that something unpleasant will happen

dangerous adjective able to or likely to cause hurt or harm > **dangerously** adverb

dangle verb **1** to hang loosely **2** to display as an enticement

Danish adjective **1** belonging or relating to Denmark ▷ noun **2** main language spoken in Denmark

dank adjective unpleasantly damp and chilly

dapper adjective (of a man) neat in appearance

dappled adjective marked with spots of a different colour

dare verb **1** to be courageous enough to (try to do something) **2** to challenge to do something risky ▷ noun **3** challenge to do something risky

daredevil noun recklessly bold person

daring adjective **1** willing to take risks ▷ noun **2** courage to do dangerous things

dark adjective **1** having little or no light **2** (of a colour) reflecting little light **3** (of hair or skin) brown or black **4** gloomy or sad **5** sinister or evil ▷ noun **6** absence of light **7** night > **darkly** adverb > **darkness** noun: The room was plunged into darkness

darken verb to become or make (something) darker

darkroom noun darkened room for processing photographic film

darling noun **1** much-loved person **2** favourite ▷ adjective **3** much-loved

darn verb **1** to mend (a garment) with a series of interwoven stitches ▷ *noun* **2** patch of darned work

dart *noun* **1** small narrow pointed missile that is thrown or shot, especially in the game of darts **2** sudden quick movement **3** tapered tuck made in dressmaking **4 darts** game in which darts are thrown at a circular numbered board ▷ *verb* **5** to move or direct quickly and suddenly

dash *verb* **1** to move quickly **2** to hurl or crash **3** to frustrate (someone's hopes) ▷ *noun* **4** sudden quick movement **5** small amount **6** mixture of style and courage **7** punctuation mark (-) indicating a change of subject **8** longer symbol used in Morse code

dashboard *noun* instrument panel in a vehicle

dashing *adjective* stylish and attractive

dasyure [**dass**-ee-your] *noun* small marsupial that lives in Australia and eats meat

data *noun* **1** information consisting of observations, measurements or facts **2** numbers, digits, etc, stored by a computer

database *noun* ICT store of information that can be easily handled by a computer

date *noun* **1** specified day of the month **2** particular day or year when an event happened **3** (*informal*) appointment, especially with a person to whom you are sexually attracted **4** (*informal*) person with whom you have a date **5** dark-brown sweet-tasting fruit of the date

palm ▷ *verb* **6** to mark with the date **7** (*informal*) to go on a date (with) **8** to assign a date of occurrence to **9** to become old-fashioned **10 date from** to originate from

dated *adjective* old-fashioned

datum *noun* singular form of **data**

daub *verb* to smear or spread quickly or clumsily

daughter *noun* **1** female child **2** woman who comes from a certain place or is connected with a certain thing

daughter-in-law daughters-in-law *noun* son's wife

daunt *verb* to make (someone) feel worried and intimidated about their prospects of success > **daunting** *adjective* worrying or intimidating

dawn *noun* **1** daybreak **2** beginning (of something) ▷ *verb* **3** to begin to grow light **4** to begin to develop or appear **5 dawn on** *verb* to become apparent (to someone)

day *noun* **1** period of 24 hours **2** period of light between sunrise and sunset **3** part of a day occupied with regular activity, especially work **4** period or point in time **5** time of success **6 call it a day** to stop work or other activity

daybreak *noun* time in the morning when light first appears

daydream *noun* **1** pleasant fantasy indulged in while awake ▷ *verb* **2** to indulge in idle fantasy

daylight *noun* light from the sun

day-to-day *adjective* routine

day trip *noun* journey for pleasure to a place and back again on the same day

daze *noun* **in a daze** confused and bewildered

dazed *adjective* stunned and unable to think clearly

dazzle *verb* **1** to impress greatly **2** to blind temporarily by sudden excessive light ▷ *noun* **3** bright light that dazzles ▷ **dazzling** *adjective*: *a dazzling smile*

de- *prefix* indicating **1** removal: *dethrone* **2** reversal: *declassify* **3** departure: *decamp*

deacon *noun* (Christianity) **1** ordained minister ranking immediately below a priest **2** (in some Protestant churches) lay official who assists the minister ▷ **deaconess** *noun*

dead *adjective* **1** no longer alive **2** no longer in use **3** numb: *My leg has gone dead* **4** complete, absolute: *dead silence* **5** (informal) very tired **6** (of a place) lacking activity ▷ *noun* **7** period during which coldness or darkness is most intense: *in the dead of night* ▷ *adverb* **8** extremely **9** suddenly: *I stopped dead*

dead end *noun* **1** road with one end blocked off **2** situation in which further progress is impossible

deadline *noun* time or date before which something must be completed

deadlock *noun* point in a dispute at which no agreement can be reached

deadly deadlier, deadliest *adjective* **1** likely to cause death **2** (informal) extremely boring ▷ *adverb* **3** extremely

deadpan *adjective, adverb* showing no emotion or expression

deaf *adjective* **1** unable to hear **2** **deaf to** refusing to listen to or take notice of ▷ **deafness** *noun* condition of being unable to hear

deafening *adjective* very loud

deal deals, dealing, dealt *noun* **1** agreement or transaction **2** kind of treatment: *a fair deal* **3** **a great deal (of)** a large amount (of) ▷ *verb* **4** to inflict (a blow) on **5** (Cards) to give out (cards) to the players ▷ **deal in** *verb* to buy or sell (goods) ▷ **deal out** *verb* to distribute ▷ **deal with** *verb* **1** to take action on **2** to be concerned with

dealer *noun* person or firm whose business involves buying or selling things

dealings *plural noun* transactions or business relations

dean *noun* **1** chief administrative official of a college or university faculty **2** chief administrator of a cathedral

dear *noun* **1** someone regarded with affection ▷ *adjective* **2** much-loved **3** costly ▷ **dearly** *adverb*

dearth [dirth] *noun* inadequate amount or scarcity

death *noun* **1** permanent end of life in a person or animal **2** instance of this **3** ending or destruction

debacle [day-**bah**-kl] *noun* (formal) disastrous failure

debase *verb* to lower in value, quality or character

debatable *adjective* not absolutely certain

debate *noun* **1** discussion ▷ *verb* **2** to discuss formally **3** to consider (a course of action)

debilitating *adjective* (formal) causing weakness: *a debilitating illness*

debit noun **1** acknowledgment of a sum owing by entry on the left side of an account ▷ verb **2** to charge (an account) with a debt

debrief verb to receive a report from (a soldier, diplomat, etc) after an event > **debriefing** noun: The mission was followed by a full debriefing

debris [**deb**-ree] noun fragments of something destroyed

debt noun something owed, especially money

debtor noun person who owes money

debut [**day**-byoo] noun first public appearance of a performer

debutante [**day**-byoo-tont] noun young upper-class woman being formally presented to society

dec- or **deca-** prefix ten: decathlon

decade noun period of ten years

decadence noun deterioration in morality or culture > **decadent** adjective: a decadent rock 'n' roll lifestyle

decaffeinated [dee-**kaf**-fin-ate-id] adjective (of coffee, tea or cola) with caffeine removed

decanter noun stoppered bottle for wine or spirits

decapitate verb to behead

decathlon noun athletic contest with ten different events

decay verb **1** to become weaker or more corrupt **2** to rot ▷ noun **3** process of decaying **4** state brought about by this process

deceased (formal) adjective **1** dead ▷ noun **2** the deceased the dead person

deceit noun behaviour intended to deceive > **deceitful** adjective: a very deceitful little girl

deceive verb to mislead (someone) by lying

decelerate verb to slow down > **deceleration** noun: a deceleration in the rate of growth

December noun twelfth and last month of the year

decency noun behaviour that is respectable and follows accepted moral standards

decent adjective **1** (of a person) polite and morally acceptable **2** fitting or proper **3** conforming to conventions of sexual behaviour **4** (informal) kind > **decently** adverb

decentralize or **decentralise** verb to reorganize into smaller local units > **decentralization** noun: the decentralization of health care

deception noun **1** deceiving **2** something that deceives, trick

deceptive adjective likely or designed to deceive > **deceptively** adverb

decibel noun unit for measuring the intensity of sound

decide verb **1** to (cause to) reach a decision **2** to settle (a contest or question)

deciduous adjective (of a tree) shedding its leaves annually

decimal noun **1** fraction written in the form of a dot followed by one or more numbers ▷ adjective **2** relating to or using powers of ten **3** expressed as a decimal

decimate verb to destroy or kill a large proportion of

decipher verb to work out the meaning of (something illegible or in code)

decision noun **1** judgment, conclusion or resolution **2** act of making up your mind **3** firmness of purpose

decisive [dis-**sigh**-siv] *adjective* **1** having a definite influence **2** having the ability to make quick decisions > **decisively** *adverb* > **decisiveness** *noun*

deck *noun* **1** area of a ship that forms a floor **2** similar area in a bus > **deck out** *verb* to make more attractive by decorating

deck chair *noun* light folding chair, made from canvas and wood and used outdoors

declaration *noun* firm, forceful statement, often an official announcement: *a declaration of war*

declare *verb* **1** to state firmly and forcefully **2** to announce officially **3** to acknowledge for tax purposes

decline *verb* **1** to become smaller, weaker or less important **2** to refuse politely to accept or do **3** (*Grammar*) to list the inflections of (a noun, pronoun or adjective) > *noun* **4** gradual weakening or loss

decode *verb* to convert from code into ordinary language

decommission *verb* to dismantle (a nuclear reactor, weapon, etc) which is no longer needed

decompose *verb* to be broken down through chemical or bacterial action > **decomposition** *noun*: *the decomposition of plant tissue*

decor [**day**-core] *noun* style in which a room or house is decorated

decorate *verb* **1** to make more attractive by adding something ornamental **2** to paint or wallpaper **3** to award a (military) medal to

decoration *noun* **1** addition that makes something more attractive **2** way in which a room or building is decorated **3** official honour or medal awarded to someone

decorative *adjective* intended to look attractive

decorator *noun* person whose job is painting and putting up wallpaper in rooms and buildings

decorum [dik-**core**-um] *noun* (*formal*) polite and socially correct behaviour

decoy *noun* **1** person or thing used to lure someone into danger **2** dummy bird or animal, used to lure again within shooting range > *verb* **3** to lure away by means of a trick

decrease *verb* **1** to make or become less > *noun* **2** lessening or reduction **3** amount by which something has decreased > **decreasing** *adjective*: *decreasing investment in training*

decree decrees, decreeing, decreed *noun* **1** law made by someone in authority **2** court judgment > *verb* **3** to order by decree

dedicate *verb* **1** to commit (yourself or your time) wholly to a special purpose or cause **2** to inscribe or address (a book etc) to someone as a tribute

deduce *verb* to reach (a conclusion) by reasoning from evidence

deduct *verb* to subtract

deduction *noun* **1** deducting **2** something that is deducted **3** deducing **4** conclusion reached by deducing

deed noun 1 something that is done 2 legal document

deem verb to consider or judge

deep adjective 1 extending or situated far down, inwards, backwards or sideways 2 of a specified dimension downwards, inwards or backwards 3 difficult to understand 4 of great intensity 5 (of a colour) strong or dark 6 (Music) low in pitch 7 **deep in** absorbed in (an activity) ▷ noun 8 **the deep** (poetic) the sea > **deeply** adverb

deepen verb to make or become deeper or more intense

deer noun large wild animal, the male of which has antlers

▌ WORD TIP
The plural of deer is deer

deface verb to deliberately spoil the appearance of

default noun 1 failure to do something 2 (Computers) instruction to a computer to select a particular option unless the user specifies otherwise 3 **by default** happening because something else has not happened 4 **in default of** in the absence of ▷ verb 5 to fail to fulfil an obligation

defeat verb 1 to win a victory over 2 to thwart or frustrate ▷ noun 3 defeating

defecate verb to discharge waste from the body through the anus

defect noun 1 imperfection or blemish ▷ verb 2 to desert one's cause or country to join the opposing forces > **defection** noun

defective adjective imperfect or faulty

defence noun 1 resistance against attack 2 argument in support of

something 3 country's military resources 4 defendant's case in a court of law

defend verb 1 to protect from harm or danger 2 to support in the face of criticism 3 to represent (a defendant) in court

defendant noun person accused of a crime

defender noun 1 person who supports someone or something in the face of criticism 2 (Sport) player whose chief task is to stop the opposition scoring

defensible adjective capable of being defended because believed to be right

defensive adjective 1 intended for defence 2 overanxious to protect yourself against (threatened) criticism > **defensively** adverb > **defensiveness** noun: There was a note of defensiveness in her voice

defer defers, deferring, deferred verb 1 to delay (something) until a future time 2 **defer to** to comply with the wishes (of)

deference noun polite and respectful behaviour > **deferential** adjective: He was always deferential to his elders > **deferentially** adverb

defiance noun open resistance to authority or opposition > **defiant** adjective: The players are in defiant mood > **defiantly** adverb

deficiency deficiencies noun 1 state of being deficient 2 lack or shortage

deficient adjective 1 lacking some essential thing or quality 2 inadequate in quality or quantity

deficit noun amount by which a sum of money is too small

define verb 1 to state precisely the meaning of 2 to show clearly the outline of

definite adjective 1 firm, clear and precise 2 having precise limits 3 known for certain > **definitely** adverb

definition noun 1 statement of the meaning of a word or phrase 2 quality of being clear and distinct

definitive adjective 1 providing an unquestionable conclusion 2 being the best example of something > **definitively** adverb

deflate verb 1 to (cause to) collapse through the release of air 2 to take away the self-esteem or conceit from 3 (Economics) to cause deflation of (an economy)

deflect verb to (cause to) turn aside from a course > **deflection** noun: the deflection of light

deforestation noun destruction of all the trees in an area

deformed adjective disfigured or abnormally shaped

defraud verb to cheat out of money, property, etc

defrost verb 1 to make or become free of ice 2 to thaw (frozen food) by removing it from a freezer

deft adjective quick and skilful in movement > **deftly** adverb

defunct adjective no longer existing or operative

defuse verb 1 to remove the fuse of (an explosive device) 2 to remove the tension from (a situation)

defy defies, defying, defied verb 1 to resist openly and boldly 2 to make impossible: The condition of the refugees defied description

degenerate adjective 1 having deteriorated to a lower mental, moral or physical level ▷ noun 2 degenerate person ▷ verb 3 to become degenerate > **degeneration** noun: the moral degeneration of society

degradation noun 1 state of poverty and misery 2 state of humiliation or corruption

degrade verb 1 to reduce to dishonour or disgrace 2 to reduce in status or quality 3 (Chemistry) to decompose into smaller molecules

degree noun 1 stage in a scale of relative amount or intensity 2 academic award given by a university or college on successful completion of a course 3 unit of measurement for temperature, angles or latitude and longitude

dehydrated adjective weak through losing too much water from the body > **dehydration** noun: a runner suffering from dehydration

deign [dane] verb (formal) to agree (to do something), but as if doing someone a favour

deity deities [**dee**-it-ee, **day**-it-ee] noun 1 god or goddess 2 state of being divine

déjà vu [**day**-zhah **voo**] noun feeling of having experienced something before that is actually happening now

dejected adjective miserable and unhappy > **dejectedly** adverb > **dejection** noun: feelings of dejection and despair

delay verb 1 to put off to a later time 2 to slow up or cause to be late ▷ noun 3 act of delaying 4 interval of time between events

delectable *adjective* delightful; very attractive

delegate *noun* **1** person chosen to represent others, especially at a meeting ▷ *verb* **2** to entrust (duties or powers) to someone **3** to appoint as a delegate

delegation *noun* **1** group chosen to represent others **2** delegating

delete *verb* to remove (something written or printed) > **deletion** *noun: the deletion of superfluous words*

deliberate *adjective* **1** done on purpose or planned in advance; intentional **2** careful and unhurried ▷ *verb* **3** to think something over > **deliberately** *adverb*

deliberation *noun* careful consideration of a subject

delicacy *delicacies noun* **1** fine, graceful or subtle character **2** something particularly good to eat

delicate *adjective* **1** fine or subtle in quality or workmanship **2** having a fragile beauty **3** (of a taste etc) pleasantly subtle **4** easily damaged **5** requiring tact > **delicately** *adverb*

delicatessen *noun* shop selling imported or unusual foods, often already cooked or prepared

delicious *adjective* very appealing to taste or smell > **deliciously** *adverb*

delight *noun* **1** (source of) great pleasure ▷ *verb* **2** to please greatly **3** delight in to take great pleasure (in) > **delighted** *adjective: I was delighted at the news*

delightful *adjective* very pleasant and attractive > **delightfully** *adverb*

delinquent *noun* **1** someone, especially a young person, who repeatedly breaks the law ▷ *adjective* **2** repeatedly breaking the law > **delinquency** *noun: He had no history of delinquency*

delirious *adjective* **1** unable to speak or act in a rational way because of illness or fever **2** wildly excited and happy > **deliriously** *adverb*

deliver *verb* **1** to carry (goods etc) to a destination **2** to hand over **3** to aid in the birth of **4** to present (a lecture or speech) **5** to release or rescue **6** to strike (a blow)

delivery *deliveries noun* **1** delivering **2** something that is delivered **3** act of giving birth to a baby **4** style in public speaking

dell *noun* (literary) small wooded hollow

delta *noun* **1** fourth letter in the Greek alphabet **2** flat area at the mouth of some rivers where the main stream splits up into several branches

delude *verb* to make someone believe that something is not true

deluge [del-lyooj] *noun* **1** great flood **2** torrential rain **3** overwhelming number ▷ *verb* **4** to flood **5** to overwhelm

delusion *noun* **1** mistaken idea or belief **2** state of being deluded

de luxe *adjective* rich or sumptuous; superior in quality

delve *verb* to research deeply (for information)

demand *verb* **1** to request forcefully **2** to require as a just, urgent, etc **3** to claim as a right ▷ *noun* **4** forceful request **5** (Economics) willingness and

ability to purchase goods and services **6** something that requires special effort or sacrifice

demean verb **demean yourself** to do something unworthy of your status or character > **demeaning** adjective: demeaning sexist comments

demeanour noun way a person behaves

demented adjective mad

dementia [dim-**men**-sha] noun state of serious mental deterioration

demi- prefix half

demise [dee-**myz**] noun **1** eventual failure (of something successful) **2** (formal) death

demo demos noun (informal) demonstration; organized expression of public opinion

democracy democracies noun **1** government by the people or their elected representatives **2** state governed in this way

democrat noun **1** advocate of democracy **2 Democrat** member or supporter of the Democratic Party in the US

democratic adjective **1** of democracy **2** upholding democracy **3 Democratic** of the Democratic Party, the more liberal of the two main political parties in the US > **democratically** adverb

demography noun study of population statistics, such as births and deaths > **demographic** adjective: demographic changes since World War II

demolish verb **1** to knock down or destroy (a building) **2** to disprove (an argument) > **demolition** noun

demon noun **1** evil spirit **2** person who does something with great energy or skill > **demonic** adjective: demonic forces

demonstrate verb **1** to show or prove by reasoning or evidence **2** to display and explain the workings of **3** to reveal the existence of **4** to show support or opposition by public parades or rallies

demonstration noun **1** organized expression of public opinion **2** explanation or display of how something works **3** proof

demote verb to reduce (someone) in status or rank > **demotion** noun: The team now faces demotion from the league

demure adjective quiet, reserved and rather shy > **demurely** adverb

den noun **1** home of a wild animal **2** small secluded room in a home **3** place where people indulge in criminal or immoral activities

denial noun **1** statement that something is not true **2** rejection of a request

denigrate verb (formal) to criticize (someone or something) unfairly

denim noun **1** hard-wearing cotton fabric, usually blue **2 denims** jeans made of denim

denomination noun **1** group having a distinctive interpretation of a religious faith **2** unit in a system of weights, values or measures

denominator noun (Maths) number below the line in a fraction

denote verb **1** to be a sign of **2** to have as a literal meaning

a b c d e f g h i j k l m n o p q r s t u v w x y z

denounce verb 1 to speak strongly against 2 to give information against

dense adjective 1 closely packed 2 difficult to see through 3 (informal) stupid > **densely** adverb

density densities noun 1 degree to which something is filled or occupied 2 measure of the compactness of a substance, expressed as its mass per unit volume

dent noun 1 hollow in the surface of something, made by hitting it ▷ verb 2 to make a dent in

dental adjective of teeth or dentistry

dental floss noun waxed thread used to remove food from between the teeth

dentist noun person qualified to practise dentistry

dentistry noun branch of medicine concerned with the teeth and gums

dentures plural noun false teeth

denunciation noun severe public criticism (of someone or something)

deny denies, denying, denied verb 1 to declare (a statement) to be untrue 2 to refuse to give or allow 3 to refuse to acknowledge

deodorant noun substance applied to the body to mask the smell of perspiration

depart verb to leave

department noun 1 specialized division of a large organization 2 major subdivision of the administration of a government > **departmental** adjective: departmental reorganization

depend verb depend on 1 to put trust (in) 2 to be influenced or determined (by) 3 to rely (on) for income or support

dependable adjective reliable and trustworthy > **dependably** adverb

dependant noun person who depends on another for financial support

dependence noun state of being dependent

dependency dependencies noun 1 country controlled by another country 2 overreliance on another person or on a drug

dependent adjective depending on someone or something

depict verb 1 to produce a picture of 2 to describe in words

deplete verb 1 to use up (supplies or money) 2 to reduce in number > **depletion** noun: depletion of water supplies

deplorable adjective very bad or unpleasant

deplore verb to express or feel strong disapproval of

deploy verb to organize (troops or resources) into a position ready for immediate action > **deployment** noun: the deployment of troops

deport verb to remove (someone) forcibly from a country > **deportation** noun: thousands of migrants facing deportation

depose verb to remove (someone) from an office or position of power

deposit verb 1 to put (something) down 2 to entrust (something) for safekeeping, especially to a bank ▷ noun 3 sum of money paid into a bank account 4 money given in part payment for goods or services **5** accumulation of sediments, minerals, etc

depot [**dep**-oh] noun **1** building where goods or vehicles are kept when not in use **2** (NZ, US) bus or railway station

depraved adjective morally bad ▷ **depravity** noun: the depravity that can exist in war

depress verb **1** to make (someone) sad **2** to lower (prices or wages) ▷ **depressing** adjective: a depressing lack of progress ▷ **depressingly** adverb

depressant noun drug able to reduce nervous activity

depressed adjective **1** unhappy and gloomy **2** suffering from economic hardship: depressed industrial areas

depression noun **1** mental state in which a person has feelings of gloom and inadequacy **2** economic condition in which there is high unemployment and low output and investment **3** area of low air pressure **4** sunken place

deprive verb **deprive of** to prevent (someone) from (having or enjoying something) ▷ **deprivation** noun: sleep deprivation

depth noun **1** distance downwards, backwards or inwards **2** intensity of emotion **3** profundity of character or thought

deputation noun body of people appointed to represent others

deputy deputies noun person appointed to act on behalf of another

deranged adjective insane or uncontrolled

derby [**dah**-bee] derbies noun **1** sporting event between teams from the same area **2 The Derby** horse race held annually at Epsom, named after the 12th Earl of Derby, who founded it in 1780

derelict adjective **1** unused and falling into ruins ▷ noun **2** (formal) social outcast or tramp

deride verb to treat with contempt or ridicule

derision noun attitude of contempt or scorn towards something or someone

derivation noun the origin of something, such as a word

derivative noun **1** word, idea, etc, derived from another ▷ adjective **2** not original, but based on or copied from something else

derive verb **derive from** to take or develop (from)

derogatory [dir-**rog**-a-tree] adjective intentionally offensive

descant noun (Music) tune played or sung above a basic melody

descend verb **1** to move down (a slope etc) **2** to move to a lower level, pitch, etc **3 be descended from** to be connected by a blood relationship to **4 descend on** to visit unexpectedly **5 descend to** to stoop to (unworthy behaviour)

descendant noun person or animal descended from an individual, race or species

descent noun **1** descending **2** downward slope **3** derivation from an ancestor

describe verb **1** to give an account of (something or someone) in words **2** to trace the outline of (a circle etc)

description noun **1** statement that describes something or someone **2** sort: *flowers of every description* ▷ **descriptive** *adjective*: *his descriptive way of writing* ▷ **descriptively** *adverb*

desert¹ [dez-ert] noun region with little or no vegetation because of low rainfall

desert² [dez-zert] verb **1** to abandon (a person or place) without intending to return **2** (*Military*) to leave (a post or duty) with no intention of returning ▷ **desertion** *noun*: *the army's high rate of desertion*

deserter noun person who leaves the armed forces without permission

deserve verb to be entitled to or worthy of

deserving adjective worthy of help, praise or reward

design verb **1** to work out the structure or form of (something), by making a sketch or plans **2** to plan and make artistically **3** to intend for a specific purpose ▷ noun **4** preliminary drawing **5** arrangement or features of an artistic or decorative work **6** art of designing **7** intention: *by design*

designate [dez-zig-nate] verb **1** to give a name to **2** to select (someone) for an office or duty ▷ adjective **3** appointed but not yet in office

designation noun name

designing adjective cunning and scheming

desirable adjective **1** worth having **2** arousing sexual desire ▷ **desirability** noun: *the desirability of a home in the country*

desire verb **1** to want very much ▷ noun **2** wish or longing **3** sexual appetite **4** person or thing desired

desist verb **desist from** to stop (doing something)

desk noun **1** piece of furniture with a writing surface and drawers **2** service counter in a public building

desktop adjective **1** of a convenient size to be used on a desk or table ▷ noun **2** computer designed to be used at a desk ▷ **desktop publishing** noun ICT means of publishing reports etc using a desktop computer and a printer

desolate adjective **1** uninhabited and bleak **2** very sad ▷ verb **3** to deprive of inhabitants **4** to make (someone) very sad ▷ **desolation** noun: *a scene of desolation and ruin*

despair noun **1** total loss of hope ▷ verb **2** to lose hope ▷ **despairing** adjective: *Tom made another despairing effort to win her round*

despatch verb, noun same as **dispatch**

desperate adjective **1** in despair and reckless **2** (of an action) undertaken as a last resort **3** having a strong need or desire ▷ **desperately** adverb ▷ **desperation** noun: *a feeling of desperation and helplessness*

despicable adjective deserving contempt ▷ **despicably** adverb

despise verb to look down on with contempt

despite preposition in spite of

despondent adjective unhappy ▷ **despondency** noun: *a mood of gloom and despondency*

dessert noun sweet course served at the end of a meal

destination noun place to which someone or something is going

destined adjective certain to be or to do something

destiny destinies noun **1** future marked out for a person or thing **2** the power that predetermines the course of events

destitute adjective having no money or possessions > **destitution** noun: She ended her life in destitution

destroy verb **1** to ruin or demolish **2** to put an end to **3** to kill (an animal)

destruction noun **1** destroying **2** cause of ruin

destructive adjective (capable of) causing destruction > **destructiveness** noun: the destructiveness of their weapons

desultory [**dez**-zl-tree] adjective **1** jumping from one thing to another; disconnected **2** random > **desultorily** adverb

detach verb to disengage and separate > **detachable** adjective

detached adjective **1** (Brit, Aust, SAfr) (of a house) not joined to another house **2** showing no emotional involvement

detachment noun **1** lack of emotional involvement **2** small group of soldiers

detail noun **1** individual piece of information **2** unimportant item **3** small individual features of something, considered collectively **4** (Chiefly military) (personnel assigned) a specific duty ▷ verb **5** to list fully > **detailed** adjective: a detailed list

detain verb **1** to delay (someone) **2** to hold (someone) in custody

detect verb **1** to notice **2** to discover or find > **detectable** adjective: the disease is not detectable at birth

detection noun **1** act of noticing, discovering or sensing something **2** work of investigating crime

detective noun policeman or private agent who investigates crime

detector noun instrument used to find something

detention noun **1** imprisonment **2** form of punishment in which a pupil is detained after school

deter deters, deterring, deterred verb to discourage (someone) from doing something by instilling fear or doubt

detergent noun chemical substance for washing clothes or dishes

deteriorate verb to become worse > **deterioration** noun: a deterioration in relations between the two men

determination noun condition of being determined or resolute

determine verb **1** to settle (an argument or a question) conclusively **2** to find out the facts about (something) **3** to make a firm decision (to do something)

determined adjective firmly decided, unable to be dissuaded > **determinedly** adverb

determiner noun (Grammar) word that determines the object to which a noun phrase refers, e.g. all

deterrent noun **1** something that deters **2** weapon, especially nuclear, intended to deter attack ▷ adjective **3** tending to deter > **deterrence** noun: nuclear deterrence

detest verb to dislike (someone or something) intensely

detonate verb to make (an explosive device) explode or (of an explosive device) to explode

detour noun route that is not the most direct one

detract verb **detract from** to make (something) seem less good

detriment noun disadvantage or damage > **detrimental** adjective: foods suspected of being detrimental to health

deuce [**dyewss**] noun **1** (Tennis) score of forty all **2** playing card with two symbols or dice with two spots

devalue devalues, devaluing, devalued verb **1** to reduce the exchange value of (a currency) **2** to reduce the value of (something or someone) > **devaluation** noun: devaluation of a number of currencies

devastate verb to damage (a place) severely or destroy it > **devastation** noun: A bomb blast brought chaos and devastation to the city

devastated adjective shocked and extremely upset

develop verb **1** to grow or bring to a later, more elaborate or more advanced stage **2** to come or bring into existence **3** to build houses or factories on (an area of land) **4** to produce (photographs) by making negatives or prints from a film

developer noun **1** person who develops property **2** chemical used to develop photographs or films

development noun **1** process of growing or developing **2** product of developing **3** event that changes a situation **4** area of land that has been developed > **developmental** adjective: the developmental needs of a child

deviant adjective **1** deviating from what is considered acceptable behaviour ▷ noun **2** deviant person

deviate verb **1** to differ from others in belief or thought **2** to depart from your previous behaviour > **deviation** noun: deviation from the norm

device noun **1** machine or tool used for a specific task **2** scheme or plan **3** **leave someone to his** or **her own devices** to leave someone alone to do as he or she wishes

devil noun **1** **the Devil** (in Christianity and Islam) chief spirit of evil and enemy of God **2** evil spirit **3** evil person **4** person: poor devil **5** daring person: be a devil!

devious adjective **1** insincere and dishonest **2** indirect > **deviousness** noun: the deviousness of drug traffickers

devise verb to work out (something) in your mind

devoid adjective **devoid of** completely lacking (in)

devolution noun transfer of authority from a central government to regional governments

devote verb to apply or dedicate (one's time, money or effort) to a particular purpose

devoted adjective showing loyalty or devotion

devotee noun **1** person who is very enthusiastic about something **2** zealous follower of a religion

devotion noun **1** strong affection for or loyalty to someone or something **2** religious zeal **3** devotions prayers > **devotional** adjective: devotional music

devour verb **1** to eat (something) greedily **2** (of an emotion) to engulf and destroy (someone) **3** to read (a book or magazine) eagerly

devout adjective deeply religious > **devoutly** adverb

dew noun drops of water that form on the ground at night from vapour in the air

dexterity noun **1** skill in using your hands **2** mental quickness > **dexterous** adjective: as people grow older they become less dexterous

dharma [**dar**-ma] noun (in the Buddhist religion) ideal truth as set out in the teaching of the Buddha

diabetes [die-a-**beet**-eez] noun disorder in which an abnormal amount of urine containing an excess of sugar is excreted > **diabetic** adjective, noun: diabetic patients; suitable for diabetics

diabolical adjective (informal) extremely bad

diagnose verb to determine by diagnosis > **diagnostic** adjective: X-rays and other diagnostic tools

diagnosis [die-ag-**no**-siss] diagnoses [die-ag-**no**-seez] noun discovery and identification of diseases from the examination of symptoms

diagonal adjective **1** from corner to corner **2** slanting ▷ noun **3** diagonal line > **diagonally** adverb

diagram noun sketch showing the form or workings of something

dial dials, dialling, dialled noun **1** face of a clock or watch **2** graduated disc on a measuring instrument **3** control on a radio or television set used to change the station **4** numbered disc on the front of some telephones ▷ verb **5** to operate the dial or buttons on a telephone in order to contact (a number)

dialect noun form of a language spoken in a particular area

dialogue noun **1** conversation between two people, especially in a book, film or play **2** discussion between representatives of two nations or groups

dialysis [die-**al**-iss-iss] noun (Medicine) filtering of blood through a membrane to remove waste products

diameter noun (Maths) (length of) a straight line through the centre of a circle or sphere

diamond noun **1** exceptionally hard, usually colourless precious stone **2** (Geometry) figure with four sides of equal length forming two acute and two obtuse angles **3** playing card marked with red diamond-shaped symbols ▷ adjective **4** (of an anniversary) sixtieth

a
b
c
d
e
f
g
h
i
j
k
l
m
n
o
p
q
r
s
t
u
v
w
x
y
z

diaphragm [die-a-fram] *noun*
1 muscular partition that separates the abdominal cavity and chest cavity **2** contraceptive device placed over the neck of the womb

diarrhoea [die-a-**ree**-a] *noun* condition in which the faeces are more liquid and frequently produced than usual

diary diaries *noun* (book for) a record of daily events, appointments or observations

dice *noun* **1** small cube each of whose sides has a different number of spots (1 to 6), used in games of chance ▷ *verb* **2** to cut (food) into small cubes > **diced** *adjective*: diced carrots

> **WORD TIP**
> The plural of *dice* is dice

dictate *verb* **1** to say aloud for someone else to write down **2** dictate to to seek to impose your will on (other people) ▷ *noun* **3** authoritative command **4** guiding principle

dictator *noun* **1** ruler who has complete power **2** person in power who acts unfairly or cruelly > **dictatorship** *noun*: a military dictatorship

diction *noun* manner of pronouncing words and sounds

dictionary dictionaries *noun* **1** book consisting of an alphabetical list of words with their meanings or translations into another language **2** alphabetically ordered reference book of terms relating to a particular subject

didgeridoo *noun* Australian musical instrument made from a long hollow piece of wood

die dies, dying, died *verb* **1** (of a person, animal or plant) to cease all biological activity permanently **2** (of something inanimate) to cease to exist or function **3** be **dying for** or to do something (*informal*) to be eager for or to do something ▷ *noun* **4** dice **5** specially shaped or patterned block of metal used to cut or mould other metal

> **WORD TIP**
> The plural of *die* in sense 4 is dice

diesel *noun* **1** diesel engine **2** vehicle driven by a diesel engine **3** diesel oil

diet *noun* **1** food that a person or animal regularly eats **2** specific range of foods, to control weight or for health reasons **3** parliament of some countries ▷ *verb* **4** to follow a special diet so as to lose weight ▷ *adjective* **5** (of food) suitable for a weight-reduction diet > **dietary** *adjective*: dietary habits

dietician *noun* person trained to advise people about healthy eating

differ *verb* **1** to be unlike **2** to disagree

difference *noun* **1** state of being unlike **2** disagreement **3** remainder left after subtraction

different *adjective* **1** unlike **2** unusual > **differently** *adverb*

differentiate *verb* **1** to perceive or show the difference (between) **2** to make (one thing) distinct from other such things > **differentiation** *noun*: The differentiation between the two product ranges will increase

difficult *adjective* **1** requiring effort or skill to do or understand **2** not easily pleased

difficulty *difficulties noun* **1** problem **2** fact or quality of being difficult

diffident *adjective* lacking self-confidence > **diffidence** *noun*: *He entered the room with a certain diffidence* > **diffidently** *adverb*

diffract *verb* (*Physics*) (of rays of light or sound waves) to break up or change direction after hitting an obstacle > **diffraction** *noun*: *the diffraction of light*

diffuse *verb* **1** to spread over a wide area ▷ *adjective* **2** widely spread **3** lacking concision > **diffusion** *noun*: *rates of diffusion of molecules*

dig *verb* **1** to cut into, break up and turn over or remove (earth), esp. with a spade **2** to **dig in** or **into** to thrust or jab **3 dig up** or **out** to find by effort or searching ▷ *noun* **4** digging **5** archaeological excavation **6** thrust or poke **7** spiteful remark

digest *verb* **1** to subject to a process of digestion **2** to absorb mentally ▷ *noun* **3** shortened version of a book, report or article > **digestible** *adjective*: *Bananas are easily digestible*

digestion *noun* (body's system for) breaking down food into easily absorbed substances

digger *noun* **1** machine used for digging **2** (*Aust*) friendly name to call a man

digicam *noun* digital camera

digit [**dij**-it] *noun* **1** finger or toe **2** (*Maths*) numeral from 0 to 9

digital *adjective* **1** displaying information as numbers rather than with hands and a dial: *a digital clock* **2** transmitting or receiving information in the form of thousands of very small signals: *digital radio* > **digitally** *adverb*

dignified *adjective* full of dignity

dignitary *dignitaries noun* person of high official position

dignity *noun* **1** serious, calm and controlled behaviour or manner **2** quality of being worthy of respect **3** sense of self-importance

digression *noun* departure from the main subject in speech or writing

dilapidated *adjective* (of a building) having fallen into ruin

dilate *verb* to make or become wider or larger > **dilated** *adjective*: *dilated pupils* > **dilation** *noun*: *dilation of the blood vessels*

dilemma *noun* situation offering a choice between two equally undesirable alternatives

diligent *adjective* **1** careful and persevering in carrying out duties **2** carried out with care and perseverance > **diligence** *noun*: *They are pursuing the matter with great diligence* > **diligently** *adverb*

dill *noun* sweet-smelling herb

dilly bag *noun* (*Aust*) small bag used to carry food

dilute *verb* **1** to make (a liquid) less concentrated, especially by adding water **2** to make (a quality etc) weaker in force > **dilution** *noun*: *a dilution of his powers*

dim *dimmer, dimmest; dims, dimming, dimmed adjective* **1** badly lit **2** not clearly seen **3** unintelligent **4 take a dim view of** to disapprove of ▷ *verb* **5** to

become or make (something)
dim > **dimly** adverb > **dimness**
noun: *the dimness of an early October evening*

dimension noun **1** measurement of the size of something in a particular direction **2** aspect or factor **3** D&T The dimensions of something are also its measurements, for example its length, breadth, height or diameter

diminish verb to become or make smaller, fewer or less

diminutive adjective **1** very small ▷ noun **2** word or affix which implies smallness or lack of importance

dimmer noun device for dimming an electric light

dimple noun small natural dent, especially in the cheeks or chin

din noun loud unpleasant confused noise

dinar [dee-nahr] noun monetary unit of various Balkan, Middle Eastern and North African countries

dine verb (formal) to eat dinner

diner noun **1** person eating a meal **2** (Chiefly US) small cheap restaurant

dinghy dinghies [ding-ee] noun small boat, powered by sails, oars or a motor

dingo dingoes noun Australian wild dog

dingy dingier, dingiest [din-jee] adjective dull and drab

dinkum adjective (Aust, NZ informal) genuine or right

dinner noun main meal of the day, eaten either in the evening or at midday

dinosaur noun type of extinct prehistoric reptile, many of which were of gigantic size

dint noun by dint of by means of

diocese [die-a-siss] noun district over which a bishop has control > **diocesan** adjective: *the diocesan synod*

dip dips, dipping, dipped verb **1** to plunge (something) quickly or briefly into a liquid **2** to slope downwards **3** to switch (car headlights) from the main to the lower beam **4** to lower briefly ▷ noun **5** dipping **6** brief swim **7** liquid chemical in which farm animals are dipped to rid them of insects **8** depression in a landscape **9** creamy mixture into which pieces of food are dipped before being eaten > **dip into** verb to read passages at random from (a book or journal)

diploma noun qualification awarded by a college on successful completion of a course

diplomacy noun **1** conduct of the relations between nations by peaceful means **2** tact or skill in dealing with people

diplomat noun official engaged in diplomacy

dire adjective disastrous, urgent or terrible

direct adjective **1** (of a route) shortest or straight **2** without anyone or anything intervening **3** likely to have an immediate effect **4** honest, frank ▷ adverb **5** in a direct manner ▷ verb **6** to lead and organize **7** to tell (someone) to do something **8** to tell (someone) the way to a place **9** to address (a letter, package, remark, etc.)

10 to provide guidance to (actors, cameramen, etc) in (a play or film)

direct current noun electric current that flows in one direction only

direction noun **1** course or line along which a person or thing moves, points or lies **2** management or guidance **3 directions** instructions for doing something or for reaching a place

directive noun instruction that must be obeyed

directly adverb **1** in a direct manner **2** at once ▷ conjunction **3** as soon as

director noun **1** person or thing that directs or controls **2** member of the governing board of a business etc **3** person responsible for the artistic and technical aspects of the making of a film etc ▷ **directorial** adjective: her directorial debut

directorate noun **1** board of directors **2** position of director

directory directories noun **1** book listing names, addresses and telephone numbers **2** (Computers) area of a disk containing the names and locations of the files it currently holds

direct speech noun the reporting of what someone has said by quoting the exact words

dirge noun slow sad song of mourning

dirt noun **1** unclean substance, filth **2** earth, soil **3** obscene speech or writing **4** (informal) harmful gossip

dirty dirtier, dirtiest adjective **1** covered or marked with dirt

2 unfair or dishonest **3** obscene **4** displaying dislike or anger: a dirty look ▷ verb **5** to make (something) dirty

dis- prefix indicating **1** reversal: disconnect **2** negation or lack: dissimilar; disgrace **3** removal or release: disembowel

disability disabilities noun **1** condition of being disabled **2** something that disables someone

disable verb to make ineffective, unfit or incapable ▷ **disablement** noun: permanent total disablement

disabled adjective lacking a physical power, such as the ability to walk

disadvantage noun unfavourable or harmful circumstance

disaffected adjective having lost loyalty to or affection for someone or something

disagree disagrees, disagreeing, disagreed verb **1** to argue or have different opinions **2** to be different, conflict **3** disagree with to cause physical discomfort (to): Curry disagrees with me ▷ **disagreement** noun: a minor disagreement

disagreeable adjective **1** unpleasant **2** (of a person) unfriendly or unhelpful

disappear verb **1** to cease to be visible **2** to cease to exist ▷ **disappearance** noun: his wife's disappearance

disappoint verb to fail to meet the expectations or hopes of ▷ **disappointed** adjective: I was disappointed that she was not there ▷ **disappointing** adjective: a disappointing performance

disappointment noun 1 feeling of being disappointed 2 person or thing that disappoints

disapprove verb **disapprove of** to consider wrong or bad > **disapproval** noun: It was greeted with universal disapproval > **disapproving** adjective: a disapproving look

disarm verb 1 to deprive of weapons 2 to win the confidence or affection of 3 (of a country) to decrease the size of its armed forces

disarmament noun reducing or getting rid of military forces and weapons

disarray noun 1 confusion and lack of discipline 2 extreme untidiness

disassemble verb D&T to take (something) to pieces

disaster noun 1 occurrence that causes great distress or destruction 2 something, such as a project, that fails > **disastrous** adjective: a disastrous military campaign > **disastrously** adverb

disband verb to (cause to) cease to function as a group

disc noun 1 flat circular object 2 compact disc or gramophone record 3 (Anatomy) circular flat structure in the body, especially between the vertebrae 4 (Computers) same as **disk**

discard verb to get rid of (something or someone) as useless or undesirable

discern verb (formal) to see or to be aware of (something) clearly

discernible adjective able to be seen or recognized

discerning adjective having good judgment > **discernment** noun: his powers of discernment

discharge verb 1 to allow (a patient) to go 2 to dismiss (someone) from duty or employment 3 to fire (a gun) 4 to release or pour out (a substance or liquid) 5 (formal) to meet the demands of (a duty or responsibility) ▷ noun 6 substance that comes out from a place 7 discharging

disciple [diss-**sipe**-pl] noun follower of the doctrines of a teacher, especially Jesus Christ

discipline noun 1 practice of imposing strict rules of behaviour 2 (formal) area of academic study ▷ verb 3 to attempt to improve the behaviour of (oneself or another) by training or rules 4 to punish > **disciplinary** adjective: They took disciplinary action against him > **disciplined** adjective able to behave and work in a controlled way

disc jockey noun person who introduces and plays pop records on a radio programme or at a disco

disclose verb to make (information) known > **disclosure** noun: disclosure of information to the press

disco discos noun 1 nightclub where people dance to amplified pop records 2 occasion at which people dance to amplified pop records

discomfort noun inconvenience, distress or mild pain

disconcert verb to embarrass or upset > **disconcerting** adjective

The unfamiliar layout was a little disconcerting

disconnect *verb* **1** to undo or break the connection between (two things) **2** to stop the supply of electricity or gas of

discontent *noun* lack of contentment > **discontented** *adjective: discontented workers*

discontinue discontinues, discontinuing, discontinued *verb* to bring (something) to an end or come to an end

discord *noun* **1** lack of agreement or harmony between people **2** harsh confused sounds

discount *verb* **1** to take no account of (something) because it is considered to be unreliable, prejudiced or irrelevant **2** to deduct (an amount) from the price of something > *noun* **3** deduction from the full price of something

discourage *verb* **1** to deprive (someone) of the will to persist in something **2** to oppose (something) by expressing disapproval > **discouragement** *noun: His shoulders drooped with exhaustion and discouragement* > **discouraging** *adjective: a discouraging lack of interest*

discourse *noun* (*formal*) **1** conversation **2** formal treatment of a subject in speech or writing > *verb* **3** **discourse on** to speak or write (about something) at length

discover *verb* **1** to be the first to find or to find out about **2** to learn about for the first time **3** to find after study or search > **discoverer** *noun: the discoverer of penicillin*

discredit *verb* **1** to damage the reputation of **2** to cause (an idea) to be disbelieved or distrusted > *noun* **3** damage to someone's reputation

discreet *adjective* **1** careful to avoid embarrassment, especially by keeping confidences secret **2** unobtrusive > **discreetly** *adverb*

discrepancy discrepancies *noun* conflict or variation between facts, figures or claims

discrete *adjective* (*formal*) separate and distinct

discretion *noun* **1** quality of behaving in a discreet way **2** freedom or authority to make judgments and decide what to do > **discretionary** *adjective: Judges were given wider discretionary powers*

discriminate *verb* **1** **discriminate against** *or* **in favour of** to single out (a particular person or group) for worse or better treatment than others **2** **discriminate between** to recognize or understand the difference (between)

discus discuses *noun* heavy disc-shaped object thrown in sports competitions

discuss *verb* **1** to consider (something) by talking it over **2** to treat (a subject) in speech or writing

discussion *noun* conversation or piece of writing in which a subject is considered in detail

disdain *noun* **1** feeling of superiority and dislike > *verb* **2** to refuse with disdain > **disdainful** *adjective: He was disdainful of his opponent's chances*

disease noun unhealthy condition in people, animals or plants
> **diseased** adjective: diseased lungs

disembark verb to get off a ship, aircraft or bus

disembodied adjective 1 lacking a body 2 seeming not to be attached to or coming from anyone

disenchanted adjective disappointed and disillusioned
> **disenchantment** noun: growing disenchantment with the new regime

disfigure verb to spoil the appearance of

disgrace noun 1 condition of shame, loss of reputation or dishonour 2 shameful person or thing ▷ verb 3 to bring shame upon (yourself or others)

disgraceful adjective shameful or scandalous > **disgracefully** adverb

disgruntled adjective sulky or discontented

disguise verb 1 to change the appearance or manner in order to conceal the identity of (someone or something) 2 to misrepresent (something) in order to obscure its actual nature or meaning ▷ noun 3 mask, costume or manner that disguises 4 state of being disguised

disgust noun 1 great loathing or distaste ▷ verb 2 to sicken or fill with loathing > **disgusted** adjective: I'm disgusted with the way he was treated > **disgusting** adjective: a disgusting habit

dish noun 1 shallow container used for holding or serving food 2 particular kind of food

3 (informal) attractive person
> **dish out** verb (informal) to distribute > **dish up** verb (informal) to serve (food)

dishearten verb to weaken or destroy the hope, courage or enthusiasm of > **disheartened** adjective: She was disheartened by their hostile reaction
> **disheartening** adjective: a frustrating and disheartening experience

dishevelled adjective (of a person's hair, clothes or general appearance) disordered and untidy

dishonest adjective not honest or fair > **dishonestly** adverb

dishonesty noun behaviour which is meant to deceive people, either by not telling the truth or by cheating

disillusion verb 1 to destroy the illusions or false ideas of ▷ noun 2 state of being disillusioned
> **disillusioned** adjective: disillusioned with politics

disinfectant noun substance that destroys harmful germs

disintegrate verb (of an object) to break into fragments
> **disintegration** noun: the violent disintegration of Yugoslavia

disinterest noun lack of personal involvement in a situation

disinterested adjective free from bias or involvement

disjointed adjective having no coherence; disconnected

disk noun (Computers) a circular storage device

disk drive noun ICT part of a computer that reads and writes information on a computer disk

dislike verb 1 to consider (something or someone) unpleasant or disagreeable ▷ noun 2 feeling of not liking something or someone

dislocate verb to displace (a bone or joint) from its normal position

dislodge verb to remove (something or someone) from a previously fixed position

dismal adjective 1 gloomy and depressing 2 (informal) of poor quality > **dismally** adverb

dismantle verb to take apart piece by piece

dismay verb 1 to fill with alarm or depression ▷ noun 2 alarm mixed with sadness

dismember verb (formal) 1 to remove the limbs of 2 to cut to pieces > **dismemberment** noun

dismiss verb 1 to remove (an employee) from a job 2 to allow (someone) to leave 3 to put (something) out of your mind 4 (of a judge) to state that (a case) will not be brought to trial > **dismissal** noun: Mr Low's dismissal from his post

dismissive adjective scornful or contemptuous

disobey verb to neglect or refuse to obey

disorder noun 1 state of untidiness and disorganization 2 public violence or rioting 3 illness

disorganized or **disorganised** adjective 1 confused and badly arranged 2 not good at planning work and activities efficiently

disown verb to deny any connection with (someone)

disparaging adjective critical and scornful: disparaging remarks

disparate adjective completely different > **disparity** noun: economic disparities between North and South

dispatch verb 1 to send off to a destination or to perform a task 2 to carry out (a duty or a task) with speed 3 (old-fashioned) to kill ▷ noun 4 official communication or report, sent in haste 5 report sent to a newspaper by a correspondent

dispel dispels, dispelling, dispelled verb to destroy or remove

dispensary dispensaries noun place where medicine is dispensed

dispense verb 1 to give out 2 to prepare and distribute (medicine) 3 dispense with to do away with or manage without

dispenser noun machine or container from which something is given out: a cash dispenser

disperse verb 1 to scatter over a wide area 2 to (cause to) leave a gathering > **dispersion** or **dispersal** noun: dispersion of their forces

dispirited adjective depressed and having no enthusiasm for anything

dispiriting adjective causing loss of enthusiasm: a dispiriting defeat

displace verb 1 to move (something) from the usual location 2 to remove (someone) from office

displacement noun 1 removal of something from its usual or correct place or position 2 (Physics) weight or volume of liquid displaced by an object submerged or floating in it

display verb 1 to make visible or noticeable ▷ noun 2 displaying 3 something displayed 4 exhibition

displease verb to annoy or upset (someone) > **displeasure** noun: The train was late, much to my displeasure

disposable adjective 1 designed to be thrown away after use 2 available for use: disposable income

disposal noun 1 getting rid of something 2 **at your disposal** available for your use

dispose verb 1 to place in a certain order 2 **dispose of a** to throw away **b** to give, sell or transfer to another **c** to deal with or settle **d** to kill

disprove verb to show (an assertion or claim) to be incorrect

dispute noun 1 disagreement, argument ▷ verb 2 to argue about (something) 3 to doubt the validity of 4 to fight over possession of

disqualify disqualifies, disqualifying, disqualified verb to stop (someone) officially from taking part in something for wrongdoing > **disqualification** noun: disqualification from the race

disquiet noun 1 feeling of anxiety ▷ verb 2 to make (someone) anxious > **disquieting** adjective: He found her letter disquieting

disregard verb 1 to give little or no attention to ▷ noun 2 lack of attention or respect

disrepair noun condition of being worn out or in poor working order

disrespect noun lack of respect > **disrespectful** adjective:

accusations that he had been disrespectful to the Queen

disrupt verb to interrupt the progress of > **disruption** noun: disruption to flights in Britain > **disruptive** adjective: disruptive pupils

dissatisfied adjective not pleased or contented > **dissatisfaction** noun: I want to express my dissatisfaction with the report

dissect verb 1 to cut open (a corpse) to examine it 2 to examine critically and minutely > **dissection** noun: corpses needed for dissection

dissent verb 1 to disagree ▷ noun 2 disagreement > **dissenting** adjective: dissenting voices

dissertation noun written thesis, usually required for a higher university degree

disservice noun harmful action

dissident noun 1 person who disagrees with and criticizes the government ▷ adjective 2 disagreeing with the government

dissimilar adjective not alike; different

dissipate verb 1 to waste or squander 2 to scatter or disappear

dissipated adjective showing signs of overindulgence in alcohol and other physical pleasures

dissolve verb 1 to (cause to) become liquid 2 to break up or end officially 3 to break down emotionally: She dissolved into tears

dissuade verb to deter (someone) from doing something by persuasion

distance noun 1 space between two points 2 state of being apart 3 remoteness in manner 4 **the distance** most distant part of the visible scene ⊳ verb 5 **distance yourself** or **be distanced from** to separate yourself or be separated mentally from

distant adjective 1 far apart 2 separated by a specified distance 3 remote in manner > **distantly** adverb

distaste noun dislike or disgust

distasteful adjective unpleasant or offensive

distil distils, distilling, distilled verb 1 to subject to or obtain by distillation 2 to give off (a substance) in drops 3 to extract the essence of > **distillation** noun process of evaporating a liquid and condensing its vapour

distillery distilleries noun place where spirit drinks are made

distinct adjective 1 not the same 2 easily sensed or understood 3 clear and definite > **distinctly** adverb

distinction noun 1 act of distinguishing 2 distinguishing feature 3 state of being different 4 special honour, recognition or fame

distinctive adjective easily recognizable > **distinctively** adverb

distinguish verb 1 to be a distinctive feature of 2 to make out by hearing, seeing, etc 3 **distinguish between** to make, show or recognize a difference (between) > **distinguishable** adjective: The brothers are not easily distinguishable > **distinguished**

adjective 1 dignified in appearance 2 highly respected > **distinguishing** adjective: distinguishing features

distort verb 1 to misrepresent (the truth or facts) 2 to twist out of shape > **distorted** adjective: a distorted voice > **distortion** noun: audio signals transmitted without distortion

distract verb 1 to draw the attention of (a person) away from something 2 to entertain > **distracted** adjective unable to concentrate, preoccupied > **distractedly** adverb > **distracting** adjective: distracting noises

distraction noun 1 something that diverts the attention 2 something that serves as an entertainment

distraught [diss-**trawt**] adjective extremely anxious or agitated

distress noun 1 extreme unhappiness 2 great physical pain 3 poverty ⊳ verb 4 to upset badly

distressing adjective very worrying or upsetting

distribute verb 1 to hand out or deliver (leaflets, mail, etc) 2 to share (something) among the members of a particular group

distribution noun 1 distributing 2 arrangement or spread

distributor noun 1 wholesaler who distributes goods to retailers in a specific area 2 device in a petrol engine that sends the electric current to the spark plugs

district noun area of land regarded as an administrative or geographical unit

a
b
c
d
e
f
g
h
i
j
k
l
m
n
o
p
q
r
s
t
u
v
w
x
y
z

district nurse noun nurse who visits and treats people in their own homes

distrust verb **1** to regard as untrustworthy ▷ noun **2** feeling of suspicion or doubt > **distrustful** adjective: I'm distrustful of all politicians

disturb verb **1** to intrude on **2** to worry or make anxious **3** to change the position or shape of > **disturbing** adjective: I found what she said about him disturbing

disturbance noun **1** interruption or intrusion **2** unruly outburst in public

disuse noun state of being no longer used > **disused** adjective: a disused coal mine

ditch noun **1** narrow channel dug in the earth for drainage or irrigation ▷ verb **2** (informal) to abandon or discard

dither verb **1** to be uncertain or indecisive ▷ noun **2** state of indecision or agitation

ditto noun **1** the same ▷ adverb **2** in the same way

ditty ditties noun (old-fashioned) short simple poem or song

diva noun distinguished female singer

dive dives, diving, dived verb **1** to plunge headfirst into water **2** (of a submarine or diver) to submerge under water **3** (of a bird or aircraft) to fly in a steep nose-down descending path **4** to move quickly in a specified direction **5 dive in** or **into** to start doing (something) enthusiastically ▷ noun **6** diving **7** steep nose-down descent **8** (informal) disreputable bar or club

diverge verb **1** to separate and go in different directions **2** to deviate (from a prescribed course) > **divergence** noun: a divergence of opinion > **divergent** adjective: divergent views

diverse adjective **1** having variety, assorted **2** different in kind

diversify diversifies, diversifying, diversified verb **1** to create different forms of **2** (of an enterprise) to vary (products or operations) in order to expand or reduce the risk of loss > **diversification** noun: diversification of agriculture

diversion noun **1** official detour used by traffic when a main route is closed **2** something that distracts someone's attention **3** diverting **4** amusing pastime

divert verb **1** to change the direction of **2** to distract the attention of **3** to entertain or amuse

divide verb **1** to separate into parts **2** to share or be shared out in parts **3** to (cause to) disagree **4** to keep apart or be a boundary between **5** to calculate how many times (one number) can be contained in (another) ▷ noun **6** division or split

dividend noun **1** sum of money representing part of the profit made, paid by a company to its shareholders **2** extra benefit

divine adjective **1** of God or a god **2** godlike **3** (informal) splendid ▷ verb **4** to discover (something) by intuition or guessing > **divinely** adverb

divinity divinities noun **1** study of religion **2** god or goddess **3** state of being divine

division noun **1** dividing, sharing out **2** one of the parts into which something is divided **3** (Maths) process of dividing one number by another **4** difference of opinion

divisive adjective tending to cause disagreement

divisor noun number to be divided into another number

divorce noun **1** legal ending of a marriage **2** any separation, especially a permanent one ▷ verb **3** to legally end one's marriage (to) **4** to remove or separate > **divorced** adjective: He is divorced, with a young son

divulge verb to make (something) known

DIY abbreviation (Brit, Aust, NZ) do-it-yourself

dizzy dizzier, dizziest adjective **1** having or causing a whirling sensation **2** mentally confused ▷ verb **3** to cause to feel giddy or confused > **dizziness** noun: His complaint causes dizziness

DNA abbreviation deoxyribonucleic acid: main constituent of the chromosomes of all living things

do does, doing, did, done; dos verb **1** to perform or complete (a deed or action) **2** to be adequate: That one will do **3** to suit or improve: That style does nothing for you **4** to find the answer to (a problem or puzzle) **5** to cause or produce: It does no harm to think ahead **6** to give or grant: Do me a favour **7** to work at, as a course of study or a job **8** used to form questions: How do you know? **9** used to intensify positive statements and commands: I do like port; Do go on **10** used to form negative

statements and commands: I do not know her well; Do not get up **11** used to replace an earlier verb: He gets paid more than I do ▷ noun **12** (informal) party or celebration > **do away with** verb to get rid of > **do up** verb **1** to fasten **2** to decorate and repair > **do with** verb to find useful or benefit from: I could do with a rest > **do without** verb to manage without

docile adjective (of a person or animal) easily controlled

dock noun **1** enclosed area of water where ships are loaded, unloaded or repaired **2** enclosed space in a court of law where the accused person sits or stands **3** weed with broad leaves ▷ verb **4** to bring or be brought into dock **5** to link (two spacecraft) or (of two spacecraft) to be linked together in space **6** to deduct money from (a person's wages) **7** to remove part of (an animal's tail) by cutting through the bone

doctor noun **1** person licensed to practise medicine **2** person who has been awarded a doctorate ▷ verb **3** to alter in order to deceive **4** to poison or drug (food or drink) **5** (informal) to castrate (an animal)

doctorate noun highest academic degree in any field of knowledge > **doctoral** adjective: a doctoral thesis

doctrine noun **1** body of teachings of a religious, political or philosophical group **2** principle or body of principles that is taught or advocated > **doctrinal** adjective: doctrinal differences among religious leaders

document noun 1 piece of paper providing an official record of something 2 ICT piece of text or graphics stored in a computer as a file that can be amended or altered by document processing software ▷ verb 3 to record or report (something) in detail 4 to support (a claim) with evidence

documentary documentaries noun 1 film or television programme presenting the facts about a particular subject ▷ adjective 2 (of evidence) based on documents

dodge verb 1 to avoid (a blow, being seen, etc) by moving suddenly 2 to evade by cleverness or trickery ▷ noun 3 cunning or deceitful trick

dodgy dodgier, dodgiest adjective (informal) 1 dangerous or risky 2 untrustworthy

dodo dodos noun large flightless extinct bird

doe noun female deer, hare or rabbit

does verb third person singular of the present tense of **do**

dog noun, dogging, dogged noun 1 domesticated four-legged mammal of many different breeds 2 related wild mammal, such as the dingo or coyote 3 male animal of the dog family 4 (informal) person: you lucky dog! 5 **go to the dogs** (informal) to go to ruin physically or morally 6 **let sleeping dogs lie** to leave things undisturbed 7 **the dogs** (informal) greyhound racing ▷ verb 8 to follow (someone) closely 9 to trouble or plague

dog collar noun 1 collar for a dog 2 (informal) white collar fastened at the back, worn by members of the clergy

dog-eared adjective 1 (of a book) having pages folded down at the corner 2 shabby or worn

dogged [**dog**-gid] adjective obstinately determined > **doggedly** adverb

dogma noun doctrine or system of doctrines proclaimed by authority as true

dogmatic adjective habitually stating your opinions forcefully or arrogantly > **dogmatism** noun

doldrums plural noun 1 depressed state of mind 2 state of inactivity

dole noun (Brit, Aust, NZ informal) money received from the state while unemployed > **dole out** verb to distribute in small quantities

doll noun 1 small model of a human being, used as a toy 2 (informal) pretty girl or young woman

dollar noun standard monetary unit of the USA, Australia, New Zealand, Canada and some other countries

dollop noun (informal) lump (of food)

dolphin noun sea mammal of the whale family, with a beaklike snout

domain noun 1 field of knowledge or activity 2 land under one ruler or government 3 (Computers) group of computers with the same name on the internet 4 (NZ) public park

dome noun 1 rounded roof built on a circular base 2 something shaped like this > **domed** adjective: a domed roof

domestic adjective 1 of one's own country or a specific country 2 of the home or family **3** enjoying running a home **4** (of an animal) kept as a pet or to produce food ▷ noun **5** person whose job is to do housework in someone else's house ▷ **domestically** adverb

domesticate verb **1** to bring or keep (a wild animal or plant) under control or cultivation **2** to accustom (someone) to home life ▷ **domesticated** adjective: domesticated animals

domesticity noun (formal) home life

dominance noun power or control

dominate verb **1** to control or govern **2** to tower above (surroundings) **3** to be very significant in ▷ **dominating** adjective: dominating personalities ▷ **domination** noun: centuries of domination by the Romans

domineering adjective forceful and arrogant

dominion noun **1** control or authority **2** land governed by one ruler or government **3** (formerly) self-governing division of the British Empire

domino dominoes noun **1** small rectangular block marked with dots, used in dominoes **2** dominoes game in which dominoes with matching halves are laid together

don dons, donning, donned verb **1** to put on (clothing) ▷ noun **2** (Brit) member of the teaching staff at a university or college **3** Spanish gentleman or nobleman

donate verb to give, especially to a charity or organization

done verb past participle of **do**

donkey noun **1** long-eared member of the horse family **2** donkey's years (informal) long time

donor noun **1** (Medicine) person who provides blood or organs for use in the treatment of another person **2** person who makes a donation

doodle verb **1** to scribble or draw aimlessly ▷ noun **2** shape or picture drawn aimlessly

doom noun **1** death or a terrible fate ▷ verb **2** to destine or condemn to death or a terrible fate

doomed adjective certain to suffer an unpleasant or unhappy experience

doomsday noun the end of the world

door noun **1** hinged or sliding panel for closing the entrance to a building, room, etc **2** entrance

doorway noun opening into a building or room

dope noun **1** (informal) illegal drug, usually cannabis **2** medicine or drug **3** (informal) stupid person ▷ verb **4** to give a drug to (a person or animal), especially in order to affect the outcome of a race

dormant adjective temporarily quiet, inactive or not being used

dormitory dormitories noun large room, especially at a school, containing several beds

dormouse dormice noun small mouselike rodent with a furry tail

dosage noun size of a dose

dose noun **1** specific quantity of a medicine taken at one time **2** (informal) something unpleasant to experience ▷ *verb* **3** to give a dose to (someone)

dossier [doss-ee-ay] *noun* collection of documents about a subject or person

dot dots, dotting, dotted *noun* **1** small round mark **2** shorter symbol used in Morse code **3 on the dot** (referring to time) precisely or exactly ▷ *verb* **4** to mark with a dot **5** to scatter or spread around

dotcom or **dot.com** *noun* company that does most of its business on the internet

dote *verb* **dote on** to love (someone) to an excessive degree > **doting** *adjective: doting parents*

double *adjective* **1** as much again in number, amount, size, etc **2** composed of two equal or similar parts **3** designed for two users: *double room* **4** folded in two ▷ *adverb* **5** twice over ▷ *noun* **6** twice the number, amount, size, etc **7** person who looks almost exactly like another **8 at** or **on the double** quickly or immediately **9 doubles** game between two pairs of players ▷ *verb* **10** to make or become twice as much or as many **11** to bend or fold (material etc) **12** to play two parts or serve two roles **13** to turn sharply > **doubly** *adverb*

double bass *noun* stringed instrument, largest and lowest member of the violin family

double-cross *verb* **1** to cheat or betray ▷ *noun* **2** double-crossing

double-decker *noun* **1** bus with two passenger decks one on top

of the other ▷ *adjective* **2** (informal) having two layers

double glazing *noun* two panes of glass in a window, fitted to reduce heat loss

doubt *noun* **1** uncertainty about the truth, facts or existence of something **2** unresolved difficulty or point ▷ *verb* **3** to question the truth of **4** to distrust or be suspicious of (someone)

doubtful *adjective* **1** unlikely **2** feeling doubt

dough [rhymes with **go**] *noun* **1** thick mixture of flour and water or milk, used for making bread etc **2** (informal) money

doughnut *noun* small cake of sweetened dough fried in deep fat

dour [doo-er] *adjective* sullen and unfriendly

douse [rhymes with **mouse**] *verb* **1** to drench with water or other liquid **2** to put out (a light)

dove *noun* bird with a heavy body, small head and short legs

dovetail *noun* **1** joint containing wedge-shaped tenons ▷ *verb* **2** to fit together neatly

dowager *noun* widow possessing property or a title inherited from her husband

dowdy dowdier, dowdiest *adjective* dull and old-fashioned

down *preposition, adverb* **1** indicating movement to or position in a lower place ▷ *adverb* **2** indicating completion of an action, lessening of intensity, etc: *calm down* ▷ *adjective* **3** depressed, unhappy ▷ *verb* **4** (informal) to drink (something) quickly ▷ *noun* **5** soft fine feathers

downcast adjective 1 sad and dejected 2 (of the eyes) directed downwards

downfall noun (cause of) a sudden loss of position or reputation

downgrade verb to reduce (something or someone) in importance, status or value

downhill adjective 1 going or sloping down ▷ adverb 2 towards the bottom of a hill

download verb 1 to transfer (data, files, etc) from the memory of one computer to that of another ▷ noun 2 file transferred in such a way

downpour noun heavy fall of rain

downright adjective, adverb extreme(ly)

downstairs adverb 1 to or on a lower floor ▷ noun 2 lower or ground floor

downstream adjective, adverb in or towards the lower part of a stream

down-to-earth adjective sensible or practical

downtrodden adjective oppressed and lacking the will to resist

downturn noun decline in the economy or in the success of a company or industry

down under adverb, noun (informal) (in or to) Australia or New Zealand

downwards or **downward** adverb 1 from a higher to a lower level, condition or position 2 from an earlier time or source to a later one

downwind adverb, adjective in the same direction towards which the wind is blowing

dowry dowries noun property brought by a woman to her husband at marriage

doze verb 1 to sleep lightly or briefly 2 **doze off** to fall into a light sleep ▷ noun 3 short sleep

dozen adjective, noun twelve

Dr abbreviation 1 Doctor 2 Drive

drab drabber, drabbest adjective dull and dreary > **drabness** noun: the drabness of his office

draft noun 1 plan, sketch or drawing of something 2 preliminary outline of a book, speech, etc 3 written order for payment of money by a bank 4 (US, Aust) selection for compulsory military service ▷ verb 5 to draw up an outline or plan of 6 to send (people) from one place to another to do a specific job 7 (US, Aust) to select for compulsory military service 8 (Aust, NZ) to select (cattle or sheep) from a herd or flock

drag drags, dragging, dragged verb 1 to pull with force, especially along the ground 2 to trail on the ground 3 to persuade or force (oneself or someone else) to go somewhere 4 to search (a river) with a dragnet or hook 5 (Computers) to move (an image) on the screen by use of the mouse 6 **drag on** or **out** to last or be prolonged tediously ▷ noun 7 person or thing that slows up progress 8 (informal) tedious thing or person 9 (informal) women's clothes worn by a man

dragon noun mythical fire-breathing monster like a huge lizard

dragonfly dragonflies noun brightly coloured insect with a long slender body and two pairs of wings

dragoon noun 1 heavily armed cavalryman ▷ verb 2 to coerce or force

drain noun 1 pipe or channel that carries off water or sewage 2 cause of a continuous reduction in energy or resources ▷ verb 3 to draw off or remove liquid from 4 to flow away or filter off 5 to drink the entire contents of (a glass or cup) 6 to make constant demands on (energy or resources), exhaust

drainage noun 1 system of drains 2 process or method of draining

drake noun male duck

drama noun 1 serious play for theatre, television or radio 2 writing, producing or acting in plays 3 situation that is exciting or highly emotional

dramatic adjective 1 of or like drama 2 behaving flamboyantly > **dramatically** adverb

dramatist noun person who writes plays

drape verb 1 to cover with material, usually in folds 2 to place casually

drastic adjective strong and severe > **drastically** adverb

draught noun 1 current of cold air, especially in an enclosed space 2 portion of liquid to be drunk, especially medicine 3 gulp or swallow 4 one of the flat discs used in the game of draughts 5 draughts game for two players using a chessboard and twelve draughts each ▷ adjective 6 (of an animal) used for pulling heavy loads 7 (of beer) served straight from barrels rather than in bottles

draughtsman draughtsmen noun person employed to prepare detailed scale drawings of machinery, buildings, etc

draughty draughtier, draughtiest adjective exposed to draughts of air

draw draws, drawing, drew, drawn verb 1 to sketch (a figure, picture, etc) with a pencil or pen 2 to pull (a person or thing) closer to or further away from a place 3 to move in a specified direction: the car drew near 4 to take from a source: draw money from bank accounts 5 to attract or interest 6 to formulate or decide: to draw conclusions 7 (of two teams or contestants) to finish a game with an equal number of points ▷ noun 8 raffle or lottery 9 contest or game ending in a tie 10 event, act, etc, that attracts a large audience > **draw out** verb 1 to encourage (someone) to talk freely 2 to make (something) longer 3 (of a train) to leave a station > **draw up** verb 1 to prepare and write out (a contract) 2 (of a vehicle) to come to a stop

drawback noun disadvantage

drawbridge noun bridge that can be raised or lowered preventing or giving access to a building such as a castle

drawer noun sliding box-shaped part of a piece of furniture, used for storage

drawing noun 1 picture or plan made by means of lines on a surface 2 art of making drawings

drawing room noun (old-fashioned) room where visitors are received and entertained

drawl verb 1 to speak slowly, with long vowel sounds ▷ noun 2 drawling manner of speech

drawn verb 1 past participle of draw ▷ adjective 2 haggard, tired or tense in appearance

dread verb 1 to anticipate with apprehension or fear ▷ noun 2 great fear > **dreaded** adjective: this dreaded disease

dreadful adjective 1 very disagreeable or shocking 2 extreme > **dreadfully** adverb

dream dreams, dreaming, dreamed or dreamt noun 1 imagined series of events experienced in the mind while asleep 2 cherished hope 3 (informal) wonderful person or thing ▷ verb 4 to see imaginary pictures in the mind while asleep 5 **dream of** or **about** to have an image (of) or fantasy (about) 6 **dream of** to consider the possibility of (something) ▷ adjective 7 ideal: a dream house

Dreamtime noun (in Australian Aboriginal legends) the time when the world was being made and the first people were created

dreamy dreamier, dreamiest adjective 1 vague or impractical 2 (informal) wonderful > **dreamily** adverb

dreary drearier, dreariest adjective dull or boring

dregs plural noun 1 solid particles that settle at the bottom of some liquids 2 most despised elements

drenched adjective soaking wet

dress noun 1 one-piece garment for a woman or girl, consisting of a skirt part and a top part and sometimes sleeves 2 complete style of clothing ▷ verb 3 to put your clothes on 4 to put formal clothes on 5 to put clothes on (a child, invalid, etc) 6 to apply a protective covering to (a wound) 7 to arrange or prepare (salad, meat, etc)

dresser noun 1 piece of furniture with shelves and with cupboards, for storing or displaying dishes 2 (Theatre) person employed to assist actors with their costumes

dressing gown noun coat-shaped garment worn over pyjamas or nightdress

dressing room noun room used for changing clothes, especially backstage in a theatre

dress rehearsal noun last rehearsal of a play or show, using costumes, lighting, etc

dribble verb 1 to (allow to) flow in drops 2 to allow saliva to trickle from the mouth 3 (Sport) to propel (a ball) by repeatedly tapping it with the foot, hand or a stick ▷ noun 4 small quantity of liquid falling in drops

drift verb 1 to be carried along by currents of air or water 2 to move aimlessly from one place or activity to another ▷ noun 3 something piled up by the wind or current, such as a snowdrift 4 general movement or development 5 point or meaning: catch my drift?

drill noun 1 tool or machine for boring holes 2 strict and often repetitious training 3 (informal) correct procedure **4** machine for sowing seed in rows **5** small furrow for seed ▷ *verb* **6** to bore a hole in (something) with or as if with a drill **7** to teach by rigorous exercises or training

drink drinks, drinking, drank, drunk *verb* **1** to swallow (a liquid) **2** to consume alcohol, especially to excess ▷ *noun* **3** (portion of) a liquid suitable for drinking **4** alcohol, or its habitual or excessive consumption > **drinker** *noun: I'm not much of a coffee drinker* > **drink in** *verb* to pay close attention to > **drink to** *verb* to drink a toast to

drip drips, dripping, dripped *verb* **1** to (let) fall in drops ▷ *noun* **2** falling of drops of liquid **3** sound made by falling drops **4** (*informal*) weak dull person **5** (*Medicine*) device by which a solution is passed in small drops through a tube into a vein

drive drives, driving, drove, driven *verb* **1** to guide the movement of (a vehicle) **2** to transport in a vehicle **3** to force (someone) into a specified state **4** to push or propel **5** (*Sport*) to hit (a ball) very hard and straight ▷ *noun* **6** journey by car, van, etc **7** path for vehicles connecting a building to a public road **8** united effort towards a common goal **9** energy and ambition **10** means by which power is transmitted in a mechanism > **drive at** *verb* (*informal*) to intend or mean: *what was he driving at?* > **driver** *noun* person who drives a vehicle > **driving** *noun*

drive-in *adjective, noun* (denoting) a cinema, restaurant, etc, used by people in their cars

drivel *noun* foolish talk

drizzle *noun* **1** very light rain ▷ *verb* **2** to rain lightly > **drizzly** *adjective: drizzly rain*

dromedary dromedaries [drom-mid-er-ee] *noun* camel with a single hump

drone *verb* **1** to make a monotonous low dull sound ▷ *noun* **2** male bee > **drone on** *verb* to talk for a long time in a monotonous tone

drool *verb* to allow saliva to flow from the mouth

droop *verb* to hang downwards loosely

drop drops, dropping, dropped *verb* **1** to (allow to) fall vertically **2** to decrease in amount, strength or value **3** to mention (a hint or name) casually **4** to discontinue **5** **drop in** or **by** to pay someone a casual visit ▷ *noun* **6** small quantity of liquid forming a round shape **7** any small quantity of liquid **8** decrease in amount, strength or value **9** vertical distance that something may fall **10** **drops** liquid medication applied in small drops > **drop off** *verb* **1** (*informal*) to fall asleep **2** to grow smaller or less

droplet *noun* small drop

droppings *plural noun* faeces of certain animals, such as rabbits or birds

drought *noun* prolonged shortage of rainfall

drove *verb* **1** past tense of **drive** **2** to drive (sheep or cattle) over a long distance ▷ *noun* **3** herd of livestock being driven together

drown *verb* **1** to die or kill by immersion in liquid **2** to forget (one's sorrows) temporarily by drinking alcohol **3** to drench thoroughly **4** to make (a sound) inaudible by being louder

drowsy drowsier, drowsiest *adjective* feeling sleepy > **drowsiness**

drudgery *noun* hard boring work

drug drugs, drugging, drugged *noun* **1** substance used in the treatment or prevention of disease **2** chemical substance, especially a narcotic, taken for the effects it produces ▷ *verb* **3** to give a drug to (a person or animal) to cause sleepiness or unconsciousness **4** to mix a drug with (food or drink)

Druid *noun* member of an ancient order of Celtic priests

drum drums, drumming, drummed *noun* **1** percussion instrument sounded by striking a membrane stretched across the opening of a hollow cylinder **2** cylindrical object or container **3 the drum** (*Aust*) information or advice ▷ *verb* **4** to play (music) on a drum **5** to tap rhythmically or regularly > **drummer** *noun* person who plays a drum or drums

drumstick *noun* **1** stick used for playing a drum **2** lower joint of the leg of a cooked chicken etc

drunk *verb* **1** past participle of **drink** ▷ *adjective* **2** intoxicated with alcohol to the extent of losing control over normal functions **3** overwhelmed by a strong influence or emotion ▷ *noun* **4** person who is drunk or who frequently gets drunk

dry drier or dryer, driest; dries, drying, dried *adjective* **1** lacking moisture **2** having little or no rainfall **3** (*informal*) thirsty **4** (of wine) not sweet **5** uninteresting **6** (of humour) subtle and sarcastic **7** prohibiting the sale of alcohol: *a dry town* ▷ *verb* **8** to make or become dry **9** to preserve (food) by removing the moisture > **drily** or **dryly** *adverb* > **dryness** *noun* > **dry up** *verb* **1** to become completely dry **2** (*informal*) to forget what you were going to say or find that you have nothing left to say

dry-clean *verb* to clean (clothes etc) with chemicals rather than water

dryer or **drier** *noun* **1** apparatus for removing moisture ▷ *adjective* **2** comparative of **dry**

dual *adjective* having two parts, functions or aspects

dub dubs, dubbing, dubbed *verb* **1** to give (a person or place) a name or nickname **2** to provide (a film) with a new soundtrack, especially in a different language **3** to provide (a film or tape) with a soundtrack

dubious [**dew**-bee-uss] *adjective* feeling or causing doubt > **dubiously** *adverb*

duchess *noun* **1** woman who holds the rank of duke **2** wife or widow of a duke

duchy duchies *noun* territory of a duke or duchess

duck ducks, ducking, ducked *noun* **1** water bird with short legs, webbed feet and a broad blunt bill **2** its flesh, used as food **3** female of this bird **4** (*Cricket*) score of nothing ▷ *verb* **5** to move (the head or body) quickly downwards, to avoid being seen or to dodge a blow **6** to plunge suddenly under water **7** (*informal*) to dodge (a duty or responsibility)

duckling *noun* young duck

duct *noun* **1** tube, pipe or channel through which liquid or gas is conveyed **2** bodily passage conveying secretions or excretions

dud (*informal*) *noun* **1** ineffectual person or thing ▷ *adjective* **2** bad or useless

due *adjective* **1** expected or scheduled to be present or arrive **2** owed as a debt **3** fitting, proper **4 due to** attributable to or caused by ▷ *noun* **5** something that is owed or required **6 dues** charges for membership of a club or organization ▷ *adverb* **7** directly or exactly: *due south*

duel *duels, duelling, duelled noun* **1** formal fight with deadly weapons between two people, to settle a quarrel ▷ *verb* **2** to fight in a duel

duet *noun* piece of music for two performers

dug *verb* past of **dig**

dugong *noun* whalelike mammal of tropical waters

dugout *noun* **1** (*Brit*) (at a sports ground) covered bench where managers and substitutes sit **2** canoe made by hollowing out a log **3** (*Military*) covered excavation to provide shelter

duke *noun* **1** nobleman of the highest rank **2** prince or ruler of a small principality or duchy

dull *adjective* **1** not interesting **2** (of an ache) not acute **3** (of weather) not bright or clear **4** lacking in spirit **5** not very intelligent **6** (of a blade) not sharp ▷ *verb* **7** to make or become dull > **dullness** *noun*: *the dullness of their routine* > **dully** *adverb*

duly *adverb* **1** in a proper manner **2** at the proper time

dumb *adjective* **1** lacking the power to speak **2** silent **3** (*informal*) stupid

dumbfounded *adjective* speechless with astonishment

dummy *dummies noun* **1** figure representing the human form, used for displaying clothes etc **2** copy of an object, often lacking some essential feature of the original **3** rubber teat for a baby to suck **4** (*informal*) stupid person ▷ *adjective* **5** imitation or substitute

dump *verb* **1** to drop or let fall in a careless manner **2** (*informal*) to get rid of (someone or something no longer wanted) ▷ *noun* **3** place where waste materials are left **4** (*informal*) dirty unattractive place **5** (*Military*) place where weapons or supplies are stored

dumpling *noun* **1** small ball of dough cooked and served with stew **2** round pastry case filled with fruit

dunce *noun* person who is stupid or slow to learn

dune *noun* mound or ridge of drifted sand

dung *noun* faeces from animals such as cattle

dungarees *plural noun* trousers which have a bib covering the chest and straps over the shoulders

dungeon noun underground prison cell

dunk verb **1** to dip (a biscuit or bread) in a drink or soup before eating it **2** to put (something) in liquid

duo duos noun **1** pair of performers **2** (informal) pair of closely connected people

dupe verb **1** to deceive or cheat ▷ noun **2** person who is easily deceived

duplicate adjective **1** copied exactly from an original ▷ noun **2** exact copy ▷ verb **3** to make an exact copy of **4** to do again (something that has already been done) > **duplication** noun: unnecessary duplication of work

durable adjective long-lasting > **durability** noun: a material renowned for its durability

duration noun length of time that something lasts

duress noun compulsion by use of force or threats

during preposition throughout or within the limit of (a period of time)

dusk noun time just before nightfall, when it is almost dark

dust noun **1** small dry particles of earth, sand or dirt ▷ verb **2** to remove dust from (furniture) by wiping **3** to sprinkle (something) with a powdery substance

dustbin noun large container for household rubbish

duster noun cloth used for dusting

dustman dustmen noun (Brit) man whose job is to collect household rubbish

dusty dustier, dustiest adjective covered with dust

Dutch adjective **1** of the Netherlands ▷ noun **2** main language spoken in the Netherlands **go Dutch** (informal) to share the expenses on an outing

dutiful adjective doing what is expected > **dutifully** adverb

duty duties noun **1** work or a task performed as part of your job **2** task that a person feels morally bound to do **3** government tax on imports **4 on duty** at work

duty-free adjective untaxed and therefore cheaper than normal: duty-free vodka

duvet [doo-vay] noun kind of quilt used in bed instead of a top sheet and blankets

DVD abbreviation Digital Versatile (or Video) Disk

dwarf dwarfs or dwarves; dwarfs, dwarfing, dwarfed noun **1** person who is smaller than average **2** (in folklore) small ugly manlike creature, often possessing magical powers ▷ adjective **3** (of an animal or plant) much smaller than the usual size for the species ▷ verb **4** to cause (someone or something) to seem small by being much larger

dwell dwells, dwelling, dwelled or dwelt verb (literary) to live as a permanent resident > **dwell on** verb to think, speak or write at length about

dwelling noun place of residence

dwindle verb to grow less in size, strength or number

dye dyes, dyeing, dyed noun **1** colouring substance **2** colour

a
b
c
d
e
f
g
h
i
j
k
l
m
n
o
p
q
r
s
t
u
v
w
x
y
z

produced by dyeing ▷ *verb* **3** to colour (hair or fabric) by applying a dye

dying *verb* present participle of **die**¹

dyke or **dike** *noun* wall built to prevent flooding

dynamic *adjective* **1** full of energy, ambition and new ideas **2** (*Physics*) of energy or forces that produce motion > **dynamically** *adverb*

dynamics *plural noun* **1** SCIENCE study of the forces that change or produce the motion of bodies or particles **2** MUSIC **a** various degrees of loudness needed in a performance **b** symbols used to indicate this

dynamite *noun* **1** explosive made of nitroglycerine **2** (*informal*) dangerous or exciting person or thing ▷ *verb* **3** to blow (something) up with dynamite

dynamo dynamos *noun* device for converting mechanical energy into electrical energy

dynasty dynasties *noun* sequence of hereditary rulers

dysentery *noun* infection of the intestine causing severe diarrhoea

dyslexia *noun* disorder causing impaired ability to read > **dyslexic** *adjective*: *a dyslexic child*

e

each *adjective, pronoun* every (one) taken separately

> **WORD TIP**
> Wherever you use *each other* you could also use *one another*

eager *adjective* showing or feeling great desire, keen > **eagerly** *adverb* enthusiastically > **eagerness** *noun*: *an eagerness to learn*

eagle *noun* **1** large bird of prey with keen eyesight **2** (*Golf*) score of two strokes under par for a hole

ear *noun* **1** organ of hearing, especially the external part of it **2** head of corn

eardrum *noun* thin piece of skin inside the ear which enables you to hear sounds

earl *noun* British nobleman ranking next below a marquess

early earlier, earliest *adjective, adverb* **1** before the expected or usual time **2** in the first part of a period **3** in a period far back in time

earmark *verb* to set (something) aside for a specific purpose

earn *verb* **1** to obtain (something) by work or merit **2** (of investments etc) to gain (interest) > **earner** *noun*: *a wage earner*

earnest *adjective* **1** serious and sincere ▷ *noun* **2** in earnest seriously > **earnestly** *adverb*

earnings *plural noun* money earned

earphone *noun* receiver for a radio etc, held to or put in the ear

earring *noun* piece of jewellery worn in the ear lobe

earshot *noun* hearing range

earth *noun* **1** planet that we live on **2** land, the ground **3** soil **4** fox's hole **5** wire connecting an electrical apparatus with the earth ▷ *verb* **6** to connect (a circuit) to earth

earthenware *noun* pottery made of baked clay

earthly *adjective* concerned with life on earth rather than heaven or life after death

earthquake *noun* violent vibration of the earth's surface

earthworm *noun* worm that burrows in the soil

earthy earthier, earthiest *adjective* **1** coarse or crude **2** of or like earth

earwig *noun* small insect with a pincer-like tail

ease *noun* **1** freedom from difficulty, discomfort or worry **2** rest or leisure ▷ *verb* **3** to give bodily or mental ease to (someone or something) **4** to lessen (severity, tension, pain, etc); relieve **5** to move carefully or gradually

easel *noun* frame to support an artist's canvas or a blackboard

easily *adverb* **1** without difficulty **2** without a doubt: *The song is easily one of their finest*

east *noun* **1** (direction towards) the part of the horizon where the sun rises **2** region lying in this direction ▷ *adjective* **3** to or in the east **4** (of a wind) from the east ▷ *adverb* **5** in, to or towards the east

Easter *noun* Christian spring festival celebrating the Resurrection of Jesus Christ

easterly *adjective* **1** to or towards the east **2** (of a wind) blowing from the east

eastern *adjective* in or from the east: *a remote eastern corner of the country*

eastward *adjective, adverb* towards the east

easy easier, easiest *adjective* **1** not needing much work or effort **2** free from pain, care or anxiety **3** easy-going

> **WORD TIP**
> Although *easy* is an adjective, it can be used as an adverb in fixed phrases like *take it easy*

eat eats, eating, ate, eaten *verb* **1** to take (food) into the mouth and swallow it **2** to have a meal > **eat away** *verb* (also **eat away at**) to destroy (something) slowly

eaves *plural noun* overhanging edges of a roof

eavesdrop eavesdrops, eavesdropping, eavesdropped *verb* to listen secretly to a private conversation

ebb *verb* **1** (of tide water) to flow back **2** to fall away or decline ▷ *noun* **3** flowing back of the tide **4 at a low ebb** in a state of weakness

ebony *noun* **1** hard black wood ▷ *adjective* **2** deep black

e-book *noun* **1** electronic book ▷ *verb* **2** book (airline tickets, appointments, etc.) on the internet

ebullient *adjective* full of enthusiasm or excitement > **ebullience** *noun*

EC *abbreviation* European Community: a former name for the European Union

eccentric *adjective* **1** odd or unconventional ▷ *noun* **2** eccentric person > **eccentrically** *adverb*: *eccentrically dressed* > **eccentricity** *noun*: *unusual to the point of eccentricity*

ecclesiastical [ik-leez-ee-**ass**-ti-kl] *adjective* of the Christian Church or clergy

echelon [**esh**-a-lon] *noun* level of power or responsibility

echidna or echidnae [ik-**kid**-na] *noun* (Aust) Australian spiny egg-laying mammal (also **spiny anteater**)

echo echoes, echoing, echoed *noun* **1** repetition of sounds by reflection of sound waves off a surface **2** close imitation ▷ *verb* **3** to be repeated as an echo **4** to imitate (what someone else has said)

eclipse *noun* temporary obscuring of one star or planet by another

eco- *prefix* of ecology or the environment

ecology *noun* study of the relationships between living things and their environment > **ecological** *adjective* **1** of ecology **2** intended to protect the environment > **ecologically** *adverb*: *ecologically sound* > **ecologist** *noun* person who studies ecology

economic *adjective* **1** HISTORY concerning the management of

the money, industry and trade in a country **2** profitable **3** (*informal*) inexpensive or cheap

economical *adjective* spending money carefully and sensibly > **economically** *adverb*: *an economically depressed area*

economics *noun* **1** HISTORY the study of the production and distribution of goods, services and wealth in a society and the organization of its money, industry and trade ▷ *plural* **2** financial aspects

economist *noun* specialist in economics

economy economies *noun* **1** system that a country uses to organize and manage its money, industry and trade **2** wealth that a country gets from business and industry **3** careful use of money or resources to avoid waste

ecosystem *noun* system involving interactions between a community and its environment

ecstasy ecstasies *noun* **1** state of intense delight **2** (*informal*) powerful drug that can produce hallucinations > **ecstatic** *adjective* very happy and excited > **ecstatically** *adverb*: *ecstatically happy*

eczema [**ek**-sim-a] *noun* skin disease that causes the skin surface to become rough and itchy

eddy eddies, eddying, eddied *noun* **1** circular movement of air, water, etc ▷ *verb* **2** to move with a circular motion

edge *noun* **1** border or line where something ends or begins **2** cutting side of a blade

3 have the edge on to have an advantage over (someone) **4 on edge** nervous or irritable ▷ *verb* **5** to provide an edge or border for (something) **6** to push (one's way) gradually

edgy edgier, edgiest *adjective* nervous or irritable

edible *adjective* fit to be eaten

edifice [ed-if-iss] *noun* large building

edit *verb* **1** to make changes, cuts and corrections (to a piece of writing, book, film, etc) so that it is fit for publication or broadcast **2** to be in charge of (a newspaper, magazine, etc) or a section of it

edition *noun* number of copies of a new publication printed at one time

editor *noun* LIBRARY **1** person who edits **2** person in charge of a newspaper or magazine or a section of it

editorial *noun* **1** newspaper article stating the opinion of the editor ▷ *adjective* **2** relating to editing or editors > **editorially** *adverb*

educate *verb* to teach (someone)

educated *adjective* having a high standard of learning and culture

education *noun* **1** gaining knowledge and understanding through learning **2** system of teaching people at school or university > **educational** *adjective*: *educational materials*; *It would be very educational* > **educationally** *adverb*

eel *noun* snakelike fish

eerie eerier, eeriest *adjective* uncannily frightening or disturbing > **eerily** *adverb*: *eerily quiet*

effect *noun* **1** change or result caused by someone or something **2** overall impression **3 take effect** to start to happen or start to produce results: *The law will take effect next year*

> **WORD TIP**
> Remember that *effect* is a noun and *affect* is a verb

effective *adjective* **1** producing a desired result **2** coming into operation or beginning officially > **effectively** *adverb*: *to function effectively*

effeminate *adjective* (of a man) displaying characteristics thought to be typical of a woman

efficient *adjective* functioning effectively and with little waste of effort > **efficiency** *noun* ability to function effectively and with little waste of effort > **efficiently** *adverb* effectively and with little waste of effort

effigy effigies [**ef**-fij-ee] *noun* statue or model of a person

effluent *noun* liquid waste that comes out of factories or sewage works

effluvium effluvia *noun* unpleasant smell or gas given off by something

effort *noun* **1** physical or mental exertion **2** attempt

effortless *adjective* done easily and well > **effortlessly** *adverb* easily and well

e.g. *abbreviation* (Latin) for example

egalitarian *adjective* favouring equality for all people

egg *noun* **1** oval or round object laid by the females of birds and other creatures, containing a developing embryo **2** hen's egg used as food

a b c d e f g h i j k l m n o p q r s t u v w x y z

3 cell produced in a female animal's body that can develop into a baby if it is fertilized ▷ **egg on** verb to encourage (someone) to do something foolish or daring

eggplant noun (US, Canadian, Aust, NZ) dark purple pear-shaped vegetable, aubergine

ego egos [**ee-goh**] noun self-esteem

egocentric adjective only thinking of oneself

egoism or **egotism** noun **1** excessive concern for one's own interests **2** excessively high opinion of oneself ▷ **egoist** or **egotist** noun egotistical person ▷ **egotistic, egotistical** or **egoistic** adjective having an excessive concern for one's own interests

Egyptian [ij-**jip**-shn] adjective **1** belonging or relating to Egypt ▷ noun **2** someone from Egypt

Eid-ul-Adha noun annual Muslim festival marking the end of pilgrimage to Mecca known as the hajj

eight adjective, noun the number 8 ▷ **eighth** adjective, noun

eighteen adjective, noun the number 18 ▷ **eighteenth** adjective, noun

eighty eighties adjective, noun the number 80 ▷ **eightieth** adjective, noun

either adjective, pronoun **1** one or the other (of two) **2** each of two ▷ conjunction **3** used preceding two or more possibilities joined by or ▷ adverb **4** likewise: I don't eat meat and he doesn't either

ejaculate verb **1** to discharge semen **2** to utter (something)

abruptly ▷ **ejaculation** noun act of ejaculating

eject verb to force out or expel (someone or something) ▷ **ejection** noun: the ejection of hecklers from the meeting

elaborate adjective **1** with a lot of fine detail; fancy ▷ verb **2** to add more information or detail about (something) ▷ **elaborately** adverb: elaborately costumed dolls ▷ **elaboration** noun adding more detail about something

eland [**eel**-and] noun large antelope of southern Africa

elapse verb (of time) to pass by

elastic adjective **1** able to stretch easily **2** adapting easily to change ▷ noun **3** rubber material that stretches and returns to its original shape ▷ **elasticity** noun: to restore the skin's elasticity

elated adjective extremely happy and excited ▷ **elation** noun great happiness

elbow noun **1** joint between the upper arm and the forearm ▷ verb **2** to shove or strike (someone) with the elbow

elder adjective **1** (of a brother, son, daughter, etc) older ▷ noun **2** older person **3** small tree with white flowers and black berries ▷ **eldest** adjective (of a brother, son, daughter, etc) oldest

elderly adjective (fairly) old

elect verb **1** to choose (someone) by voting **2** to decide (to do something) ▷ adjective **3** appointed but not yet in office: president elect

election noun **1** choosing of representatives by voting **2** act of choosing > **electoral** adjective: electoral reform

electorate noun people who have the right to vote

electric adjective **1** powered or produced by electricity **2** exciting or tense

electrical adjective using or producing electricity > **electrically** adverb

electrician noun person trained to install and repair electrical equipment

electricity noun **1** form of energy associated with stationary or moving electrons or other charged particles **2** electric current or charge

electrified adjective connected to a supply of electricity

electrifying adjective very exciting

electro- prefix operated by or caused by electricity

electrocute verb to kill or injure (someone) by electricity > **electrocution** noun: death by electrocution

electrode noun conductor through which an electric current enters or leaves a battery, vacuum tube, etc

electrolysis [il-ek-**trol**-iss-iss] noun SCIENCE process of passing an electric current through a substance in order to produce chemical changes in it

electron noun elementary particle in all atoms that has a negative electrical charge

electronic adjective ICT having transistors or silicon chips which control an electric current > **electronically** adverb

electronics noun technology concerned with the development of electronic devices and circuits

elegant adjective pleasing or graceful in dress, style or design > **elegance** noun: understated elegance > **elegantly** adverb

elegy [**el**-lij-ee] noun mournful poem, especially a lament for the dead

element noun **1** component part **2** substance that cannot be separated into other substances by ordinary chemical techniques **3** section of people within a larger group: the rowdy element **4** heating wire in an electric kettle, stove, etc **5 in your element** in a situation where you are happiest **6 elements a** basic principles of something **b** weather conditions, especially wind, rain and cold

elemental adjective simple and basic, but powerful

elementary adjective simple and straightforward

elephant noun huge four-footed thick-skinned animal with ivory tusks and a long trunk

elevate verb **1** to raise (someone) in rank or status **2** to lift (something) up

elevation noun **1** raising of someone or something to a higher level or position **2** height above sea level

eleven adjective, noun **1** the number 11 > noun **2** (Sport) team of eleven people > **eleventh** adjective, noun

elf noun (in folklore) small mischievous fairy

elicit verb **1** to bring about (a response or reaction) **2** to find

a
b
c
d
e
f
g
h
i
j
k
l
m
n
o
p
q
r
s
t
u
v
w
x
y
z

out (information) by careful questioning

eligible adjective **1** meeting the requirements or qualifications needed **2** desirable as a spouse > **eligibility** noun: eligibility for benefits

eliminate verb to get rid of (something) > **elimination** noun: the elimination of chemical weapons

elite [ill-**eet**] noun most powerful, rich or gifted members of a group

Elizabethan adjective of the reign of Elizabeth I of England (1558–1603)

elk noun large deer of N Europe and Asia

ellipse noun a regular oval shape, like a circle seen from an angle

elm noun tall tree with broad leaves

elocution noun art of speaking clearly in public

elongated adjective long and thin

elope verb (of two people) to run away secretly to get married

eloquent adjective able to speak or write skilfully and with ease > **eloquence** noun fluent powerful use of language > **eloquently** adverb

else adjective, adverb **1** in addition or more: what else can I do? **2** other or different: It was unlike anything else that had happened

elsewhere adverb in or to another place

elude verb **1** to escape from (someone or something) by cleverness or quickness **2** to baffle (someone)

elusive adjective difficult to catch or remember

elves noun plural of elf

em- prefix another form of the prefix **en-**

> **WORD TIP**
> em- is the form used before the letters b, m and p

emaciated [im-**mace**-ee-ate-id] adjective extremely thin and weak, because of illness or lack of food

email or **e-mail** noun **1** sending of messages between computer terminals ▷ verb **2** to communicate with (someone) in this way

emancipation noun freeing someone from harmful or unpleasant restrictions

embargo embargoes, embargoing, embargoed noun **1** order by a government prohibiting trade with a country ▷ verb **2** to put an embargo on (goods)

embark verb **1** to board a ship or aircraft **2** (followed by on) to begin (a new project)

embarrass verb to cause (someone) to feel self-conscious or ashamed > **embarrassed** adjective: an embarrassed silence > **embarrassing** adjective: an embarrassing situation > **embarrassment** noun: We apologize for any embarrassment this may have caused

embassy embassies noun **1** offices or official residence of an ambassador **2** ambassador and his staff

embed verb fix firmly in something solid > **embedded** adjective **1** fixed firmly and deeply **2** (of a journalist) assigned to accompany an active military unit

ember noun glowing piece of wood or coal in a dying fire

embittered *adjective* feeling anger as a result of misfortune

emblazoned *adjective* decorated (with something)

emblem *noun* object or design that symbolizes a quality, type or group

embody embodies, embodying, embodied *verb* 1 to be an example or expression of (a quality or idea) 2 to comprise or include (a number of things) > **embodiment** *noun: the embodiment of vulnerability*

embossed *adjective* (of a design or pattern) standing out from a surface

embrace *verb* 1 to clasp (someone) in your arms; hug 2 to accept (an idea) eagerly ▷ *noun* 3 act of embracing

embroider *verb* to decorate (fabric) with needlework > **embroidery** *noun*

embroiled *adjective* deeply involved and entangled (in an argument or conflict)

embryo [em-bree-oh] *noun* unborn creature in the early stages of development > **embryonic** *adjective* at an early stage

emerald *noun* 1 bright green precious stone ▷ *adjective* 2 bright green

emerge *verb* 1 to come into view 2 (followed by *from*) to come out of (a difficult or bad experience) 3 to become known > **emergence** *noun* coming into existence > **emergent** *adjective* coming into existence

emergency emergencies *noun* sudden unforeseen occurrence needing immediate action

emigrant *noun* person who goes and settles in another country

emigrate *verb* to go and settle in another country > **emigration** *noun* HISTORY process of emigrating

eminent *adjective* well-known and respected > **eminence** *noun* position of superiority or fame > **eminently** *adverb* very: *eminently reasonable*

emir [em-**meer**] *noun* Muslim ruler

emission *noun* release of something such as gas or radiation into the atmosphere

emit emits, emitting, emitted *verb* 1 to give out (heat, light or a smell) 2 to utter (a sound): *She emitted a long, low whistle*

emoticon [i-**mote**-i-kon] *noun* (Computers) symbol depicting a smile or other facial expression, used in email

emotion *noun* PSHE strong feeling

emotional *adjective* PSHE readily affected by or appealing to the emotions > **emotionally** *adverb*

emotive *adjective* tending to arouse emotion

empathize or **empathise** *verb* (followed by *with*) to understand the feelings of (someone) > **empathy** *noun* ability to understand someone else's feelings as if they were one's own

emperor *noun* ruler of an empire

emphasis emphases *noun* 1 special importance or significance 2 stress on a word or phrase in speech

emphasize or **emphasise** *verb* to make it known that (something) is very important

emphatic *adjective* showing emphasis ▷ **emphatically** *adverb*

empire *noun* **1** group of countries under the rule of one state or person **2** large organization that is directed by one person or group

employ *verb* **1** to hire (someone) **2** to provide work or occupation for (someone) **3** to use (something)

employee *noun* person who works for another person or for an organization

employer *noun* person or organization that employs someone

employment *noun* **1** state of being employed **2** work done by a person to earn money

empower *verb* to enable or authorize (someone) to do something

empress *noun* woman who rules an empire, or the wife of an emperor

empty emptier, emptiest; empties, emptying, emptied *adjective* **1** containing nothing **2** unoccupied **3** without purpose or value **4** (of words) insincere ▷ *verb* **5** to make (something) empty > **empties** *plural noun* empty boxes, bottles, etc > **emptiness** *noun: the emptiness of the desert*

emu emu *noun* large Australian flightless bird with long legs

emulate *verb* to attempt to equal or surpass (someone or something) by imitating > **emulation** *noun: a role model worthy of emulation*

emulsion *noun* a water-based paint

en- *prefix* **1** to surround or cover: *enclose; encrusted* **2** to cause to be in a certain state or condition: *enamoured; endanger*

enable *verb* to provide (someone) with the means, opportunity or authority (to do something)

enact *verb* **1** to establish (a law or bill) by law **2** to perform (a story or play) by acting > **enactment** *noun: the enactment of the Bill of Rights*

enamel enamels, enamelling, enamelled *noun* **1** glasslike coating applied to metal etc to preserve the surface ▷ *verb* **2** to cover (an object) with enamel > **enamelled** *adjective* covered with enamel

enamoured *adjective* **be enamoured of** to like (someone or something) very much

encapsulate *verb* to contain or represent (facts or ideas) in a small space

encased *adjective* surrounded or covered with a substance: *encased in plaster*

enchanted *adjective* fascinated or charmed

enchanting *adjective* attractive, delightful or charming

encircle *verb* to form a circle around (something or someone)

enclave *noun* part of a country entirely surrounded by foreign territory

enclose *verb* **1** to surround (an object or area) completely **2** to include (something) along with something else > **enclosed** *adjective* **1** surrounded completely **2** included

enclosure *noun* area of land surrounded by a wall or fence and used for a particular purpose

encompass verb to include all of (a number of things)

encore interjection **1** again, once more ▷ noun **2** short extra performance due to enthusiastic demand

encounter verb **1** to meet (someone) unexpectedly **2** to be faced with (a difficulty) ▷ noun **3** unexpected meeting

encourage verb **1** to inspire (someone) with confidence **2** to spur (someone) on > **encouragement** noun: My friends gave me a great deal of encouragement > **encouraging** adjective: The results have been encouraging

encroach verb (followed by on) to intrude gradually on (a person's rights or land) > **encroachment** noun intruding gradually on something

encrusted adjective covered with a layer of something: a necklace encrusted with gold

encyclopedia or **encyclopaedia** noun book or set of books containing facts about many subjects, usu. in alphabetical order

encyclopedic or **encyclopaedic** adjective knowing or giving information about many different things

end noun **1** furthest point or part **2** limit **3** last part of something **4** fragment **5** death or destruction **6** purpose **7** (Sport) either of the two defended areas of a playing field **8 make ends meet** to have just enough money for your needs ▷ verb **9** to come or bring (something) to a finish

endanger verb to put (something) in danger

endear verb (followed by to) to cause (someone) to be liked > **endearing** adjective: an endearing personality > **endearingly** adverb

endeavour verb **1** to try ▷ noun **2** effort

endless adjective having or seeming to have no end > **endlessly** adverb

endorse verb **1** to give approval to (someone or something) **2** to sign the back of (a cheque) **3** to record a conviction on (a driving licence)

endowed adjective **endowed with** provided with (a quality or ability)

endurance noun act or power of enduring

endure verb **1** to bear (hardship) patiently **2** to last for a long time > **enduring** adjective: an enduring friendship

enema [en-im-a] noun liquid put into a person's rectum to cause their bowels to empty

enemy enemies noun hostile person or nation; opponent

energetic adjective having energy or enthusiasm; lively > **energetically** adverb with great energy

energy noun **1** capacity for intense activity **2** capacity to do work and overcome resistance **3** source of power, such as electricity

enforce verb to cause (a law or rule) to be obeyed > **enforceable** adjective: legally enforceable contracts > **enforcement** noun: stricter enforcement of existing laws

a
b
c
d
e
f
g
h
i
j
k
l
m
n
o
p
q
r
s
t
u
v
w
x
y
z

engage verb 1 to take part or participate 2 to involve (a person or his or her attention) intensely

engaged adjective 1 having agreed to be married 2 in use

engagement noun appointment with someone

engine noun 1 any machine that converts energy into mechanical work 2 railway locomotive

engineer noun 1 person trained in any branch of engineering ▷ verb 2 to plan (an event or situation) in a clever manner

engineering noun profession of applying scientific principles to the design and construction of engines, cars, buildings or machines

English noun 1 official language of Britain, Ireland, Australia, New Zealand, South Africa, Canada, the US and several other countries 2 **the English** the people of England ▷ adjective 3 relating to England

Englishman Englishmen noun a man from England > **Englishwoman** noun

engrave verb 1 to carve (a design) onto a hard surface > **engraver** noun

engraving noun print made from an engraved plate

engrossed adjective having all your attention taken up: engrossed in a video game

engulf verb to cover or surround (something) completely

enhance verb to increase the quality, value or attractiveness of (something) > **enhancement** noun increase in quality, value or attractiveness

enigma noun puzzling thing or person

enigmatic adjective mysterious, puzzling or difficult to understand > **enigmatically** adverb

enjoy verb 1 to take joy in (something) 2 to experience (something)

enjoyable adjective giving pleasure or satisfaction

enjoyment noun pleasure or satisfaction from doing something enjoyable

enlarge verb 1 to make (something) larger 2 (followed by on) to speak or write about (a subject) in greater detail

enlargement noun 1 making something bigger 2 something, especially a photograph, that has been made bigger

enlighten verb to give information to (someone) > **enlightening** adjective: an enlightening talk > **enlightenment** noun

enlightened adjective well informed and willing to consider different opinions

enlist verb 1 to enter the armed forces 2 to obtain support or help from (someone)

enliven verb to make (something) lively or cheerful

en masse [on mass] adverb (French) in a group, all together

enormity enormities noun 1 great wickedness 2 gross offence 3 (informal) great size

enormous adjective very big, vast > **enormously** adverb very

enough adjective 1 as much or as many as necessary ▷ noun 2 sufficient quantity ▷ adverb

3 sufficiently **4** fairly or quite: *That's a common enough experience*

enquire *verb* to seek information or ask (about)

enquiry *noun* **1** question **2** investigation

enrage *verb* to make (someone) very angry > **enraged** *adjective* very angry

enrich *verb* to improve the quality of (something) > **enriched** *adjective* improved in quality > **enrichment** *noun*: *the enrichment of society*

enrol enrols, enrolling, enrolled *verb* (to cause) to become a member > **enrolment** *noun* act of enrolling

en route *adverb* (French) on the way

ensconced *adjective* settled firmly or comfortably

ensemble [on-**som**-bl] *noun* **1** all the parts of something taken together **2** company of actors or musicians **3** (*Music*) group of musicians playing together

enshrine *verb* to cherish or treasure (something)

ensign *noun* **1** naval flag **2** (*US*) naval officer

ensue ensues, ensuing, ensued *verb* to come next or result > **ensuing** *adjective* following or resulting

ensure *verb* to make certain or sure (that something happens)

entangled *adjective* involved: *entangled in international politics*

enter *verb* **1** to come or go into (a place) **2** to join (an organization) **3** to become involved in or take part in (a competition or examination) **4** to record (an item) in a journal etc

enterprise *noun* **1** company or firm **2** bold or difficult undertaking > **enterprising** *adjective* full of boldness and initiative

entertain *verb* **1** to amuse (people) **2** to receive (people) as guests > **entertainer** *noun* person who amuses audiences, e.g. a comedian or singer > **entertaining** *adjective* amusing > **entertainment** *noun* anything that people watch for pleasure, e.g. shows and films

enthral enthrals, enthralling, enthralled [en-**thrawl**] *verb* to hold the attention of (someone) > **enthralling** *adjective* fascinating

enthuse *verb* to show enthusiasm

enthusiasm *noun* ardent interest, eagerness

enthusiastic *adjective* showing great excitement, eagerness or approval > **enthusiastically** *adverb*

entice *verb* to tempt (someone) to do something

enticing *adjective* extremely attractive and tempting

entire *adjective* including every detail, part or aspect of something > **entirely** *adverb* wholly and completely > **entirety** *noun*: *this message will now be repeated in its entirety*

entitle *verb* to give a right to (someone) > **entitlement** *noun*: *They lose their entitlement to benefit when they start work*

entity entities *noun* separate distinct thing

entourage [on-toor-ahzh] *noun* group of people who follow or

a
b
c
d
e
f
g
h
i
j
k
l
m
n
o
p
q
r
s
t
u
v
w
x
y
z

travel with a famous or important person

entrails plural noun **1** intestines **2** innermost parts of something

entrance¹ noun **1** way into a place **2** act of entering **3** right of entering

entrance² verb **1** to delight (someone) **2** to put (someone) into a trance > **entrancing** adjective fascinating

entrant noun person who enters a university, contest, etc

entrenched adjective (of a belief, custom or power) firmly established

entrepreneur noun business person who attempts to make a profit by risk and initiative > **entrepreneurial** adjective: his entrepreneurial spirit

entrust verb to put (something) into the care or protection of (someone)

entry entries noun **1** entrance, way in **2** entering **3** item entered in a journal etc

envelop verb to wrap (something) up, enclose (something)

envelope noun folded gummed paper cover for a letter

enviable adjective arousing envy, fortunate

envious adjective full of envy > **enviously** adverb

environment [en-**vire**-on-ment] noun external conditions and surroundings in which people, animals, or plants live > **environmental** adjective: environmental hazards such as wind and sun > **environmentally** adverb: environmentally friendly goods

WORD TIP
There is an n before the m in environment

environmentalist noun person concerned with the protection of the natural environment

envisage verb to conceive of (something) as a possibility

envoy noun **1** messenger **2** diplomat ranking below an ambassador

envy envies, envying, envied noun **1** feeling of discontent aroused by another's good fortune ▷ verb **2** to grudge (someone) his or her good fortune, success, or qualities

enzyme noun a chemical substance, usually a protein, produced by cells in the body

ephemeral adjective short-lived

epic noun **1** long poem, book or film about heroic events or actions ▷ adjective **2** very impressive or ambitious

epidemic noun **1** widespread occurrence of a disease **2** rapid spread of something

epigram noun short witty remark or poem

epigraph noun **1** quotation at the start of a book **2** inscription

epilepsy noun disorder of the nervous system causing loss of consciousness and sometimes convulsions > **epileptic** adjective **1** of or having epilepsy ▷ noun **2** person who has epilepsy

episode noun **1** incident in a series of incidents **2** section of a serialized book, television programme, etc

epistle noun letter, especially of an apostle

epitaph noun commemorative inscription on a tomb

epithet noun descriptive word or name

epitome [ip-**pit**-a-mee] noun typical example

> **WORD TIP**
> Do not use *epitome* to mean 'the peak of something'. It means 'the most typical example of something'

epoch [**ee**-pok] noun long period of time

eponymous [ip-**pon**-im-uss] adjective after whom a book, play, etc is named: *the eponymous hero of 'Eric the Viking'*

equal equals, equalling, equalled adjective 1 identical in size, quantity, degree, etc 2 having identical rights or status 3 evenly balanced 4 (followed by to) having the necessary ability (for) ▷ noun 5 person or thing equal to another ▷ verb 6 to be equal to (something) > **equality** noun state of being equal > **equally** adverb

equate verb to make or regard (something) as equivalent to something else: *You can't equate lives with money*

equation noun [MATHS] mathematical statement that two expressions are equal

equator noun imaginary circle round the earth, lying halfway between the North and South poles > **equatorial** adjective near or at the equator

equestrian adjective relating to horses and riding

equilateral adjective [MATHS] (of a triangle) having equal sides

equilibrium noun steadiness or stability

equine adjective relating to horses

equinox noun time of year when day and night are of equal length

equip equips, equipping, equipped verb to provide (someone or something) with supplies, components, etc

equipment noun set of tools or devices used for a particular purpose; apparatus

equitable adjective fair and reasonable

equity noun fairness

equivalent adjective 1 equal in use, size, value or effect ▷ noun 2 something that has the same use, size, value or effect as something else > **equivalence** noun state of being equivalent

era noun period of time considered as distinctive

eradicate verb to destroy (something) completely > **eradication** noun: *the eradication of corruption*

erase verb to remove (something) > **eraser** noun object for erasing something written

erect verb 1 to build (something) ▷ adjective 2 in a straight and upright position; vertical > **erection** noun 1 process of erecting something 2 something that has been erected 3 stiff swollen penis in an upright position

ermine noun expensive white fur

erode verb to wear (something) away

erosion noun [GEOGRAPHY] gradual wearing away and destruction of something: *soil erosion*

erotic adjective involving or arousing sexual desire > **erotically** adverb

err verb to make a mistake

errand noun short trip to do something for someone

erratic adjective irregular or unpredictable > **erratically** adverb

erroneous adjective incorrect, mistaken > **erroneously** adverb

error noun mistake, inaccuracy or misjudgment

erudite adjective having great academic knowledge

erupt verb 1 (of a volcano) to throw out a lot of hot lava and ash suddenly and violently 2 to burst forth suddenly and violently > **eruption** noun: the volcanic eruption of Tambora

escalate verb to increase in extent or intensity

escalator noun moving staircase

escapade noun mischievous adventure

escape verb 1 to get free of (someone or something) 2 to avoid (something unpleasant or difficult): escape attention 3 (of a gas, liquid, etc) to leak gradually > noun 4 act of escaping 5 means of relaxation

escapee noun person who has escaped

escapism noun taking refuge in fantasy to avoid unpleasant reality > **escapist** adjective: escapist fantasy

eschew [iss-**chew**] verb to avoid or keep away from (something)

escort noun 1 people or vehicles accompanying another person for protection or as an honour 2 person who accompanies a person of the opposite sex to a social event > verb 3 to act as an escort to (someone)

Eskimo Eskimos noun (offensive) a name that was formerly used for the Inuit people and their language

especially adverb particularly

espionage [ess-pyon-ahzh] noun spying

espouse verb to adopt or give support to (a cause etc)

espresso noun strong coffee made by forcing steam or boiling water through ground coffee beans

> **WORD TIP**
> The second letter of espresso is s and not x

essay noun 1 short literary composition 2 short piece of writing on a subject done as an exercise by a student

essence noun 1 most important feature of a thing which gives it its identity 2 concentrated liquid used to flavour food

essential adjective 1 vitally important 2 basic or fundamental > noun 3 something fundamental or indispensable > **essentially** adverb fundamentally

establish verb 1 to set (something) up on a permanent basis 2 to make (oneself) secure or permanent in a certain place, job, etc 3 to prove (a fact) > **established** adjective: the established names of Paris fashion

establishment noun 1 act of establishing 2 commercial or other business institution 3 the **Establishment** group of people having authority within a society

estate noun 1 large area of privately owned land in the country and all the property on it **2** large area of property development, especially of new houses or factories **3** property of a deceased person

estate agent noun person who works for a company that sells houses and land

esteem noun **1** high regard ▷ verb **2** to think highly of (someone or something) > **esteemed** adjective greatly admired and respected

estimate verb **1** MATHS to calculate (an amount or quantity) roughly **2** to form an opinion about (something) ▷ noun **3** approximate calculation **4** statement from a workman etc of the likely charge for a job **5** opinion

estimation noun considered opinion

estranged adjective no longer living with your husband or wife

estrogen noun female sex hormone that regulates the reproductive cycle

estuary estuaries noun GEOGRAPHY mouth of a river

etc abbreviation et cetera

et cetera [et **set**-ra] phrase (Latin) **1** and the rest; and others **2** or the like

> **WORD TIP**
> As etc means 'and the rest', you should not write and etc

etch verb **1** to cut (a design or pattern) on a surface by using acid or a sharp tool **2** to imprint (something) vividly onto someone's mind > **etched** adjective having a design made by etching

etching noun picture printed from a metal plate that has had a design cut into it

eternal adjective lasting forever, or seeming to last forever > **eternally** adverb

eternity eternities noun **1** infinite time **2** timeless existence after death **3** period of time that seems to go on forever

ether noun colourless sweet-smelling liquid used as an anaesthetic

ethereal [eth-**eer**-ee-al] adjective extremely delicate

ethical adjective in agreement with accepted principles of behaviour that are thought to be right > **ethically** adverb

ethics noun **1** code of behaviour ▷ plural noun **2** study of morals

Ethiopian [eeth-ee-**oh**-pee-an] adjective **1** belonging to or relating to Ethiopia ▷ noun **2** someone from Ethiopia

ethnic adjective **1** relating to a people or group that shares a culture, religion, or language **2** belonging or relating to such a group, especially one that is a minority group in a particular place > **ethnically** adverb

ethos [**eeth**-oss] noun distinctive spirit and attitudes of a people, culture, etc

etiquette noun conventional code of conduct

etymology noun study of the sources and development of words

EU abbreviation European Union

eucalyptus or **eucalypt** eucalyptuses or eucalypts noun tree, mainly grown in Australia, that provides timber, gum, and medicinal oil from the leaves

Eucharist [**yew**-kar-ist] noun religious ceremony in which

Christians remember and celebrate Christ's last meal with his disciples

eunuch *noun* castrated man, especially (formerly) a guard in a harem

euphemism *noun* inoffensive word or phrase substituted for one considered offensive or upsetting > **euphemistic** *adjective*: *a euphemistic way of saying that someone has been lying* > **euphemistically** *adverb*

euphoria *noun* sense of elation > **euphoric** *adjective* intensely happy and excited

euro euros *noun* unit of the single currency of the European Union

Europe *noun* second smallest continent, having Asia to the east, the Arctic to the north, the Atlantic to the west, and the Mediterranean and Africa to the south

European *noun* 1 someone from Europe ▷ *adjective* 2 of or relating to Europe

European Union *noun* economic and political association of a number of European nations

euthanasia *noun* act of killing someone painlessly, especially to relieve his or her suffering

evacuate *verb* 1 to send (someone) away from a place of danger 2 to empty (a place) > **evacuation** *noun*: *the evacuation of the sick and wounded* > **evacuee** *noun* person who has been sent away from a place of danger

evade *verb* 1 to get away from or avoid (a problem or question) 2 to elude (someone or something)

evaluate *verb* to find or judge the value of (something)

> **evaluation** *noun* assessing the strengths and weaknesses of something

evangelical *adjective* of certain Protestant sects which maintain the doctrine of salvation by faith

evangelist *noun* travelling preacher > **evangelism** *noun* teaching and spreading of the Christian gospel > **evangelize** *verb* to preach the gospel

evaporate *verb* SCIENCE to change from a liquid or solid to a vapour > **evaporation** *noun*: *the evaporation of the sweat on the skin*

evasion *noun* deliberately avoiding doing something: *evasion of arrest*

evasive *adjective* deliberately trying to avoid talking about or doing something

eve *noun* 1 evening or day before some special event 2 period immediately before an event

even *adjective* 1 flat or smooth 2 (followed by with) on the same level (as) 3 equally balanced 4 divisible by two ▷ *adverb* 5 equally 6 simply 7 nevertheless > **evenly** *adverb*

evening *noun* 1 end of the day or early part of the night ▷ *adjective* 2 of or in the evening

event *noun* 1 anything that takes place; happening 2 planned and organized occasion 3 contest in a sporting programme

eventful *adjective* full of exciting incidents

eventual *adjective* ultimate

eventuality eventualities *noun* possible event

eventually *adverb* at the end of a situation or process

ever adverb 1 at any time 2 always

evergreen noun, adjective (tree or shrub) having leaves throughout the year

everlasting adjective never coming to an end

every adjective 1 each without exception 2 all possible

everybody pronoun every person

everyday adjective usual or ordinary

everyone pronoun every person

everything pronoun 1 all or the whole of something 2 the most important thing: *When I was 20, friends were everything to me*

everywhere adverb in all places

evict verb to legally expel (someone) from his or her home > **eviction** noun: *They were facing eviction*

evidence noun 1 reason for belief 2 matter produced before a law court to prove or disprove a point 3 sign, indication 4 **in evidence** conspicuous

evident adjective easily seen or understood > **evidently** adverb

evil noun 1 wickedness 2 wicked deed ▷ adjective 3 harmful 4 morally bad 5 very unpleasant

evoke verb to call or summon up (a memory, feeling, etc)

evolution noun gradual change in the characteristics of living things over successive generations, especially to a more complex form > **evolutionary** adjective: *an evolutionary process*

evolve verb 1 to develop gradually 2 (of an animal or plant species) to undergo evolution

ewe noun female sheep

ex- prefix former: *ex-wife*

exacerbate [ig-**zass**-er-bate] verb to make (pain, emotion or a situation) worse

exact adjective 1 correct and complete in every detail 2 precise, as opposed to approximate ▷ verb 3 to demand (something) from someone > **exactly** adverb

exaggerate verb 1 to regard or represent (something) as greater than is true 2 to make (something) greater or more noticeable > **exaggeration** noun act of exaggerating

exalted adjective very important

exam noun short for **examination**

examination noun 1 examining 2 test of a candidate's knowledge or skill

examine verb 1 to look at (something or someone) closely 2 to test the knowledge of (someone) 3 to ask questions of (someone)

examiner noun person who sets or marks an examination

example noun 1 specimen typical of its group; sample 2 person or thing worthy of imitation 3 punishment regarded as a warning to others

exasperate verb to cause great irritation to (someone) > **exasperating** adjective infuriating > **exasperation** noun: *He clenched his fist in exasperation*

excavate verb 1 to remove earth from the ground by digging 2 to dig up (buried objects) from a piece of land to learn about the past > **excavation** noun: *the excavation of a bronze-age boat*

exceed verb 1 to be greater than (something) 2 to go beyond (a limit) > **exceedingly** adverb very

excel excels, excelling, excelled *verb* to be outstandingly good at something

Excellency Excellencies *noun* title used to address a high-ranking official, such as an ambassador

excellent *adjective* exceptionally good; superb > **excellence** *noun*: *the top award for excellence*

except *preposition* **1** (sometimes followed by *for*) other than, not including **2** **except that** but for the fact that ▷ *verb* **3** not to include > **exception** *noun* **1** excepting **2** thing that is excluded from or does not conform to the general rule > **exceptional** *adjective* **1** not ordinary **2** much above the average > **exceptionally** *adverb*

excerpt *noun* passage taken from a book, speech, etc

excess *noun* **1** state or act of exceeding the permitted limits **2** immoderate amount **3** amount by which a thing exceeds the permitted limits

excessive *adjective* too great in amount or degree > **excessively** *adverb* too

exchange *verb* **1** to give or receive (something) in return for something else ▷ *noun* **2** act of exchanging **3** thing given or received in place of another **4** centre in which telephone lines are interconnected **5** (*Finance*) place where securities or commodities are traded **6** transfer of sums of money of equal value between different currencies

Exchequer *noun* (*Brit*) government department in charge of state money

excise *noun* **1** tax on goods produced for the home market ▷ *verb* **2** to cut (something) out or away

excitable *adjective* easily excited

excite *verb* **1** to arouse (someone) to strong emotion; thrill **2** to arouse or evoke (an emotion) > **excited** *adjective* happy and unable to relax > **excitedly** *adverb* > **excitement** *noun* state of being excited > **exciting** *adjective*: *The race is very exciting*

exclaim *verb* to speak suddenly, cry out

exclamation *noun* (ENGLISH) word or phrase spoken suddenly to express a strong feeling

exclamation mark *noun* punctuation mark (!) used after exclamations

exclude *verb* **1** to keep or leave (someone) out **2** to leave (something) out of consideration > **exclusion** *noun*: *women's exclusion from political power*

exclusive *adjective* **1** excluding everything else **2** not shared **3** catering for a privileged minority ▷ *noun* **4** story reported in only one newspaper > **exclusively** *adverb*

excrement *noun* waste matter discharged from the body

excrete *verb* to discharge (waste matter) from the body > **excretion** *noun*: *the excretion of this drug from the body*

excruciating *adjective* **1** agonizing **2** hard to bear > **excruciatingly** *adverb*

excursion *noun* short journey, especially for pleasure

excuse *noun* **1** explanation offered to justify a fault etc ▷ *verb* **2** to put forward a reason or justification for (a fault etc) **3** to forgive (a person) or overlook (a fault etc) **4** to free (someone) from a duty or responsibility **5** to allow (someone) to leave

execute verb **1** to kill (someone) as a punishment for a crime **2** to carry out or perform (a plan or an action) ▷ **execution** noun: *execution by lethal injection* ▷ **executioner** noun person who executes criminals

executive noun **1** person employed by a company at a senior level **2** (in an organization) committee having authority to make decisions and ensure that they are carried out ▷ adjective **3** concerned with making important decisions and ensuring that they are carried out

executor noun person appointed to perform the instructions of a will

exemplary adjective **1** being a good example **2** serving as a warning

exemplify exemplifies, exemplifying, exemplified verb to be a typical example of (something)

exempt adjective **1** not subject to an obligation or rule ▷ verb **2** to release (someone) from an obligation or rule ▷ **exemption** noun being excused from an obligation or rule

exercise noun **1** [PE] activity to train the body or mind **2** set of movements or tasks designed to improve or test a person's ability **3** performance of a function ▷ verb **4** to make use of (something):

to exercise your rights **5** to take exercise or perform exercises

exert verb **1** to use (influence, authority, etc) forcefully or effectively **2** **exert yourself** to make a special effort ▷ **exertion** noun vigorous physical effort or exercise

exhale verb to breathe out

exhaust verb **1** to tire (someone) out **2** to use up (a supply of something) **3** to discuss (a subject) thoroughly ▷ noun **4** gases ejected from an engine as waste products **5** pipe through which an engine's exhaust fumes pass ▷ **exhaustion** noun **1** extreme tiredness **2** exhausting

exhaustive adjective thorough and complete ▷ **exhaustively** adverb

exhibit verb **1** to display (things) to the public **2** to show (a quality or feeling) ▷ noun **3** object exhibited to the public

exhibition noun [ART] **1** public display of art, skills, etc **2** exhibiting

exhibitor noun person whose work is being shown in an exhibition

exhilarating adjective exciting and thrilling

exile noun **1** prolonged, usually enforced, absence from your country **2** person banished or living away from his or her country ▷ verb **3** to expel (someone) from his or her country

exist verb **1** to have being or reality **2** to live

existence noun **1** state of being or existing **2** way of living or being: *an idyllic existence*

a b c d e f g h i j k l m n o p q r s t u v w x y z

exit noun 1 way out 2 going out 3 actor's going off stage ▷ verb 4 to go out 5 to go offstage: used as a stage direction

exodus [eks-so-duss] noun departure of a large number of people

exotic adjective 1 having a strange allure or beauty 2 originating in a foreign country

expand verb 1 to become larger or make (something) larger 2 (followed by on) to give more details about (something) > **expansion** noun: the rapid expansion of private health insurance

expanse noun uninterrupted wide area

expansive adjective 1 wide or extensive 2 friendly and talkative

expatriate [eks-**pat**-ree-it] adjective 1 living outside your native country ▷ noun 2 person living outside his or her native country

expect verb 1 to regard (something) as probable 2 to look forward to or await (someone or something) 3 to require (something) as an obligation

expectancy noun feeling of anticipation

expectant adjective 1 expecting or hopeful 2 pregnant > **expectantly** adverb

expectation noun 1 act or state of expecting 2 something looked forward to 3 attitude of anticipation or hope

expedient noun 1 something that achieves a particular purpose ▷ adjective 2 suitable to the circumstances, appropriate > **expediency** noun doing what

is convenient rather than what is morally right

expedition noun 1 organized journey, especially for exploration 2 people and equipment comprising an expedition 3 pleasure trip or excursion > **expeditionary** adjective relating to an expedition, especially a military one

expel expels, expelling, expelled verb 1 to force out (a gas or liquid) from a place 2 to dismiss (someone) from a school etc permanently

expend verb to spend or use up (energy, time or money)

expendable adjective no longer useful or necessary, and therefore able to be got rid of

expenditure noun 1 something expended, especially money 2 amount expended

expense noun 1 cost 2 (cause of) spending 3 **expenses** money spent while doing something connected with work and paid back by your employer

expensive adjective high-priced > **expensively** adverb

experience noun 1 direct personal participation 2 particular incident, feeling, etc that a person has undergone 3 accumulated knowledge ▷ verb 4 to participate in or undergo (something) 5 to be affected by (an emotion)

experiment noun 1 test to provide evidence to prove or disprove a theory 2 attempt at something new ▷ verb 3 to carry out an experiment > **experimental** adjective: an experimental air-conditioning

system > **experimentally**
adverb > **experimentation**
noun: the ethical aspects of animal
experimentation

expert noun 1 person with
extensive skill or knowledge
in a particular field; authority
▷ adjective 2 skilful or
knowledgeable > **expertly** adverb

expertise [eks-per-**teez**] noun
special skill or knowledge

expire verb 1 to finish or run out
2 (literary) to die > **expiry** noun end,
especially of a contract period

explain verb 1 to make
(something) clear and intelligible
2 to account for (something)
> **explanation** noun: There was no
apparent explanation for the crash
> **explanatory** adjective: a series of
explanatory notes

explicit adjective 1 precisely and
clearly expressed 2 shown in
realistic detail > **explicitly** adverb:
She has been talking very explicitly
about AIDS to these groups

explode verb 1 to burst with
great violence, blow up 2 to
react suddenly with emotion 3 to
increase rapidly

exploit verb 1 to take advantage
of (someone) for your own
purposes 2 to make the best use
of (something) ▷ noun 3 notable
feat or deed > **exploitation** noun:
the exploitation of the famine by local
politicians

explore verb 1 to think carefully
about (an idea) 2 to travel into
(unfamiliar regions), especially for
scientific purposes > **exploration**
noun act of exploring
> **exploratory** adjective:
exploratory surgery > **explorer**

noun person who explores
unfamiliar regions

explosion noun sudden violent
burst of energy, for example one
caused by a bomb

explosive adjective 1 tending to
explode ▷ noun 2 substance that
causes explosions

exponent noun 1 person who
advocates an idea, cause, etc
2 skilful performer, especially a
musician

export noun 1 selling or shipping
of goods to a foreign country
2 product shipped or sold to a
foreign country ▷ verb 3 to sell or
ship (goods) to a foreign country
> **exporter** noun country, firm or
person that sells or ships goods to
a foreign country

expose verb 1 to uncover or reveal
(something) 2 to make (someone)
vulnerable, leave (someone)
unprotected 3 to subject (a
photographic film) to light

exposition noun detailed
explanation of a particular subject

exposure noun 1 exposing 2 lack
of shelter from the weather,
especially the cold 3 appearance
before the public, as on television

express verb 1 to put (an idea or
feeling) into words 2 to show
(an emotion) 3 to indicate (a
quantity) by a symbol or formula
▷ adjective 4 of or for rapid
transportation of people, mail,
etc ▷ noun 5 fast train or bus
stopping at only a few stations
▷ adverb 6 by express delivery

expression noun 1 ENGLISH
expressing 2 word or phrase
3 showing or communication
of emotion 4 look on the face

that indicates mood **5** (Maths) variable, function, or some combination of these

expressive adjective **1** showing feelings clearly **2** full of expression

expressway noun (Aust) road designed for fast-moving traffic

expulsion noun act of officially banning someone from a place or institution: *the high number of school expulsions*

exquisite adjective **1** of extreme beauty or delicacy **2** intense in feeling

extend verb **1** to continue and stretch into the distance **2** to draw (something) out, stretch (something) **3** to last for a certain time **4** to increase in size or scope **5** to offer (something): *extend your sympathy* ▷ **extension** noun **1** room or rooms added to an existing building **2** additional telephone connected to the same line as another **3** extending

extensive adjective having a large extent or widespread ▷ **extensively** adverb: *to travel extensively*

extent noun range over which something extends; area

exterior noun **1** part or surface on the outside **2** outward appearance ▷ adjective **3** of, on or coming from the outside

exterminate verb to destroy (animals or people) completely ▷ **extermination** noun: *the extermination of hundreds of thousands of their countrymen*

external adjective of, situated on or coming from the outside ▷ **externally** adverb: *Vitamins must be applied externally to the skin*

extinct adjective **1** having died out **2** (of a volcano) no longer liable to erupt ▷ **extinction** noun: *to save a species from extinction*

extinguish verb to put out (a fire or light)

extortionate adjective (of prices) excessive

extra adjective **1** more than is usual, expected or needed; additional ▷ noun **2** additional person or thing **3** something for which an additional charge is made **4** (Films) actor hired for crowd scenes ▷ adverb **5** unusually or exceptionally

extra- prefix outside or beyond an area or scope: *extrasensory*; *extraterritorial*

extract verb **1** to take or get (something) out, often by force **2** to get (information) from someone with difficulty ▷ noun **3** something extracted, such as a passage from a book etc **4** preparation containing the concentrated essence of a substance: *beef extract* ▷ **extraction** noun **1** country or people that your family originally comes from: *of Australian extraction* **2** process of taking or getting something out of a place

extraordinary adjective unusual or surprising ▷ **extraordinarily** adverb

extravagant adjective **1** spending money excessively **2** going beyond reasonable limits ▷ **extravagance** noun excessive spending ▷ **extravagantly** adverb

extravaganza noun elaborate and lavish entertainment, display, etc

extreme adjective **1** of a high or the highest degree or intensity

2 severe **3** immoderate **4** farthest or outermost ▷ *noun* **5** either of the two limits of a scale or range ▷ *adverb* very

extremist *noun* **1** person who favours immoderate methods ▷ *adjective* **2** holding extreme opinions > **extremism** *noun*: right-wing extremism

extremity extremities *noun* **1** farthest point **2** extremities hands and feet or fingers and toes

extricate *verb* to free (someone) from complication or difficulty

extrovert *noun* an active, lively and sociable person

exuberant *adjective* high-spirited > **exuberance** *noun*: a burst of exuberance > **exuberantly** *adverb*

exude *verb* to make (something) apparent by mood or behaviour: exude confidence

eye eyes, eyeing or eying, eyed *noun* **1** organ of sight **2** ability to judge or appreciate: a good eye for detail **3** hole at one end of a sewing needle through which you pass thread ▷ *verb* **4** to look at (something) carefully or warily

eyeball *noun* ball-shaped part of the eye

eyebrow *noun* line of hair on the bony ridge above the eye

eyelash *noun* short hair that grows out from the eyelid

eyelid *noun* fold of skin that covers the eye when it is closed

eyesight *noun* ability to see

eyesore *noun* ugly object

eyewitness *noun* person who was present at an event and can describe what happened

eyrie *noun* nest of an eagle

f

fable *noun* **1** story with a moral **2** false or fictitious account **3** legend

fabled *adjective* made famous in legend

fabric *noun* **1** cloth **2** walls, roof and basic structure of a building **3** structure, laws and customs of society

fabricate *verb* **1** to make up (a story or lie) **2** to make or build (something) > **fabrication** *noun*: The story is a complete fabrication

fabulous *adjective* **1** (informal) wonderful or very impressive **2** astounding **3** not real but told of in stories and legends

facade [fas-**sahd**] *noun* **1** front of a building **2** (false) outward appearance

face *noun* **1** front of the head **2** facial expression **3** distorted expression **4** outward appearance **5** front or side, especially the most important side **6** dial of a clock **7** dignity, self-respect ▷ *verb* **8** to be opposite (something or someone) **9** to look or turn towards (something or someone) **10** to be confronted by (something) > **face up to** *verb* to accept (an unpleasant fact or reality)

faceless *adjective* impersonal, anonymous

face-lift noun **1** operation to tighten facial skin, to remove wrinkles **2** improvement, new look

facet noun **1** aspect **2** cut surface of a precious stone

facetious [fas-**see**-shuss] adjective witty or amusing but in a rather silly or inappropriate way

facial adjective **1** of the face ▷ noun **2** beauty treatment for the face

facilitate verb to make (something) easier

facility facilities noun **1** talent, ability **2** facilities means or equipment for an activity

fact noun **1** event or thing known to have happened or existed **2** provable truth **3** in fact actually or really >**factual** adjective: factual errors >**factually** adverb: It was factually incorrect

faction noun (dissenting) minority group within a larger body

fact of life noun **1** something inescapable **2** facts of life details of sex and reproduction

factor noun **1** something that helps to cause a result **2** (Maths) one of two or more whole numbers that when multiplied together give a given number. For example, 2 and 5 are factors of 10

factory factories noun building or group of buildings where goods are manufactured

faculty faculties noun **1** physical or mental ability **2** department in a university or college

fad noun temporary fashion

fade verb **1** to lose or cause something to lose brightness, colour or strength **2** to vanish slowly

faeces [**fee**-seez] plural noun solid waste matter excreted from a person's or animal's body

fag noun (Brit informal) cigarette

Fahrenheit [**far**-ren-hite] noun a scale of temperature in which the freezing point of water is 32° and the boiling point is 212°

fail verb **1** to be unsuccessful **2** to stop working **3** to be or to judge someone to be below the required standard in a test **4** to disappoint or be useless to (someone) **5** to neglect to do or be unable to do (something) ▷ noun **6** instance of not passing an exam or test **7** without fail **a** regularly **b** definitely

failing noun **1** weak point ▷ preposition **2** in the absence of

failure noun **1** act or instance of failing **2** unsuccessful person or thing **3** someone's failure to do something fact of someone not having done something

faint adjective **1** (of sound, colour or image) not easy to hear or see owing to a lack of volume, brightness or definition **2** dizzy or weak **3** slight ▷ verb **4** to lose consciousness temporarily; to black out or pass out ▷ noun **5** temporary loss of consciousness >**faintly** adverb

fair adjective **1** unbiased, reasonable and just **2** quite large: a fair amount of money **3** quite good: a fair attempt **4** having light coloured hair or pale skin **5** (of weather) fine ▷ noun **6** travelling entertainment with sideshows, rides and amusements **7** exhibition of goods produced by a particular industry ▷ adverb **8** fairly >**fairness** noun

fairground noun open space used for a fair

fairway noun (Golf) smooth area between the tee and the green

fairy fairies noun (in stories) small, supernatural creature with magic powers

fairy tale or **story** noun
1 story about fairies or magic
2 unbelievable story or explanation

faith noun 1 confidence or trust
2 religion

faithful adjective 1 loyal 2 accurate and reliable > **faithfully** adverb
> **faithfulness** noun

fake noun 1 imitation of something meant to trick people into thinking that it is genuine; copy or sham ▷ adjective 2 imitation and not genuine; artificial > noun
3 to pretend to have (an illness, emotion, etc); feign 4 to cause (something not genuine) to appear real or more valuable by fraud

falcon noun small bird of prey that can be trained to hunt other birds or small animals

fall falls, falling, fell, fallen verb 1 to lose balance and tumble towards the ground 2 to drop from a higher to a lower place through the force of gravity 3 to land 4 to go down or decrease in number or quality 5 to pass into a specified condition; become: fall ill 6 (of a soldier) to be killed 7 to occur or happen ▷ noun 8 act of falling
9 thing or amount that falls
10 decrease or reduction in value or number 11 decline in power or influence 12 (US) autumn 13 falls waterfall > **fall down** verb (of an

argument or idea) to fail > **fall for** verb 1 (informal) to fall in love with
2 to be deceived by (a lie or trick)
> **fall out** verb to quarrel; have a disagreement > **fall through** verb (of an arrangement or plan) to fail or be abandoned

fallacy fallacies noun 1 false belief
2 unsound reasoning > **fallacious** adjective: It is a fallacious argument

fallopian tube noun one of two tubes in a woman's or female mammal's body along which the eggs pass from the ovaries to the uterus

fallout noun radioactive particles that fall to the earth after a nuclear explosion

fallow adjective (of land) ploughed but not planted so as to recover and regain fertility

false adjective 1 untrue or incorrect
2 artificial, fake 3 deceptive: false promises > **falsely** adverb
> **falseness** noun: the obvious falseness of their position > **falsity** noun: efforts to establish the truth or falsity of these claims

falsehood noun 1 quality of being untrue 2 lie

falsify falsifies, falsifying, falsified verb to alter fraudulently
> **falsification** noun: deliberate falsification of evidence

falter verb 1 to be hesitant, weak or unsure 2 to lose power momentarily 3 to talk hesitantly
4 to move unsteadily

fame noun state of being widely known or recognized

famed adjective very well-known; famous

familiar adjective 1 well-known
2 too informal and friendly

3 intimate, friendly **4** (followed by *with*) acquainted **> familiarity** *noun* **> familiarize** *verb* to acquaint (someone) fully with a particular subject **> familiarly** *adverb*

family families *noun* **1** group consisting of parents and their children **2** group descended from a common ancestor **3** group of related objects or beings **> adjective 4** suitable for parents and children together **> familial** *adjective*: *social and familial relationships*

family planning *noun* practice of controlling the number of children you have, usually by using contraception

famine *noun* severe shortage of food

famished *adjective* (*informal*) very hungry

famous *adjective* very well-known

famously *adverb* (*old-fashioned*, *informal*) excellently

fan fans, fanning, fanned *noun* **1** (*informal*) enthusiastic follower of a pop star, sport or hobby **2** hand-held or mechanical device used to create a cooling draught **> verb 3** to blow or cool (someone or something) with a fan **> fan out** *verb* to spread out like a fan

fanatic *noun* person who is very extreme in their support for a cause or in their enthusiasm for a particular activity **> fanaticism** *noun*: *the evils of religious fanaticism*

fanatical *adjective* extreme and obsessive in your support or enthusiasm for something **> fanatically** *adverb*

fancy fancies, fancying, fancied; fancier, fanciest *verb*

1 (*informal*) to have a wish for; want **2** (*informal*) to be sexually attracted to **3** to suppose **4** **fancy yourself** (*informal*) to have a high opinion of yourself **> noun 5** sudden irrational liking or desire **6** uncontrolled imagination **> adjective 7** not plain; elaborate

fancy dress *noun* party costume representing a historical figure, animal etc

fanfare *noun* short loud tune played on brass instruments

fang *noun* long pointed tooth

fantail *noun* **1** a pigeon with a large tail that can be opened out like a fan **2** small Australian and New Zealand bird with a fan-shaped tail

fantasize or **fantasise** *verb* to imagine pleasant but unlikely events or situations; daydream

fantastic *adjective* **1** (*informal*) very good **2** unrealistic or absurd **3** extremely large in degree or amount **4** strange and difficult to believe **> fantastically** *adverb*

fantasy fantasies *noun* **1** imagined story or situation; daydream **2** far-fetched notion **3** imagination unrestricted by reality **4** fiction with a large fantasy content

far farther, farthest; further, furthest *adverb* **1** at, to or from a great distance **2** at or to a remote time **3** very much: *far more important* **4** **so far** up to now **> adjective 5** a long way away in space or time **6** further away or more distant

WORD TIP
When you are talking about a physical distance you can use *farther* and *farthest* or *further*

and **furthest**. If you are talking about extra effort or time, use *further* and *furthest*: *a further delay is likely*

farce *noun* **1** humorous play in which ridiculous and unlikely situations occur **2** disorganised and ridiculous or ludicrous situation ▷ **farcical** *adjective* ludicrous ▷ **farcically** *adverb*

fare *noun* **1** charge for a passenger's journey **2** passenger **3** food provided ▷ *verb* **4** to get on (in a particular way): *We fared badly*

Far East *noun* the countries of East Asia, including China, Japan and Malaysia ▷ **Far Eastern** *adjective*

farewell *interjection* **1** goodbye ▷ *noun, adjective* **2** (related to) leaving: *a farewell speech*

far-fetched *adjective* unlikely to be true

farm *noun* **1** area of land together with the buildings on it that forms a unit and is used for growing crops or rearing livestock ▷ *verb* **2** to run a farm by rearing livestock and/or cultivating the land **3** to cultivate (land) **4** to rear (livestock) ▷ **farming** *noun*

farmhouse *noun* the main house on a farm

farmyard *noun* area surrounded by farm buildings

fascia [**fay**-shya] -**ciae** or -**cias** *noun* **1** outer surface of a dashboard **2** flat surface above a shop window **3** mobile phone casing with spaces for the buttons

fascinate *verb* **1** to attract and interest (someone) strongly **2** to make motionless from fear or awe ▷ **fascinating**

adjective: *a fascinating place to visit* ▷ **fascination** *noun*: *her fascination with politics*

fascism [**fash**-iz-zum] *noun* extreme right-wing political ideology or system of government with a powerful dictator and state control of most activities. Nationalism is encouraged and political opposition not allowed ▷ **fascist** *adjective, noun*

fashion *noun* **1** style of dress or way of behaving that is popular at a particular time; vogue **2** way something happens or is done ▷ *verb* **3** to make or shape (something): *a curtain I had fashioned into a skirt*

fashionable *adjective* currently popular; in vogue ▷ **fashionably** *adverb*

fast *adjective* **1** (capable of) acting or moving quickly **2** done in or lasting a short time **3** (of a clock or watch) showing a time later than the correct time ▷ *adverb* **4** quickly **5** soundly, deeply: *fast asleep* **6** tightly and firmly ▷ *adjective* **7** (of colour or dye) not likely to run when wet ▷ *verb* **8** to go without food, especially for religious reasons ▷ *noun* **9** period of fasting

fasten *verb* **1** to close (something), do (something) up or fix (something) in place **2** to close or do up

fast food *noun* hot food, such as hamburgers, that is prepared and served quickly after you have ordered it

fastidious *adjective* **1** very fussy about details **2** excessively concerned with cleanliness

fast-track adjective **1** taking the quickest but most competitive route to success: fast-track executives ▷ verb **2** to speed up the progress of (a project or person)

fat fatter, fattest; fats adjective **1** carrying too much weight on your body; overweight **2** (of meat) containing a lot of fat **3** thick ▷ noun **4** extra flesh on the body **5** greasy solid or liquid substance obtained from animals or plants and often used in cooking > **fatness** noun > **fatty** adjective containing fat

fatal adjective **1** causing death **2** very damaging; disastrous > **fatally** adverb

fatality fatalities noun death caused by an accident or disaster

fate noun **1** power supposed by some to control events; destiny or providence **2** fortune that awaits a person or thing

fateful adjective having an important, often disastrous, effect

father noun **1** male parent **2** man who starts, creates or invents something: the father of Italian painting **3 Father** a God **b** form of address for a priest in some Christian churches ▷ verb **4** to be the father of (a child) > **fatherhood** noun: the joys of fatherhood > **fatherly** adjective: a few words of fatherly advice

father-in-law fathers-in-law noun father of your husband or wife

fathom noun **1** unit of length, used in navigation, equal to six feet (1.83 metres) ▷ verb **2** to understand

fatigue fatigues, fatiguing, fatigued [fat-**eeg**] noun **1** extreme physical or mental tiredness **2** weakening of a material due to stress ▷ verb **3** to tire out

fault noun **1** responsibility for something wrong **2** weakness, defect or flaw **3** mistake or error **4** (Geology) large crack in rock caused by movement of the earth's crust **5** (Tennis, Squash etc) incorrect and invalid serve ▷ verb **6** to criticize > **faultless** adjective: an almost faultless performance > **faulty** adjective: faulty wiring

favour noun **1** approving attitude **2** act of goodwill or generosity **3 in favour of a** feeling approval for **b** to the benefit of **4 in someone's favour** of help or advantage to someone ▷ verb **5** to prefer (someone or something) **6** to support or recommend (something)

favourable adjective **1** encouraging or advantageous: a favourable review **2** useful or beneficial: favourable weather conditions **3** giving consent: They got a favourable response from the bank > **favourably** adverb

favourite adjective **1** most liked ▷ noun **2** preferred person or thing **3** (Sport) competitor expected to win

favouritism noun practice of giving special treatment to a person or group

fawn adjective **1** light yellowish-brown ▷ noun **2** young deer ▷ verb **3 fawn on** to seek the approval of (someone) by flattering them

fax noun **1** exact copy of a document sent electronically along a telephone line **2** electronic system for sending exact copies of documents by telephone ▷ *verb* **3** to send (a document) by this system

fear *noun* **1** distress or alarm caused by approaching danger or pain **2** thought that something undesirable or unpleasant might happen ▷ *verb* **3** to be afraid of (something or someone) **4** to be afraid (that something may happen) > **fear for** *verb* to feel anxious about the safety of (someone or something)

fearful *adjective* **1** feeling fear **2** (*informal*) very unpleasant > **fearfully** *adverb*

fearsome *adjective* terrible or frightening

feasible *adjective* able to be done; possible > **feasibility** *noun*: *the feasibility of constructing a new bypass* > **feasibly** *adverb*

feast *noun* **1** large and special meal for a lot of people **2** annual religious celebration ▷ *verb* **3** to eat a feast **4 feast on** to eat a large amount of (something)

feat *noun* impressive and difficult achievement

feather *noun* one of the light fluffy things covering a bird's body > **feathered** *adjective* > **feathery** *adjective*

feature *noun* **1** interesting or important part or characteristic of something **2** part of your face, such as your eyes or nose **3** special article or programme dealing with a particular subject **4** main film in a cinema programme ▷ *verb* **5** to have (someone or something) as a feature or to

be a feature in (something) > **featureless** *adjective*: *a featureless landscape*

February *noun* second month of the year

fed *verb* past of **feed**

federal *adjective* relating to a system of government in which a group of states is controlled by a central government, but each state has its own local powers

federation *noun* group of organizations or states that have joined together for a common purpose

fed up *adjective* (*informal*) bored or dissatisfied

fee *noun* charge or payment for a job, service or activity

feeble *adjective* **1** lacking physical or mental power **2** unconvincing

feed feeds, feeding, fed *verb* **1** to give food to (a person or animal) **2** to give (something) to (a person or animal) as food **3** to eat **4** to supply (what is needed): *The information was fed into a computer database* ▷ *noun* **5** act of feeding **6** food, especially for babies or animals

feedback *noun* **1** comments and information about the quality or success of something **2** condition in which some of the power, sound or information produced by electronic equipment goes back into it

feel feels, feeling, felt *verb* **1** to experience (an emotion, sensation or effect of something) **2** to believe **3** to become aware of (something or someone) by touch **4** to touch (something) **5** (of things) to give the impression of being (cold, hard, soft, etc) **6 feel like** to wish for or want (something) ▷ noun **7** way something feels **8** act of feeling **9** impression **10** instinctive aptitude

feeler noun organ of touch in some animals; antenna

feeling noun **1** emotion or reaction **2** physical sensation **3** ability to experience physical sensations **4** opinion **5** impression **6** sympathy or understanding **7 feelings** emotions or beliefs

feet noun plural of **foot**

feign [fane] verb to pretend to experience (something)

feline adjective **1** belonging or relating to the cat family **2** catlike

fell verb **1** past tense of **fall 2** to cut down (a tree)

fellow noun **1** (old-fashioned) man or boy **2** senior member of a learned society or a university college **3** comrade, associate or person in the same group or condition ▷ adjective **4** (of a person) in the same group or condition: his fellow editors

fellowship noun **1** feeling of friendliness and companionship experienced by those doing something together **2** group with shared aims or interests **3** paid research post in a college or university

felt verb **1** past of **feel** ▷ noun **2** matted fabric made by bonding fibres by pressure

female noun **1** person or animal that belongs to the sex that can have babies or young ▷ adjective **2** concerning or relating to females

feminine adjective **1** having qualities traditionally regarded as suitable for, or typical of, women **2** relating to women **3** belonging to a particular class of nouns, adjectives, pronouns or endings in some languages ▷ **femininity** noun: Pink emphasizes femininity

feminism noun belief that women should have the same rights and opportunities as men ▷ **feminist** noun, adjective

fen noun (Brit) low-lying, flat marshy land

fence noun **1** wooden or wire barrier between two areas of land **2** barrier or hedge for horses to jump over in horse racing or show jumping ▷ verb **3** to surround (an area of land) with a fence **4** to fight with swords as a sport ▷ **fencer** noun

fend verb **fend for yourself** to look after yourself ▷ **fend off** verb to defend yourself against (a verbal or physical attack or attacker)

ferment verb (of wine, beer or fruit) to change chemically, often producing alcohol ▷ **fermentation** noun: chemicals produced during fermentation

fern noun plant with long feathery leaves and no flowers

ferocious adjective violent and fierce ▷ **ferociously** adverb ▷ **ferocity** noun

ferret noun **1** small, fierce animal related to the weasel and kept for hunting rats and rabbits ▷ verb **2** to search around ▷ **ferret out** verb to find out (information) by searching

ferry ferries, ferrying, ferried noun **1** boat for transporting people and vehicles ▷ *verb* **2** to carry (people or goods) by ferry

fertile *adjective* **1** capable of producing young, crops or vegetation **2** creative: *a fertile mind* ▷ **fertility** *noun*

fertilize or **fertilise** *verb* **1** to cause (an animal or plant) to begin the process of reproduction by supplying sperm or pollen **2** to feed (soil or land) with nutrients ▷ **fertilization** *noun*

fertilizer or **fertiliser** *noun* substance added to the soil to improve plant growth

fervent or **fervid** *adjective* intensely passionate, enthusiastic and sincere ▷ **fervently** *adverb*

fervour *noun* very strong feeling for or belief in something

fester *verb* **1** (of a situation or problem) to grow worse and increasingly hostile **2** (of a wound) to become infected and form pus

festival *noun* **1** organized series of events or performances **2** day or period of celebration

festive *adjective* full of happiness and celebration

festivity *festivities noun* happy celebration

festooned *adjective* **festooned with** adorned with

fetch *verb* **1** to go to get (someone or something) **2** to be sold for (a sum of money)

fetching *adjective* attractive

fete [fate] *noun* **1** outdoor event with competitions, displays and goods for sale ▷ *verb* **2** to honour or entertain (someone) regally

feud *noun* **1** long-term and very bitter quarrel, especially between families ▷ *verb* **2** to carry on a feud

feudalism *noun* social and political system that was common in the Middle Ages in Europe. Under this system, ordinary people were given land and protection by a lord, and in return they worked and fought for him ▷ **feudal** *adjective* relating to or resembling feudalism

fever *noun* **1** (illness causing) high body temperature **2** nervous excitement

feverish *adjective* **1** suffering from fever **2** in a state of nervous excitement ▷ **feverishly** *adverb*

few *adjective, pronoun* **1** not many **2 a few** small number (of) **3** quite a few or a good few several

> **WORD TIP**
> You use *fewer* to talk about things that can be counted: *fewer than five visits*. When you are talking about amounts that can't be counted you should use *less*

fiancé [fee-**on**-say] *noun* man engaged to be married

fiancée [fee-**on**-say] *noun* woman engaged to be married

fiasco *fiascos noun* event or attempt that fails completely, especially in a ridiculous or disorganized way

fib *fibs, fibbing, fibbed noun* **1** small, unimportant lie ▷ *verb* **2** to tell a small lie

fibre *noun* **1** thread that can be spun into yarn **2** part of plants that can be eaten but not digested; it helps food pass quickly through the body ▷ **fibrous** *adjective*: *fibrous material*

fickle adjective changeable, inconstant

fiction noun 1 stories about people and events that have been invented by the author 2 invented story

fiddle verb 1 (often followed by with) to move or touch something restlessly 2 to falsify (accounts) ▷ noun 3 (informal) dishonest action or scheme 4 violin >**fiddler** noun

fiddly fiddlier, fiddliest adjective awkward to do or use

fidelity noun faithfulness

fidget verb 1 to move about restlessly ▷ noun 2 someone who fidgets >**fidgety** adjective

field noun 1 enclosed piece of land where crops are grown or animals are kept 2 marked off area for sports: a hockey field 3 area rich in a specified natural resource: an oil field 4 subject or area of interest; sphere ▷ verb 5 (Sport) to catch and return (a ball) 6 to deal with (a question) successfully

fielder noun (Sport) player whose task is to field the ball

field marshal noun army officer of the highest rank

fieldwork noun study of something in the environment where it naturally lives or occurs, rather than in a class or laboratory

fiend [feend] noun 1 evil spirit 2 cruel or wicked person 3 (informal) person devoted to something: fitness fiend

fierce adjective 1 wild or aggressive 2 intense or strong >**fiercely** adverb >**fierceness** noun

fiery fierier, fieriest adjective 1 consisting of or like fire 2 showing great anger, energy or passion

fifteen adjective, noun the number 15 >**fifteenth** adjective, noun

fifth adjective, noun 1 (coming as) number 5 in a series ▷ noun 2 one of five equal parts

fifty fifties adjective, noun the number 50 >**fiftieth** adjective, noun

fifty-fifty adverb 1 divided equally into two portions ▷ adjective 2 just as likely not to happen as to happen: You've got a fifty-fifty chance of being right

fig noun 1 soft, sweet fruit full of tiny seeds. It grows in hot countries and is often eaten dried 2 tree bearing it

fight fights, fighting, fought verb 1 to take part in a battle, a war, a boxing match or some other form of physical combat 2 to battle against (someone) 3 to struggle to overcome someone or obtain something 4 to carry on (a battle or contest) 5 to make (one's way) somewhere with difficulty ▷ noun 6 situation in which people hit or try to hurt each other 7 determined attempt to prevent or achieve something: the fight for independence >**fighter** noun 1 boxer 2 determined person 3 aircraft designed to destroy other aircraft > **fight off** verb 1 to drive away (an attacker) 2 to struggle to overcome

figurative adjective (of language) abstract, imaginative or symbolic >**figuratively** adverb

figure noun 1 written number 2 amount expressed in numbers 3 (Maths) geometrical shape

4 diagram or table in a written text **5** shape of a person whom you cannot see clearly **6** shape of your body **7** person **8** representation of a human form in painting or sculpture ▷ *verb* **9** (usually followed by *in*) to be included (in) **10** (*informal*) to guess or conclude ▷ **figure out** *verb* to solve (something) or to understand (something or someone)

figurehead *noun* **1** someone who is the leader in name of a movement or organization but who has no real power **2** carved wooden model of a person or creature decorating the front of a sailing ship

figure of speech *noun* expression such as a simile or idiom in which words do not have their literal meaning

file *noun* **1** box or folder used to keep documents in order **2** documents in a file **3** information about a person or subject **4** line of people one behind the other **5** (*Computers*) organized collection of related material **6** tool with a rough surface, used for smoothing or shaping hard material ▷ *verb* **7** to place (a document) in a file **8** to place (a legal document) on an official record **9** to bring (a lawsuit), especially for divorce **10** to walk or march in a line **11** to smooth or shape (something) with a file

file sharing *noun* sharing computer data on a network, esp. the internet

fill *verb* **1** to make (something) full or to become full **2** to occupy (a space or gap) completely **3** to plug (a gap) **4** to satisfy (a need) **5** to hold and perform the duties of (a position) **6** to appoint someone to (a job or position) ▷ *noun* **7** **have your fill** to have enough for your needs or wants ▷ **fill in** *verb* **1** to complete (a form) **2** to update (someone)

fillet *noun* **1** boneless piece of meat or fish ▷ *verb* **2** to remove the bones from (meat or fish)

filling *noun* **1** soft food mixture inside a sandwich, cake or pie **2** small amount of metal or plastic put into a hole in a tooth by a dentist ▷ *adjective* **3** (of food) substantial and satisfying

filly fillies *noun* young female horse

film *noun* **1** series of moving pictures projected onto a screen and shown at the cinema or on television **2** thin flexible strip of plastic used in a camera to record images when exposed to light **3** thin sheet or layer ▷ *verb* **4** to record (someone or something) using a movie or video camera **5** to make a film of (a scene, story, etc) ▷ *adjective* **6** connected with films or the cinema

filter *noun* **1** device that allows some substances, lights or sounds to pass through it, but not others ▷ *verb* **2** to pass (a substance) through a filter **3** to pass slowly or faintly ▷ **filtration** *noun*

filth *noun* **1** disgusting dirt **2** offensive material or language > **filthy** *adjective* > **filthiness** *noun*

fin *noun* **1a** thin, flat structure sticking out of a fish's body and helping it to balance and swim **2** part of the tail of an aircraft that sticks up

final *adjective* **1** last in a series or happening at the end of something **2** (of a decision) having no possibility of further change, action or discussion ▷ *noun* **3** the last game or contest in a series which decides the overall winner **4** finals last and most important examinations in a university or college course

finale [fin-**nah**-lee] *noun* last section of a piece of music or show

finalist *noun* competitor in a final

finalize or **finalise** *verb* to complete the remaining details of something

finally *adverb* **1** eventually or at last **2** lastly or in conclusion

finance *verb* **1** to provide or obtain funds for (a project or purchase) ▷ *noun* **2** management of money, loans or investments **3** funds for paying for something **4** finances money resources

financial *adjective* relating to or involving money ▷ **financially** *adverb*

financier *noun* person or organization providing the funds for a project or for business

finch *noun* small songbird with a short strong beak

find finds, finding, found *verb* **1** to discover or come across (something or someone) by chance or after a search **2** to realize **3** to consider (someone or something) to have a particular quality **4** (Law) to pronounce (the defendant) guilty or not guilty **5** to provide (money or time), especially with difficulty ▷ *noun* **6** valuable or useful person

or thing ▷ **finder** *noun* ▷ **find out** *verb* **1** to learn or discover something either by chance or after research **2** to learn about something bad, criminal or negligent done by (someone)

findings *plural noun* conclusions from an investigation

fine *adjective* **1** very good **2** (of weather) clear and dry **3** in good health **4** satisfactory **5** of delicate workmanship **6** very narrow or thin **7** subtle or abstruse: *a fine distinction* **8** (of a net or sieve) having very small holes **9** (of dust or powder) consisting of very small particles ▷ *adverb* **10** very well ▷ *noun* **11** payment imposed as a penalty or punishment ▷ *verb* **12** to impose a fine on (a person or organization)

finery *noun* very beautiful clothing and jewellery

finesse [fin-**ness**] *noun* **1** delicate skill **2** subtlety and tact

finger *noun* **1** one of the four long jointed parts of the hand **2** part of a glove that covers a finger ▷ *verb* **3** to touch or handle (something) with your fingers

fingernail *noun* any of the hard coverings on the upper part of the ends of your fingers

fingerprint *noun* mark made showing the pattern on the skin at the tip of a person's finger

finish *verb* **1** to reach the end (of) **2** to come to an end or stop **3** to use (something) up ▷ *noun* **4** end or last part **5** texture or appearance of the surface of something

finite *adjective* having limits in space, time or size

Finn *noun* someone from Finland

Finnish *adjective* **1** belonging or relating to Finland ▷ *noun* **2** the main language spoken in Finland

fir *noun* tall pointed evergreen tree that has needle-like leaves and produces cones

fire *noun* **1** flames produced when something burns **2** pile or mass of burning material **3** piece of equipment used as a heater **4** incident involving undesirable destructive burning **5** shooting of guns **6** open fire to begin shooting ▷ *verb* **7** to operate (a weapon) so that a bullet or missile is released **8** (*informal*) to dismiss from employment **9** to bake (ceramics etc) in a kiln

firearm *noun* gun

fire brigade *noun* organized body of people whose job is to put out fires

fire engine *noun* vehicle carrying equipment for putting out fires

fire escape *noun* metal staircase or ladder down the outside of a building for escape in the event of fire

fire extinguisher *noun* metal cylinder containing water or foam for spraying onto a fire to put it out

firefighter *noun* member of a fire brigade

firefly fireflies *noun* insect that glows in the dark

fireplace *noun* opening beneath a chimney where a fire can be lit

fireproof *adjective* resistant to fire

fire station *noun* building where firefighters are stationed

firework *noun* small container of gunpowder and other chemicals which produces spectacular explosions and coloured sparks when lit

firing squad *noun* group of soldiers ordered to shoot a person condemned to death

firm *adjective* **1** not soft or yielding **2** securely in position **3** definite **4** having or showing determination and authority ▷ *adverb* **5** in an unyielding manner: *hold firm* ▷ *noun* **6** business; company > **firmly** *adverb* > **firmness** *noun*

first *adjective* **1** earliest in time or order **2** graded or ranked above all others ▷ *noun* **3** person or thing coming before all others **4** outset or beginning **5** first-class honours degree at university **6** lowest forward gear in a car or other vehicle ▷ *adverb* **7** before anything else **8** for the first time > **firstly** *adverb*

first aid *noun* immediate medical assistance given to an injured person

first-class *adjective* **1** of the highest quality or standard **2** (*Travel*) (of a ticket, seat, accommodation) relating to the best and most expensive facilities **3** (of postage) quicker but more expensive

first-hand *adjective* **1** obtained directly from the original source ▷ *adverb* **2** directly from the original source

First Lady *noun* the wife of the president of a country

first-rate *adjective* excellent

fiscal *adjective* of government or public money, especially taxes

fish fishes, fishing, fished *noun* **1** cold-blooded creature living in water that has a spine, gills, fins and a scaly skin **2** the flesh of such a creature eaten as food ▷ *verb* **3** to try to catch fish **4 fish for** to try to get (information) in an indirect way ▷ **fishing** *noun*

fishery fisheries *noun* area of the sea used for fishing

fishmonger *noun* seller of fish

fishy fishier, fishiest *adjective* **1** smelling of fish **2** (*informal*) suspicious or questionable

fission *noun* **1** splitting **2** splitting of an atomic nucleus with the release of a large amount of energy; nuclear fission

fissure [fish-er] *noun* deep crack, especially in rock

fist *noun* clenched hand with the fingers curled tightly towards the palm

fit fits, fitting, fitted; fitter, fittest *verb* **1** to be of the correct size or shape (for) **2** to fix or put (something) in place **3** to be appropriate or suitable for (a situation, person or thing) **4** to correspond with the facts or circumstances **5** to adjust (something) to make it the right size and shape ▷ *noun* **6** way in which something fits **7** sudden attack or convulsion, such as an epileptic seizure **8** sudden short burst or spell of laughter, coughing or panic ▷ *adjective* **9** suitable or appropriate **10** in good health **11** worthy or deserving ▷ **fit in** *verb* **1** to make a place or time for (someone or something) **2** to conform or cause to belong ▷ **fitness** *noun* ▷ **fit out** *verb* to provide (someone or something) with the necessary equipment

fitful *adjective* happening at irregular intervals and not continuous: *a fitful breeze* ▷ **fitfully** *adverb*

fitter *noun* person who assembles or installs machinery

fitting *adjective* **1** appropriate or suitable ▷ *noun* **2** accessory or part **3** session trying on clothes that are being adjusted to ensure a correct fit **4 fittings** furnishings and accessories in a building

five *adjective, noun* the number 5

fix *verb* **1** to mend or repair **2** to place permanently **3** to settle definitely **4** to direct (your attention) steadily **5** to arrange or organize **6** (*informal*) to influence the outcome of (something) unfairly ▷ *noun* **7** (*informal*) **a** difficult situation **b** unfair or dishonest arrangement **c** injection of a drug such as heroin ▷ **fixed** *adjective* ▷ **fixedly** *adverb* steadily ▷ **fix up** *verb* **1** to arrange **2** (often followed by *with*) to provide

fixation *noun* extreme and obsessive interest in something

fixture *noun* **1** permanently fitted piece of household equipment **2** sports match or the date fixed for it

fizz *verb* **1** to make a hissing or bubbling noise **2** to give off small bubbles

fizzle *verb* to make a weak hissing or bubbling sound ▷ **fizzle out** *verb* (*informal*) to come to nothing, fail

fizzy fizzier, fizziest *adjective* (of drink) bubbly, owing to the presence of carbon dioxide

fjord [fee-**ord**] *noun* long narrow inlet of the sea between cliffs, especially in Norway

flab *noun* (*informal*) unsightly body fat

flabbergasted *adjective* completely astonished

flabby flabbier, flabbiest *adjective* having flabby flesh

flag flags, flagging, flagged *noun* **1** rectangular or square piece of cloth which has a particular colour and design, and is used as the symbol of a nation or as a signal **2** flat paving-stone ▷ *verb* **3** to lose enthusiasm or vigour **4** to mark with a flag or sticker > **flag down** *verb* to signal (a vehicle) to stop by waving the arm

flagrant [**flayg**-rant] *adjective* openly outrageous > **flagrantly** *adverb*

flagship *noun* ship carrying the commander of the fleet

flail *verb* to wave about wildly

flair *noun* **1** natural ability **2** stylishness

flak *noun* **1** anti-aircraft fire **2** (*informal*) severe criticism

flake *noun* **1** small thin piece, especially chipped off something ▷ *verb* **2** to peel off in flakes > **flaked** *adjective*: flaked almonds > **flake out** *verb* (*informal*) to collapse or fall asleep from exhaustion > **flaky** *adjective*: flaky pastry

flamboyant *adjective* **1** behaving in a very noticeable, extravagant way **2** very bright and showy > **flamboyance** *noun*

flame *noun* **1** luminous burning gas coming from burning material **2** old flame (*informal*) former boyfriend or girlfriend

flamenco *noun* type of rhythmical Spanish dancing or the guitar music that accompanies it

flamingo flamingos or flamingoes *noun* long-legged wading bird with pink or white feathers and a long neck

flammable *adjective* easily set on fire

flan *noun* open sweet or savoury tart with a pastry or cake base

flank *noun* **1** part of the side between the hips and ribs **2** side of a body of troops ▷ *verb* **3** to be at or to move along the side of

flannel *noun* **1** (*Brit*) small piece of cloth for washing the face **2** soft woollen fabric for clothing **3** flannels trousers made of flannel

flap flaps, flapping, flapped *verb* **1** to move back and forwards or up and down with a snapping sound ▷ *noun* **2** action or sound of flapping **3** piece of something such as paper, fabric or skin, attached by one edge only

flare *noun* **1** device that produces a brightly coloured flame, used especially as an emergency signal **2** flares flared trousers ▷ *verb* **3** to start to burn much more vigorously **4** (*informal*) (of temper, violence or trouble) to break out suddenly **5** (of a skirt or trousers) to become wider towards the bottom > **flared** *adjective* (of a skirt or trousers) becoming wider towards the bottom

flash *noun* **1** sudden short burst of light or flame **2** burst (of intuition or emotion) **3** very short time **4** brief unscheduled news announcement ▷ *verb* **5** to give out or to cause something to give out light suddenly or repeatedly **6** to move very fast **7** (*informal*) to show (something) briefly or arrogantly

flashback *noun* scene in a book, play or film, that returns to earlier events

flash drive *noun* portable computer hard drive and data storage device

flashlight *noun* (US) torch

flashy flashier, flashiest *adjective* expensive-looking and showy, in a vulgar way

flask *noun* **1** flat bottle for carrying alcoholic drink in the pocket **2** narrow-necked bottle

flat flats; flats, flatting, flatted; flatter, flattest *noun* **1** self-contained set of rooms, usually on one level, for living in **2** (*Music*) note or key a semitone lower than that described by the same letter. It is represented by the symbol (♭) **3** punctured tyre **4** mud bank exposed at low tide ▷ *verb* **5** (*Aust, NZ*) to live in a flat ▷ *adjective* **6** level and horizontal **7** even and smooth **8** (of a tyre or ball) deflated **9** outright **10** fixed **11** without variation or emotion **12** (of a drink) no longer fizzy **13** (of a battery) with no electrical charge **14** (*Music*) below the true pitch ▷ *adverb* **15** in or into a flat position **16** completely or absolutely **17** (of a rate or price) unvarying **18** (*Music*) too low in pitch > **flatly** *adverb* > **flatness** *noun*

flatfish *noun* sea fish, such as the sole, which has a flat body

▌**WORD TIP**
The plural of *flatfish* is *flatfish*

flathead *noun* common Australian edible fish

flatscreen *noun* slim lightweight TV set or computer with a flat screen

flatten *verb* to become or make (something) flat or flatter

flatter *verb* **1** to praise (someone) insincerely **2** to make (someone) appear more attractive **3** flatter yourself to believe something good about yourself that others doubt > **flattered** *adjective* feeling pleased and special > **flattering** *adjective*: *a flattering colour*

flattery *noun* flattering words or behaviour

flatting *noun* **go flatting** (*NZ*) to leave home and live with others in a shared house or flat

flatulence *noun* condition of having too much gas in your stomach or intestines

flaunt *verb* to display (yourself or your possessions) arrogantly

flautist *noun* flute player

flavour *noun* **1** distinctive taste **2** distinctive characteristic or quality ▷ *verb* **3** to add flavour to (food) > **flavouring** *noun* substance used to flavour food

flaw *noun* **1** fault or mark **2** mistake that makes a plan or argument invalid > **flawed** *adjective* > **flawless** *adjective*

flax *noun* plant used for making rope and cloth

flay *verb* **1** to strip the skin off (a dead animal) **2** to criticize (someone) severely

flea *noun* small wingless jumping bloodsucking insect

fleck *noun* small mark, streak or speck ▷ **flecked** *adjective*: *The wall was flecked with blood*

fled *verb* past of **flee**

fledgling *noun* 1 young bird ▷ *adjective* 2 new or inexperienced

flee flees, fleeing, fled *verb* to run away (from)

fleece *noun* 1 sheep's coat of wool 2 sheepskin used as a lining for coats etc 3 warm polyester fabric 4 (*Brit*) jacket or top made of this fabric ▷ *verb* 5 to defraud or overcharge (someone)

fleet *noun* group of ships or vehicles owned by the same organization or travelling together

fleeting *adjective* lasting for a very short time ▷ **fleetingly** *adverb*

Flemish *noun* language spoken in many parts of Belgium

flesh *noun* 1 soft part of a human or animal body 2 (*informal*) excess fat 3 meat of animals as opposed to fish or fowl 4 thick soft part of a fruit or vegetable 5 human body as opposed to the soul ▷ **fleshy** *adjective* 1 plump 2 like flesh

flew *verb* past tense of **fly**

flex *noun* 1 flexible insulated electric cable ▷ *verb* 2 to bend (your muscles)

flexible *adjective* 1 easily bent 2 adaptable ▷ **flexibility** *noun*

flick *verb* 1 to move (something) with a quick jerk of your finger 2 to move with a short sudden movement, often repeatedly ▷ *noun* 3 quick or sharp movement

flicker *verb* 1 to shine unsteadily or intermittently ▷ *noun* 2 unsteady brief light 3 momentary feeling

flight *noun* 1 journey by air 2 act or manner of flying through the air 3 ability to fly 4 aircraft flying on a scheduled journey 5 set of stairs between two landings 6 act of running away

flight attendant *noun* person who looks after passengers on an aircraft

flightless *adjective* (of certain birds or insects) unable to fly

flimsy flimsier, flimsiest *adjective* 1 not strong or substantial 2 thin 3 not very convincing

flinch *verb* to draw back or wince, as from pain

fling flings, flinging, flung *verb* 1 to throw, send or move forcefully or hurriedly ▷ *noun* 2 spell of self-indulgent enjoyment 3 brief romantic or sexual relationship

flint *noun* 1 hard grey stone 2 piece of this

flip flips, flipping, flipped *verb* 1 to turn (something small or light) over or move (something) with a quick movement 2 to hit (something) sharply with your finger or thumb ▷ **flip through** *verb* to look at (a book or magazine) quickly or idly

flippant *adjective* showing an inappropriate lack of seriousness ▷ **flippancy** *noun* ▷ **flippantly** *adverb*

flipper *noun* 1 broad, flat limb of a sea animal adapted for swimming 2 one of a pair of broad, flat pieces of rubber that you can attach to your feet to help you swim

flirt *verb* 1 to behave as if sexually attracted to someone but without serious intentions ▷ *noun* 2 person who flirts ▷ **flirtation** *noun*

a b c d e f g h i j k l m n o p q r s t u v w x y z

> **flirtatious** adjective > **flirt with** verb to consider lightly; toy with

flit flits, flitting, flitted verb **1** (informal) to depart hurriedly and secretly ▷ noun **2** act of flitting

float verb **1** to be supported by a liquid **2** to move lightly and freely, supported by the air **3** to launch (a company) as a public company, with shares available on the stock market ▷ noun **4** light object used to help someone or something to float **5** indicator on a fishing line that moves where a fish bites **6** decorated truck in a procession **7** (Brit) small delivery vehicle **8** sum of money used for minor expenses or to provide change > **floating** adjective **1** moving about, changing: floating population **2** (of a voter) not committed to any party

flock noun **1** group (of birds, sheep or goats) **2** (Christianity) congregation

flog flogs, flogging, flogged verb **1** to beat (someone) with a whip or stick **2** (Brit, NZ, S Afr informal) to sell **3** (NZ informal) to steal > **flogging** noun

flood noun **1** large amount of water covering an area that is usually dry ▷ verb **2** to cover (something) or to become covered with water **3** to come in large numbers or quantities

floodgates plural noun **open the floodgates** to give a lot of people the opportunity to do something they could not do before

floodlight noun powerful outdoor lamp used to light up public buildings and sports grounds > **floodlit** adjective

floor noun **1** the part of a room you walk on **2** one of the levels of a building **3** flat bottom surface of something **4** (right to speak in) a legislative hall ▷ verb **5** (informal) (of a remark or question) to cause (someone) to be disconcerted and unable to respond adequately

floorboard noun one of the long planks of wood from which a floor is made

flop flops, flopping, flopped verb **1** to bend, fall or collapse loosely or carelessly **2** (informal) to fail ▷ noun **3** (informal) failure

floppy floppier, floppiest adjective tending to hang loosely downwards

floppy disk or **disc** noun (Computers) flexible magnetic disk on which computer data is stored

floral adjective made from or decorated with flowers

florid adjective **1** highly elaborate and extravagant; ornate: florid language **2** with a red or flushed complexion

florist noun person or shop selling flowers

floss noun **1** See **dental floss 2** fine silky fibres

flotation noun **1** launching of a business enterprise as a public company, with shares available on the stock market **2** act of floating

flotilla noun small fleet or fleet of small ships

flotsam noun wreckage or rubbish floating at sea or washed up on the shore

flounce verb **1** to walk with exaggerated movements suggesting anger or impatience about something: *She flounced out of the office* ▷ noun **2** ornamental frill

flounder verb **1** to move with difficulty, as in mud **2** to find it difficult to decide what to do or say ▷ noun **3** edible flatfish

WORD TIP
The plural of *flounder* in sense 3 can be either *flounder* or *flounders*

flour noun powder made by grinding grain, usually wheat, and used for baking and cooking > **floured** adjective > **floury** adjective

flourish verb **1** to be active, successful, healthy or widespread **2** to wave (something) dramatically ▷ noun **3** bold sweeping or waving motion > **flourishing** adjective: *Business is flourishing*

flout verb to deliberately disobey (a rule, law, etc)

flow verb **1** (of liquid) to move in a stream **2** (of blood or electricity) to circulate **3** to hang loosely ▷ noun **4** act, rate or manner of flowing **5** continuous stream of something

flow chart noun diagram showing the sequence of steps that lead to various results

flower noun **1** part of a plant containing the reproductive organs from which the fruit or seeds develop **2** plant grown for its colourful flowers ▷ verb **3** to produce flowers, bloom

flowery adjective (of language or style) elaborate

flown verb past participle of *fly*

flu noun illness similar to a very bad cold, which causes headaches,

sore throat, weakness and aching muscles. Short for *influenza*

fluctuate verb to change frequently and erratically: *fluctuating between feeling well and not so well* > **fluctuation** noun

flue noun passage or pipe which takes fumes and smoke away from a stove or boiler

fluent adjective **1** able to speak a foreign language correctly and without hesitation **2** able to speak or write easily and without hesitation **3** spoken or written with ease > **fluency** noun > **fluently** adverb

fluff noun **1** soft, light woolly threads or fibres bunched together **2** (often followed by *up*) to brush or shake (something) to make it seem larger and lighter > **fluffy** adjective

fluid noun **1** liquid ▷ adjective **2** (of movement) smooth and flowing > **fluidity** noun

fluke noun accidental success or stroke of luck

flung verb past of *fling*

fluorescent adjective **1** having a very bright appearance when light is shone on it, as if it is shining itself: *fluorescent yellow dye* **2** (of a light or lamp) in the form of a tube and shining with a hard bright light

fluoride noun mixture of chemicals that is meant to prevent tooth decay

flurry flurries noun short rush of activity or movement

flush verb **1** to blush or to cause (someone) to blush **2** to send water through (a toilet or pipe) so as to clean it **3** to drive (someone or something) out of a hiding place ▷ noun **1** rosy red colour; blush **5** pleasure and excitement **6** (in card games) a hand all of one suit ▷ adjective **7** level with the surrounding surface **8** (informal) having plenty of money ▷ **flushed** adjective pleased and excited

flustered adjective confused, nervous and rushed

flute noun **1** wind instrument consisting of a tube with sound holes and a hole for blowing across. It is held sideways **2** tall narrow wineglass

fluted adjective having decorative grooves

flutter verb **1** to flap or wave with small, quick movements **2** to move (something) quickly and irregularly **3** (of the heart) to beat abnormally quickly ▷ noun **4** nervous agitation **5** (informal) small bet

flux noun state of constant change

fly flies, flying, flew, flown **1** insect with two pairs of wings **2** (often plural) (Brit) fastening at the front of trousers **3** flap forming the entrance to a tent ▷ verb **4** to move through the air on wings or in an aircraft **5** to pilot (a plane) **6** to float, flutter or be displayed in the air **7** to transport (someone or something) or to be transported by aircraft **8** to move quickly or suddenly **9** (of time) to pass rapidly **10** to flee ▷ adjective **11** (informal) sharp and cunning ▷ **flying** adjective, noun

fly-fishing noun method of freshwater fishing using imitation flies as bait

flying fox noun **1** large fruit-eating bat, found in Australia and Africa **2** (Aust, NZ) cable car used to carry people over rivers and gorges

flying saucer noun unidentified disc-shaped flying object, supposedly from outer space

flyover noun structure carrying one road over another at a junction or intersection

foal noun **1** young horse ▷ verb **2** to give birth to a foal

foam noun **1** mass of tiny bubbles **2** light spongy material used, for example, in furniture or packaging ▷ verb **3** to produce foam

fob off verb to stop (someone) asking questions or complaining by offering excuses, telling them half truths or giving them something of inferior quality

focus focuses or focusses, focusing or focussing, focused or focussed; focuses or foci verb **1** to adjust (your eyes, a camera or a lens, etc) in order to see or view something clearly **2** focus on a to concentrate on b to look at ▷ noun **3** centre of interest or activity

fodder noun food for farm animals or horses

foe noun enemy

foetus foetuses noun an unborn child or animal in the womb ▷ **foetal** adjective: foetal development

fog fogs, fogging, fogged noun **1** thick mist of water droplets suspended in the air ▷ verb **2** (often followed by up) to cover or become covered with steam ▷ **foggy** adjective: a foggy morning

foil *verb* **1** to ruin (someone's plan) ▷ *noun* **2** metal in a thin sheet, especially for wrapping food **3** anything or anyone that shows up the qualities of something or someone else by contrast **4** thin, light sword with a button on the tip, used in fencing

foist *verb* (followed by *on*, *upon*) to force or impose (something on someone)

fold *verb* **1** to bend (something) so that one part covers another **2** to cross (your arms) **3** (*Cooking*) to mix gently **4** (*informal*) (of business) to fail or go bankrupt ▷ *noun* **5** mark, crease or hollow made by folding **6** folded piece or part **7** small enclosed area for sheep **8** church or its members

folder *noun* piece of folded cardboard for holding loose papers

foliage *noun* leaves

folk *noun* **1** people in general **2** race of people **3** *plural noun* **3** (*informal*) relatives ▷ *adjective* **4** (of music, dance or art) traditional or representative of the ordinary local people

folklore *noun* traditional stories and beliefs of a community

follicle *noun* small pouchlike structure or cavity in the body, especially one from which a hair grows

follow *verb* **1** to go or come after (someone or something) **2** to be a logical or natural consequence of (something) **3** to keep to the course, track or direction of (a road, river or sign) **4** to act in accordance with (instructions or advice) **5** to accept the ideas or beliefs of (someone) **6** to understand (an explanation, plot or story) **7** to have a keen interest in (something) **8** to be true or logical in consequence > **follow up 1** to investigate (a matter, suggestion or discovery) **2** to do a second, often similar, thing after (a first)

follower *noun* disciple or supporter

folly follies *noun* **1** foolishness **2** foolish action or idea **3** useless extravagant building

fond *adjective* **1** tender or loving **2** (of a hope or belief) foolish **3** fond of having a liking for > **fondly** *adverb* > **fondness** *noun*

fondle *verb* to stroke tenderly

font *noun* **1** bowl in a church that holds water for baptisms **2** set of printing type of one style and size

food *noun* **1** what people and animals eat **2** substance that provides nourishment for plants

food chain *noun* a series of living things which are linked because each one feeds on the next one in the series. For example, a plant may be eaten by a rabbit which may be eaten by a fox

food group *noun* category of food based on its nutritional content

foodstuff *noun* substance used as food

food technology *noun* study of foods, what they consist of and their effect on the body

fool *noun* **1** person who behaves in a silly or stupid way **2** dessert of puréed fruit mixed with cream ▷ *verb* **3** to deceive (someone)

foolhardy *adjective* recklessly adventurous > **foolhardiness**

noun: *the foolhardiness of travelling across the world by bike*

foolish *adjective* unwise, silly or absurd **> foolishly** *adverb* **> foolishness** *noun*: *He felt ashamed of his foolishness*

foolproof *adjective* unable to fail

foosball *noun* (US & Canadian) same as **table football**

foot feet *noun* **1** part of the leg below the ankle **2** lowest part of anything: *the foot of the mountain* **3** unit of length equal to twelve inches or about 30.5 centimetres **4** (*Poetry*) basic unit of rhythm containing two or three syllables **> adjective 5** (of a brake, pedal or pump) operated by your foot **> verb 6 foot it** (*informal*) to walk **7 foot the bill** to pay the entire cost

footage *noun* amount or length of film

football *noun* **1** any of various games in which the ball can be kicked, such as soccer, rugby, Australian Rules and American football **2** ball used in any of these games **> footballer** *noun*

foothills *plural noun* hills at the foot of a mountain

foothold *noun* **1** place where you can put your foot when climbing **2** secure position from which progress may be made

footing *noun* **1** secure grip by or for the feet **2** basis or foundation of a relationship or situation

footman footmen *noun* male servant in a large house who wears a uniform

footnote *noun* note printed at the foot of a page

footpath *noun* **1** narrow path for walkers only **2** (*Aust*) raised

space alongside a road, for pedestrians

footprint *noun* mark left by a foot

footstep *noun* **1** step taken when walking **2** sound made by walking

for *preposition* **1** indicating the person or thing receiving or benefitting from something: *a gift for you* **2** indicating the destination of something: *the train for Liverpool* **3** indicating a length of time or distance: *for three weeks*; *for five miles* **4** indicating the reason, cause or purpose of something: *This is my excuse for going to Italy* **5** indicating the person or thing represented by someone: *playing for his country*

forage *verb* to search about (for food)

foray *noun* **1** brief attempt to do or get something **2** brief raid or attack

forbid forbids, forbidding, forbade, forbidden *verb* to prohibit or refuse to allow: *He forbade her to leave the house* **> forbidden** *adjective*

force *verb* **1** to make (someone) do something; compel **2** to break open **> noun 3** strength or power **4** compulsion **5** (*Physics*) Force is a pushing or pulling influence that changes a body from a state of rest to one of motion, or changes its rate of motion **6** mental or moral strength **7** person or thing with strength or influence **8** vehemence or intensity **9** group of people organized for a particular task or duty **10 in force a** having legal validity **b** in great numbers

forceful *adjective* powerful and convincing **> forcefully** *adverb*

forceps *plural noun* pair of long tongs or pincers used by a doctor

forcible *adjective* **1** involving physical force or violence **2** strong and convincing > **forcibly** *adverb*

ford *noun* **1** shallow place where a river may be crossed ▷ *verb* **2** to cross (a river) at a ford

fore *adjective* **1** in, at or towards the front ▷ *noun* **2 come to the fore** to become important or popular: *Environmental issues have come to the fore lately*

forearm *noun* arm from the wrist to the elbow

forebear *noun* ancestor

foreboding *noun* feeling that something bad is about to happen

forecast forecasts, forecasting, forecast *or* forecasted *verb* **1** to predict (weather, events, etc) ▷ *noun* **2** prediction

forecourt *noun* courtyard or open space in front of a building

forefather *noun* ancestor

forefinger *noun* finger next to the thumb

forefront *noun* leading or most active position

forego foregoes, foregoing, forewent, foregone *verb* to do without or give up (something)

foregoing *adjective* (formal) going before; preceding

foregone conclusion *noun* inevitable result

foreground *noun* part of a view, especially in a picture, nearest the observer

forehand *noun* (Tennis, Squash, Badminton) stroke made with the palm of your hand facing in the direction that you hit the ball

forehead *noun* area of your face above your eyebrows and below your hairline

foreign *adjective* **1** belonging to or involving countries other than your own **2** unfamiliar or uncharacteristic **3** in an abnormal place or position: *foreign matter* > **foreigner** *noun*

foreman foremen *noun* **1** person in charge of a group of workers **2** leader of a jury

foremost *adjective, adverb* first in time, place or importance

forensic *adjective* **1** relating to or involving the scientific examination of objects involved in a crime **2** relating to or involving the legal profession

forerunner *noun* something or someone that precedes, influences or is an early sign of subsequent developments in an area

foresee foresees, foreseeing, foresaw, foreseen *verb* to see or know beforehand; predict > **foreseeable** *adjective: He will continue as chairman for the foreseeable future*

foresight *noun* ability to anticipate and provide for future needs

foreskin *noun* fold of skin covering the tip of the penis

forest *noun* large area of trees growing close together

forestry *noun* **1** science of planting and caring for trees **2** management of forests

foretaste *noun* early limited experience of something to come

foretell foretells, foretelling, foretold *verb* to predict (something)

forever or **for ever** adverb permanently or continually

forewarn verb to warn (someone) beforehand

foreword noun introduction to a book

forfeit [for-fit] verb **1** to lose (something) as a penalty ▷ noun **2** thing lost or given up as a penalty

forge noun **1** place where a blacksmith works making metal goods by hand; smithy **2** furnace for melting metal ▷ verb **3** to make an illegal copy of (a painting, document or money, etc) **4** to shape (metal) by heating and hammering it **5** to create (a relationship etc) ▷ **forge ahead** verb to progress quickly

forgery forgeries noun **1** illegal copy of something **2** crime of forging money, documents or paintings

forget forgets, forgetting, forgot, forgotten verb **1** to fail to remember (something) **2** to neglect **3** to leave (something) behind by mistake **4** **forget yourself** to behave in an unacceptable way ▷ **forgetful** adjective tending to forget ▷ **forgetfulness** noun

forget-me-not noun plant with clusters of small blue flowers

forgive forgives, forgiving, forgave, forgiven verb to cease to blame or hold resentment against (someone); pardon ▷ **forgiveness** noun ▷ **forgiving** adjective

forgo verb same as **forego**

fork noun **1** tool for eating food, with prongs and a handle **2** large similarly-shaped garden tool **3** point where a road, river, etc divides into two branches **4** one of the branches ▷ verb **5** to pick up, dig, etc (something) with a fork **6** to branch **7** to take one or other branch at a fork in the road ▷ **forked** adjective ▷ **fork out** verb (informal) to pay

forlorn adjective **1** lonely and unhappy **2** (of a hope or attempt) desperate and without any expectation of success ▷ **forlornly** adverb

form noun **1** type or kind **2** shape or appearance **3** mode in which something appears **4** printed document with spaces for details **5** physical or mental condition **6** previous record of an athlete, racehorse, etc **7** class in school ▷ verb **8** to come into existence; be made **9** to bring (something) into existence; make **10** to make (something) up: *events that were to form the basis of her novel* **11** to acquire or develop (something)

formal adjective **1** correct, serious and conforming to accepted conventions: *a very formal letter of apology* **2** of or for formal occasions **3** stiff in manner **4** organized **5** official and publicly recognized: *the first formal agreement of its kind* ▷ **formally** adverb

formaldehyde [for-**mal**-de-hide] noun a poisonous, strong-smelling gas, used for preserving specimens in biology

formality formalities noun **1** requirement of custom or etiquette **2** necessary procedure without real importance

format formats, formatting, formatted *noun* **1** style in which something is arranged ▷ *verb* **2** to arrange (something) in a format

formation *noun* **1** process of developing and creating something **2** structure or shape of something **3** arrangement of people or things acting as a unit

formative *adjective* having an important and lasting influence on character and development

former *adjective* **1** happening or existing before now or in the past ▷ *noun* **2 the former** first mentioned of two > **formerly** *adverb*

formidable *adjective* **1** frightening because difficult to overcome or manage **2** extremely impressive > **formidably** *adverb*

formula formulae or formulas *noun* **1** group of numbers, letters or symbols expressing a scientific or mathematical rule **2** list of quantities of substances that when mixed make another substance, for example in chemistry **3** method or rule for doing or producing something

formulate *verb* to create and express (a plan or thought) in a clear and precise way

fornication *noun* (*formal*) sin of having sex with someone without being married to them

forsake forsakes, forsaking, forsook, forsaken *verb* to give up or abandon (someone)

fort *noun* **1** strong building built for defence **2 hold the fort** (*informal*) to keep things going during someone's absence

forte [for-tay] *noun* **1** something that someone does really well; speciality ▷ *adverb* **2** (*Music*) loudly

forth *adverb* forwards, out or away

forthcoming *adjective* **1** about to appear or happen **2** available **3** (of a person) communicative

forthright *adjective* direct and outspoken

fortification *noun* building, wall or ditch used to protect a place

fortitude *noun* calm and patient courage in times of trouble or when suffering

fortnight *noun* two weeks > **fortnightly** *adverb, adjective*

fortress *noun* large fort or fortified town

fortuitous [for-**tyew**-it-uss] *adjective* happening by chance or good luck > **fortuitously** *adverb*

fortunate *adjective* **1** having good luck; lucky **2** occurring by good luck > **fortunately** *adverb*

fortune *noun* **1** luck, especially when favourable **2** wealth, large sum of money **3** (often plural) person's destiny

forty forties *adjective, noun* the number 40 > **fortieth** *adjective, noun*

forum forums or fora *noun* **1** place, meeting or medium in which people can exchange ideas and discuss public issues **2** square in Roman towns where people met to discuss business and politics

forward *adverb* **1** towards or at a place further ahead in space or time **2** towards the front ▷ *adjective* **3** directed or moving ahead **4** in, at or near the front **5** presumptuous **6** well developed or advanced **7** relating to the future ▷ noun **8** attacking player in various team games, such as soccer or hockey ▷ verb **9** to send (a letter etc) on to an ultimate destination > **forwards** adverb **1** towards or at a place further ahead in space or time **2** towards the front

fossick verb (Aust, NZ) to search, especially for gold or precious stones

fossil noun the remains or impression of an animal or plant from a previous age, preserved in rock > **fossilize** verb to turn into a fossil

fossil fuel noun fuel such as coal, oil or natural gas, formed by the rotting of animals and plants from millions of years ago

foster verb **1** to bring up (someone else's child) without becoming the legal parent **2** to promote the growth or development of > **foster child** noun > **foster home** noun > **foster parent** noun

fought verb past of **fight**

foul adjective **1** dirty, wicked or obscene ▷ verb **2** to make (something) dirty or polluted, especially with faeces **3** (Sport) to break the rules to the disadvantage of (an opponent) ▷ noun **4** (Sport) act of breaking the rules

found verb **1** past of **find 2** to start or set up (an organization or institution) **3** to lay the foundation of

foundation noun **1** basis or base **2** part of a building or wall below the ground **3** act of founding **4** organization set up by money left in someone's will for research or charity **5** cosmetic used as a base for make-up

founder noun **1** person responsible for setting up an institution or organization ▷ verb **2** to break down or fail **3** (of a ship) to sink

foundry foundries noun factory where metal is melted and cast

fountain noun **1** jet of water **2** structure from which such a jet spurts

fountain pen noun pen supplied with ink from a container inside it

four adjective, noun **1** the number 4 ▷ noun **2 on all fours** on hands and knees

four-poster noun bed with four posts supporting a canopy and curtains

fourteen adjective, noun the number 14 > **fourteenth** adjective, noun

fourth adjective, noun **1** (coming as) number 4 in a series ▷ noun **2** quarter

fowl noun bird such as chicken or duck that is kept for its meat or eggs or hunted for its meat

fox foxes, foxing, foxed noun **1** dog-like wild animal with reddish-brown fur, a pointed face and ears, and a thick tail **2** cunning person ▷ verb **3** (informal) to puzzle or perplex (someone)

foxglove noun tall plant with purple or white trumpet-shaped flowers

foxhound noun breed of dog used for hunting foxes

foyer [foy-ay] noun large area just inside the main doors of a theatre, cinema or hotel

fracas [frak-ah] noun noisy quarrel

WORD TIP
The plural of *fracas* is *fracas*

fraction noun **1** part of a whole number **2** tiny amount, fragment or piece of something ▷ **fractional** adjective ▷ **fractionally** adverb

fractious adjective easily upset or angered

fracture noun **1** crack or break in something, especially a bone ▷ verb **2** to break

fragile adjective **1** easily broken or damaged **2** in a weakened physical state ▷ **fragility** noun

fragment noun **1** small piece broken off something ▷ verb **2** to break into pieces ▷ **fragmentation** noun ▷ **fragmented** adjective

fragmentary adjective made up of small pieces or parts that are not connected: *fragmentary notes in a journal*

fragrance noun **1** sweet or pleasant smell **2** perfume or scent

fragrant adjective smelling sweet or pleasant

frail adjective **1** physically weak **2** easily damaged ▷ **frailty** noun physical or moral weakness

frame noun **1** structure surrounding a door, window or picture **2** structure giving shape or support **3** person's build **4** one of the many separate photographs of which a cinema film is made up **5** frames the part of a pair of glasses that holds the lenses ▷ verb **6** to put (a picture) into a frame **7** to put (something) into words; express **8** (informal) to incriminate (a person) on a false charge

framework noun **1** supporting structure **2** set of rules, beliefs or ideas which you use to decide what to do

franc noun monetary unit of Switzerland, various African countries, and formerly of France and Belgium

franchise noun **1** right to vote **2** authorization to sell a company's goods

frank adjective **1** open, honest and straightforward in what you say ▷ noun **2** official mark on a letter permitting delivery ▷ verb **3** to put such a mark on (a letter) ▷ **frankly** adverb ▷ **frankness** noun

frantic adjective **1** made wild and uncontrolled through anxiety or fear **2** hurried and disorganized ▷ **frantically** adverb

fraternal adjective of a brother, brotherly

fraternity fraternities noun **1** brotherhood **2** group of people with shared interests, aims, etc **3** (US) male social club at college

fraud noun **1** crime of getting money by deceit or trickery **2** something that deceives people in an illegal or immoral way **3** person who is not what they pretend to be

fraudulent adjective dishonest or deceitful

fraught [frawt] adjective **1** tense or anxious **2** fraught with involving, filled with

fray verb **1** to become or make (something) ragged at the edge **2** to become strained ▷ noun **3** (Brit, Aust, NZ) noisy quarrel or fight

a b c d e f g h i j k l m n o p q r s t u v w x y z

freak noun **1** abnormal person or thing ▷ adjective **2** very unusual and unlikely to happen

freckle noun small brown spot on the skin > **freckled** adjective marked with freckles

free freer, freest; frees, freeing, freed adjective **1** (of a person or group) able to act at will; not forced, restrained or imprisoned **2** (of an activity or event) not controlled or limited: the free flow of aid; free trade **3** (of an object, event or activity) costing nothing **4** (of a person) not busy **5** (of a place, seat or space) not in use ▷ verb **6** to release or liberate (someone or something) **7** to make (something or someone) available or usable

freedom noun **1** being free **2** right or privilege of unlimited access: the freedom of the city

freehold noun right to own a house or piece of land for life without conditions

freelance adjective **1** self-employed ▷ adverb **2** as a self-employed person ▷ noun **3** a self-employed person doing specific pieces of work for various employers

freely adverb without restriction

free-range adjective kept or produced in natural conditions

freestyle noun a sports competition, especially swimming, in which competitors can use any style or method

freeway noun (US, Aust) motorway

free will noun of your own free will by choice and without pressure being exerted

freeze freezes, freezing, froze, frozen verb **1** (of a liquid) to become solid because of the cold **2** to preserve (food etc) by extreme cold **3** to be very cold **4** to become suddenly very still or quiet with fear, shock, etc **5** (Drama) to stop (the action in a film) at a particular frame **6** to fix (prices or wages) at a particular level ▷ noun **7** period of very cold weather **8** official action taken to prevent wages or prices from rising

freezer noun large refrigerator which freezes and stores food for a long time

freezing adjective (informal) very cold

freight [frate] noun **1** cargo transported by lorries, ships, etc **2** commercial transport of goods **3** cost of this

French adjective **1** belonging or relating to France ▷ noun **2** language of France, also spoken in parts of Belgium, Canada and Switzerland

French bean noun green pod eaten as a vegetable, which grows on a climbing plant with white or mauve flowers

French horn noun brass wind instrument with a coiled tube

Frenchman Frenchmen noun man from France > **Frenchwoman** noun

French window noun one of a pair of glass doors that lead into a garden or onto a balcony

frenetic [frin-**net**-ik] adjective wild and excited > **frenetically** adverb

frenzy frenzies noun wild and uncontrolled state > **frenzied** adjective

frequency frequencies noun
1 how often something happens
2 (Physics) the rate at which
a sound wave or radio wave
vibrates

frequent adjective 1 happening
often ▷ verb 2 to visit (a place)
often > **frequently** adverb

fresco frescoes or frescos noun
picture painted on wet plaster
on a wall

fresh adjective 1 newly made,
acquired, etc 2 original 3 further,
additional 4 (of food) not
preserved 5 (of water) not
salty 6 (of weather) brisk or
invigorating 7 not tired 8 **fresh
from** having recently experienced
(something) > **freshly** adverb
> **freshness** noun

freshwater adjective 1 (of a lake
or pool) containing water that
is not salty 2 (of a fish or animal)
living in a river, lake or pool that
is not salty

fret frets, fretting, fretted verb 1 to
be worried ▷ noun 2 small bar on
the fingerboard of a guitar etc

Freudian slip noun something
that you say or do that reveals
your unconscious thoughts

friar noun member of a male
Roman Catholic religious order

friction noun 1 force that stops
things from moving freely when
they rub against each other
2 rubbing 3 clash of wills or
personalities

Friday noun day between Friday
and Sunday

fridge noun electrically cooled
container in which you store food
and drinks to keep them fresh;
refrigerator

friend noun person you know well
and like

friendly friendlies; friendlier,
friendliest adjective 1 showing or
expressing liking 2 not hostile,
on the same side 3 (Sport)
match played for its own sake
and not as part of a competition
> **friendliness** noun

friendship noun 1 relationship
that you have with a friend 2 state
of being friends with someone

frieze [freeze] noun decorative
band on a wall

frigate [frig-it] noun medium-
sized fast warship

fright noun 1 sudden fear or alarm
2 sudden alarming shock

frighten verb to scare or terrify
(someone) > **frightened** adjective
> **frightening** adjective

frightful adjective 1 horrifying
2 (informal) very great
> **frightfully** adverb (informal) very

frigid [frij-id] adjective 1 (of a
woman) sexually unresponsive
2 cold and unfriendly

frill noun strip of cloth with many
folds, attached to something
as a decoration > **frilly** adjective
decorated with frills or lace

fringe noun 1 hair that is cut to
hang down over your forehead
2 ornamental edge of hanging
threads, tassels, etc 3 outer
edge 4 less important parts of
an activity or group ▷ adjective
5 (of theatre) unofficial or
unconventional > **fringed**
adjective

frisk verb (informal) to search (a
person) for concealed weapons etc

frisky friskier, friskiest adjective
lively or high-spirited

fritter noun piece of food fried in batter ▷ **fritter away** verb to waste

frivolous adjective 1 not serious or sensible 2 enjoyable but trivial > **frivolity** noun

frizzy frizzier, frizziest adjective (of hair) having small, tight wiry curls

frock noun (old-fashioned) dress

frog noun small amphibious creature with smooth skin, prominent eyes, and long back legs which it uses for jumping

frolic frolics, frolicking, frolicked verb to run around and play in a lively way

from preposition 1 indicating the origin or source of something or someone: a call from a public telephone; people from a city 100 miles away 2 indicating a starting point or point of departure: She fled from the room 3 indicating the start of a range: a score from one to five 4 indicating a cause: the wreckage from the bomb blast 5 indicating a sum or amount that is reduced by another sum or amount: The money is deducted from her salary every month

frond noun long feathery leaf

front noun 1 part of something that faces forward 2 position directly before or ahead 3 place where two armies are fighting 4 (Meteorology) dividing line between a mass of cold air and a mass of warm air 5 outward appearance 6 (informal) cover for another, usually criminal, activity 7 particular field of activity: on the economic front 8 **in front** ahead or further forward 9 **in front**

of a in the presence of b before ▷ adjective 10 of or at the front > **frontal** adjective (formal): the frontal region of the brain

frontage noun wall of a building facing onto a street, river or public place; facade

frontier noun border between two countries

frontispiece noun illustration facing the title page of a book

frost noun 1 white frozen dew or mist 2 atmospheric temperature below freezing point

frostbite noun damage to your fingers, toes or ears caused by extreme cold

frosty frostier, frostiest adjective 1 below freezing 2 unfriendly > **frostily** adverb

froth noun 1 mass of small bubbles ▷ verb 2 to foam > **frothy** adjective

frown verb 1 to wrinkle your brows in worry, anger or thought ▷ noun 2 cross, frowning expression

froze verb past tense of **freeze**

frozen verb 1 past participle of **freeze** ▷ adjective 2 extremely cold

fructose noun type of sugar found in many fruits and in honey

frugal adjective 1 spending very little money; thrifty 2 (of a meal) small and cheap > **frugality** noun > **frugally** adverb

fruit noun 1 part of a plant containing seeds, especially if edible 2 (often plural) good result of an action or effort

fruitful adjective useful or productive

fruitless adjective useless or unproductive

fruit machine noun coin-operated gambling machine

fruit salad noun mixture of pieces of different fruits served in a juice as a dessert

fruity fruitier, fruitiest adjective **1** of or like fruit **2** (of a voice) rich and deep

frustrate verb **1** to make (someone) angry or upset by not allowing or preventing [t]hem from doing what they [w]ant **2** to hinder or prevent (a [pl]an) > **frustrated** adjective: [frus]trated motorists, desperate [to ge]t moving > **frustrating** [adjec]tive: a frustrating day at work > **frustration** noun: his frustration [at bein]g left out of the team

[fry ver]b frying, fried verb to cook [in oil co]oked in fat or oil

[fuchsia] [fyew]-sha] noun plant or [shrub wit]h pink, purple or white [flowers th]at hang downwards

[fudge noun] **1** soft brown sweet [made with] butter, milk and sugar [> verb to a]void making a firm [or clear] decision about

[fuel noun fu]el, fuelled noun [substance suc]h as coal or petrol [that is burned] to provide heat [or power used, for] to provide (a [machine or indust]ry) with fuel [*the*] *atmosphere*

[full-]house

[fugitive] noun person [someone] with from arrest

[furniture,]

[noun] m adjectives [suffix meaning of:] careful [doable] which [grand] to fill:
[of furniture]

fulcrum fulcrums or fulcra noun the point at which something is balancing or pivoting

fulfil fulfils, fulfilling, fulfilled verb **1** to carry out or achieve (a promise, duty, dream or hope) **2** (of work or activity) to satisfy (someone or yourself) completely > **fulfilling** adjective: a happy and fulfilling life > **fulfilment** noun: It was the fulfilment of a dream

full adjective **1** containing as much or as many as possible **2** complete, whole **3** (of clothes) loose and made from a lot of fabric **4** having had enough to eat **5** (of a figure) plump **6** (of a sound or flavour) rich and strong > adverb **7** completely **8** directly > noun **9** in full completely > **fullness** noun > **fully** adverb

full-blooded adjective vigorous or enthusiastic

full-blown adjective fully developed

full moon noun phase of the moon when it looks round and complete

full stop noun punctuation mark (.) used at the end of a sentence and after abbreviations or initials

full-time adjective **1** involving work for the whole of each normal working week > noun **2** (Sport) the end of a match > adverb **3** during the whole of each normal working week

fully-fledged adjective completely developed: I was a fully-fledged and mature human being

fulsome adjective exaggerated and elaborate, and often sounding insincere

fumble verb to handle something awkwardly

a
b
c
d
e
f
g
h
i
j
k
l
m
n
o
p
q
r
s
t
u
v
w
x
y
z

fume verb to be very angry > **fumes**
plural noun gases, vapours or
smoke which are released from
certain chemicals or burning
substances and which smell
unpleasant and may be toxic

fun noun 1 enjoyment or
amusement 2 **make fun of** to
mock or tease (someone)

function noun 1 purpose
something exists for 2 role or job
3 way something works 4 large
or formal social event 5 (Maths)
quantity whose value depends
on the varying value of another
> verb 6 to operate or work
7 **function as** to fill the role of

functional adjective 1 relating
to the way something works
2 practical rather than decorative
3 in working order

fund noun 1 stock of money for
a special purpose 2 supply or
store 3 **funds** money resources
> verb 4 to provide money
for (something or someone)
> **funding** noun: Where are they
going to get the funding?

fundamental adjective 1 essential
or primary 2 basic > noun 3 basic
rule or fact > **fundamentally**
adverb

fundi noun (S Afr) expert or boffin

funeral noun ceremony or
religious service for the burial or
cremation of a dead person

funereal [fyew-**neer**-ee-al]
adjective gloomy or sombre

funfair noun place or event
provided for outdoor
entertainment, having stalls and
rides on machines

fungicide noun substance that
destroys fungi

fungus fungi or funguses noun
organism such as a mushroom,
toadstool or mould that does not
have leaves and grows on other
living things > **fungal** adjective: a
fungal infection

funk verb 1 (old-fashioned, informal)
to avoid (doing something)
through fear > noun 2 style of
music with a strong rhythm based
on jazz and blues

funnel funnels, funnelling,
funnelled noun 1 tube with a cone
shape at the top for pouring liquids
into a narrow opening 2 metal
chimney on a ship or steam engine
> verb 3 to move or cause to move
through or as if through a funnel

funny funnier, funniest adjective
1 odd, strange or puzzling
2 causing amusement or laughter
> **funnily** adverb

fur noun 1 soft thick body hair of
many animals 2 animal skin with
the fur left on 3 coat made from
this > **furry** adjective: a furry to...

furious adjective 1 very angry
2 involving great energy, effort...
speed > **furiously** adverb

furlong noun unit of length eq...
to 220 yards (201.168 metres)

furnace noun enclosed cham...
containing a very hot fire us...
example, in the steel indust...
melting ore

furnish verb 1 to provide (a...
or room) with furniture 2 t...
supply or provide (someo...
something)

furnishings plural noun fu...
carpets and fittings

furniture noun large mov...
articles such as chairs an...
wardrobes: a few pieces o...

furore[fyew-**ror**-ee] *noun* angry and excited reaction

furrow *noun* **1** long, shallow trench made by a plough **2** groove, especially a wrinkle on the forehead ▷ *verb* **3 furrow your brow** to frown

further *adverb, adjective* **1** a comparative form of **far** ▷ *adjective* **2** additional or more **3** more distant ▷ *adverb* **4** in addition **5** to a greater distance or extent ▷ *verb* **6** to assist the progress of (something)

further education *noun* (Brit) education beyond school other than at a university

furthermore *adverb* (formal) besides

furthest 1 *adverb, adjective* a superlative form of **far** ▷ *adjective* **2** most distant ▷ *adverb* **3** to the greatest distance or extent

furtive *adjective* sly and secretive > **furtively** *adverb*

fury *noun* violent or extreme anger

fuse *noun* **1** safety device for electric circuits, containing a wire that melts and breaks the connection when the circuit is overloaded **2** long cord attached to some types of simple bomb which is lit to detonate the bomb ▷ *verb* **3** to stop working or cause (something) to stop working as a result of a blown fuse **4** to join or combine

fuselage[**few**-zill-lahzh] *noun* body of an aircraft

fusion *noun* **1** something new created by a mixture of qualities, ideas or things **2** the joining together of two or more things to form one thing **3** the melting together of two substances **4** combination of the nucleus of two atoms with the release of energy

fuss *noun* **1** needless activity, worry or attentiveness **2** complaint or objection ▷ *verb* **3** to show unnecessary concern or attention over unimportant things

fussy fussier, fussiest *adjective* **1** inclined to fuss **2** overparticular **3** overelaborate

futile *adjective* having no chance of success: *a futile attempt to calm the storm* > **futility** *noun*: *the futility of war*

future *noun* **1** time to come **2** what will happen **3** prospects ▷ *adjective* **4** yet to come or be **5** of or relating to time to come **6** (of a verb tense) indicating that the action specified has not yet taken place

futuristic *adjective* (of a design) very modern and strange, as if belonging to a time in the future

fuzz *noun* mass of fine or curly hairs or fibres

g

g symbol **1** gram(s) **2** (acceleration due to) gravity

gabble verb **1** to speak rapidly and indistinctly ▷ noun **2** rapid indistinct speech

gable noun triangular upper part of a wall between sloping roofs

gadget noun small mechanical device or appliance > **gadgetry** noun gadgets

Gaelic [**gal**-lik, **gay**-lik] noun any of the Celtic languages of Ireland and the Scottish Highlands

gaffe noun social blunder

gaffer noun (Brit informal) foreman or boss

gag gags, gagging, gagged verb **1** to choke and nearly vomit **2** to stop up the mouth of (someone) with a strip of cloth **3** to deprive (someone) of free speech ▷ noun **5** (informal) joke

gaggle noun **1** (informal) disorderly crowd **2** flock of geese

gaiety noun **1** cheerfulness **2** merrymaking

gaily adverb merrily

gain verb **1** to acquire or obtain (something) **2** (followed by from) to get an advantage from a situation **3** (of a watch or clock) to be or become too fast ▷ noun **4** profit or advantage

5 increase > **gain on** or **upon** verb to get nearer to or catch up with (someone)

gait noun manner of walking

gala [**gah**-la] noun **1** festival **2** competitive sporting event

galah noun (Aust) **1** cockatoo with a pink breast and a grey back and wings **2** (informal) stupid person

galaxy galaxies noun system of stars

gale noun strong wind

gall [**gawl**] noun **1** (informal) impudence ▷ verb **2** to annoy (someone)

gallant adjective **1** brave and noble **2** (of a man) attentive to women > **gallantly** adverb > **gallantry** noun **1** showy, attentive treatment of women **2** bravery

gall bladder noun organ next to the liver that stores bile

galleon noun large three-masted sailing ship of the 15th–17th centuries

gallery galleries noun **1** [ART] room or building for displaying works of art **2** balcony in a church, theatre, etc

galley noun **1** kitchen of a ship or aircraft **2** (History) ship propelled by oars, usually rowed by slaves

Gallic adjective (literary) French

gallon noun liquid measure of eight pints, equal to 4.55 litres

gallop noun **1** horse's fastest pace **2** galloping ▷ verb **3** to go or ride at a gallop **4** to move or progress rapidly

gallows noun wooden structure used for hanging criminals

gallstone noun small painful lump formed in the gall bladder or its ducts

galore adverb in abundance: chocolates galore

galoshes plural noun (Brit, Aust, NZ) waterproof shoes for wearing on top of ordinary shoes

galvanized or **galvanised** adjective (of metal) coated with zinc by an electrical process to protect it from rust

gambit noun 1 opening line or move intended to secure an advantage 2 (Chess) opening move involving the sacrifice of a pawn

gamble verb 1 to bet money on the result of a game or race; wager 2 to risk losing (something) in the hope of gaining an advantage ▷ noun 3 risky undertaking ▷ **gambler** noun person who gambles regularly ▷ **gambling** noun activity of betting money

game noun 1 amusement or pastime 2 contest for amusement 3 single period of play in a contest 4 animals or birds hunted for sport or food 5 scheme or trick ▷ adjective 6 willing to try something unusual or difficult ▷ **gamely** adverb: He gamely defended the decision ▷ **gaming** noun gambling

gamekeeper noun (Brit, Aust, SAfr) person employed to look after game animals and birds on a country estate

games console noun electronic device enabling computer games to be played on a TV screen

gammon noun cured or smoked ham

gamut [**gam**-mut] noun whole range or scale (of music, emotions, etc)

gander noun male goose

gang noun group of people who join together for some purpose, e.g. to commit a crime ▷ **gang up on** verb to join together to oppose (someone)

gangplank noun portable bridge for boarding or leaving a ship

gangrene noun decay of body tissue as a result of disease or injury ▷ **gangrenous** adjective: gangrenous limbs

gangster noun member of a criminal gang

gannet noun large sea bird

gaol [**jayl**] noun same as **jail**

gap noun 1 break or opening 2 great difference: the gap between fantasy and reality

gape verb 1 to stare with the mouth open in surprise 2 to be wide open ▷ **gaping** adjective: gaping holes in the wall

garage noun 1 building where cars are kept 2 place for the refuelling, sale and repair of cars

garb noun (formal) clothes

garbage noun 1 rubbish, especially household rubbish 2 nonsense

garbled adjective (of a story etc) jumbled and confused

garden noun 1 piece of land for growing flowers, fruit or vegetables 2 **gardens** ornamental park ▷ **gardener** noun person who looks after a garden as a job or hobby ▷ **gardening** noun looking after a garden as a job or hobby

gargle verb to wash the throat with a liquid by breathing out slowly through the liquid

gargoyle noun waterspout carved in the form of a grotesque face, especially on a church

garish adjective crudely bright or colourful

garland noun circle of flowers worn or hung as a decoration

garlic noun pungent bulb of a plant of the onion family, used in cooking

garment noun article of clothing

garnet noun red semiprecious stone

garnish verb 1 to decorate (food) ▷ noun 2 decoration for food

garret noun attic in a house

garrison noun 1 troops stationed in a town or fort 2 fortified place

garrotte [gar-**rot**] verb to strangle (someone) with a piece of wire

garter noun band worn round the leg to hold up a sock or stocking

gas gases; gasses; gassing; gassed noun 1 airlike substance that is not liquid or solid 2 fossil fuel in the form of a gas, used for heating 3 (Chiefly US) petrol ▷ verb 4 to poison (people or animals) with gas ▷ adjective 5 of or like gas 6 filled with gas

> **WORD TIP**
> The plural of the noun *gas* is *gases*. The verb forms of *gas* are spelt with a double *s*

gas chamber noun airtight room which is filled with poison gas to kill people or animals

gash verb 1 to make a long deep cut in (something) ▷ noun 2 long deep cut

gas mask noun mask with a chemical filter to protect the wearer against poison gas

gasoline noun (US) petrol

gasp verb 1 to draw in breath sharply or with difficulty ▷ noun 2 convulsive intake of breath

gastric adjective of the stomach

gate noun 1 movable barrier, usually hinged, in a wall or fence 2 number of people attending a sporting event

gateau gateaux [**gat**-toe] noun rich layered cake with cream in it

gatecrash verb to enter (a party) uninvited

gateway noun 1 entrance with a gate 2 means of access: *New York is the great gateway to America*

gather verb 1 to come together in a group; assemble 2 to collect (a number of things) gradually 3 to increase (something) gradually 4 to learn (something) from information given

gathering noun meeting of people who have come together for a particular purpose

gauche [**gohsh**] adjective socially awkward

gaudy gaudier, gaudiest [**gaw-dee**] adjective vulgarly bright or colourful

gauge [**gayj**] verb 1 to estimate or calculate (something) ▷ noun 2 measuring instrument 3 scale or standard of measurement 4 distance between the rails of a railway track

gaunt adjective lean and haggard

gauntlet noun 1 heavy glove with a long cuff 2 **run the gauntlet** to be exposed to criticism or unpleasant treatment 3 **throw down the gauntlet** to offer a challenge

gave verb past tense of **give**

gay adjective 1 homosexual 2 (old-fashioned) carefree and merry ▷ noun 3 homosexual person

> **WORD TIP**
> The most common meaning

of *gay* now is 'homosexual'. In some older books it may have its old-fashioned meaning of 'lively and full of fun'. The noun *gaiety* is related to this older meaning of *gay*. The noun that means 'the state of being homosexual' is *gayness*

gaze verb to look fixedly

gazelle noun small graceful antelope

gazette noun official publication containing announcements

GB abbreviation Great Britain

GCSE abbreviation (in Britain) General Certificate of Secondary Education

gear noun **1** set of toothed wheels connecting with another or with a rack to change the direction or speed of transmitted motion **2** mechanism for transmitting motion by gears **3** setting of a gear to suit engine speed: *first gear* **4** clothing or belongings **5** equipment ▷ verb **6** (followed by to) to prepare (someone) or organize (something) for a particular event or purpose

geek noun (informal) **1** boring, unattractive person **2** person highly knowledgeable in computing > **geeky** adjective

geese noun plural of **goose**

gel gels, gelling, gelled [jell] noun **1** jelly-like substance, especially one used to set a hairstyle ▷ verb **2** to form a gel **3** (informal) to take on a definite form

gelatine [jel-at-teen] or **gelatin** noun **1** substance made by boiling animal bones **2** edible jelly made of this

gelding noun castrated horse

gem noun **1** precious stone or jewel **2** highly valued person or thing

Gemini [jem-in-nye] noun third sign of the zodiac, represented by a pair of twins

gemsbok gemsbok or gemsboks noun (SAfr) oryx, a type of large antelope with straight horns

gen noun (informal) information

gender noun **1** [PSHE] state of being male or female **2** (Grammar) classification of nouns in certain languages as masculine, feminine or neuter

gene [jean] noun part of a cell which determines inherited characteristics

general adjective **1** common or widespread **2** of or affecting all or most **3** not specific **4** including or dealing with various or miscellaneous items **5** highest in authority or rank: *general manager* ▷ noun **6** very senior army officer **7 in general** mostly or usually > **generally** adverb usually

general election noun election in which everyone old enough to vote can vote for the candidate they want to represent them in Parliament

generalize or **generalise** verb to say that something is true in most cases, ignoring minor details > **generalization** noun: *That's rather a sweeping generalization*

general practitioner noun doctor who works in the community rather than in a hospital

generate verb to produce (something) or bring (something) into being

generation noun **1** all the people born about the same time

2 average time between two generations (about 30 years)

generator noun machine for converting mechanical energy into electrical energy

generic [jin-**ner**-ik] adjective of a class, group or genus > **generically** adverb

generous adjective **1** (PSHE) very willing to give money or time **2** very large; ample > **generosity** noun (PSHE) state of being generous > **generously** adverb

genesis [**jen**-iss-iss] noun (formal) beginning or origin

genetic [jin-**net**-tik] adjective relating to genes or genetics > **genetically** adverb > **genetics** noun study of heredity and variation in organisms

genial [**jean**-ee-al] adjective cheerful and friendly > **genially** adverb in a cheerful and friendly manner

genie [**jean**-ee] noun (in fairy tales) servant who appears by magic and grants wishes

genitals or **genitalia** [jen-it-**ail**-ya] plural noun external sexual organs

genius geniuses [**jean**-yuss] noun (person with) exceptional ability in a particular field

genocide [**jen**-no-side] noun murder of a race of people

genome [**jee**-nome] noun all of the genes contained in a single cell of an organism

genre [**zhohn**-ra] noun (ENGLISH) style of literary, musical or artistic work

genteel adjective very polite and refined

gentile adjective, noun non-Jewish (person)

gentility noun excessive politeness and refinement

gentle adjective **1** mild or kindly **2** not rough or severe **3** gradual **4** easily controlled, tame > **gentleness** noun: the gentleness with which she treated her pregnant mother > **gently** adverb

gentleman gentlemen noun **1** polite well-bred man **2** man of high social position **3** polite name for a man > **gentlemanly** adjective (of a man) having good manners

gentry plural noun people just below the nobility in social rank

genuine adjective **1** not fake, authentic **2** sincere > **genuinely** adverb > **genuineness** noun: the genuineness of their intentions

genus genera [**jean**-uss] noun (Biology) group into which a family of animals or plants is divided

geo- prefix earth: geography; geologist

geography noun study of the earth's physical features, climate, population, etc > **geographical** or **geographic** adjective relating to geography > **geographically** adverb in a geographical sense

geology noun study of the earth's origin, structure and composition > **geological** adjective relating to geology > **geologist** noun person who studies geology

geometry noun branch of mathematics dealing with points, lines, curves and surfaces > **geometric** or **geometrical** adjective **1** consisting of regular lines and shapes, such as squares, triangles and circles **2** involving geometry > **geometrically** *adverb* in a geometric pattern

Georgian *adjective* of the time of any of the four kings of Britain called George, esp. 1714–1830

geranium *noun* cultivated plant with red, pink or white flowers

gerbil [jer-bill] *noun* burrowing desert rodent of Asia and Africa

geriatrics *noun* branch of medicine dealing with old age and its diseases > **geriatric** *adjective, noun* old (person)

germ *noun* **1** very small organism that causes disease **2** (*formal*) beginning from which something may develop

German *noun* **1** language of Germany, Austria and part of Switzerland **2** person from Germany ▷ *adjective* **3** of Germany or its language > **Germanic** *adjective* typical of Germany or the German people

German measles *noun* contagious disease accompanied by a cough, sore throat, and red spots

germinate *verb* **1** (of a seed) to start to grow **2** (of an idea or plan) to start to develop > **germination** *noun*: *the germination of a seed*

gerrymander *verb* to alter political boundaries in an area to give unfair advantage to a particular party and make it more likely that its candidate(s) will do well in elections > **gerrymandering** *noun*

gestation *noun* period of carrying of young in the womb between conception and birth

gesticulate *verb* to make expressive movements with the hands and arms > **gesticulation** *noun*

gesture *noun* **1** movement to convey meaning **2** thing said or done to show your feelings ▷ *verb* **3** to move the hands or head in order to communicate a message or feeling

get gets, getting, got *verb* **1** to obtain or receive (something) **2** to bring or fetch (something) **3** to become as specified: *to get wet* **4** to understand (something), often followed by (to) to) **5** (often followed by to) to come to or arrive at (a place) **6** to go on board (a plane, bus, etc) **7** to persuade (someone) to do something > **get across** *verb* to cause (something) to be understood > **get at** *verb* **1** to imply or mean (something) **2** to criticize (someone) > **get away with** *verb* not to be found out or punished for doing (something dishonest) > **get by** *verb* to manage in spite of difficulties > **get on** *verb* **1** (of two people) to like each other's company **2** to do (a task) > **get over with** *verb* to be finished with (something unpleasant) > **get through to** *verb* **1** to make (someone) understand what you are saying **2** to contact (someone) by telephone

getaway *noun* escape made by criminals

get-together *noun* (*informal*) informal meeting or party

geyser [geez-er] *noun* **1** spring that discharges steam and hot water **2** (*Brit, SAfr*) domestic gas water heater

Ghanaian [gah-**nay**-an] adjective **1** of Ghana ▷ noun **2** person from Ghana

ghastly ghastlier, ghastliest adjective extremely horrible and unpleasant

gherkin noun small pickled cucumber

ghetto ghettoes or ghettos noun part of a city where many poor people of a particular race live

ghost noun spirit of a dead person, believed to haunt people or places

ghoulish [**gool**-ish] adjective very interested in unpleasant things such as death and murder

giant noun **1** mythical being of superhuman size ▷ adjective **2** much larger than other similar things: giant prawns

gibberish noun speech that makes no sense at all

gibbon [**gib**-bon] noun ape with very long arms

gibe [jibe] noun same as **jibe**

gidday or **g'day** interjection (Aust & NZ) expression of greeting

giddy giddier, giddiest adjective feeling unsteady on your feet, usually because of illness
> **giddily** adverb dizzily

gift noun **1** present **2** natural talent
> **gifted** adjective talented

gig noun **1** rock or jazz concert **2** light two-wheeled horse-drawn carriage

gigantic adjective enormous

giggle verb **1** to laugh in a nervous or embarrassed way ▷ noun **2** short nervous laugh > **giggly** adjective laughing in a nervous or embarrassed way

gilded adjective covered with a thin layer of gold

gill[1] [jill] noun liquid measure of quarter of a pint, equal to 0.142 litres

gill[2] [gil] noun organ on the sides of a fish that it uses for breathing

gilt adjective **1** covered with a thin layer of gold ▷ noun **2** thin layer of gold used as decoration

gimmick noun something designed to attract attention or publicity
> **gimmicky** adjective designed to attract attention or publicity

gin noun strong, colourless alcoholic drink made from grain and juniper berries

ginger noun **1** plant root with a hot spicy flavour, used in cooking ▷ adjective **2** bright orange or red: ginger hair

gingerbread noun moist cake flavoured with ginger

gingerly adverb cautiously

gingham noun checked cotton cloth

gipsy noun same as **Gypsy**

giraffe noun a tall four-legged African mammal with a very long neck

girder noun large metal beam used in the construction of a bridge or a building

girdle noun woman's corset

girl noun female child > **girlhood** noun period of being a girl
> **girlish** adjective like a young girl

girlfriend noun girl or woman with whom a person is romantically or sexually involved

giro giros [**jire**-oh] noun **1** (in some countries) system of transferring money within a post office or bank directly from one account to another **2** (Brit informal) social security payment by giro cheque

girth noun measurement round something

gist [**jist**] noun substance or main point of a matter

give gives, giving, gave, given verb **1** to present (something) to another person **2** to utter or emit (something) **3** to organize or host (a party or meal) **4** to yield or break under pressure ▷ noun **5** resilience or elasticity > **give in** verb to admit defeat > **given** verb **1** the past participle of **give** ▷ adjective **2** fixed or specified: My style can change at any given moment > **give out** verb to stop working: the electricity gave out > **give up** verb **1** to stop doing (something) **2** to admit defeat **3** to let the police know where (someone) is hiding

glacé [**glass**-say] adjective preserved in a thick sugary syrup: glacé cherries

glacier noun slow-moving mass of ice formed by accumulated snow > **glaciation** noun (Geography) condition of being covered with sheet ice

glad gladder, gladdest adjective **1** pleased and happy **2 glad to** very willing to (do something) > **gladly** adverb > **gladness** noun: a night of joy and gladness

glade noun open space in a forest

gladiator noun (in ancient Rome) man trained to fight in arenas to provide entertainment

gladiolus gladioli noun garden plant with sword-shaped leaves

glamour noun alluring charm or fascination > **glamorous** adjective alluring

glance verb **1** to look rapidly or briefly ▷ noun **2** brief look

> **glance off** verb to strike and be deflected off (an object) at an oblique angle

gland noun organ that produces and secretes substances in the body > **glandular** adjective: glandular tissue

glare verb **1** to stare angrily ▷ noun **2** angry stare **3** unpleasant brightness

glass noun **1** hard, transparent substance that is easily broken, used to make windows and bottles **2** tumbler > **glassy** adjective **1** like glass **2** expressionless

glasses plural noun spectacles

glaze verb **1** to fit a sheet of glass into the frame of (a window) **2** to cover (pottery or food) with a smooth shiny surface ▷ noun **3** smooth shiny surface on pottery or food > **glaze over** verb (of eyes) to become dull and expressionless, as when someone is bored

glazed adjective (of a facial expression) looking bored

gleam noun **1** brief beam or glow of light **2** brief or faint indication ▷ verb **3** to shine and reflect light

glean verb to gather (facts etc) bit by bit

glee noun (old-fashioned) triumph and delight > **gleeful** adjective happy and excited, often at someone else's bad luck > **gleefully** adverb in a gleeful manner

glen noun deep narrow valley, especially in Scotland

glide verb **1** to move easily and smoothly **2** (of an aircraft) to move without the use of engines

glider noun aircraft without an engine which floats on air currents

glimmer verb 1 to shine faintly, flicker ▷ noun 2 faint gleam 3 faint indication

glimpse noun 1 brief or incomplete view ▷ verb 2 to catch a glimpse of (someone or something)

glint verb 1 to gleam brightly ▷ noun 2 quick flash of light 3 brightness in someone's eye expressing some emotion: *a glint of mischief*

glisten verb to gleam by reflecting light

glitter verb 1 to shine with bright flashes ▷ noun 2 sparkle or brilliance 3 tiny pieces of shiny decorative material

gloat verb to cruelly show your pleasure about your own success or someone else's failure

global adjective worldwide

globalization noun trend towards the existence of a single world market dominated by multinational companies

global warming noun increase in the overall temperature worldwide believed to be caused by the greenhouse effect

globe noun 1 sphere with a map of the earth on it 2 spherical object 3 (SAfr) light bulb 4 **the globe** GEOGRAPHY the earth

gloom noun 1 melancholy or depression 2 darkness > **gloomy** adjective 1 melancholy or unhappy 2 dark or dim > **gloomily** adverb

glorify glorifies, glorifying, glorified verb to make (something) seem more worthy than it is > **glorification** noun: *the glorification of violence*

glorious adjective 1 brilliantly beautiful 2 delightful 3 involving great fame and success > **gloriously** adverb

glory glories, glorying, gloried noun 1 praise or honour 2 something considered splendid or admirable ▷ verb 3 (followed by in) to take great delight in (something)

glory box noun (Aust, NZ old-fashioned) chest in which a young woman stores household goods and linen for her marriage

gloss noun 1 bright shine on a surface 2 attractive appearance that may hide less attractive qualities > **gloss over** verb to try to cover up or pass over (a fault or error)

glossary glossaries noun list of words with their explanations or translations, usually found at the back of a book

glossy glossier, glossiest adjective 1 smooth and shiny 2 (of a magazine) printed on shiny paper

glove noun covering for the hand with individual sheaths for each finger and the thumb

glow verb 1 to shine with a dull steady light 2 to have a strong feeling of pleasure or happiness ▷ noun 3 dull steady light 4 strong feeling of pleasure or happiness

glower [rhymes with **power**] verb, noun (to) scowl

glowing adjective (of a description, report, etc) full of praise

glucose noun kind of sugar found in fruit

glue glues, gluing or glueing, glued noun 1 substance used for sticking things together ▷ verb 2 to stick (objects) together using glue

glum glummer, glummest
adjective sullen or gloomy
> **glumly** *adverb*

glut *noun* excessive supply

gluten [gloo-ten] *noun* sticky
protein found in cereal grain

glutton *noun* **1** greedy person
2 person with a great capacity for
something > **gluttony** *noun* state
of being greedy

gnarled *adjective* rough, twisted
and knobbly

gnat *noun* small biting two-
winged fly

gnaw gnaws, gnawing, gnawed
verb **1** to bite or chew (something)
steadily **2** (followed by *at*) to
cause constant distress to
(someone)

gnome *noun* imaginary creature
like a little old man

gnu [noo] *noun* oxlike S African
antelope

go goes, going, went, gone *verb*
1 to move to or from a place **2** to
depart **3** to be, do or become as
specified: *She felt she was going mad*
4 (often followed by *with*) to blend
or harmonize with (something)
5 to fail or break down **6** to be
got rid of > *noun* **7** attempt > **go
back on** *verb* to break (a promise
etc) > **go down** *verb* to get a
particular kind of reception: *His
speech went down well* > **go for**
verb **1** to like (something) very
much **2** to attack (someone)
> **go off** *verb* **1** (of a bomb) to
explode **2** (*informal*) to stop liking
(someone or something) > **go
on** *verb* **1** to continue (doing
something) **2** to keep talking
about (something) in a rather
boring way **3** to be happening

> **go through** *verb* **1** to experience
(an unpleasant event) **2** (of a law
or agreement) to be approved and
become official > **go through
with** *verb* to do (something) even
though it is unpleasant

goad *verb* to provoke (someone) to
take some kind of action, usually
in anger

go-ahead *noun* permission to do
something

goal *noun* **1** (*Sport*) posts through
which the ball or puck has to be
propelled to score **2** score made in
this way **3** aim or purpose

goalkeeper *noun* (*Sport*) player
whose task is to stop shots
entering the goal

goanna *noun* large Australian
lizard

goat *noun* animal like a sheep with
coarse hair, a beard and horns

go-away bird *noun* (*SAfr*) grey
lourie, a type of bird that lives in
open grassland

gob *noun* (*Brit, Aust, NZ informal*)
mouth

gobble *verb* **1** to eat (food) hastily
and greedily **2** to make the rapid
gurgling cry of the male turkey

gobbledygook or
gobbledegook *noun* language
or jargon that is impossible to
understand

goblet *noun* drinking cup without
handles

goblin *noun* ugly mischievous
creature in fairy stories

god *noun* **1** spirit or being
worshipped as having
supernatural power **2** object of
worship, idol **3** God (in religions
such as Islam, Christianity and
Judaism) the Supreme Being,

creator and ruler of the universe **4 the gods** top balcony in a theatre

godchild godchildren noun child for whom a person stands as godparent ▷ **goddaughter** noun girl for whom a person stands as godparent ▷ **godson** noun boy for whom a person stands as godparent

goddess noun female god

godparent noun person who promises at a child's baptism to bring the child up as a Christian ▷ **godfather** noun **1** male godparent **2** head of a criminal, especially Mafia, organization ▷ **godmother** noun female godparent

godsend noun something unexpected but welcome

goggles plural noun protective spectacles

going noun condition of the ground for walking or riding over

gold noun **1** yellow precious metal **2** coins or articles made of this ▷ adjective **3** gold-coloured

golden adjective **1** made of gold **2** gold-coloured **3** very successful or promising

golden rule noun important principle

golden wedding noun fiftieth wedding anniversary

goldfish noun orange fish kept in ponds or aquariums

> **WORD TIP**
> The plural of goldfish is goldfish

goldsmith noun person whose job is making jewellery out of gold

golf noun outdoor game in which a ball is struck with clubs into a series of holes ▷ **golfer** noun person who plays golf

golf course noun area of grassy land where people play golf

gondola noun long narrow boat used in Venice

gone verb past participle of **go**

gong noun flat circular piece of metal that produces a note when struck

good better, best adjective **1** pleasant, acceptable or satisfactory **2** kind, thoughtful and loving **3** skilful or successful: good at art **4** well-behaved **5** used to emphasize something: a good few million pounds **6** as good as virtually ▷ noun **7** benefit **8** positive moral qualities **9 for good** permanently

> **WORD TIP**
> Good is an adjective, and should not be used as an adverb. You should say that a person did well, not did good

goodbye interjection, noun expression used on parting

Good Friday noun Friday before Easter, when Christians remember the crucifixion of Christ

good-natured adjective friendly, pleasant and even-tempered

goodness noun **1** quality of being kind ▷ interjection **2** exclamation of surprise

goodwill noun kindly feeling

goody goodies noun **1** (informal) hero in a book or film **2** enjoyable thing

goose geese noun web-footed bird like a large duck

gooseberry gooseberries noun edible yellowy-green berry

gore noun **1** blood from a wound ▷ verb **2** to pierce (someone) with horns

gorge noun **1** deep narrow valley ▷ verb **gorge yourself** to eat greedily

gorgeous adjective **1** strikingly beautiful or attractive **2** (informal) very pleasant

gorilla noun very large strong ape with very dark fur

gorse noun prickly yellow-flowered shrub

gory gorier, goriest adjective **1** horrific or bloodthirsty **2** involving bloodshed

gosling noun young goose

gospel noun **1 Gospel** any of the first four books of the New Testament **2** unquestionable truth **3** Black religious music originating in the churches of the Southern US

gossip gossips, gossiping, gossiped noun **1** idle talk, especially about other people **2** person who engages in gossip ▷ verb **3** to engage in gossip

got verb **1** past of **get 2 have got** to possess **3 have got to** to need or be required to

gouge [gowj] verb **1** to scoop or force (something) out **2** to cut a hole or groove in something

goulash [goo-lash] noun rich stew seasoned with paprika, originally from Hungary

gourd [goord] noun fleshy fruit of a climbing plant

gourmet [goor-may] noun person who enjoys good food and drink and knows a lot about it

gout [gowt] noun disease causing inflammation of the joints, especially in the toes

govern verb **1** to control (a country) **2** to influence (a situation)

governess noun woman teacher in a private household

government noun HISTORY **1** group of people who govern a country **2** control and organization of a country > **governmental** adjective: a governmental agency

governor noun **1** person who controls and organizes a state or an institution **2** (Aust) representative of the King or Queen in a State

governor general governors general noun chief representative of the King or Queen in Australia, New Zealand and other Commonwealth countries

gown noun **1** woman's long formal dress **2** official robe worn by judges, clergymen, etc

GP abbreviation general practitioner

grab grabs, grabbing, grabbed verb **1** to grasp (something) suddenly, snatch (something) ▷ noun **2** sudden snatch

grace noun **1** beauty and elegance; poise **2** polite kind behaviour **3** short prayer of thanks for a meal **4 Grace** title of a duke, duchess or archbishop ▷ verb **5** to kindly agree to be present at (an event) > **graceful** adjective: graceful ballerinas > **gracefully** adverb

gracious adjective **1** kind, polite and pleasant ▷ interjection **2 good gracious!** exclamation of surprise > **graciously** adverb

grade noun **1** place on a scale of quality, rank or size **2** mark or rating ▷ verb **3** to arrange (things) in grades

gradient noun (degree of) slope

a b c d e f g h i j k l m n o p q r s t u v w x y z

gradual adjective occurring, developing or moving in small stages > **gradually** adverb happening or changing slowly over a long period of time

graduate verb 1 to receive a degree or diploma 2 to progress gradually from one thing towards another ▷ noun 3 holder of a degree > **graduation** noun: They asked what his plans were after graduation

graffiti [graf-**fee**-tee] noun words or drawings scribbled or sprayed on walls etc

> **WORD TIP**
>
> Although graffiti is a plural in Italian, the language it comes from, in English it can be either a singular or a plural noun

graft noun 1 surgical transplant of skin or tissue 2 shoot of a plant set in the stalk of another 3 (informal) hard work 4 to transplant (living tissue) surgically 5 to insert (a plant shoot) in another stalk

grain noun 1 seedlike fruit of a cereal plant 2 cereal plants in general 3 small hard particle 4 very small amount 5 arrangement of fibres, as in wood 6 texture or pattern resulting from this 7 **go against the grain** to be contrary to your natural inclination

gram or **gramme** noun metric unit of mass equal to one thousandth of a kilogram

grammar noun branch of linguistics dealing with the form, function and order of words

grammar school noun 1 (Brit) especially formerly, a secondary school providing an education with a strong academic bias 2 (Aust) private school, usually one controlled by a church

grammatical adjective according to the rules of grammar > **grammatically** adverb

gran noun (Brit, Aust, NZ informal) grandmother

granary granaries noun 1 storehouse for grain ▷ adjective 2 (Granary®) (of bread) containing whole grains of wheat

grand adjective 1 large or impressive, imposing 2 dignified or haughty 3 (informal) excellent 4 (of a total) final ▷ noun 5 (informal) thousand pounds or dollars > **grandly** adverb in a manner intended to impress

grandad or **granddad** noun (informal) grandfather

grandchild grandchildren noun child of your son or daughter

granddaughter noun female grandchild

grandeur noun magnificence

grandfather noun male grandparent

grandfather clock noun tall standing clock with a pendulum and wooden case

grandiose adjective intended to be very impressive but seeming ridiculous

grandma noun (informal) grandmother

grandmother noun female grandparent

grandparent noun parent of your father or mother

grand piano noun large harp-shaped piano with the strings set horizontally

grandson noun male grandchild

grandstand noun terraced block of seats giving the best view at a sports ground

granite [gran-nit] noun very hard rock often used in building

granny grannies noun (informal) grandmother

grant verb 1 to allow someone to have (something) 2 to admit the truth of (something) 3 take for granted a to accept (something) as true without proof b to take advantage of (someone) without due appreciation ▷ noun 4 sum of money provided by a government for a specific purpose, such as education

granule noun small grain

grape noun small juicy green or purple berry, eaten raw or used to produce wine, raisins, currants or sultanas

grapefruit noun large round yellow citrus fruit

grapevine noun 1 grape-bearing vine 2 (informal) unofficial way of spreading news

graph noun [MATHS] diagram in which a line shows how two sets of numbers or measurements are related

-graph suffix writer or recorder of some sort or something made by writing, drawing or recording: telegraph; autograph

graphic adjective 1 vividly descriptive 2 of or using drawing, painting, etc
> **graphically** adverb in a vividly descriptive fashion > **graphics** plural noun [ICT] diagrams, graphs, etc, especially as used on a television programme or computer screen

graphite noun soft black form of carbon, used in pencil leads

grapple verb (followed by with) 1 to try to cope with (something difficult) 2 to come to grips with (a person)

grasp verb 1 to grip (something) firmly 2 to understand (something) ▷ noun 3 grip or clasp 4 understanding

grass noun common green plant that grows on lawns and in parks > **grassy** adjective covered in grass

grasshopper noun jumping insect with long hind legs

grate verb 1 to rub (food) into small bits against a grater 2 to scrape with a harsh rasping noise (followed by on) to annoy (someone) ▷ noun 4 framework of metal bars for holding fuel in a fireplace

grateful adjective feeling or showing gratitude; thankful > **gratefully** adverb thankfully

grater noun small metal tool used for grating food

gratify gratifies, gratifying, gratified verb 1 to satisfy or please (someone) 2 to indulge (a desire or whim)

grating adjective 1 harsh or rasping ▷ noun 2 framework of metal bars covering an opening

gratis adverb, adjective free, for nothing

gratitude noun feeling of being thankful for a favour or gift; appreciation

gratuitous adjective unjustified: gratuitous violence > **gratuitously** adverb unnecessarily

grave[1] noun 1 hole for burying a corpse ▷ adjective 2 serious and solemn > **gravely** adverb

grave² [rhymes with **halve**] noun accent (`) over a vowel to indicate a special pronunciation

gravel noun mixture of small stones and coarse sand

gravestone noun stone marking a grave

graveyard noun area of land where corpses are buried

gravitate verb to be drawn towards something

gravitation noun force that causes objects to be attracted to each other > **gravitational** adjective: the earth's gravitational pull

gravity noun 1 force of attraction of one object for another, especially of objects to the earth 2 seriousness or importance

gravy noun 1 juices from meat in cooking 2 sauce made from these

graze verb 1 (of animals) to feed on grass 2 to scratch or scrape (a body part) ▷ noun 3 slight scratch or scrape

grease noun 1 soft melted animal fat 2 any thick oily substance ▷ verb 3 to apply grease to (something) > **greasy** adjective covered with or containing grease

great adjective 1 large in size or number 2 important 3 (informal) excellent > **greatly** adverb: People would benefit greatly from a pollution-free environment > **greatness** noun: Abraham Lincoln achieved greatness

Great Britain noun largest of the British Isles, consisting of England, Scotland and Wales

Great Dane noun very large dog with short smooth hair

great-grandfather noun father's or mother's grandfather

great-grandmother noun father's or mother's grandmother

greed noun excessive desire for food, wealth, etc

greedy greedier, greediest adjective wanting more of something than you really need > **greedily** adverb > **greediness** noun being greedy

Greek noun 1 language of Greece 2 person from Greece ▷ adjective 3 of Greece, the Greeks or the Greek language

green adjective 1 of a colour between blue and yellow 2 **Green** of or concerned with environmental issues 3 (informal) young and inexperienced ▷ noun 4 colour between blue and yellow 5 area of grass in the middle of a village 6 grassy area on which putting or bowls is played 7 area of smooth short grass around each hole on a golf course 8 **Green** person concerned with environmental issues 9 **greens** green vegetables > **greenery** noun vegetation

greenfly greenfly or greenflies noun small green insect that damages plants

greengrocer noun (Brit) shopkeeper selling vegetables and fruit

greenhouse noun glass building for growing plants that need to be kept warm

greenhouse effect noun rise in the temperature of the earth caused by heat absorbed from the sun being unable to leave the atmosphere

green paper noun (Brit, Aust, NZ) report published by the government containing proposals to be discussed before decisions are made about them

greenstone noun (NZ) type of green jade used for Māori ornaments

greet verb **1** to meet (someone) with expressions of welcome **2** to react to (something) in a specified manner: *This decision was greeted with dismay*

greeting noun something friendly that you say to someone you meet

gregarious adjective fond of company

grenade noun small bomb thrown by hand or fired from a rifle

grevillea noun Australian evergreen tree or shrub

grew verb past tense of **grow**

grey adjective **1** of a colour between black and white **2** dull or boring ▷ noun **3** grey colour ▷ **greying** adjective (of hair) turning grey ▷ **greyness** noun: *winter's greyness*

greyed out adjective (of an item on a computer screen) unavailable

greyhound noun swift slender dog used in racing

grid noun **1** network of horizontal and vertical lines, bars, etc **2** national network of electricity supply cables

grief noun deep sadness; sorrow

grievance noun cause for complaint

grieve verb to feel grief or cause (someone) to feel grief

grievous adjective very serious ▷ **grievously** adverb: *grievously injured*

grill noun **1** device on a cooker that radiates heat downwards

2 a metal frame on which you cook food over a fire **3** grilled food ▷ verb **4** to cook (food) under a grill **5** to question (someone) relentlessly

grille or **grill** noun grating over an opening

grim grimmer, grimmest adjective **1** (of a person) very serious or stern **2** (of a place) unattractive and depressing **3** (of a situation or piece of news) very unpleasant and worrying ▷ **grimly** adverb in a grim manner

grimace noun ugly or distorted facial expression of pain, disgust, etc ▷ verb **2** to make a grimace

grime noun ingrained dirt ▷ **grimy** adjective: *a grimy industrial city*

grin grins, grinning, grinned verb **1** to smile broadly, showing the teeth ▷ noun **2** broad smile

grind grinds, grinding, ground verb **1** to crush or rub (something) to a powder; powder **2** to scrape (the teeth) together with a harsh noise

grip grips, gripping, gripped noun **1** firm hold or grasp **2** control over a situation **3** a handle on a bat or a racket ▷ verb **4** to grasp or hold (something) tightly

grisly grislier, grisliest adjective horrifying or ghastly

grit grits, gritting, gritted noun **1** rough particles of sand ▷ verb **2** to spread grit on (an icy road) **3** grit your teeth to decide to carry on in a difficult situation ▷ **gritty** adjective **1** containing or covered with grit **2** brave and determined **3** (of a drama) realistic

grizzled adjective grey-haired

grizzly bear noun large greyish-brown American bear

groan noun **1** deep sound of grief or pain ▷ verb **2** to utter a groan

grocer noun shopkeeper who sells many kinds of food and other household goods

grocery groceries noun **1** business or premises of a grocer **2** groceries goods sold by a grocer

grog noun (Brit, Aust, NZ informal) any alcoholic drink

groin noun place where the legs join the abdomen

groom noun **1** person who looks after horses **2** bridegroom ▷ verb **3** to brush or clean (a horse) **4** to train (someone) for a future role

groove noun long narrow channel in a surface > **grooved** adjective having deep grooves on the surface

grope verb (followed by for) **1** to search for (something you cannot see) with your hands **2** to try to think of (something such as the solution to a problem)

gross adjective **1** extremely bad: a gross betrayal **2** (of speech or behaviour) vulgar **3** (informal) disgusting or repulsive **4** total, without deductions **5** (of weight) including container weight ▷ noun **6** twelve dozen ▷ verb **7** to earn (an amount of money) in total > **grossly** adverb: grossly overweight

grotesque [grow-**tesk**] adjective **1** very strange and ugly **2** exaggerated and absurd > **grotesquely** adverb

grotto grottoes or grottos noun small picturesque cave

ground noun **1** surface of the earth **2** soil **3** area used for a specific purpose: rugby ground **4** position in an argument or controversy

5 grounds a enclosed land round a house **b** reason or motive ▷ verb **6** (followed by in) to base or establish (something) on something else **7** to ban (an aircraft) from flying ▷ verb **8** past of **grind**

ground floor noun floor of a building level with the ground

grounding noun basic knowledge of a subject

groundless adjective without reason

group noun **1** number of people or things regarded as a unit **2** small band of musicians or singers ▷ verb **3** to place or form (people or things) into a group

grouping noun number of things or people that are linked together in some way

grouse noun stocky game bird

WORD TIP
The plural of grouse is grouse

grove noun (literary) small group of trees

grovel grovels, grovelling, grovelled [**grov**-el] verb to behave humbly in order to win a superior's favour

grow grows, growing, grew, grown verb **1** to develop physically **2** (of a plant) to exist **3** to cultivate (plants) **4** to increase in size or degree **5** to become gradually: It was growing dark > **grow on** verb (informal) to gradually become liked by (someone) > **grow up** verb to mature

growl verb **1** to make a low rumbling sound **2** to utter (something) with a growl ▷ noun **3** growling sound

grown-up adjective, noun adult

growth noun 1 growing 2 increase 3 SCIENCE process by which something develops to its full size 4 tumour

grub noun 1 legless insect larva 2 (informal) food

grubby grubbier, grubbiest adjective dirty

grudge verb 1 to be unwilling to give or allow (someone something) ▷ noun 2 resentment

grudging adjective done or felt unwillingly: grudging admiration > **grudgingly** adverb unwillingly

gruel noun thin porridge

gruelling adjective exhausting or severe

gruesome adjective causing horror and disgust

gruff adjective rough or surly in manner or voice

grumble verb 1 to complain ▷ noun 2 complaint

grumpy grumpier, grumpiest adjective bad-tempered and fed-up

grunt verb 1 to make a low short gruff sound, like a pig ▷ noun 2 pig's sound 3 gruff noise

guarantee guarantees, guaranteeing, guaranteed noun 1 formal assurance, especially in writing, that a product will meet certain standards 2 something that makes a specified condition or outcome certain ▷ verb 3 to make certain (that something will happen) > **guarantor** noun person who gives or is bound by a guarantee

guard verb 1 to watch over (someone or something) to protect or to prevent escape ▷ noun 2 person or group that guards 3 official in charge of a train 4 screen for enclosing anything dangerous > **guard against** verb to take precautions against (something)

guardian noun 1 keeper or protector 2 person legally responsible for a child, mentally ill person, etc > **guardianship** noun position of being a guardian

guernsey noun 1 (Aust, NZ) jersey 2 (Aust) sleeveless top worn by an Australian Rules football player

guerrilla or **guerilla** noun member of an unofficial armed force fighting regular forces

guess verb 1 to form or express an opinion that something is the case, without having much information ▷ noun 2 MATHS estimate or conclusion reached by guessing

guest noun 1 person entertained at another's house or at another's expense 2 invited performer or speaker 3 customer at a hotel or restaurant

guffaw noun 1 crude noisy laugh ▷ verb 2 to laugh in this way

guidance noun leadership, instruction or advice

guide noun 1 person who conducts tour expeditions 2 person who shows the way 3 book of instruction or information 4 **Guide** member of an organization for girls equivalent to the Scouts ▷ verb 5 to act as a guide for (someone) 6 to control, supervise or influence (someone)

guidebook noun book that gives information about a place

guide dog noun dog trained to lead a blind person

guideline noun set principle for doing something

guild noun organization or club

guile [gile] noun cunning or deceit > **guileless** adjective open and honest

guillotine noun machine for beheading people

guilt noun 1 fact or state of having done wrong 2 remorse for wrongdoing

guilty guiltier, guiltiest adjective 1 responsible for an offence or misdeed 2 feeling or showing guilt > **guiltily** adverb

guinea noun old British unit of money, worth 21 shillings

guinea pig noun 1 small furry animal without a tail, often kept as a pet 2 person used to try something out on

guise [rhymes with size] noun misleading appearance

guitar noun stringed instrument with a flat back and a long neck, played by plucking or strumming > **guitarist** noun person who plays the guitar

gulf noun 1 large deep bay 2 large difference in opinion or belief

gull noun long-winged sea bird

gullet noun muscular tube through which food passes from the mouth to the stomach

gullible adjective easily tricked > **gullibility** noun being gullible

gully gullies noun channel cut by running water

gulp verb 1 to swallow (food or drink) hastily 2 to gasp > noun 3 large quantity of food or drink swallowed at one time

gum noun 1 firm flesh in which the teeth are set 2 sticky substance obtained from certain trees 3 adhesive 4 chewing gum

gumboots plural noun (Chiefly Brit) Wellington boots

gum tree noun eucalyptus tree

gun noun weapon that fires bullets or shells > **gunboat** noun small warship

gunfire noun repeated firing of guns

gunpowder noun explosive powder made from a mixture of potassium nitrate and other substances

gunshot noun shot or range of a gun

gunyah noun (Aust) hut or shelter in the bush

guppy guppies noun small colourful aquarium fish

gurdwara noun Sikh place of worship

gurgle verb, noun (to make) a bubbling noise

guru noun 1 Hindu or Sikh religious teacher or leader 2 leader, adviser or expert

gush verb 1 to flow out in large quantities 2 to express admiration in an exaggerated way > **gushing** adjective: He delivered a gushing speech

gust noun sudden blast of wind > **gusty** adjective

gusto noun enjoyment or zest

gut guts, gutting, gutted noun 1 intestine 2 guts a internal organs b (informal) courage ▷ verb 3 to remove the guts from (a dead fish) 4 (of a fire) to destroy the inside of (a building)

gutter noun shallow channel for carrying away water from a roof or roadside > **guttering** noun material for gutters

guttural *adjective* (of a sound) produced at the back of the throat

guy *noun* **1** (*informal*) man or boy **2** crude model of Guy Fawkes burnt on Nov. 5th (*Guy Fawkes Day*) **3** rope or chain to steady or secure something

guzzle *verb* to eat or drink (something) greedily

gym *noun* PE **1** gymnasium **2** gymnastics

gymkhana [jim-**kah**-na] *noun* horse-riding competition

gymnasium *noun* large room with equipment for physical training

gymnast *noun* expert in gymnastics > **gymnastic** *adjective: gymnastic exercises*

gymnastics *plural noun* exercises to develop strength and agility

gynaecology [guy-nee-**kol**-la-jee] *noun* branch of medical science concerned with the female reproductive system > **gynaecological** *adjective: a routine gynaecological examination* > **gynaecologist** *noun* doctor who specializes in gynaecology

Gypsy *Gypsies noun* member of a travelling people found throughout Europe

gyrate [jire-**rate**] *verb* to move round in a circle

h

habit *noun* **1** something that you do often **2** something that you keep doing and find it difficult to stop doing **3** loose, dress-like costume of a monk or nun

habitat *noun* natural home of an animal or plant

hack *verb* **1** to cut or chop violently *noun* **2** (inferior) writer or journalist

hacker *noun* (*informal*) someone who uses a computer to break into the computer system of a company or government

hackles *plural noun* **1** hairs on the back of an animal which rise when it is angry **2 make your hackles rise** to make you feel angry or hostile

hackneyed *adjective* (of a word or phrase) unoriginal and overused

hacksaw *noun* small saw with a narrow blade set in a frame

haddock *noun* edible sea fish of the North Atlantic

 WORD TIP
The plural of *haddock* is *haddock*

haemoglobin [hee-moh-**globe**-in] *noun* substance in red blood cells which carries oxygen round the body

haemorrhage [**hem**-or-ij] *noun* **1** (instance of) heavy bleeding ▷ *verb* **2** to bleed heavily

haemorrhoids [hem-or-oydz] *plural noun* painful lumps around the anus that are caused by swollen veins; piles

hag *noun* (*offensive*) ugly old woman

haggard *adjective* looking tired and ill

haggis *noun* Scottish dish made from the internal organs of a sheep, boiled together with oatmeal and spices in a bag traditionally made from the sheep's stomach

haggle *verb* to bargain or wrangle over a price

hail *noun* **1** frozen rain **2** large number of insults, missiles, blows or other things ▷ *verb* **3** to fall as or like hail **4** to call out to (someone); greet **5** to stop (a taxi) by waving **6** to acknowledge (someone or something) publicly ▷ **hail from** *verb* to come originally from

hair *noun* **1** soft, threadlike strand that grows with others from the skin of animals and humans **2** such strands collectively, especially on the head

haircut *noun* the cutting of someone's hair; also the style in which it is cut

hairdo hairdos *noun* (*informal*) hairstyle

hairdresser *noun* **1** person trained to cut and style hair **2** shop where people go to have their hair cut ▷ **hairdressing** *noun*, *adjective*

hairline *noun* **1** the edge of the area at the top of the forehead where your hair starts ▷ *adjective* **2** (of a crack) very fine or narrow

hairpin *noun* U-shaped wire used to hold the hair in place

hair-raising *adjective* very frightening or exciting

hairstyle *noun* cut and arrangement of a person's hair

hairy hairier, hairiest *adjective* **1** covered with hair **2** (*informal*) difficult, exciting and rather frightening

hajj *noun* pilgrimage a Muslim makes to Mecca

haka hakas *noun* (*NZ*) **1** ceremonial Māori dance with chanting **2** similar dance performed by a sports team before a match

hake *noun* edible sea fish related to the cod

> **WORD TIP**
> The plural of *hake* is hake

hakea [hah-kee-a] *noun* Australian tree or shrub with hard, woody fruit

halcyon [hal-see-on] *adjective* (*Literary*) **1** peaceful and happy **2** halcyon days time of peace and happiness

half halves *noun* **1** either of two equal parts that make up a whole **2** (*informal*) half-pint of beer, cider, etc **3** half-price ticket ▷ *adjective* **4** denoting one of two equal parts ▷ *adverb* **5** to the extent of half **6** partially or partly: *I half expected him to explode in anger*

half-baked *adjective* (*informal*) (of an idea, theory or plan) not properly thought out

half board *noun* (at a hotel) breakfast and dinner but not lunch

half-brother *noun* brother related through one parent only

half-hearted *adjective* unenthusiastic

half-pie *adjective* (*NZ informal*) incomplete

half-sister noun sister related through one parent only

half-timbered adjective (of a house) having a framework of wooden beams that are exposed and visible in the walls

half-time noun (Sport) short rest period between two halves of a game

halfway adverb, adjective at or up to half the distance between two points in place or time; midway

halibut halibut or halibuts noun large edible flatfish of N Atlantic

hall noun 1 entrance passage 2 large room or building for public meetings, dances, etc 3 (Brit) large country house

hallmark noun 1 typical feature or quality 2 mark indicating the standard of tested gold and silver ▷ verb 3 to stamp with a hallmark

hallowed adjective respected as being holy

Halloween or **Hallowe'en** noun October 31, celebrated by children by dressing up as ghosts, witches, etc

hallucinate verb to see or experience strange things in your mind because of illness or drugs > **hallucination** noun: Drugs can cause hallucinations > **hallucinatory** adjective: a hallucinatory state

halo haloes or halos [**hay**-loh] noun ring of light round the head of a holy figure

halt verb 1 to come or bring something to a stop ▷ noun 2 temporary stop

halter noun strap round a horse's head with a rope to lead it with

halve verb 1 to divide (something) in half 2 to reduce (something) or be reduced by half

ham noun 1 smoked or salted meat from a pig's thigh 2 bad actor who overacts 3 amateur radio operator

hamburger noun minced beef shaped into a flat disc, cooked and usually served in a bread roll

hammer noun 1 tool with a heavy metal head and a wooden handle, used to drive in nails etc 2 heavy metal ball on a wire, thrown as a sport ▷ verb 3 to hit (something) repeatedly with a hammer or your fist 4 (informal) to punish or defeat (someone) utterly 5 **hammer something into someone** to keep repeating something to someone in the hope that they will remember it

hammock noun hanging bed made of canvas or net

hamper noun 1 large wicker basket with a lid 2 selection of food and drink packed as a gift ▷ verb 3 to make it difficult for (someone or something) to move or progress

hamster noun small furry rodent with a short tail and cheek pouches that is often kept as a pet

WORD TIP
There is no p in hamster

hamstring noun tendon at the back of your knee ▷ verb

hand noun 1 part of your body at the end of your arm, consisting of a palm, four fingers and a thumb 2 style of handwriting 3 round of applause 4 pointer on a dial, especially on a clock 5 cards dealt to a player in a card game

6 manual worker **7** unit of length of four inches (10.16 centimetres) used to measure horses **8** help **9 have a hand in** to be involved in **10 give someone a hand** to help someone **11 to hand, at hand, on hand** nearby **12 on the one hand** way of introducing the first part of an argument or discussion when giving two contrasting points of view **13 on the other hand** way of introducing the second part of an argument or discussion when giving two contrasting points of view **14 out of hand** beyond control ▷ *verb* **15** to pass or give > **hand down** *verb* to pass from one generation to another

handbag *noun* woman's small bag for carrying personal articles in

handbook *noun* small reference or instruction book

handcuff *noun* one of a linked pair of metal rings designed to be locked round a prisoner's wrists by the police

handful *noun* **1** amount that can be held in the hand **2** small number **3** (*informal*) person or animal that is difficult to control

handicap handicaps, handicapping, handicapped *noun* **1** physical or mental disability **2** something that makes progress difficult **3** contest in which the competitors are given advantages or disadvantages according to their skill in an attempt to equalize their chances of winning **4** advantage or disadvantage given ▷ *verb* **5** to make it difficult for (someone) to do something

handicraft *noun* activity such as embroidery or pottery which

involves making things with your hands; also the items produced

handiwork *noun* result of someone's work or activity

handkerchief *noun* small square of fabric used for blowing your nose

handle *noun* **1** part of an object that is designed for holding when you use it **2** a small lever or knob used to open and close a door or window ▷ *verb* **3** to hold, feel or move with your hands **4** to control or deal with

handlebars *plural noun* curved metal bar used to steer a cycle

handout *noun* **1** clothing, food or money given to a needy person **2** written information given out at a talk etc

hand-picked *adjective* carefully chosen

handset *noun* part (of a telephone) that you speak into and listen with

handshake *noun* the grasping and shaking of a person's hand by another person as a gesture of greeting, taking leave or agreement

handsome *adjective* **1** (especially of a man) good-looking **2** large or generous > **handsomely** *adverb*

handwriting *noun* (style of) writing by hand

handy handier, handiest *adjective* **1** convenient, useful or conveniently near **2** skilful

hang hangs, hanging, hung *verb* **1** to attach (something) or be attached at the top with the lower part free **2** (*past*) hanged) to kill (someone) by suspending them by a rope around the neck ▷ *noun*

3 get the hang of (informal) to begin to understand **> hang about** or **hang around** verb **1** (informal) to wait somewhere **2 hang about with** to spend a lot of time with **> hang back** verb to hesitate or be reluctant **> hang on** verb **1** (often followed by to) to hold tightly **2** (informal) to wait **> hang out** verb (informal) to spend a lot of time **> hang over** verb (of a future event or possibility) to worry or frighten (someone) **> hang up** verb to put down the receiver ending a telephone call

hangar noun large shed for storing aircraft

hanger noun curved piece of wood, wire or plastic, with a hook, for hanging up clothes (also **coat hanger**)

hanger-on hangers-on noun unwelcome follower of an important person

hang-glider noun aircraft without an engine and consisting of a large frame covered in fabric, from which the pilot hangs in a harness **> hang-gliding** noun

hangi noun (NZ) Māori oven consisting of a hole in the ground lined with hot stones

hangover noun headache and sickness after drinking too much alcohol

hang-up noun (informal) emotional reaction

hanker verb (followed by after, for) to want very much **> hankering** noun: He has a hankering to go back to acting

hanky hankies noun (informal) handkerchief

Hanukkah or **Chanukah** [hah-na-ka] noun eight-day Jewish festival of lights

haphazard adjective not organized or planned **> haphazardly** adverb: Clothes, toys and books lay haphazardly around

hapless adjective (literary) unlucky

happen verb **1** to take place; occur **2** to chance (to be or do something)

happiness noun feeling of great contentment or pleasure

happy happier, happiest adjective **1** feeling or causing joy **2** satisfied that something is right **3** willing **4** lucky or fortunate **> happily** adverb

happy-go-lucky adjective carefree and cheerful

harangue verb **1** to talk to (someone) at length angrily, passionately and forcefully about something **> noun 2** a long, angry, passionate and forceful speech

harass verb to annoy or trouble (someone) constantly **> harassed** adjective: a harassed mother trying to soothe a crying baby **> harassment** noun: Intimidation and harassment are common

harbinger [har-binj-a] noun someone or something that announces the approach of something: I hate to be the harbinger of doom

harbour noun **1** sheltered port **> verb 2** to hide (someone) secretly in your house; shelter **3** to have (a feeling, hope or grudge) for a long time

hard adjective **1** firm, solid or rigid **2** difficult **3** requiring a lot of effort

4 unkind, unfeeling **5** causing pain, sorrow or hardship **6** (of water) containing calcium salts which stop soap lathering freely **7** (of a drug) strong and addictive **8** (of evidence or facts) provable and indisputable **9** (of drink or liquor) strong and alcoholic ▷ *adverb* **10** with great energy or effort **11** with great intensity **12** to the extent of becoming firm, solid or rigid: *The ground was baked hard* > **hardness** *noun*

hard and fast *adjective* fixed and unchangeable: *hard and fast rules*

hardback *noun* a book with a stiff cover

hard core *noun* (in an organization) group of people most resistant to change

harden *verb* to become hard or get harder > **hardening** *noun*

hard labour *noun* difficult and exhausting physical work; used in some countries as a punishment for a crime

hardly *adverb* **1** scarcely or not at all **2** with difficulty

> **WORD TIP**
> You should not use *hardly* with a negative word like *not* or *no*: *he could hardly hear her*, not *he could not hardly hear her*

hard-nosed *adjective* tough, practical and realistic

hard of hearing *adjective* unable to hear well

hardship *noun* **1** suffering **2** difficult circumstances

hard shoulder *noun* area at the edge of a motorway where you can park in the event of a breakdown

hard up *adjective* (*informal*) short of money

hardware *noun* **1** metal tools and implements **2** machinery used in a computer system **3** heavy military equipment, such as tanks and missiles

hard-wearing *adjective* strong, well-made and long-lasting

hardwood *noun* strong, hard wood from a tree such as oak or ash; also the tree itself

hardy *hardier, hardiest adjective* able to stand difficult conditions > **hardiness** *noun*

hare *hares, haring, hared noun* **1** animal like a large rabbit, with longer ears and legs ▷ *verb* **2** (usually followed by *off*) to run (away) quickly

harem *noun* group of wives or mistresses of one man, especially in Muslim societies; also the place where these women live

hark *verb* (*old-fashioned*) to listen > **hark back** *verb* to return to (an earlier subject)

harlequin *noun* **1** stock comic character with a diamond-patterned costume and mask ▷ *adjective* **2** in many colours

harm *verb* **1** to injure or damage ▷ *noun* **2** injury or damage

harmful *adjective* causing injury or damage

harmless *adjective* **1** safe to use or be near **2** unlikely to cause problems or annoyance > **harmlessly** *adverb*

harmonic *adjective* using musical harmony

harmonica *noun* small musical instrument which you play by blowing and sucking while moving it across your lips; mouth organ

harmonious [har-moh-nee-uss] *adjective* **1** peaceful, friendly and free from disagreement **2** attractively and agreeably combined > **harmoniously** *adverb*

harmony harmonies *noun* **1** peaceful agreement and cooperation **2** pleasant combination of notes sounded at the same time **3** (*Music*) the structure and relationship of chords in a piece of music

harness *noun* **1** arrangement of straps for attaching a horse to a cart or plough **2** set of straps fastened round someone's body to attach something: *a safety harness* > *verb* **3** to bring (something) under control in order to make use of it

harp *noun* large triangular stringed instrument played with the fingers > **harpist** *noun*

harpoon *noun* **1** barbed spear attached to a rope used for hunting whales > *verb* **2** to spear (a whale or large fish) with a harpoon

harpsichord *noun* stringed keyboard instrument

harrowing *adjective* very distressing

harsh *adjective* **1** severe and difficult to cope with **2** unkind, unsympathetic **3** extremely hard, bright or rough > **harshly** *adverb* > **harshness** *noun*: *the harshness of prison life*

harvest *noun* **1** (season for) the gathering of crops **2** crops gathered > *verb* **3** to gather (a ripened crop) > **harvester** *noun*

has-been *noun* (*informal*) person who is no longer popular or successful

hash *noun* **1** the character (#) **2** dish of diced cooked meat and vegetables reheated **3** (*informal*) hashish **4 make a hash of** (*informal*) to do (a job) badly

hashish [hash-eesh] *noun* drug made from the cannabis plant. It is usually smoked, and is illegal in many countries

hassle (*informal*) *noun* **1** trouble or bother > *verb* **2** to bother (someone) with repeated requests to do something; pester

haste *noun* **1** (excessive) quickness **2 make haste** to hurry or rush

hasten *verb* **1** to hurry **2** to cause (something) to happen earlier than otherwise

hasty hastier, hastiest *adjective* (too) quick > **hastily** *adverb* (too) quickly

hat *noun* **1** covering for the head, often with a brim **2 keep something under your hat** to keep something secret

hatch *verb* **1** (of a bird or reptile) to come out of the egg **2** (of an egg) to break open allowing a young bird or reptile to come out **3** to devise (a plot) > *noun* **4** covered opening in a wall, floor or ceiling

hatchback *noun* car with a rear door that opens upwards

hatchet *noun* **1** small axe **2 bury the hatchet** to make peace

hate *verb* **1** to dislike (someone or something) intensely > *noun* **2** intense dislike

hateful *adjective* causing or deserving hate

hatred *noun* intense dislike

hat trick *noun* three achievements in a row, especially in sport

haughty haughtier, haughtiest *adjective* proud, arrogant
> **haughtily** *adverb*

haul *verb* 1 to pull or drag (something or someone) with effort ▷ *noun* 2 amount gained by effort or theft 3 **long haul** something that takes a lot of time and effort

haulage *noun* business or cost of transporting goods

haunches *plural noun* buttocks and thighs

haunt *verb* 1 (of a ghost) to visit (a building or place) regularly 2 (of a memory or fear) to worry or trouble (someone) continually ▷ *noun* 3 place visited frequently

haunted *adjective* 1 frequented by ghosts 2 very worried or troubled

haunting *adjective* memorably beautiful or sad

have has, having, had *verb* 1 to possess or hold 2 to receive, take or obtain 3 to experience or be affected by 4 (followed by to) to be obliged to; must: I had to go 5 to cause to be done 6 to give birth to (a baby, foal, kittens, etc) 7 used to form past tenses (with a past participle): We have looked; She had done enough 8 **be had** to be tricked or deceived 9 **have out** to settle a matter by argument > **have on** *verb* 1 to wear (clothing) 2 (informal) to tease or trick (someone) > **have up** *verb* to bring (someone) to trial

haven *noun* place of safety

havoc *noun* disorder and confusion

hawk *noun* 1 bird of prey with a short hooked bill and very good eyesight 2 (Politics) supporter or advocate of warlike policies ▷ *verb* 3 to offer (goods) for sale in the street or door-to-door 4 to clear phlegm from your throat noisily

hawthorn *noun* thorny shrub or tree producing white blossom and red berries

hay *noun* grass cut and dried as animal feed

hay fever *noun* allergy to pollen and grass, causing sneezing and watering eyes

haystack *noun* large firmly built pile of hay

hazard *noun* 1 something that could be dangerous ▷ *verb* 2 to put (something) at risk 3 to make (a guess) > **hazardous** *adjective*: *hazardous waste*

haze *noun* mist, often caused by heat

hazel *noun* 1 small tree producing edible nuts ▷ *adjective* 2 (of eyes) greenish-brown

hazy hazier, haziest *adjective* 1 not clear, misty 2 confused or vague

he *pronoun* refers to 1 male person or animal 2 a person or animal of unknown or unspecified sex; he or she ▷ *noun* 3 male person or animal

head *noun* 1 part of your body containing your eyes, mouth, nose and brain 2 mind and mental abilities 3 upper or most forward part of anything 4 most important end of something 5 person in charge of a group, organization or school 6 pus-filled tip of a spot or boil 7 white froth on beer 8 (of a computer or tape recorder) the part that can read or write information 9 (pl head) person or animal considered as a

unit 10 can't make head nor tail of can't understand **11 off your head** (*informal*) foolish or insane ▷ *adjective* **12** chief or principal ▷ *verb* **13** to be at the top or front of **14** to be in charge of **15** to move (in a particular direction) **16** to hit (a ball) with your head **17** to provide (something) with a heading > **head off** *verb* **1** to make (someone or something) change direction **2** to prevent (something) from happening > **heads** *adverb* (*informal*) with the side of a coin which has a portrait of a head on it uppermost

headache *noun* **1** pain in your head **2** (*informal*) cause of worry or annoyance

header *noun* **1** (*Football*) hitting a ball with your head **2** headlong fall

heading *noun* title written or printed at the top of a page

headland *noun* narrow piece of land jutting out into the sea

headlight *noun* powerful light on the front of a vehicle

headline *noun* **1** title at the top of a newspaper article, especially on the front page **2 headlines** main points of a news broadcast

headmaster *noun* male head teacher of a school

headmistress *noun* female head teacher of a school

headphones *plural noun* pair of small speakers which you wear over your ears to listen to a radio, CD player, etc without other people hearing

headquarters *plural noun* centre from which the operations of an organization are directed

headroom *noun* amount of space below a roof, arch, bridge, etc under which an object must pass or fit

headstone *noun* memorial stone on a grave

headstrong *adjective* self-willed and obstinate

head teacher *noun* the teacher who is in charge of a school

headway *noun* progress

headwind *noun* wind blowing against you, hindering rather than helping your progress

heady headier, headiest *adjective* intoxicating or exciting

heal *verb* to become well or make (someone) well > **healer** *noun*

health *noun* **1** condition of your body and the extent to which it is free from illness **2** state of being well; fitness

health food *noun* food believed to be good for you, especially food that is free from additives

healthy healthier, healthiest *adjective* **1** (of a person or animal) having good health **2** (of a food or activity) good for you **3** (of an organization or system) functioning well; sound > **healthily** *adverb*

heap *noun* **1** pile of things one on top of another **2** (*informal*) large number or quantity ▷ *verb* **3** to gather (things) into a pile **4** (followed by *on*) to give a lot of (something) to (someone): *He was quick to heap praise on his secretary*

hear hears, hearing, heard *verb* **1** to pick up (a sound) with your ears **2** to listen to **3** to learn or be informed **4** (*Law*) to try (a case) > **hearer** *noun* > **hear!**

hear! exclamation of approval or agreement > **hear out** verb to listen to everything said by (someone) without interrupting

hearing noun 1 ability to hear 2 trial of a case

hearsay noun gossip, rumour

hearse noun funeral car used to carry a coffin

heart noun 1 organ that pumps blood round your body 2 centre of emotions, especially love 3 courage, spirit 4 central or most important part 5 shape representing a heart, used especially as a symbol of love 6 playing card with red heart-shaped symbols 7 **by heart** from memory

heartache noun very great sadness and emotional suffering

heart attack noun serious medical condition in which the heart suddenly beats irregularly or stops completely

heartbreak noun intense grief > **heartbreaking** adjective: the heartbreaking story of a little boy > **heartbroken** adjective suffering intense grief

heartburn noun burning sensation in the chest caused by indigestion

heartening adjective encouraging or uplifting

heart failure noun serious condition in which someone's heart does not work as well as it should, sometimes stopping completely

heartfelt adjective felt sincerely or strongly

hearth noun floor of a fireplace

heartless adjective cruel and unkind

heart-rending adjective causing great sorrow

heart-throb noun (informal) very attractive man, especially a film or pop star

heart-to-heart noun discussion in which two people talk about their deepest feelings

hearty adjective, heartiest adjective 1 friendly and enthusiastic 2 substantial and nourishing 3 strongly felt > **heartily** adverb: I'm heartily sick of it

heat noun 1 warmth or state of being hot 2 temperature 3 hot weather 4 preliminary eliminating contest or race to decide who will take part in the later stages 5 **on** or **in heat** (of some female animals) ready for mating ▷ verb 6 to make (something) hot or become hot

heath noun (Brit) area of open land covered with rough grass or heather

heathen adjective, noun (old-fashioned) person who does not believe in one of the established religions

heather noun low-growing plant with small purple, pinkish or white flowers, that grows on heaths and moorland

heating noun equipment used to heat a building; also the process and cost of running such equipment

heatwave noun period of time when the weather is much hotter than usual

heave heaves, heaving, heaved verb 1 to lift, move or throw (something heavy) with effort 2 to utter (a sigh) 3 to rise and

fall 4 to vomit ▷ noun **5** instance of heaving

heaven noun **1** place believed to be the home of God, where good people go when they die **2** wonderful place or state **3 the heavens** (literary) sky

heavenly adjective **1** of or like heaven **2** (informal) wonderful or beautiful

heavy heavier, heaviest adjective **1** great in weight or force **2** great in degree or amount **3** solid and thick in appearance **4** using a lot of something quickly **5** (informal) serious and difficult to deal with or understand **6 with a heavy heart** with sadness or sorrow > **heavily** adverb > **heaviness** noun

heavy-duty adjective (of equipment or material) strong and hard-wearing

heavy-handed adjective showing a lack of care or thought and using too much authority

heavyweight noun **1** a boxer in the heaviest weight group **2** important person with a lot of influence

Hebrew noun **1** ancient language of the Hebrews **2** its modern form, used in Israel **3** Hebrew-speaking Jew living in Israel in past times ▷ adjective **4** relating to the Hebrews and their customs

heckle verb to interrupt (a public speaker) with comments, questions or taunts > **heckler** noun

hectare noun one hundred acres or 10 000 square metres (2.471 acres)

hectic adjective rushed or busy

hedge noun **1** row of bushes forming a barrier or boundary ▷ verb **2** to avoid answering a question or dealing with a problem **3 hedge your bets** to avoid the risk of losing completely by supporting two or more people or courses of action

hedgehog noun small brown animal with a protective covering of sharp spikes covering its back

hedonism noun belief that pleasure is the most important thing in life > **hedonist** noun > **hedonistic** adjective: her hedonistic lifestyle

heed noun **1** careful attention ▷ verb **2** to pay careful attention to

heel noun **1** back part of your foot **2** the part of a shoe or sock that goes under your heel **3 down at heel** shabby and untidy ▷ verb **4** to repair the heel of (a shoe)

heeler noun (Aust) dog that herds cattle by biting at their heels

hefty heftier, heftiest adjective of great size, force or weight

height noun **1** distance from base to top **2** distance above sea level **3** a high position or place **4** highest degree or point; peak

heighten verb to make (something) higher or more intense or to become higher or more intense

heinous adjective evil and shocking

heir noun person entitled to inherit property or title

heiress noun a woman who has inherited or is likely to inherit a large amount of money or property

heirloom noun object that has belonged to a family for generations

helicopter noun aircraft with rotating blades above it which enable it to take off vertically, hover and fly

helium [**heel**-ee-um] noun (Chemistry) colourless odourless gas that is lighter than air and is used to fill balloons

hell noun **1** place believed to be where wicked people go when they die **2** terrible place or state

hellbent adjective (followed by on) determined to

hellish adjective (informal) very unpleasant

hello interjection expression of greeting

helm noun **1** position from which a boat is steered; also the tiller or wheel for steering **2 at the helm** in a position of leadership or control

helmet noun hard hat worn to protect your head

help verb **1** to make something easier, better or quicker for (someone) **2** to improve (a situation) **3** to stop yourself from: I can't help smiling **4 help yourself** to take something, especially food or drink, without being served ▷ noun **5** assistance or support > **helper** noun

helpful adjective providing help or relief > **helpfully** adverb

helping noun single portion of food

helpless adjective weak, incapable or powerless > **helplessly** adverb > **helplessness** noun

hem hems, hemming, hemmed noun **1** edge (of a piece of clothing, curtain, etc) which has been turned over and sewn in place ▷ verb **2** to provide (something) with a hem > **hem in** verb to surround and prevent (someone) from moving

hemisphere noun one half of the earth, a brain or a sphere > **hemispherical** adjective

hemp noun tall plant, some varieties of which are used to make rope, and others to produce the drug cannabis

hen noun **1** female chicken **2** female of any bird

hence (formal) conjunction **1** for this reason ▷ adverb **2** from this time

henceforth adverb from now on

henchman henchmen noun person employed by someone powerful to carry out orders

hepatitis noun inflammation of the liver

her pronoun **1** refers to a female person or animal, or anything thought of as feminine; used as the object of a verb or preposition ▷ adjective **2** belonging to her

herald noun **1** (in the past) a messenger or announcer of important news ▷ verb **2** to be a sign of (a future event)

herb noun plant whose leaves are used in medicine or to flavour food > **herbal** adjective: herbal remedies > **herbalist** noun person who grows or specializes in the use of medicinal herbs

herbivore noun animal that eats only plants > **herbivorous** [her-**biv**-or-uss] adjective: A few beetles are herbivorous

herd noun **1** large group of animals feeding and living together

2 large crowd of people ▷ *verb* **3** to collect (animals or people) into a herd

here *adverb* in, at or to this place or point

hereafter *adverb* **1** (*formal*) after this point or time ▷ *noun* **2** the **hereafter** life after death

hereby *adverb* (*formal*) by means of this or as a result of this

hereditary *adjective* passed on to a child from a parent

heredity [hir-**red**-it-ee] *noun* passing on of characteristics from one generation to another through genes

herein *adverb* (*formal*) in this place or document

heresy heresies [**herr**-iss-ee] *noun* belief or behaviour considered wrong because it goes against accepted opinion or belief, especially religious belief

herewith *adverb* (*formal*) with this letter or document

heritage *noun* possessions or traditions that have been passed from one generation to another

hermit *noun* person living in solitude, especially for religious reasons

hernia *noun* medical condition in which part of the intestine or another organ sticks through a weak point in the surrounding tissue

hero heroes *noun* **1** main male character in a film, book, etc **2** person who has done something brave or good

heroic *adjective* **1** brave, courageous and determined **2** of or like a hero > **heroically** *adverb*

heroin *noun* highly addictive drug derived from morphine

heroine *noun* **1** main female character in a film, book, etc **2** woman or girl who has done something brave or good

heroism [**herr**-oh-izz-um] *noun* great courage and bravery

heron *noun* wading bird with very long legs and a long beak and neck

herpes [**her**-peez] *noun* any of several inflammatory skin diseases, including shingles and cold sores

herring herrings or herring *noun* silvery food fish of northern seas

hers *pronoun* object or objects belonging to or relating to a woman, girl or female animal that has already been mentioned

herself *pronoun* **1** used as an object of a verb or pronoun when the woman, girl or female animal that does an action is also the woman, girl or female animal that is directly affected by it: *She pulled herself out of the water* **2** used to emphasize *she*: *She herself knew nothing about it*

hertz *noun* (*Physics*) unit of frequency equal to one cycle per second

> **WORD TIP**
> The plural of *hertz* is *hertz*

hesitant *adjective* undecided or uncertain about doing something > **hesitantly** *adverb*

hesitate *verb* **1** to pause or show uncertainty **2** to be reluctant (to do something) > **hesitation** *noun*: *"I know," he replied, without hesitation*

hessian *noun* thick coarse fabric used for making sacks

heterosexual adjective **1** (of a person) sexually attracted to members of the opposite sex ▷ noun **2** person who is sexually attracted to people of the opposite sex

hewn adjective carved from a substance

hexagon noun six-sided shape > **hexagonal** adjective: Choose between square and hexagonal tiles

heyday noun period of greatest success

hi interjection (informal) expression of greeting

hiatus hiatuses [hie-**ay**-tuss] noun (formal) pause or interruption

hibernate verb (of an animal) to spend the winter in a state resembling deep sleep > **hibernation** noun: The snakes have come out of hibernation

hibiscus hibiscuses noun type of tropical shrub with brightly coloured flowers

hiccup hiccups, hiccuping, hiccuped noun **1** one of a series of short, uncontrolled intakes of breath, each accompanied by a gulping sound in your throat that you sometimes get, especially if you have been eating or drinking too quickly **2** (informal) small problem; hitch ▷ verb **3** to make a hiccup

hide hides, hiding, hid, hidden verb **1** to put (yourself or an object) somewhere very difficult to see or find in order to avoid discovery; conceal **2** to keep (something) secret ▷ noun **3** place of concealment, especially for a bird-watcher **4** skin of an animal > **hiding** noun **1** state of

concealment: in hiding **2** (informal) severe beating

hideous [hid-ee-uss] adjective very ugly or unpleasant > **hideously** adverb

hide-out noun hiding place

hierarchy hierarchies [hire-ark-ee] noun system in which people or things are ranked according to how important they are > **hierarchical** adjective: a hierarchical society

hi-fi noun set of stereo equipment on which you can play compact discs and tapes

high adjective **1** of a great height; tall **2** far above ground or sea level **3** greater than usual in degree, quantity or intensity **4** of great importance, quality or rank **5** (of a sound or note) close to the top of a range **6** (informal) under the influence of alcohol or drugs ▷ adverb **7** at or to a high level ▷ noun **8** a high point or level: Morale reached a new high **9** on a **high** (informal) in a very excited and optimistic mood

highbrow adjective concerned with serious, intellectual subjects

higher education noun education at colleges and universities

high jump noun athletics event involving jumping over a high bar

highlands plural noun mountainous or hilly areas

highlight verb **1** to give emphasis to ▷ noun **2** most interesting part or feature **3** lighter area of a painting, showing where light shines on things **4** lightened streak in the hair

highly adverb **1** extremely **2** very well

high-minded adjective having strong moral principles

Highness noun title used to address or refer to a royal person

high-pitched adjective (of sound) high or rather shrill

high-rise adjective (of a building) having many storeys

high school noun secondary school

high tide noun the time when the sea is at its highest level

highway noun **1** public road **2** (US, Aust, NZ) main road

highwayman highwaymen noun (formerly) a robber, usually on horseback, who robbed travellers at gunpoint

hijack verb to seize control of (an aircraft or other vehicle) during a journey ▷ **hijacker** noun ▷ **hijacking** noun: an attempted hijacking

hike noun **1** long walk in the country, especially for pleasure ▷ verb **2** to go for a long walk ▷ **hiker** noun

hilarious adjective very funny ▷ **hilariously** adverb

hilarity noun great amusement and laughter

hill noun **1** raised part of land, higher than the land surrounding it, but less high than a mountain ▷ **hilly** adjective: a hilly area

hillbilly hillbillies noun (US) unsophisticated country person

hilt noun handle of a sword or knife

him pronoun refers to a male person or animal; used as the object of a verb or preposition

himself pronoun **1** used as an object of a verb or pronoun when the man, boy or male animal that does an action is also the man, boy or male animal that is directly affected by it: He pulled himself out of the water **2** used to emphasize he: He himself knew nothing about it

hind adjective **1** situated at the back ▷ noun **2** female deer

hinder verb to get in the way of (someone or something); hamper

Hindi [hin-dee] noun language spoken in northern India

hindrance noun **1** someone or something that causes difficulties or is an obstruction **2** act of hindering

hindsight noun ability to understand an event after it has taken place: With hindsight, I realized how odd he is

Hindu noun **1** person who practises Hinduism ▷ adjective **2** of Hinduism ▷ **Hinduism** noun dominant religion of India, which involves the worship of many gods and a belief in reincarnation

hinge noun **1** movable joint which attaches a door or window to its frame ▷ verb **2** (followed by on) to depend (on)

hint noun **1** indirect suggestion, clue or helpful piece of advice **2** small amount ▷ verb **3** to suggest indirectly

hinterland noun land lying behind a coast or near a city, especially a port

hip noun either side of the body between the pelvis and the thigh

hippo hippos noun (informal) hippopotamus

hippopotamus hippopotamuses or hippopotami noun large African animal with thick wrinkled skin, living near rivers

hippy hippies noun (esp. in the 1960s) someone rejecting conventional society and trying to live a life based on peace and love

hire verb **1** to pay to have temporary use of **2** to employ (someone) to do a job ▷ noun **3** temporary use in exchange for money

hirsute [her-suit] adjective (formal) hairy

his adjective **1** belonging to him ▷ pronoun **2** object or objects belonging to or relating to a man, boy or male animal that has already been mentioned

hiss verb **1** to make a long s sound, especially to show disapproval or aggression ▷ noun **2** sound like that of a long s

histogram noun statistical graph in which the frequency of values is represented by vertical bars of varying heights and widths

historian noun person who studies and writes about history

historic adjective famous or significant in history

historical adjective **1** occurring in the past **2** based on history > **historically** adverb

history histories noun **1** study of the past **2** past events and developments **3** record or account of past events and developments **4** record of someone's past

histrionic adjective excessively dramatic > **histrionics** plural noun excessively dramatic behaviour

hit hits, hitting, hit verb **1** to strike (someone or something) forcefully **2** to come into violent contact with (something or someone) **3** to affect (someone) badly **4** to reach (a point or place) **5** **hit it off** (informal) to get on well together ▷ noun **6** instance of hitting **7** successful record, film, etc **8** (Computers) single visit to a website > **hit on** verb to think of (an idea)

hit and miss adjective sometimes successful and sometimes not

hit-and-run adjective (of a car accident) in which the driver responsible for the accident drives away without stopping

hitch noun **1** minor problem ▷ verb **2** (informal) to travel by getting lifts from passing vehicles **3** to attach > **hitch up** verb to pull (something) up with a jerk

hitchhike verb to travel by getting lifts from passing vehicles > **hitchhiker** noun > **hitchhiking** noun

hi tech adjective using very advanced technology

hither adverb **1** (old-fashioned) to or towards this place **2** **hither and thither** in all directions

hitherto adverb (formal) until this time

HIV abbreviation human immunodeficiency virus: cause of AIDS

hive noun **1** same as **beehive** **2** **hive of activity** place where people are busy > **hive off** verb to separate (something) from a larger group

hoard verb **1** to save or store (objects or food); stockpile ▷ noun **2** store of things that has been saved or hidden; stash > **hoarder** noun

> **WORD TIP**
> Do not confuse hoard with horde

hoarding noun large board for displaying advertisements by the side of the road

hoarse adjective **1** (of a voice) rough and unclear **2** having a rough and unclear voice > **hoarsely** adverb

hoax noun **1** trick or attempt to deceive someone ▷ verb **2** to deceive or play a trick on > **hoaxer** noun

hob noun (Brit) a surface on top of a cooker containing rings, hotplates or gas burners for cooking things

hobble verb **1** to walk lamely **2** to tie the legs of (a horse) together to restrict its movement

hobby hobbies noun something that you do for enjoyment in your spare time

hock noun **1** joint in the back leg of an animal such as a horse that corresponds to the human ankle **2** white German wine > **in hock** (informal) in debt ▷ verb **3** (informal) pawn

hockey noun **1** team game played on a field with a ball and curved sticks **2** (US) ice hockey

hoe noun hoes, hoeing, hoed **1** long-handled tool with a small square blade, used for loosening soil or weeding ▷ verb **2** to scrape or weed with a hoe

hog hogs, hogging, hogged noun **1** castrated male pig **2** go the **whole hog** to do something completely or thoroughly in a bold or extravagant way ▷ verb

3 (informal) to take more than your share of (something) or keep (something) for too long

hoist verb **1** to raise or lift (something) up ▷ noun **2** device for lifting things

hokey-pokey noun (NZ) brittle toffee sold in lumps

hold holds, holding, held verb **1** to keep or support (something) in or with your hands or arms **2** to have or possess (power, office or an opinion) **3** to arrange for (a meeting, party, election, etc) to take place **4** to consider (someone or something) to be as specified: *Who are you holding responsible?* **5** to have space for (an amount or number) **6** (informal) to wait, especially on the telephone **7** to keep back or reserve (tickets or an order) **8** to maintain (something) in a specified position or state ▷ noun **9** act or way of holding **10** controlling influence **11** cargo compartment on a ship or aircraft > **hold back** verb to prevent or keep control of a > **hold down** verb to keep (something) or keep it under control: *How could I have children and hold down a job like this?* > **holder** noun > **hold on to** verb to continue to hold (something) in spite of difficulties > **hold out** verb to stand firm and resist opposition in difficult circumstances > **hold up** verb to delay

holdall noun large strong travelling bag

hole noun **1** gap, opening or hollow **2** animal's burrow **3** (informal) weakness or error (in a theory or argument) **4** (informal) difficult situation **5** (*Golf*) small holes into which you have to hit the ball ▷ *verb* **6** to make holes in **7** to hit (a golf ball) into the target hole

Holi *noun* Hindu festival celebrated in spring

holiday *noun* **1** time spent away from home for rest or recreation **2** day or other period of rest from work or studies ▷ *verb* **3** to take a holiday (somewhere)

holidaymaker *noun* a person who is away from home on holiday

holiness *noun* **1** state of being holy **2 Your Holiness** or **His Holiness** title used to address or refer to the Pope

hollow *adjective* **1** having a hole or space inside **2** (of a sound) as if echoing in a hollow place **3** without any real value or worth ▷ *noun* **4** space **5** dip in the land ▷ *verb* **6** to form a hollow in **7** to make (something) by forming such a hollow

holly hollies *noun* evergreen tree with prickly leaves and red berries

holocaust *noun* destruction or loss of life on a massive scale

holster *noun* leather case for a hand gun, hung from a belt

holy holier, holiest *adjective* **1** relating to God or a god **2** (of a person) religious and living a very pure and good life

homage *noun* act of respect or honour towards someone or something

home *noun* **1** place where you live **2** place for the care of the elderly, orphans, etc ▷ *adjective* **3** connected with or involving your home or country **4** (*Sport*) played on your own ground ▷ *adverb* **5** to or at home

homeland *noun* native country

homeless *adjective* **1** having nowhere to live ▷ *plural noun* **2** people who have nowhere to live > **homelessness** *noun*

homely homelier, homeliest *adjective* simple, ordinary and comfortable

homeopathy [home-ee-**op**-ath-ee] *noun* treatment of disease by small doses of a drug that produces symptoms of the disease in healthy people > **homeopath** *noun* person who practises homeopathy > **homeopathic** *adjective*

homeowner *noun* person who owns the home in which he or she lives

homesick *adjective* unhappy because of being away from home and missing family and friends > **homesickness** *noun*

homespun *adjective* not sophisticated or complicated: *The book is simple homespun philosophy*

homestead *noun* house and its land and other buildings, especially a farm

home truths *plural noun* unpleasant facts told to a person about himself or herself

homeward *adjective* **1** towards home ▷ *adverb* **2** towards home

homework *noun* **1** school work done at home **2** preparatory research and work

homicide *noun* **1** killing of a human being **2** person who kills someone > **homicidal** adjective: a homicidal maniac

homing adjective **1** (of a device) capable of guiding itself to a target **2** (of a pigeon or instinct) with or relating to the ability to find home

homophone noun word pronounced the same as another, but with a different meaning or spelling. For example, write and right

Homo sapiens [hoe-moh **sap**-ee-enz] noun (formal) scientific name for human beings as a species

homosexual adjective **1** (of a person) sexually attracted to members of the same sex ▷ noun **2** person who is sexually attracted to people of the same sex > **homosexuality** noun

hone verb **1** to sharpen (a tool) **2** to improve and develop (a skill, ability or quality)

honest adjective **1** truthful and trustworthy **2** open and sincere > **honestly** adverb

honesty noun quality of being honest

honey noun **1** sweet edible sticky substance made by bees from nectar **2** term of endearment

honeycomb noun waxy structure of six-sided cells in which honey is stored by bees in a beehive

honeyeater noun small Australian bird that feeds on nectar from flowers

honeymoon noun holiday taken by a couple who have just got married

honeysuckle noun climbing shrub with sweet-smelling flowers

hongi [**hong**-ee] noun (NZ) Māori greeting in which people touch noses

honk noun **1** sound made by a car horn **2** sound made by a goose ▷ verb **3** to make this sound **4** to cause (a horn) to make this sound

honorary adjective **1** (of a degree or title) held or given only as an honour **2** (of a job) unpaid

honour noun **1** sense of honesty and fairness **2** respect **3** award given out of respect **4** pleasure or privilege **5** honours class of university degree of a higher standard than a pass or ordinary degree ▷ verb **6** to give praise and attention to **7** to give an award to (someone) out of respect **8** to pay (a cheque or bill) **9** to keep (a promise)

honourable adjective worthy of respect or esteem

hood noun **1** loose head covering, often attached to a coat or jacket **2** folding roof of a convertible car or a pram **3** (US, Aust) car bonnet

-hood suffix added at the end of words to form nouns that indicate a state or condition: childhood; priesthood

hoof hooves or hoofs noun horny covering of the foot of a horse, deer, etc

hook noun **1** curved piece of metal, plastic, etc, used to catch, hang, hold or pull something **2** curving movement, for example of the fist in boxing, or of a golf ball **3** let someone off the hook to cause someone to get out of a punishment or difficult situation ▷ verb **4** to fasten or catch (something) with or as if with a hook

hooked adjective 1 bent like a hook 2 (followed by on) (informal) addicted (to) or obsessed (with)

hooligan noun destructive and violent young person > **hooliganism** noun

hoop noun large ring, often used as a toy

hooray interjection same as **hurray**

hoot noun 1 sound of a car horn 2 cry of an owl 3 similar sound to that of an owl ▷ verb 4 to sound (a car horn) 5 to make a long oo sound like an owl

Hoover ® noun 1 vacuum cleaner ▷ verb 2 **hoover** to clean with a vacuum cleaner

hooves noun a plural of **hoof**

hop hops, hopping, hopped verb 1 to jump on one foot 2 to move in short jumps 3 (informal) to move quickly ▷ noun 4 instance of hopping 5 (often plural) climbing plant, the dried flowers of which are used to make beer

hope verb 1 to want (something to happen or be true) ▷ noun 2 wish or feeling of desire and expectation

hopeless adjective 1 having no hope 2 certain to fail or be unsuccessful 3 unable to do something well; useless: I'm hopeless at remembering birthdays > **hopelessly** adverb > **hopelessness** noun

hopper noun large, funnel-shaped container for storing substances such as grain or sand

horde noun large crowd

horizon noun 1 apparent line that divides the earth and the sky

2 **horizons** limits of what you want to do or are interested in: Travel broadens your horizons

horizontal adjective flat and parallel to the horizon > **horizontally** adverb

hormone noun 1 substance secreted by certain glands which stimulates certain organs of the body 2 synthetic substance with the same effect > **hormonal** adjective: hormonal changes

horn noun 1 one of a pair of bony growths sticking out of the heads of cattle, sheep, etc 2 substance of which horns are made 3 musical instrument with a tube or pipe of brass fitted with a mouthpiece 4 device on a vehicle sounded as a warning

hornet noun type of large wasp with a severe sting

horoscope noun prediction about a person's future based on the positions of the planets, sun and moon at his or her birth

horrendous adjective very unpleasant and shocking

horrible adjective 1 disagreeable and unpleasant 2 causing shock, fear or disgust > **horribly** adverb

horrid adjective disagreeable and unpleasant

horrific adjective causing horror: a horrific attack

horrify horrifies, horrifying, horrified verb to cause (someone) to feel horror or shock > **horrified** adjective: He had been horrified at the discovery > **horrifying** adjective: a horrifying experience

horror noun terror or hatred

horse noun 1 large animal with hooves, a mane and a tail, used for riding and pulling carts etc **2** piece of gymnastic equipment used for vaulting over

horseback noun **1 on horseback** riding a horse ▷ adjective **2** on a horse or on horses

horsepower noun unit of power (equivalent to 745.7 watts), used to measure the power of an engine

horseradish noun strong-tasting root of a plant, often made into a sauce

horseshoe noun protective U-shaped piece of iron nailed to a horse's hoof, regarded as a symbol of good luck

horsey or **horsy** horsier, horsiest adjective very keen on horses

horticulture noun art or science of growing flowers, fruit and vegetables ▷ **horticultural** adjective

hose hoses, hosing, hosed noun **1** flexible pipe along which liquid or gas can be passed ▷ verb **2** to wash or water (something) with a hose

hosiery noun stockings, socks and tights collectively

hospice [**hoss**-piss] noun nursing home for people who are dying

hospitable adjective welcoming to strangers or guests

hospital noun place where people who are sick or injured are looked after and treated

host noun **1** person who entertains guests **2** place or country providing the facilities for an event **3** compere of a show **4** animal or plant on which a parasite lives **5** large number ▷ verb **6** to be the host of (an event or party)

hostage noun person who is illegally held prisoner and threatened with injury or death unless certain demands are met by other people

hostel noun building providing accommodation at a low cost for a specific group of people such as students, travellers, homeless people, etc

hostess noun woman who entertains guests

hostile adjective **1** unfriendly **2** (followed by to) opposed (to) **3** relating to or involving the enemies of a country

hostility hostilities noun **1** unfriendly and aggressive feelings or behaviour **2 hostilities** acts of warfare

hot hotter, hottest adjective **1** having a high temperature **2** strong, spicy **3** (of news) very recent **4** (of a temper) quick to rouse **5** liked very much: *a hot favourite* **6** dangerous or difficult to deal with **7** (informal) stolen ▷ **hotly** adverb

hotbed noun any place encouraging a particular activity: *hotbeds of unrest*

hot dog noun long roll split lengthways with a hot sausage inside

hotel noun building where people stay, paying for their room and meals

hothouse noun **1** greenhouse **2** place or situation of intense intellectual or emotional activity: *a hothouse of radical socialist ideas*

hot seat noun **in the hot seat** (informal) having to make difficult decisions for which you will be held responsible

hound noun **1** hunting dog ▷ verb **2** to pursue (someone) relentlessly

hour noun **1** unit of time equal to sixty minutes and a twenty-fourth part of a day **2** time **3** hours period regularly appointed for work or business

house houses, housing, housed noun **1** building used as a home **2** building used for some specific purpose: the opera house **3** business firm **4** law-making body or the hall where it meets **5** family or dynasty **6** theatre or cinema audience ▷ verb **7** to give accommodation to **8** to contain or cover

houseboat noun boat tied up at a particular place on a river or canal and used as a home

household noun **1** all the people living in a house ▷ adjective **2** household name very well-known person

housekeeper noun person employed to run someone else's household

House of Commons noun the more powerful of the two parts of the British Parliament. Its members are elected by the public

House of Lords noun the less powerful of the two parts of the British Parliament. Its members are unelected

House of Representatives noun **1** (in Australia) the larger of the two parts of the Federal Parliament **2** (n New Zealand) the Parliament

housewife housewives noun married woman who runs her own household and does not have a paid job

housing noun **1** houses and flats or apartments **2** the providing of houses

hovel noun small house or hut that is dirty or badly in need of repair

hover verb **1** (of a bird etc) to hang in the air **2** to stand around in a state of indecision

hovercraft hovercrafts noun vehicle which can travel over both land and sea on a cushion of air

how adverb **1** in what way, by what means **2** to what degree: I know how hard it is; How much is it for the weekend? **3** used to emphasize: How odd!

however adverb **1** nevertheless **2** by whatever means **3** no matter how: However much it hurt, he could do it

howl verb **1** (of a wolf, dog or person) to make a long, loud wailing noise ▷ noun **2** loud wailing cry **3** loud burst of laughter

HQ noun an abbreviation for **headquarters**

hub noun **1** centre of a wheel, through which the axle passes **2** the most important or active part of a place or organization

hubbub noun great noise or confusion

huddle verb **1** to keep your arms and legs close to your body, often in response to cold or fear **2** (of people or animals) to crowd closely together ▷ noun **3** small group

hue noun colour, shade

huff noun in a huff in an angry and resentful mood > **huffy** adjective > **huffily** adverb: "There's no need to be sarcastic," he replied huffily

hug hugs, hugging, hugged *verb* **1** to clasp (someone) tightly in your arms as a gesture of affection **2** to keep close to (the ground, kerb, etc) ▷ *noun* **3** tight or fond embrace

huge *adjective* very big ▷ **hugely** *adverb*: *a hugely successful career*

hui hui or huis [**hoo**-ee] *noun* (NZ) **1** meeting of Māori people **2** (*informal*) party

hulk *noun* **1** large heavy person or thing **2** body of an abandoned ship ▷ **hulking** *adjective* bulky, unwieldy

hull *noun* main body of a boat that sits in the water

hum hums, humming, hummed *verb* **1** to make a low continuous low noise **2** to sing with the lips closed **3** (*informal*) (of a place) be very busy ▷ *noun* **4** humming sound

human *adjective* **1** of or typical of people ▷ *noun* **2** person; human being ▷ **humanly** *adverb* by human powers or means

human being *noun* man, woman or child

humane *adjective* kind or merciful ▷ **humanely** *adverb*

humanism *noun* belief in mankind's ability to achieve happiness and fulfilment without the need for religion ▷ **humanist** *noun*

humanitarian *noun* **1** person who works for the welfare of mankind or who has the interests of humankind at heart ▷ *adjective* **2** concerned with the welfare of mankind ▷ **humanitarianism** *noun*

humanity humanities *noun* **1** human race **2** the quality of being human **3** kindness or mercy **4 humanities** study of literature, philosophy and the arts

human rights *plural noun* rights of individuals to freedom and justice

humble *adjective* **1** conscious of your failings **2** modest, unpretentious **3** unimportant ▷ *verb* **4** to cause (someone) to feel humble; humiliate ▷ **humbly** *adverb*

humbug *noun* **1** (*Brit*) hard striped peppermint sweet **2** speech or writing that is obviously dishonest or untrue

humdrum *adjective* ordinary, dull

humid *adjective* damp and hot

humidity *noun* amount of moisture in the air, or the state of being humid

humiliate *verb* to make (someone) feel ashamed or appear stupid in front of other people ▷ **humiliating** *adjective*: *a degrading and humiliating experience* ▷ **humiliation** *noun*

humility *noun* quality of being humble

hummingbird *noun* very small American bird whose powerful wings make a humming noise as they beat

humour *noun* **1** quality of being funny **2** ability to say amusing things or find things amusing **3** state of mind; mood ▷ *verb* **4** to be kind and indulgent to

hump *noun* **1** raised piece of ground **2** large lump on the back of an animal or person ▷ *verb* **3** (*informal*) to carry or heave **4 get** or **take the hump** (*informal*) to be annoyed, sulk

hunch noun **1** feeling or suspicion not based on facts ▷ verb **2** to draw (one's) shoulders up or together

hunchback noun (old-fashioned) person with an abnormal curvature of the spine

hundred adjective, noun **1** the number 100 ▷ noun **2 hundreds** large but unspecified number; lots ▷ **hundredth** adjective, noun

Hungarian adjective **1** belonging or relating to Hungary ▷ noun **2** person from Hungary **3** main language spoken in Hungary

hunger noun **1** need or desire to eat **2** desire or craving ▷ **hunger for** verb to want very much

hunger strike noun refusal to eat, as a means of protest

hungry hungrier, hungriest adjective needing or wanting to eat ▷ **hungrily** adverb

hunk noun **1** large piece **2** (informal) sexually attractive man

hunt verb **1** to seek out and kill (wild animals) for food or sport **2** (followed by for) to search (for) ▷ noun **3** instance of hunting ▷ **hunter** noun person or animal that hunts wild animals for food or sport ▷ **hunting** adjective, noun

huntaway noun (Aust, NZ) sheepdog trained to drive sheep by barking

hurdle noun **1** (Sport) light barrier for jumping over in some races **2** problem or difficulty **3 hurdles** race involving hurdles ▷ **hurdler** noun

hurl verb **1** to throw (something) forcefully **2** to utter (insults) forcefully

hurray or **hurrah** interjection exclamation of joy or applause

hurricane noun very violent wind or storm

hurry hurries, hurrying, hurried verb **1** to move or do something as quickly as possible **2** to cause (something or someone) to move or do something more quickly than otherwise ▷ noun **3** haste or rush ▷ **hurried** adjective ▷ **hurriedly** adverb

hurt hurts, hurting, hurt verb **1** to injure or cause physical pain to **2** to be painful **3** to make (someone) unhappy or hurt by being unkind or thoughtless towards them ▷ noun **4** physical or mental pain ▷ **hurtful** adjective unkind: a hurtful remark

hurtle verb **1** to move quickly and violently

husband noun **1** woman's partner in marriage ▷ verb **2** to use (resources) economically

husbandry noun **1** farming **2** management of resources

hush verb **1** to be silent or make (someone) silent ▷ noun **2** stillness or silence ▷ **hushed** adjective ▷ **hush up** verb to suppress information about

husk noun dry outer covering of certain seeds and fruits

husky huskier, huskiest; huskies adjective **1** (of voice) slightly hoarse ▷ noun **2** Arctic sledge dog with thick hair and a curled tail ▷ **huskily** adverb

hustle verb **1** to push (someone) about; jostle ▷ noun **2** lively activity or bustle

hut noun small house, shelter or shed

hutch noun wooden box with wire mesh at one side, for keeping pet rabbits etc

hyacinth noun sweet-smelling spring flower that grows from a bulb

hybrid noun **1** plant or animal that has been bred from two different types of plant or animal **2** anything that is a mixture of two other things ▷ adjective **3** of mixed origin

hydra hydras or hydrae noun microscopic freshwater creature that has a slender tubular body and tentacles round the mouth

hydrangea noun ornamental shrub with clusters of pink, blue or white flowers

hydraulic adjective operated by pressure forced through a pipe by a liquid such as water or oil ▷ **hydraulically** adverb > **hydraulics** noun study of the mechanical properties of fluids as they apply to practical engineering

hydro- prefix **1** water: hydroelectric **2** containing hydrogen: hydrochloric acid

hydrogen noun (Chemistry) light flammable colourless gas that combines with oxygen to form water

hyena noun wild doglike animal of Africa and Asia that hunts in packs

hygiene noun practice of keeping yourself and your surroundings clean, especially to stop the spread of disease > **hygienic** adjective > **hygienically** adverb

hymn noun Christian song in praise of God

hyper- prefix very much, over or excessively: hyperactive

hyperactive adjective (of a person) unable to relax and always in a state of restless activity

hyperbole [hie-**per**-bol-ee] noun deliberate exaggeration for effect

hyperlink (Computers) noun link from a hypertext file that gives users instant access to related material in another file ▷ verb link (files) in this way

hypertension noun (formal) high blood pressure

hypertext noun computer software and hardware that allows users to store and view text and move between related items easily

hyphen noun punctuation mark (-) indicating that two words or syllables are connected > **hyphenate** verb to separate (words or syllables) with a hyphen > **hyphenated** adjective (of two words or syllables) having a hyphen between them > **hyphenation** noun

hypnosis noun artificially induced state of relaxation in which the mind is more than usually receptive to suggestion

hypnotize or **hypnotise** verb to put (someone) into a state in which they seem to be asleep but can respond to questions and suggestions

hypochondria noun undue preoccupation with your health > **hypochondriac** noun person who continually worries about their health

hypocrisy hypocrisies [hip-**ok**-rass-ee] *noun* pretence that you have beliefs or qualities that you do not really have, so that you seem a better person than you are > **hypocrite** [**hip**-oh-krit] *noun* person who pretends to be what he or she is not > **hypocritical** *adjective* > **hypocritically** *adverb*

hypodermic *noun* syringe or needle used to inject a drug beneath the skin

hypothermia *noun* condition in which a person's body temperature is dangerously low as a result of prolonged exposure to severe cold

hypothesis hypotheses [hie-**poth**-iss-iss] *noun* explanation or theory which has not been proved to be correct

hypothetical *adjective* based on assumption rather than on fact or reality > **hypothetically** *adverb*

hysterectomy hysterectomies *noun* surgical removal of the womb

hysteria *noun* state of uncontrolled excitement or panic

hysterical *adjective* in a state of uncontrolled excitement or panic > **hysterically** *adverb*

◆ i

I *pronoun* used by a speaker or writer to refer to himself or herself as the subject of a verb

ibis ibises [**ibe**-iss] *noun* large wading bird with long legs

-ible *suffix* another form of the suffix **-able**

-ic or **-ical** *suffix* used to form adjectives: *ironic; ironical*

ice *noun* **1** frozen water **2** (*Chiefly Brit*) ice cream **3 break the ice** to create a relaxed atmosphere, especially between people meeting for the first time ▷ *verb* **4** (followed by *up, over*) to become covered with ice **5** to cover (a cake) with icing

Ice Age *noun* period lasting thousands of years when much of the earth's surface was covered in ice

iceberg *noun* large floating mass of ice

icecap *noun* mass of ice permanently covering an area

ice cream *noun* sweet creamy frozen food

ice cube *noun* small square block of ice added to a drink to cool it

ice hockey *noun* type of hockey played on ice

Icelandic *noun* main language spoken in Iceland

ice-skate *verb* to move about on ice wearing ice-skates > **ice-skater** *noun*

icicle *noun* piece of ice shaped like a pointed stick hanging down where water has dripped

icing *noun* mixture of powdered sugar and water or egg whites, used to decorate cakes

icon *noun* **1** picture on a computer screen representing a program that can be activated by clicking on it **2** picture of Christ or another religious figure, regarded as holy

ICT *abbreviation* information and communications technology

icy *adjective* icier, iciest **1** very cold **2** covered with ice **3** unfriendly and cold > **icily** *adverb*

id *noun* (*Psychology*) basic instincts and unconscious thoughts

idea *noun* **1** plan or thought formed in the mind **2** belief or opinion **3** knowledge

ideal *adjective* **1** most suitable **2** perfect > *noun* **3** principle or idea that you try to achieve because it seems perfect to you **4** perfect example (of a person or thing)

idealism *noun* tendency to seek perfection in everything > **idealist** *noun* > **idealistic** *adjective*

idealize or **idealise** *verb* to regard or portray (someone or something) as perfect or nearly perfect > **idealization** *noun*

ideally *adverb* **1** if everything were perfect; in an ideal world: *Ideally, they'd have their own home* **2** perfectly

identical *adjective* exactly the same > **identically** *adverb*

identification *noun* **1** act of identifying **2** document such as a driver's licence or passport, which proves who you are

identify identifies, identifying, identified *verb* to recognize (someone or something) as being or prove (someone or something) to be a particular person or thing > **identifiable** *adjective: a clearly identifiable cause of stress* > **identify with** *verb* to understand and sympathize with the feelings and attitudes of (a person or group)

identity identities *noun* characteristics that make you who you are

ideology ideologies *noun* body of ideas and beliefs of a group, nation, etc > **ideological** *adjective* > **ideologically** *adverb*

idiom *noun* group of words whose meaning together is different from all the words taken individually. For example, 'It is raining cats and dogs' is an idiom

idiosyncrasy idiosyncrasies *noun* personal peculiarity of mind, habit or behaviour > **idiosyncratic** *adjective*

idiot *noun* foolish or stupid person

idiotic *adjective* extremely foolish or silly > **idiotically** *adverb*

idle *adjective* **1** not doing anything **2** not willing to work; lazy **3** not being used **4** useless or meaningless: *an idle threat* > *verb* **5** (of an engine) to run slowly out of gear > **idleness** *noun* > **idly** *adverb*

idol *noun* **1** famous person who is loved and admired by fans **2** picture or statue which is worshipped as if it were a god

idyll [**id-ill**] *noun* scene or time of great peace and happiness

> **idyllic** adjective: an idyllic place to stay

i.e. abbreviation (Latin) that is to say

if conjunction **1** on the condition that **2** whether **3** even though

igloo igloos noun dome-shaped Inuit house made of snow and ice

igneous [ig-nee-uss] adjective (technical) (of rock) formed as molten rock cools and hardens

ignite verb to set fire to (something) or catch fire

ignition noun system that ignites the fuel-and-air mixture to start an engine

ignominious adjective shameful or considered wrong > **ignominiously** adverb

ignoramus ignoramuses noun ignorant person

ignorant adjective **1** lacking knowledge **2** (informal) rude through lack of knowledge of good manners > **ignorance** noun > **ignorantly** adverb

ignore verb to refuse to notice (someone or something); disregard

iguana noun large tropical American lizard

il- prefix not or the opposite of: the form of in- that is used before the letter l: illegible

ill adjective **1** not in good health **2** harmful or unpleasant: ill effects ▷ noun **3** ills difficulties or problems ▷ adverb **4** badly **5** hardly, with difficulty: I can ill afford to lose him

ill at ease adjective uncomfortable or unable to relax

illegal adjective against the law > **illegality** noun > **illegally** adverb

illegible adjective (of writing) unclear and difficult or impossible to read

illegitimate adjective **1** born of parents not married to each other **2** not lawful > **illegitimacy** noun

ill-fated adjective doomed to end unhappily

illicit adjective **1** illegal **2** forbidden or disapproved of by society

illiterate adjective **1** unable to read or write ▷ noun **2** someone who is unable to read or write > **illiteracy** noun

illness noun **1** experience of being ill **2** particular disease

illogical adjective **1** not reasonable or sensible **2** not logical > **illogically** adverb

ill-treat verb to treat (someone or something) badly, causing hurt, harm or damage > **ill-treatment** noun

illuminate verb **1** to light (something) up **2** to make (something) clear; explain **3** (History) to decorate (a manuscript) with brightly coloured pictures > **illuminating** adjective

illumination noun **1** lighting **2** illuminations coloured lights put up to decorate a town

illusion noun **1** false belief **2** deceptive impression of reality which fools the eye

illusory adjective seeming to be true, but actually false

illustrate verb **1** to explain (something) by use of examples **2** to provide (a book or text) with pictures **3** to be an example of > **illustrative** adjective: illustrative examples > **illustrator** noun

illustration noun 1 picture or diagram 2 example

illustrious adjective famous and distinguished

ill will noun feeling of hostility

im- prefix not or the opposite of: the form of in- used before the letters b, m and p: imbalance; immature; impatient

IM abbreviation instant messaging

image noun 1 mental picture of someone or something 2 impression people have of a person, organization, etc 3 representation of a person or thing in a work of art

imagery noun descriptive language used in a poem or book

imaginary adjective existing only in the imagination

imagination noun 1 the ability to form new and exciting ideas 2 ability to make mental images of things that you may not have seen

imaginative adjective having or showing a lot of creative mental ability > **imaginatively** adverb

imagine verb 1 to form a mental image of 2 to think, believe or guess > **imaginable** adjective: hats of every imaginable shape and size

imam noun 1 leader of prayers in a mosque 2 title of some Islamic leaders

imbalance noun lack of balance or proportion

imbecile [imb-ess-eel] noun stupid person

imitate verb to copy > **imitative** adjective > **imitator** noun

imitation noun 1 copy of an original 2 instance of imitating

immaculate adjective 1 completely clean or tidy 2 without any mistakes at all > **immaculately** adverb

immaterial adjective not important or not relevant

immature adjective 1 not fully developed 2 lacking the wisdom and good sense expected of a person of this age > **immaturity** noun

immediate adjective 1 occurring at once 2 next or nearest in time, space or relationship > **immediacy** noun

immediately adverb 1 straight away 2 just: immediately behind the house

immemorial adjective **since** or **from time immemorial** longer than anyone can remember

immense adjective extremely large > **immensely** adverb to a very great degree > **immensity** noun

immerse verb 1 to involve (someone) deeply; engross 2 to plunge (something or someone) into liquid > **immersion** noun: damage due to immersion in water

immigrant noun someone who has come to live permanently in a new country > **immigrate** verb to come to live > **immigration** noun coming to a foreign country in order to live there

imminent adjective about to happen > **imminently** adverb > **imminence** noun

immobile adjective 1 not moving 2 unable to move > **immobility** noun: Weeks of immobility had left every muscle stiff

immoral adjective morally wrong; corrupt > **immorality** noun

WORD TIP
Do not confuse *immoral* and *amoral*. You use *immoral* to talk about people who are aware of moral standards, but go against them. *Amoral* applies to people with no moral standards

immortal *adjective* **1** living forever **2** famous for all time > **immortalize** *verb*

immortality *noun* state of living forever and never dying

immovable or **immoveable** *adjective* fixed and unable to be moved > **immovably** *adverb*

immune *adjective* **1** protected against a specific disease **2** (followed by *to*) secure (against)

immune system *noun* body's system of defence against disease

imp *noun* **1** (in folklore) mischievous small creature with magical powers > **impish** *adjective*

impact *noun* **1** strong effect **2** (force of) a collision

impair *verb* to weaken or damage (something) > **impairment** *noun*

impale *verb* to pierce with a sharp object

impart *verb* (*formal*) to pass on (information)

impartial *adjective* not favouring one side or the other; fair and objective > **impartially** *adverb* > **impartiality** *noun*

impasse [am-pass] *noun* situation in which progress is impossible

impassioned *adjective* full of emotion

impassive *adjective* showing no emotion, calm > **impassively** *adverb*

impasto *noun* (*Art*) technique of painting with thick paint so that brush strokes or palette knife marks can be seen

impatient *adjective* **1** irritable at any delay or difficulty **2** restless (to have or do something) > **impatiently** *adverb* > **impatience** *noun*

impeccable *adjective* excellent and without any faults > **impeccably** *adverb*

impede *verb* to hinder (someone) in action or progress

impediment *noun* something that makes action, speech or progress difficult

impelled *adjective* driven (to do something)

impending *adjective* (esp. of something bad) about to happen

impenetrable *adjective* **1** impossible to get through **2** impossible to understand

imperative *adjective* **1** extremely urgent or important; vital ▷ *noun* **2** (*Grammar*) form of a verb that is used for giving orders

imperfect *adjective* **1** having faults or mistakes **2** (*Grammar*) indicating a tense of verbs describing continuous, incomplete or repeated past actions ▷ *noun* **3** (*Grammar*) tense of verbs describing continuous, incomplete or repeated past actions > **imperfection** *noun* > **imperfectly** *adverb*

imperial *adjective* **1** relating to an empire, emperor or empress **2** denoting a system of weights and measures that uses inches, feet and yards, ounces and pounds, pints and gallons > **imperialism** *noun* system of rule in which a rich and powerful

nation controls other nations
> **imperialist** adjective, noun

imperious adjective proud and domineering > **imperiously** adverb

impersonal adjective **1** lacking human warmth or sympathy **2** not relating to any particular person; objective **3** (Grammar) (of a verb) without a personal subject, as in It is snowing
> **impersonally** adverb

impersonate verb to pretend to be (another person)
> **impersonation** noun
> **impersonator** noun

impertinent adjective disrespectful or rude
> **impertinently** adverb
> **impertinence** noun

impetuous adjective hasty and lacking in forethought; rash > **impetuosity** noun
> **impetuously** adverb

impetus [imp-it-uss] noun **1** incentive, impulse **2** (Physics) force that starts a body moving

impinge verb **impinge on** or **upon** to affect or restrict

implacable adjective not prepared to be appeased; unyielding > **implacability** noun
> **implacably** adverb

implant verb **1** to put (something) into someone's body, usually by surgical operation **2** to fix (something) firmly in someone's mind ▷ noun **3** (Medicine) something put into someone's body, usually by surgical operation

implausible adjective very unlikely
> **implausibly** adverb

implement verb **1** to carry out (a plan, instructions, etc)

▷ noun **2** tool or instrument
> **implementation** noun: We need to discuss the implementation of the new plan

implicate verb to show (someone) to be involved in something, especially a crime

implication noun something suggested indirectly or implied

implicit adjective **1** expressed indirectly **2** absolute and unquestioning: implicit support
> **implicitly** adverb

implore verb to beg (someone) earnestly

imply implies, implying, implied verb to suggest or hint (that something is the case)

import verb **1** to bring in (goods) from another country ▷ noun **2** something imported
> **importation** noun > **importer** noun

important adjective **1** very valuable, necessary or significant **2** having influence or power
> **importance** noun value, necessity or significance: the importance of having a balanced diet
> **importantly** adverb

impose verb **1** to force the acceptance of (something) **2** (often followed by on) to take unfair advantage (of)
> **imposition** noun unreasonable demand

imposing adjective grand and impressive

impossible adjective not able to be done or to happen
> **impossibility** noun
> **impossibly** adverb

imposter or **impostor** noun person who pretends to be

someone else in order to get things they want

impotent [**imp**-a-tent] *adjective* 1 powerless 2 (of a man) incapable of having or maintaining an erection during sexual intercourse > **impotence** *noun* > **impotently** *adverb*

impound *verb* to take legal possession of; confiscate

impoverished *adjective* poor

impractical *adjective* not practical, sensible or realistic

impregnable *adjective* impossible to break into

impregnated *adjective* saturated or soaked

impresario impresarios *noun* person who runs theatre performances, concerts, etc

impress *verb* 1 to cause (someone) to feel admiration or respect 2 to stress or emphasize 3 **impress something on someone** to make someone understand the importance of something

impression *noun* 1 effect, especially a strong or favourable one 2 vague idea 3 impersonation for entertainment 4 mark made by pressing

impressionable *adjective* easily impressed or influenced

impressionism *noun* style of painting which is concerned with the impressions created by light and shapes, rather than with exact details > **impressionist** *noun*

impressive *adjective* making a strong impression, especially through size, importance, or quality

imprint *noun* 1 lasting effect (on the mind) 2 mark left by

something causing pressure ▷ *verb* 3 to fix (something in someone's memory) 4 to produce (a mark) by printing or stamping

imprison *verb* to put (someone) in prison > **imprisonment** *noun*

improbable *adjective* not likely to be true or to happen > **improbability** *noun* > **improbably** *adverb*

impromptu *adjective* without planning or preparation

improper *adjective* 1 indecent or shocking 2 illegal or dishonest 3 not suitable or correct > **improperly** *adverb* > **impropriety** *noun (formal)* unsuitable or slightly improper behaviour

improve *verb* to become better or to make (something) better > **improvement** *noun: There's no sign of any improvement yet*

improvise *verb* 1 to make use of whatever materials are available 2 to make up (a piece of music, speech, etc) as you go along > **improvisation** *noun* > **improvised** *adjective: They're making do with improvised shelters*

impudent *adjective* cheeky and disrespectful > **impudence** *noun* > **impudently** *adverb*

impulse *noun* 1 sudden urge to do something 2 (*Physics*) short electrical signal passing along a wire or nerve or through the air 3 **on impulse** suddenly and without planning > **impulsive** *adjective* 1 (of a person) tending to do things on the spur of the moment without thinking about them carefully 2 (of an action, decision, etc) carried out or

taken on the spur of the moment without too much thinking
> **impulsively** adverb

impure adjective **1** having dirty or unwanted substances mixed in **2** immoral, obscene

impurity impurities noun **1** quality of being impure **2** trace of dirt or another substance that should not be present

in preposition **1** indicating inside (something): *in the box* **2** indicating a state or situation, etc: *in a mess* **3** indicating a time or manner: *in the afternoon; in a husky voice* ▷ adverb **4** indicating position inside, entry into, etc: *She stayed in; come in* ▷ adjective **5** fashionable

in- prefix **1** added to the beginning of some words to form a word with the opposite meaning: *insincere* **2** in, into or in the course of: *infiltrate*

inability noun lack of means or skill to do something

inaccessible adjective impossible or very difficult to reach

inaccurate adjective not correct

inadequate adjective **1** not enough **2** not good enough > **inadequacy** noun > **inadequately** adverb

inadvertent adjective unintentional > **inadvertently** adverb

inane adjective silly or stupid > **inanely** adverb > **inanity** noun

inanimate adjective not living

inappropriate adjective not suitable > **inappropriately** adverb

inarticulate adjective unable to express yourself clearly or well

inasmuch as conjunction because or in so far as

inaudible adjective not loud enough to be heard > **inaudibly** adverb

inaugurate verb **1** to open (a building), especially with ceremony **2** to begin to use (a new system) **3** to formally establish (a new leader) in office > **inaugural** adjective > **inauguration** noun

inborn adjective existing from birth; natural

incandescent adjective glowing with heat > **incandescence** noun

incapable adjective **1** (followed by *of*) unable (to do something) **2** incompetent

incarcerate verb to imprison > **incarceration** noun

incarnate adjective in human form > **incarnation** noun

incendiary [in-**send**-ya-ree] adjective (of a bomb, attack, etc) designed to cause fires

incense noun substance that gives off a sweet perfume when burned

incensed adjective extremely angry

incentive noun something that encourages effort or action

inception noun (formal) beginning

incessant adjective never stopping > **incessantly** adverb

incest noun sexual intercourse between two people too closely related to marry > **incestuous** adjective: *an incestuous relationship*

inch noun **1** unit of length equal to about 2.54 centimetres ▷ verb **2** to move slowly and gradually

incident noun event

incidental adjective occurring as a minor part of something > **incidentally** adverb

incinerate verb to burn
> **incineration** noun

incinerator noun special container for burning rubbish

incipient adjective just starting to appear or happen

incision noun a sharp cut, made especially by a surgeon operating on a patient

incisive adjective direct and forceful

incite verb **1** to stir up (trouble, violence, criminal behaviour, etc) **2** to provoke (someone) into doing something > **incitement** noun

inclination noun **1** liking, tendency or preference **2** slope

incline verb **1** to make (someone) likely (to do something) **2 be inclined** to tend (to do something) ▷ noun **3** slope

include verb to have (something or someone) as part of something or make them part of it > **including** preposition: everybody, including me

inclusion noun act of making (something or someone) part of something

inclusive adjective including everything (specified)
> **inclusively** adverb

incognito [in-kog-**nee**-toe] adjective, adverb in disguise or with a false identity

incoherent adjective unclear and impossible to understand
> **incoherence** noun
> **incoherently** adverb

income noun amount of money earned from work, investments, etc

income tax noun tax on annual income

incoming adjective **1** coming in **2** about to come into office

incomparable adjective beyond comparison; unequalled
> **incomparably** adverb

incompatible adjective unable to live or exist together because of differences > **incompatibility** noun

incompetent adjective not having the necessary ability or skill to do something > **incompetence** noun > **incompetently** adverb

incomplete adjective not complete or finished
> **incompletely** adverb

incomprehensible adjective not able to be understood

inconceivable adjective impossible to believe

inconclusive adjective not leading to a decision or a definite result

incongruous adjective inappropriate or out of place
> **incongruously** adverb

inconsequential adjective unimportant or insignificant

inconsistent adjective not always behaving in the same way; unpredictable > **inconsistency** noun > **inconsistently** adverb

inconspicuous adjective not easily seen or obvious
> **inconspicuously** adverb

incontinent adjective unable to control your bladder or bowels
> **incontinence** noun

inconvenience noun **1** trouble or difficulty ▷ verb **2** to cause (someone) trouble or difficulty
> **inconvenient** adjective
> **inconveniently** adverb

incorporate verb to include (something or someone) as part

of a larger unit ▷ **incorporation**
noun
incorrect adjective wrong or
untrue ▷ **incorrectly** adverb
increase verb **1** to become or
make (something) greater in
size, number, etc ▷ noun **2** rise
in number, size, etc **3** amount
by which something increases
▷ **increasingly** adverb
incredible adjective **1** hard to
believe or imagine **2** (informal)
marvellous; amazing
▷ **incredibly** adverb
incredulous adjective not able to
believe something ▷ **incredulity**
noun ▷ **incredulously** adverb
increment noun increase in
money or value, especially
a regular salary increase
▷ **incremental** adjective
incriminate verb to make
(someone) seem guilty of a
crime ▷ **incriminating** adjective:
incriminating evidence
incubate [in-cube-ate] verb (of
eggs) to be kept warm until ready
to hatch ▷ **incubation** noun
▷ **incubator** noun piece of hospital
equipment in which sick or weak
newborn babies are kept warm
incumbent adjective **1** it is
incumbent on it is the duty of
(someone to do something)
▷ noun **2** person holding a
particular office or position
incur incurs, incurring, incurred
verb to cause (something
unpleasant) to happen
incurable adjective not able to be
cured ▷ **incurably** adverb
indebted adjective grateful (to
someone for help or favours)
▷ **indebtedness** noun

indecent adjective **1** morally or
sexually offensive **2** unsuitable
or unseemly: indecent haste
▷ **indecency** noun ▷ **indecently**
adverb
indeed adverb really or certainly
indefatigable adjective never
getting tired
indefinite adjective **1** without
exact limits: for an indefinite period
2 vague, unclear ▷ **indefinitely**
adverb
indefinite article noun
grammatical term for a or an
indelible adjective impossible to
erase or remove ▷ **indelibly** adverb
indemnity indemnities noun
(formal) insurance against loss
or damage
indentation noun dent or groove
in a surface or edge
independence noun **1** not relying
on anyone else **2** self-rule
independent adjective **1** free
from the control or influence of
others **2** separate **3** financially
self-reliant **4** capable of acting
for yourself or on your own
▷ noun **5** politician who does
not represent any political party
▷ **independently** adverb
indeterminate adjective not
certain and not fixed
index noun (pl indexes, indices
[in-diss-eez]) **1** alphabetical list
of names or subjects dealt with
in a book **2** alphabetical list of all
the books in a library, arranged by
title, author or subject ▷ verb **3** to
provide (a book) with an index
index finger noun finger next to
your thumb
Indian adjective **1** belonging
or relating to India ▷ noun

2 someone from India **3** Native American

indicate verb **1** to be a sign or symptom of **2** to point (something) out **3** to state (something) briefly **4** (of a measuring instrument) to show a reading of **5** (of a driver) to give a signal showing which way you are going to turn

indication noun a sign of what someone feels or what is likely to happen

indicative adjective **1 indicative of** suggesting ▷ noun **2** (Grammar) indicative mood

indicator noun **1** something acting as a sign or indication **2** flashing light on a vehicle showing the driver's intention to turn **3** (Chemistry) substance that shows if another substance is an acid or alkali by changing colour when it comes into contact with it

indict [in-**dite**] verb to charge (someone) officially with a crime > **indictable** adjective: an indictable offence > **indictment** noun

indifferent adjective **1** (often followed by to) showing no interest or concern (in) **2** of poor quality > **indifference** noun > **indifferently** adverb

indigenous [in-**dij**-in-uss] adjective born in or native to a country

indigestion noun discomfort or pain caused by difficulty in digesting food > **indigestible** adjective difficult to digest

indignant adjective angry at something unfair or wrong > **indignantly** adverb

indignation noun anger at something unfair or wrong

indignity indignities noun something causing embarrassment or humiliation

indigo noun, adjective deep violet-blue

indirect adjective not direct > **indirectly** adverb

indiscriminate adjective showing lack of careful thought or choice > **indiscriminately** adverb

indispensable adjective absolutely essential

indistinct adjective not clear > **indistinctly** adverb

individual adjective **1** relating to one particular person or thing **2** separate; distinct **3** distinctive or unusual ▷ noun **4** single person or thing > **individually** adverb

individualist noun someone who likes to do things in their own way > **individualistic** adjective: a very individualistic society

individuality noun quality of being different from all other things, and therefore interesting and noticeable

indomitable adjective (formal) too strong to be defeated or discouraged

Indonesian adjective **1** belonging to or relating to Indonesia ▷ noun **2** someone from Indonesia **3** official language of Indonesia

indoor adjective inside a building

indoors adverb inside a building

induce verb **1** to cause (a state or condition) **2** to persuade or influence (someone to do something) **3** (Medicine) to cause (a woman) to go into labour or bring on (labour) by the use of drugs etc

inducement *noun* something used to persuade someone to do something

indulge *verb* 1 to allow yourself to do something that you enjoy 2 to allow (someone) to have or do what they want

indulgence *noun* 1 something allowed because it gives pleasure 2 act of indulging yourself or someone else

indulgent *adjective* showing kindness, generosity and understanding towards someone, often to an excessive degree > **indulgently** *adverb*

industrial *adjective* relating to industry

industrial action *noun* any action, such as striking or working to rule, that is used by workers as a way of protesting about their pay and conditions with the aim of bringing about change

industrialist *noun* person who owns or controls a lot of factories

Industrial Revolution *noun* the transformation of Britain and other countries in the eighteenth and nineteenth century into industrial nations, through greater use of machinery

industrious *adjective* hard-working

industry industries *noun* 1 work and processes involved in manufacturing things in factories 2 all the people and processes involved in manufacturing a particular thing

inedible *adjective* not fit to be eaten

inefficient *adjective* badly organized, wasteful and slow > **inefficiency** *noun* > **inefficiently** *adverb*

inept *adjective* clumsy or lacking skill > **ineptitude** *noun*

inequality inequalities *noun* difference in size, status, wealth or position, between different things, groups or people

inert *adjective* 1 without the power of motion or resistance 2 chemically unreactive > **inertness** *noun*

inertia *noun* feeling of unwillingness to do anything

inevitable *adjective* unavoidable, sure to happen > **inevitability** *noun* > **inevitably** *adverb*

inexhaustible *adjective* incapable of running out or being used up

inexorable *adjective* unable to be prevented from continuing or progressing > **inexorably** *adverb*

inexpensive *adjective* not costing much

inexperienced *adjective* lacking experience of a situation or activity > **inexperience** *noun*

inexplicable *adjective* impossible to explain > **inexplicably** *adverb*

inextricably *adverb* without possibility of separation

infallible *adjective* never wrong > **infallibility** *noun*

infamous [in-fam-uss] *adjective* well-known for something bad

infant *noun* very young child

infantry *noun* soldiers who fight on foot

infatuated *adjective* feeling such intense love or passion for someone that you cannot think sensibly about them > **infatuation** *noun* intense unreasoning passion

infect *verb* to give (someone or something) a disease

infection *noun* **1** disease caused by germs **2** being infected

infectious *adjective* **1** (of a disease) spreading without actual contact **2** spreading from person to person: *infectious enthusiasm*

infer infers, inferring, inferred *verb* to work (something) out from evidence > **inference** *noun* conclusion

> **WORD TIP**
> Do not use *infer* to mean the same as *imply*.

inferior *adjective* **1** lower in quality, position or status ▷ *noun* **2** person of lower position or status > **inferiority** *noun*

infernal *adjective* **1** (old-fashioned, informal) very irritating **2** relating to hell

inferno infernos *noun* intense raging fire

infertile *adjective* **1** (of soil) poor in quality and not good for growing plants **2** unable to produce children or young > **infertility** *noun*

infested *adjective* inhabited or overrun by a large number of animals or insects > **infestation** *noun*

infidelity infidelities *noun* being unfaithful to your husband, wife or partner

infighting *noun* quarrelling within a group

infiltrate *verb* to become part of (an organization) gradually and secretly with the aim of finding out information about its activities > **infiltration** *noun* > **infiltrator** *noun*

infinite [**in**-fin-it] *adjective* without any limit or end > **infinitely** *adverb*

infinitive *noun* (Grammar) form of a verb not showing tense, person or number, e.g. *to sleep*

infinity *noun* endless space, time or number

infirmary infirmaries *nouns* hospital

inflamed *adjective* (of part of the body) red, swollen and painful because of infection

inflammable *adjective* easily set on fire

inflammation *noun* painful redness or swelling of part of the body

inflammatory *adjective* likely to provoke anger

inflate *verb* to fill (something) with air or gas > **inflatable** *adjective* able to be inflated

inflation *noun* increase in prices and fall in the value of money > **inflationary** *adjective*

inflection or **inflexion** *noun* (Grammar) change in the form of a word according to function, tense, number, etc

inflexible *adjective* **1** unwilling to be persuaded, obstinate **2** (of a policy etc) firmly fixed, unalterable

inflict *verb* to impose (something unpleasant) on

influence *noun* **1** power of a person to have an effect over others **2** effect of a person or thing on another ▷ *verb* **3** to have an effect on

influential *adjective* having a lot of influence

influenza *noun* (formal) flu

influx noun arrival or entry of many people or things

inform verb 1 to tell (someone) of something 2 to give information to the police revealing the involvement of a particular person in a crime > **informant** noun person who gives information

informal adjective 1 relaxed and friendly 2 appropriate for everyday life or use > **informality** noun > **informally** adverb

information noun knowledge or facts

informative adjective giving useful information

informer noun person who gives information to the police revealing the involvement of a particular person in a crime

infrastructure noun basic facilities, services and equipment needed for a country or organization to function properly

infringe verb 1 to break (a law or agreement) 2 to interfere with (people's rights), preventing them from using them > **infringement** noun

infuriate verb to make (someone) very angry > **infuriating** adjective

infuse verb 1 to fill (someone with an emotion or quality) 2 to leave (something) to soak in hot water so that the water absorbs its flavours, etc > **infusion** noun

ingenious [in-**jean**-ee-uss] adjective showing cleverness and originality > **ingeniously** adverb

ingenuity [in-jen-**new**-it-ee] noun cleverness and originality at inventing things or working out plans

ingot noun oblong block of metal, especially gold

ingrained adjective firmly fixed

ingredient noun one of the things from which a dish or mixture is made

inhabit verb to live in

inhabitant noun person who lives in a place

inhale verb to breathe in (air, smoke, etc) > **inhalation** noun

inherent adjective forming an inseparable part of something > **inherently** adverb

inherit verb 1 to receive (money etc) from someone who has died 2 to receive (a characteristic) from an earlier generation > **inheritance** noun > **inheritor** noun

inhibit verb 1 to prevent (someone) from doing something 2 to hinder or prevent (something) from happening

inhibited adjective finding it difficult to relax and show emotions

inhibition noun feeling of fear or embarrassment that stops you from behaving naturally

inhospitable adjective 1 difficult to live in; harsh 2 not welcoming or friendly

inhuman adjective 1 cruel or brutal 2 not human

inhumane adjective cruel or brutal > **inhumanity** noun

inimitable adjective impossible to imitate; unique

initial adjective 1 first or at the beginning ▷ noun 2 first letter, especially of a person's name > **initially** adverb

initiate verb 1 to begin or set (something) up 2 to admit (someone) into a closed group, especially by means of a special ceremony > **initiation** noun > **initiator** noun

initiative noun **1** attempt to get something done **2** first step, commencing move **3** ability to act independently

inject verb **1** to put (a substance) into someone's body with a syringe **2** to introduce (a new element) > **injection** noun: I was given an injection

injunction noun court order not to do something

injure verb to hurt (a person or animal)

injury injuries noun hurt or damage

injustice noun **1** lack of justice and fairness **2** unfair action **3 do someone an injustice** to criticize someone unfairly

ink noun coloured liquid used for writing or printing

inkling noun slight idea or suspicion

inlaid adjective decorated with small pieces of wood, metal or stone

inland adjective, adverb in or towards the interior of a country, away from the sea

in-laws plural noun the family of your husband or wife

inlet noun **1** narrow strip of water extending from the sea into the land **2** valve etc through which liquid or gas enters

inmate noun person living in an institution such as a prison

inn noun pub or small hotel, especially in the country

innards plural noun (informal) internal parts

innate adjective being part of someone's nature; inborn > **innately** adverb

inner adjective happening or located inside

innermost adjective deepest and most secret

innings noun (Sport) player's or side's turn of batting

innocent adjective **1** not guilty of a crime **2** without experience of evil **3** without malicious intent > **innocence** noun > **innocently** adverb

innocuous adjective not harmful

innovation noun **1** new idea or method **2** introduction of new ideas or methods > **innovative** adjective fresh and new

innuendo innuendos or innuendoes noun indirect reference to something rude or unpleasant

innumerable adjective too many to be counted

input noun **1** resources put into a project etc **2** data fed into a computer

inquest noun official inquiry into a sudden death

inquire verb to seek information or ask (about) > **inquiring** adjective

inquisition noun **1** thorough official investigation, often using harsh methods of questioning

inquisitive adjective curious and keen to find out about things > **inquisitively** adverb

inroads plural noun **make inroads into** to start affecting or reducing (something)

insane adjective **1** mentally ill **2** stupidly irresponsible > **insanely** adverb > **insanity** noun

insatiable [in-**saysh**-a-bl] *adjective* unable to be satisfied > **insatiably** *adverb*

inscribe *verb* 1 to write or carve (words) on something 2 to write on or carve (something) with words

inscription *noun* words written or carved on something

inscrutable *adjective* revealing nothing or giving nothing away

insect *noun* small animal with six legs and usually wings

insecticide *noun* substance for killing insects

insecure *adjective* 1 anxious, not confident 2 not safe or well-protected > **insecurity** *noun*

insensitive *adjective* unaware of or ignoring other people's feelings > **insensitivity** *noun*

insert *verb* 1 to put (something) inside or include (something) > **insertion** *noun*

inshore *adjective* 1 close to the shore 2 towards the shore ▷ *adverb* 3 towards the shore

inside *preposition* 1 in or into the interior of ▷ *adjective* 2 on or relating to the inside 3 by or from someone within an organization: *inside information* ▷ *adverb* 4 on, in or into the inside; indoors ▷ *noun* 5 inner side, surface or part 6 **inside out** with the inside facing outwards 7 **know something inside out** to know something thoroughly 8 (*informal*) **insides** stomach and bowels

WORD TIP
Do not use *of* after *inside*. You should write *she was waiting inside the school* and not *inside of the school*

insider *noun* member of a group who has privileged knowledge about it

insidious *adjective* dangerous and developing slowly without being noticed ▷ **insidiously** *adverb*

insight *noun* deep understanding

insignia *plural noun* badge or emblem of a particular organization

insignificant *adjective* small and unimportant > **insignificance** *noun*

insincere *adjective* pretending to have certain feelings; not genuine > **insincerely** *adverb* > **insincerity** *noun*

insinuate *verb* 1 to suggest (something unpleasant) indirectly; hint at 2 to work (yourself) into a position gradually and cleverly > **insinuation** *noun*

insipid *adjective* lacking interest, spirit or flavour

insist *verb* to demand or state firmly

insolent *adjective* rude and disrespectful > **insolence** *noun* > **insolently** *adverb*

insoluble *adjective* 1 impossible to solve 2 impossible to be dissolved

insolvent *adjective* unable to pay your debts > **insolvency** *noun*

insomnia *noun* difficulty in sleeping > **insomniac** *noun* person who has difficulty in sleeping

inspect *verb* to check (someone or something) closely or officially > **inspection** *noun*

inspector *noun* 1 person who inspects 2 high-ranking police officer

a
b
c
d
e
f
g
h
i
j
k
l
m
n
o
p
q
r
s
t
u
v
w
x
y
z

inspire verb 1 to fill (someone) with enthusiasm; stimulate 2 to arouse (an emotion) > **inspiration** noun 1 creative influence or stimulus 2 brilliant idea > **inspired** adjective > **inspiring** adjective

instability noun lack of stability

install verb 1 to put in and prepare (equipment) for use 2 to place (a person) formally in a position or rank 3 to settle (yourself) in a place > **installation** noun 1 installing 2 equipment installed 3 place containing equipment for a particular purpose: oil installations

instalment noun one of a series of successive parts

instance noun 1 particular example 2 **for instance** as an example

instant noun 1 very brief time 2 particular moment ▷ adjective 3 happening at once; immediate 4 (of foods) requiring little preparation > **instantly** adverb

instantaneous adjective happening at once > **instantaneously** adverb

instead adverb in place of something

instigate verb to cause (something) to happen > **instigation** noun: The search was carried out at the instigation of the president > **instigator** noun

instil instils, instilling, instilled verb to introduce (an idea etc) gradually into someone's mind

instinct noun natural tendency to behave in a certain way > **instinctive** adjective > **instinctively** adverb

institute noun 1 organization set up for a specific purpose, especially for teaching ▷ verb 2 (formal) to start or establish (a rule or system)

institution noun 1 long-established custom 2 large important organization such as a university or bank > **institutional** adjective

instruct verb 1 to tell (someone) to do something 2 to teach (someone) how to do something > **instruction** noun 2 **instructive** adjective informative or helpful > **instructor** noun: a driving instructor

instrument noun 1 tool or device used for a particular job 2 object, such as a piano or flute, played to make music 3 measuring device to show height, speed, etc

instrumental adjective 1 (followed by in) having an important role (in doing something) 2 (of music) played by or composed for musical instruments

insufficient adjective not enough > **insufficiently** adverb

insular adjective not open to new ideas; narrow-minded > **insularity** noun

insulate verb 1 to cover (something) with a layer to keep it warm or to stop electricity passing through it 2 to protect (someone) from harmful things > **insulation** noun > **insulator** noun

insulin noun hormone produced in the pancreas that controls the amount of sugar in the blood

insult verb 1 to behave rudely to (someone); offend ▷ noun 2 rude remark or action which offends you > **insulting** *adjective*

insure *verb* **1** to protect (something or yourself) by paying for insurance **2 insure against** to take action to prevent (something) from happening or to provide protection if it does happen

insurrection *noun* rebellion

intact *adjective* not changed or damaged in any way

intake *noun* amount or number of something taken in

integral *adjective* being an essential part of a whole

integrate *verb* **1** (of a person) to become part of a group or community **2** to combine (things) so that they become part of a whole > **integration** *noun*

integrity *noun* **1** quality of being honest and following your principles **2** quality of being united

intellect *noun* ability to think and reason

intellectual *adjective* **1** involving thought, ideas and understanding **2** clever, intelligent ▷ *noun* **3** person who enjoys thinking about complicated ideas > **intellectually** *adverb*

intelligence *noun* **1** quality of being able to understand and to learn things quickly and well **2** information about the aims and activities, especially military or terrorist ones, of an organization, government, etc **3** people or department collecting such information

intelligent *adjective* **1** able to understand, learn and think things out quickly **2** (of a

computerized device) able to react to events > **intelligently** *adverb*

intelligentsia *noun* intellectual or cultured people in a society

intelligible *adjective* able to be understood > **intelligibility** *noun*

intend *verb* **1** to propose or plan (to do something) **2 be intended to do something** to have something as your purpose or task

intense *adjective* **1** very great in strength or amount **2** deeply emotional > **intensely** *adverb* > **intensity** *noun*

intensify intensifies, intensifying, intensified *verb* to become or make (something) greater or stronger > **intensification** *noun*

intensive *adjective* using or needing a lot of energy or effort over a short time

intent *noun* **1** (*formal*) intention ▷ *adjective* **2 intent on doing something** determined to do something > **intently** *adverb*

intention *noun* plan

intentional *adjective* done on purpose; deliberate > **intentionally** *adverb*

inter- *prefix* between or among: *international*

interact *verb* to act, work or communicate together > **interaction** *noun*

interactive *adjective* (of television, a computer, game, etc) reacting to decisions taken by the viewer, user or player

intercept *verb* to seize or stop (someone or something) on their way somewhere

interchange *noun* act or process of exchanging things or ideas > **interchangeable** *adjective*

intercom noun internal communication system resembling a telephone

intercourse noun act of having sex

interest noun 1 desire to know or hear more about something 2 something in which you are interested 3 (often plural) advantage or benefit 4 reason for wanting something to happen 5 sum paid for the use of borrowed money 6 (often plural) right or share ▷ verb 7 to attract the attention of (someone) because they want to know or hear more

interesting adjective of interest > **interestingly** adverb

interface noun 1 area where two things interact or link 2 user interface presentation on screen of a computer program and how easy it is to operate

interfere verb 1 to try to influence other people's affairs when it is not really your business to do so 2 (followed by with) to clash (with) or get in the way (of) > **interference** noun > **interfering** adjective

interim adjective temporary or provisional

interior noun 1 inside 2 inland region ▷ adjective 3 inside or inner

interjection noun word or phrase spoken suddenly to express surprise, pain or anger

interlude noun short rest or break in an activity or event

intermediary intermediaries noun someone who tries to get two groups of people to come to an agreement

intermediate adjective occurring in the middle, between two other stages

interminable adjective seemingly endless because boring > **interminably** adverb

intermission noun interval between parts of a play, film, etc

intermittent adjective occurring at intervals > **intermittently** adverb

internal adjective happening inside a person, place or object > **internally** adverb

international adjective 1 of or involving two or more countries ▷ noun 2 game or match between teams of different countries > **internationally** adverb

internet or **Internet** noun worldwide computer communication network

interplay noun the way two things react with one another

interpret verb 1 to explain the meaning of 2 to translate orally what someone says in one language into another language for the benefit of others 3 to convey the meaning of (a poem, song, etc) in performance > **interpretation** noun > **interpreter** noun

interrogate verb to question (someone) closely > **interrogation** noun > **interrogator** noun

interrupt verb 1 to start talking while someone else is talking 2 to break into (a conversation etc) 3 to stop (a process or activity) temporarily > **interruption** noun

intersect verb (of roads) to meet and cross > **intersection** noun

interspersed adjective scattered (among, between or on)

interval noun **1** time between two particular moments or events **2** break between parts of a play, concert, etc **3** difference in pitch between musical notes **4 at intervals a** repeatedly **b** with spaces left between

intervene verb to step into a situation, especially to prevent conflict ▷ **intervention** noun

intervening adjective (of time) in between

interview noun **1** formal discussion, especially between an employer and someone trying to get a job **2** questioning of a usually well-known person about his or her career, views, etc, by a reporter ▷ verb **3** to conduct an interview with ▷ **interviewee** noun someone interviewed ▷ **interviewer** noun someone conducting an interview

intestine noun (often plural) tube that carries food from your stomach to your bowels, and in which the food is digested

intimate adjective **1** having a close personal relationship **2** personal or private **3** (of knowledge) extensive and detailed **4** having a quiet and friendly atmosphere ▷ verb **5** to hint or suggest ▷ **intimacy** noun: the intimacy of the relationship between the players ▷ **intimately** adverb ▷ **intimation** noun: the first intimation that something could be amiss

intimidate verb to frighten (someone) deliberately with the aim of influencing their behaviour ▷ **intimidated** adjective

frightened > **intimidating** adjective frightening: I found it quite intimidating ▷ **intimidation** noun

into preposition **1** indicating motion towards the inside of something: into the valley **2** indicating the result of change or division: turned into a madman; cut into pieces **3** indicating destination: Their car crashed into a tree **4** (informal) interested in: Nowadays I'm really into healthy food

intolerable adjective more than can be endured ▷ **intolerably** adverb

intonation noun the way that your voice rises and falls as you speak

intoxicated adjective **1** drunk **2** overexcited

intra- prefix within or inside: intra-European conflicts

intractable adjective (formal) stubborn and difficult to deal with

intransitive adjective (of a verb) not taking a direct object

intravenous [in-tra-**vee**-nuss] adjective given into a vein ▷ **intravenously** adverb

intrepid adjective fearless or bold ▷ **intrepidity** noun ▷ **intrepidly** adverb

intricate adjective **1** involved or complicated **2** full of fine detail ▷ **intricacy** noun: the intricacy of the design ▷ **intricately** adverb

intrigue intrigues, intriguing, intrigued verb **1** to make (someone) interested or curious **2** to plot secretly ▷ noun **3** secret planning or plotting ▷ **intriguing** adjective

intrinsic adjective essential to the basic nature of something ▷ **intrinsically** adverb

introduce verb 1 to present (someone) by name (to another person) 2 to say a few explanatory words at the beginning of (a radio or television programme) 3 to make (someone) aware of or get them interested in something for the first time 4 to insert (something) > **introductory** adjective

introduction noun 1 act of presenting a person or thing for the first time 2 piece of writing at the beginning of a book, usually telling you what the book is about

introvert noun person concerned more with his or her thoughts and feelings than with the outside world > **introversion** noun > **introverted** adjective

intrude verb to come in or join in without being invited: I don't want to intrude on your parents > **intrusion** noun > **intrusive** adjective

intuition noun feeling you have about something that you cannot explain > **intuitive** adjective > **intuitively** adverb

Inuit noun 1 member of a group of people who live in Northern Canada, Greenland, Alaska and Eastern Siberia, formerly known as Eskimos 2 language spoken by the Inuit people

inundated adjective 1 overwhelmed (with letters, requests, etc) 2 flooded

invade verb 1 to enter (a country) by force 2 to disturb (someone's privacy) > **invader** noun

invalid¹ noun disabled or chronically ill person > **invalidity** noun

invalid² adjective 1 (of an argument etc) not valid because based on a mistake 2 not acceptable legally > **invalidate** verb to make (something) invalid > **invalidity** noun

invaluable adjective extremely useful

invariably adverb almost always

invasion noun 1 entry by force; invading 2 intrusion: an invasion of privacy

invective noun (formal) abusive language used by someone who is angry

invent verb 1 to think up or create (something new) 2 to make up (a story, excuse, etc) > **invention** noun 1 something invented 2 ability to invent > **inventive** adjective creative and resourceful > **inventiveness** noun > **inventor** noun

inventory inventories noun detailed list of all the objects in a place

inverse adjective 1 reversed in effect, sequence, direction, etc > noun 2 exact opposite > **inversely** adverb

invertebrate noun (technical) animal with no backbone

inverted adjective upside down or back to front

inverted commas plural noun the punctuation marks " " or ' ', used to show where speech begins and ends; quotation marks

invest verb 1 to pay (money) into a bank or buy shares with it in the expectation of making a profit 2 to spend (money, time, etc) on something in the hope of making it a success > **invest in**

verb to buy > **investment** *noun*
> **investor** *noun*

investigate *verb* to try to find out all the facts about (something) > **investigation** *noun* > **investigative** *adjective* > **investigator** *noun*

inveterate *adjective* firmly established in a habit or condition and unlikely to stop

invincible *adjective* impossible to defeat > **invincibility** *noun*

invisible *adjective* not able to be seen > **invisibility** *noun* > **invisibly** *adverb*

invite *verb* **1** to ask (someone) to an event **2** to ask (someone to do something) > **invitation** *noun* > **inviting** *adjective* tempting or attractive

invoice *noun* **1** bill for goods or services supplied ▷ *verb* **2** to present (someone) with a bill for goods or services supplied

invoke *verb* to use (a law) to justify something

involuntary *adjective* sudden and uncontrollable; unintentional > **involuntarily** *adverb*

involve *verb* **1** to include (someone or something) as a necessary part **2** to affect or concern > **involvement** *noun*

inward *adjective* **1** directed towards the inside or middle **2** situated within **3** spiritual or mental ▷ *adverb* **4** towards the inside or middle > **inwardly** *adverb*

iodine *noun* (*Chemistry*) bluish-black substance used in medicine and photography

ion *noun* electrically charged atom

iota *noun* very small amount

IQ *abbreviation* intelligence quotient: level of intelligence shown by the results of a special test

ir- *prefix* not or the opposite of; the form of *in-* used before the letter r: *irrational*

Iranian *adjective* **1** belonging or relating to Iran ▷ *noun* **2** someone from Iran **3** main language spoken in Iran; Farsi

Iraqi *adjective* **1** belonging or relating to Iraq ▷ *noun* **2** someone from Iraq

irate *adjective* very angry

iris *noun* **1** round, coloured part of your eye **2** tall plant with purple, yellow or white flowers

Irish *adjective* **1** belonging or relating to the Irish Republic, or to the whole of Ireland ▷ *noun* **2** language spoken in some parts of Ireland

Irishman Irishmen *noun* man from Ireland

irk *verb* to irritate or annoy > **irksome** *adjective* irritating or annoying

iron *noun* **1** hard dark metal used to make steel, and things like gates and fences. Small amounts of iron are found in blood **2** device that heats up in order to press clothes **3** metal-headed golf club **4 irons** chains or restraints ▷ *adjective* **5** made of iron **6** strong, inflexible: *iron will* ▷ *verb* **7** to smooth (clothes or fabric) with an iron > **ironing** *noun* clothes to be ironed > **iron out** *verb* to solve (difficulties)

Iron Age *noun* era about three thousand years ago when people first started to make tools out of iron

ironbark *noun* Australian eucalypt with a hard, rough bark

irony ironies *noun* **1** mildly sarcastic use of words to imply the opposite of what is said **2** aspect of a situation that is odd or amusing because it is the opposite of what you would expect

irrational *adjective* not based on or not using logical reasoning > **irrationality** *noun* > **irrationally** *adverb*

irregular *adjective* **1** not regular or even **2** not conforming to accepted practice **3** (of a word) not following the typical pattern of formation in a language > **irregularity** *noun* > **irregularly** *adverb*

irrelevant *adjective* not directly connected with the matter in hand > **irrelevance** *noun* > **irrelevantly** *adverb*

irrepressible *adjective* unfailingly lively and cheerful

irresistible *adjective* too attractive or strong to resist > **irresistibly** *adverb*

irrespective of *preposition* without taking account of

irresponsible *adjective* not giving enough thought or taking enough care about the consequences of your actions or attitudes > **irresponsibly** *adverb*

irrigate *verb* to supply (land) with water by artificial channels or pipes > **irrigation** *noun*

irritate *verb* **1** to annoy **2** to cause (a body part) to itch or become inflamed > **irritable** *adjective* easily annoyed > **irritably** *adverb*

> **irritant** *noun, adjective* (person or thing) causing irritation > **irritation** *noun*

is *verb* third person singular present tense of **be**

-ish *suffix* used to form adjectives that mean 'fairly' or 'rather': *smallish; greenish*

Islam *noun* Muslim religion teaching that there is one God and that Mohammed is his prophet. The holy book of Islam is the Koran > **Islamic** *adjective*

island *noun* piece of land surrounded by water > **islander** *noun* person who lives on an island

isle *noun* (literary) island

-ism *suffix* **1** used to form nouns that refer to an action or condition: *criticism; heroism* **2** used to form nouns that refer to a political or economic system or a system of beliefs: *Marxism; Sikhism* **3** used to form nouns that refer to a type of prejudice: *racism; sexism*

isolate *verb* to set (someone) apart > **isolated** *adjective* > **isolation** *noun*

isosceles triangle [ice-**soss**-ill-eez] *noun* triangle with two sides of equal length

ISP *abbreviation* internet service provider

Israeli Israelis *adjective* **1** belonging or relating to Israel ▷ *noun* **2** someone from Israel

issue issues, issuing, issued *noun* **1** important subject that people are talking about **2** particular edition of a magazine or newspaper **3** reason for quarrelling ▷ *verb* **4** to make (a statement etc) publicly **5** to supply (someone) officially (with) **6** to produce and make available

-ist *suffix* **1** used to form nouns and adjectives which refer to someone who is involved in a certain activity or who believes in a certain system or religion: *chemist*; *motorist*; *Buddhist* **2** used to form nouns and adjectives which refer to someone who has a certain prejudice: *racist*

isthmus isthmuses [**iss**-muss] *noun* narrow strip of land with water on either side connecting two areas of land

it *pronoun* **1** refers to any inanimate object **2** refers to a baby or animal whose sex is unknown or unimportant **3** refers to a thing mentioned or being discussed **4** used as the subject of impersonal verbs: *It's windy* > **it's 1** it is **2** it has

Italian *adjective* **1** belonging or relating to Italy > *noun* **2** someone from Italy **3** main language spoken in Italy

italic *adjective* (of printing type) sloping to the right > **italics** *plural noun* this type, used for emphasis

itch *verb* **1** to have an itch **2** be **itching to do something** to be impatient to do something > *noun* **3** skin irritation causing a desire to scratch > **itchy** *adjective*

item *noun* **1** single thing in a list or collection **2** newspaper or magazine article

itinerary itineraries *noun* detailed plan of a journey

-itis *suffix* added to names of parts of the body to refer to a condition involving inflammation of that part: *appendicitis*; *tonsillitis*

its *adjective, pronoun* belonging to it

itself *pronoun* **1** used as an object of a verb or pronoun when the thing that does an action is also the thing directly affected by it: *It switches itself off* **2** used for emphasis: *The site itself forms a large rectangle*

-ity *suffix* used to form nouns that refer to a state or condition: *continuity*; *technicality*

-ive *suffix* used to form adjectives and some nouns: *massive*; *detective*

ivory *noun* **1** hard white bony substance forming the tusks of elephants > *adjective* **2** yellowish-white

ivy ivies *noun* evergreen climbing plant

iwi [**ee**-wee] *noun* (NZ) Māori tribe

-ize or **-ise** *suffix* used to form verbs. Most verbs can be spelt with either ending, though there are some that can only be spelt with '-ise', for example *advertise*, *improvise* and *revise*

j

jab jabs, jabbing, jabbed *verb* **1** to poke (something) sharply ▷ *noun* **2** quick punch or poke **3** (*informal*) injection

jabiru *noun* white and green Australian stork with red legs

jack *noun* **1** device for raising a motor vehicle or other heavy object **2** playing card with a picture of a pageboy, whose value is between a ten and a queen **3** (*Bowls*) small white bowl aimed at by the players **4** socket in electrical equipment into which a plug fits > **jack up** *verb* **1** to raise (a motor vehicle) with a jack **2** to increase (prices or salaries) **3** (*NZ informal*) to organize by dishonest means

jackal *noun* doglike wild animal of Africa and Asia

jackaroo *noun* (*Aust*) trainee on a sheep or cattle station

jackdaw *noun* bird like a small crow with black and grey feathers

jacket *noun* **1** short coat **2** skin of a baked potato **3** outer paper cover on a hardback book

jackpot *noun* **1** largest prize that may be won in a gambling game **2** **hit the jackpot** (*informal*) to be very successful through luck

jade *noun* **1** hard green stone used for making jewellery and ornaments ▷ *adjective* **2** bluish-green

jagged [jag-gid] *adjective* having an uneven edge with sharp points

jaguar *noun* large member of the cat family, with spots on its back

jail or **gaol** *noun* **1** prison ▷ *verb* **2** to send to prison > **jailer** *noun* person who is in charge of the prisoners in a jail

jam jams, jamming, jammed *verb* **1** to pack tightly into a place **2** to crowd or congest **3** to make or become stuck **4** (*Radio*) to block (a radio signal) and prevent it from being heard properly **5** **jam on the brakes** to apply the brakes fiercely ▷ *noun* **6** hold-up of traffic **7** (*informal*) awkward situation **8** food made from fruit boiled with sugar

Jamaican [jam-**may**-kn] *adjective* **1** belonging to or relating to Jamaica ▷ *noun* **2** someone from Jamaica

jamboree *noun* large gathering of people enjoying themselves

jandal® *noun* (*NZ*) sandal with a strap between the big toe and other toes and over the foot

jangle *verb* **1** to (cause to) make a harsh ringing noise **2** (of nerves) to be upset or irritated

janitor *noun* caretaker of a school or other building

January *noun* first month of the year

Japanese *adjective* **1** belonging or relating to Japan ▷ *noun* **2** someone from Japan **3** main language spoken in Japan

jar jars, jarring, jarred *noun* **1** wide-mouthed container, usually round and made of glass ▷ *verb* **2** to have a disturbing or unpleasant effect

3 to jolt or bump ▷ *noun* **4** jolt or shock

jargon *noun* words that are used in special or technical ways by particular groups of people, often making the language difficult to understand

jarrah *noun* Australian eucalypt tree that produces valuable timber

jasmine *noun* climbing plant with sweet-smelling yellow or white flowers

jaundice *noun* disease affecting the liver, causing yellowness of the skin

jaundiced *adjective* (of an attitude or opinion) bitter or cynical

jaunt *noun* short journey for pleasure

jaunty jauntier, jauntiest *adjective* expressing cheerfulness and self-confidence: *a jaunty tune* > **jauntily** *adverb*

javelin *noun* light spear thrown in sports competitions

jaw *noun* **1** one of the bones in which the teeth are set **2** jaws **a** mouth **b** gripping part of a tool

jay *noun* bird with a pinkish body and blue-and-black wings

jazz *noun* kind of music with an exciting rhythm, usually involving improvisation > **jazz up** *verb* (*informal*) to make (something) more lively or colourful

jazzy jazzier, jazziest *adjective* (*informal*) flashy or showy

jealous *adjective* **1** fearful of losing a partner or possession to a rival **2** envious **3** suspiciously watchful > **jealously** *adverb* > **jealousy** *noun* feeling of anger or bitterness caused by desire for another's possessions or abilities

jeans *plural noun* casual denim trousers

Jeep ® *noun* four-wheel-drive motor vehicle

jeer *verb* **1** (followed by *at*) to insult (someone) in a loud, unpleasant way ▷ *noun* **2** rude or insulting remark > **jeering** *adjective*

Jehovah [ji-**hove**-ah] *noun* name of God in the Old Testament

jelly jellies *noun* **1** soft food made of liquid set with gelatine **2** jam made from fruit juice and sugar

jellyfish *noun* small jelly-like sea animal with tentacles which may sting

WORD TIP

The plural of *jellyfish* is jellyfish

jeopardize or **jeopardise** [**jep**-par-dyz] *verb* to place (something) in danger

jeopardy *noun* danger: *Setbacks have put the whole project in jeopardy*

jerk *verb* **1** to move suddenly and sharply ▷ *noun* **2** sudden sharp movement **3** (*informal*) stupid or ignorant person

jerkin *noun* short sleeveless jacket

jersey *noun* **1** knitted jumper **2** machine-knitted fabric **3** Jersey breed of dairy cow that produces very rich milk

jest *verb* **1** to speak jokingly **2** *noun* joke

jester *noun* (*History*) professional clown at a royal court

jet *noun*, jets, jetting, jetted *verb* **1** to fly by jet aircraft ▷ *noun* **2** aircraft driven by jet propulsion **3** stream of liquid or gas, especially one forced from a small hole **4** nozzle from which gas or liquid is forced **5** hard black mineral

jet boat noun motorboat propelled by a jet of water

jet lag noun tiredness and confusion felt by people after a long flight across different time zones

jettison verb 1 to abandon (something) 2 to throw (something) overboard

jetty jetties noun wooden platform at the edge of the sea or a river, where boats can be moored

Jew [joo] RE noun 1 person whose religion is Judaism 2 descendant of the ancient Hebrews > **Jewish** adjective

jewel noun 1 precious stone 2 special person or thing > **jewelled** adjective

jeweller noun person who makes jewellery or who sells and repairs jewellery and watches

jewellery noun ornaments that people wear, made of valuable metals and sometimes decorated with precious stones

jib jibs, jibbing, jibbed noun 1 triangular sail set in front of a mast 2 projecting arm of a crane or derrick > **jib at** verb to object to (a proposal etc)

jibe noun 1 an insulting remark > verb 2 to make insulting or taunting remarks

jig jigs, jigging, jigged noun 1 type of lively folk dance; also the music that accompanies it > verb 2 to dance or jump around in a lively bouncy manner

jiggle verb to move up and down with short jerky movements

jigsaw noun 1 picture cut into interlocking pieces, which the user tries to fit together again 2 mechanical saw for cutting along curved lines

jihad noun Islamic holy war against those who reject the teachings of Islam

jilt verb to leave or reject (one's lover) > **jilted** adjective

jingle noun 1 catchy verse or song used in a radio or television advert 2 gentle ringing sound > verb 3 to make a gentle ringing sound

jinks plural noun **high jinks** noisy and mischievous behaviour

jinx noun person or thing that is thought to bring bad luck

jinxed adjective considered to be unlucky

jitters plural noun (informal) **the jitters** worried nervousness: I had the jitters during my speech > **jittery** adjective nervous

job noun 1 occupation or paid employment 2 task to be done 3 (informal) difficult task 4 (Brit, Aust, NZ informal) crime, especially robbery 5 **just the job** exactly right or exactly what is required

job centre noun government office where people can find out about job vacancies

jobless adjective without any work

jockey noun 1 (professional) rider of racehorses > verb 2 **jockey for position** to manoeuvre in order to obtain an advantage

jocular adjective intended to make people laugh: a jocular remark > **jocularly** adverb

jodhpurs [jod-purz] plural noun riding trousers, loose-fitting above the knee but tight below

joey noun (Aust) young kangaroo

jog jogs, jogging, jogged verb 1 to run at a gentle pace, often as a form of exercise **2** to nudge (something) slightly **3 jog someone's memory** to remind someone of something ▷ *noun* **4** slow run > **jogger** *noun* person who jogs for exercise > **jogging** *noun* activity of running at a gentle pace for exercise

join *verb* **1** to become a member (of) **2** to come into someone's company **3** to take part (in) **4** to come or bring together ▷ *noun* **5** place where two things are joined > **join up** *verb* to enlist in the armed services

joiner *noun* person who makes wooden furniture, doors and window frames

joinery *noun* work done by a joiner

joint *adjective* **1** shared by two or more ▷ *noun* **2** place where bones meet but can move **3** junction of two or more parts or objects **4** piece of meat for roasting **5** (*informal*) house or place, especially a disreputable bar or nightclub **6** (*informal*) marijuana cigarette **7 out of joint a** disorganized **b** (of a bone) knocked out of its normal position ▷ *verb* **8** to divide meat into joints > **jointed** *adjective* **1** having joints that move **2** (of a large piece of meat) cut into pieces and ready to cook > **jointly** *adverb*

joist *noun* horizontal beam that helps support a floor or ceiling

joke *noun* **1** thing said or done to cause laughter **2** ridiculous person or thing that is not worthy of respect: *The decision was a joke* ▷ *verb* **3** to make jokes > **jokingly** *adverb*

joker *noun* **1** person who jokes **2** extra card in a pack of cards, counted as any other in some games

jolly jollier, jolliest; jollies, jollying, jollied *adjective* **1** (of a person) happy and cheerful **2** (of an occasion) merry and festive ▷ *verb* **3 jolly along** to try to keep (someone) cheerful by flattery or coaxing ▷ *adverb* **4** (*informal*) very: *I'm going to have a jolly good try*

jolt *noun* **1** unpleasant surprise or shock **2** sudden jerk or bump ▷ *verb* **3** to surprise or shock **4** to bump against (someone or something) with a sudden violent movement

jostle *verb* to knock or push against roughly

jot jots, jotting, jotted *verb* **1** (followed by *down*) to write a brief note of ▷ *noun* **2** very small amount > **jottings** *plural noun* notes jotted down

jotter *noun* notebook

joule [**jool**] *noun* (*Physics*) unit of work or energy

journal *noun* **1** magazine that deals with a particular subject, trade or profession **2** diary which someone keeps regularly

journalism *noun* work of collecting, writing and publishing news in newspapers, magazines and on television and radio > **journalist** *noun* person whose job is writing for newspapers and magazines > **journalistic** *adjective*

journey *noun* **1** act or process of travelling from one place to another ▷ *verb* **2** to travel: *He intended to journey up the Amazon*

joust (*History*) noun **1** competition in medieval times between knights fighting on horseback, using lances ▷ verb **2** to fight on horseback using lances

jovial adjective happy and cheerful > **joviality** noun cheerful friendliness > **jovially** adverb

joy noun **1** feeling of great delight or pleasure **2** something or someone that causes happiness **3** (*informal*) success or luck: *Any joy with your insurance claim?*

joyful adjective **1** causing pleasure and happiness **2** extremely happy > **joyfully** adverb

joyous adjective (*formal*) extremely happy and enthusiastic > **joyously** adverb

joyride noun drive in a stolen car for pleasure > **joyrider** noun > **joyriding** noun

joystick noun control device for an aircraft or computer

jube noun (*Aust, NZ informal*) a fruit-flavoured jelly sweet

jubilant adjective feeling or expressing great joy or triumph > **jubilantly** adverb

jubilation noun feeling of great happiness or triumph

jubilee noun special anniversary, especially 25th (*silver jubilee*) or 50th (*golden jubilee*)

Judaism [joo-day-i-zm] noun RE religion of the Jews, based on the Old Testament and the Talmud > **Judaic** adjective

judder verb **1** to shake and vibrate noisily and violently ▷ noun **2** violent vibration

judder bar noun (*NZ*) raised strip across a road designed to slow down vehicles

judge noun **1** public official who tries cases and passes sentence in a court of law **2** person who decides the outcome of a contest ▷ verb **3** to act as a judge **4** to form an opinion about (someone or something) **5** to decide the result of (a competition)

judgment or **judgement** noun **1** opinion reached after careful thought **2** verdict of a judge **3** ability to make sensible decisions or achieve a balanced viewpoint

judicial adjective relating to the legal system: *an independent judicial inquiry* > **judicially** adverb

judiciary judiciaries noun branch of government concerned with justice and the legal system

judicious adjective well-judged and sensible > **judiciously** adverb

judo noun sport, originating from Japan, in which two opponents try to force each other to the ground using special throwing techniques

jug noun container for liquids, with a handle and small spout

juggernaut noun (*Brit*) large heavy truck

juggle verb **1** to throw and catch (several objects) so that most are in the air at the same time **2** to keep (several activities) in progress at the same time > **juggler** noun person who juggles in order to entertain people

jugular or **jugular vein** noun one of three large veins of the neck that return blood from the head to the heart

juice noun **1** liquid part of vegetables, fruit or meat **2 juices** fluids in the body: *gastric juices*

juicy juicier, juiciest *adjective* **1** full of juice **2** interesting, exciting or scandalous: *juicy gossip*
> **juiciness** noun

jukebox noun coin-operated machine found in cafés and pubs, on which CDs or videos can be played

July noun seventh month of the year

jumble noun **1** untidy muddle of things **2** articles for a jumble sale
> *verb* **3** (followed by *up*) to mix (things) untidily

jumble sale noun event at which cheap second-hand items are sold to raise money, often for a charity

jumbo *adjective* **1** (*informal*) very large: *jumbo packs of elastic bands*
> *noun* **2** large jet airliner

jumbuck noun (*Aust old-fashioned*) sheep

jump *verb* **1** to leap or spring into the air using the leg muscles **2** to move quickly and suddenly **3** to make a sudden sharp movement of surprise **4** to increase suddenly: *The number of crimes jumped by 10% last year* **5 jump the gun** to do something before the proper or right time **6 jump the queue** not to wait your turn > *noun* **7** act of jumping **8** sudden rise **9** break in continuity > **jump at** *verb* to accept (a chance etc) gladly > **jump on** *verb* to criticize (someone) suddenly and forcefully

jumper noun sweater or pullover

jumpy jumpier, jumpiest *adjective* nervous and worried

junction noun place where routes, railway lines or roads meet

June noun sixth month of the year

jungle noun **1** tropical forest of dense tangled vegetation **2** confusion or mess: *a jungle of complex rules*

junior *adjective* **1** holding a low-ranking position in an organization **2** younger **3** relating to childhood: *a junior school* > *noun* **4** person who holds an unimportant position in an organization

juniper noun evergreen shrub with purple berries used in cooking and medicine

junk noun **1** discarded or useless objects **2** rubbish **3** flat-bottomed Chinese sailing boat

junk food noun food of low nutritional value

junkie noun (*informal*) drug addict

Jupiter noun largest planet in the solar system and fifth from the sun

jurisdiction noun (*formal*) **1** right or power to apply laws and make legal judgments: *The Court did not have the jurisdiction to examine the case* **2** power or authority: *The airport was under French jurisdiction*

juror noun member of a jury

jury juries noun group of people in a court of law who have been chosen to listen to the facts of a case on trial, and to decide whether the accused person is guilty or not

just *adverb* **1** very recently **2** at this instant **3** merely, only **4** exactly **5** barely: *They only just won* **6** really **7 just now** (*SAfr*) in a little while
> *adjective* **8** fair or impartial in

k

action or judgment **9** proper or right > **justly** adverb > **justness** noun

justice noun **1** fairness and reasonableness: *There is no justice in this world!* **2** administration of law in a country **3** judge or magistrate

justify justifies, justifying, justified verb **1** to prove (a decision, action or idea) to be reasonable or necessary: *This decision was fully justified by economic conditions* **2** ICT to adjust (text) so that the margins are straight > **justifiable** adjective acceptable or reasonable > **justifiably** adverb > **justification** noun acceptable or reasonable explanation for something

jut juts, jutting, jutted verb to stick out beyond or above a surface or edge

jute noun strong fibre made from the bark of an Asian plant, used to make rope and sacking

juvenile adjective **1** young **2** of or suitable for young people **3** immature and rather silly > noun **4** young person or child

juxtapose verb to put (things or ideas) close together in order to emphasize the differences > **juxtaposition** noun

kaffir kaffir noun (*S Afr offensive*) Black person

kai noun (*NZ informal*) food

kaleidoscope [kal-**eye**-dos-skope] noun tube-shaped toy containing loose coloured pieces reflected by mirrors so that changing patterns form when the tube is twisted > **kaleidoscopic** adjective colourful and constantly changing

kamikaze [kam-mee-**kah**-zee] noun **1** (in World War II) Japanese pilot who performed a suicide mission > adjective **2** (of an action) undertaken in the knowledge that it will kill or injure the person performing it

kangaroo kangaroos noun Australian animal which moves by jumping with its powerful hind legs

karate noun Japanese system of unarmed combat using blows with the feet, hands, elbows and legs

karma noun (*Buddhism, Hinduism*) person's actions affecting his or her fate in future lives

Karoo Karoos noun (*S Afr*) area of very dry land

karri karris noun **1** Australian eucalypt **2** its wood, used for building

katipo katipos noun small poisonous New Zealand spider

kauri kauri or kauris noun (NZ) large New Zealand tree that produces wood used for building and making furniture

kayak [ky-ak] noun 1 Inuit canoe made of sealskins stretched over a frame 2 fibreglass or canvas-covered canoe of this design

kea keas [kay-ah] noun (NZ) 1 large greenish New Zealand parrot 2 **the Keas** youngest members of the Scouts

kebab noun 1 dish of small pieces of meat grilled on skewers 2 grilled minced lamb served in a split slice of unleavened bread

keel noun main lengthways timber or steel support along the base of a ship ▷ **keel over** verb 1 to turn upside down 2 (informal) to collapse suddenly

keen adjective 1 eager or enthusiastic 2 intense or strong 3 intellectually acute 4 (of the senses) capable of recognizing small distinctions 5 sharp ▷ **keenly** adverb ▷ **keenness** noun: keenness to please

keep keeps, keeping, kept verb 1 to have or retain possession of (something or someone) 2 to store (something) 3 to stay or cause (something or someone) to stay in, on or at a place or position 4 to continue or persist 5 to detain (someone) 6 to look after or provide for (something or someone) ▷ noun 7 cost of food and everyday expenses ▷ **keep up** verb to maintain (something) at the current level ▷ **keep up with** verb to move at a pace set by (someone)

keeper noun 1 person who looks after animals in a zoo 2 person in charge of a museum or collection 3 short for **goalkeeper**

keeping noun 1 care or charge 2 **in** or **out of keeping with** appropriate or inappropriate for

keepsake noun gift treasured for the sake of the giver

keg noun small metal beer barrel

kelpie noun Australian sheepdog with a smooth coat and upright ears

kennel noun 1 hutlike shelter for a dog 2 **kennels** place for breeding, boarding or training dogs

Kenyan [keen-yan] adjective 1 belonging or relating to Kenya ▷ noun 2 someone from Kenya

kerb noun edging to a pavement

kernel noun 1 seed of a nut, cereal or fruit; stone 2 central and essential part of something

kerosene noun (US, Canadian, Aust, NZ) liquid mixture distilled from petroleum and used as a fuel or solvent

kestrel noun type of small falcon

ketchup noun thick cold sauce, usually made of tomatoes

kettle noun container with a spout and handle used for boiling water

key noun 1 device for locking and unlocking a lock by moving a bolt 2 device turned to wind a clock, operate a machine, etc 3 any of a set of levers or buttons pressed to use a typewriter, computer or musical keyboard instrument 4 (Music) set of related notes 5 something crucial in providing an explanation or interpretation 6 means of achieving a desired end **7** list of explanations of codes, symbols, etc ▷ *adjective* **8** of great importance ▷ *verb* **9** to type in (text) using a keyboard

keyboard *noun* **1** set of keys on a piano, computer, etc **2** musical instrument played using a keyboard

Key Stage *noun* in England and Wales, one of the four age-group divisions to which each level of the National Curriculum applies (5–7; 7–11; 11–14; 14–16)

kg *symbol* kilogram(s)

khaki *adjective* **1** dull yellowish-brown ▷ *noun* **2** hard-wearing fabric of this colour used for military uniforms

khanda [**kun**-dah] *noun* sword used by Sikhs in the Amrit ceremony

kia ora [kee-a **aw**-ra] *interjection* (NZ) Māori greeting

kibbutz kibbutzim [kib-**boots**] *noun* farm or factory in Israel where the workers live together and share everything

kick *verb* **1** to drive, push or strike (something or someone) with the foot **2** (of a gun) to recoil when fired **3** (followed by *against*) (*informal*) to object (to something) or resist (something) **4** (*informal*) to free yourself of (an addiction) **5** (*Rugby*) to score (a goal) with a kick ▷ *noun* **6** thrust or blow with the foot **7** recoil of a gun when fired **8** (*informal*) excitement or thrill ▷ **kick off** *verb* **1** to start a game of soccer **2** (*informal*) to begin ▷ **kick up** *verb* (*informal*) to create (a fuss)

kid kids, kidding, kidded *noun* **1** (*informal*) child **2** young goat

3 leather made from the skin of a young goat or an animal) ▷ *verb* **4** (*informal*) to tease or deceive (someone)

kidnap kidnaps, kidnapping, kidnapped *verb* to take (someone) away by force and hold (him or her) to ransom ▷ **kidnapper** *noun* person who kidnaps someone ▷ **kidnapping** *noun*

kidney *noun* **1** either of the pair of organs that remove waste products from the blood **2** animal kidney used as food

kill *verb* **1** to cause the death of (a person or an animal) **2** (*informal*) to cause (someone) pain or discomfort **3** to put an end to (a conversation or an activity) **4** to pass (time) ▷ *noun* **5** act of killing **6** animals or birds killed in a hunt ▷ **killer** *noun* person who kills someone ▷ **killing** (*informal*) *adjective* **1** very tiring **2** very funny ▷ *noun* **3** sudden financial success

kiln *noun* oven for baking or drying pottery, bricks, etc

kilo kilos *noun* short for **kilogram**

kilogram or **kilogramme** *noun* one thousand grams

kilohertz *noun* one thousand hertz

WORD TIP

⚠ The plural of *kilohertz* is *kilohertz*

kilojoule *noun* (*Physics*) one thousand joules

kilometre *noun* one thousand metres

kilowatt *noun* (*Electricity*) one thousand watts

kilt *noun* knee-length pleated tartan skirt worn originally by Scottish Highlanders

kimono kimonos *noun* loose wide-sleeved Japanese robe, fastened with a sash

kin or **kinsfolk** *plural noun* person's relatives collectively

kind *adjective* **1** considerate, friendly and helpful ▷ *noun* **2** class or group with common characteristics **3** essential nature or character **4** **in kind a** (of payment) in goods rather than money **b** having something similar **5** **kind of** to a certain extent. ▷ **kindness** *noun*: We have been treated with such kindness

kindergarten *noun* class or school for children under six years old

kindle *verb* **1** to set (a fire) alight **2** (of a fire) to start to burn **3** to arouse (a feeling) or (of a feeling) to be aroused

kindling *noun* dry wood or straw for starting fires

kindred *adjective* **1** having similar qualities **2** related by blood or marriage ▷ *plural noun* **3** same as **kin**

kinetic energy *noun* energy produced when something moves

king *noun* **1** male ruler of a monarchy **2** ruler or chief **3** best or most important of its kind **4** piece in chess that must be defended **5** playing card with a picture of a king on it

kingdom *noun* **1** country ruled by a king or queen **2** division of the natural world

kingfisher *noun* small bird, often with a bright-coloured plumage, that dives for fish

king-size or **king-sized** *adjective* larger than standard size

kink *noun* **1** twist or bend in rope, wire, hair, etc **2** (*informal*) quirk in someone's personality

kinky kinkier, kinkiest *adjective* **1** (*informal*) having peculiar sexual tastes **2** full of kinks

kinship *noun* family relationship to other people

kiosk [kee-osk] *noun* **1** small booth selling drinks, cigarettes, newspapers, etc **2** public telephone box

kip kips, kipping, kipped *noun, verb* (*informal*) (to) sleep

kipper *noun* cleaned, salted and smoked herring

kirk *noun* (Scot) church

kiss *verb* **1** to touch (someone) with the lips in affection or greeting **2** to join lips with (someone) in love or desire ▷ *noun* **3** touch with the lips

kiss of life *noun* method of reviving someone by blowing air into his or her lungs

kit *noun* **1** outfit or equipment for a specific purpose **2** set of pieces of equipment sold ready to be put together **3** (NZ) flax basket ▷ **kit out** *verb* to provide (someone) with clothes or equipment needed for a particular activity

kitchen *noun* room used for cooking

kite *noun* **1** light frame covered with a thin material flown on a string in the wind **2** large hawk with a forked tail

kitset *noun* (NZ) set of parts for putting together to make a house or a piece of furniture

kitten *noun* young cat

kitty kitties *noun* **1** fund of money given by a group of people to pay for things together **2** total amount bet in certain gambling games

a
b
c
d
e
f
g
h
i
j
k
l
m
n
o
p
q
r
s
t
u
v
w
x
y
z

kiwi kiwi or kiwis [**kee**-wee] *noun*
1 New Zealand bird with a long
beak and no tail, which cannot fly
2 (*informal*) New Zealander

kiwi fruit *noun* edible fruit with a
fuzzy brownish skin and green flesh

kloof (*SAfr*) mountain pass
or gorge

km *symbol* kilometre(s)

knack *noun* 1 skilful way of doing
something 2 innate ability

knead *verb* 1 to work (dough) into
a smooth mixture with the hands
2 to squeeze or press (something)
with the hands

knee *noun* 1 joint between the
thigh and lower leg 2 lap 3 part
of a garment covering the
knee ▷ *verb* 4 to strike or push
(someone) with the knee

kneecap kneecaps, kneecapping,
kneecapped *noun* 1 bone in front
of the knee ▷ *verb* 2 to shoot
(someone) in the kneecap

kneel kneels, kneeling, knelt *verb*
to fall or rest on one's knees

knell *noun* 1 sound of a bell,
especially at a funeral or death
2 sign of something bad about
to happen

knickers *plural noun* woman's or
girl's undergarment covering the
lower trunk and having holes for
the legs; pants

knick-knack *noun* small
ornament

knife knives; knifes, knifing, knifed
noun 1 cutting tool or weapon
consisting of a sharp-edged blade
with a handle ▷ *verb* 2 to cut
(something) or stab (someone)
with a knife

knight *noun* 1 man who has been
given a knighthood 2 (*History*)

man who served a monarch or
lord as a mounted soldier 3 chess
piece shaped like a horse's head
▷ *verb* 4 to award a knighthood
to (a man) > **knighthood** *noun*
honorary title given to a man by
the British sovereign

knit knits, knitting, knitted *verb*
1 to make (a garment) by working
lengths of wool together using
needles or a machine 2 to join
closely together 3 to draw (one's
eyebrows) together > **knitting**
noun 1 garment being knitted
2 the activity of knitting

knob *noun* 1 rounded switch
on a machine such as a radio
2 rounded handle on a door or
drawer 3 small amount (of butter)

knobkerrie *noun* (*SAfr*) club with a
rounded end

knock *verb* 1 to give a blow or
push to (someone or something)
2 to tap on (something) with
the knuckles 3 to make or drive
(someone or something) into
a certain position by striking
4 (*informal*) to criticize (someone)
5 (of an engine) to make a
regular banging noise as a result
of a fault ▷ *noun* 6 blow or rap
7 knocking sound > **knock about**
or **around** *verb* 1 to wander or
spend time aimlessly 2 to hit or
kick (someone) brutally > **knock
back** *verb* (*informal*) 1 to drink (a
drink) quickly 2 to cost (someone)
a certain amount 3 to reject or
refuse (something) > **knock down**
verb 1 to demolish (a building)
2 to reduce (a price) > **knock
off** *verb* 1 (*informal*) to cease
work 2 (*informal*) to make or do
(something) hurriedly or easily

3 to take (a specified amount) off a price **4** (*Brit, Aust, NZ informal*) to steal (something) > **knock out** *verb* **1** to hit (someone) so hard that he or she becomes unconscious **2** (*informal*) to overwhelm or amaze (someone) **3** to defeat (a competitor) in a knockout competition > **knock up** *verb* **1** (*informal*) to put (something) together quickly **2** (*informal*) to waken (someone)

knocker *noun* metal fitting for knocking on a door

knockout *noun* **1** blow so hard that it makes an opponent unconscious **2** competition in which competitors are eliminated in each round until only the winner is left **3** (*informal*) extremely attractive person or thing

knoll [rhymes with **roll**] *noun* small rounded hill

knot knots, knotting, knotted *noun* **1** fastening made by looping and pulling tight strands of string, cord or rope **2** tangle (of hair) **3** small cluster or huddled group (of people) **4** round lump or spot in timber **5** feeling of tightness in the stomach, caused by tension or nervousness **6** unit of speed used by ships, equal to one nautical mile (1.85 kilometres) per hour > *verb* **7** to tie (something) with or into a knot

know knows, knowing, knew, known *verb* **1** to be or feel certain of the truth of (information etc) **2** to be acquainted with (a person or place) **3** to have a grasp of or understand (a skill or language)

4 to be aware of (a fact) > *noun* **5** **in the know** (*informal*) informed or aware of something few people know about

know-how *noun* (*informal*) ability to do something difficult or technical

knowing *adjective* suggesting secret knowledge > **knowingly** *adverb* **1** deliberately **2** in a way that suggests secret knowledge

knowledge *noun* **1** facts or experiences known by a person **2** state of knowing **3** specific information on a subject

knowledgeable or **knowledgable** *adjective* intelligent or well-informed

knuckle *noun* **1** bone at the finger joint **2** knee joint of a calf or pig **3** **near the knuckle** (*informal*) rather rude or offensive > **knuckle under** *verb* to yield or give in

koala *noun* Australian animal with grey fur that lives in trees

kohanga reo or **kohanga** *noun* (*NZ*) infant class where children are taught in Māori

> **WORD TIP**
> The plural of *kohanga reo* is *kohanga reo*.

kookaburra *noun* large Australian kingfisher with a cackling cry

kopje or **koppie** [**kop**-i] *noun* (*S Afr*) small hill

Koran [kaw-**rahn**] *noun* sacred book of Islam

Korean [kor-**ree**-an] *adjective* **1** relating or belonging to Korea > *noun* **2** someone from Korea **3** main language spoken in Korea

kosher [**koh**-sher] *adjective* **1** (of food) prepared according to

Jewish law **2** (*informal*) correct or genuine ▷ *noun* **3** kosher food

kowhai kowhais [**ko**-wigh] *noun* small New Zealand tree with clusters of yellow flowers

kraal *noun* S African village surrounded by a strong fence

kudu *noun* (SAfr) large African antelope with curled horns

kumara kumaras [**koo**-mih-rah] *noun* (NZ) tropical root vegetable with yellow flesh

kumquat [**kumm**-kwott] *noun* citrus fruit resembling a tiny orange

kung fu [kung foo] *noun* Chinese martial art combining hand, foot and weapon techniques

kura kaupapa Māori *noun* (NZ) primary school where the teaching is done in Māori

Kurd *noun* member of a group of people who live mainly in eastern Turkey, northern Iraq and western Iran

Kurdish *adjective* **1** belonging or relating to the Kurds ▷ *noun* **2** language spoken by the Kurds

l *symbol* litre

lab *noun* (*informal*) short for **laboratory**

label labels, labelling, labelled *noun* **1** piece of paper or plastic attached to something as an identification ▷ *verb* **2** to put a label on (something)

laboratory laboratories *noun* SCIENCE building or room designed for scientific research or for the teaching of practical science

laborious *adjective* involving great prolonged effort > **laboriously** *adverb*

Labor Party *noun* (Aust) main left-wing political party in Australia

labour or **labor** (US & Aust) *noun* **1** physical work or exertion **2** workers in industry **3** final stage of pregnancy, leading to childbirth ▷ *verb* **4** (*old-fashioned*) to work hard > **labourer** *noun* person who labours, especially someone doing manual work for wages

labrador *noun* large retriever dog with a usually gold or black coat

labyrinth [**lab**-er-inth] *noun* complicated network of passages

lace *noun* **1** delicate decorative fabric made from threads woven into an open weblike pattern

2 cord drawn through eyelets and tied ▷ *verb* **3** to fasten (shoes) with laces **4** to add a small amount of alcohol, a drug, etc to (food or drink) > **lacy** *adjective* fine, like lace

lack *noun* **1** shortage or absence of something needed or wanted ▷ *verb* **2** not to be present when or where needed **3** to need or be short of (something)

lacklustre *adjective* lacking brilliance or vitality

laconic *adjective* using only a few words

lacquer *noun* hard varnish for wood or metal

lacrosse *noun* sport in which teams catch and throw a ball using long sticks with a net at the end, in an attempt to score goals

lad *noun* boy or young man

ladder *noun* **1** frame of two poles connected by horizontal steps used for climbing **2** line of stitches that have come undone in tights or stockings ▷ *verb* **3** to have such a line of undone stitches in (one's tights or stockings)

laden *adjective* (often followed by *with*) carrying a lot (of something): *I came home laden with cardboard boxes*

ladle *noun* **1** spoon with a long handle and a large bowl, used for serving food ▷ *verb* **2** to serve out (soup etc)

lady *ladies noun* **1** woman regarded as having characteristics of good breeding or high rank **2** polite term of address for a woman **3 Lady** title of some female members of the British nobility

ladybird *noun* small red flying beetle with black spots

lady-in-waiting *ladies-in-waiting noun* female servant of a queen or princess

ladylike *adjective* polite and dignified

Ladyship *noun* **Your Ladyship** term of address for a woman with the title *Lady*

lag *lags, lagging, lagged verb* to wrap (a boiler, pipes, etc) with insulating material > **lag behind** *verb* to make slower progress than other people

lager *noun* light-coloured beer

lagoon *noun* area of water cut off from the open sea by coral reefs or sand bars

laid *verb* past of **lay¹**

lain *verb* past participle of **lie²**

lair *noun* resting place of a wild animal

laird *noun* landowner in Scotland

lake *noun* area of fresh water surrounded by land

lama *noun* Buddhist priest or monk

lamb *noun* **1** young sheep **2** its meat

lame *adjective* **1** having an injured or disabled leg or foot **2** (of an excuse) unconvincing; feeble > **lamely** *adverb* in an unconvincing manner > **lameness** *noun* state of being lame

lament *verb* **1** to feel or express sorrow for (something) ▷ *noun* **2** passionate expression of grief **3** song or poem expressing grief at someone's death

lamentable *adjective* very disappointing

laminated adjective consisting of several thin sheets or layers stuck together: laminated glass

lamp noun device that produces light from electricity, oil or gas

lamppost noun post supporting a lamp in the street

lampshade noun decorative covering over an electric light bulb that prevents the bulb giving out too harsh a light

lance noun 1 long spear used by a mounted soldier ▷ verb 2 to pierce (a boil or abscess) with a sharp instrument

land noun 1 solid part of the earth's surface 2 ground, especially with reference to its type or use 3 country or region ▷ verb 4 to come to earth after a flight, jump or fall 5 (informal) to succeed in getting (something) 6 to catch (a fish) 7 (followed by with) to cause (someone) to have to deal with something unpleasant

landing noun 1 floor area at the top of a flight of stairs 2 bringing or coming to land

landlady landladies noun woman who owns a house or small hotel and who lets rooms to people

landlord noun man who owns a house or small hotel and who lets rooms to people

landmark noun 1 prominent feature of a landscape 2 event, decision, etc considered as an important development

landowner noun person who owns land, especially a large area of the countryside

landscape noun 1 GEOGRAPHY extensive piece of inland scenery seen from one place 2 ART picture of it

landslide noun 1 falling of soil, rock, etc down the side of a mountain 2 overwhelming electoral victory

lane noun 1 narrow road, especially in the country 2 one of the strips on a road marked with lines to guide drivers

language noun 1 system of sounds, symbols, etc for communicating thought 2 particular system used by a nation or people 3 style in which a person expresses himself or herself: His language is often obscure

languid adjective lacking energy or enthusiasm > **languidly** adverb

languish verb to suffer neglect or hardship

lanky lankier, lankiest adjective ungracefully tall and thin

lantana [lan-**tay**-na] noun (Aust) shrub with orange or yellow flowers, considered a weed in Australia

lantern noun light in a transparent protective case

lap laps, lapping, lapped noun 1 part between the waist and knees of a person when sitting 2 single circuit of a racecourse or track ▷ verb 3 to overtake (an opponent) in a race so as to be one or more circuits ahead 4 (of waves) to beat softly against a shore etc > **lap up** verb (of an animal) to drink (liquid) by scooping up with the tongue

lapel [lap-**pel**] noun part of the front of a coat or jacket folded back towards the shoulders

lapse noun **1** slight mistake **2** instance of bad behaviour by someone usually well-behaved **3** period of time between two events ▷ verb **4** lapse into to give way to (a regrettable kind of behaviour); fall into: *the offenders lapsed into a sullen silence* **5** to end or become invalid, especially through disuse

laptop noun **1** [ICT] computer small enough to fit on a user's lap

lard noun fat from a pig, used in cooking

larder noun storeroom for food

large adjective **1** great in size, number or extent ▷ noun **2 at large** (of a prisoner) escaped from prison ▷ **largely** adverb to a great extent: *the public are largely unaware of this*

lark noun **1** small brown songbird, skylark **2** (informal) harmless piece of mischief or fun

larrikin noun (Aust, NZ informal) mischievous or unruly person

larva larvae noun insect in an immature stage, often resembling a worm

laryngitis noun inflammation of the larynx, causing loss of voice

larynx larynxes or larynges noun part of the throat containing the vocal cords

lasagne [laz-**zan**-ya] noun dish made from layers of pasta in wide flat sheets, meat and cheese

laser [**lay**-zer] noun device that produces a very narrow intense beam of light, used for cutting very hard materials and in surgery etc

lash noun **1** eyelash **2** strip of leather at the end of a whip **3** sharp blow with a whip ▷ **lash out** verb (followed by at) to make a sudden physical or verbal attack on (someone)

lass noun (Scot, N English) girl

lasso lassoes or lassos, lassoing, lassoed [lass-**oo**] noun **1** rope with a noose for catching cattle and horses ▷ verb **2** to catch (an animal) with a lasso

last adjective, adverb **1** coming at the end or after all others **2** most recent(ly) ▷ adjective **3** only remaining ▷ verb **4** to continue to exist or happen **5** to remain fresh, uninjured or unaltered ▷ **lastly** adverb: *Lastly, I would like to ask about your future plans*

last-ditch adjective done as a final resort

latch noun **1** fastening for a door with a bar and lever **2** lock that can only be opened from the outside with a key ▷ **latch onto** verb to become attached to (a person or idea)

late adjective **1** after the normal or expected time **2** towards the end of a period **3** recently dead ▷ adverb **4** after the normal or expected time ▷ **lately** adverb in recent times

latent adjective hidden and not yet developed

lateral [**lat**-ter-al] adjective of or relating to the side or sides

lathe noun machine for turning wood or metal while it is being shaped

lather noun froth of soap and water

Latin noun **1** language of the ancient Romans **2** member of a people who speak languages closely related to Latin, such

as French, Italian, Spanish and
Portuguese

Latin America noun parts of South
and Central America whose official
language is Spanish or Portuguese
▷ **Latin American** noun, adjective

latitude noun GEOGRAPHY
distance north or south of the
equator measured in degrees

latrine noun hole or trench in the
ground used as a toilet at a camp

latter adjective, noun **1** second of
two ▷ adjective **2** second or end
part of something: *the latter part of
his career* ▷ **latterly** adverb (formal)
recently

> **WORD TIP**
>
> You use *latter* to talk about the
> second of two items. To talk
> about the last of three or more
> items you should use *last-named*

lattice [**lat-iss**] noun structure
made of strips crossed over each
other diagonally with holes in
between

laudable adjective praiseworthy
▷ **laudably** adverb in a
praiseworthy manner

laugh verb **1** to make a noise
with the voice that expresses
amusement or happiness ▷ noun
2 act or instance of laughing
▷ **laughable** adjective ridiculously
inadequate ▷ **laughter** noun
sound or action of laughing

laughing stock noun person who
has been made to seem ridiculous

launch verb **1** to put (a ship or
boat) into the water, especially
for the first time **2** to put (a new
product) on the market **3** to send
(a missile or spacecraft) into space
or the air ▷ noun **4** launching
5 open motorboat

launch pad or **launching pad**
noun place from which space
rockets take off

launder verb (old-fashioned) to
wash and iron (clothes and linen)

laundry laundries noun **1** clothes
etc for washing or that have
recently been washed **2** business
that washes and irons clothes
and sheets

laurel noun evergreen tree with
shiny leaves

lava noun molten rock thrown
out by volcanoes, which hardens
as it cools

lavatory lavatories noun toilet

lavender noun **1** shrub with
fragrant flowers ▷ adjective
2 bluish-purple

lavish adjective **1** giving or
spending generously ▷ verb
2 (followed by on) to give (money,
affection, etc) generously: *he
lavished praise on our contribution*
▷ **lavishly** adverb

law noun **1** system of rules
developed by a government,
which regulate what people may
and may not do and deals with
people who break these rules
2 one of these rules **3** profession
of people such as lawyers, whose
job involves the application of
the laws of a country **4** scientific
fact that explains how things
work in the physical world
▷ **lawful** adjective allowed by law
▷ **lawfully** adverb as allowed by
the law ▷ **lawless** adjective having
no regard for the law

law-abiding adjective obeying
the laws

lawn noun **1** area of cultivated
grass **2** fine linen or cotton fabric

lawnmower noun machine for cutting grass

lawsuit noun court case brought by one person or group against another

lawyer noun person who is qualified in law, and who advises people about the law and represents them in court

lax adjective not strict

laxative noun medicine taken to stop constipation

lay lays, laying, laid verb 1 to put (something) down so that it lies somewhere 2 (of a bird or reptile) to produce (an egg) out of its body 3 to arrange (a table) for a meal 4 to set (a trap) for someone 5 to put (emphasis) on something to indicate that it is very important 6 past tense of **lie** 7 **lay odds on** to bet that (something) will happen ▷ adjective 8 of people who are involved with a Christian church but are not members of the clergy > **lay off** verb 1 to dismiss (staff) during a slack period 2 (informal) to stop doing something annoying > **lay on** verb to provide (a meal or entertainment)

> **WORD TIP**
> People often get confused about lay and lie. The verb to lay (past tense laid) takes an object: lay the table please; the Queen laid a wreath. The verb to lie (past tense lay) does not take an object: the book was lying on the table; I lay on the bed

lay-by noun 1 stopping place for traffic beside a road 2 (Aust, NZ) system whereby a customer pays a deposit on an item in a shop so that it will be kept for him or her until the rest of the price is paid

layer noun single thickness of something, such as a cover or coating on a surface

layman laymen noun 1 person who is not a member of the clergy 2 person without specialist knowledge

layout noun arrangement, especially of matter for printing or of a building

laze verb to be idle or lazy

lazy lazier, laziest adjective idle and not inclined to work or make much effort > **lazily** adverb > **laziness** noun the state of being idle

lb abbreviation pound (weight)

lbw abbreviation (Cricket) leg before wicket

leach verb to remove (minerals) from rocks by a liquid passing through the rock

lead¹ leads, leading, led verb 1 to guide or conduct (someone) somewhere 2 to cause (someone) to feel, think or behave in a certain way 3 to control or direct (a group of people) 4 **lead to** to result in (something happening) ▷ noun 5 clue that might the police to solve a crime 6 length of leather or chain attached to a dog's collar to control it > **leading** adjective 1 principal 2 in the first position

lead² noun soft heavy grey metal

leaden adjective 1 heavy and slow-moving 2 dull grey

leader noun 1 person who leads 2 article in a newspaper expressing editorial views > **leadership** noun 1 group of people in charge of an organization **2** ability to be a good leader

leaf leaves; leafs, leafing, leafed *noun* flat usually green blade attached to the stem of a plant > **leaf through** *verb* to turn the pages of (a book, magazine or newspaper) without reading them > **leafy** *adjective*: tall leafy trees

leaflet *noun* sheet of printed matter for distribution

league *noun* **1** association promoting the interests of its members **2** PE association of sports clubs organizing competitions between its members **3** (*obsolete*) measure of distance, about three miles

leak *noun* **1** hole or defect that allows the escape or entrance of liquid, gas, radiation, etc **2** disclosure of secrets ▷ *verb* **3** to let liquid etc in or out **4** (of a liquid etc) to find its way through a leak **5** to disclose (secret information) > **leakage** *noun* escape of liquid etc from a pipe or container > **leaky** *adjective*: the leaky roof

lean leans, leaning, leant or leaned; leaner, leanest *verb* **1** to bend or slope from an upright position: He leaned forward ▷ *adjective* **2** thin but healthy-looking **3** (of meat) lacking fat **4** (of a period) during which food or money is in short supply > **lean on** or **upon** *verb* **1** to rest against (something) **2** to depend on (someone) > **lean towards** *verb* to have an inclination or tendency to follow (particular ideas): parents who lean towards strictness

leap leaps, leaping, leapt or leaped *verb* **1** to make a sudden powerful jump ▷ *noun* **2** sudden powerful jump

leap year *noun* year with February 29th as an extra day

learn learns, learning, learnt or learned *verb* **1** to gain skill or knowledge by study, practice or teaching **2** to memorize (something) **3** to find out about or discover (something) > **learned** *adjective* having a lot of knowledge gained from years of study > **learner** *noun* person who is learning about something > **learning** *noun* knowledge got by study

lease *noun* **1** contract by which property is rented for a stated time by the owner to a tenant ▷ *verb* **2** to let or rent (property) by lease

leash *noun* lead for a dog

least *adjective* **1** superlative of **little 2** smallest ▷ *noun* **3** smallest possible amount **4** at least no fewer or less than (a specified number or amount) ▷ *adverb* **5** in the smallest degree

leather *noun* material made from specially treated animal skins > **leathery** *adjective* like leather; tough

leave leaves, leaving, left *verb* **1** to go away from (a place) **2** to allow (someone) to remain somewhere, accidentally or deliberately **3** to stop being part of (a job or organization) **4** to arrange for (money or possessions) to be given to someone after one's death **5** to cause (a number) to remain after subtracting one number from another ▷ *noun* **6** period of holiday or absence from work or duty

Lebanese adjective **1** of Lebanon ▷ noun **2** person from Lebanon

lecherous [letch-er-uss] adjective constantly thinking about sex

lectern noun sloping reading desk, especially in a church

lecture noun **1** informative talk to an audience on a subject **2** lengthy scolding ▷ verb **3** to teach in a college or university

lecturer noun teacher in a college or university

led past tense and past participle of **lead**¹

ledge noun **1** narrow shelf sticking out from a wall **2** shelflike projection from a cliff etc

ledger noun book of debit and credit accounts of a firm

lee noun **1** sheltered part or side ▷ adjective **2** denoting the side of a ship away from the wind

leech noun small worm that lives in water and feeds by sucking the blood from other animals

leek noun vegetable of the onion family with a long bulb and thick stem

leer verb **1** to look or grin at someone in a sneering or suggestive manner ▷ noun **2** sneering or suggestive look or grin

leeway noun room for free movement within limits

left adjective **1** of the side that faces west when the front faces north ▷ adverb **2** on or towards the left ▷ noun **3** left side or part **4** (Politics) people and political groups supporting socialism or communism rather than capitalism ▷ verb **5** past of **leave**

> **leftist** noun, adjective (person) of the political left

left-handed adjective more adept with the left hand than with the right

leftovers plural noun unused bits of food or material

left-wing adjective supporting socialism or communism rather than capitalism > **left-winger** noun

leg noun **1** one of the limbs on which a person or animal walks, runs or stands **2** part of a garment covering the leg **3** one of the parts of an object such as a table that rest on the floor and support its weight **4** stage of a journey **5** (Sport) one of two matches played between two sports teams

legacy legacies noun **1** thing left in a will **2** something that exists as a result of a previous event or time: the legacy of a Catholic upbringing

legal adjective **1** allowed by the law **2** relating to law or lawyers > **legally** adverb

legal aid noun system providing the services of a lawyer free, or very cheaply, to people who cannot afford the full fees

legality noun (of an action) fact of being allowed by the law: they challenged the legality of the scheme

legalize or **legalise** verb to make (something) legal > **legalization** noun: the legalization of drugs

legend noun **1** traditional story or myth **2** famous person or event > **legendary** adjective **1** famous **2** of or in legend

leggings plural noun **1** close-fitting trousers for women or children

2 protective or waterproof covering worn over trousers

legible *adjective* easily read

legion *noun* **1** large military force **2** large number **3** infantry unit in the Roman army

legislate *verb* (*formal*) to make laws

legislation *noun* law or set of laws created by a government

legislative *adjective* of the making of new laws

legislator *noun* (*formal*) maker of laws

legislature *noun* (*formal*) parliament in a country, which is responsible for making new laws

legitimate *adjective* reasonable or acceptable according to existing laws or standards > **legitimacy** *noun* state of being reasonable or acceptable > **legitimately** *adverb*: *the government has been legitimately elected by the people*

leisure *noun* **1** time for relaxation or hobbies **2** at (one's) leisure when one has time > **leisurely** *adjective* **1** deliberate, unhurried ▷ *adverb* **1** slowly

lekker *adjective* (*S Afr informal*) **1** attractive or nice **2** tasty

lemming *noun* small rodent of cold northern regions, reputed to run into the sea and drown during mass migrations

lemon *noun* sour-tasting yellow oval fruit that grows on trees ▷ *adjective* **2** pale-yellow

lemonade *noun* lemon-flavoured soft drink, often fizzy

lend lends, lending, lent *verb* **1** to give someone the temporary use of (something) **2** (of a bank etc) to provide (money) temporarily,

often for interest > **lender** *noun*: *mortgage lenders*

length *noun* **1** extent or measurement from end to end **2** period of time for which something happens **3** quality of being long **4** piece of something narrow and long **5** at length for a long time

lengthen *verb* to make (something) longer

lengthways or **lengthwise** *adverb* horizontally from one end to the other

lengthy lengthier, lengthiest *adjective* lasting for a long time

lenient [lee-nee-ent] *adjective* tolerant, not strict or severe > **leniency** *noun*: *the judge rejected pleas for leniency* > **leniently** *adverb*

lens *noun* **1** piece of glass or similar material with one or both sides curved, used to bring together or spread light rays in cameras, spectacles, telescopes, etc **2** transparent structure in the eye that focuses light

lent *verb* past of **lend**

lentil *noun* small dried red or brown seed, cooked and eaten in soups and curries

Leo *noun* fifth sign of the zodiac, represented by a lion

leopard *noun* wild Asian or African big cat, with yellow fur and black or brown spots

leotard *noun* tight-fitting costume covering the body and sometimes the legs, worn for dancing or exercise

leper *noun* person suffering from leprosy

leprosy *noun* disease attacking the nerves and skin, resulting in loss of feeling in the affected parts

lesbian noun homosexual woman > **lesbianism** noun female homosexuality

lesion noun injury or wound

less adjective 1 smaller in extent, degree or duration 2 not so much 3 comparative of **little** ▷ adverb 4 to a smaller extent or degree ▷ preposition 5 after deducting, minus

-less suffix without: hopeless

lessen verb to be reduced in amount, size or quality; decrease

lesser adjective not as great in quantity, size or worth

> **WORD TIP**
> You use less to talk about things that can't be counted: less time. When you are talking about amounts that can be counted you should use fewer

lesson noun 1 single period of instruction in a subject 2 experience that makes you understand something important

lest conjunction so as to prevent any possibility

let lets, letting, let verb 1 to allow (someone) to do something 2 used as an auxiliary to express a proposal, command, threat, or assumption: let's go 3 to grant the use of (a house or flat) for rent 4 **let oneself in for** to agree to do (something one does not really want to do) > **let down** verb 1 to fail (someone); disappoint 2 to deflate > **let off** verb 1 to excuse (someone) from a punishment 2 to light (a firework) or detonate (an explosive) ▷ noun 1 (Tennis) minor infringement or

obstruction of the ball requiring a replay of the point 2 hindrance

lethal adjective deadly: a lethal weapon

lethargy noun lack of energy and enthusiasm > **lethargic** adjective having no energy or enthusiasm

letter noun 1 written message, usually sent by post 2 alphabetical symbol

letter box noun 1 slot in a door through which letters are delivered 2 box in a street or post office where letters are posted

lettering noun writing, especially the type of letters used: bold lettering

lettuce noun plant with large green leaves used in salads

leukaemia or **leukemia** [loo-kee-mee-a] noun disease caused by uncontrolled overproduction of white blood cells

level levels, levelling, levelled adjective 1 (of a surface) smooth, flat and parallel to the ground ▷ verb 2 to make (a piece of land) flat 3 to direct (a criticism, accusation, etc) at someone ▷ adverb 4 **draw level with** to get closer to (someone) so that one is moving next to him or her ▷ noun 5 point on a scale measuring the amount, importance or difficulty of something 6 height that a liquid comes up to in a container > **level off** or **level out** verb to stop increasing or decreasing

level crossing noun point where a railway line and road cross

level-headed adjective not apt to be carried away by emotion

lever noun 1 handle used to operate machinery 2 bar used to move a heavy object or to open something

leverage noun 1 action or power of a lever 2 knowledge or influence that can be used to make someone do something

leveret [**lev**-ver-it] noun young hare

levy levies, levying, levied [**lev**-vee] verb 1 to impose and collect (a tax) ▷ noun 2 (formal) amount of money that one pays in tax

lewd adjective lustful or indecent

lexicography noun the profession of writing dictionaries > **lexicographer** noun writer of dictionaries

liability liabilities noun 1 responsibility for wrongdoing 2 (informal) person who causes a lot of problems or embarrassment 3 liabilities business debts

liable adjective 1 (followed by to) likely (to happen) 2 (followed by for) legally responsible (for something)

liaise verb to establish and maintain communication with (a person or organization)

liaison noun communication and contact between groups

liar noun person who tells lies

libel libels, libelling, libelled noun 1 published statement falsely damaging a person's reputation ▷ verb 2 to falsely damage the reputation of (someone) > **libellous** adjective: he claimed the articles were libellous

liberal adjective 1 tolerant of a wide range of behaviour, standards or opinions 2 generous (with something) 3 (of a quantity) large ▷ noun

4 person who has liberal ideas or opinions > **liberalism** noun belief in democratic reforms and individual freedom > **liberally** adverb in large quantities

Liberal Democrat or **Lib Dem** noun member of the Liberal Democrats, a British political party favouring a mixed economy and individual freedom

liberate verb to free (people) from prison or from an unpleasant situation > **liberation** noun: the women's liberation movement > **liberator** noun person who sets people free

liberty noun freedom to choose how one wants to live, without government restrictions

libido libidos [lib-**ee**-doe] noun sexual drive

Libra noun seventh sign of the zodiac, represented by a pair of scales

librarian noun (LIBRARY) person in charge of a library

library libraries noun 1 building where books are kept for people to come and read or borrow 2 collection of books, records, etc for consultation or borrowing

Libyan adjective 1 of Libya ▷ noun 2 person from Libya

lice noun a plural of **louse**

licence noun 1 official document giving official permission to do something 2 freedom to do what one wants, especially when considered irresponsible

WORD TIP
The noun licence ends in ce

license verb to give official permission for (an activity) to be carried out

WORD TIP

The verb license ends in se

lichen noun green moss-like growth on rocks or tree trunks

lick verb 1 to pass the tongue over (something) ▷ noun 2 licking

lid noun movable cover for a container

lie¹ lies, lying, lied verb 1 to say something that is not true ▷ noun 2 something said that is not true

lie² lies, lying, lay, lain verb 1 to be in a horizontal position 2 to be situated

WORD TIP

The past tense of this verb lie is lay. Do not confuse it with the verb to lay (past tense laid) meaning 'put'

lieu [lyew] noun in lieu of instead of

lieutenant [lef-ten-ant] noun junior officer in the army or navy

life lives noun 1 quality of being able to grow and develop, which is present in people, plants and animals 2 period between birth and death or between birth and the present time 3 amount of time something is active or functions 4 liveliness or high spirits 5 imprisonment for the rest of your life or until granted parole

life assurance noun insurance that provides a sum of money in the event of the policy holder's death

lifeblood noun most essential part of something

lifeboat noun 1 boat kept on shore, used for rescuing people at sea 2 small boat kept on a ship, used if the ship starts to sink

life expectancy noun number of years a person can expect to live

lifeguard noun person whose job is to rescue people in difficulty at sea or in a swimming pool

life jacket noun sleeveless inflatable jacket that keeps a person afloat in water

lifeless adjective 1 dead 2 not lively or exciting

lifelike adjective (of a picture or sculpture) looking very real or alive

lifeline noun 1 means of contact or support 2 rope used in rescuing a person in danger

lifelong adjective lasting all of a person's life

lifesaver noun (Aust, NZ) person whose job is to rescue people who are in difficulty at sea

life span noun 1 length of time during which a person is alive 2 length of time a product or organization exists or is useful

lifetime noun length of time a person is alive

lift verb 1 to move (something) upwards in position, status, volume, etc 2 to remove or cancel (a ban) 3 (informal) to steal (something) ▷ noun 4 cage raised and lowered in a vertical shaft to transport people or goods 5 ride in a car etc as a passenger

ligament noun band of tissue joining bones

light lights, lighting, lighted or lit; lighter, lightest noun 1 brightness from the sun, fire or lamps, by which things are visible 2 lamp or other device that gives out brightness 3 match or lighter to light a cigarette: have you got

a light? ▷ adjective **4** (of a place)
bright **5** (of a colour) pale **6** (of an
object) not weighing much **7** (of
a task) fairly easy **8** (of books or
music) not serious or profound
▷ verb **9** to cause (a fire) to start
burning **10** to cause (a place) to be
filled with light ▷ **lightly** adverb:
cook the onions until lightly browned
> **lightness** noun: the lightness
of the large bedroom > **light on**
or **upon** verb (literary) (of eyes, gaze,
person) to find (something) by
chance

light bulb noun glass part of an
electric lamp

lighten verb **1** to become less dark
2 to make (something) less heavy

lighter noun device for lighting
cigarettes etc

light-headed adjective feeling
faint, dizzy

light-hearted adjective cheerful
and carefree

lighthouse noun tower by the
sea with a powerful light to
guide ships

lighting noun **1** way that a
room or building is lit **2** DRAMA
apparatus for and use of artificial
light in theatres, films, etc

lightning noun bright flashes
of light in the sky, produced
by natural electricity during a
thunderstorm

lightweight noun, adjective
1 not weighing much ▷ noun
2 boxer weighing up to 135lb
(professional) or 60kg (amateur)

light year noun (Astronomy)
distance light travels in one year,
about six million million miles

likable or **likeable** adjective
pleasant and friendly

like preposition, adjective, noun
1 indicating similarity, comparison,
etc **2** feel **like** to want to do or
to have (something): I feel like a
walk ▷ verb **3** to find (something or
someone) pleasant

-like suffix resembling or similar to:
a balloonlike object

likelihood noun probability

likely adjective probable

liken verb to compare (one thing)
to another

likeness noun resemblance

likewise adverb similarly

liking noun fondness for (someone
or something)

lilac noun **1** shrub with pale mauve
or white flowers ▷ adjective
2 light-purple

lilt noun pleasing musical quality
in speaking > **lilting** adjective: a
lilting northern accent

lily lilies noun plant that grows
from a bulb and has large, often
white, flowers

limb noun **1** arm, leg or wing
2 main branch of a tree **3** go out
on a **limb** to say or do something
risky

limber up verb to stretch your
muscles in preparation for doing
sport

limbo noun **1** West Indian dance in
which dancers lean backwards to
pass under a bar **2** in **limbo** not
knowing the result or next stage
of something and powerless to
influence it

lime noun **1** calcium compound
used as a fertilizer or in making
cement **2** small green citrus
fruit **3** deciduous tree with
heart-shaped leaves and fragrant
flowers

limelight noun glare of publicity

limerick [**lim**-mer-ik] noun humorous verse of five lines

limestone noun white rock used in building

limit noun **1** boundary or extreme beyond which something cannot go: the speed limit ▷ verb **2** to prevent (something) from becoming bigger, spreading or making progress > **limited** adjective rather small in amount or extent

limitation noun **1** reducing or controlling of something **2** limitations limits of the abilities of someone or something

limousine noun large luxurious car, usually driven by a chauffeur

limp verb **1** to walk with an uneven step because of an injured leg or foot ▷ noun **2** limping walk ▷ adjective **3** without firmness or stiffness

limpet noun shellfish that sticks tightly to rocks

line noun **1** long narrow mark **2** telephone connection **3** railway track **4** course or direction of movement **5** attitude towards something **6** kind of work someone does **7** row or queue of people **8** type of product **9** row of words **10** lines words of a theatrical part ▷ verb **11** to cover the inside of (something) > **line up** verb **1** to stand in a line **2** to arrange (something) for a special occasion

lineage [**lin**-ee-ij] noun all the people from whom someone is directly descended

linear [**lin**-ee-er] adjective arranged in a line or in a strict sequence, or happening at a constant rate

line dancing noun form of dancing performed by rows of people to country and western music

linen noun [D&T] **1** cloth or thread made from flax **2** sheets, tablecloths, etc

liner noun large passenger ship or aircraft

linesman linesmen noun (in some sports) an official who helps the referee or umpire

-ling suffix small: duckling

linger verb to remain for a long time

lingerie [**lan**-zher-ee] noun women's underwear or nightwear

lingo lingoes noun (informal) foreign or unfamiliar language

linguist noun person who studies foreign languages or the way language works

lining noun any material used to line the inside of something

link noun **1** relationship or connection between two things: the link between sunbathing and skin cancer **2** person or thing forming a connection **3** any of the rings forming a chain ▷ verb **4** to join (people, places or things) together > **linkage** noun: there is no formal linkage between the two agreements

lino noun short for **linoleum**

linoleum noun floor covering with a shiny surface

lint noun soft material for dressing a wound

lion noun large animal of the cat family, the male of which has a shaggy mane

lip *noun* **1** either of the fleshy edges of the mouth **2** rim of a jug etc

lip-read lip-reads, lip-reading, lip-read *verb* to understand speech by following lip movements; a skill often used by deaf people > **lip-reading** *noun*

lipstick *noun* cosmetic in stick form, for colouring the lips

liqueur [lik-**cure**] *noun* flavoured and sweetened alcoholic spirit, usually drunk after a meal

liquid [SCIENCE] *noun* **1** substance in a physical state which can change shape but not size ▷ *adjective* **2** of or being a liquid **3** (of assets) in the form of money or easily converted into money

liquidate *verb* **1** to dissolve (a company) and share its assets among creditors (*informal*) **2** to wipe out or kill (someone) > **liquidation** *noun*: *the company went into liquidation* > **liquidator** *noun* official appointed to liquidate a business

liquor *noun* any strong alcoholic drink

liquorice [lik-ker-iss] *noun* **1** root used to flavour sweets **2** sweets flavoured with liquorice

lira lire *noun* unit of currency of Turkey and formerly of Italy

lisp *noun* **1** speech defect in which {s} and {z} are pronounced {th} ▷ *verb* **2** to speak with a lisp

list *noun* **1** item-by-item record of names or things, usually written one below another ▷ *verb* **2** to make a list of (a number of things) **3** (of a ship) to lean to one side

listen *verb* to heed or pay attention (to something) > **listener** *noun*: *I'm a regular listener to her show*

listless *adjective* lacking interest or energy > **listlessly** *adverb* without interest or energy

lit *verb* past of **light**

litany litanies *noun* **1** prayer with responses from the congregation **2** any tedious recital

literacy *noun* ability to read and write

literal *adjective* **1** according to the explicit meaning of a word or text, not figurative **2** (of a translation) word for word > **literally** *adverb*: *the views are literally breath-taking*

> **WORD TIP**
> Be careful when you use *literally*. It can emphasize something without changing the meaning: *the house was literally only five minutes walk away*. However, it can make nonsense of some things: *he literally swept me off my feet*. This sentence is ridiculous unless *he actually took a broom and swept the speaker over*

literary *adjective* of or knowledgeable about literature

literature *noun* **1** written works such as novels, plays and poetry **2** books and writings of a country, period or subject

lithe *adjective* flexible or supple

litmus *noun* (Chemistry) blue dye turned red by acids and restored to blue by alkalis

litmus test *noun* something regarded as a simple and accurate test of a particular thing

litre *noun* unit of liquid measure equal to 1000 cubic centimetres or 1.76 pints

litter *noun* **1** untidy rubbish dropped in public places **2** group of young animals produced at one birth **3** dry material to absorb a cat's excrement ▷ *verb* **4** to scatter things about untidily in (a place)

little *adjective* **1** small or smaller than average ▷ *adverb* **2** not a lot or not often ▷ *noun* **3** small amount, extent or duration

live¹ *verb* **1** to be alive **2** to reside > **live down** *verb* to wait till people forget (a past mistake or misdeed) > **live up to** *verb* to meet (one's expectations)

live² *adjective* **1** living; alive **2** (of a broadcast) transmitted during the actual performance **3** (of a wire, circuit, etc) carrying an electric current **4** causing interest or controversy **5** capable of exploding

livelihood *noun* occupation or employment

lively *adjective* full of life or vigour; energetic > **liveliness** *noun* vigour and enthusiasm

liven up *verb* to make (things) more lively

liver *noun* **1** large organ in the body that cleans the blood and aids digestion **2** animal liver as food

livestock *noun* farm animals

livid *adjective* **1** (*informal*) angry or furious **2** bluish-grey

living *adjective* **1** alive ▷ *noun* **2** for a living in order to earn money to live: *What does he do for a living?*

living room *noun* room in a house used for relaxation and entertainment

lizard *noun* four-footed reptile with a long body and tail

llama *noun* woolly animal of the camel family found in S America

load *noun* **1** something being carried **2** loads (*informal*) lots ▷ *verb* **3** to put a load onto (an animal) or into (a vehicle)

loaf loaves; loafs, loafing, loafed *noun* **1** shaped mass of baked bread ▷ *verb* **2** to be lazy and not do any work

loan *noun* **1** sum of money borrowed **2** lending ▷ *verb* **3** to lend (something) to someone

loath or **loth** [rhymes with **both**] *adjective* unwilling or reluctant (to do something)

loathe *verb* to hate or be disgusted by (someone or something) > **loathing** *noun*: *She looked at him with loathing* > **loathsome** *adjective*: *a loathsome spectacle*

lob lobs, lobbing, lobbed (*Sport*) *noun* **1** ball struck or thrown high in the air ▷ *verb* **2** to strike or throw (a ball) high in the air

lobby lobbies, lobbying, lobbied *noun* **1** corridor into which rooms open **2** group which tries to influence an organization ▷ *verb* **3** to try to influence (an MP or organization) in the formulation of policy > **lobbyist** *noun* person who lobbies an MP or organization

lobe *noun* **1** any rounded part of something **2** soft hanging part of the ear

lobster *noun* shellfish with a long tail and claws, which turns red when boiled

local *adjective* **1** of the area close to your home **2** (of an anaesthetic) producing loss of feeling in one part of the body ▷ *noun* **3** person belonging to a particular district **4** (*informal*) pub close to your home > **locally** adverb: cards designed by someone locally

locality localities noun neighbourhood or area

localized or **localised** adjective existing or happening in only one place: localized pain

locate verb 1 to discover the whereabouts of (someone or something) 2 to situate (something) in a place

location noun 1 GEOGRAPHY site or position 2 site of a film production away from the studio 3 (SAfr) Black African or coloured township

loch noun (Scot) lake

lock noun 1 appliance for fastening a door, case, etc 2 section of a canal shut off by gates between which the water level can be altered to aid boats moving from one level to another 3 small bunch of hair ▷ verb 4 to close and fasten (something) with a lock 5 to move into place and become firmly fixed there

locker noun small cupboard with a lock

locket noun small hinged pendant for a portrait etc, worn on a chain round the neck

locksmith noun person who makes and mends locks

locomotive noun railway engine

locust noun destructive African insect that flies in swarms and eats crops

lodge noun 1 small house in the grounds of a large country house 2 small house used for holidays ▷ verb 3 to live in another's house at a fixed charge 4 to stick or

become stuck (in a place) 5 to make (a complaint) formally

lodger noun person who lives in someone's house and pays rent

lodgings plural noun rented room or rooms in another person's house

loft noun space between the top storey and roof of a building

lofty loftier, loftiest adjective 1 of great height 2 very noble or important 3 proud and superior

log logs, logging, logged noun 1 portion of a felled tree stripped of branches 2 detailed record of a journey of a ship, aircraft, etc ▷ verb 3 to make a record of (something) in a ship's log

> **log in** verb to gain access (to a computer system) by keying in a special command > **log out** verb to leave (a computer system) by keying in a special command

logic noun 1 way of reasoning involving a series of statements, each of which must be true if the statement before it is true 2 any sensible thinking or reasonable decision

logical adjective 1 (of an argument) using logic 2 (of a course of action or a decision) sensible or reasonable in the circumstances > **logically** adverb: to look at things logically

logistics noun detailed planning and organization of a large, especially military, operation

logo logos [loh-go] noun emblem used by a company or other organization

-logy suffix study of something: biology; geology

loin noun 1 piece of meat from the back or sides of an animal

2 loins (*old-fashioned*) front part of the body between the waist and the thighs, especially the sexual parts

loiter *verb* to stand or wait aimlessly or idly

loll *verb* **1** to lounge lazily **2** (of a head or tongue) to hang loosely

lollipop *noun* hard sweet on a small wooden stick

lolly lollies *noun* **1** lollipop or ice lolly **2** (*Aust, NZ*) sweet

lolly scramble *noun* (*NZ*) sweets scattered on the ground for children to collect

lone *adjective* solitary or single

lonely lonelier, loneliest *adjective* **1** sad because alone **2** (of a place) isolated and unfrequented > **loneliness** *noun: a fear of loneliness*

loner *noun* (*informal*) person who prefers to be alone

lonesome *adjective* lonely and sad

long *adjective* **1** having length, especially great length, in space or time > *adverb* **2** for an extensive period **3 as long as** only if **4 before long** soon **5 no longer** not any more > *verb* **6** (followed by *for*) to have a strong desire for (something) > **longing** *noun* yearning

longevity [lon-**jev**-it-ee] *noun* long life

longhand *noun* ordinary writing, not shorthand or typing

longitude *noun* (GEOGRAPHY) distance east or west from a line passing through Greenwich, measured in degrees

long jump *noun* athletics event involving jumping as far as possible after taking a long run

long-range *adjective* **1** extending into the future **2** (of vehicles, weapons, etc) designed to cover great distances

long-sighted *adjective* able to see distant objects in focus but not nearby ones

long-standing *adjective* existing for a long time

long-suffering *adjective* enduring trouble or unhappiness without complaint

long-term *adjective* lasting or effective for a long time

long-winded *adjective* speaking or writing at tedious length

loo *noun* (*informal*) toilet

look *verb* **1** (followed by *at*) to direct the eyes or attention towards (something or someone) **2** to have the appearance of being (as specified) **3** to search (for something or someone) > *noun* **4** instance of looking; glance **5** facial expression **6 looks** attractiveness > **look after** *verb* to take care of (someone or something) > **look down on** *verb* to treat (someone) as inferior or unimportant > **look forward to** *verb* to anticipate (something) with pleasure > **look out** *verb* to be careful > **look up** *verb* **1** to discover or confirm (information) by checking in a book **2** (of a situation) to improve **3** to visit (someone) after a long gap > **look up to** *verb* to respect (someone)

lookalike *noun* person who is the double of another

lookout *noun* **1** person who is watching for danger; guard **2** place for watching **3 on the**

a b c d e f g h i j k l m n o p q r s t u v w x y z

lookout watching or waiting expectantly (for something)

loom *noun* **1** machine for weaving cloth ▷ *verb* **2** to appear suddenly and unclearly or threateningly **3** to seem ominously close

loony loonies (*informal*) *adjective* **1** foolish or insane ▷ *noun* **2** foolish or insane person

loop *noun* **1** rounded shape made by a curved line or rope crossing itself ▷ *verb* **2** to fasten (something) with a loop

loophole *noun* means of evading a rule without breaking it

loose *adjective* **1** not tight, fastened, fixed or tense **2** **at a loose end** bored, with nothing to do ▷ *adverb* **3** free from captivity > **loosely** *adverb*

> **WORD TIP**
> The adjective and adverb *loose* is spelt with two os. Do not confuse it with the verb *lose*

loosen *verb* to make (something) looser

loot *verb* **1** to steal goods from (shops and houses) during a battle or riot ▷ *noun* **2** stolen money and goods

lop lops, lopping, lopped *verb* to chop (something) off with one quick stroke

lopsided *adjective* greater in height, weight or size on one side

lord *noun* **1** male member of the British nobility **2Lord a** God or Jesus **b** (in Britain) title given to certain male officials and peers ▷ *verb* **3lord it over** to act in a superior manner towards (someone)

Lordship *noun* (in Britain) title of some male officials and peers

lore *noun* all the traditional knowledge and stories about a subject

lorikeet *noun* small brightly coloured Australian parrot

lorry lorries *noun* (*Brit, SAfr*) large vehicle for transporting goods by road

lory lories [**law-ree**] *noun* small, brightly coloured parrot found in Australia

lose loses, losing, lost *verb* **1** to come to be without (something), especially by accident or carelessness **2** to be deprived of (something) **3** to be deprived of (a relative or friend) through his or her death **4** to be defeated in (a competition etc) **5** (of a business) to spend more (money) than it earns **6** to be or become engrossed: *lost in thought* > **loser** *noun* **1** person or thing that loses **2** (*informal*) person who seems destined to fail

> **WORD TIP**
> The verb *lose* is spelt with one *o*. Do not confuse it with the adjective and adverb *loose*

loss *noun* **1** losing **2at a loss** confused or bewildered

lost *verb* **1** past of **lose** ▷ *adjective* **2** unable to find your way **3** unable to be found

lot *noun* **1** item at auction **2a lot a** a great number or quantity: *a lot of noise* **b** very much or very often: *He's out a lot* **3the lot, the whole lot** the whole amount or number: *He bet all his wages and lost the lot* **4lots** great numbers or quantities: *We took lots of photos*

lotion *noun* medical or cosmetic liquid for use on the skin

lottery lotteries *noun* method of raising money by selling tickets that win prizes by chance

lotus *noun* large water lily of Africa and Asia

loud *adjective* **1** having a high volume of sound **2** (of clothing) too bright > **loudly** *adverb* > **loudness** *noun: she was startled at their loudness*

loudspeaker *noun* piece of equipment that makes your voice louder when you speak into a microphone connected to it

lounge *noun* **1** living room in a private house **2** more expensive bar in a pub ▷ *verb* **3** to sit, lie or stand in a relaxed manner

lourie [rhymes with **Māori**] *noun* (S Afr) one of two types of bird found in South Africa: the grey lourie, which lives in open grassland, and the more brightly coloured species, which lives in forests

louse lice *noun* small insect that lives on people's bodies

lousy lousier, lousiest *adjective* (*informal*) **1** mean or unpleasant **2** bad, inferior **3** unwell

lout *noun* young man who behaves in an aggressive and rude way

lovable or **loveable** *adjective* having very attractive qualities and therefore easy to love

love *verb* **1** to have a great affection for (someone) **2** to enjoy (something) very much **3** would love to to want very much to (do something): *I would love to live there* ▷ *noun* **4** great affection **5** (Tennis, squash, etc) score of nothing **6** in love feeling a strong emotional and sexual attraction

(for someone) **7** make love (often followed by to) to have sexual intercourse with (someone) > **loving** *adjective* affectionate, tender > **lovingly** *adverb*

love affair *noun* romantic or sexual relationship between two people who are not married to each other

love life *noun* person's romantic or sexual relationships

lovely lovelier, loveliest *adjective* very beautiful, attractive and pleasant > **loveliness** *noun: a vision of loveliness*

lover *noun* **1** person having a sexual relationship outside marriage **2** person who loves a specified person or thing

low *adjective* **1** not tall or high **2** of little or less than the usual amount, degree, quality or cost **3** coarse or vulgar **4** not loud **5** deep in pitch ▷ *adverb* **6** in or to a low position, level or degree ▷ *noun* **7** low position, level or degree

lowboy *noun* (Aust, NZ) small wardrobe or chest of drawers

lower *verb* **1** to move (something) downwards **2** to lessen (something)

lowlands *plural noun* area of flat low land > **lowland** *adjective: lowland areas*

lowly lowlier, lowliest *adjective* low in importance, rank or status

low tide *noun* time, usually twice a day, when the sea is at its lowest level

loyal *adjective* faithful to your friends, country or government > **loyally** *adverb* > **loyalty** *noun: an oath of loyalty to the monarchy*

loyalist noun person who remains firm in support for a government or ruler

lozenge noun 1 medicated tablet held in the mouth until it dissolves 2 diamond-shaped figure

LP noun long-playing record

LSD noun lysergic acid diethylamide, a very powerful drug that causes hallucinations

Ltd abbreviation (Brit) Limited (Liability)

lubra noun (Aust) Australian Aboriginal woman

lubricate [loo-brik-ate] verb to oil or grease (something) to lessen friction > **lubricant** noun lubricating substance, such as oil > **lubrication** noun: use linseed oil for lubrication

lucid adjective 1 (of writing or speech) clear and easily understood 2 (of a person) able to think clearly

luck noun fortune, good or bad

luckless adjective having bad luck

lucky adjective having or bringing good luck > **luckily** adverb fortunately

lucrative adjective very profitable

ludicrous adjective absurd or ridiculous

lug lugs, lugging, lugged verb to carry or drag (something) with great effort

luggage noun traveller's cases, bags, etc

lukewarm adjective 1 moderately warm, tepid 2 indifferent or half-hearted

lull verb 1 to calm the fears or suspicions of (someone) by deception ▷ noun 2 brief time of quiet in a storm etc

lullaby lullabies noun quiet song to send a child to sleep

lumber noun 1 (Brit) unwanted disused household articles 2 (Chiefly US) sawn timber ▷ verb 3 to move heavily and awkwardly 4 (informal) to burden (someone) with something unpleasant

luminary luminaries noun (literary) famous person

luminous adjective glowing in the dark, usually because treated with a special substance > **luminosity** noun 1 brightness 2 (of a person's skin) healthy glow

lump noun 1 shapeless piece or mass 2 swelling 3 (informal) awkward or stupid person ▷ verb 4 to consider (people or things) as a single group 5 **lump it** (informal) to tolerate or put up with something > **lumpy** adjective containing or covered with lumps

lump sum noun large sum of money paid at one time

lunacy noun 1 extremely foolish or eccentric behaviour 2 (old-fashioned) severe mental illness

lunar adjective relating to the moon

lunatic adjective 1 foolish and irresponsible ▷ noun 2 foolish or annoying person 3 (old-fashioned) insane person

lunch noun 1 meal taken in the middle of the day ▷ verb 2 to eat lunch

luncheon noun (formal) lunch

lung noun organ that allows an animal or bird to breathe air: humans have two lungs in the chest

lunge noun 1 sudden forward motion 2 thrust with a sword ▷ verb 3 to move with a lunge

lurch verb 1 to make a sudden jerky movement ▷ noun 2 lurching movement 3 **leave someone in the lurch** to abandon someone in difficulties

lure verb 1 to tempt or attract (someone) by the promise of reward ▷ noun 2 person or thing that lures

lurid adjective 1 vivid in shocking detail, sensational 2 glaring in colour

lurk verb to lie hidden or move stealthily, especially for sinister purposes

luscious [lush-uss] adjective extremely pleasurable to taste or smell

lush adjective (of grass etc) growing thickly and healthily

lust noun 1 strong sexual desire 2 any strong desire ▷ verb 3 (followed by after) to have a strong desire for (someone or something) > **lustful** adjective

lustre noun gloss, sheen

lute noun ancient guitar-like musical instrument with a body shaped like a half pear

luxuriant adjective (of plants or gardens) large, healthy and growing strongly

luxurious adjective very expensive and full of luxury; splendid > **luxuriously** adverb: luxuriously furnished

luxury luxuries noun 1 enjoyment of rich, very comfortable living 2 enjoyable but not essential thing

-ly suffix 1 forming adjectives that describe a quality: friendly 2 forming adjectives that refer to how often something happens: yearly 3 forming adverbs that refer to how something is done: quickly; nicely

lying noun 1 telling lies ▷ verb 2 present participle of **lie¹**, **lie²**

lynch verb (of a crowd) to put (someone) to death without a trial

lynx lynxes noun wildcat with tufted ears and a short tail

lyre noun ancient musical instrument like a U-shaped harp

lyric adjective (of poetry) expressing personal emotion in songlike style > **lyrical** adjective poetic and romantic

m

m *symbol* **1** metre(s) **2** mile(s)

macabre [mak-**kahb**-ra] *adjective* strange and horrible, gruesome

macadamia *noun* Australian tree with edible nuts

macaroni *noun* pasta in short tube shapes

macaroon *noun* small biscuit or cake made with ground almonds

mace *noun* ornamental pole carried by an official during ceremonies as a symbol of authority

machete [mash-**ett**-ee] *noun* broad heavy knife used for cutting or as a weapon

machine *noun* **1** D&T apparatus, usually powered by electricity, designed to perform a particular task ▷ *verb* **2** to make or produce (something) by machine

machine gun *noun* automatic gun that fires rapidly and continuously

machinery *noun* machines or machine parts collectively

machismo [mak-**izz**-moh] *noun* exaggerated or strong masculinity

macho [**match**-oh] *adjective* strongly or exaggeratedly masculine

mackerel *noun* edible sea fish with blue and silver stripes

mackintosh *noun* raincoat made from specially treated waterproof cloth

mad madder, maddest *adjective* **1** mentally deranged; insane **2** very foolish **3** (*informal*) angry **4** (followed by *about*) very enthusiastic (about someone or something) ▷ **madly** *adverb* in a fast excited way ▷ **madness** *noun*: driven to the brink of madness

madam *noun* polite form of address to a woman

maddening *adjective* irritating or frustrating

madrigal *noun* song sung by several people without instruments

Mafia *noun* international secret criminal organization founded in Sicily

magazine *noun* **1** LIBRARY weekly or monthly publication with articles and photographs **2** compartment in a gun for cartridges

magenta [maj-**jen**-ta] *noun, adjective* deep purplish-red

maggot *noun* larva of an insect

magic *noun* **1** in fairy stories, a special power that can make impossible things happen **2** art of performing tricks to entertain people ▷ **magical** *adjective* **1** of, using or like magic **2** (*informal*) wonderful, marvellous ▷ **magically** *adverb* by or as if by magic

magician *noun* **1** person who performs tricks as entertainment **2** in fairy stories, a man with magical powers

magistrate *noun* official who acts as a judge in a law court that deals with less serious crimes

magnanimous *adjective* noble and generous

magnate *noun* influential or wealthy person, especially in industry

magnet *noun* piece of iron or steel capable of attracting iron and pointing north when suspended

magnificent *adjective* extremely beautiful or impressive > **magnificence** *noun*: *the magnificence of the Swiss mountains* > **magnificently** *adverb*

magnify magnifies, magnifying, magnified *verb* (of a microscope or lens) to make (something) appear bigger than it actually is > **magnification** *noun* **1** act of magnifying **2** degree to which something is magnified

magnifying glass *noun* lens which makes things appear bigger than they really are

magnitude *noun* relative importance or size

magnolia *noun* shrub or tree with showy white or pink flowers

magpie *noun* black-and-white bird

mahogany *noun* hard reddish-brown wood of several tropical trees

maid or **maidservant** *noun* female servant

maiden *noun* **1** (*literary*) young unmarried woman ▷ *adjective* **2** first: *maiden voyage*

maiden name *noun* woman's surname before marriage

mail *noun* **1** letters and packages delivered by the post office ▷ *verb* **2** to send (a letter) by mail

mail order *noun* system of buying goods by post

maim *verb* to injure (someone) very badly for life

main *adjective* **1** chief or principal ▷ *noun* **2** principal pipe or line carrying water, gas or electricity **3 mains** main distribution network for water, gas or electricity > **mainly** *adverb* for the most part, chiefly

mainframe *noun* (*Computers*) high-speed general-purpose computer

mainland *noun* stretch of land which forms the main part of a country

mainstay *noun* most important part of something

mainstream *noun* most ordinary and conventional group of people or ideas in a society

maintain *verb* **1** to keep (something) going or keep (something) at a particular rate or level **2** to support (someone) financially **3** to assert that (something) is true

maintenance *noun* **1** process of keeping something in good condition **2** money that a person sends regularly to someone to provide for the things he or she needs

maize *noun* type of corn with spikes of yellow grains

majesty *noun* **1** great dignity and impressiveness **2 His Majesty, Her Majesty** way of referring to a king or queen

major *adjective* **1** greater in number, quality or extent **2** significant or serious **3** MUSIC denoting the key in which most European music is written ▷ *noun* **4** middle-ranking army officer

majority majorities *noun* **1** greater number **2** number by which the votes on one side exceed those on the other

> **WORD TIP**
> You should use *majority* only to talk about things that can be counted: *the majority of car owners.* To talk about an amount that cannot be counted you should use *most: most of the harvest was saved*

make makes, making, made *verb* **1** to create, construct or establish (something) **2** to force (someone) to do something **3** to bring about or produce (something) **4** to perform (an action) **5** **make do** to manage with an inferior alternative ▷ *noun* **6** brand, type or style >**maker** *noun* manufacturer >**make up** *verb* **1** to form or constitute (something) **2** to invent (a story) **3** (followed by *for*) to compensate for (something) that you have done wrong) **4** to apply cosmetics to (oneself or someone else) **5** **make it up** to settle a quarrel >**making** *noun* **1** creation or production **2** **in the making** gradually becoming (something): *a captain in the making*

make-up *noun* **1** cosmetics **2** character or personality

maladjusted *adjective* (*Psychology*) unable to meet the demands of society

malaise [mal-**laze**] *noun* vague feeling of unease, illness or depression

malaria *noun* infectious disease caused by the bite of some mosquitoes

Malaysian *adjective* **1** of Malaysia ▷ *noun* **2** person from Malaysia

male *adjective* **1** of the sex which can fertilize female reproductive cells ▷ *noun* **2** male person or animal

male chauvinist *noun* man who thinks that men are better than women

malevolent [mal-**lev**-a-lent] *adjective* wishing evil to others; spiteful >**malevolence** *noun: a streak of malevolence*

malfunction *verb* **1** to function imperfectly or fail to function ▷ *noun* **2** defective functioning or failure to function

malice [mal-iss] *noun* desire to cause harm to others

malicious *adjective* intended to harm: *malicious gossip*

malign [mal-**line**] *verb* to say unpleasant and untrue things about (someone)

malignant [mal-**lig**-nant] *adjective* (of a tumour) harmful and uncontrollable

mallard *noun* wild duck, the male of which has a green head

mallee *noun* (*Aust*) low-growing eucalypt in dry regions

mallet *noun* wooden hammer with a square head

malnutrition *noun* inadequate nutrition

malodorous [mal-**lode**-or-uss] *adjective* bad-smelling

malpractice *noun* immoral, illegal or unethical professional conduct

malt *noun* grain, such as barley, prepared for use in making beer or whisky

mammal *noun* SCIENCE animal of the type that suckles its young

mammoth noun **1** extinct elephant-like mammal ▷ adjective **2** colossal

man noun; mans, manning, manned noun **1** adult male **2** humankind: *one of the hardest substances known to man* **3** men people: *all men are equal* ▷ verb **4** to be in charge of or operate (something)

mana noun (NZ) authority or influence

manacles [**man**-a-klz] plural noun metal rings or clamps attached to a prisoner's wrists or ankles

manage verb **1** to succeed in doing something **2** to be in charge of or administer (an organization or business)

manageable adjective able to be dealt with

management noun **1** managers collectively **2** administration or organization

manager noun person responsible for running a business or organization

> **WORD TIP**
> In business, the word *manager* can apply to either a man or a woman

manageress noun woman responsible for running a business or organization

managing director noun company director responsible for the way the company is managed

mandarin noun kind of small orange

mandate noun authorization or instruction from an electorate to its representative or government

mandatory adjective compulsory

mandir [**mun**-dir] noun Hindu temple

mandolin noun musical instrument with four pairs of strings

mane noun long hair on the neck of a horse, lion, etc

manger noun eating trough in a stable or barn

mangle verb **1** to destroy (something) by crushing and twisting ▷ noun **2** machine with rollers for squeezing water from washed clothes

mango mangoes or mangos noun tropical fruit with sweet juicy yellow flesh

manhole noun hole with a cover, through which a person can enter a drain or sewer

manhood noun state of being a man rather than a boy

mania noun **1** extreme enthusiasm: *my wife's mania for plant collecting* **2** mental illness

maniac noun mad person who is violent and dangerous

manic adjective **1** energetic and excited **2** affected by mania

manicure noun cosmetic care of the fingernails and hands > **manicurist** noun person whose job is the cosmetic care of fingernails and hands

manifest adjective **1** easily noticed, obvious ▷ verb **2** to show or reveal (something): *Fear can manifest itself in many ways*

manifestation noun sign that something is happening or exists: *a manifestation of stress*

manifesto manifestoes or manifestos noun declaration of policy as issued by a political party

manipulate verb **1** to control or influence (people or events) to produce a particular result **2** to control (a piece of equipment) in a skilful way > **manipulation** *noun*: political manipulation > **manipulative** *adjective* influencing people to produce a desired result > **manipulator** *noun* person who manipulates people

mankind *noun* human beings collectively

manly manlier, manliest *adjective* possessing qualities that are typically masculine

manna *noun* **appear like manna from heaven** to appear suddenly as if by a miracle to help someone in a difficult situation

manner *noun* **1** way a thing happens or is done **2** person's bearing or behaviour **3 manners** (polite) social behaviour

mannerism *noun* person's distinctive habit or trait

manoeuvre [man-**noo**-ver] *noun* **1** skilful movement **2** contrived, complicated and possibly deceptive plan or action > *verb* **3** to skilfully move (something) into a place

manor *noun* (Brit) large country house and its lands

manpower *noun* available number of workers

mansion *noun* large house

manslaughter *noun* (Law) unlawful but unintentional killing of a person

mantelpiece *noun* shelf above a fireplace

mantle *noun* (literary) responsibilities and duties which go with a particular job or position

mantra *noun* word or short piece of sacred text or prayer continually repeated to help concentration

manual *adjective* **1** of or done with the hands **2** by human labour rather than automatic means > *noun* **3** instruction book explaining how to use a machine > **manually** *adverb*

manufacture [D&T] *verb* **1** to process or make (goods) on a large scale using machinery **2** to invent or concoct (an excuse etc)

manure *noun* animal excrement used as a fertilizer

manuscript *noun* handwritten or typed document, especially a version of a book before it is printed

Manx *adjective* of the Isle of Man

many *adjective* **1** numerous > *pronoun* **2** large number

Māori *noun* **1** person descended from the people who lived in New Zealand before Europeans arrived **2** language of the Māoris

map maps, mapping, mapped *noun* representation of the earth's surface or some part of it, showing geographical features > **map out** *verb* to work out (a plan)

maple *noun* tree with broad leaves, a variety of which (sugar maple) yields sugar

mar mars, marring, marred *verb* to spoil (something)

marae *noun* (NZ) **1** enclosed space in front of a Māori meeting house **2** Māori meeting house and its buildings

marathon *noun* **1** long-distance race of 26 miles 385 yards (42.195

kilometres) ▷ *adjective* **2** (of a task) large and taking a long time

marble *noun* **1** kind of limestone with a mottled appearance, which can be highly polished **2** small glass ball used in a children's game **3 marbles** game of rolling these at one another

march *verb* **1** to walk with a military step **2** to walk quickly in a determined way ▷ *noun* **3** organized protest in which a large group of people walk somewhere together

mare *noun* female horse

margarine *noun* butter substitute made from animal or vegetable fats

margin *noun* **1** blank space at each side of a printed or written page **2** additional amount or one greater than necessary **3 win by a large margin** to win (a contest) by a large or small amount

marginal *adjective* **1** insignificant, unimportant **2** (*Politics*) (of a constituency) won by only a small margin > **marginally** *adverb* to only a small extent

marigold *noun* plant with yellow or orange flowers

marijuana [mar-ree-**wah**-na] *noun* dried flowers and leaves of the cannabis plant, used as a drug, especially in cigarettes

marina *noun* harbour for yachts and other pleasure boats

marinate *verb* to soak (fish or meat) in a seasoned liquid before cooking

marine *adjective* **1** of the sea or shipping ▷ *noun* **2** (especially in Britain and the US) soldier trained for land and sea combat

marital *adjective* relating to marriage

maritime *adjective* relating to shipping

marjoram *noun* herb used for seasoning food and in salads

mark *noun* **1** line, dot, scar, etc visible on a surface **2** written or printed symbol **3** letter or number used to grade academic work **4** unit of currency formerly used in Germany ▷ *verb* **5** to make a mark on (a surface) **6** to be a sign of (something) **7** to grade (academic work) **8** to stay close to (a sporting opponent) to hamper his or her play

marked *adjective* noticeable > **markedly** *adverb*

market *noun* **1** place where goods or animals are bought and sold **2** place with many small stalls selling different goods **3** demand for goods ▷ *verb* **4** to sell (a product) in an organized way

marketing *noun* part of a business that controls the way that goods or services are sold

market research *noun* research into consumers' needs and purchases

marksman marksmen *noun* person skilled at shooting

marlin *noun* (Aust) large fish found in tropical seas that has a very long narrow jaw

marmalade *noun* jam made from citrus fruits

maroon *adjective* reddish-purple

marooned *adjective* **1** abandoned ashore, especially on an island **2** isolated without resources

marquee *noun* large tent used for a party or exhibition

marriage noun 1 state of being married; matrimony 2 RE wedding

marrow noun long thick striped green vegetable with whitish flesh

marry marries, marrying, married verb 1 to take (someone) as a husband or wife 2 to join (a couple) in marriage > **married** adjective: a married man

Mars noun fourth planet from the sun in the solar system

marsh noun low-lying wet land

marshal marshals, marshalling, marshalled noun 1 official who organizes ceremonies or events > verb 2 to gather (things or people) together and organize them

marshmallow noun spongy pink or white sweet

marsupial [mar-**soop**-ee-al] noun animal that carries its young in a pouch, such as a kangaroo

martial art noun any of various philosophies and techniques of self-defence, originating in the Far East, such as karate

Martian [**marsh**-an] noun supposed inhabitant of Mars

martyr noun 1 person who dies or suffers for his or her beliefs > verb 2 to make a martyr of (someone) > **martyrdom** noun: They see martyrdom as the ultimate glory

marvel marvels, marvelling, marvelled verb 1 to be filled with wonder > noun 2 wonderful thing

marvellous adjective wonderful or excellent > **marvellously** adverb

Marxism noun political philosophy of Karl Marx, which states that society will develop towards communism through the struggle between different social classes > **Marxist** noun 1 person who believes in Marxism > adjective 2 believing in Marxism

marzipan noun paste of ground almonds, sugar, and egg whites, put on top of cakes or used to make small sweets

mascara noun cosmetic for darkening and lengthening the eyelashes

mascot noun person, animal or thing supposed to bring good luck

masculine adjective 1 typical of men rather than women 2 (Grammar) of the gender of nouns that includes some male animate things > **masculinity** noun: the link between masculinity and violence

mash verb to crush (cooked vegetables) into a soft mass

mask noun 1 covering for the face, as a disguise or protection > verb 2 to hide or disguise (something)

masochism [mass-oh-kiz-zum] noun condition in which pleasure is obtained from feeling pain or from being humiliated > **masochist** noun someone who gets pleasure from his or her own suffering

mason noun person who works with stone

masonry noun pieces of stone forming part of a wall or building

masquerade [mask-er-**aid**] verb (followed by as) to pretend to be (someone or something else)

mass noun 1 large quantity 2 (Physics) amount of matter in an object 3 **the masses** ordinary people ▷ *adjective* **4** involving many people ▷ *verb* **5** to gather together in a large group

massacre [**mass**-a-ker] *noun* **1** indiscriminate killing of large numbers of people ▷ *verb* **2** to kill (people) in large numbers

massage [**mass**-ahzh] *noun* **1** rubbing and kneading of parts of the body to reduce pain or stiffness ▷ *verb* **2** to give a massage to (someone)

massive *adjective* large and heavy > **massively** *adverb* extremely

mass-produce *verb* to manufacture (standardized goods) in large quantities

mast *noun* tall pole for supporting something, especially a ship's sails

master *noun* **1** person in control, such as an employer or an owner of slaves or animals **2** male teacher ▷ *adjective* **3** overall or controlling **4** main or principal ▷ *verb* **5** to acquire knowledge of or skill in (something) **6** to succeed in controlling (a difficult situation)

masterful *adjective* showing control and authority

masterly *adjective* showing great skill

mastermind *verb* **1** to plan and direct (a complex task) ▷ *noun* **2** person who plans and directs a complex task

masterpiece *noun* outstanding work of art

masturbate *verb* to stroke or rub one's genitals for sexual pleasure > **masturbation** *noun* masturbating

mat *noun* piece of fabric used as a floor covering or to protect a surface

matador *noun* man who kills the bull in bullfights

match *noun* **1** contest in a game or sport **2** small stick with a tip that produces a flame when scraped on a rough surface ▷ *verb* **3** to be exactly like, equal to, or in harmony with (something)

mate *noun* **1** (*informal*) friend **2** sexual partner of an animal **3** officer in a merchant ship ▷ *verb* **4** (of animals) to be paired for reproduction

material *noun* **1** substance of which a thing is made **2** cloth **3** information on which a piece of work may be based **4 materials** equipment needed for an activity ▷ *adjective* **5** involving possessions or money > **materially** *adverb* considerably

materialism *noun* excessive interest in or desire for money and possessions > **materialistic** *adjective: a materialistic society*

materialize or **materialise** *verb* to happen in fact or appear

maternal *adjective* **1** of a mother **2** related through one's mother

maternity *adjective* of or for pregnant women

mathematics *noun* study of numbers, quantities and shapes > **mathematical** *adjective: mathematical calculations* > **mathematically** *adverb: mathematically minded* > **mathematician** *noun* person trained in the study of numbers, quantities and shapes

maths *noun* (*informal*) mathematics

Matilda *noun* **1** (*Aust old-fashioned*) swagman's bundle of belongings

a
b
c
d
e
f
g
h
i
j
k
l
m
n
o
p
q
r
s
t
u
v
w
x
y
z

2 waltz Matilda (*Aust*) to travel about carrying your bundle of belongings

matinée [**mat**-in-nay] *noun* afternoon performance in a theatre or cinema

matrimony *noun* (*formal*) marriage > **matrimonial** *adjective*: *the matrimonial home*

matrix matrices [**may**-trix] *noun* **1** substance or situation in which something originates, takes form or is enclosed **2** (*Maths*) rectangular array of numbers or elements

matron *noun* **1** (*Brit*) **a** (in a nursing home or, formerly, in a hospital) senior nurse in charge of the nursing staff **b** (in a boarding school) woman responsible for looking after the health of the children **2** a staid or dignified married woman

matt *adjective* dull, not shiny

matted *adjective* (of hair) tangled, with strands sticking together

matter *noun* **1** substance of which something is made **2** physical substance **3** event, situation or subject **4** written material in general **5 what's the matter?** what is wrong? > *verb* **6** to be of importance

matter-of-fact *adjective* showing no emotion

matting *noun* thick woven material such as rope or straw, used as a floor covering

mattress *noun* large stuffed flat case, often with springs, used on or as a bed

mature *adjective* **1** fully developed or grown-up > *verb* **2** to become mature **3** (of a bill or bond)

to become due for payment > **maturely** *adverb* in a mature fashion > **maturity** *noun* state of being mature

maudlin *adjective* foolishly or tearfully sentimental

maul *verb* (of an animal) to attack (someone) savagely

mausoleum [maw-so-**lee**-um] *noun* stately tomb

mauve *adjective* pale purple

maxim *noun* general truth or principle

maximize or **maximise** *verb* to increase (something) to a maximum

maximum *adjective, noun* greatest possible (amount or number)

may *verb* used as an auxiliary to express possibility, permission, opportunity, etc

maybe *adverb* perhaps, possibly

mayhem *noun* violent destruction or confusion

mayonnaise *noun* thick salad dressing made with egg yolks, oil and vinegar

mayor *noun* person elected to lead and represent the people of a town

maze *noun* complex network of paths or lines designed to puzzle

MBE *abbreviation* (in Britain) Member of the Order of the British Empire

MD *abbreviation* **1** Doctor of Medicine **2** managing director

me *pronoun* objective form of I

meadow *noun* piece of grassland

meagre *adjective* scanty or insufficient

meal *noun* **1** occasion when food is served and eaten **2** the food itself

mealie *noun* (*S Afr*) maize

mean means, meaning, meant verb **1** to intend to convey or express (something) **2** to signify or denote (something) **3** to intend (to do something) **4** to have importance as specified: *It would mean a lot to them to win* ▷ adjective **5** miserly, ungenerous or petty **6** unkind or cruel ▷ noun **7** (*Maths*) average of a set of numbers ▷**meanly** adverb ▷**meanness** noun: *his meanness over money*

meander [mee-**and**-er] verb to follow a winding course

meaning noun **1** sense, significance **2** worth, purpose: *a challenge that gives meaning to life* ▷**meaningful** adjective: *a meaningful event* ▷**meaningfully** adverb: *He glanced meaningfully at the other policeman* ▷**meaningless** adjective: *a meaningless existence*

means test noun inquiry into a person's means to decide on eligibility for financial aid

meantime noun intervening period

meanwhile adverb **1** during the intervening period ▷ noun **2** intervening period

measles noun infectious disease producing red spots

measly adjective (*informal*) meagre

measure noun **1** [MATHS] unit of size or quantity **2** certain amount (of something): *a measure of agreement* **3** measures actions taken ▷ verb **4** [MATHS] to determine the size or quantity of (something) **5** [MATHS] to be (a specified amount) in size or quantity

measured adjective **1** slow and steady **2** carefully considered

measurement noun **1** measuring **2** size

meat noun animal flesh as food ▷**meaty** adjective (tasting) of or like meat

Mecca noun **1** holy city of Islam **2** place that attracts visitors

WORD TIP
Most Muslims dislike this form and use the Arabic *Makkah*

mechanic noun person skilled in repairing or operating machinery

mechanical adjective **1** of or done by machines **2** (of an action) without thought or feeling ▷**mechanically** adverb

mechanism noun **1** piece of machinery **2** process or technique

medal noun piece of metal with an inscription etc, given as a reward or memento

medallion noun disc-shaped ornament worn on a chain round the neck

medallist noun winner of a medal

meddle verb to interfere annoyingly

media plural noun television, radio and newspapers collectively

WORD TIP
Although *media* is a plural noun, it is becoming more common for it to be used as a singular: *the media is obsessed with violence*

mediaeval adjective same as **medieval**

median adjective, noun (*Geometry*) middle (point or line)

mediate verb to intervene in a dispute to bring about agreement ▷**mediation** noun: *United Nations mediation between the two sides* ▷**mediator** noun: *acting as* *mediator between the rebels and the authorities*

medical *adjective* **1** of or relating to the science of medicine ▷ *noun* **2** (*informal*) medical examination ▷ **medically** *adverb*: *medically qualified*

medication *noun* medicinal substance

medicinal [med-**diss**-in-al] *adjective* relating to the treatment of illness

medicine *noun* **1** substance used to treat disease **1** PE science of preventing, diagnosing or curing disease

medieval [med-ee-**eve**-al] *adjective* of the Middle Ages

mediocre [mee-dee-**oak**-er] *adjective* of rather poor quality ▷ **mediocrity** [mee-dee-**ok**-rit-ee] *noun: the mediocrity of most contemporary literature*

meditate *verb* **1** to reflect deeply, especially on spiritual matters **2** (*followed by* on) to think about or plan (something) ▷ **meditation** *noun* act of meditating

Mediterranean *noun* **1** large sea between southern Europe and northern Africa ▷ *adjective* **2** of the Mediterranean or the European countries adjoining it

medium *noun* mediums or media *adjective* **1** midway between extremes, average ▷ *noun* **2** means of communicating news or information to the public, such as radio or newspapers **3** person who can supposedly communicate with the dead

medley *noun* **1** miscellaneous mixture **2** musical sequence of different tunes

meek *adjective* submissive or humble ▷ **meekly** *adverb* ▷ **meekness** *noun* submissiveness or humility

meet meets, meeting, met *verb* **1** to come together with (someone) **2** to come into contact with (someone) **3** to be at the place of arrival of (someone) **4** to satisfy (a need etc) **5** to experience (a situation, attitude or problem) **6 meet with, be met with** to get (a particular reaction): *I was met with silence*

meeting *noun* **1** event in which people discuss proposals and make decisions together **2** act of meeting someone

megabyte *noun* (*Computers*) ICT 2^{20} or 1 048 576 bytes

melaleuca [mel-a-**loo**-ka] *noun* Australian shrub or tree with a white trunk and black branches

melancholy [**mel**-an-kol-lee] *noun* **1** sadness or gloom ▷ *adjective* **2** sad or gloomy

mêlée [**mel**-lay] *noun* noisy confused fight or crowd

mellow *adjective* **1** of (light) soft, not harsh **2** (of a sound) smooth and pleasant to listen to ▷ *verb* **3** to become more pleasant or relaxed

melodic [mel-**lod**-ik] *adjective* relating to melody

melodious [mel-**lode**-ee-uss] *adjective* pleasing to the ear

melodrama *noun* play full of extravagant action and emotion

melodramatic *adjective* behaving in an exaggerated, emotional way; theatrical

melody melodies *noun* MUSIC series of musical notes which make a tune

...d juicy fruit

...liquid or
...ecome liquid

...one of the people
...ging to a group
...aking up a body
adjective **3** (of a
...tate) belonging to an
...onal organization

...r of Parliament* noun
...on elected to parliament

...embership *noun* **1** state
of being a member of an
organization **2** people belonging
to an organization

membrane *noun* thin flexible
tissue in a plant or animal body

memento mementos *noun* thing
serving to remind, souvenir

memo memos *noun* short for
memorandum

memoirs [mem-wahrz] *plural
noun* biography or historical
account based on personal
knowledge

memorable *adjective* worth
remembering, noteworthy
> **memorably** *adverb*

memorandum memorandums
or memoranda *noun* **1** written
record or communication within
a business **2** note of things to be
remembered

memorial *noun* **1** something
serving to commemorate a
person or thing ▷ *adjective*
2 serving as a memorial

memory memories *noun* **1** ability
to remember **2** particular
recollection **3** [ICT] part of a
computer that stores information

men *noun* plural of **man**

menace *noun* **1** someone or
something likely to cause
serious harm **2** quality of
being threatening ▷ *verb*
3 to threaten or endanger
(someone) > **menacingly** *adverb*
threateningly

menagerie [min-naj-er-ee] *noun*
collection of wild animals for
exhibition

mend *verb* to repair or patch
(something)

menial [mean-nee-al] *adjective*
involving boring work of low
status

meningitis [men-in-jite-iss] *noun*
inflammation of the membranes
of the brain

menopause *noun* time when a
woman's menstrual cycle ceases

menorah [mi-naw-rah] *noun*
candelabra that usually has
seven parts and is used in Jewish
temples

menstruate *verb* (of a woman) to
have an approximately monthly
discharge of blood from the
womb > **menstrual** *adjective*: *the
menstrual cycle* > **menstruation**
noun approximately monthly
discharge of blood and cellular
debris from the womb of a
woman who is not pregnant

-ment *suffix* state or feeling:
contentment; *resentment*

mental *adjective* **1** of, in or done by
the mind **2** of or for mental illness
> **mentally** *adverb*

mentality mentalities *noun* way
of thinking

mention *verb* **1** to refer to
(something) briefly ▷ *noun* **2** brief
reference to a person or thing

mentor *noun* adviser or guide

menu noun 1 list of dishes to be served, or from which to order 2 (*Computers*) list of options displayed on a screen

MEP abbreviation Member of the European Parliament

mercenary mercenaries adjective 1 mainly interested in getting money ▷ noun 2 soldier paid to fight for a foreign country

merchandise noun goods that are sold

merchant noun person engaged in trade, wholesale trader

merchant navy noun ships or crew engaged in a nation's commercial shipping

merciful adjective 1 compassionate, kind 2 considered to be fortunate as a relief from suffering: *Death came as a merciful release* >**mercifully** adverb

merciless adjective showing no kindness or forgiveness; heartless >**mercilessly** adverb

mercury noun silvery liquid metal

mercy mercies noun compassionate treatment of an offender or enemy who is in one's power

mere merest adjective nothing more than: *mere chance* >**merely** adverb

merge verb to combine or blend

meringue [mer-**rang**] noun baked mixture of egg whites and sugar

merino merinos noun breed of sheep, common in Australia and New Zealand, with fine soft wool

merit noun 1 excellence or worth 2 merits admirable qualities ▷ verb 3 to deserve (something)

mermaid noun imaginary sea creature with the upper part

of a woman and the l of a fish

merry merrier, merriest 1 cheerful or jolly 2 (*infor* slightly drunk >**merrily** *He laughed merrily*

merry-go-round noun roundabout

mesh noun network or net

mess noun 1 untidy or dirty confusion 2 trouble or difficulty 3 place where members of the armed forces eat ▷ verb 4 (followe by *about*) to potter about >**mess up** verb to spoil (something) or do (something) wrong

message noun 1 communication sent 2 meaning or moral

message board noun internet discussion forum

messaging noun sending messages between mobile phones, using letters and numbers to produce shortened forms of words

messenger noun someone who takes a message to someone for someone else

Messiah noun 1 Jews' promised deliverer 2 Christ

Messrs [**mess**-erz] noun plural of Mr

met verb past of **meet**

metabolism [met-**tab**-oh-liz-zum] noun chemical processes of a living body >**metabolic** adjective: *people with a low metabolic rate*

metal noun chemical element, such as iron or copper, that is malleable and capable of conducting heat and electricity >**metallic** adjective made of or resembling metal

metamorphic *adjective* (of rocks) changed in texture or structure by heat and pressure

metamorphosis metamorphoses [met-a-**more**-foss-is] *noun* change of form or character

metaphor *noun* figure of speech in which a word is used to refer to something it does not mean literally in order to suggest a resemblance: *He is a lion in battle* ▷ **metaphorical** *adjective*: talking in metaphorical terms ▷ **metaphorically** *adverb*: speaking metaphorically

meteor *noun* piece of rock or metal that burns very brightly when it enters the earth's atmosphere from space

meteoric [meet-ee-**or**-rik] *adjective* (of someone's rise to power or success) happening very quickly

meteorite *noun* meteor that has fallen to earth

meteorology *noun* study of the earth's atmosphere, especially for weather forecasting ▷ **meteorological** *adjective* relating to the weather or weather forecasting

meter *noun* instrument for measuring and recording something, such as the consumption of gas or electricity

methane *noun* colourless inflammable gas

method *noun* **1** way or manner **2** SCIENCE technique

methodical *adjective* orderly ▷ **methodically** *adverb*

Methodist *noun* **1** member of any of the Protestant churches

originated by John Wesley and his followers ▷ *adjective* **2** of Methodists or their Church

meticulous *adjective* very careful about details > **meticulously** *adverb*

metre *noun* **1** MATHS basic unit of length equal to about 1.094 yards (100 centimetres) **2** rhythm of poetry

metric *adjective* relating to the decimal system of weights and measures based on the metre

metropolis metropolises [mit-**trop**-oh-liss] *noun* chief city of a country or region

metropolitan *adjective* of a metropolis

mettle *noun* **on your mettle** ready to do something as well as you can in a test or challenge

mew *noun* **1** cry of a cat ▷ *verb* **2** to utter this cry

Mexican *adjective* **1** of Mexico ▷ *noun* **2** person from Mexico

mg *symbol* milligram(s)

miasma miasmas or miasmata [mee-**azz**-ma] *noun* unwholesome or foreboding atmosphere

mice *noun* plural of **mouse**

micro- *prefix* very small

microchip *noun* small wafer of silicon containing electronic circuits

microphone *noun* instrument for amplifying or transmitting sounds

microprocessor *noun* integrated circuit acting as the central processing unit in a small computer

microscope *noun* instrument with lens(es) that produces a magnified image of a very small object

microscopic *adjective* very small

microwave *noun*
1 electromagnetic wave with a wavelength of a few centimetres, used in radar and cooking
2 microwave oven ▷ *verb* **3** to cook (food) in a microwave oven

mid- *prefix* middle: *mid-Atlantic; the mid-70s*

midday *noun* noon

middle *adjective* **1** equally distant from two extremes **2** medium, intermediate ▷ *noun* **3** middle point or part

middle age *noun* period of life between about 40 and 60 years old > **middle-aged** *adjective* aged between about 40 and 60 years old

Middle Ages *plural noun* period from about 1000 AD to the 15th century

middle class *noun* social class of business and professional people > **middle-class** *adjective* belonging to the middle class

Middle East *noun* area around the eastern Mediterranean up to and including Iran

Middle English *noun* the form of the English language that existed from about 1100 AD until about 1450 AD

middle-of-the-road *adjective* (of opinions) moderate

middle school *noun* in England and Wales, a school for children aged between about 8 and 12

middling *adjective* of average quality or ability

midge *noun* small mosquito-like insect

midget *noun* very small person or thing

midnight *noun* twelve o'clock at night

midriff *noun* middle part of the body

midst *noun* **in the midst of** in the middle of

midsummer *adjective* of or relating to the period in the middle of summer

midway *adverb* halfway

midwife midwives *noun* trained nurse who assists at childbirth > **midwifery** *noun* work of a midwife

might *verb* **1** past tense of **may**: *I might stay a while; You might like to go and see it* ▷ *noun* **2** (*literary*) power or strength

mightily *adverb* (*old-fashioned*) to a great degree or extent

mighty mightier, mightiest *adjective* (*literary*) powerful or strong

migraine [*mee*-grain] *noun* severe headache, often with nausea and visual disturbances

migrate *verb* **1** to move from one place to settle in another **2** (of animals) to move at a particular season to a different place > **migration** *noun*: *the migration of Soviet Jews to Israel* > **migratory** *adjective* (of an animal) migrating every year

mike *noun* (*informal*) microphone

mild *adjective* **1** not strongly flavoured **2** gentle **3** calm or temperate > **mildly** *adverb*: *to put it mildly*

mildew *noun* destructive fungus on plants or things exposed to damp

mile *noun* unit of length equal to 1760 yards or 1.609 kilometres

mileage *noun* **1** distance travelled in miles **2** miles travelled by a motor vehicle per gallon of petrol **3** (*informal*) usefulness of something

militant *adjective* **1** aggressive or vigorous in support of a cause ▷ *noun* **2** person who tries to bring about extreme political or social change > **militancy** *noun: the rise of trade-union militancy*

military *adjective* **1** of or for soldiers, armies or war ▷ *noun* **2** armed services > **militarily** *adverb*

militia [mill-**ish**-a] *noun* military force of trained citizens for use in emergency only

milk *noun* **1** white fluid produced by female mammals to feed their young **2** milk of cows, goats, etc, used by humans as food ▷ *verb* **3** to draw milk from the udders of (a cow or goat) **4** to exploit (a person or situation)

milk teeth *noun* first set of teeth in young children

milky *adjective* milkier, milkiest **1** pale creamy white **2** containing a lot of milk

Milky Way *noun* luminous band of stars stretching across the night sky

mill *noun* **1** building where grain is crushed to make flour **2** factory for making materials such as steel, wool or cotton **3** small device for grinding coffee or spices into powder

millennium millennia or millenniums *noun* period of a thousand years

miller *noun* person who works in a mill

milligram *noun* thousandth of a gram

millilitre *noun* thousandth of a litre

millimetre *noun* thousandth part of a metre

million *adjective, noun* **1** one thousand thousands; 1,000,000 **2** millions large but unspecified number; lots > **millionth** *adjective, noun: the millionth truck; a millionth of a second*

millionaire *noun* person who owns at least a million pounds, dollars, etc

millstone *noun* **millstone round your neck** unpleasant problem or responsibility that you cannot escape from

mime *noun* **1** acting without the use of words ▷ *verb* **2** to describe or express (something) in mime

mimic mimics, mimicking, mimicked *verb* **1** to imitate (a person or manner), especially in an amusing way ▷ *noun* **2** person who is good at mimicking > **mimicry** *noun* action of mimicking someone

minaret *noun* tall slender tower of a mosque

mince *verb* **1** to cut or grind (meat) into very small pieces **2** to walk in an affected manner ▷ *noun* **3** minced meat

mind *noun* **1** ability to think **2** memory or attention **3 change your mind** to change a decision that you have made ▷ *verb* **4** to take offence at (something) **5** to take care of (a child or an object)

mindful *adjective* (followed by *of*) heedful of (something)

mindless *adjective* stupid and destructive

mine *pronoun* **1** belonging to me ▷ *noun* **2** deep hole for digging out coal, ores, etc **3** bomb placed under the ground or in water ▷ *verb* **4** to dig (minerals) from a mine > **miner** *noun* person who works in a mine > **mining** *noun*: traditional industries such as coal mining

minefield *noun* area of land or water containing mines

mineral *noun* (D&T) naturally occurring inorganic substance, such as metal

mineral water *noun* water that comes from a natural spring

minestrone [min-ness-**strone**-ee] *noun* soup containing vegetables and pasta

minesweeper *noun* ship for clearing away mines

mingle *verb* to mix or blend

mini- *prefix* smaller or less important: *a TV mini-series*

miniature *noun* **1** small portrait, model or copy ▷ *adjective* **2** small-scale

minibus *noun* small bus

minim *noun* (MUSIC) musical note half the length of a semibreve. In the United States and Canada, a minim is known as a half note

minimal *adjective* minimum > **minimally** *adverb* to the minimum degree

minimize or **minimise** *verb* to reduce (something) to a minimum

minimum *adjective, noun* least possible (amount or number)

minister *noun* **1** head of a government department **2** (in a Protestant church) member of the clergy

ministerial *adjective* of a government minister

ministry ministries *noun* **1** ministers collectively **2** government department

mink *noun* **1** stoatlike animal **2** its highly valued fur

minnow *noun* very small freshwater fish

minor *adjective* **1** lesser **2** (MUSIC) (*Music*) (of a scale) having a semitone between the second and third notes ▷ *noun* **3** person regarded legally as a child

minority minorities *noun* **1** lesser number **2** group in a minority in any state

minstrel *noun* medieval singer or musician

mint *noun* **1** herb used for flavouring in cooking **2** peppermint-flavoured sweet **3** place where money is coined ▷ *verb* **4** to make (coins) ▷ *adjective* **5** in mint condition in very good condition, like new

minus (MATHS) *preposition* **1** indicating subtraction ▷ *adjective* **2** less than zero ▷ *noun* **3** sign (-) denoting subtraction or a number less than zero

minuscule [min-niss-skyool] *adjective* very small indeed

minute[1] [min-it] *noun* **1** 60th part of an hour or degree **2** moment **3** minutes record of the proceedings of a meeting ▷ *verb* **4** to write the official notes of (a meeting)

minute[2] [my-**newt**] *adjective* extremely small > **minutely** *adverb* in great detail

minutiae [my-**new**-shee-eye] *plural noun* trifling or precise details

miracle *noun* 1 RE wonderful and surprising event, believed to have been caused by God 2 any very surprising and fortunate event > **miraculous** *adjective*: *He made a miraculous recovery* > **miraculously** *adverb*

mirage [mir-**rahzh**] *noun* optical illusion, especially one caused by hot air

mire *noun* (*literary*) swampy ground or mud

mirror *noun* 1 coated glass surface for reflecting images ▷ *verb* 2 to reflect (something) in or as if in a mirror

mirth *noun* (*literary*) laughter, merriment or gaiety

mis- *prefix* wrong(ly), bad(ly)

misbehave *verb* to be naughty or behave badly > **misbehaviour** *noun* naughty or bad behaviour

miscarriage *noun* 1 spontaneous premature expulsion of a fetus from the womb 2 failure: *a miscarriage of justice*

miscellaneous [miss-**sell**-lane-ee-uss] *adjective* mixed or assorted

mischief *noun* eagerness to have fun by teasing people or playing tricks > **mischievous** *adjective* full of mischief

misconception *noun* wrong idea or belief

misconduct *noun* bad or unacceptable behaviour by a professional person

misdemeanour *noun* minor wrongdoing

miser *noun* person who hoards money and hates spending it

> **miserly** *adjective* reluctant to spend money; mean

miserable *adjective* 1 very unhappy and sad; dejected 2 causing misery > **miserably** *adverb*

misery *noun* miseries *noun* great unhappiness

misfire *verb* (of a plan) to fail to turn out as intended

misfit *noun* person not suited to his or her social environment

misfortune *noun* piece of bad luck

misgiving *noun* feeling of fear or doubt

misguided *adjective* mistaken or unwise

misinform *verb* to give incorrect information to (someone) > **misinformation** *noun* incorrect information

misinterpret *verb* to make an incorrect interpretation of

misjudge *verb* to judge (someone or something) wrongly or unfairly

mislay mislays, mislaying, mislaid *verb* to lose (something) temporarily

mislead misleads, misleading, misled *verb* to give false or confusing information to (someone)

misplaced *adjective* (of a feeling) inappropriate or directed at the wrong thing or person: *misplaced loyalty*

misprint *noun* printing error

misrepresent *verb* to represent (someone) wrongly or inaccurately > **misrepresentation** *noun*: *misrepresentation of the facts*

miss *verb* 1 to fail to notice, hear, hit, reach, find or catch (something) **2** not to be in time for (a bus, train or plane) **3** to notice or regret the absence of (someone or something) **4** to fail to take advantage of (a chance or opportunity) ▷ noun **5** fact or instance of missing

missile noun object or weapon thrown, shot or launched at a target

mission noun **1** specific task or duty **2** group of people sent on a mission **3** journey made by a military aeroplane or space rocket to carry out a task **4** building in which missionaries work

missionary missionaries noun person sent abroad to do religious and social work

missive noun (old-fashioned) letter

mist noun **1** thin fog ▷ verb **2** (of eyes) to become blurred with tears **3** (followed by up, over) (of a glass) to become opaque because covered with condensation

mistake mistakes, mistaking, mistook, mistaken noun **1** error or blunder ▷ verb **2** to confuse (a person or thing) with another

mistaken adjective **1** (of a person) wrong: I was mistaken about you **2** (of a belief or opinion) incorrect >**mistakenly** adverb incorrectly

Mister noun polite form of address to a man

mistletoe noun evergreen plant with white berries growing as a parasite on trees, used as a Christmas decoration

mistook verb past of **mistake**

mistreat verb to treat (a person or animal) badly

mistress noun **1** woman who has a continuing sexual relationship

with a married man **2** female employer of a servant **3** female teacher

mistrust verb **1** to have doubts or suspicions about (someone) ▷ noun **2** lack of trust

misty mistier, mistiest adjective full of or covered with mist

misunderstand misunderstands, misunderstanding, misunderstood verb to fail to understand (someone) properly >**misunderstanding** noun slight quarrel or disagreement

misuse noun **1** incorrect, improper or careless use ▷ verb **2** to use (something) wrongly

mite noun very tiny creature that lives in the fur of animals

mitigating adjective (formal) (of circumstances) making a crime easier to understand or justify

mitten noun glove with one section for the thumb and one for the four fingers together

mix verb to combine or blend (things) into one mass >**mix up** verb to confuse (two things or people)

mixed adjective **1** consisting of several things of the same general kind **2** involving people from two or more different races: mixed marriages **3** (of education or accommodation) for both males and females

mixed up adjective **1** confused **2** (followed by in) involved in (a crime or a scandal)

mixer noun machine used for mixing things together

mixture noun **1** several different things mixed together **2** substance consisting of other substances that have been stirred or shaken together

mix-up noun mistake in something that was planned

ml symbol millilitre(s)

mm symbol millimetre(s)

moa noun large extinct flightless New Zealand bird

moan noun 1 low cry of pain 2 (informal) grumble ▷ verb 3 to make a low cry of pain 4 (informal) to grumble

moat noun deep wide ditch, especially round a castle

mob mobs, mobbing, mobbed noun 1 disorderly crowd ▷ verb 2 to surround (someone) in a disorderly crowd

mobile adjective 1 able to move or be moved freely and easily: a mobile library 2 [PE] able to travel or move about from one place to another ▷ noun 3 same as **mobile phone** 4 hanging structure designed to move in air currents > **mobility** noun condition of being mobile

mobile phone noun cordless phone powered by batteries

moccasin noun soft leather shoe

mock verb 1 to make fun of, mimic or ridicule (someone) ▷ adjective 2 sham or imitation 3 (of an examination) done as a practice before the real examination

mockery noun expression of scorn or ridicule

mode noun 1 method or manner 2 (Maths) biggest in a set of groups

model models, modelling, modelled noun 1 (miniature) representation 2 pattern 3 person or thing worthy of imitation 4 person who poses

for an artist or photographer 5 person who wears clothes to display them to prospective buyers ▷ adjective 6 denoting a (miniature) representation of something 7 excellent: a model pupil ▷ verb 8 to display (clothes) by wearing them 9 to make (shapes or figures) out of clay or wood 10 **model yourself on** to copy the behaviour of (someone that you admire)

modem [mode-em] noun [ICT] device for connecting two computers by a telephone line

moderate adjective 1 not extreme 2 average ▷ noun 3 person of moderate views ▷ verb 4 to become less violent or extreme or make (something) less violent or extreme > **moderately** adverb > **moderation** noun: a man of fairness and moderation

modern adjective 1 of present or recent times 2 up-to-date > **modernity** noun: the clash between tradition and modernity

modernize or **modernise** verb to bring (something) up to date

modest adjective 1 not vain or boastful 2 quite small in size or amount 3 shy and easily embarrassed > **modestly** adverb in a modest manner > **modesty** noun quality of being modest

modify modifies, modifying, modified verb to change (something) slightly in order to improve it > **modification** noun small change made to improve something

module noun 1 one of the parts that when put together form a whole unit or object 2 [ICT] part

a b c d e f g h i j k l m n o p q r s t u v w x y z

of a machine or system that
does a particular task **3** part of
a spacecraft that can do certain
things away from the main body
>**modular** adjective: the course is
modular in structure

mohair noun very soft, fluffy wool
obtained from angora goats

moist adjective slightly wet

moisten verb to make
(something) moist

moisture noun tiny drops of water
in the air or on the ground

molar noun large back tooth used
for grinding

mole noun **1** small dark raised spot
on the skin **2** small burrowing
animal with black fur **3** (informal)
member of an organization who
is working as a spy for a rival
organization

molecule [**mol**-lik-kyool] noun the
smallest amount of a substance
that can exist >**molecular**
[mol-**lek**-yew-lar] adjective: the
molecular structure of fuel

molest verb to touch (a child) in
a sexual way >**molester** noun: a
child molester

mollify mollifies, mollifying,
mollified verb to make (someone)
less upset or angry

mollusc noun soft-bodied, usually
hard-shelled, animal, such as a
snail or oyster

molten adjective liquefied or melted

moment noun **1** very short space
of time; second **2** point in time
3 at the moment now

momentary adjective lasting only
a moment >**momentarily** adverb

WORD TIP
Some Americans say
momentarily when they mean

'very soon', rather than 'for a
moment'

momentous [moh-**men**-tuss]
adjective of great significance

momentum noun **1** ability to
keep developing: the campaign is
gaining momentum **2** impetus of a
moving body

monarch noun sovereign ruler
of a state

monarchy monarchies noun
government by or a state ruled by
a sovereign

monastery monasteries noun
residence of a community of
monks >**monastic** adjective of
monks, nuns or monasteries

Monday noun day between
Sunday and Tuesday

money noun medium of exchange,
coins or banknotes

mongrel noun dog of mixed breed

monitor noun **1** person or device
that checks, controls, warns or
keeps a record of something **2** ICT
visual display unit of a computer
3 (Brit, Aust, NZ) pupil assisting a
teacher with duties >verb **4** to
watch and check on (something)

monk noun member of an all-male
religious community bound
by vows

monkey noun animal that has a
long tail and climbs trees

mono- prefix single: monosyllable

monocle noun eyeglass for one
eye only

monogamy noun custom of being
married to one person at a time
>**monogamous** adjective being
married to one person at a time

monologue noun long speech
by one person during a play or a
conversation

monopoly monopolies *noun* exclusive possession of or right to do something

monotone *noun* unvaried pitch in speech or sound

monotonous *adjective* tedious due to lack of variety
> **monotony** *noun*: to break the monotony

monotreme *noun* Australian mammal with a single opening in its body for the passage of eggs, sperm, faeces and urine

monounsaturated *adjective* (of an oil) made mainly from vegetable fat
> **monounsaturate** *noun*

monsoon *noun* season of very heavy rain in South-east Asia

monster *noun* **1** large imaginary frightening beast **2** very wicked person ▷ *adjective* **3** huge

monstrosity monstrosities *noun* large ugly thing

monstrous *adjective* extremely shocking or unfair
> **monstrously** *adverb*

montage [mon-tahzh] *noun* picture or film consisting of a combination of several different items arranged to produce an unusual effect

month *noun* one of the twelve divisions of the calendar year

monthly monthlies *adjective* happening or payable once a month

monument *noun* something, especially a building or statue, that commemorates something

monumental *adjective* **1** (of a building or sculpture) very large and important **2** very large or extreme

moo *verb* to make the long deep cry of a cow

mood *noun* temporary (gloomy) state of mind

moody moodier, moodiest *adjective* **1** sullen or gloomy **2** changeable in mood

moon *noun* natural satellite of the earth

moonlight moonlights, moonlighting, moonlighted *noun* **1** light from the moon ▷ *verb* **2** (*informal*) to work at a secondary job, especially illegally

moor *noun* **1** high area of open land ▷ *verb* **2** to secure (a ship) with ropes etc

mooring *noun* place for mooring a ship

moose *noun* large N American deer

WORD TIP
The plural of *moose* is *moose*

moot *verb* to bring (something) up for discussion

mop mops, mopping, mopped *noun* **1** long stick with twists of cotton or a sponge on the end, used for washing floors **2** thick mass of hair ▷ *verb* **3** to clean (a surface) with or as if with a mop

mope *verb* to feel miserable and not interested in anything

moped *noun* type of small motorcycle

mopoke *noun* small spotted owl found in Australia and New Zealand

moral *adjective* **1** concerned with right and wrong conduct ▷ *noun* **2** lesson to be obtained from a story or event **3** RE **morals** values based on beliefs about the correct and acceptable way to behave > **morality** *noun* **1** good moral conduct **2** moral goodness or badness ▷ **morally** adverb

morale [mor-**rahl**] noun degree of confidence or hope of a person or group

morbid adjective unduly interested in death or unpleasant events

more adjective **1** greater in amount or degree **2** comparative of **much, many 3** additional or further ▷ adverb **4** to a greater extent **5** in addition ▷ pronoun **6** greater or additional amount or number

moreover adverb in addition to what has already been said

morepork noun (NZ) same as **mopoke**

morgue noun building where dead bodies are kept before being buried or cremated

moribund adjective without force or vitality

morning noun **1** part of the day before noon **2** part of the day between midnight and noon

Moroccan [mor-**rok**-an] adjective **1** of Morocco ▷ noun **2** person from Morocco

moron noun (informal) foolish or stupid person ▷ **moronic** adjective: moronic vandalism

morose [mor-**rohss**] adjective sullen or moody

morphine noun drug extracted from opium, used as an anaesthetic and sedative

Morse or **Morse code** noun code used for sending messages in which each letter is represented by a series of dots and dashes

morsel noun small piece of food

mortal adjective **1** unable to live forever **2** (of a wound) causing death ▷ noun **3** human being

mortality noun **1** state of being mortal **2** great loss of life **3** death rate

mortar noun **1** small cannon with a short range **2** mixture of lime, sand and water for holding bricks and stones together

mortgage noun **1** loan from a bank or a building society to buy a house ▷ verb **2** to use (one's house) as a guarantee to a company in order to borrow money from them

mortifying adjective embarrassing or humiliating

mortuary mortuaries noun building where corpses are kept before burial or cremation

mosaic [mow-**zay**-ik] noun design or decoration using small pieces of coloured stone or glass

Moslem noun, adjective same as **Muslim**

mosque noun Muslim temple

mosquito mosquitoes or mosquitos noun blood-sucking flying insect

moss noun small flowerless plant growing in masses on moist surfaces ▷ **mossy** adjective: a mossy wall

most noun **1** greatest number or degree ▷ adjective **2** greatest in number or degree **3** superlative of **much, many** ▷ adverb **4** in the greatest degree

mostly adverb for the most part, generally

MOT noun (in Britain) compulsory annual test of the roadworthiness of vehicles over a certain age

motel noun roadside hotel for motorists

moth *noun* insect like a butterfly which usually flies at night

mother *noun* **1** female parent ▷ *verb* **2** to look after (someone) as a mother

motherhood *noun* state of being a mother

mother-in-law mothers-in-law *noun* mother of your husband or wife

motif [moh-**teef**] *noun* (recurring) theme or design

motion *noun* **1** process, action or way of moving **2** action or gesture **3** proposal in a meeting ▷ *verb* **4** to direct (someone) by gesture

motionless *adjective* not moving

motivate *verb* **1** to inspire (someone) to behave in a particular way **2** to make (someone) feel determined to do something > **motivated** *adjective*: highly motivated employees > **motivation** *noun*: his lack of motivation at work

motive *noun* HISTORY reason for a course of action

motley *adjective* miscellaneous

motor *noun* **1** engine, especially of a vehicle **2** machine that converts electrical energy into mechanical energy ▷ *verb* **3** to travel by car

motorboat *noun* boat with an engine

motorcycle *noun* two-wheeled vehicle with an engine that is ridden like a bicycle > **motorcyclist** *noun* person who rides a motorcycle

motoring *adjective* relating to cars and driving: a motoring correspondent

motorist *noun* person who drives a car

motorway *noun* main road for fast-moving traffic

mottled *adjective* marked with blotches

motto mottoes or mottos *noun* saying expressing an ideal or rule of conduct

mould *noun* **1** hollow container in which metal etc is cast **2** fungal growth caused by dampness ▷ *verb* **3** to shape (a substance) **4** to influence or direct (someone or something) > **mouldy** *adjective* covered with mould

moult *verb* to shed feathers, hair or skin to make way for new growth

mound *noun* **1** heap, especially of earth or stones **2** small hill

mount *verb* **1** to climb or ascend (something) **2** to get up on (a horse etc) **3** to increase or accumulate **4** to fix (an object) in a particular place to display it **5** to organize (a campaign or event) ▷ *noun* **6** mountain

mountain *noun* **1** hill of great size **2** large heap

mountaineer *noun* person who climbs mountains

mountainous *adjective* full of mountains

mourn *verb* to feel or express sorrow for (a dead person or lost thing)

mourner *noun* person attending a funeral

mournful *adjective* sad or dismal

mourning *noun* conventional symbols of grief for death, such as the wearing of black

mouse mice *noun* **1** small long-tailed rodent **2** (Computers) hand-held device for moving the cursor without keying

a
b
c
d
e
f
g
h
i
j
k
l
m
n
o
p
q
r
s
t
u
v
w
x
y
z

mousse noun dish of flavoured cream, whipped and set

moustache noun hair on a man's upper lip

mouth noun **1** opening in the head for eating and issuing sounds **2** entrance to a cave or a hole **3** point where a river enters the sea ▷ verb **1** to form (words) with the lips without speaking

mouthpiece noun **1** part of a telephone into which a person speaks **2** part of a wind instrument into which the player blows **3** spokesperson

movable or **moveable** adjective able to be moved from one place to another

move verb **1** to change in place or position **2** to change the place or position of (something) **3** to change (one's house etc) **4** to stir the emotions of (someone) **5** to suggest (a proposal) formally ▷ noun **6** moving **7** act of putting a piece or counter in a game in a different position: It's your move next

movement noun **1** [DRAMA] action or process of moving **2** group with a common aim: the peace movement **3** division of a piece of classical music **4** movements (formal) everything that you do during a period of time

moving adjective causing you to feel deep sadness or emotion ▷ movingly adverb

mow mows, mowing, mowed, mown verb to cut (grass or crops) ▷ mow down verb to kill (people) in large numbers ▷ mower noun machine for cutting grass

MP abbreviation Member of Parliament

MP3 player noun device that plays audio or video files, often used for listening to music downloaded from the internet

mpg abbreviation miles per gallon

mph abbreviation miles per hour

Mr title used before a man's name

Mrs title used before a married woman's name

Ms [mizz] title used instead of Miss or Mrs

MSP abbreviation (in Britain) Member of the Scottish Parliament

much adjective **1** large amount or degree of ▷ noun **2** large amount or degree ▷ adverb **3** to a great degree **4** often: He didn't talk much about the war

muck noun **1** (informal) dirt, filth **2** manure ▷ **muck about** verb (informal) to behave stupidly and waste time ▷ **mucky** adjective (informal) very dirty

mucus [mew-kuss] noun liquid produced in parts of the body, e.g. the nose

mud noun wet soft earth

muddle verb **1** to confuse (someone) **2** to mix (things) up ▷ noun **3** state of confusion

muddy muddier, muddiest adjective **1** covered in mud **2** (of a colour) dull and not clear

muesli [mewz-lee] noun mixture of grain, nuts and dried fruit, eaten with milk

muffin noun a small round cake eaten hot

muffled adjective (of a sound) quiet or difficult to hear: a muffled explosion

mug mugs, mugging, mugged noun 1 large drinking cup 2 (informal) gullible person ▷ verb 3 (informal) to attack and rob (someone) > **mugger** noun person who attacks and robs someone > **mugging** noun act of attacking and robbing someone

muggy muggier, muggiest adjective (of weather) unpleasantly warm and damp

mule noun offspring of a horse and a donkey

mulga noun 1 Australian acacia shrub growing in desert regions 2 (Aust informal) the outback

WORD TIP
The plural of mulga is mulga

mull verb **mull over** to think (something) over or ponder (something)

mullet noun common edible fish found in Australian and New Zealand waters

mulloway noun large edible fish found in Australian waters

multi- prefix many: multicultural; multistorey

multimedia noun 1 ICT (Computing) sound, pictures, film and ordinary text used to convey information 2 TV, computers and books used as teaching aids

multinational adjective very large company with branches in many countries

multiple adjective 1 having many parts ▷ noun 2 quantity which contains another an exact number of times

multiple sclerosis [skler-**roe**-siss] noun serious disease that attacks the nervous system, affecting the ability to move

multiplication noun 1 MATHS process of multiplying one number by another 2 large increase in number

multiplicity noun large number or great variety

multiply multiplies, multiplying, multiplied verb 1 to increase in number, quantity or degree 2 MATHS to add (a number or quantity) to itself a given number of times

multitude noun (formal) very large number of people or things

mum noun (informal) mother

mumble verb to speak indistinctly, mutter

mummy mummies noun 1 child's word for **mother** 2 body embalmed and wrapped for burial in ancient Egypt

mumps noun infectious disease with swelling in the glands of the neck

munch verb to chew (food) noisily and steadily

mundane adjective very ordinary and not interesting or unusual

municipal adjective relating to a city or town

munitions plural noun military stores

mural noun picture painted on a wall

murder noun 1 unlawful intentional killing of a human being ▷ verb 2 to kill (someone) in this way > **murderer** noun person who has murdered someone > **murderous** adjective 1 likely to murder someone 2 (of an attack or other action) resulting in the death of many people

murky murkier, murkiest *adjective* dark or gloomy

murmur *verb* **1** to speak in a quiet indistinct way ▷ *noun* **2** something that someone says that can hardly be heard

muscle *noun* PE tissue in the body which produces movement by contracting > **muscle in on** *verb* (*informal*) to force your way into (a situation in which one is not welcome)

muscular *adjective* **1** with well-developed muscles **2** of muscles

muse *verb* (*literary*) to think about something for a long time

museum *noun* building where natural, artistic, historical or scientific objects are exhibited and preserved

mush *noun* soft pulpy mass

mushroom *noun* **1** edible fungus with a stem and cap ▷ *verb* **2** to grow rapidly

mushy mushier, mushiest *adjective* **1** (of a fruit or vegetable) too soft **2** (*informal*) (of a story) too sentimental

music *noun* **1** art form using a melodious and harmonious combination of notes **2** written or printed form of this

musical *adjective* **1** of or like music **2** talented in or fond of music ▷ *noun* **3** play or film with songs and dancing > **musically** *adverb*

musician *noun* MUSIC person who plays a musical instrument

musk *noun* scent obtained from a gland of the musk deer or produced synthetically > **musky** *adjective* (of a smell) strong, warm and sweet

musket *noun* (*History*) long-barrelled gun

Muslim or **Moslem** *noun* RE **1** follower of the religion of Islam ▷ *adjective* **2** of or relating to Islam

muslin *noun* fine cotton fabric

mussel *noun* edible shellfish with a dark hinged shell

must *verb* **1** used as an auxiliary to express obligation, certainty or resolution ▷ *noun* **2** essential or necessary thing

mustard *noun* paste made from the powdered seeds of a plant, used as a condiment

muster *verb* to gather together (energy, support, etc)

musty mustier, mustiest *adjective* smelling mouldy and stale

mutate *verb* to change and develop in a new way, especially genetically > **mutant** *noun, adjective*: *New species are merely mutants of earlier ones; mutant genes*

mute *adjective* (*formal*) not giving out sound or speech

muted *adjective* **1** (of sound or colour) softened **2** (of a reaction) subdued

muti [**moo**-ti] *noun* (*S Afr informal*) medicine, especially herbal medicine

mutilate [**mew**-till-ate] *verb* **1** to deprive (something) of a limb or other part **2** to damage (a book or text) > **mutilation** *noun*: *cases of torture and mutilation*

mutiny mutinies, mutinying, mutinied [**mew**-tin-ee] *noun* **1** rebellion against authority, especially by soldiers or sailors ▷ *verb* **2** to commit mutiny

mutter verb **1** to speak indistinctly **2** to grumble

mutton noun flesh of a sheep, used as food

mutton bird noun **1** (Aust) sea bird with dark plumage **2** (NZ) any of a number of migratory sea birds, the young of which are a Māori delicacy

mutual [mew-chew-al] adjective **1** felt or expressed by each of two people about the other **2** common to both or all ▷ **mutually** adverb: a mutually supportive relationship

> **WORD TIP**
> It used to be that mutual could only be used of something that was shared between two people or groups. Nowadays you can use it to mean 'shared between two or more people or groups'

muzzle noun **1** animal's mouth and nose **2** cover for a dog's muzzle to prevent biting **3** open end of a gun ▷ verb **4** to put a muzzle on (a dog)

my adjective belonging to me

mynah bird noun tropical bird that can mimic human speech

myriad [mir-ree-ad] adjective **1** very many ▷ noun **2** large indefinite number

myrrh [mur] noun fragrant substance used in perfume and incense

myself pronoun emphatic or reflexive form of I, me

mysterious adjective **1** strange and not well understood **2** secretive ▷ **mysteriously** adverb

mystery mysteries noun something that is not understood or known about

mystic noun **1** person who seeks spiritual knowledge ▷ adjective **2** mystical ▷ **mystical** adjective having a spiritual or religious significance beyond human understanding ▷ **mysticism** noun religious practice in which people search for truth and closeness to God through meditation and prayer

mystify verb mystifies, mystifying, mystified to bewilder or puzzle (someone)

mystique [miss-steek] noun atmosphere of mystery or power

myth noun **1** ENGLISH tale with supernatural characters, usually of how the world and humankind began **2** untrue idea or explanation

mythical adjective imaginary, untrue or existing only in myths

mythology noun myths collectively ▷ **mythological** adjective: a mythological beast

n

naartjie [nahr-chee] *noun* (*S Afr*) tangerine

nag nags, nagging, nagged *verb* **1** to scold or find fault constantly **2** to be a constant source of discomfort or worry to ▷ *noun* **3** person who nags >**nagging** *adjective, noun*

nail *noun* **1** pointed piece of metal with a head, hit with a hammer to join two objects together **2** hard covering of the upper tips of the fingers and toes **3** **hit the nail on the head** to say something exactly correct ▷ *verb* **4** to attach (something) with nails **5** (*informal*) to catch or arrest

naive or **naïve** [nye-eev] *adjective* **1** innocent and easily fooled **2** simple and unsophisticated >**naively** *adverb* >**naivety** or **naïveté** [nye-**eev**-tee] *noun*

naked *adjective* **1** without clothes **2** without any covering **3** **the naked eye** the eye unassisted by binoculars, telescope, etc >**nakedness** *noun*

name *noun* **1** word by which a person or thing is known **2** reputation, especially a good one **3** **call someone names** to use insulting words to describe him or her ▷ *verb* **4** to give a name to **5** to refer to (someone or something) by name **6** to fix or specify

nameless *adjective* **1** without a name **2** unspecified **3** too horrible to be mentioned

namely *adverb* that is to say

namesake *noun* person with the same name as another

nanny nannies *noun* woman whose job is looking after young children

nap naps, napping, napped *noun* **1** short sleep ▷ *verb* **2** to have a short sleep

nape *noun* back of the neck

napkin *noun* piece of cloth or paper for wiping the mouth or protecting the clothes while eating

nappy nappies *noun* piece of absorbent material fastened round a baby's bottom to absorb urine and faeces

narcotic *noun, adjective* (of) a drug, such as morphine or opium, designed to produce numbness and drowsiness

narrate *verb* **1** to tell (a story) **2** to speak words that accompany and explain what is happening in a film or TV programme >**narration** *noun*

narrative *noun* account, story

narrator *noun* **1** a person who tells a story **2** a person who speaks the words accompanying and explaining a film or TV programme

narrow *adjective* **1** small in breadth in comparison to length **2** limited in range, extent or outlook **3** with little margin: *a narrow escape* ▷ *verb* **4** to make or become narrow **5** (often followed by *down*) to limit or restrict > **narrowly** adverb > **narrowness** noun > **narrows** plural noun narrow part of a strait, river or current

narrow-minded adjective intolerant or bigoted

nasal adjective 1 of the nose 2 (of a sound) pronounced with air passing through the nose > **nasally** adverb

nasty nastier, nastiest adjective 1 unpleasant 2 (of an injury) dangerous or painful 3 spiteful or unkind > **nastily** adverb > **nastiness** noun

nation noun people of one or more cultures or races organized as a single state

national adjective 1 typical of a particular nation > noun 2 citizen of a nation > **nationally** adverb

national anthem noun official song of a country

nationalism noun 1 policy of national independence 2 patriotism, sometimes to an excessive degree > **nationalist** noun, adjective > **nationalistic** adjective

nationality nationalities noun 1 fact of being a citizen of a particular nation 2 group of people of the same race

nationalize or **nationalise** verb to put (an industry or a company) under state control > **nationalization** noun

National Party noun major political party in Australia and New Zealand

national service noun compulsory military service

nationwide adjective, adverb happening all over a country

native adjective 1 relating to a place where a person was born 2 born in a specified place 3 (followed by to) originating (in) 4 inborn ▷ noun 5 person born in a specified place 6 indigenous animal or plant 7 member of the original race of a country

Nativity noun (Christianity) birth of Jesus Christ

natter (informal) verb 1 to talk idly or chatter ▷ noun 2 long idle chat

natural adjective 1 normal or to be expected 2 genuine or spontaneous 3 of, according to, existing in or produced by nature 4 not created by human beings 5 not synthetic ▷ noun 6 person with an inborn talent or skill > **naturally** adverb 1 of course 2 in a natural or normal way 3 instinctively

nature noun 1 whole system of the existence, forces and events of the physical world that are not controlled by human beings 2 fundamental or essential qualities 3 kind or sort

naughty naughtier, naughtiest adjective 1 disobedient or mischievous 2 mildly indecent > **naughtily** adverb > **naughtiness** noun

nausea [naw-zee-a] noun feeling of being about to vomit > **nauseous** adjective 1 as if about to vomit 2 sickening

nautical adjective of the sea or ships

naval adjective of or relating to a navy or ships

navel noun hollow in the middle of the abdomen where the umbilical cord was attached

navigate verb **1** to direct or plot the path or position of a ship, aircraft or car **2** to travel over or through ▷ **navigation** noun > **navigator** noun

navy navies noun **1** branch of a country's armed services that fights at sea **2** warships of a nation ▷ adjective **3** very dark blue (also **navy-blue**)

Nazi noun **1** member of the fascist National Socialist Party, which held power in Germany under Adolf Hitler ▷ adjective **2** of or relating to the Nazis > **Nazism** noun

NB abbreviation note well

near preposition, adverb, adjective **1** indicating a place or time not far away ▷ adjective **2** almost being the thing specified: a near disaster ▷ verb **3** to draw close (to) > **nearness** noun

nearby adjective not far away

nearly adverb almost

neat adjective **1** tidy and clean **2** smoothly or competently done **3** undiluted > **neatly** adverb > **neatness** noun

necessarily adverb inevitably or certainly

necessary adjective **1** needed to achieve the desired result: the necessary skills **2** certain or unavoidable: the necessary consequences

necessity necessities noun **1** circumstances that inevitably require a certain result **2** something needed

neck noun **1** part of the body joining the head to the shoulders **2** part of a garment round the neck **3** long narrow part of a bottle or violin ▷ verb **4** (informal) to kiss and cuddle

necklace noun **1** decorative piece of jewellery worn around the neck **2** (S Afr) burning petrol-filled tyre placed round someone's neck to kill him or her

nectar noun **1** sweet liquid collected from flowers by bees **2** drink of the gods

nectarine noun smooth-skinned peach

née [nay] preposition indicating the surname that a woman had before marrying

need verb **1** to require or be in want of **2** to be obliged (to do something) ▷ noun **3** condition of lacking something **4** requirement or necessity **5** poverty

needle noun **1** thin pointed piece of metal with an eye through which thread is passed for sewing **2** long pointed rod used in knitting **3** pointed part of a hypodermic syringe **4** small pointed part in a record player that touches the record and picks up the sound signals, stylus **5** pointer on a measuring instrument or compass **6** long narrow stiff leaf ▷ verb **7** (informal) to goad or provoke

needless adjective unnecessary > **needlessly** adverb

needy needier, neediest adjective poor and in need of financial support

negative adjective **1** expressing a denial or refusal **2** lacking positive qualities **3** (of an electrical charge) having the same electrical charge as an electron ▷ noun **4** negative word or statement

5 (*Photography*) image with a reversal of tones or colours from which positive prints are made > **negatively** *adverb*

neglect *verb* **1** to take no care of **2** to fail (to do something) through carelessness **3** to disregard ▷ *noun* **4** neglecting or being neglected > **neglectful** *adjective*

negligent *adjective* neglectful or careless > **negligence** *noun* > **negligently** *adverb*

negligible *adjective* very small or unimportant

negotiable *adjective* able to be negotiated

negotiate *verb* **1** to discuss in order to reach (an agreement) **2** to succeed in passing round or over (a place or problem) > **negotiation** *noun* > **negotiator** *noun*

Negro Negroes *noun* (*old-fashioned*) member of any of the Black peoples originating in Africa

neigh *noun* **1** loud high-pitched sound made by a horse ▷ *verb* **2** to make this sound

neighbour *noun* person who lives or is situated near another

neighbourhood *noun* **1** district **2** surroundings **3** people of a district

neighbouring *adjective* situated nearby

neither *adjective, pronoun* **1** not one nor the other ▷ *conjunction* **2** not

neo- *prefix* new, recent or a modern form of: *neoclassicism*

nephew *noun* son of your brother or sister

Neptune *noun* eighth planet from the sun in the solar system

nerve *noun* **1** cordlike bundle of fibres that conducts impulses between the brain and other parts of the body **2** bravery and determination **3** impudence **4** nerves **a** anxiety or tension **b** ability or inability to remain calm in a difficult situation

nerve-racking *adjective* very distressing or harrowing

nervous *adjective* **1** apprehensive or worried **2** of or relating to the nerves > **nervously** *adverb* > **nervousness** *noun*

nervous breakdown *noun* mental illness in which someone suffers from severe depression and needs psychiatric treatment

nervous system *noun* nerves, brain and spinal cord

nest *noun* **1** place or structure in which birds or certain animals lay eggs or give birth to young **2** secluded place **3** set of things of graduated sizes designed to fit together ▷ *verb* **4** to make or inhabit a nest

nestle *verb* **1** to snuggle **2** to be in a sheltered position

nestling *noun* bird too young to leave the nest

net nets, netting, netted *noun* **1** fabric of meshes of string, thread or wire with many openings **2** piece of net used to protect or hold things or to trap animals **3** internet ▷ *verb* **4** to catch (a fish or animal) in a net

netball *noun* team game in which a ball has to be thrown through a net hanging from a ring at the top of a pole

netting noun material made of net

nettle noun plant with stinging hairs on the leaves

network noun 1 system of intersecting lines, roads, etc 2 interconnecting group or system 3 group of broadcasting stations that all transmit the same programmes at the same time

neuron or **neurone** noun cell carrying nerve impulses in the nervous system

neurosis neuroses noun mental disorder producing hysteria, anxiety, depression or obsessive behaviour

neurotic adjective 1 emotionally unstable 2 suffering from neurosis ▷ noun 3 neurotic person

neuter adjective 1 (of grammatical inflections in some languages) neither masculine nor feminine ▷ verb 2 to remove the reproductive organs of (an animal)

neutral adjective 1 taking neither side in a war or dispute 2 of or belonging to a neutral party or country 3 (of a colour) not definite or striking ▷ noun 4 neutral person or nation 5 neutral gear > **neutrality** noun > **neutralize** verb 1 prevent something from working or taking effect 2 [SCIENCE] make a substance neither acid nor alkaline

neutron noun electrically neutral elementary particle of about the same mass as a proton

never adverb at no time

nevertheless adverb in spite of that

new adjective 1 not existing before 2 recently acquired 3 having lately come into some state 4 additional 5 (followed by to) unfamiliar > **newness** noun

newborn adjective recently or just born

newcomer noun recent arrival or participant

newly adverb recently: the newly arrived visitors

new moon noun moon when it appears as a narrow crescent at the beginning of its cycle

news noun 1 important or interesting new happenings 2 information about such events reported in the media

newsagent noun (Brit) shopkeeper who sells newspapers and magazines

newspaper noun weekly or daily publication containing news

newt noun small amphibious creature with a long slender body and tail

New Testament noun second main division of the Bible

New Year noun beginning of a calendar year

New Zealander noun person from New Zealand

next adjective, adverb 1 immediately following 2 nearest

next door adjective, adverb in or to the adjacent house

NHS abbreviation (in Britain) National Health Service

nib noun writing point of a pen

nibble verb 1 to take little bites (of) ▷ noun 2 little bite

nice adjective 1 pleasant 2 kind 3 good or satisfactory 4 subtle:

a nice distinction ▷ **nicely** *adverb*
▷ **niceness** *noun*

nicety *niceties noun* **1** subtle point **2** refinement or delicacy

niche [**neesh**] *noun* **1** hollow area in a wall **2** suitable position for a particular person

nick *verb* **1** to make a small cut in **2** (*Chiefly Brit informal*) to steal **3** (*Chiefly Brit informal*) to arrest ▷ *noun* **4** small cut **5** (*informal*) prison or police station

nickel *noun* (*Chemistry*) silvery-white metal often used in alloys **2** US coin worth five cents

nickname *noun* **1** familiar name given to a person or place ▷ *verb* **2** to call (someone or something) by a nickname

nicotine *noun* addictive substance found in tobacco

niece *noun* daughter of your brother or sister

nifty *adjective* (*informal*) neat or smart

Nigerian *adjective* **1** of Nigeria ▷ *noun* **2** person from Nigeria

niggle *verb* **1** to worry slightly **2** to continually find fault (with) ▷ *noun* **3** small worry or doubt

night *noun* time of darkness between sunset and sunrise

nightclub *noun* place for dancing, music, etc, open late at night

nightdress *noun* woman's loose dress worn in bed

nightfall *noun* time when it starts to get dark

nightie *noun* (*informal*) nightdress

nightingale *noun* small bird with a musical song usually heard at night

nightly *adjective* **1** happening every night ▷ *adverb* **2** every night

nightmare *noun* **1** very bad dream **2** very unpleasant experience ▷ **nightmarish** *adjective*

nil *noun* nothing, zero

nimble *adjective* **1** agile and quick **2** mentally alert or acute ▷ **nimbly** *adverb*

nine *adjective, noun* the number 9 ▷ **ninth** *adjective, noun*

nineteen *adjective, noun* the number 19 ▷ **nineteenth** *adjective, noun*

ninety *adjective, noun* the number 90 ▷ **ninetieth** *adjective, noun*

nip *nips, nipping, nipped verb* **1** (*informal*) to hurry **2** to pinch or squeeze **3** to bite lightly ▷ *noun* **4** pinch or light bite **5** sharp coldness

nipple *noun* projection in the centre of a breast

nirvana [near-**vah**-na] *noun* (*Buddhism, Hinduism*) absolute spiritual enlightenment and bliss

nit *noun* **1** egg or larva of a louse **2** (*informal*) short for **nitwit** ▷ **nitpicking** *adjective* (*informal*) too concerned with insignificant detail, especially to find fault

nitrogen [**nite**-roj-jen] *noun* (*Chemistry*) colourless odourless gas that forms four fifths of the air

nitwit *noun* (*informal*) stupid person

no *noes or nos interjection* **1** expresses denial, disagreement or refusal ▷ *adjective* **2** not any, not a ▷ *adverb* **3** not at all ▷ *noun* **4** negative answer or vote against something

no. *abbreviation* number

nobility *noun* **1** quality of being noble **2** class of people holding titles and high social rank

noble *adjective* **1** showing or having high moral qualities **2** of the nobility **3** impressive and magnificent ▷ *noun* **4** member of the nobility ▷ **nobly** *adverb*

nobleman noblemen *noun* member of the nobility ▷ **noblewoman** *noun*

nobody nobodies *pronoun* **1** no person ▷ *noun* **2** person of no importance

nocturnal *adjective* **1** of the night **2** active at night

nod nods, nodding, nodded *verb* **1** to lower and raise (one's head) briefly in agreement or greeting ▷ *noun* **2** act of nodding ▷ **nod off** *verb* (*informal*) to fall asleep

noise *noun* sound, usually a loud or disturbing kind

noisy noisier, noisiest *adjective* **1** making a lot of noise **2** full of noise ▷ **noisily** *adverb* ▷ **noisiness** *noun*

nomad *noun* member of a tribe with no fixed dwelling place, wanderer ▷ **nomadic** *adjective*

nominal *adjective* **1** in name only **2** very small in comparison with real worth ▷ **nominally** *adverb*

nominate *verb* **1** to suggest as a candidate **2** to appoint to an office or position ▷ **nomination** *noun*

non- *prefix* indicating **1** negation: *nonexistent* **2** refusal or failure: *noncooperation* **3** exclusion from a specified class: *nonfiction* **4** lack or absence: *nonevent*

nonchalant *adjective* casually unconcerned or indifferent ▷ **nonchalance** *noun* ▷ **nonchalantly** *adverb*

noncommissioned officer *noun* (in the armed forces) a subordinate officer, risen from the ranks

nondescript *adjective* lacking outstanding features

none *pronoun* **1** not any **2** no-one

nonfiction *noun* writing that is factual rather than about imaginary events

nonplussed *adjective* perplexed

nonsense *noun* **1** something that has or makes no sense **2** absurd language **3** foolish behaviour ▷ **nonsensical** *adjective*

nonstop *adjective, adverb* without a stop

noodles *plural noun* long thin strips of pasta

nook *noun* sheltered place

noon *noun* twelve o'clock midday

no-one or **no one** *pronoun* nobody

noose *noun* loop in the end of a rope, tied with a slipknot

nor *conjunction* and not

norm *noun* standard that is regarded as normal

normal *adjective* **1** usual, regular or typical **2** meeting standards or conventions ▷ **normality** *noun*

normally *adverb* **1** usually **2** in a normal way

north *noun* **1** direction towards the North Pole, opposite south **2** area lying in or towards the north ▷ *adjective* **3** to or in the north **4** (of a wind) from the north ▷ *adverb* **5** in, to or towards the north

North America *noun* continent consisting of Canada, the United States and Mexico ▷ **North American** *adjective*

northeast *noun* **1** direction midway between north and east **2** area lying in or towards the northeast ▷ *adjective* **3** to or in the northeast **4** (of a wind) from the northeast ▷ *adverb* **5** in, to or towards the northeast

northeasterly *adjective, adverb* **1** in, towards or from the northeast ▷ *noun* **2** wind blowing from the northeast

northeastern *adjective* in or from the northeast

northerly *adjective, adverb* **1** in, towards or from the north ▷ *noun* **2** wind blowing from the north

northern *adjective* in or from the north

North Pole *noun* northernmost point on the earth's axis

northward *adjective, adverb* in or towards the north

northwest *noun* **1** direction midway between north and west **2** area lying in or towards the northwest ▷ *adjective* **3** to or in the northwest **4** (of a wind) from the northwest ▷ *adverb* **5** in, to or towards the northwest

northwesterly *adjective, adverb* **1** in, towards or from the northwest ▷ *noun* **2** wind blowing from the northwest

northwestern *adjective* in or from the northwest

Norwegian *adjective* **1** of Norway ▷ *noun* **2** person from Norway **3** language of Norway

nose *noun* **1** organ of smell, used also in breathing **2** front part of a vehicle ▷ *verb* **3** to move forward slowly and carefully **4** to pry or snoop

nostalgia *noun* sentimental longing for the past > **nostalgic** *adjective*

nostril *noun* either of the two openings at the end of the nose

nosy nosier, nosiest *adjective* (*informal*) prying or inquisitive

not *adverb* expressing negation, refusal or denial

notable *adjective* **1** worthy of being noted, remarkable ▷ *noun* **2** person of distinction > **notably** *adverb*

notch *noun* **1** V-shaped cut **2** (*informal*) step or level ▷ *verb* **3** to make a notch in

note *noun* **1** short letter **2** brief comment or record **3** banknote **4** (symbol for) a musical sound **5** hint or mood ▷ *verb* **6** to notice or pay attention to **7** to record (something) in writing **8** to remark upon (something) > **note down** *verb* to write (something) down to have as a record

notebook *noun* book for writing in

noted *adjective* well-known

nothing *pronoun* **1** not anything **2** matter of no importance **3** figure o ▷ *adverb* **4** not at all

notice *noun* **1** observation or attention **2** sign giving warning or an announcement **3** advance warning of intention to end a contract of employment ▷ *verb* **4** to observe or become aware of **5** to point out or remark upon

noticeable *adjective* easily seen or detected, appreciable > **noticeably** *adverb*

noticeboard *noun* board where notices are displayed

notify notifies, notifying, notified *verb* to inform > **notification** *noun*

notion *noun* **1** idea or opinion **2** whim

notorious adjective well known for something bad ▷**notoriety** noun ▷**notoriously** adverb

notwithstanding preposition in spite of

nougat noun chewy sweet containing nuts and fruit

nought noun 1 figure 0 2 nothing

noun noun word that refers to a person, place or thing

nourish verb 1 to feed 2 to encourage or foster (an idea or feeling)

nourishing adjective providing the food necessary for life and growth

nourishment noun food necessary for life and growth

novel noun 1 long fictitious story in book form ▷ adjective 2 fresh, new or original

novelist noun person who writes novels

novelty novelties noun 1 newness 2 something new or unusual

November noun eleventh month of the year

novice noun 1 beginner 2 person who has entered a religious order but has not yet taken vows

now adverb 1 at or for the present time 2 immediately ▷ conjunction 3 seeing that, since

nowadays adverb in these times

nowhere adverb not anywhere

noxious adjective 1 poisonous or harmful 2 extremely unpleasant

nozzle noun projecting spout through which fluid is discharged

nuance [**new**-ahnss] noun subtle difference in colour, meaning or tone

nubile [**new**-bile] adjective (of a young woman) 1 sexually attractive 2 old enough to get married

nuclear adjective 1 of nuclear weapons or energy 2 of a nucleus, especially the nucleus of an atom

nuclear reactor noun device in which a nuclear reaction is maintained and controlled to produce nuclear energy

nucleus nuclei [**nyoo**-klee-uss] noun 1 central part of an atom or cell 2 basic central part of something

nude adjective 1 naked ▷ noun 2 naked figure in painting, sculpture or photography ▷**nudity** noun

nudge verb 1 to push gently, especially with the elbow ▷ noun 2 gentle push or touch

nudist noun person who believes in not wearing clothes ▷**nudism** noun

nugget noun 1 small lump of gold in its natural state 2 something small but valuable ▷ verb 3 (NZ, S Afr) to polish footwear

nuisance noun something or someone that causes annoyance or bother

null adjective null and void not legally valid

nulla-nulla noun wooden club used by Australian Aborigines

numb adjective 1 without feeling, as through cold, shock or fear ▷ verb 2 to make numb

numbat noun small Australian marsupial with a long snout and tongue

number noun 1 sum or quantity 2 word or symbol used to express a sum or quantity, numeral 3 numeral or string of numerals used to identify a person or thing **4** one of a series, such as a copy of a magazine **5** song or piece of music **6** group of people **7** (*Grammar*) classification of words depending on how many persons or things are referred to ▷ *verb* **8** to count **9** to give a number to **10** to amount to **11** to include in a group

numeral *noun* word or symbol used to express a sum or quantity

numerical *adjective* measured or expressed in numbers > **numerically** *adverb*

numerous *adjective* existing or happening in large numbers

nun *noun* female member of a religious order

nurse *noun* **1** person whose job is looking after sick people, usually in a hospital **2** woman whose job is looking after children ▷ *verb* **3** to look after (a sick person) **4** to breast-feed (a baby) **5** to try to cure (an ailment) **6** to harbour or foster (a feeling)

nursery nurseries *noun* **1** room where children sleep or play **2** place where children are taken care of while their parents are at work **3** place where plants are grown for sale

nursery school *noun* school for children from 3 to 5 years old

nursing home *noun* private hospital or home for old people

nurture *noun* **1** act or process of promoting the development of a child or young plant ▷ *verb* **2** to promote or encourage the development of

nut *noun* **1** fruit consisting of a hard shell and a kernel **2** small piece

of metal that screws onto a bolt **3** (*informal*) insane or eccentric person **4** (*informal*) head

nutmeg *noun* spice made from the seed of a tropical tree

nutrient *noun* substance that provides nourishment

nutrition *noun* **1** process of taking in and absorbing nutrients **2** process of being nourished > **nutritional** *adjective* > **nutritionist** *noun* professional advising on diet

nutritious or **nutritive** *adjective* nourishing

nutty nuttier, nuttiest *adjective* **1** containing or resembling nuts **2** (*informal*) insane or eccentric

nylon *noun* **1** synthetic material used for clothing etc **2** nylons (*old-fashioned*) stockings made of nylon

a
b
c
d
e
f
g
h
i
j
k
l
m
n
o
p
q
r
s
t
u
v
w
x
y
z

O

oaf noun stupid or clumsy person

oak noun 1 deciduous forest tree 2 its wood, used for furniture

OAP abbreviation (in Britain) old-age pensioner

oar noun pole with a broad blade, used for rowing a boat

oasis oases noun fertile area in a desert

oat noun 1 hard cereal grown as food 2 oats grain of this cereal

oath noun solemn promise, especially to be truthful in court

oatmeal noun rough flour made from oats

OBE abbreviation (in Britain) Officer of the Order of the British Empire

obedient adjective obeying or willing to obey > **obedience** noun: unquestioning obedience > **obediently** adverb

obelisk [ob-bill-isk] noun four-sided stone column tapering to a pyramid at the top, built in honour of a person or event

obese [oh-**beess**] adjective very fat > **obesity** noun: Obesity rates among children are increasing

obey verb to carry out instructions or orders

obituary obituaries noun announcement of someone's death, especially in a newspaper

object noun 1 physical thing 2 focus of thoughts or action 3 aim or purpose 4 (Grammar) word that a verb or preposition affects ▷ verb 5 to express disapproval

objection noun 1 expression or feeling of opposition or disapproval 2 reason for opposing something

objectionable adjective unpleasant and offensive

objective noun 1 aim or purpose ▷ adjective 2 not biased 3 existing in the real world outside the human mind > **objectively** adverb > **objectivity** noun: The press strives for balance and objectivity

obligation noun duty

obligatory adjective required by a rule or law

oblige verb 1 to compel (someone) morally or by law to do something 2 to do a favour for (someone)

oblique [oh-**bleak**] adjective 1 slanting 2 indirect > **obliquely** adverb

obliterate verb to destroy every trace of > **obliteration** noun: the obliteration of three rainforests

oblivion noun 1 state of being forgotten 2 state of being unaware or unconscious

oblong adjective 1 having two long sides, two short sides and four right angles ▷ noun 2 oblong figure

obnoxious adjective offensive

oboe noun double-reeded woodwind instrument > **oboist** noun

obscene adjective 1 portraying sex offensively 2 disgusting > **obscenely** adverb

obscure *adjective* **1** not well known **2** hard to understand **3** indistinct ▷ *verb* **4** to make (something) obscure > **obscurity** *noun: She was plucked from obscurity*

observance *noun* observing of a custom

observant *adjective* quick to notice things

observation *noun* **1** action or habit of observing **2** remark

observatory *noun* building equipped for studying the weather and the stars

observe *verb* **1** to see or notice **2** to watch (someone or something) carefully **3** to remark **4** to act according to (a law or custom) > **observable** *adjective: This had no observable effect on their behaviour*

obsession *noun* something that preoccupies a person to the exclusion of other things > **obsessional** *adjective: She became almost obsessional about the way she looked*

obsolete *adjective* no longer in use

obstacle *noun* something that makes progress difficult

obstetrics *noun* branch of medicine concerned with pregnancy and childbirth > **obstetric** *adjective: obstetric care* > **obstetrician** *noun: an appointment to see the obstetrician*

obstinate *adjective* **1** stubborn **2** difficult to remove or change > **obstinacy** *noun: the streak of obstinacy in me that would not let me stop* > **obstinately** *adverb*

obstruct *verb* to block with an obstacle > **obstruction** *noun: vehicles causing an obstruction* > **obstructive** *adjective: She was* obstructive and refused to follow procedure

obtain *verb* to acquire intentionally > **obtainable** *adjective: It's obtainable from most health shops*

obtrusive *adjective* unpleasantly noticeable

obtuse *adjective* **1** mentally slow **2** (*Maths*) (of an angle) between 90° and 180° **3** not pointed

obvious *adjective* easy to see or understand, evident > **obviously** *adverb*

occasion *noun* **1** time at which a particular thing happens **2** reason: *no occasion for complaint* **3** special event ▷ *verb* (*formal*) **4** to cause

occasional *adjective* happening sometimes > **occasionally** *adverb*

occult *adjective* **1** relating to the supernatural ▷ *noun* **2 the occult** knowledge or study of the supernatural

occupancy occupancies *noun* (length of) a person's stay in a specified place

occupant *noun* person occupying a specified place

occupation *noun* **1** profession **2** activity that occupies your time **3** control of a country by a foreign military power **4** being occupied > **occupational** *adjective: occupational health and safety issues*

occupy occupies, occupying, occupied *verb* **1** to live or work in (a building) **2** to take up the attention of (someone) **3** to take up (space or time) **4** to take possession of (a place) by force > **occupier** *noun: the occupier of the flat*

a b c d e f g h i j k l m n o p q r s t u v w x y z

occur occurs, occurring, occurred *verb* **1** to happen **2** to exist **3 occur to** to come to the mind of

occurrence *noun* **1** something that occurs **2** fact of occurring

ocean *noun* **1** vast area of sea between continents **2** (*literary*) sea > **oceanic** *adjective*: *oceanic islands*

o'clock *adverb* used after a number to specify an hour

octagon *noun* geometric figure with eight sides > **octagonal** *adjective*: *an octagonal box*

octave *noun* (*Music*) (interval between the first and) eighth note of a scale

October *noun* tenth month of the year

octopus octopuses *noun* sea creature with a soft body and eight tentacles

odd *adjective* **1** unusual **2** occasional **3** not divisible by two **4** not part of a set > *noun plural* **5 odds** (ratio showing) the probability of something happening > **oddly** *adverb* > **oddness** *noun*: *the oddness of his opinions*

oddity oddities *noun* odd person or thing

oddments *plural noun* things left over

odds and ends *plural noun* small miscellaneous items

ode *noun* lyric poem, usually addressed to a particular subject

odious *adjective* offensive

odour *noun* particular smell > **odorous** *adjective*: *odorous air emissions*

odyssey [odd-iss-ee] *noun* long eventful journey

oesophagus oesophagi [ee-**soff**-a-guss] *noun* passage between the mouth and stomach

oestrogen [**ee**-stra-jen] *noun* female hormone that controls the reproductive system

of *preposition* **1** belonging to **2** consisting of **3** connected with **4** characteristic of

off *preposition* **1** away from > *adverb* **2** away **3** (of a machine) **3** not operating **4** cancelled **5** (of food) gone bad

offal *noun* edible organs of an animal, such as liver or kidneys

offence *noun* **1** (cause of) hurt feelings or annoyance **2** illegal act **3 give offence** to cause to feel upset or angry **4 take offence** to feel hurt or offended

offend *verb* **1** to hurt the feelings of (a person) **2** (*formal*) to commit a crime

offensive *adjective* **1** disagreeable **2** insulting **3** aggressive > *noun* **4** position or action of attack > **offensively** *adverb*

offer *verb* **1** to present (something) for acceptance or rejection **2** to provide **3** to be willing (to do something) **4** to propose as payment > *noun* **5** instance of offering something

offering *noun* thing offered

offhand *adjective* **1** casual, curt > *adverb* **2** without preparation

office *noun* **1** room or building where people work at desks **2** department of a commercial organization **3** formal position of responsibility **4** place where tickets or information can be obtained

officer *noun* **1** person in authority in the armed services **2** member of the police force **3** person with special responsibility in an organization

official adjective **1** of a position of authority **2** approved or arranged by someone in authority ▷ noun **3** person who holds a position of authority ▷ **officially** adverb

officialdom noun officials collectively

officiate verb to act in an official role

offing noun **in the offing** likely to happen soon

off-licence noun (Brit) shop licensed to sell alcohol for drinking elsewhere

offline adjective (of a computer) not connected to the internet

offset offsets, offsetting, offset verb to cancel out or compensate for

offshoot noun something developed from something else

offshore adjective, adverb in or from the part of the sea near the shore

offside adjective, adverb (Sport) (positioned) illegally ahead of the ball ▷ noun **2** side of a vehicle that is furthest from the pavement

offspring noun immediate descendant or descendants of a person or animal

often adverb frequently, much of the time

ogle verb to stare at (someone) lustfully

ogre noun **1** giant that eats human flesh **2** monstrous or cruel person

ohm noun unit of electrical resistance

oil noun **1** viscous liquid, insoluble in water and usually

flammable **2** same as **petroleum** **3** petroleum derivative, used as a fuel or lubricant **4** oils oil-based paints used in art ▷ verb **5** to lubricate (a machine) with oil

oil painting noun picture painted using oil-based paints

oilskin noun (garment made from) waterproof material

oily oilier, oiliest adjective **1** covered with or containing oil **2** like oil

ointment noun greasy substance used for healing skin or as a cosmetic

OK or **okay** (informal) interjection **1** expression of approval ▷ noun **2** approval

old adjective **1** having lived or existed for a long time **2** of a specified age: two years old **3** former

olden adjective old: in the olden days

Old English noun form of the English language that existed from the fifth century AD until about 1100. Also known as **Anglo-Saxon**

old-fashioned adjective **1** no longer commonly used or valued **2** favouring or denoting the styles or ideas of a former time

Old Norse noun language spoken in Scandinavia and Iceland from about 700 AD to about 1350 AD and from which many English words are derived

Old Testament noun part of the Bible recording Hebrew history

oleander [ol-lee-**ann**-der] noun Mediterranean flowering evergreen shrub

olive noun **1** small green or black fruit used as food or pressed for its

oil **2** tree on which this fruit grows
▷ *adjective* **3** greyish-green

-ology *suffix* used to form
words that refer to the study of
something: *biology; geology*

Olympic Games *plural noun*
four-yearly international sports
competition

ombudsman *noun* official who
investigates complaints against
government organizations

omelette *noun* dish of eggs
beaten and fried

omen *noun* happening or object
thought to foretell success or
misfortune

ominous *adjective* worrying,
seeming to foretell misfortune
> **ominously** *adverb*

omission *noun* **1** something that
has not been included or done
2 act of missing out or failing to do
something

omit omits, omitting, omitted *verb*
1 to leave out **2** to neglect (to do
something)

omnibus omnibuses *noun*
1 several books or TV or radio
programmes made into one
2 (*old-fashioned*) bus

omnipotent *adjective* having
unlimited power > **omnipotence**
noun: the omnipotence of God

omnivore *noun* animal that
eats all kinds of food, including
meat and plants > **omnivorous**
*adjective: Brown bears are
omnivorous*

on *preposition* **1** touching or
attached to: *lying on the ground;
a puppet on a string; on the coast*
2 inside: *on a train* **3** indicating
when: *on Mondays* **4** using: *on the
phone* **5** about: *a talk on dictionary*

skills ▷ *adverb* **6** in operation:
He left the lights on **7** continuing:
He stayed on after his family left
8 forwards: *from that day on*
▷ *adjective* **9** operating: *All the
lights were on* **10** taking place:
What's on at the cinema?

once *adverb* **1** on one occasion
2 formerly ▷ *conjunction* **3** as
soon as ▷ *noun* **4** one occasion
or case **5** at once **a** immediately
b simultaneously

one *adjective, noun* **1** the number
1 ▷ *adjective* **2** single, lone **3** used
emphatically to mean *a* or
an: *They got one almighty shock*
▷ *noun* **4** single unit ▷ *pronoun*
5 any person **6** referring back to
something or someone already
mentioned or known about:
*the pretty one; His business was a
successful one*

one-off *noun* something that
happens or is made only once

onerous [**own**-er-uss] *adjective* (of
a task) difficult to carry out

oneself *pronoun* reflexive form
of one

one-sided *adjective* **1** considering
only one point of view **2** having all
the advantage on one side

one-way *adjective* moving or
allowing travel in one direction
only

ongoing *adjective* in progress,
continuing

onion *noun* strongly flavoured
edible bulb

online *adjective* relating to the
internet: *online shopping*

onlooker *noun* person who
watches without taking part

only *adjective* **1** alone of its kind
▷ *adverb* **2** exclusively **3** merely

4 no more than **5** only too extremely ▷ *conjunction* **6** but

onomatopoeia [on-a-mat-a-**pee**-a] *noun* use of a word which imitates the sound it represents, such as {*hiss*} > **onomatopoeic** *adjective*: Buzz is an onomatopoeic word

onset *noun* beginning

onslaught *noun* violent attack

onto *preposition* **1** to a position on **2** aware of: *She's onto us*

onus *onuses* [**own**-uss] *noun* (*formal*) responsibility or burden

onward *adjective* **1** directed or moving forward ▷ *adverb* **2** ahead, forward

onyx *noun* type of quartz with coloured layers

ooze *verb* **1** to flow slowly ▷ *noun* **2** soft mud at the bottom of a lake or river

opal *noun* iridescent precious stone

opaque *adjective* **1** not able to be seen through, not transparent **2** difficult to understand

open *adjective* **1** not closed **2** not covered **3** unfolded **4** ready for business **5** free from obstruction, accessible **6** frank ▷ *verb* **7** to (cause to) become open **8** to begin ▷ *noun* **9** in the open **a** outdoors **b** not secret

opening *noun* **1** opportunity **2** hole **3** first part ▷ *adjective* **4** first

open-minded *adjective* receptive to new ideas

open-plan *adjective* (of a house or office) having few interior walls

opera *noun* drama in which the text is sung to an orchestral accompaniment > **operatic**

adjective: an amateur operatic society

operate *verb* **1** to work **2** to control the working of (a machine) **3** to perform a surgical operation (on a person or animal)

operation *noun* **1** method or procedure of working **2** medical procedure in which the body is worked on to repair a damaged part **3** in operation working or being used

operational *adjective* **1** in working order **2** occurring while a plan is being carried out

operative *adjective* **1** working ▷ *noun* **2** worker with a special skill

operator *noun* **1** someone who works at a telephone exchange or on a switchboard **2** someone who operates a machine **3** someone who runs a business: *a tour operator*

opinion *noun* personal belief or judgment

opinionated *adjective* having strong opinions

opium *noun* addictive narcotic drug made from poppy seeds

opponent *noun* person you are competing, fighting or arguing against in a contest, battle or argument

opossum *noun* small marsupial of America or Australia

opportune *adjective* (*formal*) happening at a suitable time

opportunism *noun* doing whatever is advantageous without regard for principles > **opportunist** *noun: Car thieves are opportunists*

opportunity opportunities noun
1 favourable time or condition
2 good chance

oppose verb 1 to work against
2 **be opposed to** to disagree with
or disapprove of

opposed adjective 1 **opposed to**
against (something or someone)
in speech or action 2 opposite or
very different 3 **as opposed to** in
strong contrast with

opposite adjective 1 situated
on the other side 2 facing
3 completely different ▷ noun
4 person or thing that is opposite
▷ preposition 5 facing ▷ adverb
6 on the other side

opposition noun 1 obstruction
or hostility 2 group opposing
another 3 **the Opposition**
political parties not in power

oppressed adjective treated
cruelly or unfairly > **oppression**
noun: political oppression
> **oppress** verb > **oppressor** noun:
They tried to resist their oppressors by
non-violent means

oppressive adjective 1 tyrannical
2 uncomfortable or depressing
3 (of weather) hot and humid
> **oppressively** adverb

opt verb 1 to show preference (for)
or choose (to do something) 2 **opt
out** to choose not to be part (of)

optical adjective 1 concerned with
vision, light or images 2 relating
to the appearance of things: an
optical illusion

optician noun 1 person qualified
to prescribe glasses 2 person who
supplies and fits glasses

optimism noun tendency to take
the most hopeful view > **optimist**
noun: Optimists predict the economy

will grow steadily > **optimistic**
adjective: She was in a jovial and
optimistic mood > **optimistically**
adverb

optimum optima or optimums
noun 1 best possible conditions
▷ adjective 2 most favourable

option noun 1 choice 2 thing
chosen 3 right to buy or sell
something at a specified price
within a given time

opulent [op-pew-lent] adjective
having or indicating wealth
> **opulence** noun: the elegant
opulence of the German embassy

opus opuses or opera noun artistic
creation, especially a musical
work

or conjunction 1 used to join
alternatives: tea or coffee 2 used to
introduce a warning: Do as I say or
else I'll shoot

-or suffix used to form nouns from
verbs: actor; conductor

oracle noun 1 shrine of an ancient
god 2 prophecy, often obscure,
revealed at a shrine 3 person
believed to make infallible
predictions

oral adjective 1 spoken 2 (of a drug)
to be taken by mouth ▷ noun
3 spoken examination > **orally**
adverb

orange noun 1 reddish-yellow
citrus fruit ▷ adjective 2 reddish-
yellow

orang-utan or **orang-utang**
noun large reddish-brown ape
with long arms

orator [or-rat-tor] noun skilful
public speaker

oratory oratories [or-rat-tree]
noun 1 art of making speeches
2 small private chapel

orbit noun **1** curved path of a planet, satellite or spacecraft around another body **2** sphere of influence ▷ verb **3** to move in an orbit around **4** to put (a satellite or spacecraft) into orbit

orchard noun area where fruit trees are grown

orchestra noun **1** large group of musicians, especially playing a variety of instruments **2** area of a theatre in front of the stage, reserved for the musicians > **orchestral** adjective: an orchestral concert

orchestrate verb **1** to arrange (music) for orchestra **2** to organize (something) to produce a particular result > **orchestration** noun: Mahler's imaginative orchestration

orchid noun plant with flowers that have unusual lip-shaped petals

ordain verb to make (someone) a member of the clergy

ordeal noun painful or difficult experience

order noun **1** instruction to be carried out **2** methodical arrangement or sequence **3** established social system **4** condition of a law-abiding society **5** request for goods to be supplied **6** kind, sort **7** religious society of monks or nuns **8** in order so that it is possible ▷ verb **9** to command or instruct (to do something) **10** to request (something) to be supplied in return for payment

orderly orderlies adjective **1** well-organized **2** well-behaved ▷ noun **3** male hospital attendant

ordinarily adverb usually

ordinary adjective **1** usual or normal **2** dull or commonplace

ordination noun act of making someone a member of the clergy

ordnance noun weapons and military supplies

ore noun (rock containing) a mineral which yields metal

oregano [or-rig-**gah**-no] noun sweet-smelling herb used in cooking

organ noun **1** part of an animal or plant that has a particular function, such as the heart or lungs **2** musical keyboard instrument in which notes are produced by forcing air through pipes

organic adjective **1** of or produced from animals or plants **2** grown without artificial fertilizers or pesticides **3** (Chemistry) relating to compounds of carbon > **organically** adverb

organism noun any living animal or plant

organist noun organ player

organization noun **1** group of people working together **2** act of organizing > **organizational** adjective: organizational skills

organize or **organise** verb **1** to plan and arrange (something) **2** to arrange systematically > **organized** adjective: organized resistance > **organizer** noun: She is a good organizer

orgasm noun most intense point of sexual pleasure

orgy orgies noun **1** party involving promiscuous sexual activity **2** unrestrained indulgence: an orgy of destruction

orient verb **1** to position (yourself) according to your surroundings **2** to position (a map) in relation to the points of the compass

Oriental adjective relating to eastern or south-eastern Asia: *Oriental carpets*

orientation noun **1** activities and aims that a person or organization is interested in **2** position of an object with relation to the points of the compass or other specific directions

oriented or **orientated** adjective interested (in) or directed (toward something): *Medical care needs to be oriented towards prevention* > **-oriented** or **-orientated** suffix: *career-oriented women*

orienteering noun sport in which competitors hike over a course using a compass and map

origin noun **1** point from which something develops **2** ancestry

original adjective **1** first or earliest **2** new, not copied or based on something else **3** able to think up new ideas ⊳ noun **4** first version, from which others are copied > **originality** noun: *ideas of startling originality* > **originally** adverb

originate verb to come or bring into existence > **originator** noun: *the originator of the theory of relativity*

ornament noun **1** decorative object ⊳ verb **2** to decorate

ornamental adjective designed to be attractive rather than useful

ornamentation noun decoration on a building, a piece of furniture or a work of art

ornate adjective highly decorated, elaborate

ornithology noun study of birds > **ornithological** adjective: *an ornithological society* > **ornithologist** noun: *a keen amateur ornithologist*

orphan noun **1** child whose parents are dead ⊳ verb **2** to cause (someone) to become an orphan

orphanage noun children's home for orphans

orthodox adjective conforming to established views > **orthodoxy** noun: *He rebelled against religious orthodoxy*

osmosis noun **1** movement of a liquid through a membrane from a lower to a higher concentration **2** process of subtle influence

osprey noun large fish-eating bird of prey

ostensible adjective apparent, seeming **ostensibly** adverb

ostentatious adjective **1** intended to impress people, for example by looking expensive **2** flaunting your wealth or making a show of your importance > **ostentation** noun: *a notable lack of ostentation* > **ostentatiously** adverb

ostinato noun (Music) musical phrase that is continuously repeated throughout a piece

ostrich ostriches noun large African bird that runs fast but cannot fly

other adjective **1** different from the ones specified or understood **2** additional **3 the other day** a few days ago ⊳ noun **4** other person or thing

otherwise conjunction **1** or else, if not ▷ adverb **2** differently, in another way

otter noun small brown freshwater mammal that eats fish

ouch interjection exclamation of sudden pain

ought verb used to express **1** obligation: *You ought to pay* **2** advisability: *You ought to diet* **3** probability: *You ought to know by then*

ounce noun unit of weight equal to one sixteenth of a pound (28.4 grams)

our adjective belonging to us

ours pronoun thing(s) belonging to us

ourselves pronoun emphatic and reflexive form of **we, us**

oust verb to force (someone) out of a position

out adverb **1** towards the outside of a place: *Two dogs rushed out of the house* **2** not at home **3** in the open air: *They are playing out in bright sunshine* **4** no longer shining or burning: *The lights went out* ▷ adjective **5** on strike: *1000 construction workers are out in sympathy* **6** unacceptable or unfashionable: *Miniskirts are out* **7** incorrect: *Logan's timing was out in the first two rounds*

out- prefix **1** surpassing: *outlive; outdistance* **2** on the outside or away from the centre: *outpost*

out-and-out adjective entire or complete: *an out-and-out lie*

outback noun remote bush country of Australia

outboard motor noun engine externally attached to the stern of a boat

outbreak noun sudden occurrence (of something unpleasant)

outburst noun sudden expression of emotion

outcast noun person rejected by a particular group

outclassed adjective surpassed in quality

outcome noun result

outcrop noun part of a rock formation that sticks out of the earth

outcry outcries noun vehemence or widespread protest

outdated adjective no longer in fashion

outdo outdoes, outdoing, outdid, outdone verb to be more successful or better than (someone or something) in performance

outdoor adjective happening or used outside

outdoors adverb **1** in(to) the open air ▷ noun **2** the open air

outer adjective on the outside

outer space noun space beyond the earth's atmosphere

outfit noun **1** matching set of clothes **2** (informal) group of people working together

outgoing adjective **1** leaving **2** sociable ▷ noun **3** outgoings expenses

outgrow outgrows, outgrowing, outgrew, outgrown verb to become too large or too old for

outhouse noun building near a main building

outing noun leisure trip

outlandish adjective extremely unconventional

outlaw verb **1** to make (something) illegal ▷ noun

2 (*History*) criminal deprived of legal protection

outlay outlays *noun* expenditure

outlet *noun* **1** means of expressing emotion **2** market for a product **3** place where a product is sold **4** opening or way out

outline *noun* **1** short general explanation **2** line defining the shape of something ▷ *verb* **3** to give the main features or general idea of (something) **4** to show the general shape of an object but not its details

outlive *verb* to live longer than someone

outlook *noun* **1** attitude **2** probable outcome

outlying *adjective* distant from the main area

outmoded *adjective* no longer fashionable or accepted

outnumber *verb* to exceed in number

out of *preposition* **1** because of: *She went along out of curiosity* **2** from (a material or source): *old instruments made out of wood* **3** no longer in a specified state or condition: *out of work* **4** at or to a point outside: *The train pulled out of the station* **5** away from, not in: *out of focus*

out-of-date *adjective* old-fashioned

out of doors *adverb* outside

outpatient *noun* patient who does not stay in hospital overnight

outpost *noun* outlying settlement

output ouputs, outputting, outputted *or* output *noun* **1** amount produced **2** power, voltage or current delivered by

an electrical circuit **3** (*Computers*) data produced ▷ *verb* **4** (*Computers*) to produce (data) at the end of a process

outrage *noun* **1** great moral indignation **2** gross violation of morality ▷ *verb* **3** to cause deep indignation, anger or resentment in (someone)

outright *adjective, adverb* **1** absolute(ly) **2** open(ly) and direct(ly)

outset *noun* beginning

outshine outshines, outshining, outshone *verb* to surpass (someone) in excellence

outside *preposition, adjective, adverb* **1** indicating movement to or position on the exterior ▷ *adjective* **2** unlikely: *an outside chance* **3** coming from outside ▷ *noun* **4** external area or surface

outsider *noun* **1** person outside a specific group **2** contestant thought unlikely to win

outsize *or* **outsized** *adjective* larger than normal

outskirts *plural noun* outer areas, especially of a town

outspan *verb* (*S Afr*) relax

outspoken *adjective* **1** tending to say what you think, regardless of how others may react **2** said openly

outstanding *adjective* **1** excellent **2** still to be dealt with or paid

outstretched *adjective* extended or stretched out as far as possible

outstrip outstrips, outstripping, outstripped *verb* **1** to surpass (someone) in a particular activity **2** to go faster than (someone)

outward *adjective* **1** apparent ▷ *adverb* **2** away from somewhere ▷ **outwardly** *adverb*

outwards adverb away from a place or towards the outside: The door opened outwards

outweigh verb to be more important, significant or influential than

outwit outwits, outwitting, outwitted verb to get the better of (someone) by cunning

oval adjective **1** egg-shaped ▷ noun **2** anything that is oval in shape

ovary ovaries noun female egg-producing organ

ovation noun enthusiastic round of applause

oven noun heated compartment or container for cooking, or for drying or firing ceramics

over preposition, adverb **1** indicating position on the top of, movement to the other side of, amount greater than, etc: a room over the garage; climbing over the fence; over fifty pounds ▷ adjective **2** finished ▷ noun **3** (Cricket) series of six balls bowled from one end

over- prefix **1** too much: overeat **2** above: overlord **3** on top: overshoe

overall adjective, adverb **1** in total ▷ noun **2** overalls protective garment consisting of trousers with a jacket or bib and braces attached

overawe verb to fill (someone) with respect or fear > **overawed** adjective: He had been overawed to meet the Prime Minister

overbearing adjective unpleasantly forceful

overboard adverb **1** from a boat into the water **2** go overboard to go to extremes, especially in enthusiasm

overcast adjective (of the sky) covered by clouds

overcoat noun heavy coat

overcome overcomes, overcoming, overcame, overcome verb **1** to gain control over an effort **2** (of an emotion) to affect strongly

overcrowded adjective containing more people or things than is desirable

overdo overdoes, overdoing, overdid, overdone verb **1** to do to excess **2** to exaggerate (something)

overdose noun **1** excessive dose of a drug ▷ verb **2** to take more of a drug than is safe, either accidentally or deliberately

overdraft noun **1** overdrawing **2** amount overdrawn

overdrawn adjective **1** having taken out more money than you had in your bank account **2** (of an account) in debit

overdrive noun extra, higher gear in a vehicle, which is used at high speeds to reduce engine wear and save petrol

overdue adjective still due after the time allowed

overestimate verb to believe something or someone to be bigger, more important, or better than is the case

overflow overflows, overflowing, overflowed or overflown verb **1** to flow over (a brim) **2** to be filled beyond capacity so as to spill over ▷ noun **3** outlet that enables surplus liquid to be drained off

overgrown adjective thickly covered with plants and weeds

overhang overhangs, overhanging, overhung *verb* **1** to project or hang over beyond (something) ▷ *noun* **2** overhanging part or object

overhaul *verb* **1** to examine (a system or an idea) carefully for faults **2** to make repairs or adjustments to (a vehicle or machine)

overhead *adverb, adjective* above your head

overhear overhears, overhearing, overheard *verb* to hear (a speaker or remark) unintentionally or without the speaker's knowledge

overjoyed *adjective* extremely pleased

overlaid *adjective* **overlaid with** covered with

overland *adjective, adverb* by land

overlander *noun* (*Aust history*) man who drove cattle or sheep long distances through the outback

overlap overlaps, overlapping, overlapped *verb* **1** to share part of the same space or period of time (as) ▷ *noun* **2** area overlapping

overleaf *adverb* on the back of the current page

overload *verb* to put too large a load on or in (something)

overlook *verb* **1** to fail to notice **2** to ignore (misbehaviour or a fault)

overly *adverb* excessively

overnight *adjective, adverb* **1** (taking place) during one night **2** (happening) very quickly

overpower *verb* **1** to subdue or overcome (someone) **2** to have such a strong effect on as to make helpless or ineffective ▷ **overpowering** *adjective*: *overpowering anger*

overrate *verb* to have too high an opinion of ▷ **overrated** *adjective*: *The food here is overrated*

overreact *verb* to react more strongly or forcefully than is necessary

overriding *adjective* more important than anything else

overrule *verb* to reverse the decision of (a person with less power)

overrun overruns, overrunning, overran, overrun *verb* **1** to conquer (territory) rapidly by force of number **2** to spread over (a place) rapidly **3** to extend beyond a set limit

overseas *adverb, adjective* to, of or from a distant country

oversee oversees, overseeing, oversaw, overseen *verb* to watch over from a position of authority ▷ **overseer** *noun*: *I was promoted to overseer*

overshadow *verb* to reduce the significance of (a person or thing) by comparison

oversight *noun* mistake caused by not noticing something

overspill *noun* (*Brit*) rehousing of people from crowded cities in smaller towns

overstate *verb* to state (something) too strongly

overstep oversteps, overstepping, overstepped *verb* **overstep the mark** to go too far and behave in an unacceptable way

overt *adjective* open, not hidden ▷ **overtly** *adverb*

overtake overtakes, overtaking, overtook, overtaken *verb* to move past (a vehicle or person) travelling in the same direction

overthrow overthrows, overthrowing, overthrew, overthrown *verb* to defeat and replace (a ruler or government) by force

overtime *noun, adverb* (paid work done) in addition to your normal working hours

overtones *plural noun* additional meaning: *the political overtones of the trial*

overture *noun* 1 (Music) orchestral introduction 2 **overtures** opening moves in a new relationship

overturn *verb* 1 to turn upside down 2 to overrule (a legal decision)

overview *noun* general understanding or description of a situation

overweight *adjective* weighing more than is healthy

overwhelm *verb* 1 to overpower the thoughts, emotions or senses of (someone) 2 to overcome (people) with irresistible force > **overwhelming** *adjective*: *an overwhelming majority* > **overwhelmingly** *adverb*

overwork *verb* to work too hard or too long

overwrought *adjective* nervous and agitated

ovulate [ov-yew-late] *verb* to produce or release an egg cell from an ovary

ovum ova [oh-vum] *noun* unfertilized egg cell

owe *verb* 1 to be obliged to pay (a sum of money) to (a person) 2 to feel an obligation to do or give

owl *noun* night bird of prey

own *adjective* 1 used to emphasize possession: *my own idea* ▷ *pronoun* 2 the one or ones belonging to a particular person: *I had one of my own* 3 **on your own** a alone b without help ▷ *verb* 4 to have (something) as your possession

owner *noun* person to whom something belongs

ownership *noun* state or fact of being an owner

ox oxen *noun* castrated bull

oxide *noun* compound of oxygen and one other element

oxidize or **oxidise** *verb* to combine chemically with oxygen, as in burning or rusting > **oxidation** *noun*: *the oxidation of metals*

oxygen *noun* (Chemistry) gaseous element essential to life and combustion

oxymoron [ox-see-**more**-on] *noun* figure of speech that combines two apparently contradictory ideas: *cruel kindness*

oyster *noun* edible shellfish

oz. *abbreviation* ounce

ozone *noun* strong-smelling form of oxygen

ozone layer *noun* layer of ozone in the upper atmosphere that filters out ultraviolet radiation

p

p *abbreviation* **1** (Brit, Aust, NZ) penny **2** (Brit) pence

pa *noun* (NZ) (formerly) a fortified Māori settlement

pace *noun* **1** single step in walking **2** length of a step **3** rate of progress ▷ *verb* **4** to walk up and down, especially in anxiety **5 pace out** to cross or measure with steps

pacemaker *noun* electronic device surgically implanted in a person with heart disease to regulate the heartbeat

Pacific [pas-**sif**-ik] *noun* ocean separating North and South America from Asia and Australia

pacifist *noun* person who refuses on principle to take part in war > **pacifism** *noun*

pacify pacifies, pacifying, pacified *verb* to soothe or calm

pack *verb* **1** to put (clothes etc) together in a suitcase or bag **2** to put (goods) into containers or parcels **3** to fill with people or things ▷ *noun* **4** bag carried on a person's or animal's back **5** (Chiefly US) same as **packet 6** set of playing cards **7** group of dogs or wolves that hunt together > **pack in** *verb* (informal) to stop doing (something) > **pack up** *verb* **1** to put (your things) in a bag because you are leaving **2** (of machine) to stop working

package *noun* **1** small parcel **2** deal in which separate items are presented together as a unit ▷ *verb* **3** to put (something) into a package

packaging *noun* container or wrapping in which an item is sold or sent

packed *adjective* very full

packet *noun* **1** small container (and contents) **2** small parcel **3** (informal) large sum of money

pact *noun* formal agreement

pad pads, padding, padded *noun* **1** piece of soft material used for protection, support, absorption of liquid, etc **2** number of sheets of paper fastened at the edge **3** fleshy underpart of an animal's paw **4** place for launching rockets **5** (informal) home ▷ *verb* **6** to protect or fill (something) with soft material **7** to walk with soft steps

paddle *noun* **1** short oar with a broad blade at one or each end ▷ *verb* **2** to move (a canoe etc) with a paddle **3** to walk barefoot in shallow water

paddock *noun* small field or enclosure for horses

paddy paddies *noun* (Brit informal) fit of temper

padlock *noun* **1** detachable lock with a hinged hoop fastened over a ring on the object to be secured ▷ *verb* **2** to fasten (something) with a padlock

padre [**pah**-dray] *noun* chaplain to the armed forces

paediatrician *noun* doctor who specializes in treating children

paediatrics noun branch of medicine concerned with diseases of children > **paediatric** adjective: paediatric medicine

pagan adjective **1** not belonging to one of the world's main religions ▷ noun **2** someone who believes in a pagan religion > **paganism** noun

page pages, paging, paged noun **1** (one side of) a sheet of paper forming a book etc **2** screenful of information from a website or teletext service **3** small boy who attends a bride at her wedding **4** (History) boy in training for knighthood ▷ verb **5** to summon (someone) by bleeper or loudspeaker, in order to pass on a message

pageant noun parade or display of people in costume, usually illustrating a scene from history

pagoda noun pyramid-shaped Asian temple or tower

pail noun (contents of) a bucket

pain noun **1** physical or mental suffering **2** pains trouble or effort **3** on pain of subject to the penalty of

painful adjective causing emotional or physical pain > **painfully** adverb

painkiller noun drug that relieves pain

painstaking adjective extremely thorough and careful

paint noun **1** coloured substance, spread on a surface with a brush or roller ▷ verb **2** to colour or coat with paint **3** to use paint to make a picture of

pair noun **1** set of two things matched for use together ▷ verb **2** to group or be grouped in twos

Pakeha [pah-kee-ha] noun (NZ) New Zealander who is not of Māori descent

Pakistani [pah-kiss-**tah**-nee] adjective **1** belonging or relating to Pakistan ▷ noun **2** someone from Pakistan

pal noun (informal, old-fashioned in NZ) friend

palace noun **1** residence of a king, bishop, etc **2** large grand building

Palagi Palagi or Palagis [pa-**lang**-gee] noun (NZ) Samoan name for a Pakeha

palatable adjective pleasant to taste

palate noun **1** roof of the mouth **2** sense of taste

pale adjective **1** light, whitish **2** whitish in the face, especially through illness or shock ▷ noun **3** wooden or metal post used in fences **4** beyond the pale outside the limits of social convention ▷ verb **5** to become pale or paler

Palestinian adjective belonging or relating to the region formerly called Palestine or its people ▷ noun Arab from this region

palette noun artist's flat board for mixing colours on

pall noun **1** cloth spread over a coffin **2** dark cloud (of smoke) **3** depressing oppressive atmosphere ▷ verb **4** to become boring

palm noun **1** inner surface of the hand **2** tropical tree with long pointed leaves growing out of the top of a straight trunk ▷ verb **3** palm off to get rid of (an unwanted thing or person), especially by deceit

a b c d e f g h i j k l m n o p q r s t u v w x y z

Palm Sunday *noun* Sunday before Easter

palpable *adjective* **1** obvious: *a palpable hit* **2** so intense as to seem capable of being touched: *the tension is almost palpable* ▷ **palpably** *adverb*

paltry paltrier, paltriest *adjective* (of an amount) very small

pamper *verb* to treat (someone) with great indulgence, spoil

pamphlet *noun* thin paper-covered booklet

pan pans, panning, panned *noun* **1** wide long-handled metal container used in cooking **2** bowl of a toilet ▷ *verb* **3** to sift gravel from (a river) in a pan to search for gold **4** (*informal*) to criticize harshly **5** (of a film camera) to be moved slowly so as to cover a whole scene or follow a moving object ▷ **pan out** *verb* to work out

panacea [pan-a-**see**-a] *noun* remedy for all diseases or problems

panache [pan-**ash**] *noun* confident elegant style

pancake *noun* thin flat circle of fried batter

pancreas [**pang**-kree-ass] *noun* large gland behind the stomach that produces insulin and helps digestion

panda *noun* large black-and-white bearlike mammal from China

panda car *noun* (Brit) police patrol car

pandemonium *noun* wild confusion, uproar

pander *verb* **pander to** to indulge (a person his or her desires)

pane *noun* sheet of glass in a window or door

panel panels, panelling, panelled **1** flat distinct section of a larger surface, for example in a door **2** group of people as a team in a quiz etc **3** list of jurors, doctors, etc **4** board or surface containing switches and controls to operate equipment ▷ *verb* **5** to cover or decorate with panels ▷ **panelled** *adjective*

panelling *noun* panels collectively, especially on a wall

pang *noun* sudden sharp feeling of pain or sadness

panic panics, panicking, panicked *noun* **1** sudden overwhelming fear, often affecting a whole group of people ▷ *verb* **2** to feel or cause to feel panic

panorama *noun* wide unbroken view of a scene ▷ **panoramic** *adjective*: *panoramic views*

pansy pansies *noun* small garden flower with velvety purple, yellow or white petals

pant *verb* to breathe quickly and noisily during or after exertion

panther *noun* leopard, especially a black one

pantomime *noun* play based on a fairy tale, performed at Christmas time

pantry pantries *noun* small room or cupboard for storing food

pants *plural noun* **1** undergarment for the lower part of the body **2** (US, Canadian, Aust, NZ) trousers

papaya or **pawpaw** [pa-**pie**-ya] *noun* large sweet West Indian fruit

paper *noun* **1** material made in sheets from wood pulp or other fibres **2** printed sheets of this **3** newspaper **4** set of examination questions **5** article or essay

6 papers personal documents ▷ *verb* **7** to cover (walls) with wallpaper

paperback *noun* book with covers made of flexible card

paperwork *noun* clerical work, such as writing reports and letters

papier-mâché [**pap**-yay **mash**-ay] *noun* material made from paper mixed with paste and moulded when moist

paprika *noun* mild powdered seasoning made from red peppers

par *noun* **1** usual or average condition: *feeling under par* **2** (*Golf*) expected standard score **3** face value of stocks and shares **4 on a par with** equal to

parable *noun* story that illustrates a religious teaching

parachute *noun* **1** large fabric canopy that slows the descent of a person or object from an aircraft ▷ *verb* **2** to land or drop by parachute ▷ **parachutist** *noun*

parade *noun* **1** procession or march **2** street or promenade ▷ *verb* **3** to display or flaunt **4** to march in procession

paradise *noun* **1** heaven **2** place or situation that is near-perfect

paradox *noun* statement that seems self-contradictory but may be true ▷ **paradoxical** *adjective*: *a paradoxical effect*

paraffin *noun* (*Brit, SAfr*) liquid mixture distilled from petroleum and used as a fuel or solvent

paragon *noun* model of perfection

paragraph *noun* section of a piece of writing starting on a new line

parallel parallels, paralleling or parallelling, paralleled or

parallelled *adjective* **1** separated by an equal distance at every point **2** exactly corresponding ▷ *noun* **3** line separated from another by an equal distance at every point **4** thing with similar features to another **5** line of latitude ▷ *verb* **6** to correspond to

parallelogram *noun* (*Maths*) four-sided geometric figure with opposite sides parallel

paralyse *verb* **1** to affect with paralysis **2** to make temporarily unable to move or take action

paralysis *noun* inability to move or feel, because of damage to the nervous system

paramedic *noun* person working in support of the medical profession

parameter [par-**am**-it-er] *noun* limiting factor or boundary

paramilitary *adjective* organized on military lines

paramount *adjective* of the greatest importance

paranoia *noun* **1** mental illness causing delusions of grandeur or persecution **2** (*informal*) intense fear or suspicion

paranoid *adjective* having undue suspicion or fear of persecution

parapet *noun* low wall or railing along the edge of a balcony or roof

paraphernalia *noun* personal belongings or bits of equipment

paraphrase *verb* to put (a statement or text) into other words

parasite *noun* **1** animal or plant living in or on another **2** person who lives at the expense of others ▷ **parasitic** *adjective*: *parasitic diseases*

parasol noun umbrella-like sunshade

paratroops or **paratroopers** plural noun soldiers trained to be dropped by parachute into a battle area

parcel parcels, parcelling, parcelled noun **1** something wrapped up, package ▷ verb **2 parcel up** to wrap up **3 parcel out** to divide into parts

parched adjective **1** very hot and dry **2** (informal) thirsty

parchment noun thick smooth writing material made from animal skin

pardon verb **1** to forgive or excuse ▷ noun **2** forgiveness **3** official release from punishment for a crime

pare verb **1** to cut off the skin or top layer of **2 pare down** to reduce in size or amount

parent noun father or mother ▷ **parental** adjective: parental duties

parentage noun ancestry or family

parish noun area that has its own church and a priest or pastor

parishioner noun inhabitant of a parish

parity noun (formal) equality or equivalence

park noun **1** area of open land for recreational use by the public **2** area containing a number of related enterprises: a business park **3** (Brit) area of private land around a large country house ▷ verb **4** to stop and leave (a vehicle) temporarily ▷ **parked** adjective: parked cars ▷ **parking** noun: free parking

parliament noun law-making assembly of a country ▷ **parliamentary** adjective: parliamentary debates

parlour noun (old-fashioned) living room for receiving visitors

parochial adjective **1** narrow in outlook **2** of a parish

parody parodies, parodying, parodied noun **1** exaggerated and amusing imitation of someone else's style ▷ verb **2** to make a parody of

parole noun **1** early freeing of a prisoner on condition that he or she behaves well **2 on parole** (of a prisoner) released on condition that he or she behaves well ▷ verb **3** to place (a person) on parole

parrot noun **1** tropical bird with a short hooked beak and an ability to imitate human speech ▷ verb **2** to repeat (someone's words) without thinking

parry parries, parrying, parried verb **1** to ward off (an attack) **2** to avoid (an awkward question) in a clever way

parsley noun herb used for seasoning and decorating food

parsnip noun long tapering cream-coloured root vegetable

parson noun **1** Anglican parish priest **2** any member of the clergy

part noun **1** one of the pieces that make up a whole **2** one of several equal divisions **3** actor's role **4** component of a vehicle or machine **5** parts region or area ▷ verb **6** to divide or separate from one another **7** (of people) to leave each other **8 take someone's part** to support someone in an argument etc **9 take**

(something) in good part to respond to (teasing or criticism) with good humour ▷ **part with** verb to give away or hand over

partake partaking, partook, partaken verb 1 partake of to take (food or drink) 2 partake in to take part in

partial adjective 1 not complete 2 prejudiced 3 partial to having a liking for ▷ **partially** adverb

participate verb to become actively involved in ▷ **participant** noun: participants in the course ▷ **participation** noun: participation in religious activities

participle noun form of a verb used in compound tenses: written; writing

particle noun 1 extremely small piece or amount 2 (Physics) minute piece of matter, such as a proton or electron

particular adjective 1 relating to one person or thing, not general 2 exceptional or special 3 very exact 4 difficult to please, fastidious ▷ noun 5 particulars items of information, details ▷ **particularly** adverb

parting noun 1 occasion when one person leaves another 2 line of scalp between sections of hair combed in opposite directions 3 dividing or separating

partisan noun 1 strong supporter of a party or group 2 member of a resistance movement ▷ adjective 3 prejudiced or one-sided

partition noun 1 screen or thin wall that divides a room 2 division of a country into independent parts ▷ verb 3 to divide (something) into separate parts

partly adverb not completely

partner noun 1 either member of a couple in a relationship or activity 2 member of a business partnership ▷ verb 3 to be the partner of

part of speech noun particular grammatical class of words, such as noun or verb

partook the past tense of **partake**

partridge noun game bird of the grouse family

part-time adjective occupying or working less than the full working week

party parties noun 1 social gathering for pleasure 2 group of people travelling or working together 3 group of people with a common political aim 4 (formal) person or people forming one side in a lawsuit or dispute

pass verb 1 to go by, past or through 2 to be successful in (a test or examination) 3 to spend (time) or (of time) to go by 4 to give or hand 5 to be inherited by 6 (Sport) to hit, kick or throw (the ball) to another player 7 (of a law-making body) to agree to (a law) 8 to exceed ▷ noun 9 successful result in a test or examination 10 permit or licence 11 make a pass at (informal) to make sexual advances to ▷ **pass away** verb to die ▷ **pass out** verb (informal) to faint ▷ **pass up** verb (informal) to fail to take advantage of (something)

passable adjective 1 (just) acceptable 2 (of a road) capable of being travelled along

passage noun 1 channel or opening providing a way through

2 hall or corridor **3** section of a book etc **4** journey by sea **5** right or freedom to pass

passé [pas-say] *adjective* out-of-date

passenger *noun* **1** person travelling in a vehicle driven by someone else **2** member of a team who does not pull his or her weight

passer-by passers-by *noun* person who is passing something or someone

passing *adjective* **1** brief or transitory **2** cursory or casual

passion *noun* **1** intense sexual love **2** any strong emotion **3** great enthusiasm **4** Passion (*Christianity*) the suffering of Christ

passionate *adjective* expressing very strong feelings about something > **passionately** *adverb*

passive *adjective* **1** not playing an active part **2** submissive and receptive to outside forces **3** (*Grammar*) (of a verb) in a form indicating that the subject receives the action, e.g. {was jeered} in {he was jeered by the crowd} > **passively** *adverb* > **passivity** *noun*: *the passivity of the public under military occupation*

Passover *noun* Jewish festival commemorating the sparing of the Jews in Egypt

passport *noun* official document of nationality granting permission to travel abroad

password *noun* **1** secret word or phrase that ensures admission **2** ICT a sequence of characters that must be keyed in order to

get access to some computers or computer files

past *adjective* **1** of the time before the present **2** ended, gone by **3** (*Grammar*) (of a verb tense) indicating that the action specified took place earlier ⊳ *noun* **4** period of time before the present **5** person's earlier life, especially a disreputable period **6** (*Grammar*) past tense ⊳ *adverb* **7** by, along ⊳ *preposition* **8** beyond **9** past it (*informal*) unable to do the things you could do when younger

pasta *noun* type of food, such as spaghetti, that is made in different shapes from flour and water

paste *noun* **1** moist soft mixture, such as toothpaste **2** adhesive, especially for paper **3** (*Brit*) pastry dough **4** shiny glass used to make imitation jewellery ⊳ *verb* **5** to fasten with paste

pastel *noun* **1** coloured chalk crayon for drawing **2** picture drawn in pastels **3** pale delicate colour ⊳ *adjective* **4** pale and delicate in colour

pasteurized *adjective* (of food or drinks) treated with a special heating process to kill bacteria

pastime *noun* activity that makes time pass pleasantly

pastor *noun* member of the clergy in charge of a congregation

pastoral *adjective* **1** of or depicting country life **2** of a clergyman or his duties

past participle *noun* (*Grammar*) the form of a verb, usually ending in *ed* or *en*, that is used to make some past tenses and the passive.

For example *killed* in *she has killed the goldfish* and *broken* in *a window had been broken* are past participles

pastry pastries *noun* 1 baking dough made of flour, fat and water 2 cake or pie

past tense *noun* (*Grammar*) tense of a verb that is used mainly to refer to things that happened or existed before the time of writing or speaking

pasture *noun* grassy land for farm animals to graze on

pasty¹ pastier, pastiest [**pay**-stee] *adjective* (of a complexion) pale and unhealthy

pasty² pasties [**pass**-tee] *noun* round of pastry folded over a savoury filling

pat pats, patting, patted *verb* 1 to tap lightly ▷ *noun* 2 gentle tap or stroke 3 small shaped mass of butter etc ▷ *adjective* 4 quick, ready or glib 5 **off pat** learned thoroughly

patch *noun* 1 piece of material sewn on a garment 2 small contrasting section 3 plot of ground 4 protective pad for the eye ▷ *verb* 5 to mend with a patch > **patch up** *verb* 1 to repair clumsily 2 to make up (a quarrel)

patchwork *noun* needlework made of pieces of different materials sewn together

patchy patchier, patchiest *adjective* of uneven quality or intensity

pâté [pat-ay] *noun* spread of finely minced liver etc

patent *noun* 1 document giving the exclusive right to make or sell an invention ▷ *adjective* 2 obvious: *It's patent nonsense* ▷ *verb* 3 to obtain a patent for (an invention) > **patently** *adverb*

paternal *adjective* 1 fatherly 2 related through your father

paternity *noun* fact or state of being a father

path *noun* 1 surfaced walk or track 2 course of action

pathetic *adjective* 1 causing feelings of pity or sadness 2 distressingly inadequate > **pathetically** *adverb*

pathological *adjective* 1 of pathology 2 (*informal*) extreme and uncontrollable > **pathologically** *adverb*

pathology *noun* scientific study of diseases > **pathologist** *noun*: an *experienced pathologist*

pathos *noun* power of arousing pity or sadness

pathway *noun* path

patience *noun* 1 quality of being patient 2 card game for one

patient *adjective* 1 enduring difficulties or delays calmly ▷ *noun* 2 person receiving medical treatment > **patiently** *adverb*

patio patios *noun* paved area adjoining a house

patriarch *noun* 1 male head of a family or tribe 2 highest-ranking bishop in Orthodox Churches

patrician (*formal*) *noun* 1 member of the nobility ▷ *adjective* 2 of noble birth

patriot *noun* person who loves his or her country and supports its interests > **patriotic** *adjective*: *patriotic songs* > **patriotism** *noun*: *He joined the army out of a sense of patriotism*

patrol patrols, patrolling, patrolled *noun* 1 regular circuit by a guard **2** person or small group patrolling **3** unit of Scouts or Guides ▷ verb **4** to engage in a patrol of (a place)

patron noun **1** person who gives financial support to charities, artists, etc **2** regular customer of a shop, pub, etc

patronize or **patronise** verb **1** to treat in a condescending way **2** to be a patron of ▷ **patronizing** adjective: The tone of the interview was patronizing

patron saint noun saint regarded as the guardian of a country or group

patter verb **1** to make repeated soft tapping sounds ▷ noun **2** quick succession of taps **3** glib rapid speech

pattern noun **1** arrangement of repeated parts or decorative designs **2** regular way that something is done **3** diagram or shape used as a guide to make something

paunch noun protruding belly

pauper noun (old-fashioned) very poor person

pause verb **1** to stop for a time ▷ noun **2** stop or rest in speech or action

pave verb to form (a surface) with stone or brick

pavement noun paved path for pedestrians

pavilion noun **1** building on a playing field etc **2** building for housing an exhibition etc

paw noun **1** animal's foot with claws and pads ▷ verb **2** to scrape with the paw or hoof **3** (informal) to touch in a rough or overfamiliar way

pawn verb **1** to deposit (an article) as security for money borrowed ▷ noun **2** chessman of the lowest value **3** person manipulated by someone else

pawnbroker noun lender of money on goods deposited

pawpaw noun same as a **papaya**

pay pays, paying, paid verb **1** to give money etc in return for goods or services **2** to settle a debt or obligation **3** to compensate (for) **4** to give **5** to be profitable to ▷ noun **6** wages or salary

payable adjective due to be paid

payment noun **1** act of paying **2** money paid

payroll noun list of paid employees of an organization

PC abbreviation **1** personal computer **2** (in Britain) Police Constable **3** politically correct

PE abbreviation physical education

pea noun **1** climbing plant with seeds growing in pods **2** its seed, eaten as a vegetable

peace noun **1** calm, quietness **2** absence of anxiety **3** freedom from war **4** harmony between people

peaceful adjective quiet and calm ▷ **peacefully** adverb

peach noun **1** soft juicy fruit with a stone and a downy skin **2** (informal) very pleasing person or thing ▷ adjective **3** pinkish-orange

peacock noun large male bird with a brilliantly coloured fanlike tail

peak noun **1** pointed top, especially of a mountain **2** point of greatest development etc **3** projecting piece on the front of a cap ▷ verb **4** to form or reach a peak

▷ *adjective* **5** of or at the point of greatest demand

peal *noun* **1** long loud echoing sound, especially of bells or thunder ▷ *verb* **2** to sound with a peal or peals

peanut *noun* **1** pea-shaped nut that ripens underground **2** **peanuts** (*informal*) trifling amount of money

pear *noun* sweet juicy fruit with a narrow top and rounded base

pearl *noun* hard round shiny object found inside some oyster shells and used as a jewel

peasant *noun* person working on the land, especially in poorer countries or in the past

peat *noun* decayed vegetable material found in bogs, used as fertilizer or fuel

pebble *noun* small roundish stone

peck *verb* **1** to strike or pick up with the beak **2** (*informal*) to kiss quickly **3** **peck at** to nibble or eat reluctantly ▷ *noun* **4** pecking movement

peculiar *adjective* **1** strange **2** distinct, special **3** belonging exclusively to > **peculiarly** *adverb*

pedal pedals, pedalling, pedalled *noun* **1** foot-operated lever used to control a vehicle or machine, or to modify the tone of a musical instrument ▷ *verb* **2** to propel (a bicycle) by using its pedals

pedantic *adjective* excessively concerned with details and rules, especially in academic work

peddle *verb* to sell (goods) from door to door

pedestal *noun* base supporting a column, statue, etc

pedestrian *noun* **1** person who walks ▷ *adjective* **2** dull, uninspiring

pedestrian crossing *noun* place marked where pedestrians may cross a road

pediatrician *noun* another spelling of **paediatrician**

pediatrics *noun* another spelling of **paediatrics**

pedigree *noun* register of ancestors, especially of a purebred animal

peek *verb* **1** to glance quickly or secretly ▷ *noun* **2** a quick look at something

peel *verb* **1** to remove the skin or rind of (a vegetable or fruit) **2** (of skin or a surface) to come off in flakes ▷ *noun* **3** rind or skin

peep *verb* **1** to look slyly or quickly **2** to make a small shrill noise ▷ *noun* **3** peeping look **4** small shrill noise

peer *verb* **1** to look closely and intently ▷ *noun* **2** (feminine **peeress**) (in Britain) member of the nobility **3** person of the same status, age, etc

peerage *noun* (*Brit*) **1** whole body of peers **2** rank of a peer

peer group *noun* group of people of similar age, status, etc

peerless *adjective* so magnificent or perfect that nothing can equal it

peewee *noun* black-and-white Australian bird

peg pegs, pegging, pegged *noun* **1** pin or clip for joining, fastening, marking, etc **2** hook or knob for hanging things on **3** **off the peg** (of clothes) ready-to-wear, not tailor-made ▷ *verb* **4** to fasten with pegs **5** to stabilize (prices)

peggy square noun (NZ) small hand-knitted square

pejorative [pij-**jor**-a-tiv] adjective (of words etc) with an insulting or critical meaning

Pekinese noun small dog with a short wrinkled muzzle

> ■ **WORD TIP**
> The plural of Pekinese is Pekinese

pelican noun large water bird with a pouch beneath its bill for storing fish

pellet noun small ball of something

pelt verb 1 to throw (missiles) at 2 **pelt along** to run fast, rush 3 to rain heavily ▷ noun 4 skin of a fur-bearing animal 5 **at full pelt** at top speed

pelvis pelvises noun framework of bones at the base of the spine, to which the hips are attached
> **pelvic** adjective: the pelvic bone

pen pens, penning, penned noun 1 instrument for writing in ink 2 small enclosure for domestic animals ▷ verb 3 to write or compose 4 to enclose (animals) in a pen 5 **penned in** being or feeling trapped or confined

penal [**pee**-nal] adjective of or used in punishment

penalize or **penalise** verb 1 to impose a penalty on 2 to handicap or hinder

penalty penalties noun 1 punishment for a crime or offence 2 (Sport) handicap or disadvantage imposed for breaking a rule, such as a free shot at goal by the opposing team

penance noun voluntary self-punishment to make amends for wrongdoing

pence noun (Brit) a plural of **penny**

penchant [**pon**-shon] noun (formal) inclination or liking

pencil pencils, pencilling, pencilled noun 1 thin cylindrical instrument containing graphite, for writing or drawing ▷ verb 2 to draw, write or mark with a pencil

pendant noun ornament worn on a chain round the neck

pending (formal) preposition 1 while waiting for ▷ adjective 2 not yet decided or settled

pendulum noun suspended weight swinging to and fro, especially as a regulator for a clock

penetrate verb 1 to find or force a way into or through 2 to arrive at the meaning of

penetrating adjective 1 (of a sound) loud and unpleasant 2 quick to understand

pen friend noun friend with whom a person corresponds without meeting

penguin noun flightless black-and-white sea bird of the southern hemisphere

penicillin noun antibiotic drug effective against a wide range of diseases and infections

peninsula noun strip of land nearly surrounded by water

penis penises noun organ of copulation and urination in male mammals

penitent adjective 1 feeling sorry for having done wrong ▷ noun 2 someone who is penitent
> **penitence** noun: a gesture of penitence

penknife penknives noun small knife with blade(s) that fold into the handle

pennant noun triangular flag, especially one used by ships as a signal

penniless adjective very poor

penny pence, pennies noun **1** British bronze coin worth one hundredth of a pound **2** former British and Australian coin worth one twelfth of a shilling

pension noun regular payment to people above a certain age, retired employees, widows, etc

pensioner person receiving a pension

pensive adjective deeply thoughtful, often with a tinge of sadness

pentagon noun geometric figure with five sides

pentathlon [pen-**tath**-lon] noun sports contest in which athletes compete in five different events

penthouse noun flat built on the roof or top floor of a building

pent-up adjective (of an emotion) not released, repressed

penultimate adjective second last

peony peonies noun garden plant with showy red, pink or white flowers

people peoples, peopling, peopled plural noun **1** persons generally **2** the community **3** your family ▷ noun **4** race or nation ▷ verb **5** to provide with inhabitants

pepper noun **1** sharp hot condiment made from the fruit of an East Indian climbing plant **2** colourful tropical fruit used as a vegetable, capsicum ▷ verb **3** to season with pepper **4** to sprinkle or dot

peppermint noun **1** plant that yields an oil with a strong sharp flavour **2** sweet flavoured with this

per preposition **1** for each **2 as per** in accordance with

perceive verb **1** to become aware of (something) through the senses **2** to understand

per cent adverb in each hundred

percentage noun proportion or rate per hundred

perceptible adjective able to be perceived, recognizable

perception noun **1** act of perceiving **2** intuitive judgment

perceptive adjective able to realize or notice things that are not obvious ▷ **perceptively** adverb

perch noun **1** resting place for a bird **2** any of various edible fishes ▷ verb **3** to alight, rest or place on or as if on a perch

percolator noun coffeepot in which boiling water is forced through a tube and filters down through coffee

percussion noun **1** striking of one thing against another **2** [MUSIC] percussion instruments collectively

perennial adjective **1** lasting through many years ▷ noun **2** plant lasting more than two years

perfect adjective **1** having all the essential elements **2** faultless **3** correct or precise **4** utter or absolute **5** excellent ▷ noun **6** (Grammar) perfect tense ▷ verb **7** to improve **8** to make fully correct ▷ **perfectly** adverb

perfectionist noun person who demands the highest standards of excellence

perforated adjective pierced with holes >**perforation** noun: perforation of the eardrum

perform verb 1 to carry out (an action) 2 to act, sing or present a play before an audience 3 to fulfil (a request etc) >**performer** noun: a world-class performer

performance noun 1 act of performing 2 artistic or dramatic production 3 manner or quality of functioning: the poor performance of our economy

perfume noun 1 liquid cosmetic worn for its pleasant smell 2 fragrance > verb 3 to give a pleasant smell to >**perfumed** adjective: a perfumed envelope

perfunctory adjective done only as a matter of routine, superficial

perhaps adverb possibly, maybe

peril noun great danger >**perilous** adjective: a perilous journey >**perilously** adverb

perimeter [per-**rim**-it-er] noun (length) of the outer edge of an area

period noun 1 particular portion of time 2 single occurrence of menstruation 3 division of time at school etc when a particular subject is taught 4 (US) full stop > adjective 5 (of furniture, dress, a play, etc) dating from or in the style of an earlier time

periodical noun 1 magazine issued at regular intervals > adjective 2 periodic

peripheral [per-**if**-er-al] adjective 1 unimportant, not central 2 on or relating to the edge of an area

periphery peripheries [per-**if**-er-ee] noun 1 boundary or edge 2 fringes of a field of activity

perish verb 1 to be destroyed or die 2 to decay or rot

perjury perjuries noun (Law) act or crime of lying while under oath in a court

perk noun (informal) incidental benefit gained from a job, such as a company car > **perk up** verb to cheer up

perm noun 1 long-lasting curly hairstyle produced by treating the hair with chemicals > verb 2 to give (hair) a perm

permanent adjective lasting forever >**permanence** noun: belief in the permanence of nature >**permanently** adverb

permeable adjective (formal) able to be permeated, especially by liquid

permeate verb to penetrate or spread throughout (something)

permissible adjective allowed by the rules

permission noun authorization to do something

permissive adjective tolerant or lenient, especially in sexual matters >**permissiveness** noun: An atmosphere of permissiveness prevails

permit permits, permitting, permitted verb 1 to give permission, allow > noun 2 document giving permission to do something

permutation noun any of the ways a number of things can be arranged or combined

pernicious adjective (formal) 1 wicked 2 extremely harmful, deadly

peroxide noun 1 hydrogen peroxide used as a hair bleach

2 oxide containing a high proportion of oxygen

perpendicular adjective **1** at right angles to a line or surface **2** upright or vertical ▷ noun **3** line or plane at right angles to another

perpetrate verb to commit or be responsible for (a wrongdoing) >**perpetrator** noun: the perpetrator of this crime

perpetual adjective **1** lasting forever **2** continually repeated >**perpetually** adverb

perpetuate verb to cause to continue or be remembered

perplexed adjective puzzled or bewildered

persecute verb **1** to treat cruelly because of race, religion, etc **2** to subject to persistent harassment >**persecution** noun: political persecution >**persecutor** noun: They rose up against their persecutors

persevere verb to keep making an effort despite difficulties >**perseverance** noun: This will require enormous patience and perseverance

Persian [**per**-shn] adjective, noun old word for Iranian, used especially when referring to the older forms of the language

persimmon noun sweet red tropical fruit

persist verb **1** to continue to be or happen **2** to continue in spite of obstacles or objections >**persistence** noun: Skill only comes with practice and persistence >**persistent** adjective: persistent rain

person people or persons noun **1** human being **2** body of a human being **3** (Grammar) form of pronouns and verbs that shows if a person is speaking, spoken to, or spoken of **4** in person actually present

WORD TIP

The usual plural of person is people. Persons is much less common, and is used only in formal or official English

personal adjective **1** individual or private **2** of the body: personal hygiene **3** (of a remark etc) offensive

personality personalities noun **1** person's distinctive characteristics **2** celebrity

personification noun **1** form of imagery in which something inanimate is described as if it has human qualities **2** living example of a particular quality: the personification of evil

personify personifies, personifying, personified verb **1** to give human characteristics to **2** to be an example of, typify

personnel noun **1** people employed in an organization **2** department in an organization that appoints or keeps records of employees

perspective noun **1** view of the relative importance of situations or facts **2** method of drawing that gives the effect of solidity and relative distances and sizes

perspiration noun sweat

perspire verb to sweat

persuade verb **1** to make (someone) do something by argument, charm, etc **2** to convince

pertaining adjective (formal) **pertaining to** about or concerning

pertinent adjective relevant

perturbed adjective greatly worried

Peruvian [per-**roo**-vee-an] adjective **1** belonging or relating to Peru ▷ noun **2** someone from Peru

pervade verb to spread right through (something) > **pervasive** adjective: the pervasive influence of the army in national life

perverse adjective deliberately doing something different from what is thought normal or proper > **perversely** adverb > **perversity** noun: What sort of perversity causes people to resist so obvious a good?

pervert verb **1** to use or alter for a wrong purpose **2** to lead into abnormal (sexual) behaviour ▷ noun **3** person who practises sexual perversion

perverted adjective **1** having disgusting or unacceptable behaviour or ideas, especially sexual behaviour or ideas **2** completely wrong: a perverted sense of value

peseta [pa-**say**-ta] noun former monetary unit of Spain

peso pesos [**pay**-soh] noun main unit of currency in several South American countries

pessimism noun tendency to expect the worst in all things > **pessimist** noun: I'm a natural pessimist; I usually expect the worst > **pessimistic** adjective: a pessimistic view of life

pest noun **1** annoying person **2** insect or animal that damages crops

pester verb to annoy or nag continually

pesticide noun chemical for killing insect pests

pet pets, petting, petted noun **1** animal kept for pleasure and companionship **2** person favoured or indulged ▷ adjective **3** particularly cherished ▷ verb **4** to treat as a pet **5** to pat or stroke affectionately **6** (old-fashioned) to kiss and caress erotically

petal noun one of the brightly coloured outer parts of a flower

peter out verb to come gradually to an end

petite adjective (of a woman) small and slim

petition noun **1** formal request, especially one signed by many people and presented to a government or other authority ▷ verb **2** to present a petition to (a government or someone in authority)

petrified adjective very frightened

petrol noun flammable liquid obtained from petroleum, used as fuel in internal-combustion engines

petroleum noun thick dark oil found underground

petticoat noun woman's skirt-shaped undergarment

petty pettier, pettiest adjective **1** unimportant or trivial **2** small-minded **3** on a small scale: petty crime

petulant adjective childishly irritable or peevish > **petulance** noun: His petulance made her impatient > **petulantly** adverb

petunia noun garden plant with funnel-shaped flowers

pew noun fixed benchlike seat in a church

pewter noun greyish metal made of tin and lead

pH noun (Chemistry) measure of the acidity of a solution

phalanger noun long-tailed Australian tree-dwelling marsupial

phallus phalluses or phalli noun penis, especially as a symbol of reproductive power in primitive rites > **phallic** adjective: a phallic symbol

phantom noun **1** ghost **2** unreal vision

pharaoh [fare-oh] noun king (of ancient Egypt)

pharmaceutical adjective connected with the industrial production of medicines

pharmacist noun person who is qualified to prepare and sell medicines

pharmacy pharmacies noun **1** preparation and dispensing of drugs and medicines **2** pharmacist's shop

phase noun **1** any distinct or characteristic stage in a development or chain of events ▷ verb **2** to arrange or carry out in stages or to coincide with something else > **phase in** verb to introduce gradually > **phase out** verb to discontinue gradually

PhD abbreviation Doctor of Philosophy: degree awarded to someone who has done advanced research in a subject

pheasant noun game bird with bright plumage

phenomenal adjective extraordinarily great or good > **phenomenally** adverb

phenomenon phenomena noun **1** anything appearing or observed **2** remarkable person or thing

philanthropist noun someone who freely gives help or money to people in need > **philanthropic** adjective: philanthropic organizations > **philanthropy** noun: a retired banker well known for his philanthropy

philistine adjective, noun person who is hostile towards culture and the arts

philosophical or **philosophic** adjective **1** of philosophy **2** calm in the face of difficulties or disappointments

philosophy philosophies noun **1** study of the meaning of life, knowledge, thought, etc **2** theory or set of ideas held by a particular philosopher **3** person's outlook on life > **philosopher** noun

phishing [fish-ing] noun practice of tricking computer users into revealing their financial data in order to defraud them

phlegm [flem] noun thick yellowish substance formed in the nose and throat during a cold

phobia noun intense and unreasoning fear or dislike > **phobic** adjective: He is phobic about getting in lifts

-phobia suffix fear of: claustrophobia

phoenix noun legendary bird said to set fire to itself and rise anew from its ashes

phone (informal) noun **1** telephone ▷ verb **2** to call or talk to (a person) by telephone

-phone suffix giving off sound: telephone

phoney phoneys, phonies; phonier, phoniest (informal) adjective **1** not genuine **2** insincere ▷ noun **3** phoney person or thing photo | 402

photo photos noun short for **photograph**

photo- prefix light or using light: photography

photocopy photocopies, photocopying, photocopied noun **1** photographic reproduction ▷ verb **2** to make a photocopy of ▷ **photocopier** noun

photogenic adjective always looking attractive in photographs

photograph noun **1** picture made by the chemical action of light on sensitive film ▷ verb **2** to take a photograph of

photographic adjective **1** connected with photography **2** (of a person's memory) able to retain facts or appearances in precise detail

photosynthesis noun process by which a green plant uses sunlight to build up carbohydrate reserves

phrasal verb noun phrase consisting of a verb and an adverb or preposition, with a meaning different from the parts, such as {take in} meaning {deceive}

phrase noun **1** group of words forming a unit of meaning, especially within a sentence **2** short effective expression ▷ verb **3** to express in words

physical adjective **1** of the body, as contrasted with the mind or spirit **2** of material things or nature **3** of physics ▷ **physically** adverb

physical education noun training and practice in sports and gymnastics

physician noun doctor of medicine

physics noun science of the properties of matter and energy

▷ **physicist** noun: a nuclear physicist

physio- prefix to do with the body or natural functions: physiotherapy

physiology noun science of the normal function of living things

physiotherapy noun treatment of disease or injury by physical means such as massage, rather than by drugs ▷ **physiotherapist** noun: She sees a physiotherapist once a week

physique noun person's bodily build and muscular development

pi noun (Maths) a number, approximately 3.142 and symbolized by the Greek letter π. It is the ratio of the circumference of a circle to its diameter

piano pianos noun **1** musical instrument with strings which are struck by hammers worked by a keyboard (also **pianoforte**) ▷ adverb **2** (Music) quietly ▷ **pianist** noun

piccolo piccolos noun small flute

pick verb **1** to choose **2** to remove (flowers or fruit) from a plant **3** to take hold of and move with the fingers **4** to provoke (a fight etc) deliberately **5** to open (a lock) by means other than a key ▷ noun **6** choice **7** best part **8** tool with a curved iron crossbar and wooden shaft, for breaking up hard ground or rocks ▷ **pick on** verb to continually treat someone unfairly ▷ **pick out** verb **1** to select for use or special consideration **2** to recognize (a person or thing) ▷ **pick up** verb **1** to raise or lift **2** to collect **3** to improve

pickaxe noun large pick

picket noun **1** person or group standing outside a workplace to deter would-be workers during a strike ▷ verb 2 to form a picket outside (a workplace)

pickings plural noun money easily acquired

pickle noun 1 food preserved in vinegar or salt water 2 (*informal*) awkward situation ▷ verb 3 to preserve in vinegar or salt water

pickpocket noun thief who steals from someone's pocket

picnic picnics, picnicking, picnicked noun 1 informal meal out of doors ▷ verb 2 to have a picnic

pictorial adjective of or in painting or pictures

picture noun 1 drawing or painting 2 photograph 3 mental image 4 beautiful or picturesque object 5 image on a TV screen 6 **the pictures** cinema ▷ verb 7 to visualize or imagine 8 to represent in a picture

picturesque adjective 1 (of a place or view) pleasant to look at 2 (of language) forceful or vivid

pie noun dish of meat, fruit, etc baked in pastry

piece noun 1 separate bit or part 2 instance: *a piece of luck* 3 example or specimen 4 literary or musical composition 5 coin 6 small object used in draughts, chess, etc ▷ verb 7 **piece together** to make or assemble bit by bit

piecemeal adverb bit by bit

pier noun 1 platform on stilts sticking out into the sea 2 pillar, especially one supporting a bridge

pierce verb 1 to make a hole in or through with a sharp instrument 2 to make a way through

piercing adjective 1 (of a sound) shrill and high-pitched 2 (of eyes or a stare) intense and penetrating

piety pieties noun deep devotion to God and religion

pig noun 1 animal kept and killed for pork, ham and bacon 2 (*informal*) greedy, dirty or rude person

pigeon noun bird with a heavy body and short legs, sometimes trained to carry messages

pigeonhole noun 1 compartment for papers in a desk etc ▷ verb 2 to classify

piggyback noun 1 ride on someone's shoulders ▷ adverb 2 carried on someone's shoulders

piglet noun young pig

pigment noun colouring matter, paint or dye ▷ **pigmentation** noun: *the pigmentation of the skin*

pigsty pigsties noun hut with a small enclosed area where pigs are kept

pigtail noun plait of hair hanging from the back or either side of the head

pike noun 1 large freshwater fish with strong teeth 2 (*History*) pointed metal blade attached to a long pole, used as a weapon

pilchard noun small edible fish of the herring family

pile noun 1 number of things lying on top of each other 2 (*informal*) large amount 3 fibres of a carpet or a fabric, especially velvet, that stand up from the weave ▷ verb 4 to collect into a pile

pile-up noun (*informal*) traffic accident involving several vehicles

pilfer verb to steal (minor items) in small quantities

pilgrim noun RE person who journeys to a holy place
> **pilgrimage** noun: the pilgrimage to Mecca

pill noun **1** small ball of medicine swallowed whole **2 the pill** pill taken by a woman to prevent pregnancy

pillage verb **1** to steal property by violence in war ▷ noun **2** violent seizure of goods, especially in war

pillar noun **1** upright post, usually supporting a roof **2** strong supporter

pillar box noun (in Britain) red pillar-shaped letter box in the street

pillory pillories, pillorying, pilloried verb to ridicule publicly

pillow noun stuffed cloth bag for supporting the head in bed

pillowcase or **pillowslip** noun removable cover for a pillow

pilot noun **1** person qualified to fly an aircraft or spacecraft **2** person employed to steer a ship entering or leaving a harbour ▷ adjective **3** experimental and preliminary ▷ verb **4** to act as the pilot of **5** to guide or lead (a project or people)

pimp noun man who gets customers for a prostitute in return for a share of his or her earnings

pimple noun small pus-filled spot on the skin > **pimply** adjective: pimply teenagers

pin pins, pinning, pinned noun **1** short thin piece of stiff wire with a point and head, for fastening things **2** wooden or metal peg or stake ▷ verb **3** to fasten with a pin **4** to seize and hold fast > **pin down** verb **1** to force (someone) to make a decision, take action, etc **2** to define clearly

PIN abbreviation personal identification number: a number used by the holder of a cash card or credit card

pinafore noun **1** apron **2** dress with a bib top

pincers plural noun **1** tool consisting of two hinged arms, for gripping **2** claws of a lobster etc

pinch verb **1** to squeeze (something) between finger and thumb **2** to cause pain by being too tight **3** (informal) to steal ▷ noun **4** act of pinching **5** as much as can be taken up between the finger and thumb **6 at a pinch** if absolutely necessary

pinched adjective (of someone's face) thin and pale

pine verb **1 pine for** to feel great longing (for) ▷ noun **2** evergreen coniferous tree with very thin leaves **3** its wood

pineapple noun large tropical fruit with juicy yellow flesh and a hard skin

Ping-Pong ® noun table tennis

pink noun **1** pale reddish colour **2** fragrant garden plant **3 in the pink** in good health ▷ adjective **4** of the colour pink

pinnacle noun **1** highest point of fame or success **2** mountain peak

pinpoint verb **1** to locate or identify exactly ▷ adjective **2** exact: pinpoint accuracy

pinstripe noun **1** very narrow stripe in fabric **2** the fabric itself

pint noun liquid measure, 1/8 gallon (.568 litre)

pioneer noun **1** explorer or early settler of a new country

2 originator or developer of something new ▷ *verb* **3** to be the pioneer or leader of

pious *adjective* deeply religious

pip *noun* **1** small seed in a fruit **2** high-pitched sound used as a time signal on radio

pipe *noun* **1** tube for conveying liquid or gas **2** tube with a small bowl at the end for smoking tobacco **3** tubular musical instrument **4** **the pipes** bagpipes ▷ *verb* **5** to convey (a liquid such as oil) by pipe

pipeline *noun* **1** long pipe for transporting oil, water, etc **2** means of communication

piper *noun* player on a pipe or bagpipes

piping *noun* **1** system of pipes **2** fancy edging on clothes etc

piranha *noun* small fierce freshwater fish of tropical America

pirate *noun* sea robber

pirouette *noun* spinning turn balanced on the toes of one foot

Pisces [pie-seez] *noun* twelfth sign of the zodiac, represented by two fish

pistil *noun* seed-bearing part of a flower

pistol *noun* short-barrelled handgun

piston *noun* cylindrical part in an engine that slides to and fro in a cylinder

pit pits, pitting, pitted *noun* **1** deep hole in the ground **2** coal mine **3** dent or depression **4** **pits** servicing and refuelling area on a motor-racing track **5** same as **orchestra pit** ▷ *verb* **6** to mark with small dents or scars

pitch *verb* **1** to throw or hurl **2** to set up (a tent) **3** to fall headlong **4** (of a ship or plane) to move with the front and back going up and down alternately **5** to set the level or tone of ▷ *noun* **6** area marked out for playing sport **7** degree or angle of slope **8** degree of highness or lowness of a (musical) sound **9** dark sticky substance obtained from tar

pitcher *noun* large jug with a narrow neck

pitfall *noun* hidden difficulty or danger

pith *noun* soft white lining of the rind of oranges etc

pitiful *adjective* **1** arousing pity **2** woeful, contemptible

pittance *noun* very small amount of money

pitted *adjective* covered in small hollows

pity pities, pitying, pitied *noun* **1** sympathy or sorrow for others' suffering **2** regrettable fact ▷ *verb* **3** to feel pity for

pivot *noun* **1** central shaft on which something turns ▷ *verb* **2** to provide with or turn on a pivot

pixie pixies *noun* (in folklore) fairy

pizza *noun* flat disc of dough covered with a wide variety of savoury toppings and baked

placard *noun* notice that is carried or displayed in public

placate *verb* to make (someone) stop feeling angry or upset

place *noun* **1** particular part of an area or space **2** particular town, building, etc **3** position or point reached **4** seat or space **5** usual position **6** **take place** to happen ▷ *verb* **7** to put in a particular place

a b c d e f g h i j k l m n o p q r s t u v w x y z

8 to identify, put in context **9** to make (an order, bet, etc)

placebo placebos or placeboes [plas-**see**-bo] noun substance given to a patient in place of a drug and from which, though it has no active ingredients, the patient may imagine they get some benefit

placenta placentas or placentae [plass-**ent**-a] noun organ formed in the womb during pregnancy, providing nutrients for the fetus

placid adjective not easily excited or upset, calm > **placidly** adverb

plagiarism noun copying ideas or passages from someone else's work and pretending it is your own > **plagiarist** noun

plague plagues, plaguing, plagued noun **1** fast-spreading fatal disease **2** (History) bubonic plague **3** overwhelming number of things that afflict or harass > verb **4** to trouble or annoy continually

plaice noun edible European flatfish

plaid noun tartan cloth or pattern

plain adjective **1** easy to see or understand **2** expressed honestly and clearly **3** without decoration or pattern **4** not beautiful **5** simple or ordinary > noun **6** large stretch of level country > adverb **7** clearly or simply: plain stupid > **plainly** adverb

plaintiff noun person who sues in a court of law

plait [platt] noun **1** intertwined length of hair > verb **2** to intertwine separate strands in a pattern

plan plans, planning, planned noun **1** way thought out to do or achieve something **2** diagram showing the layout or design of something

> verb **3** to arrange beforehand **4** to make a diagram of

plane noun **1** aeroplane **2** (Maths) flat surface **3** level of attainment etc **4** tool for smoothing wood > adjective **5** perfectly flat or level > verb **6** to smooth (wood) with a plane

planet noun large body in space that revolves round the sun or another star > **planetary** adjective: planetary systems

plank noun long flat piece of sawn timber

plankton noun minute animals and plants floating in the surface water of a sea or lake

plant noun **1** living organism that grows in the ground and has no power to move **2** equipment or machinery used in industrial processes **3** factory or other industrial premises > verb **4** to set (seeds or crops) into the ground to grow **5** to place firmly in position

plantation noun **1** estate for the cultivation of tea, tobacco, etc **2** wood of cultivated trees

plaque noun **1** flat piece of metal which is fixed to a wall and has an inscription in memory of a famous person or event **2** filmy deposit on teeth that causes decay

plasma noun clear liquid part of blood

plaster noun **1** mixture of lime, sand, etc for coating walls **2** adhesive strip of material for dressing cuts etc > verb **3** to coat (a wall or ceiling) with plaster **4** to coat thickly > **plasterer** noun

plastered adjective **1** plastered to stuck to **2** plastered with covered with

plastic noun **1** synthetic material that can be moulded when soft but sets in a hard long-lasting shape **2** credit cards etc as opposed to cash ▷ adjective **3** made of plastic **4** easily moulded, pliant

plastic surgery noun repair or reconstruction of missing or malformed parts of the body

plate noun **1** shallow dish for holding food **2** flat thin sheet of metal, glass, etc **3** thin coating of metal on another metal ▷ verb **4** to coat (a metal surface) with a thin coating of another metal

plateau plateaus or plateaux noun **1** area of level high land **2** stage when there is no change or development

platform noun **1** raised floor **2** raised area in a station from which passengers board trains **3** structure in the sea which holds machinery, stores, etc for drilling an oil well **4** programme of a political party

platinum noun (Chemistry) valuable silvery-white metal

platitude noun remark that is true but not interesting or original

platonic adjective (of a relationship) friendly or affectionate but not sexual

platoon noun smaller unit within a company of soldiers

platter noun large dish

platypus platypuses noun Australian egg-laying amphibious mammal, with dense fur, webbed feet and a ducklike bill (also **duck-billed platypus**)

plaudits plural noun expressions of approval

plausible adjective **1** apparently true or reasonable **2** persuasive but insincere ▷ **plausibility** noun: the plausibility of the theory ▷ **plausibly** adverb

play verb **1** to occupy yourself in (a game or recreation) **2** to compete against (someone) in a game or sport **3** to act (a part) on the stage **4** to perform on (a musical instrument) **5** to give out sound (a radio, CD player, etc) to give out sound ▷ noun **6** story performed on stage or broadcast **7** activities children take part in for amusement **8** playing of a game **9** conduct: fair play **10** (scope for) freedom of movement

playboy noun rich man who lives only for pleasure

playful adjective **1** friendly and light-hearted **2** lively ▷ **playfully** adverb

playground noun outdoor area for children to play in

playgroup noun regular meeting of very young children for supervised play

playing card noun one of a set of 52 cards used in card games

playing field noun extensive piece of ground for sport

playwright noun (DRAMA) author of plays

plaza noun **1** open space or square **2** modern shopping complex

plea noun **1** serious or urgent request, entreaty **2** statement of a prisoner or defendant **3** excuse

plead verb **1** to ask urgently or with deep feeling **2** to give as an excuse **3** (Law) to declare yourself to be guilty or innocent of a charge made against you

pleasant adjective pleasing or enjoyable ▷ **pleasantly** adverb

please verb 1 to give pleasure or satisfaction to (someone) ▷ adverb 2 polite word of request ▷ **pleased** adjective: I'm pleased to be going home

pleasing adjective attractive, satisfying or enjoyable

pleasure noun 1 feeling of happiness and satisfaction 2 something that causes this

pleat noun 1 fold made by doubling material back on itself ▷ verb 2 to arrange (material) in pleats

plebiscite [pleb-iss-ite] noun decision by direct voting of the people of a country

pledge noun 1 solemn promise 2 something valuable given as a guarantee that a promise will be kept or a debt paid ▷ verb 3 to promise solemnly 4 to bind by or as if by a pledge

plentiful adjective existing in large amounts or numbers ▷ **plentifully** adverb

plenty noun 1 large amount or number 2 quite enough

plethora noun excess

pleurisy noun inflammation of the membrane covering the lungs

pliable adjective 1 easily bent 2 easily influenced

pliers plural noun tool with hinged arms and jaws for gripping

plight noun difficult or dangerous situation

plinth noun slab forming the base of a statue, column, etc

plod plods, plodding, plodded verb 1 to walk with slow heavy steps 2 to work slowly but determinedly

plonk verb to put (something) down heavily and carelessly

plop plops, plopping, plopped noun 1 sound of an object falling into water without a splash ▷ verb 2 to make this sound

plot plots, plotting, plotted noun 1 secret plan to do something illegal or wrong 2 story of a film, novel, etc 3 small piece of land ▷ verb 4 to plan secretly, conspire 5 to mark the position or course of (a ship or aircraft) on a map 6 to mark and join up (points on a graph)

plough noun 1 agricultural tool for turning over soil ▷ verb 2 to turn over (earth) with a plough 3 **plough through** to move or work through slowly and laboriously

ploy noun manoeuvre designed to gain an advantage

pluck verb 1 to pull or pick off 2 to pull out the feathers of (a bird for cooking) 3 to sound the strings of (a guitar etc) with the fingers ▷ noun 4 bravery or courage

plug plugs, plugging, plugged noun 1 thing fitting into and filling a hole 2 device connecting an appliance to an electricity supply ▷ verb 3 to block or seal (a hole or gap) with a plug 4 (informal) to advertise (a product etc) by constant repetition

plum noun 1 oval usually dark red fruit with a stone in the middle ▷ adjective 2 dark purplish-red

plumage noun bird's feathers

plumber noun person who fits and repairs pipes and fixtures for water and drainage systems

plumbing noun pipes and fixtures used in water and drainage systems

plume noun feather, especially one worn as an ornament

plummet plummets, plummeting, plummeted verb to plunge downward

plump adjective moderately fat

plunder verb 1 to seize (valuables) from (a place) by force, especially in wartime ▷ noun 2 things plundered, spoils

plunge verb 1 to put or throw forcibly or suddenly (into) 2 to descend steeply 3 **plunge into** to become deeply involved in ▷ noun 4 plunging, dive

Plunket Society noun organization for the care of mothers and babies, now called the Royal New Zealand Society for the Health of Women and Children

plural adjective 1 of or consisting of more than one ▷ noun 2 word indicating more than one

pluralism noun existence and toleration of a variety of peoples, opinions, etc in a society > **pluralist** adjective: a pluralist democracy

plural noun noun name given to a noun normally used only in the plural, for example 'scissors' or 'police'

plus preposition, adjective 1 indicating addition ▷ adjective 2 more than zero 3 positive 4 advantageous ▷ noun 5 sign (+) denoting addition 6 advantage

plush noun 1 fabric with long velvety pile ▷ adjective 2 luxurious

Pluto noun smallest planet in the solar system and farthest from the sun

ply plies, plying, plied verb 1 to work at (a job or trade) 2 to use

(a tool) 3 **ply with** to supply with or subject to persistently ▷ noun 4 thickness of wool, fabric, etc

plywood noun board made of thin layers of wood glued together

p.m. abbreviation after noon

pneumatic adjective worked by or inflated with wind or air

pneumonia noun inflammation of the lungs

poach verb 1 to catch (animals) illegally on someone else's land 2 to simmer (food) gently in liquid

pocket noun 1 small bag sewn into clothing for carrying things 2 pouchlike container, especially for catching balls at the edge of a snooker table 3 isolated or distinct group or area ▷ verb 4 to put (something) into your pocket 5 to take (something) secretly or dishonestly

pocket money noun small regular allowance given to children by parents

pod noun long narrow seed case of peas, beans, etc

podcast noun 1 audio file similar to a radio broadcast which can be downloaded to a computer, MP3 player, etc. ▷ verb 2 to create such files and make them available for downloading

poddy poddies noun (Aust) calf or lamb that is being fed by hand

podium podiums or podia noun small raised platform for a conductor or speaker

poem noun imaginative piece of writing in rhythmic lines

poet noun writer of poems

poetic adjective of or like poetry > **poetically** adverb

poetry noun **1** poems **2** art of writing poems

poignant adjective sharply painful to the feelings > **poignancy** noun: the film contains moments of almost unbearable poignancy

point noun **1** main idea in a discussion, argument, etc **2** aim or purpose **3** detail or item **4** characteristic **5** particular position, stage or time **6** dot indicating decimals **7** sharp end **8** unit for recording a value or score **9** one of the direction marks of a compass **10** electrical socket **11** on the point of very shortly going to > verb **12** to show the direction or position of something or draw attention to it by extending a finger or other pointed object towards it **13** to direct or face towards

point-blank adjective **1** fired at a very close target **2** (of a remark or question) direct, blunt > adverb **3** directly without

pointed adjective **1** having a sharp end **2** (of a remark) obviously directed at a particular person > **pointedly** adverb

pointer noun helpful hint

pointless adjective meaningless or irrelevant > **pointlessly** adverb

point of view points of view noun way of considering something

poise noun calm dignified manner

poised adjective **1** absolutely ready **2** behaving with or showing poise

poison noun **1** substance that kills or injures when swallowed or absorbed > verb **2** to give poison to someone **3** to have a harmful or evil effect on

poisonous adjective **1** containing a harmful substance that could kill you or make you ill **2** (of an animal) producing a venom that can cause death or illness in anyone bitten or stung by it

poke verb **1** to jab or prod with your finger, a stick, etc **2** to thrust forward or out > noun **3** poking

poker noun **1** metal rod for stirring a fire **2** card game in which players bet on the hands dealt

polar adjective of or near either of the earth's poles

polar bear noun white bear that lives in the regions around the North Pole

pole noun **1** long rounded piece of wood etc **2** point furthest north or south on the earth's axis of rotation **3** either of the opposite ends of a magnet or electric cell

Pole noun someone from Poland

pole vault noun athletics event in which contestants jump over a high bar using a long flexible pole to lift themselves into the air

police noun **1** organized force in a state which keeps law and order > verb **2** to control or watch over with police or a similar body

policeman policemen noun member of a police force > **policewoman** noun

policy policies noun **1** plan of action adopted by a person, group or state **2** document containing an insurance contract

polio noun disease affecting the spinal cord, which often causes paralysis (also **poliomyelitis**)

polish verb **1** to make smooth and shiny by rubbing **2** to make more nearly perfect > noun **3** substance used for polishing **4** pleasing elegant style

Polish *adjective* **1** belonging or relating to Poland ▷ *noun* **2** main language spoken in Poland

polite *adjective* **1** showing consideration for others in your manners, speech, etc **2** socially correct or refined > **politely** *adverb* > **politeness** *noun*: She listened out of politeness

political *adjective* of the state, government or public administration > **politically** *adverb*

politically correct *adjective* (of language) intended to avoid any implied prejudice

politician *noun* person actively engaged in politics, especially a member of parliament

politics *noun* **1** winning and using of power to govern society **2** (study of) the art of government **3** person's beliefs about how a country should be governed

polka *noun* **1** lively 19th-century dance **2** music for this

poll *noun* **1** questioning of a random sample of people to find out general opinion **2** voting **3** number of votes recorded **4** **the polls** political election ▷ *verb* **5** to receive (votes) **6** to question (a person) in an opinion poll

pollen *noun* fine dust produced by flowers to fertilize other flowers

pollinate *verb* to fertilize by the transfer of pollen > **pollination** *noun*: without sufficient pollination, the growth of the corn is stunted

pollutant *noun* something that pollutes

pollute *verb* to contaminate with something poisonous or harmful > **polluted** *adjective*: polluted rivers

pollution *noun* harmful or poisonous substances introduced into an environment

polo *noun* game like hockey played by teams of players on horseback

polo-neck *noun* sweater with high turned-over collar

polyester *noun* man-made material used to make plastics and clothes

polygamy [pol-**ig**-a-mee] *noun* practice of having more than one husband or wife at the same time > **polygamous** *adjective*: polygamous societies

polygon *noun* geometrical figure with three or more angles and sides

polystyrene *noun* synthetic material used especially as white rigid foam for packing and insulation

polythene *noun* light plastic used for bags etc

polyunsaturated *adjective* of a group of fats that do not form cholesterol in the blood > **polyunsaturate** *noun*: spreads containing polyunsaturates

pomegranate *noun* round tropical fruit with a thick rind containing many seeds in a red pulp

pomp *noun* stately display or ceremony

pompous *adjective* foolishly serious and grand, self-important > **pomposity** *noun*: the pomposity of some politicians > **pompously** *adverb*

pond *noun* small area of still water

ponder *verb* to think thoroughly or deeply (about)

ponderous *adjective* **1** serious and dull **2** heavy and unwieldy **3** (of

movement) slow and clumsy
> **ponderously** adverb

pong noun (informal) strong unpleasant smell

pontiff noun (formal) the Pope

pony ponies noun small horse

ponytail noun long hair tied in one bunch at the back of the head

pony trekking noun leisure activity in which people ride across country on ponies

poodle noun dog with curly hair often clipped fancifully

pool noun 1 small body of still water 2 swimming pool 3 shared fund or group of workers or resources 4 game in which players try to hit coloured balls into pockets around the table using long sticks called cues ▷ verb 5 to put in a common fund

poor adjective 1 having little money and few possessions 2 less, smaller or weaker than is needed or expected 3 inferior 4 unlucky, pitiable

poorly adverb 1 in a poor manner ▷ adjective 2 not in good health

pop pops, popping, popped verb 1 to make or cause to make a small explosive sound 2 (informal) to go, put or come unexpectedly or suddenly ▷ noun 3 music of general appeal, especially to young people 4 small explosive sound 5 (Brit) nonalcoholic fizzy drink

popcorn noun grains of maize heated until they puff up and burst

Pope noun head of the Roman Catholic Church

poplar noun tall slender tree

poppy poppies noun plant with a large red flower

populace noun (formal) the ordinary people

popular adjective 1 widely liked and admired 2 of or for the public in general > **popularity** noun: the growing popularity of Chilean wines > **popularly** adverb

populate verb 1 to live in, inhabit 2 to fill with inhabitants

population noun 1 all the people who live in a particular place 2 the number of people living in a particular place

pop-up noun (Computers) image that appears above the open window on a computer screen

porcelain noun 1 fine china 2 objects made of it

porch noun covered approach to the entrance of a building

porcupine noun animal covered with long pointed quills

pore noun 1 tiny opening in the skin or in the surface of a plant ▷ verb 2 **pore over** to examine or study intently

pork noun pig meat

pornography noun writing, films or pictures designed to be sexually exciting > **pornographic** adjective: pornographic magazines

porpoise noun fishlike sea mammal

porridge noun breakfast food made of oatmeal cooked in water or milk

port noun 1 (town with) a harbour 2 left side of a ship or aircraft when facing the front of it 3 strong sweet wine, usually red

-port suffix carrying: transport

portable adjective easily carried

porter noun 1 man who carries luggage 2 hospital worker who transfers patients between rooms **3** doorman or gatekeeper of a building

portfolio portfolios noun **1** (flat case for carrying) examples of an artist's work **2** area of responsibility of a government minister **3** list of investments held by an investor

porthole noun small round window in a ship or aircraft

portion noun **1** part or share **2** helping of food for one person **3** destiny or fate

portrait noun **1** picture of a person **2** lifelike description

portray verb to describe or represent by artistic means, as in writing or film > **portrayal** noun: his portrayal of Hamlet

Portuguese adjective **1** of Portugal, its people or their language ▷ noun **2** person from Portugal **3** language of Portugal and Brazil

pose verb **1** to place in or take up a particular position to be photographed or drawn **2** to raise (a problem) **3** to ask (a question) **4 pose as** to pretend to be ▷ noun **5** position while posing **6** behaviour adopted for effect

poser noun **1** puzzling question **2** a person who behaves in a showy way to impress others

posh adjective (informal) **1** smart, luxurious **2** upper-class

position noun **1** place or usual or expected place **2** way in which something is placed or arranged **4** attitude, point of view **5** job ▷ verb **6** to place

positive adjective **1** feeling no doubts, certain **2** confident, hopeful **3** helpful, providing

encouragement **4** absolute, downright **5** (Maths) greater than zero **6** (of an electrical charge) having a deficiency of electrons > **positively** adverb

possess verb **1** to have or own (something) **2** (of a feeling, belief, etc) to have complete control of, dominate > **possessor** noun: the proud possessor of a new car

possession noun **1** state of possessing; ownership **2 possessions** things a person possesses

possessive adjective **1** wanting all the attention or love of another person **2** (of a word) indicating the person or thing that something belongs to

possibility possibilities noun something that might be true or might happen

possible adjective **1** able to exist, happen or be done **2** worthy of consideration ▷ noun **3** person or thing that might be suitable or chosen

possum noun **1** same as **opossum 2** (Aust, NZ) phalanger, a marsupial with thick fur and a long tail

post noun **1** official system of delivering letters and parcels **2** (single collection or delivery of) letters and parcels sent by this system **3** length of wood, concrete, etc fixed upright to support or mark something **4** job ▷ verb **5** to send by post **6** to put up (a notice) in a public place **7** to send (a person) to a new place to work **8** to supply someone regularly with the latest information

post- *prefix* after, later than: *postwar*

postage *noun* charge for sending a letter or parcel by post

postal order *noun* (Brit) written money order sent by post and cashed at a post office by the person who receives it

postbox *noun* metal box with a hole in it which you put letters into for collection by the postman

postcard *noun* card for sending a message by post without an envelope

postcode *noun* system of letters and numbers used to aid the sorting of mail

poster *noun* large picture or notice stuck on a wall

posterior *noun* **1** buttocks ▷ *adjective* **2** behind, at the back of

posterity *noun* (formal) future generations, descendants

posthumous [poss-tume-uss] *adjective* occurring after a person's death: *a posthumous award for bravery* > **posthumously** *adverb*

postman postmen *noun* person who collects and delivers post

postmortem *noun* medical examination of a body to establish the cause of death

post office *noun* **1** place where postal business is conducted **2** Post Office (Brit) government department responsible for postal services

postpone *verb* to put off to a later time > **postponement** *noun*: *the postponement was due to the weather*

posture *noun* **1** position or way in which someone stands, walks, etc ▷ *verb* **2** to behave in an exaggerated way to get attention

posy posies *noun* small bunch of flowers

pot pots, potting, potted *noun* **1** round deep container **2** teapot ▷ *verb* **3** to put (a plant) in soil in a flowerpot

potassium nitrate *noun* white chemical compound used to make gunpowder, fireworks and fertilizers (also **saltpetre**)

potato potatoes *noun* roundish starchy vegetable that grows underground

potent *adjective* **1** effective or powerful **2** (of a male) capable of having sexual intercourse > **potency** *noun*: *the potency of the wine*

potential *adjective* **1** possible but not yet actual ▷ *noun* **2** ability or talent not yet fully used > **potentially** *adverb*

potential energy *noun* energy stored in something

pothole *noun* **1** hole in the surface of a road **2** deep hole in a limestone area

potion *noun* dose of medicine or poison

potted *adjective* **1** grown in a pot **2** (of meat or fish) cooked or preserved in a pot

potter *noun* **1** person who makes pottery ▷ *verb* **2** potter about, around or away to be busy in a pleasant but aimless way

pottery potteries *noun* **1** articles made from baked clay **2** craft of making pottery

potty potties; pottier, pottiest *noun* **1** bowl used by a small child as a toilet ▷ *adjective* **2** (*informal*) crazy or silly

pouch *noun* **1** small bag **2** baglike pocket of skin on an animal

poultry *noun* domestic fowls

pounce *verb* **1** **pounce on** to spring upon suddenly to attack or capture ▷ *noun* **2** pouncing

pound *noun* **1** monetary unit of Britain and some other countries **2** unit of weight equal to 0.454 kg **3** enclosure for stray animals or officially removed vehicles ▷ *verb* **4** to hit heavily and repeatedly **5** to crush to pieces or powder **6** (of the heart) to throb heavily **7** to run heavily

pour *verb* **1** to flow or cause to flow out in a stream **2** to rain heavily **3** to come or go in large numbers

pout *verb* **1** to thrust out (the lips) sullenly or provocatively ▷ *noun* **2** pouting look

poverty *noun* **1** state of being without enough food or money **2** lack of, scarcity

powder *noun* **1** substance in the form of tiny loose particles **2** medicine or cosmetic in this form ▷ *verb* **3** to cover or sprinkle with powder > **powdery** *adjective*

power *noun* **1** ability to do or act **2** strength **3** position of authority or control **4** (*Maths*) product from continuous multiplication of a number by itself **5** (*Physics*) rate at which work is done **6** electricity supply **7** particular form of energy: *nuclear power* ▷ *verb* **8** to supply with power

powerful *adjective* strong, influential or effective: *a powerful car* > **powerfully** *adverb*

powerless *adjective* unable to control or influence events

power station *noun* installation for generating and distributing electric power

practicable *adjective* **1** capable of being done successfully **2** usable

practical *adjective* **1** involving experience or actual use rather than theory **2** sensible, useful and effective **3** good at making or doing things **4** in effect though not in name ▷ *noun* **5** examination in which something has to be done or made > **practicality** *noun*: *the practicalities of everyday life*

practically *adverb* **1** almost but not completely or exactly **2** in a practical way

practice *noun* **1** something done regularly or habitually **2** repetition of something so as to gain skill **3** doctor's or lawyer's place of work

practise *verb* **1** to do repeatedly so as to gain skill **2** to take part in, follow (a religion etc) **3** to work at: *to practise medicine* **4** to do habitually

practised *adjective* expert or skilled as a result of long experience

practitioner *noun* person who practises a profession

pragmatic *adjective* concerned with practical consequences rather than theory > **pragmatically** *adverb* > **pragmatism** *noun*: *a reputation for clear thinking and pragmatism*

prairie *noun* large treeless area of grassland, especially in N America and Canada

a b c d e f g h i j k l m n o p q r s t u v w x y z

praise verb 1 to express approval or admiration of (someone or something) 2 to express honour and thanks to (one's God) ▷ noun 3 something said or written to show approval or admiration

pram noun four-wheeled carriage for a baby, pushed by hand

prance verb to walk with exaggerated bouncing steps

prank noun mischievous trick

prattle verb 1 to chatter in a childish or foolish way ▷ noun 2 childish or foolish talk

prawn noun edible shellfish like a large shrimp

pray verb 1 to say prayers (to God) 2 to ask earnestly

prayer noun 1 thanks or appeal addressed to God 2 set form of words used in praying 3 earnest request

pre- prefix before, beforehand: prenatal; prerecorded; preshrunk

preach verb 1 to give a talk on a religious theme as part of a church service 2 to speak in support of (an idea, principle, etc)

precarious adjective (of a position or situation) dangerous or insecure > **precariously** adverb

precaution noun action taken in advance to prevent something bad happening > **precautionary** adjective: the curfew is a precautionary measure

precede verb to go or be before (someone or something) in time, place or rank > **preceding** adjective coming before: the preceding day

precedence [press-ee-denss] noun formal order of rank or position

precedent noun previous case or occurrence regarded as an example to be followed

precinct noun 1 (Brit, Aust, S Afr) area in a town closed to traffic 2 (Brit, Aust, S Afr) enclosed area round a building 3 (US) administrative area of a city 4 surrounding region

precious adjective 1 of great value and importance 2 loved and treasured

precipice noun very steep face of cliff or rockface

precipitate verb (formal) to cause to happen suddenly

precipitation (formal) noun rain, snow, sleet or hail

precise adjective 1 exact, accurate in every detail 2 strict in observing rules or standards > **precisely** adverb > **precision** noun: The work requires great precision

preclude verb (formal) to make impossible to happen

precocious adjective having developed or matured early or too soon

preconceived adjective (of an idea) formed without real experience or reliable information > **preconception** noun: preconceptions about the sort of people who study computing

precondition noun something that must happen or exist before something else can

precursor noun something that precedes and is a signal of something else, forerunner

predator noun animal that kills and eats other animals > **predatory** adjective: predatory birds

predecessor noun 1 person who precedes another in an office or position 2 ancestor

predetermined adjective decided in advance

predicament noun embarrassing or difficult situation

predict verb to tell about in advance; prophesy ▷ **predictable** adjective: a predictable outcome ▷ **prediction** noun forecast or prophesy: He was unwilling to make a prediction

predominant adjective more important or more noticeable than anything else in a particular set of people or things ▷ **predominantly** adverb

predominate verb to be the main or controlling element ▷ **predominance** noun: the predominance of English on the internet

pre-eminent adjective excelling all others, outstanding ▷ **pre-eminence** noun: London's pre-eminence among European financial centres

pre-empt verb (formal) to prevent an action by doing something which makes it pointless or impossible

preen verb (of a bird) to clean or trim (feathers) with the beak

preface [pref-iss] noun 1 introduction to a book ▷ verb 2 to serve as an introduction to (a book, speech, etc)

prefect noun senior pupil in a school, with limited power over others

prefer prefers, preferring, preferred verb to like better

preference noun 1 liking for one thing above another or above the rest 2 person or thing preferred

preferential adjective showing preference

prefix noun letter or group of letters put at the beginning of a word to make a new word, such as {un-} in {unhappy}

pregnant adjective carrying a fetus in the womb ▷ **pregnancy** noun: Cut out all alcohol during pregnancy

prehistoric adjective of the period before written history begins

prejudice noun 1 unreasonable or unfair dislike or preference ▷ verb 2 to cause (someone) to have a prejudice ▷ **prejudiced** adjective: racially prejudiced ▷ **prejudicial** adjective: rumours considered prejudicial to security

preliminary preliminaries adjective 1 happening before and in preparation, introductory ▷ noun 2 preliminary remark, contest, etc

prelude noun event preceding and introducing something else

premature adjective 1 happening or done before the normal or expected time 2 (of a baby) born before the end of the normal period of pregnancy ▷ **prematurely** adverb

premeditated adjective planned in advance

première noun first performance of a play, film, etc

premise noun statement assumed to be true and used as the basis of reasoning

premium noun 1 additional sum of money, as on a wage or charge 2 (regular) sum paid for insurance

premonition noun feeling that something unpleasant is going to happen

preoccupation noun something that holds the attention completely

preoccupied adjective absorbed in something, especially your own thoughts

preparation noun 1 preparing 2 D&T something done to get ready for a particular purpose or event

preparatory [prip-**par**-a-tree] adjective preparing for

prepare verb to make or get ready

prepared adjective 1 willing 2 ready

preposition noun word used before a noun or pronoun to show its relationship with other words, such as {by} in {go by bus}

preposterous adjective utterly absurd

prerequisite noun (formal) something required before something else is possible

prerogative noun (formal) special power or privilege

prescribe verb to recommend the use of (a medicine)

prescription noun written instructions from a doctor for the making up and use of a medicine

presence noun 1 fact of being in a specified place 2 impressive dignified appearance

present adjective 1 being in a specified place 2 existing or happening now 3 (Grammar) (of a verb tense) indicating that the action specified is taking place now ▷ noun 4 present time or tense 5 something given to bring pleasure to another person ▷ verb 6 to introduce formally or publicly 7 to introduce and compere (a TV or radio show) 8 to cause: present a difficulty 9 to give or offer formally

presentable adjective attractive, neat, fit for people to see

presentation noun 1 act of presenting or a way of presenting something 2 manner of presenting 3 formal ceremony in which an award is made 4 talk or demonstration

present-day adjective existing or happening now: present-day farming practices

presently adverb 1 soon 2 (US, Scot) at the moment

present participle noun (Grammar) the form of a verb that ends in -ing, used to form some tenses and to form adjectives and nouns from a verb

present tense noun (Grammar) tense of a verb that is used mainly to talk about things that happen or exist at the time of writing or speaking

preservative noun chemical that prevents decay

preserve verb 1 to keep from being damaged, changed or ended 2 to treat (food) to prevent it decaying ▷ noun 3 area of interest restricted to a particular person or group 4 fruit preserved by cooking in sugar > **preservation** noun: the preservation of natural resources

preside verb to be in charge, especially of a meeting

president noun 1 head of state in many countries 2 head of a society, institution, etc > **presidential** adjective: presidential elections

press verb 1 to apply force or weight to 2 to squeeze 3 to smooth by applying pressure or heat **4** to urge (someone) insistently **5** to crowd or push ▷ *noun* **6 the press a** news media collectively, especially newspapers **b** journalists collectively **7** printing machine

press conference *noun* interview for reporters given by a person

pressing *adjective* urgent

pressure *noun* **1** force produced by pressing **2** urgent claims or demands **3** (*Physics*) force applied to a surface per unit of area ▷ *verb* **4** to persuade forcefully

pressurize or **pressurise** *verb* to put pressure on (someone) in an attempt to persuade them to do something

prestige *noun* high status or respect resulting from success or achievements > **prestigious** *adjective*: one of the country's most prestigious schools

presumably *adverb* one supposes (that)

presume *verb* **1** to take (something) for granted **2** to dare (to)

presumptuous *adjective* doing things you have no right to do

pretence *noun* behaviour intended to deceive

pretend *verb* to claim or give the appearance of (something untrue) to deceive or in play

pretender *noun* person who makes a false or disputed claim to a position of power

pretension *noun* false claim to merit or importance

pretentious *adjective* making (unjustified) claims to special merit or importance

pretext *noun* false reason given to hide the real one

pretty prettier, prettiest *adjective* **1** pleasing to look at ▷ *adverb* **2** fairly, moderately: I'm pretty certain > **prettily** *adverb* > **prettiness** *noun*: the prettiness of the village

prevail *verb* **1** to gain mastery **2** to be generally established

prevalent *adjective* widespread, common > **prevalence** *noun*: the prevalence of asthma in Britain

prevent *verb* to keep from happening or doing > **preventable** *adjective*: preventable illnesses > **prevention** *noun*: crime prevention

preventive *adjective* intended to help prevent things such as disease or crime

preview *noun* **1** advance showing of a film or exhibition before it is shown to the public **2** ICT part of a computer program which allows the user to look at what has been keyed or added to a document or spreadsheet as it will appear when it is printed

previous *adjective* coming or happening before > **previously** *adverb*

prey *noun* **1** animal hunted and killed for food by another animal **2** victim ▷ *verb* **3 prey on a** to hunt and kill for food **b** to worry or obsess

price *noun* **1** amount of money for which a thing is bought or sold **2** unpleasant thing that must be endured to get something desirable ▷ *verb* **3** to fix or ask the price of

priceless *adjective* **1** very valuable **2** (informal) very funny

pricey pricier, priciest *adjective* (*informal*) expensive

prick *verb* **1** to pierce lightly with a sharp point **2** to cause to feel mental pain ▷ *noun* **3** sudden sharp pain caused by pricking **4** mark made by pricking

prickle *noun* **1** thorn or spike on a plant ▷ *verb* **2** to feel a tingling or pricking sensation

pride *noun* **1** feeling of pleasure and satisfaction when you have done well **2** too high an opinion of yourself **3** sense of dignity and self-respect **4** something that causes you to feel pride **5** group of lions ▷ *verb* **6 pride yourself on** to feel pride about

priest *noun* **1** (in the Christian church) a person who can administer the sacraments and preach **2** (in some other religions) an official who performs religious ceremonies ▷ **priestly** *adjective*: *his priestly duties*

priestess *noun* a female priest in a non-Christian religion

priesthood *noun* position of being a priest

prim primmer, primmest *adjective* formal, proper and rather prudish

primaeval *adjective* same as **primeval**

primarily *adverb* chiefly or mainly

primary *adjective* **1** chief, most important **2** being the first stage, elementary

primary colours *plural noun* (in physics) red, green and blue or (in art) red, yellow and blue, from which all other colours can be produced by mixing

primary school *noun* school for children from five to eleven years

or (in New Zealand) between five to thirteen years

primate *noun* **1** member of an order of mammals including monkeys and humans **2** archbishop

prime *adjective* **1** main, most important **2** of the highest quality ▷ *noun* **3** time when someone is at his or her best or most vigorous ▷ *verb* **4** to give (someone) information in advance to prepare them for something **5** to prepare (a gun, pump, etc) for use

Prime Minister *noun* leader of a government

primeval [prime-**ee**-val] *adjective* of the earliest age of the world

primitive *adjective* **1** of an early simple stage of development **2** basic, crude

primrose *noun* pale yellow spring flower

prince *noun* **1** male member of a royal family, especially the son of the king or queen **2** male ruler of a small country

princess *noun* female member of a royal family, especially the daughter of the king or queen

principal *adjective* **1** main, most important ▷ *noun* **2** head of a school or college **3** person taking a leading part in something **4** sum of money lent on which interest is paid ▷ **principally** *adverb*

> **WORD TIP**
> Do not confuse *principal* with *principle*

principality principalities *noun* territory ruled by a prince

principle *noun* **1** moral rule guiding behaviour **2** general or basic truth **3** scientific law concerning the working of something

WORD TIP
Do not confuse *principle* with *principal*

print *verb* **1** to reproduce (a newspaper, book, etc) in large quantities by mechanical or electronic means **2** to reproduce (text or pictures) by pressing ink onto paper etc **3** to write in letters that are not joined up **4** to stamp (fabric) with a design **5** (*Photography*) to produce (pictures) from negatives ▷ *noun* **6** printed words etc **7** printed copy of a painting **8** printed lettering **9** photograph **10** printed fabric **11** mark left on a surface by something that has pressed against it

printer *noun* **1** person or company that prints (books, etc) **2** machine that prints **3** ICT machine connected to a computer that prints out results on paper

printing *noun* **1** process of producing printed matter **2** printed text **3** all the copies of a book printed at one time **4** form of writing in which the letters are not joined together

print-out *noun* printed information from a computer

prior *adjective* **1** earlier **2** prior to before ▷ *noun* **3** head monk in a priory

prioritize or **prioritise** *verb* to arrange (items to be attended to) in order of their relative importance

priority priorities *noun* **1** most important thing that must be dealt with first **2** right to be or go before others

priory priories *noun* place where certain orders of monks or nuns live

prise *verb* to force open by levering

prism *noun* transparent block usually with triangular ends and rectangular sides, used to disperse light into a spectrum or refract it in optical instruments

prison *noun* building where criminals and accused people are held

prisoner *noun* person held captive

pristine *adjective* clean, new and unused

private *adjective* **1** for the use of one person or group only **2** secret **3** personal or unconnected with your work **4** owned or paid for by individuals rather than by the government **5** quiet, not likely to be disturbed ▷ *noun* **6** soldier of the lowest rank > **privacy** *noun: an invasion of privacy* > **privately** *adverb*

private school *noun* school that does not receive money from the government, and parents pay for their children to attend

privatize or **privatise** *verb* to sell (a publicly owned company) to individuals or a private company > **privatization** *noun: the privatization of public transport*

privilege *noun* advantage or favour that only some people have

privy *adjective* sharing knowledge of something secret

prize *noun* **1** reward given for success in a competition etc ▷ *adjective* **2** winning or likely to win a prize ▷ *verb* **3** to value highly **4** same as **prise**

pro pros adverb, preposition **1** in favour of ▷ noun plural **2 pros and cons** arguments for and against ▷ noun **3** (informal) professional

pro- prefix **1** in favour of: pro-Russian **2** instead of: pronoun

probability probabilities noun **1** condition of being probable **2** event or other thing that is likely to happen or be true **3** (Maths) measure of the likelihood of an event happening

probable adjective likely to happen or be true

probably adverb in all likelihood

probation noun **1** system of dealing with law-breakers, especially juvenile ones, by placing them under supervision **2** period when someone is assessed for suitability for a job etc > **probationary** adjective: a probationary period of two years

probe verb **1** to search into or examine closely ▷ noun **2** surgical instrument used to examine a wound, cavity, etc

problem noun **1** something difficult to deal with or solve **2** question or puzzle set for solution > **problematic** adjective: Getting there will be problematic

procedure noun way of doing something, especially the correct or usual one > **procedural** adjective: The judge rejected the case on procedural grounds

proceed verb **1** to start or continue doing **2** (formal) to walk or go

proceedings plural noun **1** organized or related series of events **2** minutes of a meeting **3** legal action

process noun **1** series of actions or changes **2** method of doing or producing something ▷ verb **3** to handle or prepare by a special method of manufacture

procession noun line of people or vehicles moving forward together in order

processor noun (ICT) central chip in a computer which controls its operations

proclaim verb to declare publicly > **proclamation** noun: a proclamation of independence

procure verb to get or provide

prod prods, prodding, prodded verb **1** to poke with something pointed ▷ noun **2** prodding

prodigy prodigies noun person with some marvellous talent

produce verb **1** to bring (something) into existence **2** to present to view **3** to make or manufacture ▷ noun **4** food grown for sale

producer noun **1** person with control over the making of a film, record, etc **2** person or company that produces something

product noun **1** something produced **2** number resulting from multiplication

production noun **1** process of manufacturing or growing something in large quantities **2** amount of goods manufactured or food grown by a country or company **3** presentation of a play, opera, etc

productive adjective **1** producing large quantities **2** useful, profitable

productivity noun rate at which things are produced or dealt with

profane *adjective* showing disrespect for religion or holy things

profess *verb* (*formal*) **1** to claim (something to be true), sometimes falsely **2** to declare or express (something)

profession *noun* **1** type of work, such as being a doctor, that needs special training **2** all the people employed in a profession: *the legal profession*

professional *adjective* **1** working in a profession **2** taking part in an activity, such as sport or music, for money **3** very competent ▷ *noun* **4** person who works in a profession **5** person paid to take part in sport, music, etc >**professionally** *adverb*

professor *noun* teacher of the highest rank in a university >**professorial** *adjective*: *professorial posts*

proficient *adjective* skilled, expert >**proficiency** *noun*: *proficiency in English*

profile *noun* **1** outline, especially of the face, as seen from the side **2** brief biographical sketch

profit *noun* **1** money gained **2** benefit obtained ▷ *verb* **3** to gain or benefit

profound *adjective* **1** showing or needing great knowledge **2** strongly felt, intense >**profoundly** *adverb* >**profundity** *noun*: *His work lacks depth and profundity*

profuse *adjective* plentiful >**profusely** *adverb* >**profusion** *noun*: *a profusion of wild flowers*

program programs, programming, programmed *noun*

1 sequence of coded instructions for a computer ▷ *verb* **2** to arrange (data) so that it can be processed by a computer **3** to feed a program into (a computer) >**programmer** *noun*

programme *noun* **1** planned series of events **2** broadcast on radio or television **3** list of items or performers in an entertainment

progress *noun* **1** improvement, development **2** movement forward **3 in progress** taking place ▷ *verb* **4** to become more advanced or skilful **5** to move forward >**progression** *noun*: *Both drugs slow the progression of the disease*

progressive *adjective* **1** favouring political or social reform **2** happening gradually

prohibit *verb* to forbid or prevent from happening

prohibitive *adjective* (of prices) too high to be affordable >**prohibitively** *adverb*

project *noun* **1** planned scheme to do or examine something over a period ▷ *verb* **2** to make a forecast based on known data **3** to make (a film or slide) appear on a screen **4** to communicate (an impression) **5** to stick out beyond a surface or edge >**projection** *noun*: *sales projections*

projector *noun* apparatus for projecting photographic images, films or slides on a screen

proletariat [pro-lit-**air**-ee-at] *noun* (*formal*) working class >**proletarian** *adjective*: *proletarian revolution*

proliferate *verb* to increase rapidly in numbers

> **proliferation** noun: the proliferation of nuclear weapons

prolific adjective very productive
> **prolifically** adverb

prologue noun introduction to a play or book

prolong verb to make (something) last longer > **prolonged** adjective: prolonged negotiations

prom noun (informal) concert at which some of the audience stand (also **promenade concert**)

promenade noun (Chiefly Brit) paved walkway along the seafront at a holiday resort

prominent adjective 1 very noticeable 2 famous, widely known > **prominence** noun: He came to prominence during the war > **prominently** adverb

promiscuous adjective having many casual sexual relationships > **promiscuity** noun: male promiscuity

promise verb 1 to say that you will definitely do or not do something 2 to show signs of, seem likely ▷ noun 3 undertaking to do or not to do something 4 indication of future success

promontory promontories noun point of high land jutting out into the sea

promote verb 1 to help to make (something) happen or increase 2 to raise to a higher rank or position 3 to encourage the sale of (a product) by advertising > **promotion** noun: promotion through the ranks > **promotional** adjective: promotional material

prompt verb 1 to cause (an action) 2 to remind (an actor or speaker) of words that he or she has forgotten ▷ adjective 3 done without delay ▷ adverb 4 exactly: six o'clock prompt > **promptly** adverb

prone adjective 1 **prone to** likely to do or be affected by (something) 2 lying face downwards

prong noun one spike of a fork or similar instrument

pronoun noun word, such as {she} or {it}, used to replace a noun

pronounce verb 1 to form the sounds of (words or letters), especially clearly or in a particular way 2 to declare formally or officially

pronounced adjective very noticeable

pronouncement noun formal announcement

pronunciation noun way in which a word or language is pronounced

proof noun 1 evidence that shows that something is true or has happened 2 copy of something printed, such as the pages of a book, for checking before final production ▷ adjective 3 able to withstand: proof against criticism 4 denoting the strength of an alcoholic drink: seventy proof

prop props, propping, propped verb 1 to support (something) so that it stays upright or in place ▷ noun 2 pole, beam, etc used as a support 3 movable object used on the set of a film or play

propaganda noun (organized promotion of) information to assist or damage the cause of a government or movement

propagate verb 1 to spread (information and ideas) 2 to

reproduce, breed or grow
> **propagation** noun: the
propagation of true Buddhism

propel propels, propelling,
propelled verb to cause to move
forward

propeller noun revolving shaft
with blades for driving a ship or
aircraft

propensity propensities noun
(formal) natural tendency

proper adjective 1 real or genuine
2 suited to a particular purpose
3 correct in behaviour 4 (Brit, Aust,
NZ informal) complete > **properly**
adverb

proper noun noun name of a
person, place or institution

property properties noun
1 something owned 2 possessions
collectively 3 land or buildings
owned by somebody 4 quality or
attribute

prophecy prophecies noun
1 prediction 2 message revealing
God's will

prophesy prophesies,
prophesying, prophesied verb
to foretell

prophet noun 1 person
supposedly chosen by God to
spread His word 2 person who
predicts the future

prophetic adjective correctly
predicting what will happen
> **prophetically** adverb

proportion noun 1 relative size
or extent 2 correct relation
between connected parts
3 part considered with respect
to the whole 4 **proportions**
dimensions or size 5 **in**
proportion a comparable in size,
rate of increase, etc **b** without

exaggerating > verb 6 to adjust in
relative amount or size

proportional or **proportionate**
adjective being in proportion
> **proportionally** or
proportionately adverb

proportional representation
noun system of voting in
elections in which the number of
representatives of each party is
in proportion to the number of
people who voted for it

proposal noun 1 plan that
has been suggested 2 offer of
marriage

propose verb 1 to put forward
(a plan) for consideration 2 to
nominate (someone) for a
position 3 to intend or plan (to do)
4 to make an offer of marriage

proposition noun 1 offer
2 statement or assertion
3 (informal) thing to be dealt with

proprietor noun owner of a
business establishment

propriety noun (formal) correct
conduct

propulsion noun 1 method by
which something is propelled
2 act of propelling or state of
being propelled

prose noun ordinary speech or
writing in contrast to poetry

prosecute verb 1 to bring
a criminal charge against
(someone) 2 to continue to do
(something) > **prosecutor** noun:
the public prosecutor

prosecution noun 1 bringing of
criminal charges against someone
2 lawyers who try to prove that a
person on trial is guilty

prospect noun 1 something
anticipated 2 **prospects**

a
b
c
d
e
f
g
h
i
j
k
l
m
n
o
p
q
r
s
t
u
v
w
x
y
z

probability of future success
▷ verb 3 to explore, especially for gold or oil ▷ **prospector** noun: a gold prospector

prospective adjective 1 future
2 expected

prospectus noun booklet giving details of a university, company, etc

prosper verb to be successful
▷ **prosperous** adjective: a prosperous family

prostitute noun person who offers sexual intercourse in return for payment
▷ **prostitution** noun

prostrate adjective 1 lying face downwards 2 physically or emotionally exhausted

protagonist noun (formal)
1 supporter of a cause 2 leading character in a play or a story

protea [**pro-tee-a**] noun African shrub with showy flowers

protect verb to defend from trouble, harm or loss
▷ **protection** noun: protection for our children

protégé or **protégée** (feminine)
[**pro**-ti-zhay] noun person who is protected and helped by another

protein noun any of a group of complex organic compounds that are essential for life

protest noun 1 declaration or demonstration of objection ▷ verb
2 to object or disagree 3 to assert formally

Protestant noun 1 follower of any of the Christian churches that split from the Roman Catholic Church in the sixteenth century
▷ adjective 2 of or relating to such a church

protestation noun strong declaration

protocol noun rules of behaviour for formal occasions

proton noun positively charged particle in the nucleus of an atom

prototype noun original or model to be copied or developed

protracted adjective lengthened or extended

protractor noun instrument for measuring angles

protrude verb to stick out or project ▷ **protrusion** noun: a protrusion of rock

proud adjective 1 feeling pleasure and satisfaction 2 feeling honoured 3 thinking yourself superior to other people
4 dignified ▷ **proudly** adverb

prove proving, proved, proved or proven verb 1 to establish the validity of 2 to demonstrate or test 3 to be found to be

proverb noun short saying that expresses a truth or gives a warning ▷ **proverbial** adjective: the proverbial man in the street

provide verb 1 to make available 2 **provide for a** to take precautions (against) **b** to support financially ▷ **provider** noun: providers of sports facilities

providence noun God or nature seen as a protective force that arranges people's lives

province noun 1 area governed as a unit of a country or empire 2 area of learning, activity, etc 3 **provinces** parts of a country outside the capital

provincial adjective 1 of a province or the provinces

2 unsophisticated and narrow-minded

provision noun **1** act of supplying something **2** something supplied **3** (Law) condition incorporated in a document **4** provisions food

provisional adjective temporary or conditional > **provisionally** adverb

proviso provisos or provisoes [pro-**vize**-oh] noun condition in an agreement

provocation noun act done deliberately to annoy someone

provocative adjective **1** intended to annoy people or make them react: a provocative speech **2** intended to make someone feel sexual desire: provocative poses

provoke verb **1** to deliberately anger **2** to cause (an adverse reaction)

prow noun bow of a vessel

prowess noun superior skill or ability

prowl verb to move stealthily around a place as if in search of prey or plunder

proximity noun (formal) **1** nearness in space or time **2** nearness or closeness in a series

proxy proxies noun **1** person authorized to act on behalf of someone else **2** authority to act on behalf of someone else

prude noun person who is excessively modest, prim or proper > **prudish** adjective: I'm not prudish but I was offended by those photos

prudent adjective cautious, discreet and sensible > **prudence** noun: A lack of prudence may lead to financial problems > **prudently** adverb

prune noun **1** dried plum ▷ verb **2** to cut off dead parts or excessive branches from (a tree or plant) **3** to shorten or reduce

pry pries, prying, pried verb to make an impertinent or uninvited inquiry (about a private matter)

PS abbreviation postscript

psalm noun sacred song

PSHE abbreviation Personal Social and Health Education: a lesson in which students are taught about social and personal issues

pseudo- prefix false, pretending or unauthentic: pseudoclassical

pseudonym noun fictitious name adopted especially by an author

psyche [**sye**-kee] noun human mind or soul

psychiatry noun branch of medicine concerned with mental disorders > **psychiatric** adjective: chronic psychiatric illnesses > **psychiatrist** noun: a psychiatrist of many years experience

psychic adjective **1** having mental powers which cannot be explained by natural laws **2** relating to the mind ▷ noun **3** person with psychic powers

psychoanalysis noun method of treating mental and emotional disorders by discussion and analysis of the person's thoughts and feelings > **psychoanalyst** noun: I saw a pyschoanalyst for several years

psychology psychologies noun **1** study of human and animal behaviour **2** (informal) person's mental make-up > **psychologist** noun: She trained as a psychologist

psychopath noun person afflicted with a personality disorder causing him or her to commit antisocial or violent acts > **psychopathic** adjective: a psychopathic killer

psychosis psychoses noun severe mental disorder in which the sufferer's contact with reality becomes distorted > **psychotic** adjective: psychotic disorders

pterodactyl [terr-roe-**dak**-til] noun extinct flying reptile with batlike wings

PTO abbreviation please turn over

pub noun building with a bar licensed to sell alcoholic drinks

puberty noun beginning of sexual maturity

pubic adjective of the lower abdomen: pubic hair

public adjective 1 of or concerning the people as a whole 2 for use by everyone 3 well-known 4 performed or made openly > noun 5 the community, people in general > **publicly** adverb

publican noun (Brit, Aust, NZ) person who owns or runs a pub

publication noun 1 publishing of a printed work 2 printed work: medical publications

publicity noun 1 process or information used to arouse public attention 2 public interest so aroused

publicize or **publicise** verb to bring to public attention

public school noun private fee-paying school in Britain

public servant noun (Aust, NZ) someone who works in the public service

public service noun (Aust, NZ) government departments responsible for the administration of the country

publish verb 1 to produce and issue (printed matter) for sale 2 to announce formally or in public > **publishing** noun

publisher noun [LIBRARY] company or person that publishes books, periodicals, music, etc

pudding noun 1 dessert, especially a cooked one served hot 2 savoury dish with pastry or batter: steak-and-kidney pudding 3 sausage-like mass of meat: black pudding

puddle noun small pool of water, especially of rain

puerile adjective silly and childish

puff noun 1 (sound of) a short blast of breath, wind, etc 2 act of inhaling cigarette smoke 3 **out of puff** out of breath > verb 4 to blow or breathe in short quick draughts 5 to take draws at (a cigarette) 6 **puff up** or **out** to swell > **puffy** adjective: dark-ringed puffy eyes

puffin noun black-and-white sea bird with a brightly-coloured beak

pug noun small snub-nosed dog

puja [**poo**-jah] noun variety of practices which make up Hindu worship

puke (informal) verb 1 to vomit > noun 2 vomited matter

pull verb 1 to exert force on (an object) to move it towards the source of the force 2 to strain or stretch 3 to remove or extract 4 to attract > noun 5 act of pulling 6 force used in pulling 7 (informal) power, influence > **pull down** verb to destroy or demolish > **pull out** verb 1 (of a vehicle or driver) to move away from the side of the road or move out to overtake 2 (of a train) to depart 3 to withdraw

4 to remove by pulling ▷ **pull through** verb to recover from a serious illness

pulley noun wheel with a grooved rim in which a belt, chain or piece of rope runs in order to lift weights by a downward pull

pullover noun sweater that is pulled on over the head

pulmonary adjective (formal) of the lungs

pulp noun **1** soft wet substance made from crushed or beaten matter **2** flesh of a fruit

pulpit noun raised platform for a preacher

pulse noun **1** regular beating of blood through the arteries at each heartbeat **2** any regular beat or vibration **3** edible seed of a pod-bearing plant such as a bean or pea ▷ verb **4** to beat, throb or vibrate

puma noun large American wild cat with a greyish-brown coat

pumice [**pumm**-iss] noun light porous stone used for scouring

pummel pummels, pummelling, pummelled verb to strike repeatedly with or as if with the fists

pump noun **1** machine used to force a liquid or gas to move in a particular direction **2** light flat-soled shoe ▷ verb **3** to raise or drive (air, liquid, etc) with a pump **4** pump into to supply in large amounts: pumping money into the economy

pumpkin noun large round fruit with an orange rind, soft flesh and many seeds

pun noun use of words to exploit double meanings for humorous effect

punch verb **1** to strike with a clenched fist ▷ noun **2** blow with a clenched fist **3** tool or machine for shaping, piercing or engraving **4** drink made from a mixture of wine, spirits, fruit, sugar and spices

punctual adjective arriving or taking place at the correct time ▷ **punctuality** noun: train punctuality ▷ **punctually** adverb

punctuate verb **1** to put punctuation marks into (a written text) **2** to interrupt at frequent intervals

punctuation noun (use of) marks such as commas, colons, etc in writing, to assist in making the sense clear

puncture noun **1** small hole made by a sharp object, especially in a tyre ▷ verb **2** to pierce a hole in (something) with a sharp object

pungent adjective having a strong sharp bitter flavour ▷ **pungency** noun: the spices that give Jamaican food its pungency

punish verb to cause (someone) to suffer or undergo a penalty for some wrongdoing

punishment noun something unpleasant done to someone because they have done something wrong

punitive [**pew**-nit-tiv] adjective relating to punishment

Punjabi [pun-**jah**-bee] adjective **1** belonging or relating to the Punjab, a state in north-western India ▷ noun **2** someone from the Punjab **3** language spoken in the Punjab

punk noun **1** aggressive style of rock music **2** follower of this music

punt noun open flat-bottomed boat propelled by a pole

puny punier, puniest adjective small and feeble

pup noun young of certain animals, such as dogs and seals

pupil noun 1 person who is taught by a teacher 2 round dark opening in the centre of the eye

puppet noun small doll or figure moved by strings or by the operator's hand

puppy puppies noun young dog

purchase verb 1 to obtain (goods) by payment ▷ noun 2 thing that is bought 3 act of buying
> **purchaser** noun: We need to find a purchaser

pure adjective 1 unmixed or untainted 2 innocent 3 complete: pure delight 4 concerned with theory only: pure mathematics

purée [pyoo-ray] noun food which has been mashed or blended to a thick, smooth consistency

purely adverb involving only one feature and not including anything else

Purgatory noun (in Roman Catholic belief) place where spirits of the dead are sent to suffer for their sins before going to Heaven

purge verb 1 to rid (something) of undesirable qualities 2 to rid (an organization, etc) of undesirable people

purify purifies, purifying, purified verb to free (something) of harmful or inferior matter
> **purification** noun: a water purification plant

purist noun person concerned with strict obedience to the traditions of a subject

puritan noun someone who believes in strict moral principles and avoids physical pleasures
> **puritanical** adjective: puritanical attitudes towards sex

purple noun 1 colour between red and blue ▷ adjective 2 of this colour

purport verb to claim (to be or do something)

purpose noun 1 reason for which something is done or exists 2 determination 3 practical advantage or use: use the time to good purpose

purr verb 1 (of cats) to make a low vibrant sound, usually when pleased ▷ noun 2 this sound

purse noun 1 small bag for money 2 (US, NZ) handbag ▷ verb 3 to draw (one's lips) together into a small round shape

purser noun ship's officer who keeps the accounts

pursue pursues, pursuing, pursued verb 1 to follow (a person, vehicle or animal) in order to capture or overtake 2 to follow (a goal) 3 to engage in > **pursuer** noun: They had to shake off their pursuers

purveyor noun (formal) person who sells or provides goods or services

pus noun yellowish matter produced by infected tissue

push verb 1 to move or try to move by steady force 2 to drive or spur (oneself or another person) to do something 3 (informal) to sell (drugs) illegally ▷ noun 4 act of pushing 5 special effort 6 the push (informal) dismissal from a job or relationship ⊳ **push off** *verb* (informal) to go away

pushchair *noun* small folding chair on wheels in which a baby or toddler can be wheeled around

pusher *noun* (informal) person who sells illegal drugs

pushing *preposition* almost or nearly (a certain age, speed, etc): *pushing sixty*

pushover *noun* (informal) **1** something that is easy **2** someone who is easily persuaded or defeated

pushy *pushier, pushiest adjective* (informal) too assertive or ambitious

pussy *pussies noun* (informal) cat

put *puts, putting, put verb* **1** to cause to be (in a position or place) **2** to cause to be (in a state or condition) **3** to lay (blame, emphasis, etc) on a person or thing **4** to express **5** to estimate or judge ⊳ *noun* **6** throw in putting the shot ⊳ **put down** *verb* **1** (informal) to belittle or humiliate **2** to put (a sick animal) to death ⊳ **put off** *verb* **1** to postpone **2** to cause to lose interest in ⊳ **put out** *verb* **1** to extinguish (a fire, light, etc) **2** to annoy or anger **3** to dislocate: *He put his back out gardening* ⊳ **put up** *verb* **1** to build or erect **2** to accommodate **3** **put up with** (informal) to endure or tolerate

putt (*Golf*) *noun* **1** stroke on the putting green to roll the ball into or near the hole ⊳ *verb* **2** to strike (the ball) in this way

putting *noun* golf played with a putter on a course of very short holes

putty *noun* adhesive used to fix glass into frames and fill cracks in woodwork

puzzle *verb* **1** to perplex and confuse or be perplexed or confused ⊳ *noun* **2** problem that cannot be easily solved **3** toy, game or question that requires skill or ingenuity to solve > **puzzled** *adjective: There was a puzzled expression on her face* > **puzzlement** *noun: He frowned in puzzlement* > **puzzling** *adjective: a number of puzzling questions*

PVC *abbreviation* polyvinyl chloride: plastic material used in clothes etc

Pygmy *Pygmies noun* **1** member of one of the very short peoples of Equatorial Africa ⊳ *adjective* **2** *pygmy* very small

pyjamas *plural noun* loose-fitting trousers and top worn in bed

pylon *noun* steel tower-like structure supporting electrical cables

pyramid *noun* **1** solid figure with a flat base and triangular sides sloping upwards to a point **2** building of this shape, especially an ancient Egyptian one

pyre *noun* pile of wood for burning a corpse on

python *noun* large nonpoisonous snake that crushes its prey

q

quack verb 1 (of a duck) to make the loud harsh sound that ducks make ▷ noun 2 sound made by a duck 3 unqualified person who claims medical knowledge

quad noun 1 see **quadrangle** 2 short for **quintuplet**

quad bike or **quad** noun vehicle like a small motorcycle with four large wheels, designed for agricultural and sporting uses

quadrangle noun rectangular courtyard with buildings on all four sides ▷ **quadrangular** adjective

quadri- prefix four: quadrilateral

quadriceps noun large muscle in four parts at the front of your thigh

quadrilateral (Maths) adjective 1 having four sides ▷ noun 2 polygon with four sides

quadruped [kwod-roo-ped] noun any animal with four legs

quadruple verb 1 (of an amount or number) to become four times as large as previously 2 to make (an amount or number) four times as large as previously; multiply by four ▷ adjective 3 four times as much or as many

quadruplet noun one of four children born at the same time to the same mother

quagmire [kwog-mire] noun soft wet area of land

quail noun 1 small game bird of the partridge family ▷ verb 2 to feel or look afraid

quaint adjective attractively unusual, especially in an old-fashioned style ▷ **quaintly** adverb

quake verb to shake and tremble with or as if with fear

Quaker noun member of a Christian sect, the Society of Friends

qualification noun 1 official record of achievement in a course or examination 2 quality or skill needed for a particular activity 3 something you add to a statement to make it less strong

qualify qualifies, qualifying, qualified verb 1 to pass the necessary examinations or tests to do a particular job or to take part in a sporting event 2 to make (someone) suitable for something 3 to moderate or restrict (a statement) by adding a detail or explanation to make it less strong ▷ **qualified** adjective

quality qualities noun 1 how good something is 2 characteristic 3 basic character or nature of something

qualm [kwahm] noun 1 pang of conscience 2 sudden sensation of misgiving

quandary quandaries noun difficult situation or dilemma

quango quangos noun body responsible for a particular area of public administration, which is financed by the government but is outside direct government control. Quango is short for 'quasi-autonomous non-governmental organization'

quantity quantities noun **1** amount you can measure or count **2** amount of something that there is: *emphasis on quantity rather than quality*

quarantine noun period or state of isolation to prevent the spread of disease between people or animals

quarrel quarrels, quarrelling, quarrelled noun **1** angry argument ▷ verb **2** to have an angry argument ▷ **quarrelsome** adjective prone to get into arguments

quarry quarries, quarrying, quarried noun **1** place where stone is dug from the surface of the earth **2** person or animal that is being hunted ▷ verb **3** to extract (stone) from a quarry

quart noun unit of liquid measure equal to two pints (1.136 litres)

quarter noun **1** one of four equal parts of something **2** (US) 25-cent piece **3** region or district of a town or city **4** fourth part of a year **5** (informal) unit of weight equal to 4 ounces **6** quarters lodgings ▷ verb **7** to divide (something) into four equal parts

quarterly quarterlies adjective **1** occurring, due or issued every three months ▷ noun **2** magazine or journal issued every three months ▷ adverb **3** once every three months

quartet noun **1** group of four performers **2** music for such a group

quartz noun kind of hard, shiny crystal used in making very accurate watches and clocks

quash verb to throw out (a decision or judgment)

quasi- [kway-zie] prefix almost but not really: *quasi-religious; a quasi-scholar*

quaver verb **1** (of a voice) to quiver or tremble ▷ noun **2** (Music) note half the length of a crotchet and an eighth the length of a semibreve. In the United States and Canada, a quaver is known as an eighth note

quay [kee] noun place where boats are tied up and loaded or unloaded

queasy queasier, queasiest adjective feeling slightly sick ▷ **queasiness** noun

queen noun **1** female monarch or a woman married to a king **2** the only female bee, wasp or ant in a colony that can lay eggs **3** the most powerful piece in chess

queen mother noun the widow of a king and the mother of the reigning monarch

queer adjective very strange

quell verb **1** to put an end to or suppress (a rebellion or riot) **2** to overcome (a feeling)

quench verb to satisfy (one's thirst)

query queries, querying, queried noun **1** question **2** question mark ▷ verb **3** to express uncertainty, doubt or an objection concerning (something); question

quest noun long and difficult search

question noun **1** a sentence which asks for information **2** problem that needs to be discussed; matter **3** difficulty or uncertainty **4** out of the question impossible

5 in question under discussion ▷ *verb* **6** to put a question or questions to (a person) **7** to express uncertainty about; query

questionable *adjective* of disputable value or authority ▷**questionably** *adverb*

question mark *noun* punctuation mark (?) written at the end of questions

questionnaire *noun* set of questions on a form, used to collect information from people

queue queues, queuing or queueing, queued *noun* **1** line of people or vehicles waiting for something ▷ *verb* **2** (often followed by *up*) to form or remain in a line while waiting

quibble *verb* **1** to make trivial objections ▷ *noun* **2** trivial objection

quiche [**keesh**] *noun* savoury tart with an egg custard filling to which vegetables etc are added

quick *adjective* **1** speedy, fast **2** lasting or taking a short time **3** happening without any delay **4** intelligent and able to understand things easily ▷ *noun* **5** area of sensitive flesh under a nail ▷ *adverb* **6** (*informal*) in a rapid manner ▷**quickly** *adverb*

quicksand *noun* area of deep wet sand that you sink into if you walk on it

quid *noun* (*Brit informal*) pound (sterling)

quiet *adjective* **1** making little or no noise **2** calm or peaceful **3** involving very little fuss or publicity ▷ *noun* **4** quietness ▷**quietly** *adverb* ▷**quietness** *noun*

WORD TIP
Do not confuse the spellings of *quiet* and the adverb *quite*

quieten *verb* (often followed by *down*) to become or make (someone) quiet

quill *noun* **1** pen made from the feather of a bird's wing or tail **2** stiff hollow spine of a hedgehog or porcupine

quilt *noun* padded covering for a bed

quilted *adjective* consisting of two layers of fabric with a layer of soft material between them

quin *noun* short for **quintuplet**

quince *noun* acid-tasting fruit used for making jam and marmalade

quintessence *noun* (*formal*) most perfect representation of a quality or state ▷**quintessential** *adjective*: It was the quintessential Hollywood party

quintet *noun* **1** group of five performers **2** music for such a group

quintuplet *noun* one of five children born at the same time to the same mother

quip quips, quipping, quipped *noun* **1** witty remark ▷ *verb* **2** to make a witty remark

quirk *noun* **1** odd habit or characteristic **2** unexpected event or development: a quirk of fate ▷**quirky** *adjective*

quit quits, quitting, quit *verb* **1** to stop (doing something) **2** to give up (a job) **3** to depart from (a place) ▷**quitter** *noun* person who lacks perseverance

quite *adverb* **1** fairly but not very: She's quite pretty **2** absolutely

or completely: *You're quite right*
3 emphasizing how large or
impressive something is: *It
was quite a party* ▷ *interjection*
4 expression of agreement

> **WORD TIP**
> Do not confuse the spellings of
> *quite* and the adjective *quiet*

quiver *verb* **1** to shake with a
tremulous movement ▷ *noun*
2 shaking or trembling **3** case
for arrows

quiz quizzes, quizzing, quizzed
noun **1** game in which the
competitors are asked questions
to test their knowledge ▷ *verb*
2 to question (someone) closely
about something

quizzical *adjective* amused and
questioning: *a quizzical look*
> **quizzically** *adverb*

quota *noun* number or quantity
of something which is officially
allowed

quotation *noun* **1** extract from a
book or speech which is quoted
2 statement of how much a piece
of work will cost

quotation marks *plural noun*
raised commas used in writing to
mark the beginning and ending of
a quotation

quote *verb* **1** to repeat (words)
exactly from (an earlier work,
speech or conversation) **2** to state
(a price) for goods or a job of work
▷ *noun* **3** quotation **4** **quotes**
(*informal*) the same as **quotation
marks**

Qur'an *noun* another spelling
of **Koran**

435 | racial

r

RAAF *abbreviation* Royal
Australian Air Force

rabbi rabbis [**rab**-bye] *noun* Jewish
spiritual leader

rabbit *noun* small burrowing
mammal with long ears

rabble *noun* disorderly crowd of
noisy people

rabid *adjective* **1** fanatical **2** having
rabies

rabies [**ray**-beez] *noun* usually
fatal viral disease transmitted by
dogs and certain other animals

raccoon *noun* small N American
mammal with a long striped tail

race *noun* **1** contest of speed
2 group of people of common
ancestry with distinguishing
physical features, such as skin
colour **3** **the races** series of
contests of speed between horses
or greyhounds over a fixed course
▷ *verb* **4** to take part in a contest
of speed with someone **5** to run
swiftly > **racer** *noun*: *a champion
powerboat racer*

racecourse *noun* grass track,
sometimes with jumps, along
which horses race

racehorse *noun* horse trained to
run in races

racial *adjective* relating to the
different races that people belong
to > **racially** *adverb*

racism or **racialism** noun hostile attitude or behaviour to members of other races, based on a belief in the innate superiority of one's own race > **racist** or **racialist** adjective, noun: a racist attack; He's a racist

rack noun **1** framework for holding particular articles, such as coats or luggage **2 go to rack and ruin** to be destroyed ▷ verb **3** to cause great suffering to **4 rack your brains** (informal) to try very hard to remember

racket noun **1** noisy disturbance **2** occupation from which money is made illegally **3** another spelling of **racquet**

racquet or **racket** noun bat with strings across it used in tennis and similar games

radar noun device for tracking distant objects by bouncing high-frequency radio pulses off them

radiant adjective **1** looking happy **2** shining **3** emitting radiation > **radiance** noun

radiate verb **1** to spread out from a centre **2** to show (an emotion or quality) to a great degree

radiation noun **1** transmission of energy from one body to another **2** particles or waves emitted in nuclear decay **3** process of radiating

radiator noun **1** (Brit) arrangement of pipes containing hot water or steam to heat a room **2** tubes containing water as cooling apparatus for a car engine **3** (Aust, NZ) electric fire

radical adjective **1** fundamental **2** thorough **3** advocating fundamental change ▷ noun **4** person advocating fundamental

(political) change > **radicalism** noun: a long tradition of radicalism > **radically** adverb

radii noun a plural of **radius**

radio radios, radioing, radioed noun **1** system of sending sound over a distance by transmitting electrical signals **2** piece of equipment for listening to radio programmes **3** communications device for sending and receiving messages using radio waves **4** broadcasting of programmes to the public by radio ▷ verb **5** to transmit (a message) by radio

radioactive adjective emitting radiation as a result of nuclear decay > **radioactivity** noun: high levels of radioactivity

radiotherapy noun treatment of disease, especially cancer, by radiation > **radiotherapist** noun

radish noun small hot-flavoured root vegetable eaten raw in salads

radium noun (Chemistry) radioactive metallic element

radius radii or radiuses noun (length of) a straight line from the centre to the circumference of a circle

RAF abbreviation (in Britain) Royal Air Force

raffia noun prepared palm fibre for weaving mats etc

raffle noun **1** lottery with goods as prizes ▷ verb **2** to offer as a prize in a raffle

raft noun floating platform of logs, planks, etc

rafter noun one of the main beams of a roof

rag noun **1** fragment of cloth **2** (informal) newspaper **3 rags** tattered clothing

rage noun 1 violent anger or passion ▷ verb 2 to feel or show intense anger 3 to proceed violently and with restraint

ragged [rag-gid] adjective 1 (of clothes) old and torn 2 untidy

raid noun 1 sudden surprise attack or search ▷ verb 2 to make a raid on 3 to sneak into (a place) in order to steal > **raider** noun

rail noun 1 horizontal bar, especially as part of a fence or track 2 railway considered as a means of transport ▷ verb 3 **rail at** or **against** to complain bitterly or loudly about

railing noun fence made of rails supported by posts

railway noun 1 track of iron rails on which trains run 2 company operating a railway

rain noun 1 water falling in drops from the clouds ▷ verb 2 to fall or pour down as rain 3 to fall rapidly and in large quantities

rainbird noun S African bird whose call is believed to be a sign that it will rain

rainbow noun arch of colours in the sky

raincoat noun water-resistant overcoat

rainfall noun amount of rain

rainforest noun dense forest in tropical and temperate areas

rainwater noun rain that has been stored

raise verb 1 to lift up 2 to set upright 3 to increase in amount or intensity 4 to collect or levy 5 to bring up (a family) 6 to put forward for consideration

raisin noun dried grape

rake noun 1 tool with a long handle and a crosspiece with teeth, used for smoothing earth or gathering leaves, hay, etc ▷ verb 2 to gather or smooth with a rake 3 to search (through) > **rake up** verb to revive memories of (a forgotten unpleasant event)

rally rallies, rallying, rallied noun 1 large gathering of people for a meeting 2 marked recovery of strength 3 (Tennis etc) lively exchange of strokes 4 car-driving competition on public roads ▷ verb 5 to bring or come together after dispersal or for a common cause 6 to regain health or strength

ram rams, ramming, rammed noun 1 adult male sheep ▷ verb 2 to strike against with force 3 to drive or force

RAM abbreviation (Computers) random access memory: storage space which can be filled with data but which loses its contents when the machine is switched off

Ramadan noun 1 9th Muslim month 2 strict fasting from dawn to dusk observed during this time

ramble verb 1 to walk without a definite route 2 to talk in a confused way ▷ noun 3 long walk in the countryside

ramifications plural noun consequences resulting from an action

ramp noun slope joining two level surfaces

rampage verb 1 to rush about violently 2 **go on the rampage** to behave violently or destructively

rampant adjective growing or spreading uncontrollably

rampart noun mound or wall for defence

ramshackle *adjective* tumbledown, rickety or makeshift

ranch *noun* large cattle farm in the American West

rancid *adjective* (of butter, bacon, etc) stale and having an offensive smell

rancour *noun* deep bitter hate > **rancorous** *adjective: a series of rancorous disputes*

rand *noun* monetary unit of S Africa

random *adjective* **1** made or done by chance or without plan **2 at random** haphazard(ly) > **randomly** *adverb*

range *noun* **1** limits of effectiveness or variation **2** distance that a missile or plane can travel **3** distance of a mark shot at **4** whole set of related things **5** chain of mountains **6** place for shooting practice or rocket testing > *verb* **7** to vary between one point and another **8** to cover or extend over **9** to roam (over)

ranger *noun* official in charge of a nature reserve etc

rank *noun* **1** relative place or position **2** status **3** social class **4** row or line **5 rank and file** ordinary people or members **6 the ranks** common soldiers > *verb* **7** to have a specific rank or position **8** to arrange in rows or lines > *adjective* **9** complete or absolute: *rank favouritism* **10** smelling offensively strong

ransack *verb* **1** to search through every part of (a place or thing) **2** to pillage or plunder

ransom *noun* money demanded in return for the release of someone who has been kidnapped

rant *verb* to talk in a loud and excited way

rap raps, rapping, rapped *verb* **1** to hit with a sharp quick blow **2** to utter (a command) abruptly **3** to perform a rhythmic monologue with musical backing > *noun* **4** quick sharp blow **5** rhythmic monologue performed to music > **rapper** *noun: rappers such as Jay-Z and 50 Cent*

rape *verb* **1** to force (someone) to submit to sexual intercourse > *noun* **2** act of raping **3** plant with oil-yielding seeds, also used as fodder > **rapist** *noun: a convicted rapist*

rapid *adjective* **1** quick, swift > *noun* **2** rapids part of a river with a fast turbulent current > **rapidity** *noun: Water rushed through with great rapidity* > **rapidly** *adverb*

rapier [**ray**-pyer] *noun* fine-bladed sword

rapport [rap-**pore**] *noun* harmony or agreement

rapt *adjective* engrossed or spellbound

rapture *noun* feeling of extreme delight > **rapturous** *adjective: a rapturous welcome* > **rapturously** *adverb*

rare *adjective* **1** uncommon **2** infrequent **3** of uncommonly high quality **4** (of meat) lightly cooked > **rarely** *adverb* seldom

rarefied [**rare**-if-ide] *adjective* **1** highly specialized, exalted **2** (of air) thin

raring *adjective* **raring to** enthusiastic, willing or ready to

rarity rarities *noun* **1** something that is valuable because it is unusual **2** state of being rare

rascal noun **1** rogue **2** naughty (young) person

rash adjective **1** hasty, reckless or incautious ▷ noun **2** eruption of spots or patches on the skin **3** outbreak of (unpleasant) occurrences ▷ **rashly** adverb

rasher noun thin slice of bacon

rasp noun **1** harsh grating noise **2** coarse file ▷ verb **3** to make a harsh grating noise

raspberry raspberries noun red juicy edible berry

rat noun **1** small rodent **2** (informal) contemptible person, especially a deserter or informer

rate noun **1** degree of speed or progress **2** proportion between two things **3** charge **4 at any rate** in any case ▷ verb **5** to consider or value **6** to estimate the value of

rather adverb **1** to some extent **2** more truly or appropriately **3** more willingly

ratify ratifies, ratifying, ratified verb to give formal approval to ▷ **ratification** noun: the ratification of the treaty

rating noun **1** valuation or assessment **2** classification **3** ratings size of the audience for a TV programme

ratio ratios noun relationship between two numbers or amounts expressed as a proportion

ration noun **1** fixed allowance of food etc **2** rations fixed daily allowance of food, such as that given to a soldier ▷ verb **3** to restrict the distribution of (something)

rational adjective **1** reasonable, sensible **2** capable of reasoning

▷ **rationality** noun: We live in an era of rationality ▷ **rationally** adverb

rationale [rash-a-**nahl**] noun reason for an action or decision

rattle verb **1** to give out a succession of short sharp sounds **2** to shake briskly causing sharp sounds **3** (informal) to confuse or fluster ▷ noun **4** short sharp sound **5** baby's toy that rattles when shaken

rattlesnake noun poisonous snake with loose horny segments on the tail that make a rattling sound

raucous adjective hoarse or harsh

ravage (formal) verb **1** to cause extensive damage to ▷ noun **2** ravages damaging effects

rave verb **1** to talk in a wild or incoherent manner **2** (informal) to write or speak (about) with great enthusiasm ▷ noun **3** (informal) large-scale party with electronic dance music **4 rave review** (informal) enthusiastic praise

raven noun **1** black bird like a large crow ▷ adjective **2** (of hair) shiny black

ravenous adjective very hungry

ravine [rav-**veen**] noun narrow steep-sided valley worn by a stream

raving adjective **1** delirious **2** (informal) exceptional: a raving beauty ▷ noun **3** ravings frenzied or wildly extravagant talk

ravioli plural noun small squares of pasta with a savoury filling

ravishing adjective lovely or entrancing

raw adjective **1** uncooked **2** not manufactured or refined **3** inexperienced **4** chilly **5** raw

deal unfair or dishonest treatment

raw material *noun* natural substance used to make something

ray *noun* **1** single line or narrow beam of light **2** small amount that makes an unpleasant situation seem slightly better: *a ray of hope* **3** large sea fish with a flat body and a whiplike tail

raze *verb* to destroy (buildings or a town) completely

razor *noun* sharp instrument for shaving

razor blade *noun* small, sharp, flat piece of metal fitted into a razor for shaving

re- *prefix* again: *re-enter; retrial*

reach *verb* **1** to arrive at or get to (a place) **2** to make a movement (towards), as if to grasp or touch **3** to succeed in touching **4** to make contact or communication with **5** to extend as far as (a point or place) ▷ *noun* **6** distance that you can reach **7** range of influence ▷ **reachable** *adjective*: *a reachable target*

react *verb* **1** to act in response (to) **2 react against** to act in an opposing or contrary manner

reaction *noun* **1** physical or emotional response to a stimulus **2** any action resisting another **3** opposition to change **4** chemical or nuclear change, combination or decomposition

reactionary *reactionaries adjective* **1** opposed to change, especially in politics ▷ *noun* **2** person opposed to change

reactor *noun* apparatus in which a nuclear reaction is maintained

and controlled to produce nuclear energy

read *reads, reading, read verb* **1** to look at and understand or take in (written or printed matter) **2** to look at and say aloud **3** to interpret in a specified way **4** (of an instrument) to register **5** to undertake a course of study in (a subject) ▷ *noun* **6** matter suitable for reading: *a good read*

reader *noun* **1** person who reads **2** textbook **3** (*Chiefly Brit*) senior university lecturer

readership *noun* readers of a publication collectively

readily *adverb* **1** willingly and eagerly **2** easily done or quickly obtainable ▷ **readiness** *noun*: *readiness to help out*

reading *noun* **1** activity of reading books **2** figure or measurement shown on a meter or gauge

readjust *verb* to adapt to a new situation

ready *readier, readiest adjective* **1** prepared for use or action **2** willing, prompt **3** easily produced or obtained: *ready cash*

ready-made *adjective* for immediate use by any customer

reaffirm *verb* to state again

real *adjective* **1** existing in fact **2** actual **3** genuine

real estate *noun* property consisting of land and houses

realism *noun* recognition of the true nature of a situation ▷ **realist** *noun*

realistic *adjective* seeing and accepting things as they really are ▷ **realistically** *adverb*

reality *noun* state of things as they are

realize or **realise** verb **1** to become aware or grasp the significance of **2** (formal) to achieve (a plan, hopes, etc) **3** to convert (property or goods) into money ▷ **realization** noun: the realization that things cannot go on like this

really adverb **1** very **2** truly ▷ interjection **3** exclamation of dismay, doubt or surprise

realm noun (formal) **1** kingdom **2** sphere of interest

reap verb **1** to cut and gather (a harvest) **2** to receive as the result of a previous activity

reappear verb to appear again > **reappearance** noun

reappraisal noun (formal) the assessment again of the value or quality of a person or thing

rear noun **1** back part **2** part of an army, procession, etc behind the others ▷ verb **3** to care for and educate (children) **4** to breed (animals) **5** (of a horse) to rise on its hind feet

rear admiral noun high-ranking naval officer

rearrange verb to organize differently

reason noun **1** cause or motive **2** faculty of rational thought **3** sanity ▷ verb **4** to think logically in forming conclusions **5 reason with** to persuade by logical argument into doing something

reasonable adjective **1** sensible **2** not excessive **3** logical > **reasonably** adverb

reasoning noun process by which you draw conclusions from facts or evidence

reassess verb to reconsider the value or importance of > **reassessment** noun: a reassessment of the company's worth

reassure verb to relieve (someone) of anxieties > **reassurance** noun: She needed some reassurance

rebate noun discount or refund

rebel rebels, rebelling, rebelled verb **1** to revolt against the ruling power **2** to reject accepted conventions ▷ noun **3** person who rebels

rebellion noun organized open resistance to authority

rebellious adjective unwilling to obey and likely to rebel against authority

rebuff verb **1** to reject or snub ▷ noun **2** blunt refusal, snub

rebuild rebuilds, rebuilding, rebuilt verb to build (a building or town again), after severe damage

rebuke verb **1** to scold sternly ▷ noun **2** stern scolding

recall verb **1** to recollect or remember **2** to order to return **3** to annul or cancel

recap recaps, recapping, recapped (informal) verb to recapitulate

recapture verb **1** to relive (a former experience or sensation) **2** to capture again

recede verb **1** to move to a more distant place **2** (of the hair) to stop growing at the front

receipt noun **1** written acknowledgment of money or goods received **2** receiving or being received **3** receipts money taken in over a particular period by a shop or business

receive verb **1** to get (something offered or sent to you) **2** to

a
b
c
d
e
f
g
h
i
j
k
l
m
n
o
p
q
r
s
t
u
v
w
x
y
z

experience **3** to greet (guests)
4 to react to: *The news was well
received*

receiver *noun* **1** part of
telephone that is held to the
ear **2** equipment in a telephone,
radio or television that converts
electrical signals into sound
3 person appointed by a court
to manage the property of a
bankrupt

recent *adjective* **1** having
happened lately **2** new
>**recently** *adverb*

reception *noun* **1** area for
receiving guests, clients, etc
2 formal party **3** manner of
receiving **4** welcome **5** (in
broadcasting) quality of signals
received

receptionist *noun* person who
receives guests, clients, etc

receptive *adjective* willing to
accept new ideas, suggestions, etc

recess *noun* **1** niche or alcove
2 holiday between sessions of
work

recession *noun* period of
economic difficulty when little is
being bought or sold

recharge *verb* to charge (a
battery) with electricity again
after it has been used

recipe *noun* **1** directions for
cooking a dish **2** method for
achieving something

recipient *noun* person who
receives something

reciprocal [ris-**sip**-pro-kl]
adjective **1** mutual **2** given or done
in return >**reciprocally** *adverb*

reciprocate *verb* **1** to give or feel
in return **2** (of a machine part) to
move backwards and forwards

recital *noun* **1** musical
performance by a soloist or
soloists **2** act of reciting

recite *verb* to repeat (a poem etc)
aloud to an audience

reckless *adjective* heedless of
danger >**recklessly** *adverb*
>**recklessness** *noun*: *a surge of
recklessness*

reckon *verb* **1** to be of the opinion
2 to consider **3** to calculate **4** to
expect **5** reckon with *or* without
to take into account or fail to take
into account

reckoning *noun* **1** counting or
calculating **2** retribution for your
actions

reclaim *verb* **1** to regain
possession of **2** to convert
(unsuitable or submerged land)
into land suitable for farming
or building on >**reclamation**
noun: *the reclamation of land from
the marshes*

recline *verb* to rest in a leaning
position

recluse *noun* person who avoids
other people >**reclusive**
adjective: *a reclusive billionaire*

recognize *or* **recognise** *verb*
1 to identify as (a person or thing)
already known **2** to accept or
be aware of (a fact or problem)
3 to acknowledge formally the
status or legality of (someone
or something) **4** to show
appreciation of (something)
>**recognition** *noun*: *Her work
has received popular recognition*
>**recognizable** *adjective*: *His
features were easily recognizable*
>**recognizably** *adverb*

recommend *verb* **1** to advise
or counsel **2** to praise or

commend **3** to make acceptable > **recommendation** noun: the committee's recommendations

reconcile verb **1** to harmonize (conflicting beliefs etc) **2** to re-establish friendly relations with (a person or people) or between (people) **3** to accept or cause to accept (an unpleasant situation) > **reconciliation** noun: hopes for a reconciliation between the two countries

reconnaissance [rik-**kon**-iss-anss] noun survey for military or engineering purposes

reconsider verb to think about again > **reconsideration** noun: reconsideration of the decision

reconstruct verb **1** to rebuild **2** to form a picture of (a past event, especially a crime) > **reconstruction** noun: post-war reconstruction

record noun [**rek**-ord] **1** document or other thing that preserves information **2** disc with indentations which a record player transforms into sound **3** best recorded achievement **4** known facts about a person's past > verb [rik-**kord**] **5** to put in writing **6** to preserve (sound, TV programmes, etc) on plastic disc, magnetic tape, etc, for reproduction on a playback device **7** to show or register

recorder noun **1** person or machine that records, especially a video, cassette or tape recorder **2** type of flute, held vertically

recording noun **1** something that has been recorded **2** process of storing sounds or visual signals for later use

recount verb to tell in detail

recoup [rik-**koop**] verb to regain or make good (a loss)

recourse noun (formal) **1** source of help **2** have recourse to to turn to a source of help or course of action

recover verb **1** (of a person) to regain health, spirits or composure **2** to regain a former condition **3** to find again or obtain the return of (something lost) **4** to get back (a loss or expense)

recovery recoveries noun **1** act of recovering from sickness, a shock or a setback **2** restoration to a former and better condition **3** regaining of something lost

recreate verb to make happen or exist again

recreation noun agreeable or refreshing occupation, relaxation or amusement > **recreational** adjective: recreational activities

recrimination noun mutual blame

recruit verb **1** to enlist (new soldiers, members, etc) > noun **2** newly enlisted soldier, member or supporter > **recruitment** noun: the recruitment of civil servants

rectangle noun oblong four-sided figure with four right angles > **rectangular** adjective: a rectangular box

rectify rectifies, rectifying, rectified verb (formal) to put right, correct

rector noun **1** clergyman in charge of a parish **2** head of certain academic institutions

rectory noun rector's house

rectum rectums or recta *noun* final section of the large intestine > **rectal** *adjective*: rectal cancer

recuperate *verb* to recover from illness > **recuperation** *noun*: powers of recuperation

recur recurs, recurring, recurred *verb* to happen again

recurring *adjective* **1** happening or occurring many times **2** [MATHS] (of a digit) repeated over and over again after the decimal point in a decimal fraction

recycle *verb* to reprocess (used materials) for further use > **recyclable** *adjective*: recyclable glass

red redder, reddest; reds *adjective* **1** of a colour varying from crimson to orange and seen in blood, fire, etc **2** flushed in the face from anger, shame, etc ▷ *noun* **3** red colour **4 in the red** (*informal*) in debt

redback *noun* small Australian spider with a poisonous bite

redcurrant *noun* small round edible red berry

redeem *verb* **1** to make up for **2** to reinstate (oneself) in someone's good opinion **3** (*Christianity*) to free from sin

redemption *noun* state of being redeemed

red-handed *adjective* (*informal*) (caught) in the act of doing something wrong or illegal

red-hot *adjective* **1** glowing red **2** extremely hot

redress (*formal*) *verb* **1** to make amends for ▷ *noun* **2** compensation or amends

red tape *noun* excessive adherence to official rules

reduce *verb* **1** to bring down or lower **2** to lessen or weaken

reduction *noun* **1** act of reducing **2** amount by which something is reduced

redundancy redundancies *noun* **1** state of being redundant **2** person or job made redundant

redundant *adjective* **1** (of a worker) no longer needed **2** superfluous

reed *noun* **1** tall grass that grows in swamps and shallow water **2** tall straight stem of this plant **3** (*Music*) vibrating cane or metal strip in certain wind instruments

reef *noun* ridge of rock or coral near the surface of the sea

reek *verb* **1** to smell strongly **2 reek of** to give a strong suggestion of ▷ *noun* **3** strong unpleasant smell

reel *noun* **1** cylindrical object on which film, tape, thread or wire is wound **2** winding apparatus, as of a fishing rod **3** lively Scottish dance ▷ *verb* **4** to move unsteadily or spin around **5** to be in a state of confusion or stress > **reel off** *verb* to recite or write fluently or quickly

re-elect *verb* to vote for (someone) to retain his or her position, for example as a Member of Parliament

refer refers, referring, referred *verb* **refer to 1** to allude (to) **2** to be relevant (to) **3** to send (to) for information **4** to submit (to) for decision

referee *noun* **1** umpire in sports, especially soccer or boxing **2** person willing to testify to someone's character etc

reference noun **1** act of referring **2** citation or direction in a book **3** written testimonial regarding character or capabilities **4** with reference to concerning

referendum referendums or referenda noun direct vote of the electorate on an important question

refine verb **1** to purify **2** to improve

refined adjective **1** cultured or polite **2** purified

refinement noun **1** improvement or elaboration **2** fineness of taste or manners

refinery refineries noun place where sugar, oil, etc is refined

reflect verb **1** (of a surface or object) to throw back light, heat or sound **2** (of a mirror) to form an image of (something) by reflection **3** to show **4** to consider carefully

reflection noun **1** act of reflecting **2** return of rays of heat, light, etc from a surface **3** image of an object given back by a mirror etc **4** conscious thought or meditation **5** (Maths) transformation of a shape in which right or left, or top and bottom, are reversed

reflex noun **1** involuntary response to a stimulus or situation ▷ adjective **2** (of a muscular action) involuntary **3** reflected **4** (of an angle) more than 180°

reflexive adjective (Grammar) denoting a verb whose subject is the same as its object: He's done himself

reform noun **1** improvement ▷ verb **2** to improve (a law or institution)

by correcting abuses **3** to give up or cause to give up a bad habit or way of life ▷ **reformer** noun: reformers of the legal system

reformation noun **1** act or instance of something being reformed **2** Reformation religious movement in 16th-century Europe that resulted in the establishment of the Protestant Churches

refract verb to change the course of (light etc) passing from one medium to another ▷ **refraction** noun: the refraction of light on the waves

refrain verb **1** refrain from to keep yourself from doing **2** noun frequently repeated part of a song

refresh verb **1** to revive or reinvigorate, as through food, drink or rest **2** to stimulate (the memory)

refreshing adjective **1** having a reviving effect **2** pleasantly different or new

refreshment noun something that refreshes, especially food or drink

refrigerator noun full name for fridge

refuel refuels, refuelling, refuelled verb to supply or be supplied with fresh fuel

refuge noun **1** (source of) shelter or protection **2** place, person or thing that offers protection or help

refugee noun person who seeks refuge, especially in a foreign country

refund verb **1** to give back (money) ▷ noun **2** return of money **3** amount returned

refurbish verb (formal) to renovate and brighten up > **refurbishment** noun: The office is in need of complete refurbishment

refusal noun denial of anything demanded or offered

refuse¹ [rif-**yooz**] verb **1** to be determined not (to do something) **2** to decline to give or allow (something) to (someone)

refuse² [**ref**-yoos] noun rubbish or useless matter

refute verb to prove (a statement or theory) to be false

regain verb **1** to get back or recover **2** to reach again

regal adjective of or like a king or queen > **regally** adverb

regard verb **1** to look upon or think of in a specified way **2** to look closely at (something or someone) **3** to take notice of **4** as **regards** on the subject of ▷ noun **5** respect or esteem **6** attention **7** **regards** expression of goodwill

regardless adjective **1** **regardless of** taking no notice of ▷ adverb **2** in spite of everything

regatta noun meeting for yacht or boat races

regency regencies noun period when a country is ruled by a regent

regenerate verb **1** to (cause to) undergo spiritual, economic or physical renewal **2** to come or bring into existence once again > **regeneration** noun: economic regeneration

regent noun **1** ruler of a kingdom during the absence, childhood or illness of its monarch ▷ adjective **2** ruling as a regent: prince regent

reggae noun style of Jamaican popular music with a strong beat

regime [ray-**zheem**] noun **1** system of government **2** particular administration

regiment noun organized body of troops as a unit of the army > **regimental** adjective: a regimental reunion

regimented adjective very strictly controlled > **regimentation** noun: bureaucratic regimentation

region noun **1** administrative division of a country **2** area considered as a unit but with no definite boundaries **3** part of the body **4** **in the region of** approximately > **regional** adjective: regional government > **regionally** adverb

register noun **1** (book containing) an official list or record of things **2** range of a voice or instrument **3** style of speaking or writing, such as slang, used in particular circumstances ▷ verb **4** to enter (an event, person's name, ownership, etc) in a register **5** to show on a scale or other measuring instrument **6** to show on a person's face > **registration** noun: compulsory registration of dogs

registrar noun **1** keeper of official records **2** senior hospital doctor, junior to a consultant **3** senior administrative official at a university

registration number noun numbers and letters displayed on a vehicle to identify it

registry registries noun place where official records are kept

registry office noun place where births, marriages and deaths are recorded, and where people can marry without a religious ceremony

regret regrets, regretting, regretted *verb* **1** to feel sorry about **2** to express apology or distress ▷ *noun* **3** feeling of repentance, guilt or sorrow > **regretful** *adjective: a regretful smile* > **regretfully** *adverb*

regrettable *adjective* unfortunate and undesirable > **regrettably** *adverb*

regular *adjective* **1** normal, customary or usual **2** symmetrical or even **3** done or occurring according to a rule **4** periodical **5** employed continuously in the armed forces ▷ *noun* **6** regular soldier **7** (*informal*) frequent customer > **regularity** *noun: monotonous regularity* > **regularly** *adverb*

regulate *verb* **1** to control by means of rules **2** to adjust slightly

regulation *noun* **1** rule **2** regulating

regurgitate *verb* **1** to vomit **2** (of some birds and animals) to bring back (partly digested food) into the mouth **3** to reproduce (ideas, facts, etc) without understanding them

rehabilitate *verb* to help (a person) to readjust to society after illness, imprisonment, etc > **rehabilitation** *noun: the rehabilitation of young offenders*

rehearsal *noun* practice of a performance in preparation for the actual event

rehearse *verb* **1** to practise (a play, concert, etc) **2** to repeat aloud

reign *noun* **1** period of a sovereign's rule ▷ *verb* **2** to rule (a country) **3** to be supreme

rein *noun* **1 reins a** narrow straps attached to a bit to guide a horse **b** means of control **2 keep a tight rein on** to control carefully

reincarnation *noun* **1** rebirth of a soul in successive bodies **2** one of a series of such transmigrations

reindeer reindeer or reindeers *noun* deer of arctic regions with large branched antlers

reinforce *verb* **1** to give added emphasis to (an idea or feeling) **2** to make physically stronger or harder

reinforcement *noun* **1** reinforcing of something **2 reinforcements** additional soldiers sent to join an army in battle

reinstate *verb* **1** to restore to a former position **2** to cause to exist or be important again > **reinstatement** *noun: parents campaigned for her reinstatement*

reiterate *verb* (*formal*) to repeat again and again > **reiteration** *noun: a reiteration of the same old ideas*

reject *verb* **1** to refuse to accept or believe **2** to deny to (a person) the feelings hoped for **3** to discard as useless ▷ *noun* **4** person or thing rejected as not up to standard > **rejection** *noun: feelings of rejection; be prepared for lots of rejections*

rejoice *verb* to feel or express great happiness

rejoin *verb* to come together with (someone or something) again

rejuvenate *verb* to restore youth or vitality to > **rejuvenation** *noun: the whole system needs rejuvenation*

relapse verb 1 to fall back into bad habits, illness, etc ▷ noun 2 return of bad habits, illness, etc

relate verb 1 to establish a relation between 2 to have reference or relation to 3 to have an understanding (of people or ideas) 4 to tell (a story) or describe (an event)

relation noun 1 connection between things 2 relative 3 connection by blood or marriage 4 act of relating (a story) 5 relations a social or political dealings b family

relationship noun 1 dealings and feelings between people or countries 2 emotional or sexual affair 3 connection between two things

relative adjective 1 dependent on relation to something else, not absolute 2 having reference or relation (to) 3 (Grammar) referring to a word or clause earlier in the sentence ▷ noun 4 person connected by blood or marriage

relative pronoun noun pronoun that replaces a noun that links two parts of a sentence

relax verb 1 to make or become looser, less tense or less rigid 2 to ease up from effort or attention 3 to make (rules or discipline) less strict 4 to become more friendly > **relaxation** noun: rest and relaxation

relay noun 1 race between teams in which each runner races part of the distance ▷ verb 2 to pass on (a message) 3 to broadcast (a performance or event) as it happens

release verb 1 to free (a person or animal) from captivity or imprisonment 2 to free (something) from (one's grip) 3 to issue (a record, film, etc) for sale or public showing 4 to give out heat, energy, etc ▷ noun 5 setting free 6 statement to the press 7 act of issuing for sale or publication 8 newly issued film, record, etc

relegate verb 1 to put in a less important position 2 to demote (a sports team) to a lower league > **relegation** noun

relent verb 1 to change your mind about some decision 2 to become milder or less severe

relentless adjective 1 never stopping and never becoming less intense 2 merciless > **relentlessly** adverb

relevant adjective to do with the matter in hand > **relevance** noun: a fact of little relevance

reliable adjective able to be trusted, dependable > **reliability** noun: her car's reliability > **reliably** adverb

reliant adjective dependant > **reliance** noun: reliance on public transport

relic noun 1 something that has survived from the past 2 body or possession of a saint, regarded as holy 3 relics remains or traces

relief noun 1 gladness at the end or removal of pain, distress, etc 2 release from monotony or duty 3 money or food given to victims of disaster, poverty, etc

relief map noun map showing the shape and height of land by shading

relieve verb 1 to lessen (pain, distress, boredom, etc) 2 to bring assistance to (someone in need) 3 to free (someone) from an obligation 4 to take over the duties of (someone) 5 **relieve yourself** to urinate or defecate

religion noun system of belief in and worship of a supernatural power or god

religious adjective 1 of religion 2 pious or devout 3 scrupulous or conscientious

religiously adverb regularly as a duty: *he stuck religiously to the rules*

relinquish verb 1 to give up 2 to renounce (a claim or right)

relish verb 1 to savour or enjoy (an experience) to the full ▷ noun 2 liking or enjoyment 3 appetizing savoury food, such as pickle

relive verb 1 to remember (a past experience) very vividly, imagining it happening again

relocate verb to move to a new place to live or work ▷ **relocation** noun: *relocation to London*

reluctant adjective unwilling or disinclined ▷ **reluctance** noun: *he has shown reluctance to explain his position* ▷ **reluctantly** adverb

rely relies, relying, relied verb **rely on** or **upon a** to be dependent on **b** to have trust in

remain verb 1 to continue to be 2 to stay behind or in the same place 3 to be left after use or the passage of time 4 to be left to be done, said, etc

remainder noun 1 part which is left 2 amount left over after subtraction or division

remand verb 1 to send (a prisoner or accused person) back into custody or put on bail before trial ▷ noun 2 **on remand** in custody or on bail before trial

remark verb 1 to make a casual comment (on) 2 to say 3 to observe or notice ▷ noun 4 observation or comment

remarkable adjective 1 worthy of note or attention 2 striking or unusual ▷ **remarkably** adverb

remarry remarries, remarrying, remarried verb to marry again

remedial adjective 1 intended to correct a specific disability, handicap, etc 2 designed to improve someone's ability in something

remedy remedies, remedying, remedied noun 1 means of curing pain or disease 2 means of solving a problem ▷ verb 3 to put right or improve

remember verb 1 to become aware of (something forgotten) again 2 to keep (an idea, intention, etc) in your mind

remembrance noun 1 memory 2 honouring of the memory of a person or event

remind verb 1 to cause to remember 2 to put in mind (of)

reminder noun 1 something that recalls the past 2 note to remind a person of something not done

reminiscent adjective reminding or suggestive (of)

remission noun 1 reduction in the length of a prison term 2 easing of intensity, as of an illness

remit verb [**ree**-mitt] area of competence or authority

remittance noun (formal) money sent as payment

remnant noun **1** small piece, especially of fabric, left over **2** surviving trace

remorse (formal) noun feeling of sorrow and regret for something you did >**remorseful** adjective: he was genuinely remorseful

remote adjective **1** far away, distant **2** aloof **3** slight or faint >**remoteness** noun: the remoteness of the farmhouse

remote control noun control of an apparatus from a distance by an electrical device

remotely adverb used to emphasize a negative statement

removal noun removing, especially changing residence

remove verb **1** to take away **2** to take (clothing) off **3** to get rid of **4** to dismiss (someone) from office >**removable** adjective: a tin with a removable base

renaissance noun **1** revival or rebirth **2** Renaissance revival of learning in the 14th–16th centuries

renal [ree-nal] adjective of the kidneys

rename verb to give (something) a new name

render verb **1** to cause to become **2** to give or provide (aid, a service, etc) **3** to represent in painting, music or acting

rendezvous rendezvous [ron-day-voo] noun **1** appointment **2** meeting place

> **WORD TIP**
> The plural of rendezvous is rendezvous

rendition noun (formal) **1** performance **2** translation

renew verb **1** to begin again **2** to make valid again **3** to grow again **4** to restore to a former state >**renewal** noun: the renewal of my TV licence

renewable adjective **1** able to be renewed ▷ noun **2** renewables sources of alternative energy, such as wind and wave power

renounce verb (formal) **1** to give up (a belief, habit, etc) voluntarily **2** to give up (a title or claim) formally >**renunciation** noun: progress requires a renunciation of terrorism

renovate verb to restore to good condition >**renovation** noun: property which will need extensive renovation

renowned adjective well-known for something good >**renown** noun: a singer of some renown

rent verb **1** to give or have use of (land, a building, a machine, etc) in return for regular payments ▷ noun **2** regular payment for use of land, a building, machine, etc

rental noun **1** concerned with the renting out of goods and services **2** sum payable as rent

reorganize or **reorganise** verb to organize in a new and more efficient way >**reorganization** noun: the reorganization of the legal system

rep noun short for **representative**: a sales rep

repair verb **1** to restore (something damaged or broken) to good condition **2** to make up for (a mistake or injury) **3** to go to (a place) ▷ noun **4** act of repairing **5** repaired part

repay repays, repaying, repaid verb **1** to pay back or refund **2** to make a return for (something): repay

hospitality > **repayment** noun:
monthly repayments

repeal verb 1 to cancel (a law)
officially ▷ noun 2 act of repealing

repeat verb 1 to say, write or
do again 2 to tell to another
person (the secrets told to you
by someone else) 3 to happen
again ▷ noun 4 act or instance
of repeating 5 programme
broadcast again > **repeated**
adjective: repeated reminders
> **repeatedly** adverb

repel repels, repelling, repelled
verb 1 to cause (someone) to feel
disgusted 2 to force or drive back
(someone or something) 3 to
reject or spurn

repellent adjective 1 distasteful
2 resisting water etc ▷ noun
3 something that repels,
especially a chemical to repel
insects

repent verb (formal) to feel
regret for (a deed or omission)
> **repentance** noun: they showed
no repentance during the trial
> **repentant** adjective: a repentant
arms dealer

repercussions plural noun
indirect effects, often unpleasant

repertoire noun stock of plays,
songs, etc that a player or
company can give

repertory repertories noun
repertoire

repetition noun 1 act of repeating
2 thing repeated

repetitive or **repetitious**
adjective full of repetition

replace verb 1 to take the place of
2 to substitute a person or thing
for (another) 3 to put (something)
back in its rightful place

replacement noun 1 act or
process of replacement 2 person
or thing that replaces another

replay noun 1 immediate
reshowing on TV of an incident
in sport, especially in slow
motion 2 second sports match,
especially one following an earlier
draw ▷ verb 3 to play (a match,
recording, etc) again

replenish verb (formal) to make full
or complete again by supplying
what has been used up

replica noun exact copy

reply replies, replying, replied verb
1 to make answer (to) in words or
writing or by an action 2 to say
(something) in answer ▷ noun
3 answer or response

report verb 1 to give an account
of 2 to make a report (on) 3 to
make a formal complaint about
4 to present yourself (to) 5 to be
responsible (to) ▷ noun 6 account
or statement 7 rumour 8 written
statement of a child's progress
at school

reported speech noun report
of what someone said that
gives the content of the speech
without repeating the exact
words

reporter noun person who
gathers news for a newspaper,
TV, etc

repossess verb (of a lender) to
take back (property) from a
customer who is behind with
payments

represent verb 1 to act as a
delegate or substitute for (a
person, country, etc) 2 to stand as
an equivalent of 3 to be a means
of expressing 4 to display the

characteristics of **5** to portray, as in art

representation noun **1** state of being represented by someone **2** anything that represents, such as a pictorial portrait **3 representations** formal requests or complaints made to an official body

representative noun **1** person chosen to stand for a group **2** (travelling) salesperson ▷ adjective **3** typical

repress verb **1** to keep (feelings) in check **2** to restrict the freedom of > **repression** noun: political repression

repressive adjective restricting freedom by the use of force

reprieve verb **1** to postpone the execution of (a condemned person) **2** to give temporary relief to ▷ noun **3** (document granting) postponement or cancellation of a punishment **4** temporary relief

reprimand verb **1** to blame (someone) officially for a fault ▷ noun **2** official blame

reprisal noun retaliation

reproach verb **1** to express disapproval (of someone's actions) ▷ noun **2** blame **3 beyond reproach** beyond criticism > **reproachful** adjective: a reproachful look > **reproachfully** adverb

reproduce verb **1** to produce a copy of **2** to produce offspring **3** to re-create

reproduction noun **1** process of reproducing **2** facsimile, as of a painting etc **3** quality of sound from an audio system

reproductive adjective relating to the reproduction of living things

reptile noun cold-blooded egg-laying vertebrate with horny scales or plates, such as a snake or tortoise > **reptilian** adjective: reptilian creatures

republic noun **1** form of government in which the people or their elected representatives possess the supreme power **2** country in which a president is the head of state > **republican** noun, adjective: republican beliefs; a staunch republican > **republicanism** noun: the growth of republicanism in Australia

repulse verb **1** to be disgusting to **2** to drive (an army) back **3** to reject with coldness or discourtesy

repulsion noun **1** distaste or aversion **2** (Physics) force separating two objects

repulsive adjective horrible and disgusting

reputable adjective of good reputation, respectable

reputation noun estimation in which a person is held

reputed adjective supposed > **reputedly** adverb: he reputedly earns £30,000 per week

request verb **1** to ask for ▷ noun **2** asking **3** thing asked for

Requiem [rek-wee-em] noun **1** Mass for the dead **2** music for this

require verb **1** to want or need **2** to be a necessary condition

requirement noun **1** essential condition **2** specific need or want

requisite [rek-wizz-it] (formal) adjective **1** necessary, essential ▷ noun **2** essential thing

rescue rescues, rescuing, rescued verb **1** to bring (someone or something) out of danger or trouble ▷ noun **2** rescuing > **rescuer** noun: It took rescuers hours to reach the trapped men

research noun **1** systematic investigation to discover facts or collect information ▷ verb **2** to carry out investigations into (a subject) > **researcher** noun: a government researcher

resemblance noun similarity

resemble verb to be or look like

resent verb to feel bitter about > **resentment** noun: resentment against his supervisor

resentful adjective bitter and angry > **resentfully** adverb

reservation noun **1** doubt **2** exception or limitation **3** seat, room, etc that has been reserved **4** area of land reserved for use by a particular group **5** (Brit) strip of ground separating the two carriageways of a dual carriageway or motorway

reserve verb **1** to set aside, keep for future use **2** to obtain by arranging beforehand, book **3** to keep (something) for yourself ▷ noun **4** something, especially money or troops, kept for emergencies **5** area of land reserved for a particular purpose **6** (Sport) substitute **7** concealment of feelings or friendliness

reservoir noun natural or artificial lake storing water for community supplies

reshuffle noun reorganization

reside verb (formal) to live permanently (in a place)

residence noun (formal) home or house

resident noun **1** person who lives in a place ▷ adjective **2** living in a place

residential adjective **1** (of part of a town) consisting mainly of houses **2** providing living accommodation

residue noun what is left, remainder > **residual** adjective: residual radiation

resign verb **1** to give up office, a job, etc **2** to reconcile (oneself) to

resignation noun **1** resigning **2** passive endurance of difficulties

resilient adjective **1** (of a person) recovering quickly from a shock etc **2** able to return to normal shape after stretching etc > **resilience** noun: Londoners' resilience during the Blitz

resin [rezz-in] noun **1** sticky substance from plants, especially pines **2** similar synthetic substance

resist verb **1** to withstand or oppose **2** to refrain from despite temptation **3** to be proof against > **resistible** adjective

resistance noun **1** act of resisting **2** capacity to withstand something **3** (Electricity) opposition offered by a circuit to the passage of a current through it

resistant adjective **1** opposed to something and wanting to prevent it **2** not harmed or affected by

resistor noun D&T device which increases the resistance in an electrical circuit

resolute adjective firm in purpose > **resolutely** adverb

resolution noun 1 firmness of conduct or character 2 thing resolved upon 3 decision of a court or vote of an assembly 4 act of resolving

resolve verb 1 to decide with an effort of will 2 to form (a resolution) by a vote ▷ noun 3 absolute determination

resonance noun 1 echoing, especially with a deep sound 2 sound produced in one object by sound waves coming from another object

resonate verb to vibrate and produce a deep, strong sound

resort verb 1 to have recourse (to) for help etc ▷ noun 2 place for holidays 3 the use of something as a means or aid

resounding adjective 1 echoing 2 clear and emphatic

resource noun 1 thing resorted to for support 2 ingenuity 3 means of achieving something 4 **resources** a sources of economic wealth b stock that can be drawn on, funds

resourceful adjective capable and full of initiative > **resourcefulness** noun: *a person of great experience and resourcefulness*

respect noun 1 consideration 2 deference or esteem 3 point or aspect 4 reference or relation: *with respect to* 5 **in respect of** or **with respect to** in reference or relation to ▷ verb 6 to treat with

esteem 7 to show consideration for

respectable adjective 1 worthy of respect 2 fairly good > **respectability** noun: *she has lost all respectability* > **respectably** adverb

respectful adjective showing respect for someone > **respectfully** adverb

respective adjective relating separately to each of those in question > **respectively** adverb

respiration [ress-per-**ray**-shun] noun breathing

respiratory adjective of breathing

respire verb to breathe

respite noun (formal) 1 pause or interval of rest 2 delay

respond verb 1 to state or utter (something) in reply 2 to act in answer to any stimulus 3 to react favourably

respondent noun 1 person who answers a questionnaire or a request for information 2 (Law) defendant

response noun 1 answer 2 reaction to a stimulus

responsibility responsibilities noun 1 state of being responsible 2 person or thing for which you are responsible

responsible adjective 1 having control and authority 2 reporting or accountable (to) 3 sensible and dependable 4 involving responsibility > **responsibly** adverb

responsive adjective readily reacting to some influence

rest noun 1 freedom from exertion etc 2 repose 3 pause, especially in music 4 object used for support

5 what is left **6** others ▷ verb **7** to take a rest **8** to give a rest (to) **9** to be supported **10** to place for support or steadying

restaurant noun commercial establishment serving meals

restaurateur [rest-er-a-**tur**] noun person who owns or runs a restaurant

restful adjective relaxing or soothing

restless adjective finding it hard to remain still or relaxed because of boredom or impatience ▷ **restlessly** adverb ▷ **restlessness** noun: restlessness in the audience

restore verb **1** to return (a building, painting, etc) to its original condition **2** to cause to recover health or spirits **3** to return (something lost or stolen) to its owner **4** to reinforce or re-establish ▷ **restoration** noun: the restoration of old houses

restrain verb **1** to hold (someone) back from action **2** to control or restrict

restrained adjective not displaying emotion

restraint noun **1** control, especially self-control **2** something that restrains

restrict verb to confine to certain limits ▷ **restrictive** adjective

restriction noun rule or situation that limits what you can do

result noun **1** outcome or consequence **2** score **3** number obtained from a calculation **4** exam mark or grade ▷ verb **5** result from to be the outcome or consequence (of) **6** result in to end (in) ▷ **resultant** adjective: civil war and the resultant famine

resume verb **1** to begin again or go on with (something interrupted) **2** to occupy or take again ▷ **resumption** noun: a resumption of negotiations

resurgence noun rising again to vigour ▷ **resurgent** adjective: resurgent extremism

resurrect verb **1** to restore to life **2** to use once more (something discarded etc)

resurrection noun **1** rising again (especially from the dead) **2** revival **3 the Resurrection** (Christianity) the coming back to life of Jesus Christ three days after he had been killed

resuscitate [ris-**suss**-it-tate] verb to restore to consciousness ▷ **resuscitation** noun: mouth-to-mouth resuscitation

retail noun **1** selling of goods individually or in small amounts to the public ▷ adverb **2** by retail ▷ verb **3** to sell or be sold retail

retain verb to keep in your possession

retaliate verb to repay an injury or wrong in kind ▷ **retaliation** noun: retaliation for the recent bombings

retarded adjective underdeveloped, especially mentally

rethink rethinks, rethinking, rethought verb to consider again, especially with a view to changing your tactics

reticent adjective not willing to say or tell much ▷ **reticence** noun: a lack of reticence

retina retinas or retinae noun light-sensitive membrane at the back of the eye

retinue *noun* band of attendants

retire *verb* **1** to (cause to) give up office or work, especially through age **2** (*formal*) to go away or withdraw **3** to go to bed

retort *verb* **1** to reply quickly, wittily or angrily ▷ *noun* **2** quick, witty or angry reply

retract *verb* **1** to withdraw (a statement etc) **2** to draw in (a part or appendage) ▷ **retraction** *noun: a retraction of his comments*

retreat *verb* **1** to move back from a position, withdraw ▷ *noun* **2** act of or military signal for retiring or withdrawal **3** place to which anyone retires, refuge

retribution *noun* punishment or vengeance for evil deeds

retrieve *verb* **1** to fetch back again **2** to restore to a better state **3** to recover (information) from a computer ▷ **retrieval** *noun: the retrieval of confiscated items*

retriever *noun* large dog often used by hunters to bring back birds and animals which have been shot

retro- *prefix* back or backwards: *retrospective*

retrospect *noun* **in retrospect** when looking back on the past

retrospective *adjective* **1** looking back in time **2** applying from a date in the past ▷ **retrospectively** *adverb*

return *verb* **1** to go or come back **2** to give, put or send back **3** to hit, throw or play (a ball) back **4** (of a jury) to deliver (a verdict) ▷ *noun* **5** returning **6** (thing) being returned **7** profit **8** official report, as of taxable income **9** return ticket **10** **in return** in exchange

reunion *noun* meeting of people who have been apart

reunite *verb* to bring or come together again after a separation

rev revs, revving, revved (*informal*) *noun* **1** revolution (of an engine) ▷ *verb* **2** **rev up** to increase the speed of revolution of (an engine)

revamp *verb* to renovate or restore

reveal *verb* **1** to disclose or divulge (a secret) **2** to expose to view (something concealed)

revel revels, revelling, revelled *verb* **1** to take pleasure (in something) **2** to make merry

revelation *noun* **1** surprising or interesting fact made known to people **2** person or experience that proves to be different from expectations

revenge *noun* **1** retaliation for wrong done ▷ *verb* **2** to avenge (oneself or another)

revenue *noun* income, especially of a state

revered *adjective* respected and admired

reverence *noun* awe mingled with respect and esteem

Reverend *adjective* title of respect for a clergyman

reverse *verb* **1** to turn upside down or the other way round **2** to change completely **3** to move (a vehicle) backwards ▷ *noun* **4** opposite **5** back side **6** change for the worse **7** reverse gear ▷ *adjective* **8** opposite or contrary ▷ **reversal** *noun: a complete reversal of previous policy*

reversible *adjective* **1** capable of being reversed **2** (of clothing) made so that either side may be used as the outer side

revert verb (formal) **1** to return to a former state **2** to come back to a subject

review noun **1** critical assessment of a book, concert, etc **2** publication with critical articles **3** general survey ▷ verb **4** to hold or write a review of **5** to examine, reconsider or look back on

revise verb **1** to change or alter **2** to restudy (work) in preparation for an examination > **revision** noun: another revision of the report

revive verb to bring or come back to life, vigour, use, etc

revolt noun **1** uprising against authority ▷ verb **2** to rise up in rebellion **3** to cause to feel disgust

revolting adjective disgusting and horrible

revolution noun **1** overthrow of a government by the governed **2** great change **3** complete rotation

revolutionary revolutionaries adjective **1** advocating or engaged in revolution **2** radically new or different ▷ noun **3** person advocating or engaged in revolution

revolve verb **1** to move or cause to move around a centre **2** revolve around to be centred on

revolver noun small gun held in the hand

revulsion noun strong disgust

reward noun **1** something given in return for a service **2** sum of money offered for finding a criminal or missing property ▷ verb **3** to pay or give something to (someone) for a service, information, etc

rewarding adjective giving personal satisfaction, worthwhile

rewind rewinds, rewinding, rewound verb to run (a tape or film) back to an earlier point in order to replay

rhapsody rhapsodies noun freely structured emotional piece of music

rhetoric noun **1** art of effective speaking or writing **2** artificial or exaggerated language

rhetorical adjective **1** (of a question) not requiring an answer **2** (of language) intended to be grand and impressive

rheumatism noun painful inflammation of joints or muscles

rhino noun short for **rhinoceros**

rhinoceros rhinoceroses or rhinoceros noun large thick-skinned animal with one or two horns on its nose

rhododendron noun evergreen flowering shrub

rhombus rhombuses or rhombi noun parallelogram with sides of equal length but no right angles, diamond-shaped figure

rhubarb noun garden plant of which the fleshy stalks are cooked as fruit

rhyme noun **1** sameness of the final sounds at the ends of lines of verse, or in words **2** word identical to another in its final sounds **3** verse marked by rhyme ▷ verb **4** (of a rhyme) to form a rhyme with another word

rhythm noun **1** any regular movement or beat **2** arrangement of the durations of and stress on the notes of a piece of music, usually grouped into a regular pattern **3** (in poetry) arrangement of words to form a regular pattern of stresses >**rhythmic** or**rhythmical** adjective: rhythmic breathing >**rhythmically** adverb

rib noun **1** one of the curved bones forming the framework of the upper part of the body **2** cut of meat including the rib(s) **3** curved supporting part, as in the hull of a boat >**ribbed** adjective: ribbed sweaters

ribbon noun narrow band of fabric used for trimming, tying, etc

ribcage noun bony structure of ribs enclosing the lungs

rice noun **1** cereal plant grown on wet ground in warm countries **2** its seeds as food

rich adjective **1** owning a lot of money or property, wealthy **2** abounding **3** fertile **4** (of food) containing much fat or sugar **5** (of colours, smells and sounds) strong and pleasant >**richness** noun: the richness of Tibet's mineral deposits

richly adverb **1** elaborately **2** fully

rick noun **1** stack of hay etc >verb **2** to sprain or wrench (a joint)

rickets noun disease of children marked by softening of the bones, bow legs, etc, caused by vitamin D deficiency

rickety adjective shaky or unstable

rickshaw noun light two-wheeled man-drawn Asian vehicle

ricochet ricochets, ricocheting or ricochetting, ricocheted or ricochetted [**rik**-osh-ay] verb **1** (of a bullet) to rebound from a solid surface >noun **2** such a rebound

rid rids, ridding, rid verb **1** (formal) to relieve (oneself) or make a place

free of (something undesirable) **2 get rid of** to free yourself of (something undesirable)

riddle noun **1** puzzling question designed to test people's ingenuity **2** puzzling person or thing >verb **3** to pierce with many holes **4 riddled with** full of (something undesirable)

ride rides, riding, rode, ridden verb **1** to sit on and control or propel (a horse, bicycle, etc) **2** to go on horseback or in a vehicle **3** to travel over >noun **4** journey on a horse etc or in a vehicle

rider noun **1** person who rides **2** supplementary clause added to a document

ridge noun **1** long narrow hill **2** long narrow raised part on a surface **3** line where two sloping surfaces meet **4** (Meteorology) elongated area of high pressure

ridicule noun **1** treatment of a person or thing as ridiculous >verb **2** to laugh at, make fun of

ridiculous adjective deserving to be laughed at, absurd >**ridiculously** adverb

rife adjective **1** widespread or common **2 rife with** full of

rifle noun **1** firearm with a long barrel >verb **2** to search (a house or safe) and steal from it

rift noun **1** break in friendly relations **2** crack, split or cleft

rig rigs, rigging, rigged verb **1** to arrange in a dishonest way for profit or advantage >noun **2** apparatus for drilling for oil and gas >**rig up** verb to set up or build temporarily

right adjective **1** just **2** true or correct **3** proper **4** in a satisfactory condition **5** of the side that faces east when the front is turned to the north **6** of the outer side of a fabric ▷ *adverb* **7** properly **8** straight or directly **9** on or to the right side ▷ *noun* **10** claim, title, etc allowed or due **11** what is just or due **12** in the right morally or legally correct **13** Right conservative political party or group ▷ *verb* **14** to bring or come back to a normal or correct state

right angle noun angle of 90°

righteous [rye-chuss] *adjective* **1** upright, godly or virtuous **2** morally justified

rightful *adjective* **1** in accordance with what is right **2** having a legally or morally just claim > **rightfully** *adverb*

right-handed *adjective* using or for the right hand

right-wing *adjective* believing more strongly in capitalism or conservatism, or less strongly in socialism, than other members of the same party or group > **right-winger** *noun: a veteran right-winger*

rigid *adjective* **1** inflexible or strict **2** unyielding or stiff > **rigidity** *noun: the rigidity of government policy* > **rigidly** *adverb*

rigorous *adjective* harsh, severe or stern > **rigorously** *adverb*

rigour *noun* **1** harshness, severity or strictness **2** hardship

rim *noun* **1** edge or border **2** outer ring of a wheel > **rimmed** *adjective: rimmed with gold*

rimu *noun* (NZ) New Zealand tree whose wood is used for building and furniture

rind *noun* tough outer coating of fruits, cheese or bacon

ring rings, ringing, rang, rung *verb* **1** to give out a clear resonant sound, as a bell **2** to cause (a bell) to sound **3** to call (a person) by telephone **4** (of a building or place) to be filled with sound **5** to put a ring round ▷ *noun* **6** ringing **7** telephone call **8** circle of gold etc, especially for a finger **9** any circular band, coil or rim **10** circle of people **11** enclosed area, especially a circle for a circus or a roped-in square for boxing **12** group operating (illegal) control of a market > **ring off** *verb* to end a telephone call > **ring up** *verb* **1** to make a telephone call to **2** to record on a cash register

ringbark *verb* (Aust) to kill (a tree) by cutting away a strip of bark from around its trunk

ringer *noun* **1** (*informal*) person or thing apparently identical to another **2** (Aust) person who works on a sheep farm **3** (Aust, NZ) fastest shearer in a woolshed

ring-in *noun* (*informal*) **1** (Aust) person or thing that is not normally a member of a particular group **2** (Aust, NZ) someone who is brought in at the last minute as a replacement for someone else

ringleader *noun* instigator of a mutiny, riot, etc

rink *noun* **1** sheet of ice for skating or curling **2** floor for roller-skating

rinse *verb* **1** to remove soap from (washed clothes, hair, etc) by applying clean water **2** to wash lightly **3** rinsing **4** liquid to tint hair

riot *noun* **1** disorderly unruly disturbance ▷ *verb* **2** to take part in a riot **3 run riot** to behave without restraint

rip rips, ripping, ripped *verb* **1** to tear or be torn violently **2** to remove hastily or roughly **3** (*informal*) to move violently or hurriedly ▷ *noun* **4** split or tear > **rip off** (*informal*) to cheat (someone) by overcharging

RIP *abbreviation* rest in peace

ripe *adjective* **1** ready to be reaped, eaten, etc **2** matured **3** ready or suitable **4 ripe old age** an elderly but healthy age > **ripeness** *noun*

ripen *verb* **1** to make or become ripe **2** to mature

ripper *noun* (*Aust, NZ informal*) excellent person or thing

ripple *noun* **1** slight wave or ruffling of a surface **2** sound like ripples of water: *a ripple of applause* ▷ *verb* **3** to flow or form into little waves (on)

rise rising, rose, risen *verb* **1** to get up from a lying, sitting or kneeling position **2** to get out of bed, especially to begin the day **3** to move upwards **4** (of the sun or moon) to appear above the horizon **5** to reach a higher level **6** (of an amount or price) to increase **7** to rebel **8** (of a court) to adjourn ▷ *noun* **9** rising **10** upward slope **11** increase, especially of wages

riser *noun* person who rises, especially from bed

risk *noun* **1** chance of disaster or loss **2** person or thing considered as a potential hazard ▷ *verb* **3** to act in spite of the possibility of (injury or loss) **4** to expose to danger or loss

rite *noun* formal practice or custom, especially religious

ritual *noun* **1** prescribed order of rites **2** regular repeated action or behaviour ▷ *adjective* **3** concerning rites

rival rivals, rivalling, rivalled *noun* **1** person or thing that competes with or equals another for favour, success, etc ▷ *adjective* **2** in the position of a rival ▷ *verb* **3** to (try to) equal

rivalry rivalries *noun* keen competition

river *noun* **1** large natural stream of water **2** plentiful flow

rivet [**riv-vit**] *noun* **1** bolt for fastening metal plates, the end being put through holes and then beaten flat ▷ *verb* **2** to fasten with rivets **3** to cause a person's attention to be fixed, as in fascination

riveting *adjective* very interesting and exciting

road *noun* **1** way prepared for passengers, vehicles, etc **2** route in a town or city with houses along it **3** way or course: *the road to fame*

road rage *noun* aggressive behaviour by a driver as a reaction to the behaviour of another driver

road train *noun* (*Aust*) line of linked trailers pulled by a truck, used for transporting cattle or sheep

roadworks *plural noun* repairs to a road, especially blocking part of the road

roam *verb* to walk about with no fixed purpose or direction

roar *verb* **1** to make a very loud noise **2** (of lions, etc) to make loud growling cries **3** to shout (something) as in anger **4** to laugh loudly ▷ noun **5** such a sound

roast verb **1** to cook (food) by dry heat, as in an oven **2** to make or be very hot ▷ noun **3** roasted joint of meat ▷ adjective **4** roasted

rob robs, robbing, robbed verb **1** to take something from (a person or place) illegally **2** to deprive, especially of something deserved

robber noun criminal who steals money or property using force or threats > **robbery** noun: a bank robbery

robe noun long loose outer garment

robin noun small brown bird with a red breast

robot noun **1** automated machine, especially one performing functions in a human manner **2** person of machine-like efficiency **3** (S Afr) set of coloured lights at a junction to control the traffic flow > **robotic** adjective

robust adjective very strong and healthy > **robustly** adverb

rock noun **1** hard mineral substance that makes up part of the earth's crust, stone **2** large rugged mass of stone **3** hard sweet in sticks **4** style of pop music with a heavy beat **5 on the rocks a** (of a marriage) about to end **b** (of an alcoholic drink) served with ice ▷ verb **6** to (cause to) sway to and fro

rock and roll or **rock'n'roll** noun style of pop music blending rhythm and blues and country music

rocket noun **1** self-propelling device powered by the burning of explosive contents (used as a firework, weapon, etc) **2** vehicle propelled by a rocket engine, as a weapon or carrying a spacecraft **3** firework that explodes when it is high in the air ▷ verb **4** to increase rapidly

rocking chair noun chair allowing the sitter to rock backwards and forwards

rock melon noun (US, Aust, NZ) kind of melon with sweet orange flesh

rocky rockier, rockiest adjective **1** shaky or unstable **2** having many rocks

rod noun **1** slender straight bar, stick **2** cane

rodent noun animal with teeth specialized for gnawing, such as a rat, mouse or squirrel

rodeo rodeos noun display of skill by cowboys, such as bareback riding

roe noun **1** mass of eggs in a fish, sometimes eaten as food **2** small species of deer

rogue noun **1** dishonest or unprincipled person **2** mischief-loving person ▷ adjective **3** (of a wild beast) having a savage temper and living apart from the herd

role or **rôle** noun **1** task or function **2** actor's part

roll verb **1** to move along by turning over and over **2** to move along on wheels or rollers **3** to curl or make by curling into a ball or tube **4** to move along in an undulating movement **5** to smooth out with a roller **6** to rotate wholly or partially: He rolled his eyes **7** (of a ship or aircraft) to turn from side

a
b
c
d
e
f
g
h
i
j
k
l
m
n
o
p
q
r
s
t
u
v
w
x
y
z

to side about a line from nose to tail ▷ *noun* **8** act of rolling over or from side to side **9** piece of paper etc rolled up **10** small round individually baked piece of bread **11** list or register **12** continuous sound, as of drums, thunder, etc **13** swaying unsteady movement or gait ▷ **roll up** *verb* **1** to form into a cylindrical shape **2** (*informal*) to appear or arrive

roll call *noun* calling out of a list of names to check who is present

roller *noun* **1** rotating cylinder used for smoothing or supporting a thing to be moved, spreading paint, etc **2** small tube around which hair may be wound in order to make it curly

Rollerblade ® *noun* roller skate with the wheels set in one straight line

roller coaster *noun* (at a funfair) narrow railway with steep slopes

roller-skate *noun* **1** shoe with four small wheels that enable the wearer to glide swiftly over a flat surface ▷ *verb* **2** to move on roller-skates

rolling pin *noun* cylindrical roller for flattening pastry

ROM *abbreviation* (*Computers*) read only memory: storage device that holds data permanently and cannot be altered by the programmer

Roman Catholic *adjective* **1** of that section of the Christian Church that acknowledges the supremacy of the Pope ▷ *noun* **2** person who belongs to the Roman Catholic church > **Roman Catholicism** *noun*: *the spread of Roman Catholicism*

romance *noun* **1** love affair **2** mysterious or exciting quality **3** novel or film dealing with love, especially sentimentally

Romanian or **Rumanian** [roe-**may**-nee-an] *adjective* **1** belonging or relating to Romania ▷ *noun* **2** someone from Romania **3** main language spoken in Romania

romantic *adjective* **1** of or dealing with love **2** idealistic but impractical **3** (of literature, music, etc) displaying passion and imagination rather than order and form ▷ *noun* **4** romantic person or artist > **romantically** *adverb* > **romanticism** *noun*

rondavel *noun* (*SAfr*) small circular building with a conical roof

roo *noun* (*Aust informal*) kangaroo

roof *noun* outside upper covering of a building, car, etc

roofing *noun* material used for covering roofs

rooftop *noun* outside part of the roof of a building

rook *noun* **1** Eurasian bird of the crow family **2** chess piece shaped like a castle

room *noun* **1** enclosed area in a building **2** unoccupied space **3** scope or opportunity **4** **rooms** lodgings

roost *noun* **1** place where birds rest or sleep ▷ *verb* **2** to rest or sleep on a roost

root *noun* **1** part of a plant that grows down into the earth obtaining nourishment **2** plant with an edible root, such as a carrot **3** part of a tooth, hair, etc below the skin **4** source or origin **5** form of a word from which other words and forms are derived **6 roots** person's sense of belonging ▷ *verb* **7** to establish a root and start to grow **8** to dig or burrow > **root out** *verb* to get rid of completely

rooted *adjective* developed from or strongly influenced by something

rope *noun* **1** thick cord ▷ *verb* **2** to tie with a rope

rosary rosaries *noun* **1** series of prayers **2** string of beads for counting these prayers

rose *noun* **1** shrub or climbing plant with prickly stems and fragrant flowers **2** flower of this plant **3** pink colour ▷ *adjective* **4** pink ▷ *verb* **5** past tense of **rise**

rosella *noun* type of Australian parrot

rosemary *noun* **1** fragrant flowering shrub **2** its leaves as a herb

rosette *noun* large badge of coloured ribbons gathered into a circle, which is worn as a prize in a competition or to support a political party

Rosh Hashanah or **Rosh Hashana** *noun* festival celebrating the Jewish New Year

roster *noun* list of people and their turns of duty

rostrum rostrums or rostra *noun* platform or stage

rosy rosier, rosiest *adjective* **1** pink-coloured **2** hopeful or promising

rot rots, rotting, rotted *verb* **1** to decay or cause to decay **2** to deteriorate slowly, physically or mentally ▷ *noun* **3** decay

rota *noun* list of people who take it in turn to do a particular task

rotate *verb* **1** to (cause to) move round a centre or on a pivot **2** to (cause to) follow a set sequence > **rotation** *noun*: *the daily rotation of the earth*

rotor *noun* **1** revolving portion of a dynamo, motor or turbine **2** rotating device with long blades that provides thrust to lift a helicopter

rotten *adjective* **1** decaying **2** (*informal*) very bad **3** corrupt

rouble [roo-bl] *noun* monetary unit of Russia and Tajikistan

rough *adjective* **1** uneven or irregular **2** not careful or gentle **3** difficult or unpleasant **4** approximate **5** violent, stormy or boisterous **6** in preliminary form **7** lacking refinement ▷ *verb* **8** to make rough ▷ *noun* **9** rough state or area **10** (*Golf*) part of the course where the grass is uncut > **roughly** *adverb* > **roughness** *noun*: *the roughness of the surface*

roulette *noun* gambling game in which a ball is dropped onto a revolving wheel with numbered holes in it

round *adjective* **1** spherical, cylindrical, circular or curved ▷ *adverb, preposition* **2** indicating an encircling movement, presence on all sides, etc: *tied round the waist; books scattered round the room* ▷ *verb* **3** to move round ▷ *noun* **4** customary course, as of a milkman **5** game (of golf) **6** stage in a competition **7** one of several periods in a boxing match etc **8** number of drinks bought at one time **9** bullet or shell for a gun > **round up** *verb* to gather (people or animals) together

roundabout noun **1** road junction at which traffic passes round a central island **2** revolving circular platform on which people ride for amusement ▷ adjective **3** not straightforward

rounded adjective curved in shape, without any points or sharp edges

rounders noun bat-and-ball team game

round-the-clock adjective throughout the day and night

rouse [rhymes with **cows**] verb **1** to wake up **2** to provoke or excite

rouseabout noun (Aust, NZ) labourer in a shearing shed

rout noun **1** overwhelming defeat **2** disorderly retreat ▷ verb **3** to defeat and put to flight

route noun **1** roads taken to reach a destination **2** chosen way

routine noun **1** usual or regular method of procedure **2** set sequence ▷ adjective **3** ordinary or regular ▷ **routinely** adverb

roving adjective **1** wandering or roaming **2** not restricted to any particular location or area

row¹ [rhymes with **go**] noun **1** straight line of people or things ▷ verb **2** to propel (a boat) by oars

row² [rhymes with **now**] (informal) noun **1** dispute **2** disturbance **3** reprimand ▷ verb **4** to quarrel noisily

rowdy rowdier, rowdiest adjective disorderly, noisy and rough

royal adjective **1** of, befitting or supported by a king or queen **2** splendid ▷ noun **3** (informal) member of a royal family

royalist noun supporter of monarchy

royalty royalties noun **1** royal people **2** rank or power of a monarch **3** payment to an author, musician, inventor, etc

RSS abbreviation Really Simple Syndication: a way of allowing web users to receive updates on their browsers from selected websites

rub rubs, rubbing, rubbed verb **1** to apply pressure and friction to (something) with a circular or backwards-and-forwards movement **2** to clean, polish or dry by rubbing **3** to chafe or fray through rubbing ▷ **rub it in** to emphasize an unpleasant fact ▷ **rub out** verb to remove or be removed with a rubber

rubber noun **1** strong waterproof elastic material, originally made from the dried sap of a tropical tree, now usually synthetic **2** piece of rubber used for erasing writing **3** series of matches ▷ adjective **4** made of or producing rubber

rubbish noun **1** waste matter **2** anything worthless **3** nonsense

rubble noun fragments of broken stone, brick, etc

rubric noun (formal) set of instructions at the beginning of an official document

ruby rubies noun **1** red precious gemstone ▷ adjective **2** deep red

rucksack noun large pack carried on the back

rudder noun vertical hinged piece at the stern of a boat or at the rear of an aircraft, for steering

rude adjective **1** impolite or insulting **2** coarse, vulgar or obscene **3** unexpected and unpleasant **4** roughly made **5** robust > **rudely** adverb > **rudeness** noun: I was angry at her rudeness

rudimentary adjective (formal) basic, elementary

rudiments plural noun simplest and most basic stages of a subject

ruff noun **1** starched and frilled collar **2** natural collar of feathers, fur, etc on certain birds and animals

ruffle verb **1** to disturb the calm of **2** to annoy or irritate > noun **3** frill or pleat

rug noun **1** small carpet **2** thick woollen blanket

rugby noun form of football played with an oval ball which may be handled by the players. Rugby League is played with 13 players in each side, Rugby Union is played with 15 players in each side

rugged [**rug**-gid] adjective **1** rocky or steep **2** uneven and jagged **3** strong-featured **4** tough and sturdy

rugger noun (Chiefly Brit informal) rugby

ruin verb **1** to destroy or spoil completely **2** to cause (someone) to lose money > noun **3** destruction or decay **4** loss of wealth, position, etc **5** broken-down unused building

rule noun **1** statement of what is allowed, for example in a game or procedure **2** what is usual **3** government, authority or control **4** measuring device with a straight edge **5** as a rule usually > verb **6** to govern (people or a political unit) **7** to be pre-eminent or superior **8** to give a formal decision > **rule out** verb to dismiss from consideration

ruler noun **1** person who governs **2** measuring device with a straight edge

rum noun strong alcoholic drink distilled from sugar cane

Rumanian [roo-**may**-nee-an] adjective, noun another spelling of **Romanian**

rumble verb **1** to make a low continuous noise **2** (Brit informal) to discover the (disreputable) truth about > noun **3** deep resonant sound

rummage verb **1** to search untidily and at length > noun **2** untidy search through a collection of things

rumour noun **1** unproved statement **2** gossip or common talk

rump noun **1** buttocks **2** rear of an animal

run runs, running, ran, run verb **1** to move with a more rapid gait than walking **2** to take part in (a race) **3** to travel according to schedule **4** to function **5** to manage **6** to stand as a candidate for political or other office **7** to continue in a particular direction or for a specified period **8** to expose yourself to (a risk) **9** to flow **10** to spread > noun **11** act or spell of running **12** ride in a car **13** continuous period **14** series of unravelled stitches, ladder **15** (Cricket) score of one made by a batsman > **run away** verb to make your escape; flee > **run down** verb **1** to be rude about **2** to reduce in number or size **3** to stop working > **run out** verb to use up or (of a supply) to be used up ▷ **run over** verb to knock down (a person) with a moving vehicle

runaway noun person or animal that has run away

run-down adjective 1 exhausted 2 shabby or dilapidated ▷ noun **rundown** 3 reduction in number or size 4 brief overview or summary

rung noun 1 crossbar on a ladder ▷ verb 2 past participle of **ring**

runner noun 1 competitor in a race 2 messenger 3 part underneath an ice skate etc, on which it slides 4 slender horizontal stem of a plant, such as a strawberry, running along the ground and forming new roots at intervals 5 long strip of carpet or decorative cloth

runner bean noun long green pod eaten as a vegetable

runner-up runners-up noun person who comes second in a competition

running adjective 1 continuous 2 consecutive 3 (of water) flowing ▷ noun 4 act of moving or flowing quickly 5 management of a business etc

runny runnier, runniest adjective 1 tending to flow 2 exuding moisture

runt noun smallest animal in a litter

runway noun hard level roadway where aircraft take off and land

rupee noun monetary unit of India and Pakistan

rupture noun 1 breaking, breach 2 hernia ▷ verb 3 to break, burst or sever

rural adjective in or of the countryside

ruse [rooz] noun (formal) trick

rush verb 1 to move or do very quickly 2 to force (someone) to act hastily 3 to make a sudden attack upon (a person or place) ▷ noun 4 sudden quick or violent movement 5 marsh plant with a slender pithy stem 6 **rushes** first unedited prints of a scene for a film ▷ adjective 7 done with speed, hasty

rush hour noun period at the beginning and end of the working day, when many people are travelling to or from work

rusk noun hard brown crisp biscuit, used especially for feeding babies

Russian adjective 1 belonging or relating to Russia ▷ noun 2 someone from Russia 3 main language spoken in Russia

rust noun 1 reddish-brown coating formed on iron etc that has been exposed to moisture ▷ adjective 2 reddish-brown ▷ verb 3 to become coated with rust

rustic adjective simple in a way considered to be typical of the countryside

rustle verb to make a low whispering sound > **rustling** adjective: a rustling sound

rusty rustier, rustiest adjective 1 coated with rust 2 of a rust colour 3 out of practice

rut noun 1 furrow made by wheels 2 dull settled habits or way of living

ruthless adjective pitiless, merciless > **ruthlessly** adverb > **ruthlessness** noun: she has a reputation for ruthlessness

rye noun kind of grain used for fodder and bread

S

Sabbath noun day for worship and rest in some religions: Saturday for Jews, Sunday for Christians

sable noun dark fur from a small weasel-like Arctic animal

sabotage [**sab**-ot-ahj] noun 1 damage done to machinery, systems, etc in order to cause disruption ▷ verb 2 to damage in order to disrupt

sabre noun 1 heavy curved sword 2 (Fencing) light sword

sachet [**sash**-ay] noun small envelope or bag containing a single portion of something

sack noun 1 large bag without handles 2 plundering (of a captured town) 3 **the sack** (informal) dismissal ▷ verb 4 (informal) to dismiss 5 to plunder (a captured town)

sacrament noun a ceremony of the Christian Church, especially Communion

sacred [**say**-krid] adjective holy or connected with religion

sacrifice [**sak**-riff-ice] noun 1 giving up (of something valuable or important) to help someone or something else 2 thing given up 3 killing (of an animal) as an offering to a god 4 thing offered ▷ verb 5 to give up (something

valuable or important) for the good of someone or something else 6 to kill (an animal) as an offering to a god ▷ **sacrificial** adjective: sacrificial offerings

sacrilege [**sak**-ril-ij] noun behaviour that shows great disrespect for something holy or worthy of respect ▷ **sacrilegious** adjective: It would be sacrilegious to waste this

sacrosanct adjective regarded as too important to be criticized or changed

sad adjective 1 unhappy, filled with sorrow 2 causing unhappiness or sorrow: a sad story 3 very bad: a sad day for democracy 4 (Brit informal) pathetic and inadequate: What a sad person! ▷ **sadly** adverb ▷ **sadness** noun: His joy was tinged with sadness

sadden verb to make (someone) sad

saddle noun 1 rider's seat on a horse or bicycle 2 joint (of meat) ▷ verb 3 to put a saddle on (a horse) 4 to burden (with a responsibility)

sadism [**say**-dizz-um] noun gaining of pleasure from making someone suffer ▷ **sadist** noun person who gains pleasure from causing suffering ▷ **sadistic** adjective: a sadistic bully ▷ **sadistically** adverb

safari safaris noun expedition for hunting or observing wild animals, especially in Africa

safari park noun park where wild animals such as lions and elephants roam freely

safe adjective 1 not in danger 2 not harmful or dangerous ▷ noun

3 strong lockable container > **safely** adverb > **safety** noun: a threat to public safety

safeguard verb **1** to protect ▷ noun **2** protection

safekeeping noun keeping or being held in a place of safety; protection

sag sags, sagging, sagged verb to sink in the middle or hang loosely > **sagging** adjective

saga [**sah**-ga] noun **1** legend of Norse heroes **2** any long story or series of events

sage noun **1** a herb used in cooking **2** (literary) a very wise person

Sagittarius [saj-it-**tair**-ee-uss] noun ninth sign of the zodiac, represented by a half-horse half-man creature with a bow and arrow

sail noun **1** sheet of fabric that when raised on the mast of a sailing vessel catches the wind and causes it to be blown along **2** one of the arms of a windmill that move round in the wind ▷ verb **3** to travel by water **4** to begin a voyage **5** to move smoothly

sailor noun member of the crew of a ship or boat

saint noun **1** (Christianity) dead person honoured by the Church for their holy life **2** very good person

saintly adjective behaving in a very good or holy way

sake noun **1** benefit **2** purpose

salad noun mixture of raw vegetables

salami [sal-**lah**-mee] noun kind of sausage that is eaten cold

salary salaries noun regular monthly payment to an employee > **salaried** adjective with a salary

sale noun **1** exchange of goods for money **2** event at which goods are sold for unusually low prices **3** auction > **saleable** adjective fit to be sold

salesman noun man who sells products for a company > **saleswoman** noun

salient [**say**-lee-ent] adjective (formal) prominent, noticeable

saliva [sal-**live**-a] noun liquid that forms in the mouth and helps you chew food

sallow adjective (of skin) pale and unhealthy

salmon noun large silver-coloured fish with orange-pink flesh

WORD TIP
The plural of salmon is salmon

salmonella [sal-mon-**nell**-a] noun kind of bacterium that causes severe food poisoning

salon noun place where hairdressers or beauticians work

saloon noun **1** car with a fixed roof and a separate boot **2** in America, a place where alcoholic drinks are sold and drunk

salt noun **1** white substance used to flavour and preserve food **2** chemical compound formed from an acid base ▷ verb **3** to season or preserve with salt

salty saltier, saltiest adjective containing salt or tasting of salt

salute noun **1** formal sign of respect that often involves raising your right hand to your forehead **2** firing of guns as a military greeting of honour ▷ verb **3** to greet with a salute **4** to make a salute

salvage verb **1** to save from destruction or waste ▷ noun **2** any ships or cargoes that are saved or reclaimed from the sea **3** any goods that are saved from destruction

salvation noun fact or state of being saved from harm or the consequences of sin

salvo salvos or salvoes noun **1** firing of several guns or missiles at the same time **2** burst (of applause or questions)

same adjective, pronoun **1** identical, not different, unchanged **2** just mentioned

Samoan adjective **1** belonging or relating to Samoa ▷ noun **2** person from Samoa

sample noun **1** small amount of something for trying or testing **2** (Music) short extract from an existing recording mixed into a backing track to produce a new recording ▷ verb **3** to try a sample of **4** (Music) to take a short extract from (one recording) and mix it into a backing track **5** to record (a sound) and feed it into a computerized synthesizer so that it can be reproduced at any pitch

samurai [**sam**-oor-eye] noun member of an ancient Japanese warrior class

WORD TIP

The plural of samurai is samurai

sanctimonious [sank-tim-**moan**-ee-uss] adjective pretending to be religious and virtuous

sanction noun **1** official approval **2** punishment or penalty intended

to make a person, group or country obey a particular rule or law ▷ verb **3** to authorize or permit

sanctity noun quality of being important and deserving respect

sanctuary sanctuaries noun **1** place where you are safe from harm or danger **2** place where wildlife is protected

sand noun **1** substance consisting of small grains of rock. Beaches are made of sand ▷ verb **2** to smooth with sandpaper

sandal noun open shoe with straps

sandpaper noun strong paper coated with sand and used for smoothing surfaces

sandshoe noun (Brit, Aust, NZ) light canvas shoe with a rubber sole

sandstone noun type of rock formed from sand

sandwich noun **1** two slices of bread with a layer of food between ▷ verb **2** to insert between two other things: a shop sandwiched between two pubs

sandy sandier, sandiest adjective **1** covered with sand **2** (of hair) reddish-fair

sane adjective **1** of sound mind **2** sensible, rational

sanguine [**sang**-gwin] adjective (formal) cheerful and confident

sanitary adjective concerned with cleanliness and hygiene

sanitary towel noun absorbent pad worn by women during their periods

sanitation noun sanitary measures, especially drainage or sewerage

sanity noun ability to think and act in a mentally stable way

sap saps, sapping, sapped noun 1 watery liquid found in plants ▷ verb 2 to undermine, weaken or destroy

sapling noun young tree

sapphire noun blue gemstone

sarcastic adjective relating to or involving the mocking or insulting use of irony > **sarcastically** adverb: "Thanks, Mum," I said sarcastically

sarcophagus sarcophagi or sarcophaguses noun stone coffin

sardine sardines noun small sea fish of the herring family

sardonic adjective mocking or scornful > **sardonically** adverb

sari saris noun long piece of cloth draped around the body and over one shoulder, worn by Hindu women

sarmie noun (S Afr informal) sandwich

sartorial adjective (formal) relating to men's clothes

sash noun decorative strip of cloth worn round the waist or over one shoulder

Satan noun 1 the Devil 2 Great Satan radical Islamic term for the United States

satanic [sa-tan-ik] adjective caused by or influenced by Satan

satchel noun bag with a shoulder strap, for carrying books

satellite noun 1 man-made device orbiting the earth and collecting and relaying information 2 natural object in space that moves round a planet or star 3 country that is dependent on a more powerful one

satin noun silky fabric with a smooth surface on one side

satire noun 1 use of mocking or ironical humour, especially in literature, to show how foolish or bad someone or something is 2 play, novel or poem that does this > **satirical** adjective: a satirical magazine

satisfaction noun feeling of pleasure you have when you do or get something you wanted or that was necessary

satisfactory adjective acceptable or adequate > **satisfactorily** adverb

satisfy satisfies, satisfying, satisfied verb 1 to make (someone) content or pleased by doing something well enough or by giving them enough of something 2 to provide enough for 3 to convince or persuade > **satisfied** adjective: He is satisfied with my work

satisfying adjective pleasing or fulfilling

satsuma [sat-soo-ma] noun fruit like a small orange

saturated adjective 1 very wet 2 completely full

Saturday noun day between Friday and Sunday

Saturn noun sixth planet from the sun in the solar system

sauce noun one of many kinds of thin or thick, sweet or savoury liquids served with food

saucepan noun deep metal cooking pot with a handle

saucer noun small round dish put under a cup

saucy saucier, sauciest adjective cheeky in an amusing way

Saudi [rhymes with **cloudy**] *adjective* **1** belonging or relating to Saudi Arabia ▷ *noun* **2** person from Saudi Arabia

sauna *noun* **1** activity of alternately sitting in a steamy room sweating then having a cold bath or shower **2** place where you do this

saunter *verb* **1** to walk in a leisurely manner, stroll ▷ *noun* **2** leisurely walk

sausage *noun* minced meat in an edible tube-shaped skin

sauté sautés, sautéing or sautéeing, sautéed [**soh-tay**] *verb* to fry quickly in a little fat

savage *adjective* **1** wild, untamed **2** cruel and violent ▷ *noun* **3** violent and uncivilized person ▷ *verb* **4** to attack ferociously > **savagely** *adverb*

savagery *noun* cruel and violent behaviour

save *verb* **1** to rescue or preserve from harm, protect **2** to keep for the future, set aside **3** to spare or prevent (someone having to do something) **4** (*Sport*) to prevent the scoring of (a goal) ▷ *noun* **5** (*Sport*) act of preventing a goal ▷ *preposition* **6** (*formal*) (often followed by *for*) except: *I was alone save for the cat* > **saver** *noun* person who saves money

saving *noun* **1** reduction in the amount of time or money used **2** **savings** money you have saved

saviour *noun* person who rescues you

savour *verb* to enjoy fully; relish

savoury savouries *adjective* **1** salty or spicy **2** pleasant or respectable ▷ *noun* **3** (usually plural) savoury dish served before or after a meal

saw[1] saws, sawing, sawed, sawn *noun* **1** tool, with a blade with sharp teeth along one edge, for cutting wood ▷ *verb* **2** to cut with a saw

saw[2] *verb* past tense of **see**

sawdust *noun* fine, powdery wood fragments produced when you saw wood

saxophone *noun* brass wind instrument with keys and a curved body often played in jazz bands

say says, saying, said *verb* **1** to express in words, utter **2** to give as your opinion **3** to suppose ▷ *noun* **4** right or chance to speak or influence a decision

saying *noun* well-known phrase or proverb that tells you something about human life

scab *noun* **1** crust that forms over a wound **2** (*offensive*) someone that works when their colleagues are on strike; a blackleg > **scabby** *adjective*

scaffolding *noun* framework of poles and boards used by workmen to stand on when working on the outside of a building

scald [**skawld**] *verb* **1** to burn with hot liquid or steam ▷ *noun* **2** burn caused by scalding

scale *noun* **1** size or extent (of something): *the sheer scale of the disaster* **2** set of levels or numbers used for measuring things *The earthquake measured 3.5 on the Richter scale* **3** relationship between the size of something on a map, plan, or in a model and its size in the real world: *a scale of 1:10,000* **4** MUSIC upward or downward sequence of eight musical notes **5** one of the small pieces of hard skin that form the skin of fishes and reptiles **6** coating that forms in kettles etc due to hard water ▷ *verb* **7** to climb

scalene *adjective* (of a triangle) with sides that are all of different lengths

scallop *noun* edible shellfish with two flat fan-shaped shells

scalp *noun* **1** skin under the hair on your head **2** piece of skin and hair removed when someone is scalped ▷ *verb* **3** to cut off the skin and hair from someone's head in one piece

scalpel *noun* small surgical knife

scaly *adjective* covered with scales

scamper *verb* to run about quickly and lightly perhaps in play

scampi *plural noun* large prawns, often eaten fried in breadcrumbs

scan *verb* **1** to look (at something) carefully **2** to glance over (something) quickly **3** to examine or search (something) by x-raying it or by passing a radar or sonar beam over it **4** (of verse) to conform to metrical rules ▷ *noun* **5** examination or search by a scanner

scandal *noun* situation or event considered shocking and immoral ▷ **scandalous** *adjective*: *This is a scandalous waste of money*

Scandinavia [skan-din-**nay**-vee-a] *noun* name given to a group of countries in Northern Europe, including Norway, Sweden, Denmark and sometimes Finland

and Iceland ▷ **Scandinavian** *noun, adjective*

scanner *noun* **1** machine used to examine, identify or record things by means of a beam of light or X-rays **2** ICT machine that converts text or images into a form that can be stored on a computer

scant *adjective* barely enough, meagre

scapegoat *noun* someone made to bear the blame for something that may not be their fault

scar *scars, scarring, scarred noun* **1** mark left after a wound has healed **2** permanent emotional damage left by a bad experience ▷ *verb* **3** to leave a permanent mark on **4** to have a permanent effect on

scarce *adjective* **1** not enough to meet demand **2** not common, rarely found **3 make yourself scarce** (*informal*) to leave quickly ▷ **scarcity** *noun*: *the scarcity of housing*

scarcely *adverb* hardly

> **WORD TIP**
> As *scarcely* already has a negative sense, it is followed by *ever* or *any*, and not by *never* or *no*

scare *verb* **1** to frighten or be frightened ▷ *noun* **2** fright **3** panic ▷ **scared** *adjective*: *I was really scared*

scarecrow *noun* figure dressed in old clothes, set up to scare birds away from crops

scarf *scarfs* or *scarves noun* piece of material worn round the neck, head or shoulders

scarlet *adjective, noun* bright red

scary *scarier, scariest adjective* (*informal*) frightening

scathing [**skayth**-ing] adjective harshly critical: They were scathing about his idea

scatter verb 1 to throw or drop all over an area 2 to move away in different directions

scattering noun small number (of things) spread over a large area

scavenge verb to search for (anything usable) among discarded material

scenario noun 1 summary of the plot of a play or film 2 way a situation might develop in the future

scene noun 1 place where a real or imaginary event happens 2 part of a play or film in which a series of events happens in one place 3 picture or view: a village scene 4 display of emotion: Don't make a scene 5 (informal) area of activity: the fashion scene 6 **behind the scenes a** backstage **b** in secret

scenery noun 1 natural features of a landscape 2 painted backcloths or screens used on stage to represent the scene of action

scenic adjective with nice views, picturesque

scent noun 1 smell, especially a pleasant one 2 series of clues 3 perfume ▷ verb 4 to detect by smell 5 to fill with fragrance

sceptic [**skep**-tik] noun person who doubts things that are widely believed > **sceptical** adjective: She was deeply sceptical about the idea > **scepticism** noun: his scepticism about some of their claims

sceptre noun ornamental rod symbolizing royal power

schedule [**shed**-yool] noun 1 plan listing events or tasks together

with the times they are to happen; timetable 2 list ▷ verb 3 to plan and arrange (something) for a particular time

schema schemata [**skee**-ma] noun 1 (technical) outline of a plan or theory 2 mental model used by the mind to understand new experiences or view the world

scheme noun 1 plan or arrangement 2 secret plot ▷ verb 3 to plan in an underhand manner

schism [**skizz**-um] noun split or division in a group or organization

schizophrenia [skit-soe-**free**-nee-a] noun serious mental illness in which the sufferer has thoughts and feelings that do not relate to reality

scholar noun 1 a learned person 2 a student receiving a scholarship 3 (S Afr) pupil

scholarly adjective having or showing a lot of knowledge; learned

scholarship noun 1 award given to a student in recognition of their academic ability in order to finance their studies 2 academic knowledge and learning

school noun 1 place where children are educated or instruction is given in a subject 2 group of artists, thinkers, etc with shared beliefs or methods 3 shoal (of fish, whales, dolphins, etc) ▷ verb 4 to educate or train

schoolchild noun child who goes to school > **schoolboy** noun > **schoolgirl** noun

schooling noun the education you receive at school

schooner noun sailing ship

science noun 1 study of and knowledge about natural and physical phenomena 2 a branch of science, for example physics or biology

science fiction noun stories about events happening in the future or in other parts of the universe

scientific adjective 1 relating to science or to a particular science: *scientific knowledge* 2 systematic: *this scientific method* > **scientifically** adverb

scientist noun person who studies or practises a science

scintillating adjective lively and witty

scissors plural noun cutting tool with two crossed blades

scoff verb 1 to speak scornfully 2 (*informal*) to eat (food) quickly and greedily

scold verb to rebuke, reprimand or tell (someone) off

scone noun small plain cake made from flour and fat and usually eaten with butter

scoop verb (often followed by *up*) 1 to pick up or remove using a spoon, shovel or the palm of your hand ▷ noun 2 tool like a large spoon or shovel used for picking up ice cream, mashed potato and other substances 3 important news story reported in one newspaper before it appears elsewhere

scooter noun 1 light motorcycle 2 a simple vehicle consisting of a platform on wheels and a handlebar; to make it work you stand on the platform on one leg and use your other leg to push on the ground

scope noun 1 opportunity for doing something 2 range of activity

-scope suffix used to form nouns which refer to an instrument used for observing or detecting: *microscope; telescope*

scorching adjective extremely hot

score verb 1 to gain (a point, goal, run) in a game 2 to record the score obtained by the players 3 to cut a line in 4 to achieve (a success, victory) 5 (followed by *out*) to cross out ▷ noun 6 number of points, goals, or runs gained by each competitor or competing team in a game or competition 7 written version of a piece of music showing parts for each musician 8 grievance: *settle old scores* 9 (*old-fashioned*) twenty or about twenty 10 **scores** lots: *Ros entertained scores of celebrities* > **scorer** noun person who scores

scorn noun 1 open contempt ▷ verb 2 to despise 3 (*formal*) to reject with contempt

scornful adjective showing contempt; contemptuous > **scornfully** adverb

Scorpio noun eighth sign of the zodiac, represented by a scorpion

scorpion noun small lobster-shaped animal with a poisonous sting at the end of a jointed tail

Scot noun person from Scotland > **Scots** adjective Scottish

scotch noun whisky made in Scotland

Scotsman Scotsmen noun man from Scotland > **Scotswoman** Scotswomen noun

Scottish adjective belonging or relating to Scotland

scoundrel noun (old-fashioned) cheat or deceiver

scour verb **1** to clean or polish by rubbing with something rough **2** to carry out a thorough search of (a place)

scourge [rhymes with **urge**] noun **1** person or thing causing severe suffering ▷ verb **2** whip **3** to cause severe suffering to **4** to whip

scout noun **1** person sent out to see what an area is like and to find out the position of things **2** member of the Scout Association, an organization for boys which aims to develop character and promotes outdoor activities ▷ verb **3** to act as a scout **4** (especially followed by **around**) to look around (for something)

scowl verb **1** to frown in an angry or sullen way ▷ noun **2** an angry or sullen expression

scrabble verb to scrape at with the hands, feet or claws

scramble verb **1** to climb or crawl hastily or awkwardly using your hands to help you **2** to cook (eggs beaten up with milk) ▷ noun **3** motorcycle race over rough ground **4** rough climb

scrap scraps, scrapping, scrapped noun **1** small piece **2** waste metal collected for reprocessing **3** (informal) fight or quarrel **4** scraps leftover food ▷ verb **5** to get rid of

scrapbook noun book with blank pages in which you stick things such as pictures or newspaper articles

scrape verb **1** to clean (something off) using something rough or sharp: scraping the fallen snow off the track **2** to rub (against something) with a harsh noise: The chair scraped across the floorboards. ▷ noun **3** act or sound of scraping **4** mark or wound caused by scraping

scratch verb **1** to mark or cut with claws, nails or anything rough or sharp **2** to rub (skin) with nails or fingertips to relieve itching ▷ noun **3** a small cut or mark **4 from scratch** from the very beginning **5 up to scratch** up to standard

scratchcard noun ticket with a surface that you scratch off to show whether or not you have won a prize in a competition

scrawl verb **1** to write (words, etc) carelessly or hastily ▷ noun **2** careless or untidy writing

scrawny scrawnier, scrawniest adjective thin and bony

scream verb **1** to shout or cry in a loud, high-pitched voice especially when afraid or in pain ▷ noun **2** shrill piercing cry **3** (informal) very funny person or thing

screech verb **1** to give a shrill cry or a high-pitched sound ▷ noun **2** shrill cry

screen noun **1** vertical surface on which pictures or films are shown or projected **2** a movable vertical panel used to separate different parts of a room or to protect something ▷ verb **3** to show (a film or television programme) **4** to shelter or conceal (someone or something) with or as if with a screen **5** to investigate (a person or group) to check their suitability for a task

a b c d e f g h i j k l m n o p q r s t u v w x y z

screenplay noun script (of a film)

screenshot noun (Computers) copied image of a computer screen at a particular moment

screw noun **1** metal pin with a spiral ridge round its shaft and a slot for a screwdriver on its head used for fastening things together ▷ verb **2** to fasten with screws **3** to twist (something) round and round in order to fasten it onto something else: *He screwed the top on the bottle* > **screw up** verb **1** to twist or squeeze (something) into a distorted shape **2** (informal) to bungle or spoil

screwdriver noun tool for turning screws

scribble verb **1** to write (something) hastily or illegibly, **2** to make meaninglessly or illegible marks ▷ noun **3** something written or drawn quickly or roughly

scrimp verb to live cheaply, spending as little money as possible

script noun **1** text of a film, play or TV programme **2** system of writing: *Arabic script*

scripture noun sacred writings, especially the Bible > **scriptural** adjective: *scriptural references*

scroll noun **1** roll of parchment or paper **2** ornamental carving shaped like a scroll ▷ verb **3** to move (text) up or down on a VDU screen in order to find something

scrounge verb (informal) to get (something) by cadging or begging > **scrounger** noun someone who makes a habit of scrounging

scrub scrubs, scrubbing, scrubbed verb **1** to clean by rubbing, often with a hard brush and water ▷ noun **2** scrubbing: *You'll have to give them a scrub* **3** low trees and bushes **4** area of land covered with scrub

scruff noun **1** back (of your neck or collar) **2** (informal) untidy person

scruffy scruffier, scruffiest adjective dirty and untidy or shabby

scrum noun (Rugby) restarting of play in which groups of opposing forwards push against each other to gain possession of the ball

scrunchie noun a loop of elastic loosely covered with material which is used to hold hair in a ponytail

scruple noun moral principles that make you unwilling to do something that seems wrong

scrupulous adjective **1** very conscientious or honest about what one does **2** very careful or precise > **scrupulously** adverb

scrutinize or **scrutinise** verb to examine very carefully

scrutiny noun close examination

scuba diving noun sport of swimming underwater using tanks of compressed air and breathing apparatus

scuff verb **1** to drag (your feet) while walking **2** to scrape (your shoes) by doing so

scuffle noun **1** short, disorderly fight > **verb 2** to fight in a disorderly manner

scullery sculleries noun small room next to a kitchen where washing and cleaning are done

sculpt verb to carve or shape (figures and objects) using materials such as stone, wood or clay

sculptor *noun* someone who makes sculptures

sculpture *noun* **1** a work of art produced by carving or shaping materials such as stone, wood or clay **2** art of making figures or designs in wood, stone, clay, etc > **sculptural** *adjective*: *sculptural pieces*

scum *noun* **1** a layer of a dirty substance on the surface of a liquid **2** (*informal*) worthless people

scungy scungier, scungiest *adjective* (*Aust, NZ informal*) sordid or dirty

scurrilous [**skur**-ril-luss] *adjective* offensive and damaging to someone's good name

scurry scurries, scurrying, scurried *verb* to run quickly with short steps

scurvy *noun* disease caused by lack of vitamin C

scuttle *verb* **1** to run with short quick steps **2** to make a hole in (a ship) to sink it ▷ *noun* **3** fireside container for coal

scythe *noun* **1** long-handled tool with a curved blade for cutting grass ▷ *verb* **2** to cut with a scythe

sea *noun* **1** the salty water that covers three quarters of the earth's surface **2** particular area of this **3** a large mass (of people or things) **4 at sea a** in a ship on the ocean **b** confused or bewildered

seagull *noun* common bird with white, grey and black plumage that lives near the sea; gull

seahorse *noun* small fish that swims upright, with a head that looks like a horse's head

seal *noun* **1** amphibious mammal with flippers as limbs **2** official mark or stamped piece of wax on a document which shows that it is genuine **3** embossed piece of wax or lead fixed over the opening part of a container or envelope to show that it has not been tampered with **4** device used to close an opening tightly ▷ *verb* **5** to stick down (an envelope) **6** to close with or as if with a seal **7** to make (something) airtight or watertight > **seal off** *verb* to enclose or isolate (a place) completely

sea lion *noun* a type of large seal

seam *noun* **1** line of stitches joining two pieces of cloth **2** thin layer of coal or ore

seaman seamen *noun* sailor

seance [**say**-anss] *noun* meeting at which people try to communicate with the dead

search *verb* **1** to examine (someone or something) closely in order to find something **2** to look (for someone or something); seek ▷ *noun* **3** an attempt to find something

search engine *noun* (*Computers*) internet service enabling users to search for items of interest

searching *adjective* keen or thorough: *searching questions*

searchlight *noun* powerful light with a beam that can be shone in any direction

searing *adjective* (of pain) very sharp

seashore *noun* the land along the edge of the sea

seasick *adjective* feeling sick because of the movement of a boat > **seasickness** *noun*: *The crew were all suffering from seasickness*

seaside noun area next to the sea

season noun 1 any of the four periods of the year (spring, summer, autumn or winter), each having their own typical weather conditions 2 period of the year when something usually happens: *the football season* 3 fitting or proper time (for something) ▷ verb 4 to add salt, pepper or spices to (a dish)

seasonal adjective depending on or varying with the seasons: *seasonal work*

seasoned adjective very experienced: *a seasoned professional*

seasoning noun salt, herbs and other flavourings and condiments that are added to food to enhance flavour

season ticket noun ticket for something that you can use as many times as you like within a certain period

seat noun 1 something you can sit on 2 the part (of a piece of clothing) that covers your bottom 3 buttocks 4 membership of a legislative or administrative body: *his chances of winning a seat in parliament* ▷ verb 5 to cause (someone) to sit 6 to provide seating for: *The theatre seats 570 people*

seat belt noun strap fixed to an aeroplane or car seat that you fasten round yourself to hold you in

seating noun the number of seats or the way seats are arranged in a place

seaweed noun plant growing in the sea

secateurs plural noun small pruning shears

secluded adjective private, sheltered

second¹ adjective 1 following the first 2 alternate, additional ▷ noun 3 one of the sixty parts that a minute is divided into 4 moment 5 person or thing coming second 6 someone who attends to the needs of one of the participants in a duel or boxing match 7 (usually in plural) slightly defective product sold cheaply ▷ verb 8 to express formal support for (a proposal) ▷ **secondly** adverb

second² verb to transfer (a person) temporarily to another job ▷ **secondment** noun temporary transfer to another job: *She was on secondment from the local authority*

secondary adjective 1 of less importance 2 coming after or derived from what is primary or first 3 relating to the education of pupils between the ages of 11 and 18 or, in New Zealand, between 13 and 18

secondary school noun a school for pupils between the ages of eleven and eighteen

second-class adjective 1 inferior 2 cheaper, slower or less comfortable than first-class ▷ adverb 3 by second-class mail, transport, etc

second cousin noun Your second cousins are the children of your parents' first cousins

second-hand adjective 1 not bought or acquired when new but after someone else's use: *a second-hand car* ▷ adverb 2 following use by someone else: *We bought it* *second-hand* **3** indirectly: *I heard it second-hand*

second-rate *adjective* of poor quality

secret *adjective* **1** kept from the knowledge of others ▷ *noun* **2** something kept secret **3** underlying explanation: *the secret of my success* **4 in secret** without other people knowing ▷ **secrecy** *noun*: *The whole event was shrouded in secrecy* ▷ **secretly** *adverb*

secret agent *noun* spy

secretary *secretaries noun* **1** person employed by an organization to keep records, write letters and do office work **2 Secretary** head of a state department: *the Health Secretary* ▷ **secretarial** *adjective*: *secretarial work*

secrete *verb* **1** (of an organ, gland, etc) to produce and release (a substance) **2** (*formal*) to hide or conceal

secretive *adjective* inclined to keep things secret

secret service *noun* government department in charge of espionage

sect *noun* religious or political group which has broken away from a larger group

sectarian [sek-**tair**-ee-an] *adjective* strongly supporting a particular sect: *sectarian violence*

section *noun* **1** part or subdivision of something **2** cross-section ▷ *verb* **3** to cut or divide into sections

sector *noun* **1** part or subdivision (of something) **2** part of a circle enclosed by two radii and the arc which they cut off

secular *adjective* not connected with religion or the church

secure *adjective* **1** locked or well protected **2** free from danger **3** free from anxiety **4** firmly fixed ▷ *verb* **5** (*formal*) to obtain: *They secured the rights to her story* **6** to fasten (something) firmly ▷ **securely** *adverb*

security *securities noun* **1** state of being secure **2** precautions against theft, espionage or other danger **3** something given or pledged to guarantee payment of a loan **4 securities** stocks, shares, bonds or other investments ▷ *adjective* **5** relating to precautions against theft, espionage or other danger: *Security forces arrested one member*

sedate *verb* **1** calm and dignified **2** slow or unhurried ▷ *verb* **3** to give (someone) a drug to calm them down or make them sleep ▷ **sedately** *adverb* ▷ **sedation** *noun*: *under sedation*

sedative [**sed**-at-tiv] *adjective* **1** having a soothing or calming effect ▷ *noun* **2** sedative drug

sedentary [**sed**-en-tree] *adjective* done sitting down, involving little exercise

sediment *noun* **1** solid material that settles at the bottom of a liquid **2** material deposited by water, ice or wind

sedimentary *adjective* (of rocks such as sandstone and limestone) formed from fragments of compressed shells or rocks

seduce *verb* **1** to persuade into sexual intercourse **2** to tempt into wrongdoing ▷ **seduction** *noun*: *a classic tale of lust, seduction* and revenge > **seductive** adjective: a seductive offer > **seductively** adverb

see seeing, saw, seen verb 1 to observe: He saw us on TV 2 to meet or visit: I went to see my dentist 3 to understand: I see what you mean 4 to watch: She wanted to see a horror movie 5 to find out: I'll see what's happening 6 to make sure (of something): I'll see that she gets it 7 to make an effort, try: I'll see if I can find it 8 to have experience of; witness: The next couple of years saw two momentous developments 9 to accompany (someone to a place): he offered to see her home 10 **see to** to deal with: I'll see to your breakfast > noun 11 diocese of a bishop > **see through** verb to understand the real nature of

seed noun 1 the grain of a plant from which a new plant can grow 2 origin or beginning: the seeds of mistrust 3 (Sport) tennis player ranked according to his or her ability

seedling noun young plant grown from a seed **seedy** adjective shabby: a seedy hotel

seek seeks, seeking, sought verb 1 to try to find or obtain (someone or something) 2 to try (to do something): He sought to reunite the country

seem verb to appear to be: He seemed such a quiet chap

seeming adjective appearing to be real or genuine; apparent > **seemingly** adverb

seep verb to trickle through slowly; ooze

seesaw noun 1 plank balanced in the middle so that two people

seated on either end ride up and down alternately > verb 2 to move up and down

seething adjective 1 very agitated and angry 2 crowded and full of restless activity

segment noun 1 one of several sections into which something may be divided 2 one of the two parts of a circle formed when you draw a straight line across it

segregate verb to set apart > **segregated** adjective: Rival fans had broken out of their segregated area > **segregation** noun: segregation, based on race, colour or creed

seize verb 1 to take hold of forcibly or quickly 2 to take immediate advantage of > **seize on** verb to show great and sudden interest in (something): MPs have seized on a new report > **seize up** verb 1 (of body parts) to become stiff and painful 2 (of mechanical parts) to become jammed through overheating

seizure [seez-yer] noun 1 sudden violent attack of an illness, especially a heart attack 2 act of seizing or being seized: the largest seizure of drugs in US history

seldom adverb not often; rarely: They seldom speak to each other

select verb 1 to pick out or choose > adjective 2 chosen in preference to others: an invitation to a select few 3 restricted to a particular group, exclusive: one of the select band of players to have won both trophies > **selector** noun someone that selects people or things

selection noun 1 selecting: the selection of parliamentary candidates

2 things or people that have been selected **3** range from which something may be selected

selective *adjective* choosing carefully; choosy: *I am selective about what I eat* **> selectively** *adverb*

self selves *noun* **1** distinct individuality or identity of a person or thing **2** your basic nature **3** your own welfare or interests

self- *prefix* used with many main words to mean **1** done to yourself or by yourself: *self-help; self-control* **2** automatic(ally): *a self-loading rifle*

self-assured *adjective* confident

self-centred *adjective* thinking only about yourself and not about other people

self-confessed *adjective* by your own admission

self-confident *adjective* confident of your own abilities or worth **> self-confidence** *noun: her lack of self-confidence*

self-conscious *adjective* nervous, easily embarrassed and worried about what other people think of you **> self-consciously** *adverb*

self-control *noun* ability to restrain yourself and not show your feelings

self-defence *noun* knowledge of and ability to use means to protect yourself if attacked

self-employed *adjective* working for yourself, with responsibility for your own tax payments, rather than working for an employer

self-esteem *noun* your good opinion of yourself

self-evident *adjective* obvious without proof

self-indulgent *adjective* having a habit of allowing yourself treats or letting yourself do things you enjoy

self-interest *noun* personal advantage

selfish *adjective* caring too much about yourself and not enough about other people **> selfishly** *adverb* **> selfishness** *noun: I can't bear greed and selfishness*

selfless *adjective* putting other people's interests before your own; unselfish

self-made *adjective* rich and successful through your own efforts

self-raising *adjective* (of flour) containing baking powder to make baking rise

self-respect *noun* confidence and pride in your own abilities and worth

self-righteous *adjective* thinking yourself more virtuous than others **> self-righteousness** *noun: the arrogance and self-righteousness of politicians*

self-service *adjective* (of shops, cafés or garages) requiring you to serve yourself and then pay a cashier

self-sufficient *adjective* able to provide for yourself without help

sell sells, selling, sold *verb* **1** to exchange (something) for money **2** to stock or deal in **3** (of goods) to be sold **4** to sell for to be priced at **5** (*informal*) to persuade (someone) to accept (something) **6** to sell yourself to present yourself well, so that people have confidence in your ability: *You've got to sell yourself at the interview* > **seller** *noun: a newspaper seller* > **sell out** *verb* to sell your entire stock (of something)

Sellotape ® *noun* **1** type of adhesive tape ▷ *verb* **2** to stick (something) with Sellotape

semblance *noun* outward or superficial appearance: *an effort to restore a semblance of normality*

semen [see-men] *noun* sperm-carrying fluid produced by men and male animals

semi- *prefix* used with many main words to mean **1** half: *semicircle* **2** partly or almost: *semiskilled workers*

semibreve *noun* (MUSIC) musical note four beats long. In the United States and Canada, a semibreve is known as a whole note

semicircle *noun* half of a circle, or something with this shape > **semicircular** *adjective: a semicircular alcove*

semicolon *noun* the punctuation mark (;)

semidetached *adjective* (of a house) joined to another on one side

semifinal *noun* match or round before the final > **semifinalist** *noun* competitor or competing team that has reached the match or round before the final

seminar *noun* meeting of a group of students for discussion

semipermeable *adjective* (of materials) allowing certain substances with small enough molecules to go through while providing a barrier for substances with larger molecules

semiprecious *adjective* (of gemstones) having less value than precious stones

semiquaver *noun* **1** note half the length of a quaver and a sixteenth the length of a semibreve. In the United States and Canada, a quaver is known as a sixteenth note

semitone *noun* smallest interval between two notes in Western music

Senate *noun* the smaller, more important of the two councils in the government of some countries, for example Australia, Canada and the USA

senator *noun* member of a Senate

send sends, sending, sent *verb* **1** to cause (a person or thing) to go to or be taken or transmitted to a place **2** to bring into a specified state or condition: *The blow sent him tumbling to the ground* > **send for** *verb* to ask (someone) to come and see you > **send up** *verb* (*informal*) to make fun of (someone or something) by imitating

senile *adjective* mentally or physically weak because of old age > **senility** *noun: the onset of senility*

senior *adjective* **1** superior in rank or standing **2** older **3** of or for older pupils > *noun* **4** senior person > **seniority** *noun: Promotion appeared to be based on seniority*

senior citizen *noun* an elderly person, especially one receiving an old-age pension

sensation *noun* **1** physical feeling **2** general feeling or awareness

3 ability to feel things physically **4** exciting person or thing

sensational adjective **1** causing intense shock, anger or excitement **2** (informal) very good > **sensationally** adverb

sense noun **1** any of the faculties of perception or feeling (sight, hearing, touch, taste or smell) **2** feeling: a sense of guilt **3** ability to think and behave sensibly **4** meaning **5 make sense** to be understandable or seem sensible ▷ verb **6** to become aware of; perceive

senseless adjective **1** (of act) without meaning or purpose **2** (of person) unconscious

sensibility noun ability to experience deep feelings

sensible adjective **1** having or showing good sense **2** practical > **sensibly** adverb

sensitive adjective **1** responsive and able to react with understanding **2** easily hurt or offended **3** (of a subject) liable to arouse controversy or strong feelings if not dealt with carefully **4** capable of being affected or harmed **5** (of an instrument) responsive to slight changes > **sensitively** adverb > **sensitivity** noun: a matter that needs to be handled with sensitivity

sensor noun ICT device that detects or measures the presence of something, such as radiation, light or heat

sensual [**senss**-yool] adjective **1** having a strong liking for physical pleasures **2** giving pleasure to the body and senses rather than the mind

> **sensuality** noun > **sensually** adverb

sensuous adjective pleasing to the senses > **sensuously** adverb

sentence noun **1** sequence of words capable of standing alone as a statement, question or command **2** punishment passed on a criminal ▷ verb **3** to pass sentence on (a convicted person)

sentiment noun **1** feeling, attitude **2** feelings such as tenderness or sadness: There's no room for sentiment in business

sentimental adjective **1** excessively romantic or nostalgic **2** relating to a person's emotions > **sentimentalism** noun > **sentimentality** noun

sentinel noun sentry

sentry noun soldier on guard duty

separate adjective **1** not the same, different **2** set apart **3** not shared, individual ▷ verb **4** (of a couple) to stop living together **5** to act as a barrier between **6** to distinguish between **7** to divide up into parts > **separately** adverb > **separation** noun **1** separating or being separated **2** (Law) living apart of a married couple without divorce

sepia [**see**-pee-a] adjective, noun reddish-brown (pigment)

September noun ninth month of the year

septic adjective (of a wound) infected

sepulchre [**sep**-pull-ker] noun (literary) tomb or burial vault

sequel noun **1** novel, play or film that continues the story of an earlier one **2** consequence, result

sequence noun **1** string (of events) **2** arrangement of two or more things in successive order: *Do things in the right sequence*

sequin noun small, shiny metal disc sewn on clothes to decorate them

Serbian adjective **1** of Serbia ▷ noun **2** person from Serbia **3** form of Serbo-Croat spoken in Serbia

Serbo-Croat [ser-boh-**kroh**-at] adjective, noun the main language spoken in Serbia and Croatia

serenade noun **1** music played or sung outside a woman's window to a woman by a lover ▷ verb **2** to sing or play a serenade to (someone)

serene adjective calm, peaceful > **serenely** adverb > **serenity** noun: *It is a place of peace and serenity*

serf noun medieval farm labourer who could not leave the land he worked on

sergeant noun **1** noncommissioned officer in the army or air force **2** police officer ranking between constable and inspector

sergeant major noun noncommissioned army officer of the highest rank

serial noun **1** story or play produced in successive instalments: *a television serial*

serial number noun a number given on a product that identifies it and distinguishes it from other products of the same kind

series noun **1** group or succession of related things, usually arranged in order **2** set of radio or TV programmes about the same subject or characters

▌ **WORD TIP**
The plural of *series* is series

serious adjective **1** giving cause for concern: *It's a serious problem* **2** concerned with important matters **3** not cheerful, grave **4** sincere, not joking > **seriously** adverb > **seriousness** noun: *He has accepted the seriousness of the situation*

sermon noun **1** talk on a religious or moral subject given as part of a church service **2** long moralizing speech

serpent noun (literary) snake

serrated adjective having an edge like a saw with toothlike points

servant noun person employed to do household work for another

serve verb **1** to do useful work for (a person, community, country or cause) **2** to attend to (customers) **3** to dish out food or pour out drinks for (someone) **4** to provide with a service **5** to be a member of the armed forces **6** to spend (time) in prison **7** to act or be used: *the room that served as their office* **8** (Tennis etc) to put (the ball) into play **9** serve right to be the just and deserved reward for (someone) ▷ noun **10** (Tennis, Badminton) act of serving the ball

server noun ICT (Computers) computer or computer program that supplies data to other machines on a network

service noun **1** system that provides something needed by the public: *the bus service* **2** government organization: *the diplomatic service* **3** help and efforts: *services to the community* **4** overhaul of a machine or vehicle **5** formal religious ceremony **6** (*Tennis etc*) act, manner or right of serving the ball **7** set of matching plates, cups, saucers and so on; pieces of china **8 services a** armed forces **b** (on a motorway etc) garage, eating and toilet facilities **9 be of service** to help **10 in service** available for use or in use ▷ *verb* **11** to examine and repair (a machine or vehicle)

serviceman *noun* member of the armed forces > **servicewoman** *noun*

service station *noun* garage selling fuel for motor vehicles

servile *adjective* **1** too eager to obey people, fawning **2** too eager to obey; subservient; obsequious > **servility** *noun*

serving *noun* **1** helping (of food) ▷ *adjective* **2** (of spoon, dish) used for serving food **3** (of officer, soldier) on active service

session *noun* **1** period spent in an activity **2** meeting of a court, parliament, council or other official group **3** a period during which meetings are held regularly: *the end of the parliamentary session* **4** period during which an activity takes place: *a drinking session*

set sets, setting, set *noun* **1** number of things or people that belong together or form a group **2** (*Maths*) group of numbers or objects that satisfy a given condition or share a property **3** television or radio **4** (*Tennis*) a group of six or more games played as part of a match **5** scenery used in a play or film ▷ *verb* **6** to put in a specified position or state **7** to make ready **8** to make or become firm, solid or hard **9** to establish or to prescribe, assign **11** (of the sun) to go down ▷ *adjective* **12** fixed or established beforehand **13** rigid or inflexible **14 set on** determined to (do something): *He is set on becoming a wrestler* > **set about** *verb* to start > **set back** *verb* **1** to delay **2** (*informal*) to cost (someone): *A short taxi ride will set you back £12.50* > **set off** *verb* **1** to start a journey **2** to cause (something) to start a journey > **set out** *verb* **1** to start a journey **2** to give yourself the task of (doing something): *I didn't set out to be controversial* > **set up** *verb* to make all the preparations for (something): *He has set up a website*

setback *noun* anything that delays progress

settee *noun* padded seat with arms at either end for two or three people to sit on; sofa

setter *noun* long-haired gun dog

setting *noun* **1** background or surroundings **2** time and place where a film, book, etc is supposed to have taken place **3** plates and cutlery for a single place at table **4** position or level to which the controls of a machine can be adjusted

settle *verb* **1** to arrange or put in order **2** to come to rest **3** to set up home **4** to make quiet, calm or stable **5** to pay (a bill) **6 settle for** or **on** to opt for or agree to: *We settled for orange juice and coffee.* > **settle down** *verb* **1** to start living quietly in one place, especially on getting married **2** to become quiet or calm

settlement noun **1** an official agreement between people who have been involved in a conflict **2** [GEOGRAPHY] a place where people have settled and built homes **3** subsidence (of a building) **4** long wooden bench with high back and arms

settler noun someone who settles in a new country

seven adjective, noun the number 7 > **seventh** adjective, noun **1** (coming as) number 7 in a series ▷ noun **2** one of seven equal parts

seventeen adjective, noun the number 17 > **seventeenth** adjective, noun

seventy seventies adjective, noun the number 70 > **seventieth** adjective, noun

sever verb **1** to cut through or off **2** to break off (a relationship)

several adjective **1** some, a few **2** various, separate

severe adjective **1** extremely bad or unpleasant **2** stern, strict or harsh **3** plain, sober and forbidding > **severely** adverb > **severity** noun

sew sews, sewing, sewed, sewn [so] verb [D & T] to join, make or embroider items using a needle and thread or a sewing machine > **sewing** noun

sewage noun waste matter or excrement carried away in sewers

sewer noun drain to remove waste water and sewage

sewerage noun system of sewers

sex noun **1** male or female group: the two sexes **2** state of being male or female; gender: We didn't want to know the sex of the baby **3** sexual intercourse **4** sexual feelings or behaviour

sexism noun [PSHE] discrimination on the basis of a person's sex

sextet noun **1** group of six performers **2** music for such a group

sextuplet noun one of six children born to the same mother from the same pregnancy

sexual adjective **1** connected with the act of sex or with people's desire for sex: sexual attraction **2** relating to the difference between males and females: sexual equality **3** relating to the biological process by which people and animals produce young: sexual reproduction > **sexually** adverb

sexual intercourse noun physical act of sex between two people

sexuality [seks-yoo-**al**-it-ee] noun **1** the ability to experience sexual feelings **2** the state of being heterosexual, homosexual or bisexual

sexy sexier, sexiest adjective **1** sexually exciting or attractive **2** (informal) exciting or trendy

shabby shabbier, shabbiest adjective **1** old and worn in appearance **2** mean or unfair > **shabbily** adverb

shack noun rough hut

shackle noun **1** one of a pair of metal rings joined by a chain, for fastening around a person's wrists or ankles ▷ verb **2** to fasten with shackles **3** (literary) to restrict or hamper

shade noun 1 an area of darkness and coolness sheltered from direct sunlight 2 cover used to provide protection from a direct source of light 3 particular hue, tone or variety of a colour 4 **shades** (*informal*) sunglasses ▷ verb 5 to screen (something or someone) from light ▷ **shading** noun (ART) graded areas of light and dark on a painting or drawing

shadow noun 1 dark shape cast on a surface when something stands between the surface and a source of light 2 patch of shade 3 **be a shadow of your former self** to be much weaker or less impressive than you used to be ▷ verb 4 to cast a shadow over 5 to follow secretly

shadow cabinet noun those members of the main opposition party in Parliament who would be ministers if their party were in power

shadowy adjective 1 (of a place) dark and full of shadows 2 (of a figure or shape) difficult to make out

shady shadier, shadiest adjective 1 situated in or giving shade 2 of doubtful honesty or legality

shaft noun 1 long straight and narrow part (of a tool or weapon) 2 ray of light 3 revolving rod that transmits power in a machine: *the drive shaft* 4 vertical passageway: *a lift shaft* 5 one of the bars between which a horse, donkey, etc is harnessed to a cart

shaggy shaggier, shaggiest adjective 1 covered with rough hair or wool 2 (of hair, fur) long and untidy

shake shakes, shaking, shook, shaken verb 1 to move quickly up and down or back and forth 2 to move (your head) from side to side in order to say 'no' 3 to make unsteady 4 to tremble 5 to grasp (someone's hand) in greeting or agreement 6 to shock or upset ▷ noun 7 shaking 8 vibration

shaky shakier, shakiest adjective weak and unsteady ▷ **shakily** adverb

shall verb 1 used as an auxiliary verb to form the future tense or to indicate intention or inevitability 2 used as an auxiliary verb when making suggestions or asking what to do: *Shall I check?*; *Shall we eat out tonight?*

shallow adjective 1 not deep 2 not given to deep thought or understanding; superficial

sham shams, shamming, shammed noun 1 thing or person that is not genuine ▷ adjective 2 not genuine ▷ verb 3 to fake, feign

shambles noun confused and disorganized situation or event

shame noun 1 guilt and embarrassment that comes from realizing that you have done something bad or foolish 2 capacity to feel such guilt and embarrassment 3 cause of shame: *There is no shame in that* 4 cause for regret: *It's a shame you can't come* ▷ verb 5 to cause to feel shame 6 to compel by shame: *They shamed their parents into giving up cigarettes* ▷ interjection 7 (SAfr informal) exclamation of sympathy

a
b
c
d
e
f
g
h
i
j
k
l
m
n
o
p
q
r
s
t
u
v
w
x
y
z

shameful adjective causing or deserving shame ▷ **shamefully** adverb

shameless adjective with no sense of shame ▷ **shamelessly** adverb

shampoo noun **1** soapy liquid used for washing hair, carpets or upholstery **2** wash with shampoo ▷ verb **3** to wash (something) with shampoo

shamrock noun plant with three round leaves on each stem used as the national emblem of Ireland

shanghai shanghais, shanghaiing, shanghaied verb **1** to force or trick (someone) into doing something ▷ noun **2** (Aust, NZ) catapult

shanty noun **1** shack or crude dwelling **2** sailor's traditional song

shape noun **1** outward form of an object **2** pattern or mould **3** way in which something is organized **4 in good shape** in good condition or in a good state of health ▷ verb **5** to form or mould **6** to influence the development of

shapeless adjective without a definite shape

shapely adjective (of woman) having an attractive figure

shard noun broken piece of pottery or glass

share verb **1** to hold (something) jointly or to join with others in doing, using or having (something): *We shared a bottle of champagne* **2** to divide (something) up equally: *We could share the cost between us* ▷ noun **3** part of something that belongs

to or is contributed by a person **4** one of the equal parts into which the capital stock of a public company is divided > **share out** verb to divide (something) equally among a group of people

shareholder noun a person who owns shares in a company

share-milker noun (NZ) person who works on a dairy farm and shares the profit from the sale of its produce

shark noun **1** large, powerful fish with sharp teeth **2** person who cheats others

sharp adjective **1** (of knife, needle) having a fine edge or point that is good for cutting or piercing things **2** not gradual **3** clearly defined **4** quick-witted **5** shrill **6** bitter or sour in taste **7** (Music) above the true pitch ▷ adverb **8** promptly **9** (Music) too high in pitch ▷ noun **10** (Music) note, or the symbol for it (♯), that is one semitone above the natural pitch ▷ **sharply** adverb ▷ **sharpness** noun

sharpen verb to make or become sharp or sharper

shatter verb **1** to break into pieces **2** to destroy completely

shattered adjective (informal) **1** completely exhausted **2** badly upset

shattering adjective causing shock or exhaustion

shave shaves, shaving, shaved verb **1** to remove (hair) from (the face, head or body) with a razor or shaver **2** to pare away ▷ noun **3** shaving **4 close shave** (informal) narrow escape

shaven adjective shaved

shaver noun electric razor

shavings *plural noun* small, very thin pieces of wood cut off a larger piece; parings

shawl *noun* piece of cloth worn over a woman's head or shoulders or wrapped around a baby

she *pronoun* refers to **1** female person or animal previously mentioned **2** something regarded as female, such as a car, ship or nation

sheaf *sheaves noun* **1** bundle (of papers) **2** tied bundle (of reaped corn)

shear *shears, shearing, sheared, shorn verb* **1** to clip hair or wool from (a sheep) **2** to cut through

shearer *noun* someone whose job is to shear sheep

sheath *noun* **1** close-fitting cover, especially for a knife or sword **2** (*Brit, Aust, NZ*) condom

shed *sheds, shedding, shed noun* **1** building used for storage or shelter or as a workshop ▷ *verb* **2** to cast off (skin, hair or leaves) **3** to weep (tears) **4** (*formal*) to get rid of: *The firm is to shed 700 jobs* **5** to drop (a load) **6 shed light (on)** to make clearer

sheen *noun* soft shine on the surface of something

sheep *noun* (*pl* sheep) farm animal bred for wool and meat

┃ **WORD TIP**
┃ The plural of *sheep* is *sheep*

sheep-dip *noun* liquid disinfectant used to keep sheep clean and free of pests

sheepdog *noun* breed of dog often used for herding sheep

sheepish *adjective* embarrassed because of feeling foolish
> **sheepishly** *adverb*

sheepskin *noun* skin of a sheep with the fleece still on, used for making rugs and coats

sheer *adjective* **1** absolute, complete: *sheer folly* **2** perpendicular, steep: *a sheer cliff* **3** (of material) so fine as to be transparent

sheet *noun* **1** large piece of fine cloth used under blankets or duvets as bedding **2** fine rectangular piece of any material

sheikh or **sheik** [shake] *noun* Arab chief

shelf *shelves noun* flat piece of wood, metal or glass fixed horizontally and used for putting things on

shell *noun* **1** hard outer covering of an egg, nut or certain animals **2** external frame of something: *The room was just an empty shell* **3** explosive device fired from a large gun ▷ *verb* **4** to remove the shell or outer covering from (peas, nuts) **5** to fire at (a place) with artillery shells

shellfish *shellfish* or *shellfishes noun* a small, usually edible, sea creature with a shell

shelter *noun* **1** building or structure providing protection from danger or the weather **2** protection ▷ *verb* **3** to give shelter to **4** to take shelter

sheltered *adjective* **1** (of place) protected from wind and rain **2** (of life) away from unpleasant or upsetting things **3** (of accommodation for the elderly or handicapped) offering specially equipped and monitored facilities

shelve *verb* to put aside or postpone

shepherd noun **1** person who tends sheep ▷ verb **2** to guide or watch over (people)

sheriff noun **1** (in the US) chief law enforcement officer of a county **2** (in England and Wales) person appointed by the king or queen to carry out ceremonial duties **3** (in Scotland) chief judge of a district **4** (in Australia) officer of the Supreme Court

sherry sherries noun pale or dark brown fortified wine

shield noun **1** piece of armour carried on the arm to protect the body from blows or missiles **2** anything that protects ▷ verb **3** to protect

shift verb **1** to move **2** to transfer (blame or responsibility) **3** to remove or be removed **4** (of opinion, situation) to change ▷ noun **5** set period during which different groups of people work in a factory or the people assigned to a particular period: the night shift

shilling noun former British, Australian and New Zealand coin worth one-twentieth of a pound; in Britain replaced by the 5p piece

shimmer verb **1** to shine with a faint flickering light ▷ noun **2** a faint, flickering light

shin noun **1** front of the lower leg ▷ verb **2** to climb (a pole or tree) quickly, gripping with your arms and legs

shine verb shining, shone **1** to give out or reflect light **2** to aim (a light or torch) **3** to be very good (at something) ▷ noun **4** brightness or lustre

shingle noun **1** small pebble found on beaches **2** small wooden roof tile

shining adjective **1** bright, gleaming **2 shining example** very good or typical example

shiny shinier, shiniest adjective bright, polished-looking

ship ships, shipping, shipped noun **1** a large boat which carries passengers or cargo; vessel ▷ verb **2** to send or transport (something or someone) somewhere, sometimes by ship

-ship suffix used to form nouns that refer to a condition or position: fellowship

shipment noun **1** a quantity of goods transported somewhere: a shipment of olive oil **2** transporting (of cargo)

shipping noun **1** business of transporting cargo on ships **2** ships collectively

shipwreck noun **1** destruction of a ship through storm or collision **2** wrecked ship ▷ verb **3** to leave (someone) a survivor of a shipwreck

shipyard noun place where ships are built

shiralee noun (Aust old-fashioned) bundle of possessions carried by a swagman

shire noun **1** (Brit old-fashioned) county **2** (Aust) rural area with an elected council

shirk verb to avoid (duty or work)

shirt noun lightweight, blouse-like piece of clothing worn especially by men and boys, typically having a collar, sleeves and buttons down the front

shiver verb 1 to tremble, as from cold or fear ▷ noun 2 slight tremble, as from cold or fear

shoal noun large number of fish swimming together

shock noun 1 sudden upsetting experience 2 sudden violent blow or impact 3 something causing this 4 serious medical condition in which the blood cannot circulate properly brought about by physical or mental shock 5 pain and muscular spasm caused by an electric current passing through the body 6 bushy mass (of hair) ▷ verb 7 to horrify or astonish 8 to offend or scandalize > **shocked** adjective > **shocker** noun > **shocking** adjective 1 (informal) very bad 2 rude or immoral

shock absorber noun one of the devices fitted near a vehicle's wheels to help prevent it bouncing up and down

shoddy shoddier, shoddiest adjective made or done badly

shoe shoes, shoeing, shod noun 1 type of protective footwear that covers the foot, ends below the ankle and has a hard sole 2 horseshoe ▷ verb 3 to fit (a horse) with a horseshoe or horseshoes

shoestring noun **on a shoestring** using a very small amount of money

shoot shoots, shooting, shot verb 1 to hit, wound or kill (a person or animal) by firing a gun at them 2 to fire (an arrow or a bolt) from a bow or crossbow 3 to hunt 4 to send out or move rapidly: They shot back into Green Street 5 (of a plant) to sprout 6 to photograph

or film: The whole film was shot in California 7 (Sport) to take a shot at goal ▷ noun 8 new branch or sprout of a plant 9 hunting expedition

shooting noun an incident in which someone is shot

shooting star noun meteor

shop shops, shopping, shopped noun 1 place where things are sold 2 workshop: a bicycle repair shop 3 **talk shop** to discuss work, especially on a social occasion ▷ verb 4 to go to the shops to buy things 5 (Brit, Aust, NZ informal) to inform against > **shopper** noun: Christmas shoppers

shopkeeper noun someone who owns or manages a small shop

shoplifting noun practice of stealing goods from shops

shopping noun 1 goods bought from shops 2 activity of buying things

shop steward noun (in some countries) trade-union official elected to represent his or her fellow workers

shore noun 1 edge of a sea or lake ▷ verb 2 **shore up** to reinforce, strengthen or prop (something) up

shoreline noun the edge of a sea, lake or wide river

shorn verb 1 a past participle of shear ▷ adjective 2 (of grass, hair) cut very short

short adjective 1 not long: a short distance 2 not tall: He's short and plump 3 not lasting long, brief: a short time 4 deficient: short of cash 5 abrupt, rude: She was a bit short with me 6 (of a drink) consisting chiefly of a spirit 7 (of pastry) crumbly **8** *adverb* **8** abruptly ▷ *noun* **9** drink of spirits **10** short film **11** (*informal*) short circuit

shortage *noun* deficiency

shortbread or **shortcake** *noun* crumbly biscuit made with butter

short circuit *noun* electrical fault that occurs when two points accidentally become connected and the electricity travels directly between them rather than through the complete circuit

shortcoming *noun* failing or defect

shortcut *noun* quicker route or method

shorten *verb* to make or become shorter

shortfall *noun* smaller amount than needed

shorthand *noun* system of rapid writing using symbols to represent words

short-list *verb* to put on a short list

shortly *adverb* **1** soon **2** rudely

short-sighted *adjective* **1** unable to see distant things clearly **2** not taking account of possible future events

short-term *adjective* happening or having an effect within a short time or for a short time

shot *verb* **1** past of **shoot** ▷ *noun* **2** shooting **3** small lead pellets used in a shotgun **4** person with specified skill in shooting: *a good shot* **5** (*informal*) attempt: *someone who would have a shot at explaining it* **6** (*Sport*) act or instance of hitting, kicking or throwing the ball **7** photograph **8** uninterrupted film sequence **9** (*informal*) injection **10** like

a shot (*informal*) quickly and eagerly

shotgun *noun* gun for firing a lot of small pellets at once

shot put *noun* athletic event in which contestants throw a heavy metal ball as far as possible ▷ **shot-putter** *noun* person who takes part in shot putting events

should *verb* **1** ought to: *He should have done better* **2** to be likely to: *He should have heard by now* **3** (*formal*) would: *I should like to express my thanks* **4** sometimes used in subordinate clauses after that: *It is inevitable that you should go* **5** was to or were to: *if he should die prematurely*

shoulder *noun* **1** part of the body to which an arm, foreleg or wing is attached **2** part of a piece of clothing that covers your shoulders **3** cut of meat including the upper foreleg **4** side of a road ▷ *verb* **5** to bear (a burden or responsibility) **6** to put on your shoulder

shoulder blade *noun* either of the two large flat triangular bones in the upper part of your back, below your shoulders

shout *noun* **1** loud cry ▷ *verb* **2** to cry out loudly ▷ **shout down** *verb* to silence (someone) or to prevent (someone) from being heard by shouting

shove *verb* **1** to push roughly **2** (*informal*) to put ▷ *noun* **3** rough push ▷ **shove off** *verb* (*informal*) to go away

shovel shovels, shovelling, shovelled *noun* **1** tool for lifting or moving loose material ▷ *verb* **2** to lift or move (something) as with a shovel

show shows, showing, showed, shown *verb* **1** to make, be or become noticeable or visible **2** to exhibit or display: *Show me your passport* **3** to indicate or prove **4** to demonstrate: *Show me how it works* **5** to guide or lead: *I'll show you to your room* **6** to reveal or display (an emotion) ▷ *noun* **7** public exhibition **8** entertainment on television or at the theatre and so on **9** mere display or pretence > **show off** *verb* **1** (informal) to try to impress people by behaving in a flamboyant manner **2** to allow others to see (something) to invite admiration > **show up** *verb* **1** (informal) to arrive **2** to reveal or be revealed clearly **3** to expose the faults or defects of **4** (informal) to embarrass

show business *noun* the entertainment industry

showdown *noun* (informal) confrontation that settles a dispute

shower *noun* **1** device for washing that sprays you with water **2** wash under such a device **3** short period of rain, hail or snow **4** sudden fall of a lot of objects ▷ *verb* **5** to wash in a shower **6** to give (a lot of things) or present (someone) with a lot of things

showing *noun* public presentation or viewing (of a film or television programme)

showjumping *noun* competitive sport of riding horses to demonstrate skill in jumping

show-off *noun* (informal) person who tries to impress people with their knowledge or skill

showroom *noun* room in which goods for sale are on display

showy showier, showiest *adjective* large or bright and intended to impress; ostentatious > **showily** *adverb*

shrapnel *noun* **1** artillery shell filled with pellets which scatter on explosion **2** fragments from this

shred shreds, shredding, shredded *noun* **1** long narrow strip torn from something **2** small amount ▷ *verb* **3** to tear to shreds

shrew *noun* **1** small mouselike animal **2** (offensive) bad-tempered nagging woman

shrewd *adjective* clever and perceptive > **shrewdly** *adverb* > **shrewdness** *noun*: *the shrewdness of that decision*

shriek *noun* **1** shrill cry ▷ *verb* **2** to utter (with) a shriek

shrill *adjective* (of a sound) sharp and high-pitched > **shrillness** *noun* > **shrilly** *adverb*

shrimp *noun* small edible shellfish

shrine *noun* place of worship associated with a sacred person or object

shrink shrinks, shrinking, shrank, shrunk *verb* **1** to become or make smaller **2** to recoil or withdraw ▷ *noun* **3** (informal) psychiatrist > **shrinkage** *noun* decrease in size, value or weight

shrivel shrivels, shrivelling, shrivelled *verb* to shrink and wither

shroud *noun* **1** piece of cloth used to wrap a dead body **2** anything which conceals ▷ *verb* **3** to conceal: *achievements that have remained shrouded in mystery*

shrub *noun* a low, bushy plant

shrug shrugs, shrugging, shrugged *verb* 1 to raise and then drop (the shoulders) as a sign of indifference, ignorance or doubt ▷ *noun* 2 act of shrugging your shoulders

shrunken *adjective (formal)* reduced in size: *a shrunken old man*

shudder *verb* 1 to shake or tremble violently, especially with horror ▷ *noun* 2 shiver of fear or horror

shuffle *verb* 1 to walk without lifting your feet properly 2 shuffle about to move about and fidget 3 to mix (cards) up thoroughly ▷ *noun* 4 act of shuffling

shun shuns, shunning, shunned *verb* to avoid

shunt *verb* to move (objects or people) to a different position

shut shuts, shutting, shut *verb* to close > shut down to close permanently > shut up (*informal*) to stop talking

shutter *noun* 1 hinged doorlike cover for closing off a window 2 device in a camera that opens to allow light through the lens when a photograph is taken

shuttle *noun* 1 plane or other vehicle that goes to and fro between two places 2 instrument that passes the weft thread between the warp threads in weaving ▷ *adjective* 3 (of services) involving a plane, bus or train service that travels to and fro between two places

shuttlecock *noun* feathered object used as a ball in the game of badminton

shy shyer, shyest; shies, shying, shied *adjective* 1 nervous and uncomfortable in company; timid 2 shy of cautious or wary of ▷ *verb* 3 (of horse) to move away suddenly when startled or afraid 4 to shy away from to avoid (doing something) through fear or lack of confidence ▷ **shyly** *adverb* ▷ **shyness** *noun*

sibling *noun (formal)* brother or sister

sick *adjective* 1 ill 2 feel sick to feel nauseous and likely to vomit 3 be sick to vomit 4 (*informal*) (of person, story, joke) showing an unpleasant and frivolous disrespect for something said 5 sick of (*informal*) disgusted by or weary of ▷ **sickness** *noun*

sicken *verb* to make (someone) nauseated or disgusted ▷ **sickening** *adjective: a string of sickening attacks*

sickle *noun* tool with a short handle and a curved blade for cutting grass or grain

sickly sicklier, sickliest *adjective* 1 unhealthy or weak 2 causing revulsion or nausea

side *noun* 1 either of two halves into which something can be divided 2 either surface of a flat object 3 surface or edge of something, especially with neither the front nor the back 4 area immediately next to a person or thing 5 aspect or part 6 one of two opposing groups or teams 7 slope (of a hill) 8 television channel ▷ *adjective* 9 at or on the side: *the side door* 10 of lesser importance: *a side* road **11** on the side **a** as an extra **b** unofficially > **side with** verb to support (one side in a dispute)

sideboard noun a long, low cupboard for plates and glasses in a dining room

sideburns plural noun areas of hair growing on a man's cheeks in front of his ears

side effect noun (of drug) additional undesirable effect

sidekick noun (informal) close friend or associate

sideline noun **1** extra interest or source of income **2** (Sport) line marking the boundary of a playing area

sideshow noun stall at a fairground

sidestep sidesteps, sidestepping, sidestepped verb to dodge (an issue)

sidewalk noun (US) paved path for pedestrians, at the side of a road; pavement

sideways adverb **1** to or from the side **2** obliquely

siding noun short stretch of railway track beside the main tracks where engines and carriages are left when not in use

sidle verb to walk in a furtive manner

siege noun military operation in which an army surrounds a place and prevents food or help from reaching the people inside

sieve noun utensil with mesh through which a substance is sifted or strained > verb **2** to sift or strain through a sieve

sift verb **1** to pass (a substance) through a sieve to remove lumps **2** to examine (information or

evidence) to select what is important

sigh noun **1** long audible breath expressing sadness, tiredness, relief or longing > verb **2** to let out a sigh

sight noun **1** ability to see **2** range of vision **3** something seen: It was a ghastly sight **4** thing worth seeing: Tim was eager to see the sights. **5** device for guiding the eye while using a gun or optical instrument **6** (informal) a lot > verb **7** to catch sight of

> **WORD TIP**
> Do not confuse the spellings of sight and site

sighted adjective able to see

sighting noun instance of something rare or unexpected being seen

sightseeing noun visiting places that tourists usually visit > **sightseer** noun: For centuries, sightseers have flocked to this site

sign noun **1** indication of something not immediately or outwardly observable **2** gesture, mark or symbol conveying a meaning **3** notice displayed to advertise, inform or warn **4** omen > verb **5** to write (your name) on (a document or letter) to show its authenticity or your agreement **6** to communicate using sign language **7** to make a sign or gesture > **sign on** verb to register as unemployed > **sign up** verb to sign a document committing yourself to a job, course, etc

signal signals, signalling, signalled noun **1** sign or gesture to convey information **2** piece of equipment beside a railway track which tells train drivers whether to stop or not **3** sequence of electrical impulses or radio waves transmitted or received ▷ *verb* **4** to convey (information) by signal

signature *noun* **1** person's name written by himself or herself in his or her usual style when signing **2** sign at the start of a piece of music to show the key or tempo

significant *adjective* **1** important **2** having or expressing a meaning **3** (of amount) large > **significance** *noun*: *We didn't appreciate the significance of this till later* > **significantly** *adverb*

signify signifies, signifying, signified *verb* **1** to indicate or suggest **2** to be a symbol or sign for

sign language or **signing** *noun* system of communication by gestures, as used by deaf people

signpost *noun* road sign with information on it such as the name of a town and how far away it is

Sikh [seek] *noun* person who believes in Sikhism, an Indian religion which separated from Hinduism in the sixteenth century and which teaches that there is only one God > **Sikhism** *noun*

silence *noun* **1** absence of noise or speech ▷ *verb* **2** to make (someone or something) silent

silent *adjective* **1** not saying a word; uncommunicative **2** not making a sound; quiet > **silently** *adverb*

silhouette *noun* outline of a dark shape seen against a light background > **silhouetted**

adjective: *chimney-stacks silhouetted against the sky*

silicon *noun* brittle nonmetallic element widely used in chemistry and industry

silk *noun* **1** fibre made by the silkworm **2** thread or fabric made from this

silkworm *noun* larva of a particular kind of moth

silky or **silken** *adjective* of or like silk; smooth and soft

sill *noun* ledge at the bottom of a window or door

silly sillier, silliest *adjective* foolish

silt *noun* **1** mud deposited by moving water ▷ *verb* **2** silt up (of river, lake) to fill or be choked with silt

silver *noun* **1** valuable greyish-white metallic element used for making jewellery and ornaments **2** coins or articles made of silver or silver-coloured metal ▷ *adjective*, *noun* **3** greyish-white

silverbeet *noun* (Aust, NZ) leafy green vegetable with white stalks

silver fern *noun* (NZ) tall fern found in New Zealand. It is the symbol of New Zealand national sports teams

silverfish silverfishes or silverfish *noun* small silver-coloured insect with no wings

silver jubilee *noun* 25th anniversary of an important event

silver medal *noun* a medal made from silver, or something resembling this, awarded to the competitor who comes second in a competition

silver wedding *noun* 25th wedding anniversary

silvery *adjective* having the appearance or colour of silver

similar *adjective* **1** alike but not identical **2** (Geometry) (of triangles) having the same angles >**similarly** *adverb*

similarity *noun* similar quality; resemblance

simile [**sim**-ill-ee] *noun* figure of speech comparing one thing to another, using *as* or *like*: *He's as white as a sheet; She runs like a deer*

simmer *verb* **1** to cook gently at just below boiling point **2** to be in a state of suppressed rage

simple *adjective* **1** easy to understand or do **2** plain or unpretentious **3** not combined or complex **4** having some degree of mental retardation **5** no more than; mere >**simplicity** *noun* quality of being simple

simple-minded *adjective* not very intelligent or sophisticated

simplify simplifies, simplifying, simplified *verb* to make less complicated >**simplification** *noun*

simplistic *adjective* too simple or naive

simply *adverb* **1** merely or just **2** in a way that is easy to understand **3** plainly or unpretentiously

simulate *verb* **1** to make a pretence of **2** to reproduce the characteristics of **3** to have the appearance of >**simulation** *noun* >**simulator** *noun* device designed to reproduce actual conditions, for example in order to train pilots or astronauts

simultaneous *adjective* occurring at the same time >**simultaneously** *adverb*

sin sins, sinning, sinned *noun* **1** wicked and immoral behaviour **2** offence against a principle or standard, especially a religious one **3 live in sin** (old-fashioned) (of an unmarried couple) to live together as if married ▷ *verb* **4** to do something wicked and immoral

since *preposition* **1** during the period of time from: *I've been waiting here since half past three* ▷ *conjunction* **2** from the time when: *We've known each other since we were kids* **3** for the reason that: *I'm forever on a diet, since I put on weight easily* ▷ *adverb* **4** from that time: *They split up and he has since remarried*

sincere *adjective* without pretence or deceit >**sincerity** *noun*: *There is no doubting their sincerity*

sincerely *adverb* **1** genuinely **2 Yours sincerely** ending for formal letters addressed and written to a named person

sinew *noun* **1** tough fibrous tissue joining muscle to bone **2** muscles or strength

sinful *adjective* wicked and immoral

sing sings, singing, sang, sung *verb* **1** to make musical sounds with the voice **2** to perform (a song) **3** (of bird, insect) to make a humming or whistling sound >**singer** *noun* person who sings, especially professionally

singe singes, singeing, singed *verb* **1** to burn the surface of ▷ *noun* **2** a slight burn

single *adjective* **1** one only **2** unmarried **3** designed for one user: *a single bed* **4** (of a ticket) valid for an outward journey only **5** **in single file** (of people or things) arranged in one line ▷ *noun* **6** thing intended for one person **7** **single ticket** **8** recording of one or two short pieces of music on a record, CD or cassette **9** **singles** game between two players ▷ **single out** *verb* to pick out from others ▷ **singly** *adverb* on your own or one by one

single-handed *adjective* without assistance

single-minded *adjective* having one aim only

singular *adjective* **1** (of a word or form) denoting one person or thing **2** remarkable, unusual ▷ *noun* **3** singular form of a word ▷ **singularity** *noun* ▷ **singularly** *adverb*

sinister *adjective* seeming evil or harmful

sink sinks, sinking, sank, sunk *noun* **1** a basin with taps supplying water, usually in a kitchen ▷ *verb* **2** to move or cause to move downwards, especially through water: *An Indian cargo ship sank in icy seas* **3** to descend or cause to descend: *He sank into black despair* **4** to decline in value or amount **5** to become weaker **6** to dig or drill (a hole or shaft) **7** to make (a knife, your teeth) go deeply into something **8** to invest (money) ▷ **sink in** *verb* (of fact) to penetrate the mind

sinner *noun* person who has committed a sin

sinus sinuses [**sine**-uss] *noun* air passage in the skull

sip sips, sipping, sipped *verb* **1** to drink in small mouthfuls ▷ *noun* **2** amount sipped

siphon *verb* to draw (a liquid) out of something through a tube and transfer it to another place

sir *noun* **1** polite term of address for a man **2** **Sir** title of a knight or baronet

siren *noun* **1** device making a loud wailing noise as a warning **2** (*literary*) dangerously alluring woman

sirloin *noun* prime cut of loin of beef

sis or **sies** *interjection* (S Afr informal) exclamation of disgust

sister *noun* **1** girl or woman with the same parents as another person **2** female fellow-member of a group **3** senior nurse **4** nun ▷ *adjective* **5** closely related, similar

sisterhood *noun* strong feeling of companionship between women

sister-in-law sisters-in-law *noun* **1** your husband or wife's sister **2** your brother's wife

sit sits, sitting, sat *verb* **1** to have your body bent at the hips so that your weight is on your buttocks rather than your feet **2** to lower yourself to a sitting position **3** to perch **4** (of an official body) to hold a session **5** to take (an examination)

sitcom *noun* (*informal*) a television comedy series which shows characters in amusing situations; situation comedy

site *noun* **1** piece of ground where a particular thing happens or is situated **2** same as **website** ▷ *verb* **3** to provide with a site

> **WORD TIP**
> Do not confuse the spellings of *site* and *sight*

sitting noun **1** one of the times when a meal is served **2** one of the occasions when a parliament or law court meets and carries out its work

sitting room noun room in a house where people sit and relax; living room

situated adjective located

situation noun **1** state of affairs **2** (old-fashioned) location and surroundings **3** position of employment

Siva noun Hindu god and one of the Trimurti

six adjective, noun the number 6

sixteen adjective, noun the number 16 > **sixteenth** adjective, noun

sixth adjective, noun **1** (coming as) number 6 in a series ▷ noun **2** one of six equal parts

sixth sense noun instinctive awareness

sixty sixties adjective, noun the number 60 > **sixtieth** adjective, noun

sizable or **sizeable** adjective quite large

size noun **1** dimensions, bigness **2** one of a series of standard measurements of goods > **size up** verb (informal) to assess

sizzle verb to make a hissing sound like frying fat

sjambok [sham-bok] noun (SAfr) long whip made from animal hide

skate skates, skating, skated noun **1** boot with a steel blade attached to the sole for gliding over ice; ice skate **2** item of footwear with a set of wheels attached for gliding over a hard surface; roller skate **3** large edible sea fish ▷ verb **4** to glide on or as if on skates > **skate**

over or **round** verb to avoid discussing or dealing with (a matter) fully

skateboard noun narrow board on small wheels for riding on while standing up

skeleton noun **1** framework of bones inside a person's or animal's body ▷ adjective **2** (of staff, workforce) reduced to a minimum

sketch noun **1** quick, rough drawing **2** brief description **3** short humorous play ▷ verb **4** to make a sketch (of something or someone) **5** to give a brief description of

sketchy sketchier, sketchiest adjective incomplete or inadequate

skew or **skewed** adjective slanting or crooked

skewer noun **1** pin to hold meat together during cooking ▷ verb **2** to push a skewer through

ski skis, skiing, skied noun **1** one of a pair of long runners attached to boots for gliding over snow or water ▷ verb **2** to travel on skis > **skier** noun person who skis

skid skids, skidding, skidded verb **1** (of a moving vehicle) to slide sideways uncontrollably ▷ noun **2** instance of skidding

skilful adjective having or showing skill; able > **skilfully** adverb

skill noun **1** special ability or expertise **2** something requiring special training or expertise

skilled adjective **1** having the knowledge and ability to do something well **2** (of work) requiring special training

skim skims, skimming, skimmed verb **1** to remove floating matter

from the surface of (a liquid) **2** to
glide smoothly over (a surface)
3 to read (a book) quickly

skimmed milk noun milk from
which the cream has been
removed

skin skins, skinning, skinned
noun **1** outer covering of the
body **2** complexion **3** outer layer
or covering **4** film on a liquid
5 animal skin used as a material or
container ▷ verb **6** to remove the
skin of (an animal)

skinny skinnier, skinniest adjective
very thin

skip skips, skipping, skipped verb
1 to leap lightly from one foot
to the other **2** to jump over a
rope as it is swung under one
3 (informal) to pass over or omit
▷ noun **4** little jump from one
foot to the other **5** large metal
container for holding rubbish
and rubble

skipper noun (informal) captain
(of ship)

skirmish noun brief or minor fight
or argument

skirt noun **1** piece of women's
clothing that hangs down over
the legs from the waist ▷ verb **2** to
border **3** to go round **4** to avoid
dealing with (an issue)

skirting board noun narrow
board round the bottom of an
interior wall

skite (Aust, NZ informal) verb **1** to
boast ▷ noun **2** boast

skittle noun bottle-shaped object
used as a target in some games

skull noun bony part of the head
surrounding the brain

skunk noun small black-and-white
North American mammal which

lets out a foul-smelling fluid when
attacked

sky skies noun the space around
the earth which you can see when
you look upwards

skylight noun window in a roof
or ceiling

skyline noun **1** line where the
earth and sky appear to meet
2 outline of buildings, trees, etc
against the sky

skyscraper noun very tall building

slab noun thick, flat piece of
something

slack adjective **1** not tight **2** not
busy **3** not thorough; negligent
▷ noun **4** part (of rope) that is not
taut ▷ verb **5** to neglect your work
or duty > **slackness** noun

slacken verb to make or become
slack

slag slags, slagging, slagged noun
1 waste material left when ore has
been melted down to remove the
metal ▷ verb **2** slag off (informal)
to criticize

slalom noun skiing competition
in which competitors have to
twist and turn quickly to avoid
obstacles

slam slams, slamming, slammed
verb **1** to shut, put down or
hit (something) violently and
noisily ▷ noun **2** act or sound of
slamming

slander noun **1** false and
potentially damaging claim about
a person **2** crime of making such a
statement ▷ verb **3** to make false
and potentially damaging claims
about a person > **slanderous**
adjective: false or slanderous
statements that damage a person's
reputation

slang *noun* very informal language

slant *verb* **1** to lean at an angle; slope **2** to present (information) in a biased way ▷ *noun* **3** slope **4** point of view, especially a biased one

slap slaps, slapping, slapped *noun* **1** blow with the open hand or a flat object ▷ *verb* **2** to strike with the open hand or a flat object **3** (*informal*) to put (someone or something somewhere) forcefully or carelessly

slash *verb* **1** to cut with a long, sweeping stroke **2** to reduce drastically ▷ *noun* **3** a diagonal line used for separating letters, words or numbers (/); stroke

slat *noun* narrow strip of wood or metal ▷ **slatted** *adjective*: slatted wooden blinds

slate *noun* **1** rock which splits easily into thin layers **2** piece of this for covering a roof or, formerly, for writing on ▷ *verb* **3** (*informal*) to criticize (something or someone) harshly

slaughter *verb* **1** to kill (animals) for food **2** to kill (people) savagely or indiscriminately ▷ *noun* **3** mass killing; massacre

slave *noun* **1** person owned by another person and forced to work for them **2** person who is dominated by another person or by a habit ▷ *verb* **3** to work like a slave ▷ **slavery** *noun* **1** state or condition of being a slave **2** practice of owning slaves

slay slays, slaying, slew, slain *verb* (*literary*) to kill

sleazy sleazier, sleaziest *adjective* run-down or sordid

sled *noun* sledge

sledge *noun* vehicle on runners for sliding on snow

sledgehammer *noun* large, heavy hammer

sleek *adjective* **1** glossy, smooth and shiny **2** (of person) rich and elegant in appearance

sleep sleeps, sleeping, slept *noun* **1** natural state of rest in which your eyes are closed and you are unconscious **2** period spent sleeping; nap **3** put to sleep to kill (a sick or injured animal) painlessly ▷ *verb* **4** to be asleep **5** (of house, flat, etc) to have beds for (a specified number of people) ▷ **sleep together** *verb* to have sexual intercourse ▷ **sleep with** *verb* to have sexual intercourse with

sleeper *noun* **1** person who sleeps in a specified way: *I'm a very heavy sleeper* **2** bed on a train **3** railway car fitted for sleeping in **4** beam supporting the rails of a railway **5** ring worn in a pierced ear to stop the hole from closing up

sleeping bag *noun* padded bag for sleeping in

sleeping pill *noun* pill which you take to help you sleep

sleepout *noun* (*Aust*) area of veranda or porch closed off for use as a bedroom **2** (*NZ*) small building for sleeping in

sleepover *noun* (*informal*) overnight stay at someone else's house

sleepwalk *verb* to walk around while asleep

sleepy sleepier, sleepiest *adjective* **1** tired and ready to go to sleep **2** (of town or village) very quiet

> **sleepily** *adverb* > **sleepiness** *noun*

sleet *noun* mixed rain and snow or hail

sleeve *noun* **1** part of a piece of clothing that covers your arms or upper arms **2** tubelike cover **3** (of record) cover > **sleeveless** *adjective: a sleeveless pullover*

sleigh *noun* sledge

slender *adjective* **1** attractively slim **2** small in amount

sleuth [**slooth**] *noun* detective

slew *verb* **1** past tense of **slay 2** (of vehicle) to skid or swing round

slice *noun* **1** thin flat piece cut from something **2** share **3** kitchen utensil with a broad flat blade **4** (Sport) instance of hitting a ball so that it goes to one side rather than straight ahead ▷ *verb* **5** to cut into slices **6** (Sport) to hit (a ball) with a slice **7** **slice through** to cut or move through (something) quickly, like a knife

slick *adjective* **1** (of action) skilfully and quickly done **2** (of person) persuasive but insincere **3** (of book, film) well-made and attractive, but superficial ▷ *noun* **4** patch of oil on water

slide *verb* **1** slides, sliding, slid **1** to slip smoothly along (a surface) ▷ *noun* **2** small piece of photographic film which can be projected onto a screen so that you can see the picture **3** small piece of glass on which you put something for viewing under a microscope **4** structure with a steep, slippery slope for children to slide down **5** ornamental hair clip

slight *adjective* **1** small in quantity or extent **2** not important **3** slim and delicate ▷ *verb* **4** to snub ▷ *noun* **5** snub > **slightly** *adverb*

slim slimmer, slimmest; slims, slimming, slimmed *adjective* **1** not heavy or stout, thin **2** slight ▷ *verb* **3** to make or become slim by diet and exercise > **slimmer** *noun*

slime *noun* unpleasant, thick, slippery substance

slimy slimier, slimiest *adjective* **1** like slime or covered with slime **2** showing excessive and insincere helpfulness and friendliness; ingratiating

sling slings, slinging, slung *noun* **1** bandage hung from the neck to support an injured hand or arm **2** rope or strap for lifting something **3** strap with a string at each end for throwing a stone ▷ *verb* **4** to throw or put as if with a sling

slip slips, slipping, slipped *verb* **1** to slide accidentally, losing your balance **2** to go smoothly, easily or quietly: *She slipped out of the house* **3** to put something (somewhere) easily or quickly **4** to pass out of (your) mind: *It slipped my mind* ▷ *noun* **5** act of slipping **6** mistake **7** piece of clothing worn under a dress or skirt; petticoat **8** small piece of paper **9** **give someone the slip** to escape from someone > **slip up** *verb* to make a mistake

slipped disc *noun* painful condition in which one of the discs connecting the bones of your spine moves out of its position

slipper noun lose, soft shoe for indoor wear

slippery adjective **1** smooth, wet or greasy and therefore difficult to hold or walk on **2** (of a person) untrustworthy

slippery dip noun (Aust informal) children's slide at a playground or funfair

slip rail noun (Aust, NZ) fence that can be slipped out of place to make an opening

slipstream noun the flow of air behind a fast-moving object, such as a car or plane

slit slits, slitting, slit noun **1** long narrow cut or opening ▷ verb **2** to make a long, straight cut in

slither verb to slide in an uneven manner

sliver [**sliv**-ver] noun small thin piece

slob noun (informal) lazy and untidy person

slog slogs, slogging, slogged verb to work hard and steadily

slogan noun a short, easily-remembered phrase used in politics or advertising; catch-phrase

slop slops, slopping, slopped verb **1** to splash or spill ▷ noun **2** **slops** dirty water or liquid waste

slope noun **1** surface that is higher at one end than at the other; incline **2** the angle at which something slopes; gradient **3** slopes hills ▷ verb **4** (of a surface) to be higher at one end than at the other **5** to lean to one side: sloping handwriting

sloppy sloppier, sloppiest adjective **1** careless or untidy **2** foolishly sentimental >**sloppily** adverb >**sloppiness** noun

slot slots, slotting, slotted noun **1** narrow opening for putting something in **2** (informal) place in a schedule, scheme or organization ▷ verb **3** to fit into a slot

sloth [rhymes with **both**] noun **1** laziness **2** a South and Central American animal that moves very slowly and hangs upside down from the branches of trees

slouch verb to sit, stand or move with a drooping posture

slouch hat noun (Aust) hat with a wide, flexible brim, especially an Australian army hat with the left side of the brim turned up

Slovak adjective **1** belonging to or relating to Slovakia ▷ noun **2** someone from Slovakia **3** language spoken in Slovakia

slow adjective **1** taking a longer time than is usual or expected **2** not fast **3** (of a clock or watch) showing a time earlier than the correct one **4** not clever ▷ verb **5** (often followed by down, up) to become less fast **6** to reduce the speed (of) >**slowly** adverb >**slowness** noun

slow motion noun movement that is much slower than normal, especially in a film

sludge noun **1** thick mud **2** sewage

slug slugs, slugging, slugged noun **1** small, slow-moving creature with a slimy body, like a snail without a shell **2** (informal) mouthful (of an alcoholic drink) **3** bullet

sluggish adjective slow-moving, lacking energy >**sluggishly** adverb >**sluggishness** noun: the sluggishness of the economy

sluice noun 1 channel carrying off water 2 sliding gate used to control the flow of water in this; sluicegate ▷ verb 3 to pour water over or through

slum slums, slumming, slummed noun 1 squalid overcrowded house or area ▷ verb 2 to be temporarily experiencing poorer places or conditions than usual

slumber (literary) noun 1 sleep ▷ verb 2 to sleep

slump verb 1 (of prices or demand) to fall suddenly and dramatically 2 (of person) to sink or fall heavily ▷ noun 3 a sudden, severe drop in prices or demand 4 time of unemployment and economic decline

slur slurs, slurring, slurred verb 1 to pronounce or say (words) indistinctly 2 (Music) to sing or play (notes) smoothly without a break ▷ noun 3 slurring of words 4 remark intended to discredit someone 5 (Music) a slurring of notes **b** curved line indicating notes to be slurred

slurp (informal) verb 1 to eat or drink noisily ▷ noun 2 slurping sound

slush noun 1 wet, melting snow 2 (informal) sloppy sentimental talk or writing ▷ **slushy** adjective: a slushy romance

slut (offensive) 1 dirty, untidy woman 2 immoral woman

sly slyer or slier, slyest or sliest adjective 1 crafty 2 secretive and cunning 3 roguish 4 **on the sly** secretly ▷ **slyly** adverb

smack verb 1 to slap (someone) sharply 2 **smack your lips** to open and close (your lips) loudly

in enjoyment or anticipation 3 **smack of** to suggest or be reminiscent of: His tale smacks of fantasy ▷ noun 4 sharp slap 5 slapping sound 6 small fishing boat 7 (informal) heroin ▷ adverb 8 (informal) squarely or directly: smack in the middle

small adjective 1 not large in size, number or amount 2 unimportant ▷ noun 3 narrow part of the lower back > **smallness** noun: the smallness of the cell

smallpox noun serious contagious disease with blisters that leave scars

small talk noun light social conversation

smart adjective 1 neat and tidy 2 clever 3 fashionable 4 brisk ▷ verb 5 to feel or cause stinging pain ▷ **smartly** adverb > **smartness** noun

smarten verb to make or become smart

smash verb 1 to break violently and noisily 2 to strike (against something) violently 3 to destroy ▷ noun 4 act or sound of smashing 5 violent collision of vehicles 6 (informal) popular success 7 (informal) powerful overhead shot

smashing adjective (informal) excellent

smattering noun slight knowledge

smear noun 1 dirty, greasy mark or smudge 2 untrue and malicious rumour 3 (Medicine) bodily sample smeared on to a slide for examination under a microscope ▷ verb 4 to spread with a greasy or sticky substance 5 to rub so as to produce a dirty mark or smudge **6** to slander

smell smells, smelling, smelled or smelt *noun* **1** odour or scent **2** ability to perceive odours by the nose ▷ *verb* **3** to have or give off a smell: *He smelled of tobacco and garlic* **4** to have an unpleasant smell **5** to sniff (something) **6** to perceive (a scent or odour) by means of the nose **7** to detect by instinct

smelly smellier, smelliest *adjective* having a nasty smell

smelt smelts, smelting, smelted *verb* **1** a past of **smell** **2** to extract (a metal) from (an ore) by heating

smile *verb* **1** to turn up the corners of your mouth slightly because you are pleased or amused or want to convey friendliness ▷ *noun* **2** turning up of the corners of the mouth to show pleasure, amusement or friendliness

smirk *noun* **1** smug smile ▷ *verb* **2** to give a smirk

smith *noun* worker in metal

smitten *verb adjective* in love (with someone) or very enthusiastic (about them)

smock *noun* **1** loose top resembling a long blouse ▷ *verb* **2** to gather (material) by sewing in a honeycomb pattern

smog *noun* mixture of smoke and fog

smoke *noun* **1** cloudy mixture of gas and small particles sent into the air when something burns **2** act of smoking tobacco ▷ *verb* **3** to give off smoke **4** to suck in and blow out smoke from (a cigarette, cigar or pipe) **5** to use cigarettes, cigars or a pipe

habitually **6** to cure (meat, fish or cheese) by treating with smoke > **smoker** *noun: a heavy smoker* > **smoking** *noun*

smoky smokier, smokiest *adjective* full of smoke

smooth *adjective* **1** even and without roughness, holes or lumps **2** without obstructions or difficulties **3** charming and polite but possibly insincere **4** free from jolts **5** not harsh in taste ▷ *verb* **6** to make smooth > **smoothly** *adverb* > **smoothness** *noun*

smoothie *noun* thick drink made from milk, blended fruit and ice

smother *verb* **1** to kill (someone) by covering their mouth and nose so that they cannot breathe **2** to provide (someone with love and protection) to an excessive degree **3** to suppress or stifle (an emotion) **4** to cover (a dish) thickly with something

smothered *adjective* completely covered (in or with something)

smoulder *verb* **1** to burn slowly with smoke but no flame **2** (of feelings) to exist in a suppressed state

smudge *verb* **1** to make or become dirty or messy through contact with something ▷ *noun* **2** dirty or blurred mark

smug smugger, smuggest *adjective* self-satisfied > **smugly** *adverb* > **smugness** *noun*

smuggle *verb* **1** to import or export (goods) secretly and illegally **2** to take (something or someone) somewhere secretly

smuggler *noun* someone who smuggles goods illegally into a country

snack noun light quick meal

snag snags, snagging, snagged noun **1** small problem or disadvantage **2** hole in fabric caused by a sharp object **3** (Aust, NZ informal) sausage ▷ verb **4** to catch or tear (clothing on a point)

snail noun **1** small, slow-moving creature with a long, shiny body and a shell on its back **2 at a snail's pace** at a very slow speed

snail mail noun (informal) conventional post, as opposed to e-mail

snake noun **1** long, thin, scaly reptile without limbs ▷ verb **2** to move in a winding course like a snake

snap snaps, snapping, snapped verb **1** to break suddenly **2** to (cause to) make a sharp cracking sound **3** to bite (at) suddenly **4** to speak sharply and angrily **5** to take a snapshot of ▷ noun **6** act or sound of snapping **7** (informal) snapshot; photo **8** sudden brief spell of cold weather **9** card game in which the word snap is called when two similar cards are put down ▷ adjective **10** (of decision) made on the spur of the moment >**snap up** verb to take eagerly and quickly

snapper noun type of edible fish, found in waters around Australia and New Zealand

snapshot noun photograph taken quickly and casually

snare noun **1** trap for catching birds or small animals involving a noose ▷ verb **2** to catch (an animal or bird) in or as if in a snare

snarl verb **1** (of an animal) to growl with bared teeth **2** to speak or utter fiercely **3** to make tangled

▷ noun **4** act or sound of snarling **5** tangled mess

snatch verb **1** to seize or try to seize suddenly **2** to take (food, rest, etc) hurriedly ▷ noun **3** act of snatching **4** fragment (of conversation or song)

sneak verb **1** to move furtively **2** to bring, take or put furtively **3** (informal) to tell tales ▷ noun **4** someone who reports other people's bad behaviour or naughtiness to those in authority

sneakers plural noun casual shoes with rubber soles

sneaking adjective (of feeling) slight but persistent and a little worrying

sneaky adjective (informal) underhand

sneer noun **1** scornful and contemptuous expression or remark, intended to show your low opinion of someone or something ▷ verb **2** to show contempt for someone or something by giving a sneer

sneeze verb **1** to react to a tickle in the nose by involuntarily letting out air and droplets of water from the nose and mouth suddenly and noisily ▷ noun **2** act or sound of sneezing

snide adjective (of comment, remark) critical in an unfair and nasty way

sniff verb **1** to breathe in through the nose in short breaths that can be heard ▷ verb **2** to smell (something) by sniffing ▷ noun **3** act or sound of sniffing >**sniff at** verb to express contempt for

snigger noun **1** sly, disrespectful laugh, especially one partly stifled ▷ verb **2** to let out a snigger

snip snips, snipping, snipped verb **1** to cut in small quick strokes with scissors or shears ▷ noun **2** (informal) bargain **3** act or sound of snipping

snippet noun (of information, news) small piece

snob noun **1** someone who admires upper-class people and looks down on lower-class people **2** someone who believes that they are better than other people > **snobbery** noun: intellectual snobbery > **snobbish** adjective: snobbish attitudes

snooker noun game played on a large table covered with smooth green cloth. Players score points by hitting different coloured balls into side pockets using a long stick called a cue

snoop (informal) verb **1** to pry ▷ noun **2** act of snooping > **snooper** noun: the ease with which snoopers can obtain personal data about you

snooze (informal) verb **1** to sleep lightly for a short time, especially during the day ▷ noun **2** short light sleep

snore verb **1** to make snorting sounds while sleeping ▷ noun **2** sound of snoring

snorkel snorkels, snorkelling, snorkelled noun **1** tube allowing a swimmer to breathe while face down in water ▷ verb **2** to swim using a snorkel > **snorkelling** noun: We went snorkelling there

snort verb **1** to breathe out noisily through the nostrils **2** to express contempt or anger by snorting ▷ noun **3** act or sound of snorting

snout noun (of an animal) nose and jaws

snow noun **1** flakes of ice crystals which fall from the sky in cold weather ▷ verb **2** to fall as or like snow

snowball noun **1** snow shaped into a ball for throwing ▷ verb **2** to increase rapidly

snowdrift noun deep pile of snow formed by the wind

snowdrop noun small white bell-shaped spring flower

snowman snowmen noun figure shaped out of snow

snub snubs, snubbing, snubbed verb **1** to insult (someone) deliberately, especially by making an insulting remark or by ignoring them ▷ noun **2** deliberate insult ▷ adjective **3** (of a nose) short and turned-up

snuff noun **1** powdered tobacco for sniffing up the nostrils ▷ verb **2** to put out (a candle)

snug adjective **1** warm and comfortable **2** comfortably close-fitting ▷ noun **3** (in Britain and Ireland) small room in a pub > **snugly** adverb

snuggle verb to nestle into a person or thing for warmth or from affection

so adverb **1** to such an extent: Why are you so cruel? **2** very: I'm so tired **3** also; too: He laughed, and so did Jarvis **4** in such a manner: She's a good student and we'd like her to remain so **5** that is the case: Have you locked the car? If so, where were the keys? **6** so much, so many limited: There are only so many questions we can ask **7** so long **a** for a limited time **b** goodbye ▷ *conjunction* **8** therefore **9** (often followed by *that*) **a** in the case that: *He left from work late so that he could talk to the children* **b** with the result that: *We were late leaving so that it was dark when we arrived* **10** so **as to** in order to ▷ *interjection* **11** exclamation of surprise, triumph or realization: *So! You finally made it*

soak *verb* **1** to make (something) thoroughly wet **2** to put (something) in liquid or to lie in liquid so as to become thoroughly wet **3** (of liquid) to go into, permeate or saturate ▷ *noun* **4** soaking > **soak up** *verb* to absorb

soaked *adjective* extremely wet

soaking *adjective* if something is soaking, it is very wet

soap *noun* **1** substance made of natural oils and fats and used for washing **2** (informal) soap opera ▷ *verb* **3** to apply soap to (person, thing) > **soapy** *adjective*

soap opera *noun* radio or television serial dealing with people's daily lives

soar *verb* **1** (of value, price, amount) to increase suddenly **2** to rise or fly upwards > **soaring** *adjective*: *soaring temperatures*

sob sobs, sobbing, sobbed *verb* **1** to cry noisily, with gasps and short breaths **2** to say while sobbing ▷ *noun* **3** act or sound of sobbing

sober *adjective* **1** not drunk **2** serious and thoughtful **3** (of colours) plain and dull ▷ *verb* **4** to make (someone) sober or to become sober > **soberly** *adverb*

> **sober up** *verb* to become sober after being drunk

sobering *adjective* causing you to become serious and thoughtful: *the sobering lesson of the last year*

so-called *adjective* misleadingly called

soccer *noun* football played by two teams of eleven players kicking a ball in an attempt to score goals

sociable *adjective* **1** friendly or companionable **2** (of an occasion) providing companionship > **sociability** *noun*: *man's natural sociability*

social *adjective* **1** relating to society or how it is organized **2** living in a community **3** sociable **4** relating to activities that involve meeting others > **socially** *adverb*

socialism *noun* political system or ideas promoting public ownership of industries, resources and transport > **socialist** *noun, adjective*

socialize or **socialise** *verb* to meet others socially

social security *noun* **1** payments made to the unemployed, elderly or sick by the state **2** system responsible for making such payments

social work *noun* work which involves helping or advising people with serious financial or family problems > **social worker** *noun*

society societies *noun* **1** human beings considered as a group within a particular country or region **2** organization for people who have the same interest or aim: *the school debating society* **3** rich, upper-class or fashionable people collectively **4** companionship

sociology noun study of human societies ▷ **sociological** adjective: *the sociological study of social relations* ▷ **sociologist** noun

sock noun piece of clothing that covers your foot and ankle

socket noun **1** place on a wall or on a piece of electrical equipment into which you can put a plug or bulb **2** hollow part or opening into which another part fits: *eye sockets*

sod noun (literary) surface of the ground, together with the grass and roots growing in it; turf

soda noun **1** soda water **2** sodium in the form of crystals or powder, used for baking or cleaning

soda water noun fizzy drink made from water charged with carbon dioxide

sodden adjective soaked

sodium noun silvery-white chemical element which combines with other chemicals. Salt is a sodium compound

sofa noun padded seat with arms at either end for two or three people to sit on; settee

soft adjective **1** not hard, stiff, firm or rough **2** (of voice, sound) not loud or harsh; quiet **3** (of colour, light) not bright **4** (of a breeze or climate) mild **5** (of person) (too) lenient **6** (of person) weak and easily influenced **7** (of drugs) not liable to cause addiction ▷ **softly** adverb

soft drink noun any cold, nonalcoholic drink

soften verb **1** to make (something) soft or softer or to become soft

or softer **2** (of person) to become more sympathetic and less critical

software noun computer programs

soggy soggier, soggiest adjective unpleasantly wet or full of water

soil noun **1** top layer of earth in which plants grow ▷ verb **2** to make (something) dirty ▷ **soiled** adjective

solace [sol-iss] noun (literary) comfort when sad or distressed

solar adjective **1** relating or belonging to the sun **2** using the energy of the sun

solar system noun the sun and the planets, comets and asteroids that go round it

solder verb **1** to join (two pieces of metal) using molten metal ▷ noun **2** soft metal alloy used to join two metal surfaces

soldier noun **1** member of an army ▷ verb **2** to serve in an army > **soldier on** verb to persist doggedly

sole soles, soling, soled adjective **1** one and only **2** not shared, exclusive ▷ noun **3** underside of your foot or shoe **4** small edible flatfish ▷ verb **5** to put a sole on (a shoe)

solely adverb only, alone

solemn adjective **1** serious, deeply sincere **2** formal > **solemnity** noun: *the solemnity of the occasion* > **solemnly** adverb

solicitor noun (Brit, Aust, NZ) lawyer who gives legal advice to clients and prepares documents and cases

solid adjective **1** (of a substance, object) hard or firm **2** not liquid or gas **3** not hollow **4** of the same substance throughout **5** strong or substantial **6** (of person, firm) sound or reliable **7** whole or without interruption: *I cried for two solid days* ▷ *noun* **8** solid substance or object > **solidity** *noun: The extensive use of wood gives a feeling of solidity* > **solidly** *adverb*

solidarity *noun* unity and mutual support

soliloquy *noun* soliloquies *noun* speech made by a person while alone, especially in a play

solitary *adjective* **1** (of an activity) done alone **2** (of person, animal) used to being alone **3** single, lonely

solitary confinement *noun* the state of being kept alone, without company, in a prison cell; isolation

solitude *noun* state of being alone

solo solos *noun* **1** music for one performer **2** act performed by one person alone ▷ *adjective* **3** done alone: *my first solo flight* ▷ *adverb* **4** by oneself, alone

soloist *noun* musician or dancer who performs a solo

solstice *noun* either the shortest winter day or the longest summer day

soluble *adjective* **1** (of substance) able to be dissolved **2** (of problem) able to be solved > **solubility** *noun*

solution *noun* **1** answer to a problem **2** act of solving a problem **3** liquid in which a solid substance has been dissolved

solve *verb* to find the answer to (a problem)

solvent *adjective* **1** having enough money to pay your debts ▷ *noun* **2** liquid capable of dissolving

other substances > **solvency** *noun* state of having enough money to pay your debts

Somali Somalis *adjective* **1** belonging or relating to Somalia ▷ *noun* **2** person from Somalia **3** language spoken by Somalis

sombre *adjective* **1** (of colour, place) dark, gloomy **2** (of atmosphere) serious, sad or gloomy

some *adjective* **1** a number or quantity of **2** unknown or unspecified **3** a considerable number or amount of **4** (*informal*) remarkable ▷ *pronoun* **5** a number or quantity ▷ *adverb* **6** about or approximately

somebody *pronoun* some person; someone

some day *adverb* at an unknown date in the future

somehow *adverb* in some unspecified way

someone *pronoun* some person; somebody

somersault *noun* **1** forwards or backwards roll in which the head is placed on the ground and the body is brought over it ▷ *verb* **2** to perform a somersault

something *pronoun* **1** unknown or unspecified thing **2** impressive or important thing

sometime *adverb* **1** at some unspecified time ▷ *adjective* **2** former

sometimes *adverb* from time to time, now and then; occasionally

somewhat *adverb* to some extent, rather

somewhere *adverb* **1** in, to or at some unspecified or unknown place **2** some time, some number or some quantity: *somewhere between the winter of 1999 and the summer of 2004*

son *noun* male child

sonar *noun* device for calculating the depth of the sea or the position of an underwater object using sound waves

sonata *noun* piece of music, usually in three or more movements, for the piano or another instrument with or without piano

song *noun* **1** music with words that are sung to the music **2** tuneful sound made by certain birds **3 for a song** very cheaply

songbird *noun* any bird with a musical call

son-in-law sons-in-law *noun* daughter's husband

sonnet *noun* poem consisting of 14 lines with a fixed rhyme scheme

soon *adverb* in a short time

soot *noun* black powder that rises in the smoke from a fire > **sooty** *adjective*: *a black sooty substance*

soothe *verb* **1** to make (someone) calm **2** to relieve (pain etc) > **soothing** *adjective*: *soothing music*

sophisticated *adjective* **1** (of person) having refined or cultured tastes or habits **2** (of machine, device) made using advanced and complicated methods; complex > **sophistication** *noun*: *the sophistication of communications technology*

soppy soppier, soppiest *adjective* (*informal*) too sentimental

soprano sopranos *noun* **1** (singer with) the highest female or boy's voice **2** highest pitched of a family of instruments

sorcerer *noun* magician

sorceress *noun* female sorcerer

sorcery *noun* witchcraft or black magic

sordid *adjective* **1** dishonest or immoral **2** dirty or squalid

sore *adjective* **1** painful **2** resentful **3** (of need) urgent ▷ *noun* **4** painful place where your skin has become infected > **sorely** *adverb* greatly: *She will be sorely missed* > **soreness** *noun*: *Bleeding and soreness can follow*

sorghum *noun* kind of grass cultivated for grain

sorrow *noun* **1** grief or sadness **2** cause of sorrow

sorry sorrier, sorriest *adjective* **1** feeling sadness, sympathy or regret **2** pitiful or wretched

sort *noun* **1** group sharing certain qualities or characteristics; kind; type **2 out of sorts** slightly unwell or bad-tempered ▷ *verb* **3** to arrange into different groups according to kind **4** to mend, fix or solve

> **WORD TIP**
> When you use *sort* in its singular form, the adjective before it should also be singular: *that sort of car*. When you use the plural form *sorts*, the adjective before it should be plural: *those sorts of shops*

SOS *noun* signal that you are in danger and need help

so-so *adjective* (*informal*) neither good nor bad; mediocre

soufflé [soo-flay] or **souffle** *noun* light fluffy dish made with beaten egg whites and other ingredients and baked in the oven

sought [sawt] *verb* past of **seek**

soul *noun* **1** spiritual part of a human being believed by many to be immortal **2** essential part or fundamental nature **3** deep and sincere feelings **4** person regarded as typifying some quality: *Sonia was the soul of patience* **5** person: *There was not a soul there* **6** type of music combining blues, pop and gospel

sound *noun* **1** something heard; noise **2** everything heard **3** impression formed from hearing about someone or something: *I like the sound of your aunt* **4** channel or strait ▷ *verb* **5** to make a sound or cause (something) to make a sound **6** to seem to be as specified **7** to pronounce **8** to find the depth of (water etc) **9** to examine: *Sonia* (the body, heart etc) by tapping or with a stethoscope **10** to find out the views of ▷ *adjective* **11** in good condition **12** firm, substantial **13** financially reliable **14** showing good judgment **15** ethically correct **16** (of sleep) deep **17** thorough > **soundly** *adverb*: *to sleep soundly*

sound bite *noun* short, memorable sentence or phrase extracted from a longer speech, especially by a politician, for use on television or radio

sound effect *noun* sounds created artificially to make a play more realistic, especially a radio play

soundproof *adjective* **1** (of room) not penetrable by sound

▷ *verb* **2** to make (something) soundproof

soundtrack *noun* the part of a film that you hear

soup *noun* liquid food made from meat, vegetables, etc and water

sour *adjective* **1** sharp-tasting; acid **2** (of milk) gone bad **3** (of a person's temperament) bad-tempered and unfriendly ▷ *verb* **4** to make (something) sour or to become sour

source *noun* **1** origin or starting point **2** person, book, etc providing information **3** spring where a river or stream begins

> **WORD TIP**
> Do not confuse the spellings of *source* and *sauce*

sour grapes *plural noun* scornful remark or action that is born of envy

south *noun* **1** direction towards the South Pole, opposite north **2** area lying in or towards the south ▷ *adjective* **3** to or in the south **4** (of a wind) from the south ▷ *adverb* **5** in, to or towards the south

South America *noun* fourth largest continent, having the Pacific Ocean on its west side, the Atlantic on its east side and the Antarctic to the south. South America is joined to North America by the Isthmus of Panama > **South American** *adjective*

south-east *noun, adverb, adjective* halfway between south and east

south-easterly *adjective* **1** to or towards the south-east **2** (of wind) from the south-east

south-eastern adjective in or from the south-east

southerly adjective 1 to or towards the south 2 (of wind) from the south

southern adjective in or from the south > **southerner** noun person from the south of a country or area

Southern Cross noun group of stars which can be seen from the southern part of the earth, and which is represented on the national flags of Australia and New Zealand

South Pole noun southernmost point of the earth

southward adjective 1 towards the south ▷ adverb 2 towards the south

south-west noun, adverb, adjective halfway between south and west

south-westerly adjective 1 to or towards the south-west 2 (of wind) from the south-west

south-western adjective in or from the south-west

souvenir noun keepsake, memento

sovereign noun 1 king, queen or other royal ruler of a country 2 former British gold coin worth one pound ▷ adjective 3 (of a state) independent

sovereignty [sov-rin-tee] noun political power that a country has to govern itself

Soviet adjective belonging or relating to the country that used to be the Soviet Union

sow¹ sows, sowing, sowed, sown [rhymes with **know**] verb 1 to scatter or plant (seed) 2 to plant seed in (the ground) 3 to implant or introduce (undesirable feelings or attitudes)

sow² [rhymes with **cow**] noun female adult pig

soya noun plant whose edible bean (soya bean) is used for food and as a source of oil

soya bean noun type of edible Asian bean

spa noun resort with a mineral-water spring

space noun 1 unlimited expanse in which all objects exist and move 2 interval 3 blank portion 4 unoccupied area 5 the universe beyond the earth's atmosphere ▷ verb 6 to place (a series of things) at intervals

spacecraft noun vehicle for travel beyond the earth's atmosphere

spaceman spacemen noun someone who travels in space

spaceship noun a spacecraft that carries people through space

space shuttle noun vehicle for repeated space flights

spacious adjective having or providing a lot of space; roomy

spade noun 1 tool for digging 2 playing card of the suit marked with black leaf-shaped symbols

spaghetti noun long, thin pieces of pasta

spam verb spamming, spammed 1 to send unsolicited e-mail or text messages to multiple recipients ▷ noun 2 unsolicited e-mail or text messages sent in this way

span spans, spanning, spanned noun 1 the period of time between two dates or events during which something exists or functions 2 distance between two extreme points (of something) 3 distance from thumb to little finger of the expanded hand ▷ *verb* **4** to last throughout (a period of time) **5** (of bridge) to stretch across (a river, valley)

spangle *noun* **1** small, sparkling piece of metal or plastic used to decorate clothing or hair ▷ *verb* **2** to decorate with spangles

Spaniard [**span**-yard] *noun* someone from Spain

spaniel *noun* type of dog with long ears and silky hair

Spanish *adjective* **1** belonging or relating to Spain ▷ *noun* **2** main language spoken in Spain, also spoken by many people in Central and South America ▷ *plural noun* **3 the Spanish** the people of Spain

spank *verb* to slap with the open hand, on the buttocks or legs

spanner *noun* tool for gripping and turning a nut or bolt

spar *spars, sparring, sparred verb* **1** to box or fight using light blows for practice **2** to argue (with someone) ▷ *noun* **3** pole that a sail is attached to on a ship or yacht

spare *adjective* **1** extra **2** in reserve **3** (of time) free ▷ *noun* **4** duplicate kept in case of damage or loss ▷ *verb* **5** to refrain from punishing or harming (someone) **6** to save (someone) from (something unpleasant) **7** to afford to give

sparing *adjective* economical >**sparingly** *adverb*

spark *noun* **1** tiny, bright piece of burning material thrown out from a fire **2** fiery particle caused by friction **3** flash of light caused by electricity **4** trace or hint (of a particular quality) ▷ *verb* **5** to give

off sparks >**spark off** *verb* to set off or give rise to

sparkle *verb* **1** to glitter with lots of small, bright points of light **2** to be lively, intelligent and witty ▷ *noun* **3** sparkling point of light **4** vivacity or wit >**sparkling** *adjective* **1** (of wine or mineral water) slightly fizzy **2** glittering

sparrow *noun* common, small bird with brown and grey feathers

sparse *adjective* thinly scattered or spread >**sparsely** *adverb*: sparsely populated areas

spartan *adjective* simple and without luxuries; austere

spasm *noun* **1** involuntary muscular contraction **2** sudden burst of activity or feeling

spasmodic *adjective* occurring for short periods of time or at irregular intervals >**spasmodically** *adverb*

spate *noun* large number of things happening within a short period of time

spatial *adjective* of or in space

spatter *verb* **1** to scatter or be scattered in drops over (something) ▷ *noun* **2** something spattered in drops

spawn *noun* **1** jelly-like mass containing the eggs of fish or amphibians such as frogs ▷ *verb* **2** (of fish, frogs) to lay eggs **3** to give rise to

speak *speaks, speaking, spoke, spoken verb* **1** to say words; talk **2** to give a speech or lecture **3** to know how to talk in (a specified language) **4** to communicate or express in words >**speak out** *verb* to publicly state an opinion

speaker noun 1 person who speaks, especially at a formal occasion 2 loudspeaker 3 **Speaker** (in Parliament) the official chairperson whose role is to control proceedings

speakerphone noun telephone with a microphone and loudspeaker allowing more than one person to participate in a call

spear noun 1 weapon consisting of a long shaft with a sharp point 2 slender shoot ▷ verb 3 to pierce with a spear or other pointed object

spearhead verb to lead (an attack or campaign)

spec noun **on spec** (informal) as a risk or gamble

special adjective 1 distinguished from others of its kind 2 for a specific purpose 3 exceptional 4 particular

specialist noun 1 expert in a particular activity or subject ▷ adjective 2 having a skill or knowing a lot about a particular subject > **specialism** noun

speciality noun 1 special interest or skill 2 product specialized in

specialize or **specialise** verb to be a specialist > **specialization** noun: Farmers began to abandon mixed farms in favour of greater specialization

specialized or **specialised** adjective developed for a particular purpose or trained in a particular area of knowledge

specially adverb particularly

species noun group of plants or animals that are related closely enough to interbreed naturally

WORD TIP
The plural of species is species

specific adjective particular > **specifically** adverb

specification noun detailed description of something to be made or done

specify specifies, specifying, specified verb to refer to or state specifically

specimen noun 1 example or small sample (of something) that gives an idea of what the whole is like 2 sample of urine, blood, etc taken for analysis

speck noun small spot or particle

speckled adjective covered in small marks or spots

spectacle noun 1 strange, interesting or ridiculous sight 2 impressive public show

spectacular adjective impressive > **spectacularly** adverb

spectator noun person watching something; onlooker

spectra the plural of **spectrum**

spectre noun 1 ghost 2 frightening idea or image

spectrum spectra or spectrums noun 1 range of colours found in a rainbow and produced when light passes through a prism or a drop of water 2 range (of opinions, emotions) 3 entire range of anything

speculate verb 1 to weigh up and make guesses about something 2 to buy property, shares, etc in the hope of selling them at a profit > **speculation** noun

speculative adjective 1 based on guesses and opinions rather than known facts 2 (of expression) suggesting that the person

a b c d e f g h i j k l m n o p q r s t u v w x y z

concerned is weighing up and making guesses about something

speech noun **1** ability to speak **2** act or manner of speaking **3** talk given to an audience **4** group of lines spoken by one of the characters in a play **5** language or dialect

speechless adjective unable to speak because of great emotion

speed speeds, speeding, sped or speeded noun **1** fast movement or travel; swiftness; rapidity **2** rate at which something moves or happens; velocity ▷ verb **3** to go quickly **4** to drive faster than the legal limit > **speed up** verb to accelerate

speedboat noun light fast motorboat

speed limit noun maximum speed at which vehicles are legally allowed to drive on a particular road

speedway noun **1** track for motorcycle racing **2** (US, Canadian, NZ) track for motor racing

speedy speedier, speediest adjective rapid > **speedily** adverb

spell spells, spelling, spelt or spelled verb **1** to provide the letters that form (a word) in the correct order **2** (of letters) to make up (a word) **3** to indicate or suggest: This method could spell disaster ▷ noun **4** a word or sequence of words used to perform magic **5** effect of a spell **6** period of time of weather or activity > **spell out** verb to explain in detail

spellbound adjective so fascinated by something that you cannot think about anything else

spelling noun **1** way a word is spelt **2** person's ability to spell

spend spends, spending, spent verb **1** to pay out (money) **2** to use or pass (time) **3** to use up (energy)

spent adjective used: spent matches

sperm sperms or sperm noun cell produced in the sex organ of a male animal which can enter a female animal's egg and fertilize it

spew verb to come out or to send (something) out in a stream > **spew up** verb (informal) to vomit

sphere noun **1** perfectly round solid object **2** field of activity or interest > **spherical** adjective round

sphinx sphinxes noun monster with a lion's body and a human head

spice noun **1** powder or seeds from a plant added to food to give it flavour **2** something which makes life more exciting ▷ verb **3** to flavour with spices > **spice up** verb to make (something) more exciting

spicy spicier, spiciest adjective strongly flavoured with spices

spider noun small eight-legged creature which spins a web to catch insects for food

spike noun **1** sharp point **2** sharp pointed metal object **3** spikes sports shoes with spikes for greater grip ▷ verb **4** to pierce or fasten with a spike **5** to add alcohol to (a drink)

spiky spikier, spikiest adjective having sharp points

spill spills, spilling, spilled or spilt verb **1** to allow (something) accidentally to pour out of something **2** to pour from or as if from a container **3** (*informal*) to give away a secret

spillage *noun* the spilling of something, or something that has been spilt

spin spins, spinning, spun *verb* **1** to turn quickly or to cause (something) to turn quickly round a central point **2** to make thread or yarn by twisting together fibres using a spinning machine or spinning wheel **3** (of spiders) to make (a web) **4** (*informal*) to present information in a way that creates a favourable impression ▷ *noun* **5** a rapid turning motion around a central point **6** continuous spiral descent of an aircraft **7** (*informal*) short drive for pleasure **8** (*informal*) presentation of information in a way that creates a favourable impression **> spin out** *verb* to make (something) last an unusually long time; to prolong

spinach *noun* dark green leafy vegetable

spinal *adjective* relating to your spine

spine *noun* **1** backbone **2** edge of a book on which the title is printed **3** sharp point on an animal or plant

spinifex *noun* coarse spiny Australian grass

spinning wheel *noun* a wooden machine for spinning flax or wool

spin-off *noun* unexpected benefit

spinster *noun* woman who has never married

spiny *adjective* covered with spines

spiral spirals, spiralling, spiralled *noun* **1** something that forms a continuous curve winding round and round a central point so that a circle of increasingly bigger loops winds out from the middle or else a tubular shape is formed consisting of loops above loops **2** steadily accelerating increase or decrease ▷ *adjective* **3** in the shape of a spiral ▷ *verb* **4** to move in a spiral **5** to increase or decrease with steady acceleration

spire *noun* pointed part of at the top of some church towers

spirit *noun* **1** nonphysical part of a person connected with your deepest thoughts and feelings **2** nonphysical part of a person believed to live on after death **3** supernatural being; ghost **4** courage and liveliness **5** essential meaning as opposed to literal interpretation **6** liquid obtained by distillation **7** **spirits** emotional state ▷ *verb* **8** (usually followed by *away, off*) to carry (something or someone) away mysteriously

spirited *adjective* lively and courageous

spirit level *noun* glass tube containing a bubble in liquid, used to check whether a surface is level

spiritual *adjective* **1** relating to the spirit **2** relating to sacred things ▷ *noun* **3** type of religious folk song originating among Black slaves in America **> spirituality** *noun*: *People still want spirituality in their lives* **> spiritually** *adverb*

spit spits, spitting, spat *verb* **1** to eject (saliva or food) from the mouth **2** to rain slightly ▷ *noun* **3** saliva **4** sharp rod on which meat is skewered for roasting

spite noun **1** deliberate nastiness; malice **2 in spite of** in defiance of or regardless of ▷ verb **3 to spite** to annoy or hurt (someone) from spite

spiteful adjective deliberately nasty; malicious

spitting image noun (informal) person who looks very like another

splash verb **1** to scatter liquid on (something) **2** to scatter (liquid) in drops **3** (of liquid) to be scattered in drops **4** to print (a story or photograph) prominently in a newspaper ▷ noun **5** splashing sound **6** small amount (of liquid) **7** contrastive patch (of colour or light) **8** extravagant display **9** small amount of liquid added to a drink ▷ **splash out** verb (informal) to spend extravagantly

splatter verb **1** to splash ▷ noun **2** splash

spleen noun **1** organ near your stomach that filters bacteria from the blood

splendid adjective **1** excellent **2** beautiful and impressive ▷ **splendidly** adverb

splendour noun quality of being beautiful and impressive

splint noun long piece of wood or metal used as support for a broken bone

splinter noun **1** thin sharp piece broken off, especially from wood ▷ verb **2** to break into fragments

split splits, splitting, split verb **1** to break into separate pieces **2** to separate **3** to tear or crack **4** to share (something) ▷ noun **5** crack, tear or division caused by splitting

6 splits act of sitting with the legs outstretched in opposite directions ▷ **split up** verb to end a relationship or marriage

split second noun extremely short period of time

splitting adjective (of headache) very painful

splutter verb **1** to speak in a confused way because of embarrassment **2** to make hissing or spitting sounds

spoil spoils, spoiling, spoiled or spoilt verb **1** to damage **2** to harm the character of (a child) by giving or pampering them too much **3** to treat (someone) **4** to rot, go bad

spoilsport noun person who spoils people's fun

spoke verb **1** past tense of **speak** ▷ noun **2** bar joining the hub of a wheel to the rim

spokesperson noun person chosen to speak on behalf of a group ▷ **spokesman** noun ▷ **spokeswoman** noun

sponge noun **1** sea animal with a porous absorbent skeleton **2** part of the very light skeleton of a sponge, or something resembling it, used for washing and cleaning **3** type of light cake ▷ verb **4** to wipe (something) with a sponge **5** (followed by off, on) to live at the expense of (others)

sponsor verb **1** to provide financial support for (an event or training) **2** to agree to pay a sum to (a charity fund-raiser) if they successfully complete an activity **3** to put forward and support (a proposal or suggestion) ▷ noun **4** person or organization sponsoring something or someone > **sponsorship** noun: He also received corporate sponsorship from big business

spontaneous adjective 1 not planned or arranged 2 occurring through natural processes without outside influence > **spontaneity** noun ability to act without planning or prior arrangement > **spontaneously** adverb

spoof noun mildly satirical parody

spooky spookier, spookiest adjective eerie and frightening

spool noun cylindrical object onto which thread, tape or film can be wound

spoon noun 1 object shaped like a small shallow bowl with a long handle, used for eating, stirring and serving food ▷ verb 2 to lift (something) with a spoon

spoonful spoonfuls or spoonsful noun the amount held by a spoon

sporadic adjective happening at irregular intervals > **sporadically** adverb

spore noun (technical) minute reproductive body of some plants and bacteria

sporran noun pouch worn in front of a kilt

sport noun 1 any activity for pleasure, competition or exercise requiring physical effort and skill 2 such activities collectively 3 enjoyment 4 person who reacts cheerfully ▷ verb 5 to wear proudly

sporting adjective 1 relating to sport 2 behaving in a fair and decent way 3 **a sporting chance** reasonable chance of success

sports car noun fast low-built car, usually open-topped

sportsman sportsmen (feminine **sportswoman**) sportswomen noun person who plays sports > **sportsmanship** noun PE behaviour and attitudes of a good sportsman, esp. fairness, generosity, and cheerfulness when losing

sporty sportier, sportiest adjective 1 (of car) fast and flashy 2 (of person) good at sports

spot spots, spotting, spotted noun 1 small, round, coloured area on a surface 2 small lump on your skin, caused by infection or allergy; pimple 3 place or location 4 (informal) small quantity 5 (on television show) part regularly reserved for a particular performer or type of entertainment 6 **on the spot** a at the place in question b immediately c in an awkward predicament ▷ verb 7 to notice

spot check noun random examination

spotless adjective absolutely clean > **spotlessly** adverb

spotlight spotlights, spotlighting, spotlit or spotlighted noun 1 powerful light which can be directed to light up a small area ▷ verb 2 to draw the public's attention to (a situation or problem)

spot-on adjective (informal) absolutely accurate

spotted adjective having a pattern of spots

spotter noun person whose hobby is watching for things of a particular kind: a train spotter

spotty spottier, spottiest *adjective* with spots

spouse *noun* husband or wife

spout *verb* 1 to pour out in a stream or jet 2 (*informal*) to utter (a stream of words) lengthily ▷ *noun* 3 tube with a lip-like end for pouring liquid 4 stream or jet of liquid

sprain *verb* 1 to injure (a joint) by a sudden twist ▷ *noun* 2 such an injury

sprawl *verb* 1 to lie or sit with your legs and arms spread out 2 (of a place) to spread out in a straggling manner ▷ *noun* 3 something that has spread untidily over a large area > **sprawling** *adjective: a sprawling city*

spray *noun* 1 fine drops of liquid splashed or forced into the air 2 liquid kept under pressure in a can or other container 3 piece of equipment for spraying liquid 4 branch with buds, leaves, flowers or berries on it ▷ *verb* 5 to scatter in fine drops 6 to cover with a spray

spread spreads, spreading, spread *verb* 1 to open (something) out or to arrange (something) so that all or most of it can be seen easily 2 to stretch out 3 to put a thin layer of (a substance or coating) on a surface 4 to reach or affect a wider and wider area 5 to distribute (something) evenly ▷ *noun* 6 extent reached or distribution (of something) 7 wide variety 8 (*informal*) large meal 9 soft food which can be put on bread, biscuits, etc

spread-eagled *adjective* with arms and legs outstretched

spreadsheet *noun* computer program for entering and arranging figures and sums

spree *noun* period of time spent doing something enjoyable to excess: *a shopping spree*

sprig *noun* 1 twig or shoot 2 (*Aust, NZ*) stud on the sole of a soccer or rugby boot

sprightly sprightlier, sprightliest *adjective* lively and active

spring springs, springing, sprang, sprung *noun* 1 season between winter and summer 2 coil of wire which returns to its natural shape after being pressed or pulled 3 place where water comes up through the ground 4 jump 5 elasticity; bounce ▷ *verb* 6 to move suddenly upwards or forwards in a single motion; jump 7 to move suddenly and quickly 8 to result or originate (from) 9 (followed by *on*) to give a surprising piece of news, task) to (someone)

springboard *noun* 1 flexible board on which a diver or gymnast jumps to gain height 2 something that provides a helpful starting point (for an activity or enterprise)

springbok *noun* 1 S African antelope 2 person who has represented South Africa in a sports team

spring-clean *verb* to clean (a house) thoroughly

spring onion *noun* small onion with long green shoots, often eaten raw in salads

sprinkle verb to scatter (liquid or powder) in tiny drops or particles over (something)

sprinkling noun small quantity or number

sprint noun 1 short fast race 2 fast run ▷ verb 3 to run a short distance at top speed

sprinter noun athlete who runs fast over short distances

sprite noun type of fairy; elf

sprout verb 1 to produce shoots 2 to begin to grow or develop 3 (followed by up) to appear rapidly ▷ noun 4 short for Brussels sprout

spruce noun 1 kind of fir tree ▷ adjective 2 neat and smart ▷ verb 3 spruce up to make neat and smart

spunk noun (informal) 1 (old-fashioned) courage, spirit 2 (Aust, NZ) good-looking person

spur spurs, spurring, spurred verb 1 to urge on, incite (someone) ▷ noun 2 encouragement or incentive; stimulus 3 spiked wheel on the heel of a rider's boot used to urge on a horse 4 ridge sticking out from a mountain or hillside 5 on the spur of the moment on impulse

spurious adjective not genuine or real

spurn verb to refuse to accept; reject

spurt verb 1 to gush out in a jet ▷ noun 2 sudden gush 3 short sudden burst of activity or speed

spy spies, spying, spied noun 1 person employed to obtain secret information 2 person who secretly watches others ▷ verb 3 to act as a spy 4 to catch sight of

squabble verb 1 to quarrel about something trivial ▷ noun 2 a quarrel

squad noun small group of people working or training together

squadron noun section of one of the armed forces, especially the air force

squalid adjective 1 dirty and unpleasant 2 unpleasant, unwholesome and perhaps dishonest; sordid

squall noun 1 sudden strong wind ▷ verb 2 to cry noisily, yell

squalor noun bad or dirty conditions or surroundings

squander verb to waste (money or resources)

square noun 1 shape with four equal sides and four right angles 2 flat open area in a town, bordered by buildings or streets 3 product of a number multiplied by itself ▷ adjective 4 square in shape 5 in area: 10 million square feet of office space 6 in length on each side: a towel measuring a foot square 7 straight or level 8 with all accounts or debts settled ▷ verb 9 to multiply (a number) by itself 10 to make (something) square ▷ adverb 11 squarely, directly

squarely adverb 1 in a direct way 2 in an honest and frank manner

square root noun number of which a given number is the square

squash squashes, squashing, squashed verb 1 to crush (something) flat 2 to stop (a difficult or troubling situation) often by force; suppress 3 to push into a confined space 4 to humiliate (someone) with a crushing reply ▷ *noun* **5** sweet fruit drink diluted with water **6** crowd of people in a confined space **7** game played in an enclosed court with a rubber ball and long-handled rackets **8** marrow-like vegetable

squat squats, squatting, squatted; squatter, squattest *verb* **1** to crouch with your knees bent and the weight on your feet **2** to live in unused premises without any legal right to do so ▷ *noun* **3** place where squatters live ▷ *adjective* **4** short and broad

squatter *noun* **1** person who lives in unused premises without permission and without paying rent **2** (*Aust, NZ*) someone who owns a large amount of land for sheep or cattle farming **b** (*History*) someone who rented land from the King or Queen

squawk *noun* **1** (of a bird) loud harsh cry ▷ *verb* **2** (of a bird) to make a squawking noise

squeak *verb* **1** to give a short, high-pitched sound or cry ▷ *noun* **2** short, high-pitched sound or cry >**squeaky** *adjective: squeaky floorboards*

squeal *verb* **1** to give a long, high-pitched cry or sound **2** (*informal*) to inform on someone to the police ▷ *noun* **3** long high-pitched cry or sound

squeamish *adjective* easily upset by unpleasant sights or situations

squeeze *verb* **1** to grip or press firmly **2** to crush or press to extract liquid **3** to push into a confined space **4** to get (something) out of someone) by force or great effort ▷ *noun* **5** act of squeezing **6** tight fit

squelch *verb* **1** to make a wet, sucking sound, as when walking through mud ▷ *noun* **2** wet, sucking sound

squid *noun* sea creature with a long soft body and ten tentacles

squiggle *noun* wavy line >**squiggly** *adjective: a squiggly line*

squint *verb* **1** to look at something with your eyes screwed up **2** to have eyes that look in different or slightly different directions ▷ *noun* **3** eye condition in which your eyes look in different or slightly different directions

squire *noun* **1** country gentleman, usually the main landowner in a community **2** (*History*) knight's apprentice

squirm *verb* **1** to wriggle, writhe **2** to feel embarrassed

squirrel *noun* small furry animal with a bushy tail that lives in trees

squirt *verb* **1** to force (a liquid) out of a narrow opening **2** (of a liquid) to be forced out of a narrow opening ▷ *noun* **3** jet of liquid

Sri Lankan [sree-**lang**-kan] *adjective* **1** belonging or relating to Sri Lanka ▷ *noun* **2** someone from Sri Lanka

stab stabs, stabbing, stabbed *verb* **1** to push a knife or something pointed into the body of (someone) **2** to jab (at) **3 stab in the back** to behave treacherously towards (someone) ▷ *noun* **4** act of stabbing **5** sudden unpleasant sensation **6** (*informal*) attempt

stable *noun* **1** building in which horses are kept **2** establishment that breeds and trains racehorses

3 establishment that manages or trains several entertainers or athletes ▷ *adjective* **4** firmly fixed or established **5** firm in character **6** (*Science*) not subject to decay or decomposition > **stability** *noun: a time of political stability*

staccato [stak-**ah**-toe] *adjective* consisting of short abrupt sounds

stack *noun* **1** pile **2** stacks large amount ▷ *verb* **3** to pile in a stack

stadium stadiums or stadia *noun* sports ground surrounded by rows of tiered seats

staff *noun* **1** people employed in an organization ▷ *verb* **2** to provide the personnel for (an organization)

stag *noun* adult male deer

stage *noun* **1** step or period of development **2** portion of a journey **3** platform in a theatre where actors or entertainers perform **4 the stage** theatre as a profession ▷ *verb* **5** to put (a play) on stage **6** to organize and carry out (an event)

stagecoach *noun* large horse-drawn vehicle formerly used to carry passengers and mail

stagger *verb* **1** to walk unsteadily **2** to astound (someone) **3** to set (events) apart to avoid them happening at the same time > **staggered** *adjective: I was absolutely staggered and amazed* > **staggering** *adjective: The results have been quite staggering*

stagnant *adjective* (of water or air) stale from not moving

stag night *noun* party for a man who is about to get married, which only men go to

staid *adjective* serious and rather dull

stain *noun* **1** mark that is difficult to remove ▷ *verb* **2** to mark; discolour **3** to colour with a special kind of dye

stained glass *noun* coloured pieces of glass held together with strips of lead

stainless steel *noun* metal made from steel and chromium that does not rust

stair *noun* one of a flight of steps between floors

staircase *noun* flight of stairs with a handrail or banisters

stairway *noun* flight of stairs with a handrail or banisters

stake *noun* **1** pointed wooden post that can be hammered into the ground as a support or marker **2** money wagered **3** interest, usually financial, held in something **4 at stake** being risked ▷ *verb* **5** to support or mark out with stakes **6** to risk; wager **7 stake a claim to** to claim a right to > **stake out** *verb* (*informal*) (of police) to keep (a place) under surveillance

stale *adjective* **1** (of food, air) not fresh **2** (of person) lacking energy or ideas through overwork or monotony

stalemate *noun* **1** situation in which neither side in an argument or contest can win; deadlock **2** (*Chess*) position in which any of a player's moves would put his king in check and which results in a draw

stalk *noun* **1** plant's stem ▷ *verb* **2** to follow or approach stealthily **3** to pursue persistently and, sometimes, attack (a person with whom one is obsessed) **4** to walk in a stiff or haughty manner

stall noun **1** large table for the display and sale of goods ▷ plural noun **2** stalls ground-floor seats in a theatre or cinema ▷ verb **3** (of a motor vehicle or engine) to stop accidentally **4** to employ delaying tactics

stallion noun adult male horse that can be used for breeding

stamina noun enduring energy and strength

stammer verb **1** to speak or say with involuntary pauses or repetition of syllables ▷ noun **2** tendency to stammer

stamp noun **1** piece of gummed paper stuck to an envelope or parcel to show that the postage has been paid **2** small block with a pattern cut into it, which you press onto an inky pad to print a pattern or mark; also the mark made by the stamp **3** characteristic feature **4** act of bringing your foot down hard on the ground ▷ verb **5** to bring (your foot) down hard on the ground **6** to walk with heavy footsteps **7** to impress (a pattern or mark) on (something) or to mark (something) with (a pattern or mark) **8** to stick a postage stamp on > **stamp out** verb to put an end to (something) by force

stampede noun **1** sudden rush of frightened animals or of a crowd ▷ verb **2** to run or to cause to run in a wild, uncontrolled way

stance noun **1** attitude **2** manner of standing

stand stands, standing, stood verb **1** to be upright or to rise to an upright position **2** to be situated **3** to place (something) in an upright position **4** to be in a specified state or position **5** to remain unchanged or valid **6** to tolerate or bear **7** to offer oneself as a candidate **8** (informal) to treat (someone) to (something) **9** stand trial to be tried in a court of law ▷ noun **10** stall for the sale of goods **11** structure for spectators at a sports ground **12** firmly held opinion **13** (US, Aust) witness box **14** rack or piece of furniture on which things may be placed > **stand by** verb **1** to support (someone) **2** to remain with or stick to (a decision, promise) **3** to be ready and available (to do something) **4** to look on without taking any action > **stand down** verb to resign (from your job or position) > **stand for** verb **1** to represent or mean **2** (informal) to tolerate or put up with > **stand in** verb (usually followed by for) to act as a temporary replacement or substitute (for someone) > **stand out** verb to be very noticeable or to be better or more important than other similar things or people > **stand up** verb **1** stand up to **a** to remain undamaged by (rough treatment); withstand **b** to confront or challenge (a bully) **2** stand up for to support or defend (someone)

standard noun **1** level of quality **2** example against which others are judged or measured **3** moral principle **4** distinctive flag

5 upright pole ▷ adjective **6** usual, regular or average **7** accepted as correct

standard English noun form of English taught in schools, used in text books and broadsheet newspapers and spoken and written by most educated people

standardize or **standardise** verb to cause to conform to a standard ▷ **standardization** noun

stand-by noun **1** something available for use when you need it: *a useful stand-by* ▷ adjective **2** (of ticket) made available at the last minute if there are any seats left

stand-in noun substitute

standing adjective **1** permanent or regular ▷ noun **2** reputation or status **3** duration: *a friend of 20 years' standing*

standpoint noun point of view

standstill noun complete stop

stanza noun verse of a poem

staple noun **1** small, thin piece of wire or metal bent so that the two ends form prongs capable of piercing papers, carpets and other materials and fired into place using a stapler or staplegun ▷ verb **2** to fasten with staples ▷ adjective **3** (of food) forming a regular and basic part of someone's everyday diet

star stars, starring, starred noun **1** large ball of burning gas in space that appears as a point of light in the sky at night **2** shape with four, five, six or more points sticking out in a regular pattern **3** asterisk **4** famous actor, sports player or musician **5** stars astrological forecast, horoscope ▷ verb **6** (of

actor, entertainer) to be a star (in a film or show) **7** (of film, show) to have (someone) as a star ▷ adjective **8** leading, famous

starboard noun **1** right-hand side of a ship, when facing forward ▷ adjective **2** of or on this side

starch noun **1** substance used for stiffening fabric such as cotton or linen **2** carbohydrate found in foods such as bread or potatoes ▷ verb **3** to stiffen (fabric) with starch

stare verb **1** to look or gaze fixedly (at someone or something) ▷ noun **2** fixed gaze

starfish starfishes or starfish noun a flat, star-shaped sea creature with five limbs

stark adjective **1** harsh, unpleasant and plain ▷ adverb **2** absolute **3** stark naked completely naked

starling noun songbird with glossy dark speckled feathers

start verb **1** to begin **2** to set (something) in motion or to be set in motion **3** to make a sudden involuntary movement from fright **4** to establish or set up ▷ noun **5** first part of something; beginning **6** place or time of starting **7** advantage or lead in a competitive activity **8** sudden movement made from fright

starter noun **1** first course of a meal **2** device for starting a car's engine

startle verb to surprise or frighten a little ▷ **startled** adjective: *a startled rabbit* ▷ **startling** adjective: *a startling revelation*

starve verb **1** to die or suffer as a result of hunger **2** to prevent (a person or animal) from having around **3** to deprive (someone) of something needed **4** (*informal*) to be hungry **5 to be starved of** to suffer through lack of (money, affection, etc) ▷ **starvation** noun: *people dying from starvation*

stash (*informal*) verb **1** to store (something) in a secret place ▷ noun **2** secret store

state noun **1** condition of a person or thing **2** country **3** region with its own government **4** the government **5 in a state** (*informal*) in an excited or agitated condition ▷ adjective **6** of or concerning the government **7** (of ceremony) involving the ruler or leader of the country ▷ verb **8** to express in words

state house noun (*NZ*) publicly-owned house rented to a low-income tenant

stately home noun (*Brit*) very large old house which belongs or once belonged to an upper-class family

statement noun **1** something you say or write when you give facts or information in a formal way **2** printed financial account

state school noun school maintained and funded by the government or a local authority providing free education

statesman statesmen noun experienced and respected political leader

static adjective **1** never moving or changing: *The temperature remained fairly static* **2** electrical charge caused by friction. It builds up in metal objects

station noun **1** place where trains stop for passengers **2 bus station, coach station** place where some buses start their journeys **3** headquarters or local offices of the police or a fire brigade **4** building with special equipment for a particular purpose: *power station* **5** television or radio channel **6** (*old-fashioned*) position in society **7** large Australian sheep or cattle property ▷ verb **8** to send (someone) to a particular place to work or do a particular job

stationary adjective not moving

stationery noun writing materials such as paper and pens

statistic noun fact obtained by analysing numerical information ▷ **statistical** adjective: *statistical information* ▷ **statistically** adverb

statistician noun person who compiles and studies statistics

statue noun large sculpture of a human or animal figure

stature noun **1** person's height **2** reputation of a person or their achievements

status statuses noun **1** social position **2** importance given to something; prestige **3** official classification given to someone or something: *marital status*

status quo noun existing state of affairs

statute noun written law ▷ **statutory** adjective required or authorized by law

staunch adjective **1** loyal, firm ▷ verb **2** to stop (a flow of blood)

stave staves, staving, staved noun (*Music*) the five lines that music is written on > **stave off** verb to delay or prevent (something)

stay verb **1** to remain in a place or condition **2** to be living temporarily, often as a guest or visitor **3** (Scot, SAfr) to live permanently: where do you stay? ▷ noun **4** short time spent somewhere

stead noun **stand someone in good stead** to be useful to someone

steadfast adjective firm and determined > **steadfastly** adverb

steady steadier, steadiest; steadies, steadying, steadied adjective **1** regular or continuous **2** not shaky or wavering; firm **3** (of voice, gaze) calm and controlled **4** sensible and dependable ▷ verb **5** to make (something, someone or yourself) steady > **steadily** adverb

steak noun **1** thick slice of meat, especially beef **2** large piece of fish

steal steals, stealing, stole, stolen verb **1** to take (something) unlawfully or without permission **2** to move quietly and secretively

stealth noun quietness and secrecy

steam noun **1** hot vapour formed when water boils ▷ adjective **2** (of engine) operated using steam as a means of power ▷ verb **3** to give off steam **4** (of a vehicle) to move by steam power **5** to cook or treat with steam > **steamy** adjective: a steamy atmosphere

steam engine noun engine worked by steam

steamer noun **1** ship powered by steam **2** container used to cook food in steam

steed noun (literary) horse

steel noun **1** very strong metal containing mainly iron with a small amount of carbon ▷ verb **2** to prepare (yourself) for something unpleasant

steel band noun a group of people who play music on special metal drums

steep adjective **1** sloping sharply **2** (informal) (of a price) unreasonably high ▷ verb **3** to soak (something) thoroughly in liquid > **steeply** adverb

steeped adjective **steeped in** deeply affected by: an industry steeped in tradition

steeple noun a tall pointed structure on top of a church tower

steeplechase noun **1** horse race with obstacles to jump **2** track race with hurdles and a water jump

steer verb **1** to control the direction of (a vehicle or ship) **2** to influence the course or direction of (a person or conversation) ▷ noun **3** castrated male ox

stem stems, stemming, stemmed noun **1** long thin central part of a plant **2** long slender part, as of a wineglass **3** part of a word to which endings are added ▷ verb **4** to restrict or stop (the flow of something): to stem the flow of refugees **5** **stem from** to originate from

stench noun foul smell

stencil stencils, stencilling, stencilled noun **1** thin sheet with cut-out pattern through which ink or paint passes to form the pattern on the surface below

2 pattern made thus ▷ *verb* **3** to make (a pattern) with a stencil

step steps, stepping, stepped *noun* **1** act of moving and setting down your foot, as when walking **2** distance covered by a step **3** sound made by stepping **4** foot movement in a dance **5** one of a series of actions taken in order to achieve a goal **6** degree in a series or scale **7** raised flat surface, usually one of a series that you can walk up or down **8** steps stepladder ▷ *verb* **9** to move and set down the foot, as when walking **10** to walk a short distance > **step down** or **step aside** *verb* to resign from an important position > **step in** *verb* to become involved in something in order to help; intervene > **step up** *verb* to increase (the rate of something) by stages

step- *prefix* denoting a relationship created by the remarriage of a parent: *stepmother; stepson*

steppes *plural noun* wide grassy treeless plains in Russia and Ukraine

stepping stone *noun* **1** one of a series of stones for stepping on in crossing a stream **2** means of making progress towards a goal

stereo stereos *adjective* **1** (of recording, music system) having the sound directed through two speakers ▷ *noun* **2** a piece of equipment that reproduces sound from records, tapes or CDs directing the sound through two speakers

stereotype *noun* **1** fixed image or set of characteristics that people

consider to represent a particular type of person or thing ▷ *verb* **2** to make assumptions about what sort of person someone is and how they will behave, based on beliefs about group characteristics

sterile *adjective* **1** free from germs **2** unable to produce offspring or seeds **3** lacking in new ideas and enthusiasm > **sterility** *noun: an infection that can cause permanent sterility*

sterilize or **sterilise** *verb* **1** to make (something) completely clean and free from germs, usually by boiling or treating with antiseptic **2** to give (a person or animal) an operation to make them unable to have offspring

sterling *noun* **1** British money system ▷ *adjective* **2** excellent in quality

stern *adjective* **1** severe, strict ▷ *noun* **2** rear part of a ship > **sternly** *adverb*

steroid *noun* chemical both occurring naturally in your body and made artificially as a medicine. Sometimes sportsmen illegally take them as drugs to improve their performance

stethoscope *noun* medical instrument for listening to sounds made inside the body

stew *noun* **1** dish of small pieces of savoury food cooked together slowly in a liquid ▷ *verb* **2** to cook (meat, vegetables or fruit) slowly in a closed pot

steward *noun* **1** person who looks after passengers on a ship or aircraft **2** official who helps at a public event such as a race

stewardess *noun* woman who works on a ship or plane looking after passengers and serving meals

stick sticks, sticking, stuck *noun* 1 long thin piece of wood 2 such a piece of wood shaped for a special purpose: *hockey stick* 3 something like a stick: *stick of celery* 4 (*informal*) verbal abuse, criticism ▷ *verb* 5 to push (a pointed object) into (something) 6 to attach (something to something else) with glue or sticky tape 7 to become attached (to something) 8 (of a movable part) to become fixed in position and difficult to move 9 (*informal*) to put 10 to remain for a long time ▷ **stick by** *verb* to continue to help and support (someone) ▷ **stick out** *verb* 1 to extend or project beyond something else; protrude 2 to be very noticeable ▷ **stick to** *verb* to keep to (something) rather than changing to something else ▷ **stick together** *verb* to stay together and support one another ▷ **stick up** *verb* to point upwards from a surface ▷ **stick up for** *verb* (*informal*) to support or defend

sticker *noun* adhesive label or sign

sticking plaster *noun* small piece of fabric that you stick over a cut or sore to protect it

stick insect *noun* insect with a long cylindrical body and long legs, which looks like a twig

sticky stickier, stickiest *adjective* 1 covered with a substance that can stick to other things 2 (of paper, tape) with glue on one side so that you can stick it to a surface 3 (*informal*) difficult, unpleasant 4 (of weather) warm and humid

stiff *adjective* 1 not easily bent or moved 2 difficult or severe: *stiff competition for places* 3 unrelaxed or awkward 4 firm in consistency 5 containing a lot of alcohol; strong: *a stiff drink* 6 (of breeze, wind) blowing strongly ▷ *adverb* 7 (*informal*) utterly: *bored stiff* > **stiffly** *adverb* > **stiffness** *noun*

stiffen *verb* 1 to become stiff 2 to make (fabric) stiff

stifle *verb* 1 to prevent something from happening or continuing; suppress 2 to suffocate > **stifling** *adjective*: *the stifling heat*

stigma stigmas *noun* 1 mark of social disgrace 2 part of a plant that receives pollen

stile *noun* a set of steps allowing people to climb a fence

stiletto stilettos *noun* woman's shoe with a high narrow heel

still *adverb* 1 now as before or in the future as before 2 up to this or that time 3 even or yet: *still more insults* 4 quietly or without movement ▷ *adjective* 5 motionless 6 silent and calm, undisturbed 7 (of a drink) not fizzy ▷ *noun* 8 photograph from a film scene ▷ *verb* 9 to make (something) still > **stillness** *noun*

stillborn *adjective* born dead

stilt *noun* 1 one of the long upright poles on which some buildings are built, for example on wet land 2 one of a pair of poles with footrests on them for walking on above the ground

stilted *adjective* (of conversation, writing, speech) formal, unnatural and rather awkward

stimulant noun drug or other substance that makes your body work faster, increasing your heart rate and making it difficult to sleep

stimulate verb 1 to encourage (something) to begin or develop: to stimulate discussion 2 to give (someone) new ideas and enthusiasm >**stimulating** adjective: a stimulating environment >**stimulation** noun

stimulus stimuli noun something that causes a process or event to begin or develop

sting stings, stinging, stung verb 1 (of certain animals or plants) to wound by injecting with poison 2 (of part of your body) to be a source of sharp tingling pain 3 (of comment, remark) to cause (someone) to feel upset ▷ noun 4 sharp pointed organ of certain animals or plants by which poison can be injected

stink stinks, stinking, stank, stunk verb 1 to give off a strong unpleasant smell ▷ noun 2 strong unpleasant smell

stint noun 1 period of time spent doing a particular job ▷ verb 2 stint on to be mean or miserly with

stipulate verb (formal) to specify as a condition of an agreement >**stipulation** noun

stir stirs, stirring, stirred verb 1 to mix (a liquid) by moving a spoon etc around in it 2 to move slightly 3 to make (someone) feel strong emotions ▷ noun 4 excitement or shock

stirring adjective causing excitement, emotion and enthusiasm

stirrup noun one of a pair of metal loops attached to a saddle in which a rider places his or her feet

stitch verb 1 to sew or repair by sewing ▷ noun 2 one of the loops of thread that can be seen where material or a wound has been sewn 3 loop of yarn formed round a needle or hook in knitting or crochet 4 sharp pain in the side

stoat noun small wild animal of the weasel family, with brown fur that turns white in winter

stock noun 1 total amount of goods available for sale in a shop 2 supply stored for future use 3 financial shares in, or capital of, a company 4 liquid produced by boiling meat, fish, bones or vegetables 5 farm animals 6 ancestry 7 (History) **stocks** instrument of punishment consisting of a wooden frame with holes into which the hands and feet of the victim were locked ▷ verb 8 (of a shop) to keep (goods) for sale 9 to fill (a cupboard or shelf) with goods 10 to supply (a farm) with livestock or (a lake etc) with fish ▷ adjective 11 (of phrase) clichéd or hackneyed >**stock up** verb (often followed by with, on) to buy in a supply (of something)

stockbroker noun person who buys and sells stocks and shares for customers

stock exchange noun institution for the buying and selling of shares

stocking noun close-fitting covering for the foot and leg

stockman stockmen noun man who looks after sheep or cattle on a farm

stock market noun organization and activity involved in buying and selling stocks and shares

stockpile verb **1** to store a large quantity of (something) for future use ▷ noun **2** large store of something

stocktaking noun counting, checking and valuing of the goods in a shop

stocky stockier, stockiest adjective (of a person) broad and sturdy

stoke verb to keep (a fire or furnace) burning by moving or adding fuel

stomach noun **1** organ in your body which digests food **2** front part of your body below the waist; abdomen ▷ verb **3** to put up with

stone stones, stoning, stoned noun **1** material of which rocks are made **2** a small piece of rock **3** gem; jewel **4** hard central part of some fruits **5** unit of weight equal to 14 pounds or 6.350 kilograms **6** hard deposit formed in the kidney or bladder ▷ verb **7** to throw stones at **8** to remove stones from (a fruit)

stoned adjective (informal) under the influence of drugs

stony stonier, stoniest adjective **1** containing stones or like stone **2** unfeeling or hard

stool noun **1** seat with legs but without arms or a back **2** lump of excrement or faeces

stoop verb **1** to bend (the body) forward and downward **2** to walk with your body bent forward and downward **3** to degrade oneself ▷ noun **4** stooping posture

stop stops, stopping, stopped verb **1** to cease from doing (something)

2 to bring to or come to a halt **3** to prevent or restrain **4** to withhold **5** to block or plug **6** to stay or rest ▷ noun **7** stopping or being stopped **8** place where a bus, train or other vehicle stops **9** full stop **10 put a stop to** to prevent (something) from happening or continuing **11 come to a stop** to come to a halt

stoppage noun mass stopping of work on account of a disagreement with an employer

stopper noun piece of glass or cork that fits into the neck of a jar or bottle

stopwatch noun watch which can be stopped instantly for exact timing of a sporting event

storage noun **1** storing **2** space for storing

store noun **1** shop **2** supply kept for future use **3** storage place, such as a warehouse **4 in store** about to happen **5** stores stock of provisions ▷ verb **6** to collect and keep (things) for future use **7** to put (furniture etc) in a warehouse for safekeeping

storeroom noun room where things are kept until they are needed

storey storeys noun floor or level of a building

stork noun very large white and black wading bird with long red legs and a long bill

storm noun **1** violent weather with wind, rain or snow and often thunder and lightning **2** angry or excited reaction ▷ verb **3** (often followed by out) to rush violently or angrily **4** to shout angrily **5** to attack or capture (a place)

suddenly > **stormy** *adjective*
1 characterized by storms
2 involving violent emotions

story stories *noun* **1** description of a series of events told or written for entertainment **2** plot of a book or film **3** news report **4** (*informal*) lie

stout *adjective* **1** fat **2** thick, strong and sturdy **3** determined, firm and strong ▷ *noun* **4** strong dark beer > **stoutly** *adverb*

stove *noun* **1** apparatus for cooking or heating ▷ *verb* **2** a past of **stave**

stow *verb* to store or pack > **stow away** *verb* to hide on a ship or aircraft in order to travel free

straddle *verb* **1** to have one leg or part on each side of (something) **2** to be positioned across and on two sides of (something), linking the two parts: *The town straddles a river*

straight *adjective* **1** not curved or crooked **2** level or upright **3** honest or frank **4** (of spirits) undiluted **5** neat and tidy ▷ *adverb* **6** in a straight line **7** immediately **8** in a level or upright position ▷ *noun* **9** straight part, especially of a racetrack

straightaway *adverb* immediately

straighten *verb* **1** to remove any bends or curves from **2** to make (something) neat and tidy **3** to organize and sort out (a confused situation)

straightforward *adjective* **1** (of a task) easy and involving no problems **2** honest, frank

strain *noun* **1** worry and nervous tension **2** force exerted

by straining **3** injury from overexertion **4** great demand on strength or resources **5** melody or theme **6** breed or variety ▷ *verb* **7** to cause (something) to be used or tested beyond its limits **8** to injure (yourself or a muscle) by overexertion **9** to make an intense effort **10** to sieve

strained *adjective* **1** not relaxed, tense **2** not natural, forced

strait *noun* narrow channel connecting two areas of sea

straitjacket *noun* special strong jacket used to tie the arms of a violent person tightly around their body

strait-laced *adjective* prudish or puritanical

strand *noun* **1** single thread of string, wire, etc **2** element or part **3** (*literary*) shore

stranded *adjective* stuck somewhere with no means of leaving

strange *adjective* **1** odd or unusual **2** not familiar > **strangely** *adverb* > **strangeness** *noun*

stranger *noun* **1** person you have never met before **2** (followed by *to*) someone who is inexperienced in or unaccustomed to something

strangle *verb* to kill (someone) by squeezing their throat > **strangulation** *noun* strangling

strangled *adjective* (of sound, cry) unclear and muffled

stranglehold *noun* complete power or control over someone or something

strap straps, strapping, strapped *noun* **1** strip of flexible material for lifting, fastening or holding something in place ▷ *verb* **2** to fasten (something) with a strap or straps

strapping adjective tall, strong and healthy-looking

strata noun plural of **stratum**

strategic [strat-**ee**-jik] adjective 1 advantageous 2 (of weapons) aimed at an enemy's homeland > **strategically** adverb

strategy strategies noun 1 overall plan 2 art of planning, especially in war > **strategist** noun

stratum strata [**strah**-tum] noun 1 layer, especially of rock 2 social class

straw noun 1 dried stalks of grain 2 single stalk of straw 3 long thin tube used to suck up liquid into the mouth 4 **the last straw** the latest in a series of bad events and makes you feel you cannot stand any more

strawberry strawberries noun sweet fleshy red fruit with small seeds on the outside

stray verb 1 to wander away 2 (of thoughts, mind) to move on to other topics 3 to deviate from certain moral standards ▷ adjective 4 having strayed 5 scattered, random ▷ noun 6 stray animal

streak noun 1 long band of contrasting colour or substance 2 quality or characteristic 3 short stretch (of good or bad luck) ▷ verb 4 to mark (something) with streaks 5 to move rapidly 6 (informal) to run naked in public > **streaky** adjective

stream noun 1 small river 2 steady flow of something 3 schoolchildren grouped together by age and ability ▷ verb 4 to flow steadily 5 to float in the air 6 to group (pupils) in streams

streamer noun 1 strip of coloured paper that unrolls when tossed 2 long narrow flag

streamline verb 1 to give (a car, plane, etc) a smooth even shape to offer least resistance to the flow of air or water 2 to make (an organization or process) more efficient by removing parts of it

street noun public road, usually lined with buildings

strength noun 1 quality of being strong 2 quality or ability considered an advantage 3 how strong or weak something is 4 total number of people in a group 5 **on the strength of** on the basis of

strengthen verb 1 to give (something) more power, influence or support and make it more likely to succeed 2 to improve (an object) or add to its structure so that it can withstand rough treatment; reinforce

strenuous adjective involving a lot of effort or energy > **strenuously** adverb

stress noun 1 worry and nervous tension 2 emphasis 3 stronger sound in saying a word or syllable 4 (Physics) force producing strain ▷ verb 5 to emphasize 6 to put stress on (a word or syllable) > **stressful** adjective: a stressful time

stretch verb 1 to extend or be extended 2 to be able to be stretched 3 to hold out your legs or arms as far as you can 4 to pull (something soft or elastic) so that it becomes longer or bigger

5 to strain (resources or abilities) to the utmost > noun **6** act of stretching **7** continuous expanse of land or water **8** period of time

stretcher noun frame covered with canvas, on which an injured person is carried

strewn adjective untidily scattered: The costumes were strewn all over the floor

stricken adjective seriously affected by disease, grief or pain, etc

strict adjective **1** stern or severe **2** sticking closely to specified rules **3** (of absolute, sense, etc) complete, absolute

strictly adverb **1** only: I was in it strictly for the money **2** strictly speaking in fact; really

stride strides, striding, strode, stridden verb **1** to walk with long steps > noun **2** long step **3** regular pace **4** strides progress

strident adjective loud and harsh

strife noun (formal) conflict, quarrelling

strike strikes, striking, struck noun **1** stoppage of work as a protest **2** a military attack: the threat of air strikes > verb **3** to hit **4** (of an illness, disaster or enemy) to attack suddenly **5** to light (a match) by rubbing the head against something **6** (of a clock) to indicate (a time) by sounding a bell **7** (of thought, idea) to enter the mind of (someone) **8** to discover (gold, oil, etc) **9** to agree (a bargain, deal) **10** to stop work as a protest **11 be struck by** to be impressed by > **strike off** verb to remove (someone) from the official register of those

allowed to practise in their profession > **strike out** verb to cross (something) out > **strike up** verb **1** to begin (a conversation or friendship) **2** (of a band, orchestra) to begin to play

striker noun **1** striking worker **2** (in soccer) a player whose function is to attack and score goals

striking adjective impressive or very noticeable > **strikingly** adverb

string strings, stringing, strung noun **1** thin cord used for tying **2** set of objects threaded on a string **3** series of things or events **4** stretched wire or cord on a musical instrument that produces sound when vibrated **5 strings a** restrictions or conditions **b** section of an orchestra consisting of stringed instruments **6 pull strings** to use your influence > verb **7** to provide with a string or strings **8** to thread (objects, beads) on a string > **string along** verb to deceive (someone) over a period of time > **string out** verb to make (something) last longer than necessary > **string up** verb (informal) to kill (someone) by hanging

stringed adjective (of a musical instrument) having strings that are plucked or played with a bow

stringent [strin-jent] adjective (of rules and conditions) strictly controlled or enforced

stringy-bark noun any Australian eucalypt that has bark that peels off in long, tough strands

strip strips, stripping, stripped **1** long narrow piece **2** (Brit, Aust,

NZ) clothes a sports team plays in ▷ *verb* **3** to take your clothes off **4** to remove the covering from the surface of **5** **to strip someone of** to take (a title or possession) away from someone **6** to dismantle (an engine)

stripe *noun* **1** long narrow band of contrasting colour or substance **2** narrow band of material worn on a uniform to show someone's rank ▷ **striped, stripy** or **stripey** *adjective* with a pattern of stripes

stripper *noun* entertainer who performs a striptease

striptease *noun* entertainment in which a performer undresses to music

strive strives, striving, strove, striven *verb* to make a great effort (to do something)

stroke *verb* **1** to touch or caress (something) lightly with your hand ▷ *noun* **2** light touch or caress with the hand **3** serious medical condition involving a blockage in or a rupture of a blood vessel in the brain **4** blow **5** chime of a clock **6** mark made by a pen or paintbrush **7** style or method of swimming **8** **stroke of luck** piece of luck; lucky break

stroll *verb* **1** to walk in a leisurely manner; amble ▷ *noun* **2** leisurely walk

stroller *noun* (*Aust*) pushchair

strong *adjective* **1** having powerful muscles **2** not easily broken **3** great in degree or intensity **4** determined **5** (of argument) supported by evidence **6** having a specified number: *twenty strong* **7** good: *a strong candidate* **8** (of economy, currency, relationship)

stable and successful ▷ *adverb* **9** **still going strong** still healthy or doing well after a long time ▷ **strongly** *adverb*

stronghold *noun* **1** place that is held and defended by an army **2** place where an attitude or belief is strongly held

structure *noun* **1** something that has been built or constructed; construction **2** the way something is made, built or organized **3** quality of being well planned and organized: *The days have no real structure* ▷ *verb* **4** to arrange (something) into an organized pattern or system ▷ **structural** *adjective* ▷ **structurally** *adverb*

struggle *verb* **1** to try hard (to do something) but with difficulty or in difficult circumstances **2** to move about violently in an attempt to get free **3** to fight (with someone) ▷ *noun* **4** something requiring a lot of effort **5** fight

strum strums, strumming, strummed *verb* to play (a guitar or banjo) by sweeping the thumb or a plectrum across the strings

strut struts, strutting, strutted *verb* **1** to walk pompously; swagger ▷ *noun* **2** piece of wood or metal which strengthens or supports part of a building or structure

Stuart *noun* family name of the monarchs who ruled Scotland from 1371 to 1714 and England from 1603 to 1714

stub stubs, stubbing, stubbed *noun* **1** short piece (of pencil, cigarette) left after use **2** part of a cheque or ticket that you keep; counterfoil ▷ **verb 3** to strike (your toe) painfully against an object > **stub out** verb to put out (a cigarette) by pressing the end against a surface

stubble noun **1** short stalks of grain left in a field after reaping **2** short growth of hair on the chin of a man who has not shaved recently > **stubbly** adjective

stubborn adjective **1** refusing to agree or give in; obstinate **2** difficult to deal with
> **stubbornly** adverb
> **stubbornness** noun

stuck verb **1** past of **stick**
▷ adjective **2** fixed or jammed and unable to move **3** unable to get away **4** unable to continue

stuck-up adjective (informal) conceited or snobbish

stud noun **1** small piece of metal attached to a surface for decoration **2** disc-like removable fastener for clothes **3** one of several small round objects fixed to the sole of a football boot to give better grip **4** male animal, especially a stallion, kept for breeding **5** place where horses are bred

studded adjective decorated with small pieces of metal or precious stones

student noun person who studies a subject, especially at university

studied adjective (of action or response) carefully practised or planned

studio studios noun **1** workroom of an artist or photographer **2** place containing special equipment where records, films,

or radio or television programmes are made

studious [**styoo**-dee-uss] adjective inclined to spend a lot of time studying

studiously adverb carefully and deliberately

study studies, studying, studied verb **1** to spend time learning (a subject) **2** to investigate (something) by observation and research **3** to look at (something) carefully ▷ noun **4** activity of studying **5** piece of research on a particular subject **6** sketch done as practice or preparation **7** room for studying in

stuff noun **1** substance or material **2** collection of unnamed things ▷ verb **3** to push (something) somewhere quickly and roughly **4** to fill (something) with a substance or objects **5** to fill (food) with a seasoned mixture **6** to fill (an animal's skin) with material to restore the shape of the live animal

stuffing noun **1** seasoned mixture used to stuff poultry or vegetables **2** padding

stuffy stuffier, stuffiest adjective **1** lacking fresh air; airless **2** very formal and old-fashioned

stumble verb **1** to trip and nearly fall **2** to walk in an unsure way **3** to make frequent mistakes in speech > **stumble across** or **on** verb to discover (something) accidentally

stump noun **1** base of a tree left when the main trunk has been cut away **2** part of a thing left after a larger part has been removed **3** (Cricket) one of the three upright sticks forming the wicket ▷ *verb* **4** to baffle > **stump up** *verb* (*informal*) to provide (the money required)

stun stuns, stunning, stunned *verb* **1** to shock or overwhelm (someone) **2** to knock (a person or animal) unconscious with a blow to the head

stunning *adjective* very attractive or impressive

stunt *noun* **1** acrobatic or dangerous action **2** anything spectacular done to gain publicity ▷ *verb* **3** to prevent or impede the (growth or development) of

stupendous *adjective* very large or impressive > **stupendously** *adverb*

stupid *adjective* **1** lacking intelligence **2** silly or lacking in good judgment > **stupidity** *noun* > **stupidly** *adverb*

sturdy sturdier, sturdiest *adjective* strong and firm and unlikely to be damaged or injured > **sturdily** *adverb*

sturgeon *noun* fish from which caviar is obtained

stutter *noun* **1** difficulty in speaking characterized by a tendency to repeat sounds at the beginning of words and a problem completing words ▷ *verb* **2** to hesitate or repeat sounds when speaking

sty sties *noun* pen for pigs; pigsty

stye styes *noun* infection at the base of an eyelash

style *noun* **1** manner of writing, speaking or doing something **2** shape or design **3** elegance and smartness **4** current fashion ▷ *verb* **5** to shape or design

(something) > **stylize** *verb* cause to conform to an established stylistic form

stylish *adjective* smart, elegant and fashionable; chic; smart > **stylishly** *adverb*

stylized or **stylised** *adjective* D&T using a particular artistic or literary form as a basis rather than being natural or spontaneous

suave [swahv] *adjective* smooth and sophisticated in manner > **suavely** *adverb*

sub- *prefix* used with many main words to mean **1** under or beneath: submarine **2** subordinate: sublieutenant **3** falling short of: subnormal **4** forming a subdivision: subheading

subconscious *noun* **1** (*Psychoanalysis*) part of your mind that can influence you without your being aware of it ▷ *adjective* **2** happening or existing in someone's subconscious and therefore not directly realized or understood by them: *a subconscious fear of rejection* > **subconsciously** *adverb*

subcontinent *noun* large land mass that is a distinct part of a continent

subdue subdues, subduing, subdued *verb* **1** to overcome and bring under control **2** to make (a colour, light or emotion) less strong

subdued *adjective* **1** rather quiet and sad **2** not very noticeable or bright

subject *noun* **1** person or thing being discussed, dealt with or

a
b
c
d
e
f
g
h
i
j
k
l
m
n
o
p
q
r
s
t
u
v
w
x
y
z

studied **2** (*Grammar*) word or phrase that represents the person or thing performing the action of the verb in a sentence. For example, in the sentence *My cat catches birds*, *my cat* is the subject **3** area of study **4** person living under the rule of a monarch or government ▷ *adjective* **5** to **subject someone to** to cause someone to undergo or experience (something unpleasant) ▷ *adjective* **6 subject to a** affected by; liable to **b** conditional upon

subjective *adjective* based on personal feelings and prejudices rather than on fact and rational thought

subjunctive (*Grammar*) *noun* **1** form of the verb sometimes used when expressing doubt, supposition or wishes ▷ *adjective* **2** in or of that mood

sublime *adjective* **1** awe-inspiring and uplifting **2** unparalleled; supreme >**sublimely** *adverb*

submarine *noun* ship that can travel beneath the surface of the sea

submerge *verb* to go below or to put (something) below the surface of a liquid

submission *noun* **1** state of being submissive and under someone's control **2** act of submitting **3** something submitted for consideration

submissive *adjective* quiet and obedient

submit submits, submitting, submitted *verb* **1** (often followed by *to*) to surrender yourself or agree (to something) because you are not powerful enough to resist

it **2** to send in (an application or proposal) for consideration

subordinate *noun* **1** person under the authority of another ▷ *adjective* **2** of lesser rank or importance ▷ *verb* **3** to treat (something) as less important

subordinate clause *noun* ENGLISH (*Grammar*) clause which adds details to the main clause of a sentence

subscribe *verb* **1** to pay (a subscription) **2** to give support or approval (to a theory, belief, etc) >**subscriber** *noun*

subscription *noun* sum of money that you pay regularly to belong to an organization or to receive regular copies of a magazine

subsequent *adjective* occurring or coming into existence after something else: *the December uprising and the subsequent political violence* >**subsequently** *adverb*

subservient *adjective* submissive, servile >**subservience** *noun*

subside *verb* **1** to become less intense **2** to sink to a lower level

subsidence *noun* act or process of subsiding

subsidiary subsidiaries *noun* **1** company which is part of a larger company ▷ *adjective* **2** of lesser importance

subsidize or **subsidise** *verb* **1** to provide part of the cost of (something) **2** to help (someone) financially >**subsidized** *adjective*

subsidy subsidies *noun* financial aid

substance *noun* **1** solid, powder, liquid or paste **2** essential meaning of something **3** solid or meaningful quality **4** physical composition of something **5** wealth

substantial *adjective* **1** of considerable size or value **2** (of food or a meal) sufficient and nourishing **3** solid or strong

substantially *adverb* generally, essentially or mostly

substitute *verb* **1** to take the place of (something or someone) or to put (something or someone) in the place of another ▷ *noun* **2** person or thing taking the place of (another) > **substitution** *noun: the substitution of margarine for butter*

subterfuge *noun* the use of tricks or deceitful methods to achieve an objective

subtitle *noun* **1** secondary title of a book **2** subtitles printed translation or transcript that appears at the bottom of the screen for some films and television programmes ▷ *verb* **3** to provide with a subtitle or subtitles

subtle *adjective* **1** very fine, delicate or small in degree **2** using indirect methods to achieve something > **subtlety** *noun* > **subtly** *adverb*

subtract *verb* to take (one number or quantity) from another

subtraction *noun* MATHS subtracting of one number from another, or a sum in which you do this

suburb *noun* residential area on the outskirts of a city

suburban *adjective* **1** relating to a suburb or suburbs **2** dull and conventional

suburbia *noun* suburbs and their inhabitants

subversive *adjective* **1** intended to destroy or weaken a political system: *subversive activities* ▷ *noun* **2** person who tries to destroy or weaken a political system > **subversion** *noun*

subvert *verb* (formal) to cause (something) to weaken or fail

subway *noun* **1** passage under a road or railway **2** underground railway

succeed *verb* **1** to achieve the intended result **2** to turn out satisfactorily **3** to come next in order after **4** to take over a position from > **succeeding** *adjective*

success *noun* **1** achievement of something attempted **2** attainment of wealth, fame or position **3** successful person or thing

successful *adjective* having success > **successfully** *adverb*

succession *noun* **1** series of people or things following one another in order **2** act of succeeding someone to an important position **3** right by which someone succeeds to an important position **4** in succession without a break

successive *adjective* occurring one after the other without a break; consecutive

successor *noun* person who succeeds someone in a position

succinct *adjective* brief and clear > **succinctly** *adverb*

succulent *adjective* juicy and delicious > **succulence** *noun*

succumb *verb* **1** (followed by to) to give way (to something overpowering) **2** to die of (an illness)

such adjective 1 of the kind specified 2 so, so great or so much: I have such a terrible sense of guilt ▷ pronoun 3 such things 4 such as like 5 such and such something specific but not known or named

suchlike pronoun such or similar things: shampoos, talcs, toothbrushes and suchlike

suck verb 1 to draw (liquid or air) into the mouth 2 to take (something) into your mouth and lick, dissolve or roll it around with your tongue 3 (followed by in) to draw (something or someone) in by irresistible force ▷ **suck up to** verb (informal) to do things to please (someone) in order to obtain praise or approval

sucker noun 1 (informal) person who is easily fooled or cheated 2 pad, organ or device which sticks to something using suction

suckle verb 1 (of a mother) to feed (a baby) at the breast 2 (of a baby) to feed at its mother's breast ▷ **suckling** noun unweaned baby or young animal

sucrose [**soo**-kroze] noun chemical name for sugar

suction noun 1 force involved when a substance is drawn or sucked from one place to another 2 process by which two surfaces stick together when the air between them is removed: They stay there by suction

Sudanese [soo-dan-**neez**] adjective 1 belonging or relating to the Sudan ▷ noun 2 someone from the Sudan

sudden adjective happening quickly and unexpectedly ▷ **suddenly** adverb ▷ **suddenness** noun

sudoku noun puzzle in which a player enters numbers in a square made up of nine three-by-three grids, so that every column, row, and grid contains the numbers one to nine

sue sues, suing, sued verb to start legal proceedings against

suede noun thin, soft leather with a velvety finish on one side

suffer verb 1 to experience pain or misery 2 to deteriorate in condition or quality 3 to undergo or be subjected to (pain, injury) 4 to tolerate ▷ **sufferer** noun ▷ **suffer from** verb to be affected by (a condition) ▷ **suffering** noun

suffice [suf-**fice**] verb (formal) to be enough for a purpose

sufficient adjective enough, adequate ▷ **sufficiently** adverb

suffix noun letter or letters added to the end of a word to form another word, for example {-ly} and {-ness} in {smartly} and {softness}

suffocate verb 1 to be killed or kill (someone) by deprivation of oxygen 2 to feel uncomfortable from heat and lack of air ▷ **suffocation** noun

suffrage noun right to vote in political elections

suffragette noun (in Britain in the early 20th century) a woman who campaigned militantly for the right to vote

suffused adjective (literary) **suffused with** flooded with (light or colour)

sugar noun sweet substance used to sweeten food and drinks

suggest verb **1** to propose (an idea, plan) **2** to bring (something) to mind or indicate

suggestion noun **1** thing suggested **2** hint or indication

suggestive adjective **1** suggesting something indecent or sexual in nature **2 suggestive of** conveying a hint of > **suggestively** adverb

suicidal adjective **1** liable to commit suicide **2** having potentially fatal consequences; very dangerous > **suicidally** adverb

suicide noun **1** killing oneself intentionally **2** person who kills himself or herself intentionally **3** self-inflicted ruin of someone's own prospects or interests: *political suicide*

suicide bomber noun terrorist who carries out a bomb attack, knowing that he or she will be killed in the explosion

suit noun **1** set of clothes designed to be worn together **2** outfit worn for a specific purpose **3** one of the four sets into which a pack of cards is divided **4** lawsuit > verb **5** to be acceptable to or convenient for **6** (of colour, piece of clothing) to cause (someone) to look good

suitable adjective appropriate or proper > **suitability** noun: *his suitability for the role* > **suitably** adverb: *a lack of suitably qualified applicants*

suitcase noun case in which you carry your clothes when you are travelling

suite noun **1** set of connected rooms in a hotel **2** set of matching furniture or bathroom fittings **3** set of musical pieces in the same key

suited adjective right or appropriate for a particular purpose or person: *He is well suited to be minister for the arts*

suitor noun (old-fashioned) man who is courting a woman

sulk verb **1** to be silent and sullen because of resentment or bad temper > noun **2** resentful or sullen mood > **sulky** adjective

sullen adjective silent and unwilling to be sociable, in a disagreeable way > **sullenly** adverb

sulphur noun (Chemistry) pale yellow nonmetallic element which burns with a very unpleasant smell

sultan noun (of certain Muslim countries) ruler or sovereign

sultana noun **1** dried grape **2** the wife of a sultan

sum sums, summing, summed noun **1** amount of money **2** problem in arithmetic; calculation **3** total > **sum up** verb **1** to summarize **2** to form a quick opinion of

summarize or **summarise** verb to give a short account of the main points of

summary summaries noun **1** brief account giving the main points of something; précis; résumé > adjective **2** done quickly, without formalities: *Summary executions are common* > **summarily** adverb: *He was summarily dismissed*

summer noun warmest season of the year, between spring and autumn

a b c d e f g h i j k l m n o p q r s t u v w x y z

summit noun 1 top of a mountain or hill 2 highest point 3 meeting between heads of state or other high officials to discuss particular issues

summon verb 1 to order (someone) to come 2 (often followed by up) to gather (one's courage, strength, etc)

summons summonses; summonsing, summonsed noun 1 official order requiring someone to appear in court 2 an order to go to someone ▷ verb 3 to order (someone) to appear in court

sumptuous adjective lavish, magnificent

sum total noun complete or final total

sun suns, sunning, sunned noun 1 star around which the earth and other planets revolve 2 any star around which planets revolve 3 heat and light from the sun ▷ verb 4 to expose (yourself) to the sun's rays

sunbathe verb to lie in the sunshine in order to get a suntan

sunburn noun painful reddening of the skin caused by overexposure to the sun > **sunburnt** or **sunburned** adjective

sundae noun ice cream topped with fruit etc

Sunday noun day between Saturday and Monday

Sunday school noun special class held on Sundays to teach children about Christianity

sundial noun device showing the time by means of a pointer that casts a shadow on a marked dial

sundry adjective 1 several, various 2 all and sundry everybody

sunflower noun tall plant with large golden flowers

sunglasses plural noun spectacles with dark lenses that you wear to protect your eyes from the sun

sunken verb 1 a past participle of **sink** ▷ adjective 2 having sunk to the bottom of the sea, a river or lake 3 constructed below the level of the surrounding area 4 curving inwards: Her cheeks were sunken

sunlight noun bright light produced when the sun is shining > **sunlit** adjective

sunny sunnier, sunniest adjective full of or exposed to sunlight

sunrise noun 1 daily appearance of the sun above the horizon 2 time of this

sunset noun 1 daily disappearance of the sun below the horizon 2 time of this

sunshine noun light and warmth from the sun

sunstroke noun illness caused by spending too much time in hot sunshine

suntan noun browning of the skin caused by exposure to the sun > **suntanned** adjective

super adjective (informal) very nice or very good; excellent

super- prefix used with many main words to mean 1 above or over: superimpose 2 outstanding: superstar 3 of greater size or extent: supermarket

superb adjective excellent, impressive or splendid > **superbly** adverb

supercilious adjective showing arrogant pride or scorn

superego superegos *noun* (*Psychology*) part of your mind that acts as a conscience

superficial *adjective* **1** not careful or thorough **2** (of a person) without depth of character, shallow **3** of or on the surface > **superficially** *adverb*

superfluous [soo-**per**-flew-uss] *adjective* (*formal*) unnecessary or no longer needed

superhuman *adjective* beyond normal human ability or experience

superimpose *verb* to place (something) on or over something else

superintendent *noun* **1** senior police officer **2** supervisor

superior *adjective* **1** greater in quality, quantity or merit **2** higher in position or rank **3** believing oneself to be better than others ▷ *noun* **4** person of greater rank or status > **superiority** *noun*

superlative [soo-**per**-lat-iv] *adjective* **1** of outstanding quality ▷ *noun* **2** (*Grammar*) the form of an adjective or adverb that indicates the greatest degree of it: *quickest; best; easiest*

supermarket *noun* large self-service store selling food and household goods

supernatural *adjective* **1** of or relating to things beyond the laws of nature ▷ *noun* **2** the **supernatural** supernatural forces, occurrences and beings collectively

superpower *noun* extremely powerful nation

supersede *verb* to replace or supplant on account of being more modern

supersize or **supersized** *adjective* larger than standard size

supersonic *adjective* of or travelling at a speed greater than the speed of sound

superstar *noun* very famous entertainer or sports player

superstition *noun* **1** irrational beliefs founded on ignorance or fear **2** idea or practice based on the belief that certain things bring good or bad luck > **superstitious** *adjective*

supervise *verb* to watch over (an activity) in order to check that it is carried out correctly or safely > **supervision** *noun* > **supervisor** *noun*

supper *noun* light evening meal

supplant *verb* to take the place of (someone or something); oust

supple *adjective* able to bend and move easily

supplement *verb* **1** to add something to (something) in order to improve it **2** to add to (something) ▷ *noun* **3** thing added to complete something or make up for a lack **4** magazine inserted into a newspaper

supplementary *adjective* added to something else to improve it

supplier *noun* firm that provides particular goods

supply supplies, supplying, supplied *verb* **1** to provide (someone) with something **2** to provide or send (something) ▷ *noun* **3** amount available **4** supplying **5** (*Economics*) willingness and ability to provide goods and services: *All food prices are based on supply and demand* **6** **supplies** food or equipment

support verb 1 to take an active interest in and hope for the success of (a sports team, political principle, etc) 2 to bear the weight of; hold up 3 to give practical or emotional help to 4 to provide (someone) with money for the necessities of life 5 to help to prove (a theory etc) ▷ noun 6 supporting 7 means of support 8 encouragement and help 9 money > **supporter** noun person who supports a team, principle, etc

supportive adjective (of person) encouraging and helpful in troubled times

suppose verb 1 to presume to be true 2 to consider as a proposal for the sake of discussion 3 **be supposed to a** to be expected or required to: You were supposed to phone me **b** to be permitted to: We're not supposed to swim here > **supposing** or **suppose** conjunction what if

supposed adjective presumed to be true without proof; alleged > **supposedly** adverb: a supposedly safe investment

supposition noun 1 something supposed 2 supposing

suppress verb 1 to put an end to 2 to prevent publication of (information) 3 to restrain (an emotion or response) > **suppression** noun

supremacy noun 1 supreme power 2 state of being supreme

supreme adjective highest in authority, rank or degree > **supremely** adverb extremely

surcharge noun additional charge

sure adjective 1 free from uncertainty or doubt 2 reliable or accurate 3 inevitable or certain 4 **sure of** confident about ▷ adverb, interjection 5 (informal) certainly > **surely** adverb it must be true that

surf noun 1 foam caused by waves breaking on the shore ▷ verb 2 to go surfing 3 **surf the internet** to go from website to website reading the information > **surfer** noun

surface noun 1 outside or top of an object 2 superficial appearance ▷ verb 3 to come up from under the water

surfboard noun long smooth board used in surfing

surf club noun (Aust) organization of lifesavers in charge of safety on a particular beach, and which often provides leisure facilities

surfeit noun excessive amount; too much

surfing noun sport of riding towards the shore on a surfboard on the crest of a wave

surge noun 1 sudden powerful increase ▷ verb 2 to increase suddenly 3 to move forward strongly

surgeon noun doctor who performs operations

surgery surgeries noun 1 treatment involving cutting open part of the patient's body to treat the affected part 2 place where a doctor, dentist, etc can be consulted 3 occasion when a doctor or dentist is available for consultation 4 (Brit) occasion when an elected politician is available for consultation

surgical *adjective* used in or involving a medical operation ▷ **surgically** *adverb*

surly surlier, surliest *adjective* ill-tempered and rude ▷ **surliness** *noun*

surmise *verb, noun* to guess; conjecture

surmount *verb* to overcome (a problem) ▷ **surmountable** *adjective: He sees any hurdles as surmountable*

surname *noun* family name; last name

surpass *verb (formal)* to be greater than or superior to

surplus surpluses *noun* amount left over in excess of what is required

surprise *noun* **1** unexpected event **2** amazement and wonder ▷ *verb* **3** to cause (someone) to feel amazement or wonder **4** to come upon, attack or catch (someone) suddenly and unexpectedly ▷ **surprised** *adjective: I was surprised to see him there* ▷ **surprising** *adjective: a surprising choice*

surreal *adjective* very strange and dreamlike; bizarre

surrender *verb* **1** to stop fighting and give oneself up **2** to give way (to a temptation or influence) **3** to give (something) up to another ▷ *noun* **4** surrendering

surreptitious *adjective* done secretly or stealthily ▷ **surreptitiously** *adverb: I found myself surreptitiously looking through her diary*

surrogate *adjective* **1** acting as a substitute for someone or something ▷ *noun* **2** substitute

surround *verb* **1** to be or come all around (a person or thing) **2** to encircle or enclose (something or someone) with something ▷ *noun* **3** border or edging

surrounding *adjective* (of area) all around: *the surrounding countryside*

surveillance *noun* close observation

survey *verb* **1** to look at or consider (something or someone) as a whole **2** to inspect (a building) to find out what condition it is in and assess its value **3** to examine and measure (an area), often to make a map **4** to find out the opinions or habits of (a group of people) ▷ *noun* **5** detailed examination of something, often in the form of a report

surveyor *noun* person whose job is to survey buildings or land

survival *noun* managing to go on living or existing in spite of great danger or difficulties

survive *verb* **1** to continue to live or exist after a (difficult experience) **2** to live on after the death of (another) ▷ **survivor** *noun*

sus- *prefix* another form of **sub-**

susceptible *adjective* (often followed by *to*) liable to be influenced by or affected by ▷ **susceptibility** *noun: a person's susceptibility to illness*

suspect *verb* **1** to believe (someone) to be guilty of something without having any proof: *They suspected her of being a witch* **2** to think (something) to be false or questionable: *He suspected her motives* **3** to believe (something) to be the case: *She* suspected he was right ▷ noun **4** person who is suspected ▷ adjective **5** not to be trusted

suspend verb **1** to hang (something or someone) from a high place **2** to delay or stop (something) **3** to remove (someone) temporarily from a job or team

suspender noun **1** strap for holding up stockings **2** (US) braces

suspense noun state of uncertainty while awaiting news, an event, etc

suspension noun **1** delaying or stopping of something **2** temporary removal of someone from their job **3** system of springs and shock absorbers supporting the body of a vehicle **4** liquid mixture in which very small bits of a solid material are contained and are not dissolved

suspicion noun **1** feeling of not trusting a person or thing **2** belief that something is true or likely to happen without definite proof **3** slight trace

suspicious adjective **1** (of person) feeling suspicion **2** (of thing or person) causing suspicion > **suspiciously** adverb

sustain verb **1** to keep up, maintain or prolong **2** to give (someone) the energy, strength and nourishment needed to keep them going **3** to suffer (an injury or loss)

sustainable adjective **1** capable of being sustained **2** (of development, resource) capable of being maintained at a steady level without exhausting natural

resources or causing ecological damage

sustenance noun (formal) food

swab swabs, swabbing, swabbed noun **1** small piece of cotton wool used to apply medication, clean a wound, etc ▷ verb **2** to clean (something) with a mop and a lot of water **3** to clean or take specimens of (a wound) with a swab

swag noun **1** (informal) stolen property **2** swags of (Aust, NZ informal) lots of

swagger verb **1** to walk or behave arrogantly ▷ noun **2** arrogant walk or manner

swagman swagmen noun (Aust & NZ history) tramp who carried his belongings in a bundle on his back

swallow verb **1** to make (something) go down your throat and into your stomach **2** to make a gulping movement in the throat, as when nervous **3** (informal) to believe (something) gullibly **4** to refrain from showing (a feeling) **5** to engulf or absorb ▷ noun **6** small bird with long pointed wings and a forked tail **7** swallowing

swamp noun **1** watery area of land; bog ▷ verb **2** to cause (something) to fill or be covered with water **3** to overwhelm (something or someone) > **swampy** adjective

swan noun large usually white water bird with a long graceful neck

swap swaps, swapping, swapped verb **1** to exchange (something) for something else ▷ noun **2** exchange

swarm noun 1 large group of bees or other insects flying together ▷ verb 2 (of bees, insects) to fly together in a large group 3 (of people) to go somewhere quickly and at the same time 4 (of a place) to be crowded or overrun

swarthy swarthier, swarthiest adjective dark-complexioned

swashbuckling adjective having the exciting adventures of pirates, especially those depicted in films

swastika noun symbol in the shape of a cross with the arms bent over at right angles. It was the official symbol of the Nazis in Germany, but in India it is a good luck sign

swat swats, swatting, swatted verb to hit (an insect) sharply in order to kill it

swathe noun 1 long strip of cloth wrapped around something 2 long strip of land ▷ verb 3 to wrap (someone or something) in bandages or layers of cloth

swathed adjective **swathed in** wrapped in

sway verb 1 to swing to and fro or from side to side 2 to waver or to cause (someone) to waver in opinion ▷ noun 3 power or influence 4 swaying motion

swear swears, swearing, swore, sworn verb 1 to use obscene or blasphemous language 2 to state or promise an oath 3 to state earnestly > **swear by** verb to have complete confidence in > **swear in** verb to cause (someone new to a position) to take an oath promising to fulfil their duties

swearword noun word considered obscene or blasphemous which

some people use when they are angry

sweat noun 1 salty liquid given off through the pores of the skin when you are hot or afraid ▷ verb 2 to have sweat coming through the pores 3 to be anxious

sweater noun (woollen) garment for the upper part of the body

sweatshirt noun long-sleeved cotton jersey

sweaty sweatier, sweatiest adjective covered or soaked with sweat

swede noun large round root vegetable with yellow flesh and a brownish-purple skin

Swede noun someone from Sweden

Swedish adjective 1 belonging or relating to Sweden ▷ noun 2 main language spoken in Sweden

sweep sweeps, sweeping, swept verb 1 to remove dirt from (a floor) with a broom 2 to move smoothly and quickly 3 to spread rapidly 4 to move majestically 5 to carry (something or someone) away suddenly or forcefully 6 to stretch in a long wide curve ▷ noun 7 sweeping 8 sweeping motion 9 wide expanse 10 sweepstake 11 chimney sweep

sweeping adjective 1 (of curve or movement) long and wide 2 affecting a lot of people to a great extent; wide-ranging 3 (of statement) based on a general assumption rather than on careful thought; indiscriminate

sweet adjective 1 tasting of or like sugar 2 kind and charming 3 attractive and delightful 4 (of wine) with a high sugar content

a
b
c
d
e
f
g
h
i
j
k
l
m
n
o
p
q
r
s
t
u
v
w
x
y
z

5 pleasant and satisfying ▷ noun **6** things such as toffees, chocolates and mints **7** dessert > **sweetly** adverb > **sweetness** noun

sweet corn noun type of maize with sweet yellow kernels, eaten as a vegetable

sweeten verb to add sugar or another sweet substance to (food or drink)

sweetener noun sweet, artificial substance that can be used instead of sugar

sweetheart noun **1** form of address for someone you are very fond of **2** boyfriend or girlfriend

sweet pea noun climbing plant with bright fragrant flowers

sweet tooth noun strong liking for sweet foods

swell swells, swelling, swelled, swollen verb **1** to becomes larger and rounder **2** to increase in number **3** (of a sound) to become gradually louder ▷ noun **4** regular up and down movement of waves in the sea ▷ adjective **5** (US informal) excellent or fine

swelling noun **1** enlargement of part of the body, caused by injury or infection **2** increase in size

sweltering adjective uncomfortably hot

swerve verb to change direction suddenly to avoid colliding with something

swift adjective **1** moving or able to move quickly ▷ noun **2** fast-flying bird with narrow crescent-shaped wings > **swiftly** adverb > **swiftness** noun

swig swigs, swigging, swigged verb **1** to drink (something) in large mouthfuls, usually from a bottle ▷ noun **2** large mouthful of drink

swill verb **1** to rinse (something) in large amounts of water **2** to drink (something) greedily ▷ noun **3** sloppy mixture containing waste food, fed to pigs

swim swims, swimming, swam, swum verb **1** to move through water, using your arms and legs to help you **2** to be covered or flooded with liquid **3** to reel: Her head was swimming ▷ noun **4** act or period of swimming > **swimmer** noun

swimming noun activity of moving through water using your arms and legs

swimming bath noun public swimming pool

swimming costume noun clothing worn by a woman when she goes swimming

swimming pool noun (building containing) an artificial pond for swimming in

swimming trunks plural noun shorts or briefs worn by a man when he goes swimming

swimsuit noun swimming costume

swindle verb **1** to cheat (someone) out of money or property ▷ noun **2** trick in which someone is cheated out of money or property > **swindler** noun

swine noun **1** pig **2** nasty and unpleasant person

WORD TIP
The plural of swine is always swine when it refers to pigs. Both swine and swines are possible when it means people

swing swings, swinging, swung
verb **1** to move to and fro from a
fixed point **2** to move (something)
or to move in a curve **3** (of an
opinion or mood) to change
sharply **4** (informal) to be hanged
▷ noun **5** seat hanging from a
frame or a branch, which moves
backwards and forwards when
you sit on it **6** sudden or extreme
change **7** instance of swinging

swipe verb **1** to strike (at
something) with a sweeping blow
2 (informal) to steal **3** to pass (a
credit card or debit card) through
a machine that electronically
reads information stored in the
card ▷ noun **4** sweeping blow

swirl verb **1** to move quickly in
circles ▷ noun **2** whirling motion
3 twisting shape

swish verb **1** to move with a
soft whistling or hissing sound
▷ noun **2** whistling or hissing
sound ▷ adjective **3** (informal)
fashionable, smart

Swiss adjective **1** belonging or
relating to Switzerland ▷ noun
2 person from Switzerland

> **WORD TIP**
> The plural of Swiss is Swiss

switch noun **1** small control for
an electrical device or machine
2 abrupt change **3** exchange or
swap ▷ verb **4** to change abruptly
(to something) **5** to replace
(something) with something else
> **switch off** verb **1** to turn (a light
or machine) off by means of a
switch **2** to stop paying attention
> **switch on** verb to turn (a light
or machine) on by means of a
switch

switchboard noun place in an
office where telephone calls are
received and connected to the
appropriate people

swivel swivels, swivelling,
swivelled verb **1** to turn round on
a central point ▷ adjective **2** (of
chair, stool) revolving

swollen verb **1 a** past participle of
swell ▷ adjective **2** having swelled
up; enlarged or puffed up

swoon verb **1** to faint ▷ noun
2 faint

swoop verb **1** to sweep down or
pounce suddenly

swop noun, verb same as **swap**

sword noun weapon with a long
sharp blade and a short handle

swordfish swordfishes or
swordfish noun large fish with a
very long upper jaw

sworn verb **1** past participle of
swear ▷ adjective **2** bound by or as
if by an oath: sworn enemies

swot swots, swotting, swotted
(informal) verb **1** to study or revise
hard ▷ noun **2** someone who
spends too much time studying
> **swot up** verb to find out as
much about a subject as possible
in a short time

sycamore noun tree that has large
leaves with five points

syllable noun part of a word
pronounced as a unit

syllabus syllabuses or syllabi noun
list of subjects for a particular
course or examination

symbol noun shape, design or
idea that is used to represent
something

symbolic adjective having a special
meaning that is considered to
represent something else

symbolize or **symbolise**
verb **1** (of shape, design or

a
b
c
d
e
f
g
h
i
j
k
l
m
n
o
p
q
r
s
t
u
v
w
x
y
z

idea) to be a symbol of **2** to represent (something) with a symbol >**symbolism** noun **1** representation of something by symbols **2** movement in art and literature using symbols to express abstract and mystical ideas

symmetrical adjective having two halves that are mirror images of each other >**symmetrically** adverb

symmetry noun state of having two halves that are mirror images of each other

sympathetic adjective **1** feeling or showing kindness and understanding to other people **2** likeable or appealing **3** (followed by to, towards) agreeable or favourably disposed (to something) >**sympathetically** adverb

sympathize or **sympathise** verb **1** to feel or express understanding and concern **2** to have similar feelings

sympathizer or **sympathiser** noun supporter of a particular cause

sympathy sympathies noun **1** compassion for someone's pain or distress **2** agreement with someone's feelings or interests

symphony symphonies noun composition for orchestra, with several movements

symptom noun **1** something wrong with your body that is a sign of an illness **2** sign that something is wrong >**symptomatic** adjective: The price dispute was symptomatic of other problems

synagogue noun place of worship and religious instruction for Jewish people

synchronize or **synchronise** verb **1** (of two or more people) to perform (an action) at the same time **2** to set (watches) to show the same time **3** to match (the soundtrack and action of a film) precisely >**synchronization** noun

syncopation noun (Music) stressing of weak beats instead of the usual strong ones

syndicate noun group of people or firms undertaking a joint project

syndrome noun **1** medical condition characterized by a particular set of symptoms **2** set of characteristics indicating a particular problem

synod noun church council

synonym noun word with the same meaning as or a similar meaning to another

synonymous adjective **1** having the same or a very similar meaning **2** (followed by with) closely associated: the Statue of Liberty is synonymous with New York

synopsis synopses noun summary or outline of a book, play or film

syntax noun (Grammar) way in which words are arranged to form phrases and sentences

synthesis syntheses noun **1** combination of objects or ideas into a whole **2** SCIENCE artificial production of a substance >**synthetic** adjective **1** (of a substance) made artificially rather than naturally **2** not genuine; insincere

syphon verb same as **siphon**

t

Syrian [**sirr**-ee-an] *adjective*
1 belonging or relating to Syria
▷ *noun* **2** someone from Syria

syringe *noun* **1** hollow tube with a part inside that can be raised or pushed down to draw up or squirt down liquid **2** similar device, with a fine hollow needle at one end, for giving injections and taking blood samples ▷ *verb* **3** to clean (part of the body) using a syringe

syrup *noun* **1** solution of sugar in water **2** thick sweet liquid
> **syrupy** *adjective*

system *noun* **1** method or set of methods for doing something **2** set of interconnected pieces of equipment **3** (*Biology*) set of organs that together perform a function: *the immune system* **4** scheme of classification or arrangement

systematic *adjective* following a fixed plan and done in an efficient way > **systematically** *adverb*

tab *noun* small flap or projecting label

tabby *noun* cat with dark stripes on a lighter background

tabernacle *noun* **1** portable shrine of the Israelites **2** Christian place of worship not called a church **3** Jewish temple

table *noun* **1** piece of furniture with a flat top supported by legs **2** arrangement of information in columns ▷ *verb* **3** to submit (a motion) for discussion by a meeting

tablecloth *noun* a cloth used to cover a table and keep it clean

table football *noun* game like soccer played on a table with sets of miniature figures on rods allowing them to be moved to hit a ball

tablespoon *noun* large spoon for serving food

tablet *noun* **1** pill of compressed medicinal substance **2** inscribed slab of stone etc

table tennis *noun* game like tennis played on a table with small bats and a light ball

tabloid *noun* (ENGLISH) small-sized newspaper with many photographs and a concise, usually sensational style

taboo *noun* **1** social custom that some words, subjects

a
b
c
d
e
f
g
h
i
j
k
l
m
n
o
p
q
r
s
t
u
v
w
x
y
z

or actions must be avoided because embarrassing or offensive **2** religious custom that forbids people to do something ▷ *adjective* **3** forbidden by a taboo

tacit [**tass**-it] *adjective* implied but not spoken ▷ **tacitly** *adverb*

taciturn [**tass**-it-turn] *adjective* habitually not talking very much

tack *noun* **1** short nail with a large head **2** course of action: *in desperation I changed tack* ▷ *verb* **3** to fasten (something to a surface) with tacks **4** to stitch (a piece of fabric) with tacks

tackies or **takkies** *plural noun* (S Afr informal) tennis shoes or plimsolls

tackle *verb* **1** to deal with (a task) **2** to confront (an opponent) **3** (Sport) to attempt to get the ball from an opposing player ▷ *noun* **4** (Sport) act of tackling an opposing player **5** equipment for fishing

tacky tackier, tackiest *adjective* **1** slightly sticky **2** (*informal*) vulgar and tasteless

tact *noun* skill in avoiding giving offence; diplomacy ▷ **tactful** *adjective* careful not to offend people ▷ **tactfully** *adverb*: *He tactfully refrained from further comment* ▷ **tactless** *adjective*: *tactless remarks* ▷ **tactlessly** *adverb* in a tactless manner

tactic *noun* [PE] method or plan to achieve an end ▷ **tactical** *adjective*: *a tactical move* ▷ **tactically** *adverb*: *to vote tactically* ▷ **tactics** *noun* art of directing military forces in battle

tactile *adjective* of or having the sense of touch

tadpole *noun* black long-tailed larva of a frog or toad

taffeta *noun* stiff shiny silk or rayon fabric

tag tags, tagging, tagged *noun* **1** small label made of cloth, paper or plastic **2** children's game where the person being chased becomes the chaser upon being touched ▷ *verb* **3** to attach a tag to ▷ **tag along** *with verb* to accompany (someone), especially if uninvited

tail *noun* **1** part extending beyond the end of the body of an animal, bird, or fish **2** rear or last part or parts of something ▷ *verb* **3** (*informal*) to follow (someone) secretly ▷ **tail off** *verb* to become gradually less ▷ **tails** *plural noun* **1** (*informal*) man's coat with a long back split into two below the waist ▷ *adjective, adverb* **2** with the side of a coin uppermost that does not have a portrait of a head on it

tailback *noun* (Brit) queue of traffic stretching back from an obstruction

tailor *noun* **1** person who makes men's clothes ▷ *verb* **2** to adapt (something) to suit a purpose

tailor-made *adjective* perfect for a purpose

taint *verb* **1** to spoil (something) with a small amount of decay, contamination or other bad quality ▷ *noun* **2** something that taints

taipan *noun* (Aust) large poisonous Australian snake

take takes, taking, took, taken *verb* **1** to remove (something) from a place **2** to accompany (someone) somewhere **3** to use (a mode of transport or a road) to go from one place to another **4** to steal **5** to swallow (medicine) **6** to bear (something painful): *We can't take much more of this* **7** to measure (someone's temperature or pulse) **8** to require (time, resources or ability) **9** to accept > **take after** *verb* to look or behave like (a parent etc) > **take down** *verb* to write down (what someone is saying) > **take in** *verb* **1** to understand **2** to deceive or swindle > **take off** *verb* (of an aircraft) to leave the ground > **take over** *verb* to start controlling > **take to** *verb* to like (someone or something) immediately

takeaway *noun* shop or restaurant selling meals for eating elsewhere

takings *plural noun* money received by a shop, theatre or cinema, etc

talc *noun* talcum powder

talcum powder *noun* powder, usually scented, used to dry or perfume the body

tale *noun* story

talent *noun* natural ability; gift > **talented** *adjective*: *a talented pianist*

talisman *noun* object believed to have magic power

talk *verb* **1** to express ideas or feelings by means of speech **2** to gossip **3** to make an informal speech about something > *noun* **4** discussion or gossip **5** speech or lecture > **talkative** *adjective* fond of talking; chatty > **talk down to** *verb* to talk to (someone) as if you are more important or clever than him or her

tall *adjective* **1** higher than average **2** of a specified height: *a wall ten metres tall*

tally tallies, tallying, tallied *verb* **1** (of numbers or statements) to be exactly the same or give the same results or conclusions > *noun* **2** record of a debt or score

Talmud *noun* books containing the ancient Jewish ceremonies and civil laws

talon *noun* bird's hooked claw

tambourine *noun* percussion instrument like a small drum with jingling metal discs attached

tame *adjective* **1** (of animals) brought under human control **2** (of animals) not afraid of people **3** uninteresting and unexciting > *verb* **4** to make (a wild animal) tame

tamper *verb* (followed by *with*) to interfere with (something)

tampon *noun* firm piece of cotton wool inserted into the vagina to absorb the blood during menstruation

tan tans, tanning, tanned *noun* **1** brown coloration of the skin from exposure to sunlight > *verb* **2** (of skin) to go brown from exposure to sunlight **3** to convert (an animal's hide) into leather > *adjective* **4** yellowish-brown

tandem *noun* bicycle for two riders, one behind the other

tang *noun* strong sharp taste or smell > **tangy** *adjective* having a strong sharp taste or smell

tangata whenua [tang-ah-tah [fen]-noo-ah] *plural noun* (NZ) original Polynesian settlers in New Zealand

tangent noun 1 line that touches a curve without intersecting it 2 go off at a tangent to move to an unrelated and completely different line of thought or action

tangerine noun 1 small orange-like fruit of an Asian citrus tree 2 reddish orange ▷ adjective 3 reddish-orange

tangible adjective clear or definite enough to be easily seen or felt: tangible proof

tangle noun 1 confused mass or situation ▷ verb 2 to catch or trap (someone) in wires or ropes so that it is difficult to get free

tango tangos noun S American dance

taniwha [tun-ee-fah] noun (NZ) mythical Māori monster that lives in water

tank noun 1 container for liquids or gases 2 armoured fighting vehicle moving on tracks

tankard noun large beer-mug, often with a hinged lid

tanker noun ship or truck for carrying liquid in bulk

tannin noun vegetable substance used in tanning

tantalizing or **tantalising** adjective excitingly and tormentingly desirable but difficult or impossible to get: a tantalizing glimpse of riches to come

tantamount adjective

tantamount to equivalent in effect to

tantrum noun childish outburst of temper

Tanzanian [tan-zan-**nee**-an] adjective 1 of Tanzania ▷ noun 2 person from Tanzania

tap taps, tapping, tapped verb 1 to hit (something) lightly 2 to fit a device to (a telephone) in order to listen secretly to the calls ▷ noun 3 light knock 4 valve to control the flow of liquid from a pipe or cask

tap dancing noun style of dancing in which the dancers wear shoes with metal toe caps and heels that click against the floor

tape noun 1 long thin strip of fabric used for binding or fastening 2 strip of sticky plastic used for sticking things together 3 (recording made on) a cassette containing magnetic tape ▷ verb 4 to record (sounds or television pictures) using a tape recorder or a video recorder 5 to attach (things) with sticky tape

tape measure noun tape marked off in centimetres or inches for measuring

taper verb 1 to become narrower towards one end ▷ noun 2 long thin candle

tape recorder noun device for recording and reproducing sound on magnetic tape

tapestry tapestries noun fabric decorated with coloured woven designs

tar noun thick, black, sticky substance used in making roads

tarantula noun large hairy spider with a poisonous bite

target noun 1 something you aim at when firing weapons 2 goal or objective 3 person or thing at which an action or remark is directed: a target for our hatred

tariff noun 1 tax that a government collects on imported goods 2 list of fixed prices

Tarmac ® noun mixture of tar, bitumen and crushed stones used for roads etc

tarnish verb 1 to become stained or less bright 2 to damage or taint (someone's reputation)

tarot card [**tarr**-oh] noun card in a special pack used mainly in fortune-telling

tarpaulin noun sheet of heavy waterproof fabric

tarragon noun herb with narrow green leaves used in cooking

tarry tarries, tarrying verb (old-fashioned) 1 to linger or delay 2 to stay somewhere briefly

tar-seal noun (NZ) tarred road surface

tart noun 1 pie or flan with a sweet filling ▷ adjective 2 sour or sharp to taste 3 (of a remark) unpleasant and cruel

tartan noun 1 design of straight lines crossing at right angles, especially one associated with a Scottish clan 2 cloth with such a pattern

tartar noun hard deposit on the teeth

tarwhine noun edible Australian sea fish, especially a sea bream

task noun (difficult or unpleasant) piece of work to be done; duty

Tasmanian devil noun black-and-white marsupial of Tasmania that eats flesh

tassel noun decorative fringed knot of threads

taste noun 1 sense by which the flavour of a substance is distinguished in the mouth 2 distinctive flavour 3 small amount tasted 4 brief experience of something 5 liking 6 ability to appreciate what is beautiful or excellent ▷ verb 7 to distinguish the taste of (a substance) 8 to take a small amount of (something) into the mouth 9 to have a specific taste: *it tastes like chocolate* > **tasteful** adjective having or showing good taste > **tastefully** adverb: *a tastefully decorated home* > **tasteless** adjective 1 vulgar and unattractive 2 (of a remark or joke) offensive 3 (of food) having very little flavour

taste bud noun small organ on the tongue which perceives flavours

tasty tastier, tastiest adjective pleasantly flavoured

tatters plural noun **in tatters** badly torn > **tattered** adjective ragged or torn

tattoo tattoos, tattooing, tattooed noun 1 pattern made on the body by pricking the skin and staining it with indelible inks 2 military display or pageant ▷ verb 3 to make a pattern on the body of (someone) by pricking the skin and staining it with indelible inks

tatty tattier, tattiest adjective shabby or worn out

taught verb past of **teach**

taunt verb 1 to tease (someone) with jeers ▷ noun 2 jeering remark

Taurus noun second sign of the zodiac, represented by a bull

taut adjective drawn tight

tavern noun (old-fashioned) pub

tawdry tawdrier, tawdriest adjective cheap, showy and of poor quality

tawny adjective yellowish-brown

tax noun **1** amount of money that people have to pay to the government so that it can provide public services ▷ verb **2** to levy a tax on (something) **3** to make heavy demands on (someone) ▷ **taxation** noun levying of taxes

taxi taxis, taxiing, taxied noun **1** car with a driver that may be hired to take people to any specified destination ▷ verb **2** (of an aircraft) to run along the ground before taking off or after landing

tea noun **1** drink made from infusing the dried leaves of an Asian bush in boiling water **2** cup of this drink **3** leaves used to make this drink **4** (Brit, Aust, NZ) main evening meal **5** (Chiefly Brit) light afternoon meal of tea, cakes, etc **6** drink like tea, made from other plants; infusion

tea bag noun small porous bag of tea leaves, placed in boiling water to make tea

teach teaches, teaching, taught verb **1** to tell or show (someone) how to do something **2** to give lessons in (a subject) **3** to cause (someone) to learn or understand ▷ **teacher** noun person who teaches, especially in a school ▷ **teaching** noun: the teaching of English in schools

teak noun very hard wood of a large Asian tree

team noun **1** group of people forming one side in a game **2** group of people or animals working together ▷ **team up with** verb to join (someone) to work together

teamwork noun cooperative work by a team

teapot noun container with a lid, spout and handle for making and serving tea

tear tears, tearing, tore, torn noun **1** drop of fluid appearing in and falling from the eye **2** hole or split ▷ verb **3** to rip a hole in (soemthing) **4** to rush somewhere ▷ **tearful** adjective weeping or about to weep ▷ **tearfully** adverb: She smiled tearfully

tearaway noun wild or unruly person

tease verb **1** to make fun of (someone) in a provoking or playful way ▷ noun **2** person who teases

teaspoon noun small spoon for stirring tea

teat noun **1** nipple of a breast or udder **2** rubber nipple of a feeding bottle

tea tree noun (Aust, NZ) tree found in Australia and New Zealand with leaves containing tannin, like tea leaves

tech noun (informal) technical college

technical adjective **1** of or specializing in industrial, practical or mechanical arts and applied sciences **2** skilled in technical subjects **3** relating to a particular field ▷ **technically** adverb according to a strict interpretation of the rules: technically illegal

technical college noun college with courses in subjects like technology and secretarial skills

technicality technicalities noun **1** petty point based on a strict application of rules **2 technicalities** detailed methods used for a process or activity

technician noun person skilled in a particular technique

technique noun **1** method or skill used for a particular task **2** skill and ability developed through training and practice

techno- prefix craft or art: technology

technology noun **1** [D&T] application of practical or mechanical sciences to industry or commerce **2** area of activity requiring scientific methods and knowledge: computer technology > **technological** adjective: an era of rapid technological change > **technologically** adverb: technologically advanced

teddy teddies noun soft toy bear (also **teddy bear**)

tedious adjective causing fatigue or boredom

tedium noun quality of being boring and lasting for a long time

tee tees, teeing, teed noun **1** small peg from which a golf ball can be played at the start of each hole **2** area of a golf course from which the first stroke of a hole is made > **tee off** verb to make the first stroke of a hole in golf

teem verb **1** (followed by with) to be full of (people or things) **2** to rain heavily

teenager noun person aged between 13 and 19 > **teenage** adjective **1** aged between 13 and 19 **2** typical of people aged between 13 and 19: teenage fashion

teens plural noun period of being a teenager

teeter verb to wobble or move unsteadily

teeth noun plural of **tooth**

teethe verb (of a baby) to grow his or her first teeth

teetotal adjective drinking no alcohol > **teetotaller** noun person who never drinks alcohol

tele- prefix distance: telecommunications

telecommunications noun communications using telephone, radio, television, etc

telegram noun formerly, a message sent by telegraph

telegraph noun formerly, a system for sending messages over a distance along a cable

telepathy noun direct communication between people's minds > **telepathic** adjective able to communicate with other people's minds

telephone 1 device for transmitting sound over a distance along wires ▷ verb **2** to call or talk to (someone) by telephone

telephone box noun small shelter in the street containing a public telephone

telescope noun long instrument shaped like a tube with lenses that make distant objects appear larger and nearer

Teletext ® noun electronic system that broadcasts pages of information onto a television set

televise verb to broadcast (an event) on television

television noun **1** system of producing a moving image and

a b c d e f g h i j k l m n o p q r s t u v w x y z

accompanying sound on a distant screen **2** device for receiving broadcast signals and converting them into sound and pictures

tell tells, telling, told *verb* **1** to make (something) known to (someone) in words **2** to order or instruct (someone) to do something **3** to judge correctly (what is happening or what the situation is) **4** (of an unpleasant or tiring experience) to have a serious effect >**teller** *noun* bank cashier > **telling** *adjective* having a marked effect

telltale *noun* **1** person who reveals secrets > *adjective* **2** revealing

telly tellies *noun* (*informal*) television

temerity [tim-**merr**-it-tee] *noun* boldness

temp *noun* (*Brit informal*) temporary employee, especially a secretary

temper *noun* **1** outburst of anger **2** calm mental condition: *I lost my temper* **3** frame of mind ▷ *verb* **4** to make (something) less extreme

temperament *noun* person's character or disposition

temperamental *adjective* having changeable moods

temperate *adjective* (of climate) not extreme

temperature *noun* **1** SCIENCE degree of heat or cold **2** (*informal*) abnormally high body temperature

tempest *noun* (*literary*) violent storm

tempestuous *adjective* violent or strongly emotional

template *noun* pattern used to cut out shapes accurately

temple *noun* **1** RE building for worship **2** region on either side of the forehead

tempo *noun* **1** rate or pace **2** MUSIC speed of a piece of music

temporary *adjective* lasting only for a short time >**temporarily** *adverb*: *the peace agreement has temporarily halted the civil war*

tempt *verb* **1** to entice (someone) to do something **2 be tempted to do something** to want to do something you think might be wrong or harmful

temptation *noun* **1** state of being tempted **2** tempting thing

ten *adjective, noun* the number 10

tenacious *adjective* determined and not giving up easily >**tenaciously** *adverb*: *In spite of his illness, he clung tenaciously to his job* >**tenacity** *noun* determination

tenant *noun* person who rents land or a building >**tenancy** *noun*: *He took over the tenancy of the farm*

tend *verb* **1** to be inclined (to do something) **2** to take care of (someone or something)

tendency tendencies *noun* inclination to act in a certain way

tender *adjective* **1** (of meat) easy to cut or chew **2** (of a person) gentle and affectionate **3** (of a body part) painful and sore **4 at a tender age** young and inexperienced ▷ *verb* **5** to offer (an apology or your resignation) ▷ *noun* **6** a formal offer to supply goods or services at a stated cost

tendon *noun* strong tissue attaching a muscle to a bone

tendril noun slender stem by which a climbing plant clings

tenement noun (especially in Scotland or the US) building divided into several flats

tenet [**ten**-nit] noun doctrine or belief

tenner noun (Brit informal) ten-pound note

tennis noun game in which players use rackets to hit a ball back and forth over a net

tenor noun 1 singer with the second highest male voice 2 general meaning ▷ adjective 3 (of a voice or instrument) between alto and baritone

tense adjective 1 emotionally strained; anxious 2 (of a situation or period of time) causing nervousness and worry 3 stretched tight ▷ verb 4 to become tense ▷ noun 5 (Grammar) form of a verb showing the time of action

tension noun 1 emotional strain; anxiety 2 D&T degree of stretching

tent noun portable canvas shelter

tentacle noun long thin parts of an animal such as an octopus that it uses to feel and hold things

tentative adjective cautious or hesitant ▷ **tentatively** adverb cautiously or hesitantly

tenterhooks plural noun **on tenterhooks** in anxious suspense

tenuous adjective slight or flimsy

tenure noun 1 legal right to live in a place or to use land or buildings for a period of time 2 period of the holding of an office or position

tepee [**tee**-pee] noun cone-shaped tent, formerly used by Native Americans

tepid adjective slightly warm

term noun 1 word or expression 2 fixed period 3 period of the year when a school etc is open or a law court holds sessions 4 **terms** conditions of an agreement 5 type of language: *The young priest spoke of her in glowing terms* 6 **come to terms with** to learn to accept (something difficult or unpleasant) ▷ verb 7 to give a name to or describe (something)

terminal adjective 1 (of an illness) ending in death ▷ noun 2 place where people or vehicles begin or end a journey 3 point where current enters or leaves an electrical device 4 keyboard and VDU having input and output links with a computer ▷ **terminally** adverb: *terminally ill*

terminate verb to come to an end or bring (something) to an end ▷ **termination** noun: *the termination of trade*

terminology terminologies noun set of technical terms relating to a subject

terminus terminuses noun railway or bus station at the end of a line

termite noun white antlike insect that destroys timber

tern noun gull-like sea bird with a forked tail and pointed wings

ternary adjective MUSIC consisting of three parts

terrace noun 1 row of houses built as one block 2 paved area next to a building

terracotta noun brownish-red unglazed pottery

terrain noun area of ground, especially with reference to its physical character

terrapin noun small turtle-like reptile

terrestrial adjective of the earth or land

terrible adjective 1 very serious 2 (informal) very bad > **terribly** adverb very or very much: terribly upset

terrier noun a small short-bodied dog

terrific adjective 1 great or intense 2 (informal) excellent > **terrifically** adverb: terrifically repressed

terrify terrifies, terrifying, terrified verb to fill (someone) with fear

territory territories noun 1 area under the control of a particular government 2 area inhabited and defended by an animal > **territorial** adjective of the ownership of a particular area of land or water: a territorial dispute

terror noun 1 great fear 2 terrifying person or thing

terrorism noun use of violence and intimidation to achieve political ends > **terrorist** noun, adjective: terrorist attacks

terrorize or **terrorise** verb to force or oppress (someone) by fear or violence

terse adjective (of a statement) short and rather unfriendly

tertiary [tur-shar-ee] adjective 1 third in degree, order, etc 2 (of education) at university or college level

test verb 1 to try out (something) to ascertain its worth, capability or endurance 2 to ask (someone) questions to find out how much he or she knows > noun 3 deliberate action or experiment to find out whether something works or how well it works 4 set of questions or tasks given to someone to find out what he or she knows > **testing** adjective (of a situation or problem) very difficult to deal with: a testing time

testament noun (Law) will

test case noun lawsuit that establishes a precedent

testicle noun either of the two male reproductive glands

testify testifies, testifying, testified verb 1 to give evidence under oath 2 **testify to** to be evidence of

testimony testimonies noun formal statement, especially in a court of law > **testimonial** noun statement saying how good someone or something is

testis testes noun testicle

test match noun one of a series of international cricket or rugby matches

testosterone noun male hormone that produces male characteristics

test tube noun narrow round-bottomed glass tube used in scientific experiments

tetanus noun painful infectious disease caused by germs getting into wounds

tether noun 1 rope or chain for tying an animal to a spot 2 **at the end of your tether** at the limit of your endurance ▷ *verb* **3** to tie (an animal) up with rope

Teutonic [tew-**tonn**-ik] *adjective* of or like the (ancient) Germans

text *noun* **1** main written part of a book, rather than the pictures or index **2** any written material **3** novel or play studied for a course **4** text message ▷ *verb* **5** to send a text message to (someone) >**textual** *adjective*: *textual analysis of Shakespeare*

textbook *noun* book about a particular subject for students to use

textile *noun* D&T fabric or cloth, especially woven

text message *noun* message sent in text form, especially by means of a mobile phone

texture *noun* structure, feel or consistency

Thai Thais *adjective* **1** of Thailand ▷ *noun* **2** person from Thailand **3** main language spoken in Thailand

than *conjunction, preposition* used to introduce the second element of a comparison

thank *verb* to express gratitude to (someone)

thankful *adjective* grateful >**thankfully** *adverb*: *Thankfully, she was not injured*

thankless *adjective* unrewarding or unappreciated

thanks *plural noun* **1** words of gratitude **2 thanks to** because of (someone or something): *I'm as prepared as I can be, thanks to you* ▷ *interjection* **3** polite expression of gratitude

thanksgiving *noun* **1** act of thanking God, especially in prayer

or in a religious ceremony **2** (*US, Canadian*) public holiday in the autumn

thank you *interjection* expression of gratitude

that *adjective, pronoun* **1** used to refer to someone or something already mentioned, familiar or at a distance ▷ *conjunction* **2** used to introduce a clause ▷ *pronoun* **3** used to introduce a relative clause

thatch *noun* **1** roofing material of reeds or straw ▷ *verb* **2** to roof (a house) with reeds or straw

thaw *verb* **1** to make or become unfrozen **2** to become more relaxed or friendly ▷ *noun* **3** warmer weather causing snow or ice to melt

the *adjective* the definite article, used before a noun

theatre *noun* **1** DRAMA place where plays etc are performed **2** hospital operating room **3** drama and acting in general

theatrical *adjective* **1** DRAMA involving or performed in the theatre **2** exaggerated or affected >**theatrically** *adverb*

thee *pronoun* (*old-fashioned*) objective form of **thou**

theft *noun* act or an instance of stealing

their *adjective* of or associated with them >**theirs** *pronoun* (thing or person) belonging to them

> **WORD TIP**
> Be careful not to confuse *their* with *there*.

them *pronoun* refers to people or things other than the speaker or those addressed

theme noun **1** main idea or subject being discussed **2** tune, especially one played at the beginning and end of a television or radio programme

themselves pronoun emphatic and reflexive form of **they, them**

then adverb **1** at that time **2** that being so

theology noun study of religions and religious beliefs > **theologian** noun person who studies religion and the nature of God > **theological** adjective: theological books

theoretical adjective **1** based on theory rather than practice or fact **2** not proved to exist or be true > **theoretically** adverb in theory

theory theories noun **1** set of ideas to explain something **2** idea or opinion **3** in theory in an ideal or hypothetical situation

therapeutic [ther-rap-**pew**-tik] adjective **1** causing you to feel happier and more relaxed **2** (Medicine) (of treatment) designed to treat a disease or improve a person's health

therapy noun curing treatment > **therapist** noun person skilled in a particular type of therapy

there adverb **1** in or to that point or that place ▷ pronoun **2** used to say that something exists or does not exist or to draw attention to something: There are flowers on the table

WORD TIP
Be careful not to confuse there with their. A good way to remember that there is connected to the idea of place is by remembering the spelling of two other place words, here and where

thereby adverb (formal) by that means

therefore adverb consequently, that being so

thermal adjective **1** of heat **2** (of clothing) retaining heat

thermometer noun SCIENCE instrument for measuring temperature

thermostat noun device for controlling temperature, e.g. on a central-heating system

thesaurus thesauruses [thiss-**sore**-uss] noun LIBRARY reference book in which words with similar meanings are grouped together

these adjective, pronoun plural of **this**

thesis theses noun written work submitted for a university degree

they pronoun refers to **1** people or things other than the speaker or people addressed **2** people in general **3** (informal) he or she

thick adjective **1** of great or specified extent from one side to the other **2** measuring a certain amount from one side to the other **3** having a dense consistency **4** (informal) stupid or insensitive

thicken verb to become thick or thicker

thicket noun dense growth of small trees

thief thieves noun person who steals

thieving noun act of stealing

thigh noun upper part of the human leg

thimble noun cap protecting the end of the finger when sewing

thin thinner, thinnest; thins, thinning, thinned adjective **1** not thick **2** slim or lean **3** (of a liquid) containing a lot of water: thin soup ▷ verb **4** to make (something such as paint or soup) thinner by adding liquid

thing noun **1** an object rather than a plant, animal or human being **2** things possessions, clothes, etc

think thinks, thinking, thought verb **1** to consider, judge or believe (something) **2** to make use of the mind **3** to be considerate enough or remember (to do something)

third adjective, noun **1** (coming as) number three in a series ▷ noun **2** one of three equal parts

Third World noun developing countries of Africa, Asia and Latin America

thirst noun **1** desire to drink **2** craving or yearning > **thirstily** adverb: drinking her milk thirstily > **thirsty** adjective: Drink when you feel thirsty during exercise

thirteen adjective, noun the number 13 > **thirteenth** adjective, noun

thirty thirties adjective, noun the number 30 > **thirtieth** adjective, noun

this adjective, pronoun **1** used to refer to a thing or person nearby, just mentioned or about to be mentioned ▷ adjective **2** used to refer to the present time: this morning

thistle noun prickly plant with purple flowers

thong noun **1** thin strip of leather etc **2** skimpy article of underwear or beachwear that covers the genitals while leaving the buttocks bare

thorn noun prickle on a plant > **thorny** adjective **1** covered with thorns **2** (of a subject or question) difficult to discuss or answer

thorough adjective **1** complete **2** (of a person) careful or methodical > **thoroughly** adverb: I thoroughly enjoy your programme

thoroughbred noun animal of pure breed

thoroughfare noun main road in a town

those adjective, pronoun plural of **that**

thou pronoun (obsolete) singular form of **you**

though conjunction **1** despite the fact that ▷ adverb **2** nevertheless

thought verb **1** past of **think** ▷ noun **2** thinking; reflection **3** concept or idea **4** ideas typical of a time or place > **thoughtful** adjective **1** kind and considerate **2** quiet and serious because thinking about something > **thoughtfully** adverb > **thoughtless** adjective inconsiderate > **thoughtlessly** adverb

thousand adjective, noun **1** the number 1000 ▷ noun **2** thousands large but unspecified number; lots > **thousandth** adjective, noun

thrash verb **1** to beat (someone), especially with a stick or whip **2** to defeat (someone) completely > **thrash out** verb to solve (a problem) by thorough argument

thread noun **1** fine strand or yarn **2** idea or theme connecting the different parts of an argument or story **3** spiral ridge on a screw, nut or bolt ▷ *verb* **4** to pass thread, tape or cord through (something) **5** to carefully make (your way) somewhere

threadbare *adjective* (of clothing) old and thin

threat *noun* **1** declaration of intent to harm **2** dangerous person or thing **3** possibility of something unpleasant happening

threaten *verb* **1** to make or be a threat to (someone) **2** to be likely to harm (someone or something)

three *adjective, noun* the number 3

three-dimensional *adjective* having height or depth as well as length and width

threesome *noun* group of three

threshold *noun* **1** bar forming the bottom of a doorway **2** entrance **3** point at which something begins to take effect

thrice *adverb* (old-fashioned) three times

thrift *noun* wisdom and caution with money ▷ **thrifty** *adjective* inclined to save money and not waste things

thrill *noun* **1** sudden feeling of excitement **2** something causing a sudden feeling of excitement ▷ *verb* **3** to cause (someone) to feel a thrill **4** (followed by *to*) to feel a thrill because of (something) ▷ **thrilled** *adjective* extremely pleased ▷ **thrilling** *adjective* very exciting and enjoyable

thriller *noun* book, film, etc with an atmosphere of mystery or suspense

thrive thrives, thriving, thrived or throve *verb* to be healthy, happy

or successful ▷ **thriving** *adjective*: *the river's thriving population of kingfishers*

throat *noun* **1** passage from the mouth and nose to the stomach and lungs **2** front of the neck

throb throbs, throbbing, throbbed *verb* **1** (of a body part) to produce a series of strong beats or dull pains **2** to vibrate with a loud rhythmic noise

throes *plural noun* **1** violent pangs or pains **2 in the throes of** struggling to cope with (something)

thrombosis thromboses *noun* forming of a clot in a blood vessel or the heart

throne *noun* **1** ceremonial seat of a monarch or bishop **2** position of being king or queen

throng *noun* **1** large crowd ▷ *verb* **2** to go to (a place) in large numbers

throttle *noun* **1** device controlling the amount of fuel entering an engine ▷ *verb* **2** to strangle (someone)

through *preposition* **1** from end to end or side to side of **2** because of **3** during ▷ *adjective* **4** finished: *I'm through with the explaining*

WORD TIP
Do not confuse the spellings of *through* and *threw*, the past tense of *throw*

throughout *preposition, adverb* in every part (of)

throve *verb* a past tense of **thrive**

throw throws, throwing, threw, thrown *verb* **1** to hurl (something) through the air **2** to move (yourself) suddenly or with force **3** to bring (someone) into a specified state, especially suddenly: *It threw them into a panic* **4 throw a tantrum** to suddenly begin behaving in an uncontrolled way **5 throw light on** to make (something) have light on it **6 throw yourself into** to become enthusiastically involved in (an activity)

throwback noun something that has the characteristics of something that existed a long time ago: *a throwback to the fifties*

thrush noun **1** brown songbird **2** fungal disease of the mouth or vagina

thrust thrusts, thrusting, thrust verb **1** to push (something) somewhere forcefully **2** to make (your way) somewhere by pushing between people or things ▷ noun **3** sudden forceful movement **4** most important part of an activity, idea or argument

thud thuds, thudding, thudded noun **1** dull heavy sound ▷ verb **2** to make such a sound

thug noun violent man, especially a criminal

thumb noun **1** short thick finger set apart from the others ▷ verb **2** to signal with the thumb for (a lift in a vehicle)

thump noun **1** (sound of) a dull heavy blow ▷ verb **2** to strike (someone or something) heavily **3** to make a fairly loud, dull sound, as of something falling **4** (of your heart) to beat strongly and quickly

thunder noun **1** loud noise accompanying lightning **2** any loud rumbling noise ▷ verb **3** to

rumble with thunder **4** to make a loud continuous noise

thunderbolt noun lightning flash

thunderous adjective very loud

Thursday noun day between Wednesday and Friday

thus adverb (formal) **1** therefore **2** in this way

thwart verb to foil or frustrate (someone or his or her plans)

thy adjective (old-fashioned) of or associated with you (thou)

thyme [time] noun bushy herb with very small leaves

thyroid adjective, noun (of) a gland in the neck controlling body growth

tiara noun woman's semicircular jewelled headdress

Tibetan adjective of Tibet ▷ noun **2** person from Tibet

tic noun twitching of a group of muscles, especially in the face

tick noun **1** mark (✓) used to check off or indicate the correctness of something **2** recurrent tapping sound, as of a clock **3** tiny bloodsucking parasitic animal ▷ verb **4** to mark (something) with a tick **5** (of a clock) to make a ticking sound > **ticking** noun: *the endless ticking of clocks* > **tick off** (informal) to speak angrily to (someone) who has done something wrong

ticket noun card or paper entitling the holder to admission, travel, etc

tickle verb **1** to touch or stroke (someone) to produce laughter **2** to please or amuse (someone)

tidal adjective of or relating to tides

tidal wave noun very large destructive wave

tide noun 1 rise and fall of the sea caused by the gravitational pull of the sun and moon 2 current caused by this 3 widespread feeling or tendency > **tide over** verb to help (someone) through a difficult period of time

tidings plural noun (formal) news

tidy tidier, tidiest; tidies, tidying, tidied adjective 1 neat and orderly 2 (Brit, Aust, NZ informal) (of a sum of money) fairly large > verb 3 to put (a place) in order

tie ties, tying, tied verb 1 to fasten (one thing to another) with string, rope, etc 2 to make (a knot or bow) in (something) 3 to link (one thing with another) closely 4 (followed by with) to score the same as (another competitor) > noun 5 long narrow piece of material worn knotted round the neck 6 connection or feeling that links you with a person, place or organization: I had very close ties with the family

tied up adjective busy

tie-dyeing or **tye-dyeing** noun [D & T] method of dyeing clothing in patterns by tying sections of the cloth together so that they will not absorb the dye

tier noun one of a set of layers or rows that has other layers or rows above or below it

tiff noun petty quarrel

tiger noun large orange-and-black striped Asian cat

tiger snake noun fierce, very poisonous Australian snake with dark stripes across its back

tight adjective 1 stretched or drawn taut 2 closely fitting 3 secure or firm 4 (of a plan or arrangement) allowing only the minimum time or money needed to do something > adverb 5 held firmly and securely: he held me tight > **tightly** adverb: he buttoned his collar tightly > **tightness** noun: a feeling of tightness in the chest

tighten verb 1 to stretch or pull (a rope or chain) until it is straight 2 to make (a rule or system) stricter or more efficient 3 **tighten your hold on** to hold (something) more firmly

tightrope noun rope stretched taut on which acrobats perform

tights plural noun one-piece clinging garment covering the body from the waist to the feet

tiki tikis noun (NZ) small carving of an ancestor worn as a pendant in some Māori cultures

tile noun 1 flat piece of ceramic, plastic, etc used to cover a roof, floor or wall > verb 2 to cover (a surface) with tiles > **tiled** adjective covered with tiles

till conjunction, preposition 1 until > verb 2 to plough (ground) for raising crops > noun 3 drawer for money, usually in a cash register

tiller noun lever to move a rudder of a boat

tilt verb 1 to slant (something) at an angle > noun 2 slope

timber noun 1 wood as a building material 2 wooden beam in the frame of a house, boat, etc > **timbered** adjective

timbre [**tam**-ber] noun 1 [MUSIC] particular quality or characteristic of a musical instrument, voice, or sound

time noun 1 past, present and future as a continuous

whole **2** specific point in time **3** unspecified interval **4** instance or occasion **5** period with specific features ▷ *verb* **6** to note the time taken by (an activity or action) **7** to choose a time for (something) >**timer** *noun* device that measures time, especially one that is part of a machine >**timing** *noun* **1** skill in judging the right moment to do something **2** when an event actually happens

timeless *adjective* not affected by the passing of time or by changes in fashion

timely *adjective* happening at the appropriate time

time management *noun* D&T arranging and prioritizing tasks in order to work as efficiently as possible

timescale *noun* length of time during which an event takes place

timetable *noun* plan showing the times when something takes place, the departure and arrival times of trains or buses, etc

timid *adjective* **1** easily frightened **2** shy, not bold >**timidity** *noun* >**timidly** *adverb*

timpani [tim-pee-ee] *plural noun* set of kettledrums

tin *noun* **1** soft metallic element **2** (airtight) metal container

tinder *noun* dry easily-burning material used to start a fire

tinge *noun* trace: *a tinge of envy* >**tinged** *adjective: Her homecoming was tinged with sadness*

tingle *verb, noun* (to feel) a prickling or stinging sensation >**tingling** *noun* **1** prickling or stinging sensation ▷ *adjective* **2** prickling or stinging

tinker *noun* **1** travelling mender of pots and pans ▷ *verb* **2** (followed by *with*) to fiddle with (an engine etc) in an attempt to repair it

tinkle *verb* **1** to ring with a high tinny sound like a small bell ▷ *noun* **2** this sound or action

tinned *adjective* (of food) preserved by being sealed in a tin

tinsel *noun* long threads with strips of shiny paper attached, used as a decoration at Christmas

tint *noun* **1** small amount of a particular colour **2** weak dye for the hair ▷ *verb* **3** to give a tint to (one's hair) >**tinted** *adjective* having a small amount of a particular colour

tiny *tinier, tiniest adjective* very small

tip *tips, tipping, tipped noun* **1** narrow or pointed end of anything **2** money given in return for service **3** useful piece of advice or information **4** rubbish dump ▷ *verb* **5** to tilt or overturn (something) **6** to pour (something) somewhere quickly or carelessly >**tipped** *adjective: tipped for success*

tipple *noun* alcoholic drink that someone usually drinks

tipsy *tipsier, tipsiest adjective* slightly drunk

tiptoe *tiptoes, tiptoeing, tiptoed verb* to walk quietly with the heels off the ground

tirade *noun* long angry speech

tire *verb* **1** to reduce the energy of (someone), as by exertion; exhaust (someone) **2** (followed by *of*) to become weary or bored with >**tired** *adjective* exhausted

> **tiredness** noun > **tiring** adjective causing tiredness

tireless adjective energetic and determined

tiresome adjective boring and irritating

tissue noun 1 substance of an animal body or plant 2 piece of thin soft paper used as a handkerchief etc

tit noun any of various small songbirds

titanic adjective huge or very important

titillate verb to excite or stimulate (someone) pleasurably > **titillation** noun act of exciting or stimulating

title noun 1 name of a book, film, etc 2 name signifying rank or position 3 (Sport) championship > **titled** adjective having a high social rank and a title such as Lord, Lady or Sir

titter verb to laugh in a nervous or embarrassed way

TNT noun trinitrotoluene, a powerful explosive

to preposition 1 indicating movement towards, equality or comparison, etc: walking to school; forty miles to the gallon 2 used to mark the indirect object or infinitive of a verb ▷ adverb 3 to a closed position: pull the door to

WORD TIP

> The preposition to is spelt with one o, the adverb too has two os, and the number two is spelt with wo

toad noun animal like a large frog

toadstool noun poisonous fungus like a mushroom

toast noun 1 sliced bread browned by heat 2 **drink a toast to** to drink an alcoholic drink in honour of (someone) ▷ verb 3 to brown (bread) by heat 4 to warm (oneself) in front of a fire 5 to drink a toast to (someone) > **toaster** noun electrical device for toasting bread

tobacco noun dried leaves of the tobacco plant, which people smoke in pipes, cigarettes and cigars

tobacconist noun person or shop selling tobacco, cigarettes, etc

toboggan noun narrow sledge for sliding over snow

today noun 1 this day 2 the present age ▷ adverb 3 on this day 4 nowadays

toddler noun young child beginning to walk > **toddle** verb to walk with short unsteady steps

to-do to-dos noun (Brit, Aust, NZ) fuss or commotion

toe toes noun 1 movable part of your foot resembling a finger 2 part of a shoe or sock covering your toes

toff noun (Brit informal) rich or aristocratic person

toffee noun chewy sweet made of boiled sugar

toga [**toe**-ga] noun garment worn by citizens of ancient Rome

together adverb 1 with each other; jointly 2 at the same time 3 so as to be joined or fixed to each other: She clasped her hands together 4 very near to each other ▷ adjective 5 (informal) organized > **togetherness** noun feeling of closeness and friendship

WORD TIP
Two nouns joined by *together with* do not make a plural subject, so the following verb is not plural: *Jones, together with his partner, has had great success*

toil *noun* **1** hard work ▷ *verb* **2** to work hard

toilet *noun* (room with) a bowl connected to a drain for receiving and disposing of urine and faeces

toiletries *plural noun* cosmetics used for cleaning or grooming

token *noun* **1** sign or symbol: *as a token of goodwill* **2** voucher exchangeable for goods of a specified value **3** disc used as money in a slot machine ▷ *adjective* **4** not being treated as important: *a token contribution to your fees*

told *verb* past of **tell**

tolerable *adjective* **1** bearable **2** (*informal*) quite good

tolerance *noun* **1** acceptance of other people's rights to their own opinions or actions **2** ability to endure something > **tolerant** *adjective*: *tolerant of different points of view*

tolerate *verb* **1** to allow (something) to exist or happen **2** to endure (something) patiently > **toleration** *noun* act of tolerating something

toll *verb* **1** to ring (a bell) slowly and regularly, especially to announce a death ▷ *noun* **2** charge for the use of a bridge or road **3** total loss or damage from a disaster

tom *noun* male cat

tomahawk *noun* fighting axe of the Native Americans

tomato tomatoes *noun* red fruit used in salads and as a vegetable

tomb *noun* large grave for one or more corpses

tomboy *noun* girl who acts or dresses like a boy

tome *noun* large heavy book

tomorrow *adverb, noun* **1** (on) the day after today **2** (in) the future

ton *noun* **1** unit of weight equal to 2240 pounds or 1016 kilograms (*long ton*) or, in the US, 2000 pounds or 907 kilograms (*short ton*) **2 tons** (*informal*) a lot

tone *noun* **1** sound with reference to its pitch, volume, etc **2** quality of a sound or colour **3** style of a piece of writing and the ideas or opinions expressed in it ▷ *verb* **4** to harmonize (with) **5** to give tone to **6** give more firmness or strength to (the body or a part of the body) > **tonal** *adjective* involving the quality or pitch of a sound or of music • **tone down** *verb* to make (something) more moderate

tone-deaf *adjective* unable to perceive subtle differences in pitch

tongs *plural noun* large pincers for grasping and lifting

tongue *noun* **1** muscular organ in the mouth, used in speaking and tasting **2** language **3** cooked tongue of an ox **4** flap of leather on a shoe

tonic *noun* **1** medicine that makes you feel stronger, healthier and less tired **2** anything that makes you feel stronger or more cheerful

tonight *adverb, noun* (in or during) the night or evening of this day

tonne [tunn] *noun* MATHS unit of weight equal to 1000 kilograms

tonsil noun small gland in the throat

tonsillitis noun painful swelling of the tonsils caused by an infection

too adverb 1 also, as well 2 to excess

> **WORD TIP**
>
> The adverb *too* has two os, the preposition *to* is spelt with one *o*, and the number *two* is spelt with *wo*

tool noun 1 implement used by hand 2 object, skill or idea needed for a particular purpose: *a bargaining tool*

toot verb (of a car horn) to make a short hooting sound

tooth teeth noun 1 bonelike projection in the jaws for biting and chewing 2 toothlike prong or point

toothpaste noun paste used to clean the teeth

top tops, topping, topped noun 1 highest point or part 2 lid or cap 3 highest rank 4 garment for the upper part of the body 5 toy that spins on a pointed base ▷ adjective 6 at or of the top ▷ verb 7 to be at the top of (a poll or chart) 8 to be greater than (a specified amount)

top hat noun man's tall cylindrical hat

topic noun subject of a conversation, book, etc > **topical** adjective relating to current events

topping noun sauce or garnish for food

topple verb to become unsteady and fall over

top-secret adjective meant to be kept completely secret

topsy-turvy adjective in confusion

top-up card noun card used to add credit to a mobile phone

Torah noun Jewish law and teaching

torch noun 1 small portable battery-powered lamp 2 long stick with burning material wrapped round one end

torment verb 1 to cause (someone) great suffering ▷ noun 2 great suffering 3 source of suffering

torn verb 1 past participle of **tear²** ▷ adjective 2 unable to decide between two or more things

tornado tornadoes or tornados noun violent whirlwind

torpedo torpedoes, torpedoing, torpedoed noun 1 self-propelled underwater missile ▷ verb 2 to attack or destroy (a ship) with torpedoes

torrent noun 1 rushing stream 2 rapid flow of questions, abuse, etc

torrential adjective (of rain) very heavy

torrid adjective 1 very hot and dry 2 highly emotional

torso torsos noun trunk of the human body

tortoise noun slow-moving land reptile with a dome-shaped shell

tortuous adjective 1 winding or twisting 2 not straightforward

torture verb 1 to cause (someone) severe pain or mental anguish ▷ noun 2 severe physical or mental pain 3 torturing > **torturer** noun person who tortures people

Tory Tories noun member of the Conservative Party in Great Britain or Canada

toss verb **1** to throw (something) lightly **2** to throw up (a coin) to decide between alternatives by guessing which side will land uppermost **3** to move (the head) suddenly backwards, esp. when angry **4** to move repeatedly from side to side

tot tots, totting, totted noun **1** small child **2** small amount of strong alcohol such as whisky ▷ verb totting, totted **3 tot up** to add (numbers) together

total totals, totalling, totalled noun **1** whole, especially a sum of parts ▷ adjective **2** complete **3** of or being a total ▷ verb **4** to amount to (a certain figure) **5** to add together (a set of numbers or objects) > **totally** adverb: something totally different

totalitarian adjective of a dictatorial one-party government > **totalitarianism** noun principles of a totalitarian system

tote verb to carry (a gun)

totem pole noun post carved or painted with symbols and pictures by Native Americans

totter verb to move unsteadily

toucan noun tropical American bird with a large bill

touch verb **1** to come into contact with **2** to tap, feel or stroke **3** to move (someone) emotionally ▷ noun **4** sense by which an object's qualities are perceived when they come into contact with part of the body **5** gentle tap, push or caress **6** small amount: a touch of mustard **7** detail: finishing touches **8** touch and go risky or critical

touchdown noun landing of an aircraft

touching adjective emotionally moving

touchy touchier, touchiest adjective easily offended

tough adjective **1** (of a person) strong and independent and able to put up with hardship **2** (of a substance) difficult to break **3** (of a task, problem or way of life) difficult or full of hardship **4** (of policies or actions) strict and firm > **toughen** verb to become stronger or make (something) stronger > **toughness** noun: a reputation for toughness and determination

toupee [**too**-pay] noun small wig worn to cover a bald patch

tour noun **1** long journey during which you visit several places **2** short trip round a place such as a city or famous building ▷ verb **3** to make a tour of (a place)

tourism noun GEOGRAPHY tourist travel as an industry

tourist noun GEOGRAPHY person travelling for pleasure

tournament noun PE sporting competition with several stages to decide the overall winner

tourniquet [**tour**-nick-kay] noun strip of cloth tied tightly round a limb to stop bleeding

tousled adjective (of hair) ruffled and untidy

tout [rhymes with **shout**] verb **1** to seek business in a persistent manner **2** to try to sell (something) ▷ noun **3** person who sells tickets for a popular event at inflated prices

tow verb **1** (of a vehicle) to drag (another vehicle), especially by means of a rope ▷ noun **2** towing **3** in tow following closely behind

towards or **toward** preposition **1** in the direction of **2** with regard to **3** as a contribution to **4** near to

towel noun piece of thick soft cloth for drying yourself

towelling noun material used for making towels

tower noun tall structure, often forming part of a larger building > **towering** adjective: towering cliffs ▷ **tower over** verb to be much taller than

town noun **1** group of buildings larger than a village **2** central part of this

township noun (SAfr) urban settlement formerly for Black or Coloured people only

towpath noun path beside a canal or river

toxic adjective poisonous

toxin noun poison of bacterial origin

toy noun something designed to be played with > **toy with** verb **1** to consider (an idea) without being very serious about it **2** to play or fiddle with (an object)

toyi-toyi or **toy-toy** noun (SAfr) dance of political protest

trace verb **1** to track down and find **2** (EXAM TERM) to follow the course of **3** to copy (a drawing or a map) exactly by drawing on a thin sheet of transparent paper set on top of the original ▷ noun **4** track left by someone or something **5** very small amount

track noun **1** rough road or path **2** mark or trail left by the passage of anything **3** railway line **4** course for racing **5** separate section on a record, tape or CD ▷ verb **6** to follow the trail or path of (animals or people) > **track down** verb to hunt for and find (someone or something)

track record noun past accomplishments of a person or organization

tracksuit noun warm loose-fitting suit worn by athletes etc, especially during training

tract noun **1** wide area **2** pamphlet, especially a religious one **3** (Anatomy) system of organs with a particular function: the digestive tract

traction noun (Medicine) application of a steady pull on an injured limb by weights and pulleys

tractor noun motor vehicle with large rear wheels for pulling farm machinery

trade noun **1** (HISTORY) buying, selling or exchange of goods **2** person's job or craft ▷ verb **3** to buy and sell (goods) **4** to exchange (things) > **trader** noun person who trades in goods

trademark noun (legally registered) name or symbol used by a firm to distinguish its goods

tradesman tradesmen noun **1** skilled worker **2** shopkeeper

trade union noun society of workers formed to protect their interests

tradition noun custom or practice of long standing; convention > **traditional** adjective **1** (of customs or beliefs) having existed for a long time without changing **2** (of an organization or institution) using older methods rather than modern ones

> **traditionalist** noun person who supports the established customs and beliefs of his or her society

> **traditionally** adverb

traffic traffics, trafficking, trafficked noun 1 vehicles coming and going on a road 2 illegal trade in something such as drugs ▷ verb 3 (followed by in) to buy and sell (drugs or other goods) illegally

traffic lights plural noun set of coloured lights at a junction to control the traffic flow

traffic warden noun (Brit) person employed to control the movement and parking of traffic

tragedy tragedies noun 1 shocking or sad event 2 serious play, film, etc in which the hero is destroyed by a personal failing in adverse circumstances

tragic adjective 1 very sad, often involving death, suffering or disaster 2 (of a film, play or book) sad and serious > **tragically** adverb: Tragically, she died before the project was finished

trail noun 1 path, track or road 2 tracks left by a person, animal or object ▷ verb 3 to drag (something) along the ground 4 to hang down loosely 5 to move slowly, without energy or enthusiasm > **trail off** verb (of a voice) to gradually become more hesitant until it stops completely

trailer noun 1 vehicle designed to be towed by another vehicle 2 extract from a film or programme used to advertise it

train verb 1 to instruct in a skill 2 to learn the skills needed to do a particular job or activity 3 to

prepare for a sports event etc 4 to aim (a gun etc) 5 to cause (an animal) to perform or (a plant) to grow in a particular way ▷ noun 6 line of railway coaches or wagons drawn by an engine 7 sequence or series 8 long trailing back section of a dress 9 line or group of vehicles or people following behind something or someone

trainee noun person being trained

trainers plural noun sports shoes

trait noun characteristic feature

traitor noun (HISTORY) person who betrays his or her country or group

trajectory trajectories noun curving path followed by an object moving through the air

tram noun public transport vehicle powered by an overhead wire and running on rails laid in the road

tramp verb 1 to walk heavily ▷ noun 2 homeless person who travels on foot 3 long country walk

trample verb (followed by on) 1 to tread heavily on and damage 2 to show no consideration for (someone or his or her rights or feelings)

trampoline noun tough canvas sheet attached to a frame by springs, used by acrobats, etc

trance noun unconscious or dazed state

tranquil adjective calm and quiet > **tranquillity** noun: a haven of peace and tranquillity

tranquillizer or **tranquilliser** noun drug that reduces anxiety or tension

trans- prefix across, through or beyond

transaction noun business deal that involves buying and selling something

transcend verb to go beyond or be superior to (something)

transcribe verb to write down (something said)

transcript noun written copy of something spoken

transfer transfers, transferring, transferred verb 1 to move (something) from one place to another: They transferred the money to the Swiss account 2 to move (someone) to a different place or job within the same organization ▷ noun 3 movement of something from one place to another 4 design that can be transferred from one surface to another ▷ **transferable** adjective: Your Railcard is not transferable to anyone else

transfixed adjective so impressed or frightened by something that you cannot move

transform verb to change the shape or character of something ▷ **transformation** noun: He's undergone a personal transformation

transfusion noun injection of blood into the blood vessels of a patient

transient adjective lasting only for a short time ▷ **transience** noun: the transience of the club scene

transistor noun 1 semiconducting device used to amplify electric currents 2 small portable radio using transistors

transit noun 1 carrying of goods or people by vehicle from one place to another 2 in transit travelling or being taken from one place to another: damaged in transit

transition noun change from one state to another ▷ **transitional** adjective (of a period or stage) during which something changes from one form or state to another

transitive adjective (Grammar) (of a verb) requiring a direct object

transitory adjective not lasting long

translate verb to turn (something) from one language into another ▷ **translation** noun: an English translation of Faust ▷ **translator** noun person who translates from one language into another

translucent adjective letting light pass through, but not transparent

transmission noun 1 passing or sending of something to a different place or person 2 broadcasting of television or radio programmes 3 broadcast

transmit transmits, transmitting, transmitted verb 1 to pass (something) from one person or place to another 2 to send out (signals) by radio waves 3 to broadcast (a radio or television programme) ▷ **transmitter** noun piece of equipment used to broadcast radio or television programmes

transparency transparencies noun 1 transparent quality 2 colour photograph on transparent film that can be viewed by means of a projector

transparent adjective 1 able to be seen through, clear 2 easily understood or recognized

>**transparently** adverb in a transparent manner

transpire verb 1 (formal) to become known 2 (informal) to happen

> **WORD TIP**
> Some people think that it is wrong to use *transpire* to mean 'happen'. However, it is very widely used in this sense, especially in spoken English

transplant verb 1 to transfer (an organ or tissue) surgically from one part or body to another 2 to remove and transfer (a plant) to another place ▷ noun 3 surgical transplanting 4 thing transplanted

transport verb 1 to convey (goods or people) from one place to another 2 to enrapture ▷ noun GEOGRAPHY 3 business or system of transporting 4 vehicles used in transport >**transportation** noun GEOGRAPHY transporting of people and things from one place to another

transvestite noun person who enjoys wearing clothes normally worn by people of the opposite sex

trap traps, trapping, trapped noun 1 device for catching animals 2 plan for tricking or catching someone ▷ verb 3 to catch (animals) in a trap 4 to trick (someone) into something >**trapper** noun person who traps animals for their fur

trapdoor noun door in floor or roof

trapeze noun horizontal bar suspended from two ropes, used by circus acrobats

trapezium trapeziums or trapezia noun four-sided shape with two parallel sides of unequal length

trappings plural noun accessories that symbolize an office or position

trash noun 1 anything worthless 2 (US, SAfr) rubbish

trauma [traw-ma] noun emotional shock

traumatic adjective very upsetting

travel travels, travelling, travelled verb 1 to go from one place to another, through an area or for a specified distance ▷ noun 2 travelling, especially as a tourist >**traveller** noun: air travellers >**travelling** adjective: travelling entertainers >**travels** plural noun journeys to distant places

traveller's cheque noun cheque bought at home and then exchanged abroad for foreign currency

traverse verb to move over or back and forth over (an area)

travesty travesties noun grotesque imitation or mockery

trawl noun 1 net dragged at deep levels behind a fishing boat ▷ verb 2 to fish with such a net

trawler noun trawling boat

tray noun flat board, usually with a rim, for carrying food or drinks

treachery noun wilful betrayal >**treacherous** adjective 1 disloyal or untrustworthy 2 unreliable or dangerous >**treacherously** adverb in a treacherous manner

treacle noun thick dark syrup produced when sugar is refined

tread treads, treading, trod, trodden verb 1 to set your foot (on something) 2 to crush (something) by walking on it ▷ *noun* **3** way of walking or dancing **4** part of a tyre or shoe that touches the ground

treadmill *noun* **1** cylinder turned by treading on steps projecting from it **2** dreary routine

treason *noun* **1** betrayal of one's sovereign or country **2** treachery or disloyalty

treasure *noun* **1** collection of wealth, especially gold or jewels **2** valued person or thing ▷ *verb* **3** to prize or cherish (something) > **treasured** *adjective: my most treasured possessions*

treasurer *noun* official in charge of funds

Treasury *noun* government department in charge of finance

treat *verb* **1** to deal with or regard (someone or something) in a certain manner **2** to give medical treatment to (a patient or an illness) **3** to subject (something such as wood or fabric) to a chemical or industrial process **4** to provide (someone) with something as a treat ▷ *noun* **5** pleasure, entertainment, etc given or paid for by someone else > **treatment** *noun* **1** medical care **2** way of treating a person or thing

treatise [treat-izz] *noun* formal piece of writing on a particular subject

treaty treaties *noun* signed contract between states

treble *adjective* **1** triple ▷ *noun* **2** (singer with or part for) a soprano voice ▷ *verb* **3** to increase (something) three times

tree *noun* large perennial plant with a woody trunk

trek treks, trekking, trekked *noun* **1** long difficult journey, especially on foot ▷ *verb* **2** to make such a journey

trellis *noun* framework of horizontal and vertical strips of wood

tremble *verb* **1** to shake or quiver **2** to feel fear or anxiety ▷ *noun* **3** trembling > **trembling** *adjective: with trembling fingers*

tremendous *adjective* **1** huge **2** (*informal*) great in quality or amount > **tremendously** *adverb*

tremor *noun* **1** involuntary shaking **2** unsteady quality in the voice, e.g. when upset **3** minor earthquake

trench *noun* long narrow ditch, especially one used as a shelter in war

trenchant *adjective* (of writing or comments) bold and firmly expressed

trend *noun* general tendency or direction

trendy trendier, trendiest *adjective* (*informal*) consciously fashionable

trepidation *noun* fear or anxiety

trespass *verb* to go onto another's property without permission > **trespasser** *noun: Trespassers will be prosecuted*

tresses *plural noun* long flowing hair

trestle *noun* board fixed on pairs of spreading legs, used as a support

trevally trevallies *noun* (*Aust, NZ*) any of various food and game fishes

tri- *prefix* three

triad *noun* **1** group of three **2** (MUSIC) chord of three notes consisting of the tonic and the third and fifth above it

trial noun **1** (Law) investigation of a case before a judge **2** trying or testing

triangle noun **1** MATHS geometric figure with three sides **2** triangular percussion instrument >**triangular** adjective having three sides >**triangulation** noun GEOGRAPHY method of measuring an area by dividing it into triangles and calculating the areas of the triangles >**triangulate** verb

triathlon noun sports contest in which athletes compete in three different events

tribe noun group of clans or families believed to have a common ancestor >**tribal** adjective of tribes

tribulation noun great distress

tribunal noun board appointed to inquire into a specific matter

tributary tributaries noun stream or river flowing into a larger one

tribute noun **1** sign of respect or admiration **2a tribute to** positive result of (something): His success is a tribute to hard work

trice noun **in a trice** instantly

triceps noun PE muscle at the back of the upper arm

▌ **WORD TIP**
The plural of triceps is triceps

trick noun **1** deceitful or cunning action or plan **2** feat of skill or cunning done in order to entertain ▷ verb **3** to cheat or deceive (someone)

trickery noun deception

trickle verb **1** to flow in a thin stream or drops **2** to move gradually ▷ noun **3** thin stream of

liquid **4** small number or quantity of things or people

tricky trickier, trickiest adjective difficult to do or deal with

tricycle noun three-wheeled cycle

trifle noun **1** something that is not very important or valuable **2** dessert of sponge cake, fruit, custard and cream **3a trifle** a little >**trifle with** verb to toy with (someone or something)

trifling adjective insignificant

trigger noun **1** small lever releasing a catch on a gun or machine **2** action that sets off a course of events ▷ verb **3** (usually followed by off) to set (an action or process) in motion

trigonometry noun branch of mathematics dealing with relations of the sides and angles of triangles

trill noun **1** shrill warbling sound made by some birds ▷ verb **2** (of a bird trill) to sing with short high-pitched repeated notes

trillion noun **1** one million million; 1,000,000,000,000 **2** formerly, one million million million, 10¹⁸ **3 trillions** large but unspecified number; lots

trilogy trilogies noun series of three related books, plays, etc

trim trimmer, trimmest; trims, trimming, trimmed adjective **1** neat and smart ▷ verb **2** to cut or prune (something) into good shape ▷ noun **3** decoration **4** haircut that neatens the existing style >**trimmed** adjective: trimmed with flowers

trimmings plural noun extra parts added to something for decoration or as a luxury

Trimurti noun (Hinduism) three deities Brahma, Vishnu and Siva

Trinity noun (Christianity) union of God the Father, God the Son and God the Holy Spirit in one God

trinket noun small or worthless ornament or piece of jewellery

trio trios noun **1** group of three musicians who sing or play together **2** piece of music for three performers **3** any group of three

trip noun **1** journey to a place and back, especially for pleasure ▷ verb **2** to stumble or cause (someone) to stumble

tripe noun stomach of a cow used as food

triple adjective **1** having three parts ▷ verb **2** to increase (something) three times

triplet noun one of three babies born at one birth

tripod [tripe-pod] noun three-legged stand, stool, etc

tripper noun tourist

trite adjective (of a remark or idea) commonplace and unoriginal

triumph noun **1** (happiness caused by) victory or success ▷ verb **2** to be victorious or successful

triumphal adjective celebrating a triumph

triumphant adjective feeling or showing triumph

trivia plural noun trivial things or details

trivial adjective of little importance

troll noun giant or dwarf in Scandinavian folklore

trolley noun **1** small wheeled table for food and drink **2** wheeled cart for moving goods

trombone noun brass musical instrument with a sliding tube

troop noun **1** large group **2** troops soldiers ▷ verb **3** to move in a crowd

trooper noun low-ranking cavalry soldier

trophy trophies noun **1** cup, shield, etc given as a prize **2** memento of success

tropic noun **1** either of two lines of latitude at 23½°N (tropic of Cancer) or 23½°S (tropic of Capricorn) **2** the tropics part of the earth's surface between these lines

tropical adjective of or in the tropics

trot trots, trotting, trotted verb **1** (of a horse) to move at a medium pace, lifting the feet in diagonal pairs **2** (of a person) to move at a steady brisk pace ▷ noun **3** trotting

trotter noun pig's foot

trouble noun **1** (cause of) distress or anxiety **2** care or effort **3** in trouble likely to be punished for doing something wrong ▷ verb **4** to cause (someone) to worry **5** to cause inconvenience to or bother (someone) > **troubled** adjective: She was deeply troubled > **troubling** adjective worrying

troublesome adjective causing problems or difficulties

trough [troff] noun long open container, especially for animals' food or water

trounce verb to defeat (someone) utterly

troupe [troop] noun group of performers who work together and often travel around together

trousers plural noun two-legged outer garment with legs reaching usually to the ankles

trout noun game fish related to the salmon

> **WORD TIP**
> The plural of trout is trout

trowel noun hand tool with a wide blade for spreading mortar, lifting plants, etc

truant noun 1 pupil who stays away from school without permission 2 **play truant** to stay away from school without permission > **truancy** noun staying away from school without permission

truce noun temporary agreement to stop fighting

truck noun 1 railway goods wagon 2 large vehicle for transporting loads by road > **trucker** noun truck driver noun > **have no truck with** refuse to be involved with

truculent [truck-yew-lent] adjective aggressively defiant > **truculence** noun aggressive defiance

trudge verb 1 to walk heavily or wearily > noun 2 long tiring walk

true truer, truest adjective 1 in accordance with facts; accurate 2 genuine 3 **come true** to actually happen > **truly** adverb very

truffle noun 1 edible underground fungus 2 sweet flavoured with chocolate

trump noun 1 card of the suit outranking the others 2 **trumps** suit outranking the others

trumpet noun 1 valved brass instrument with a flared tube > verb 2 (of an elephant) to cry loudly

truncated adjective made shorter

truncheon noun club carried by a policeman

trundle verb to move (something) heavily on wheels

trunk noun 1 main stem of a tree 2 large case or box for clothes etc 3 person's body excluding the head and limbs 4 elephant's long nose

truss verb 1 to tie (someone) up > noun 2 supporting belt with a pad for holding a hernia in place

trust verb 1 to believe in and rely on (someone or something) 2 to consign (something) to someone's care 3 to believe that (someone) will do something successfully or properly > noun 4 confidence in the truth, reliability, etc of a person or thing 5 obligation arising from responsibility 6 arrangement in which one person administers property, money, etc on another's behalf > **trusting** adjective inclined to trust others

trustee noun person holding property on another's behalf

trustworthy adjective reliable or honest

trusty trustier, trustiest adjective faithful or reliable

truth noun 1 state of being true; reality 2 something true

truthful adjective honest > **truthfully** adverb: I answered all their questions truthfully

try tries, trying, tried verb 1 to make an effort or attempt (to do something) 2 to test or sample (something) 3 to subject (a person) to a legal process involving the hearing of evidence to decide whether they are guilty or not of a crime > noun 4 attempt or effort 5 test of something: You gave it a try **6** (*Rugby*) score gained by touching the ball down over the opponent's goal line

> **WORD TIP**
> You can use *try to* in speech and writing: *try to get here on time for once*. *Try and* is very common in speech, but you should avoid it in written work: *just try and stop me!*

trying *adjective* (*informal*) difficult or annoying

tryst *noun* arrangement to meet

tsar or **czar** [**zahr**] *noun* (*History*) Russian emperor > **tsarina** or **czarina** [zah-**ree**-na] *noun* (*History*) female tsar or the wife of a tsar

tsetse fly [**tset**-see] *noun* bloodsucking African fly whose bite transmits disease, especially sleeping sickness

T-shirt *noun* simple short-sleeved cotton shirt with no collar

tsunami *noun* large, often destructive sea wave, caused by an earthquake or volcanic eruption under the sea

tuatara *noun* large lizard-like New Zealand reptile

tub *noun* open, usually round container

tuba [**tube**-a] *noun* valved low-pitched brass instrument

tubby tubbier, tubbiest *adjective* (of a person) short and fat

tube *noun* **1** hollow cylinder **2** flexible cylinder with a cap to hold pastes > **tubing** *noun* **1** length of tube **2** system of tubes

tuberculosis [tube-berk-yew-**lohss**-iss] *noun* serious infectious disease affecting the lungs

tubular [**tube**-yew-lar] *adjective* of or shaped like a tube

TUC *abbreviation* (in Britain and S Africa) Trades Union Congress

tuck *verb* **1** to push or fold (something) into a small space **2** to push the loose ends of (a piece of fabric) inside or under something to make it tidy > *noun* **3** stitched fold > **tuck away** *verb* **1** to eat (a large amount of food) **2** to locate (something) in a quiet place where few people go

tucker *noun* (*Aust, NZ informal*) food

Tudor *noun* family name of the English monarchs who reigned from 1485 to 1603

Tuesday *noun* day between Monday and Wednesday

tuft *noun* bunch of feathers, grass, hair, etc held or growing together at the base

tug tugs, tugging, tugged *verb* **1** to pull (something) hard > *noun* **2** hard pull **3** small ship used to tow other vessels

tug of war *noun* contest in which two teams pull against one another on a rope

tuition *noun* instruction, especially received individually or in a small group

tulip *noun* brightly coloured spring flower

tumble *verb* **1** to fall, especially awkwardly or violently > *noun* **2** fall

tumbler *noun* stemless drinking glass

tummy tummies *noun* (*informal*) stomach

tumour [**tew**-mer] *noun* abnormal growth in or on the body

tumultuous [tew-**mull**-tew-uss] *adjective* (of an event or welcome) very noisy and excited

tuna *noun* large marine food fish

WORD TIP
The plural of *tuna* is *tuna*

tundra *noun* vast treeless Arctic region

tune *noun* 1 (pleasing) sequence of musical notes 2 correct musical pitch: *She sang out of tune* ▷ *verb* 3 to adjust (a musical instrument) so that it is in tune 4 to adjust (a machine) to obtain the desired performance 5 (followed by to) to turn or press the controls of a radio or television set to select (a particular station)

tuneful *adjective* having a pleasant and easily remembered tune

tuner *noun* person who tunes pianos

tunic *noun* large piece of clothing, often sleeveless and rather shapeless, covering the top part of the body and reaching to the hips, thighs or knees

Tunisian [tyoo-**niz**-ee-an] *adjective* 1 of Tunisia ▷ *noun* 2 person from Tunisia

tunnel tunnels, tunnelling, tunnelled *noun* 1 underground passage ▷ *verb* 2 to make a tunnel

turban *noun* Muslim, Hindu or Sikh man's head covering, made by winding cloth round the head

turbine *noun* machine or generator driven by gas, water, etc turning blades

turbot *noun* large European flat fish that is caught for food

WORD TIP
The plural of *turbot* is *turbot*

turbulence *noun* 1 confusion, movement or agitation 2 atmospheric instability causing gusty air currents ▷ **turbulent** *adjective* 1 (of a period of history) involving much uncertainty and possibly violent change 2 (of air or water currents) making sudden changes of direction

tureen *noun* serving dish for soup

turf turves; turfs, turfing, turfed *noun* short thick even grass ▷ **turf out** (*informal*) to throw (someone) out

turgid [**tur**-jid] *adjective* (of language) pompous

Turk *noun* person from Turkey

turkey turkeys *noun* 1 large bird bred for food 2 meat of this bird

Turkish *adjective* 1 of Turkey ▷ *noun* 2 Turkish language

turmoil *noun* agitation or confusion

turn *verb* 1 to change position or direction 2 to change the position or direction of (something) 3 to move or cause (something) to move round an axis; rotate 4 to direct (one's attention or thoughts) to someone or something 5 (usually followed by *into*) to change (something) into (something else) ▷ *noun* 6 turning 7 opportunity to do something as part of an agreed succession 8 change in the way something is happening or being done: *a turn for the worse* 9 in turn in sequence one after the other ▷ **turn down** *verb* 1 to reduce the volume or brightness (of a radio or heater) 2 to refuse or reject (a request or an offer) ▷ **turn up** *verb* 1 to arrive or appear 2 to be found 3 to increase the volume or brightness of (a radio or heater)

turncoat noun person who deserts one party or cause to join another

turning noun road or path leading off a main route

turning point noun moment when a decisive change occurs

turnip noun root vegetable with orange or white flesh

turnout noun number of people appearing at a gathering

turnover noun 1 total sales made by a business over a certain period 2 rate at which staff leave and are replaced

turnstile noun revolving gate for admitting one person at a time

turpentine noun strong-smelling colourless liquid used for cleaning and for thinning paint

turps noun turpentine oil

turquoise adjective 1 blue-green ▷ noun 2 blue-green precious stone

turret noun small tower

turtle noun sea tortoise

tusk noun long pointed tooth of an elephant, walrus, etc

tussle noun fight or scuffle

tutor noun 1 person teaching individuals or small groups ▷ verb 2 to act as a tutor to (someone)

tutorial noun period of instruction with a tutor

tutu noun short stiff skirt worn by ballerinas

TV abbreviation 1 television 2 television set

twang noun 1 sharp ringing sound 2 nasal speech ▷ verb 3 to make a twang or cause (something) to make a twang

tweak verb 1 to pinch or twist (something) sharply ▷ noun 2 tweaking

twee adjective (informal) too sentimental, sweet or pretty

tweed noun thick woollen cloth

tweet noun, verb (to) chirp

tweezers plural noun small pincer-like tool for pulling out hairs or picking up small objects

twelve adjective, noun the number 12 > **twelfth** adjective, noun

twenty twenties adjective, noun the number 20 > **twentieth** adjective, noun

twice adverb two times

twiddle verb to fiddle or twirl (something) in an idle way

twig noun small branch or shoot

twilight noun 1 soft dim light just after sunset 2 final stages of something: *the twilight of his career*

twin noun 1 one of a pair, especially of two children born at one birth ▷ adjective 2 denoting one of two similar things that are close together or happen together

twine noun 1 string or cord ▷ verb 2 to twist or coil round (something)

twinge noun sudden sharp pain or emotional pang

twinkle verb 1 to shine brightly but intermittently ▷ noun 2 flickering brightness

twirl verb to cause (something) to spin or twist round and round

twist verb 1 to turn (something) out of the natural position 2 to distort or pervert (something) 3 to wind or twine (something) 4 to injure (a body part) by turning it too sharply or in an unusual direction 5 to change the meaning of or distort (someone's words) slightly ▷ noun **6** twisting **7** unexpected development in the plot of a film, book, etc

twisted adjective **1** bent **2** (of person, mind, behaviour) unpleasantly abnormal

twit noun (informal) foolish person

twitch verb **1** to move spasmodically **2** to pull (something) sharply ▷ noun **3** little jerky movement

twitter verb (of birds) to utter chirping sounds

two adjective, noun the number 2

> **WORD TIP**
> Do not confuse the spelling of the preposition *to*, the adverb *too* and the number *two*

two-faced adjective deceitful, hypocritical

twofold adjective having two equally important parts or reasons

twosome [**too**-sum] noun two people or things that are usually seen together

two-time verb (informal) to deceive (a lover) by having an affair with someone else

two-up noun (Aust, NZ) popular gambling game in which two coins are tossed and bets are placed on whether they land heads or tails

tycoon noun powerful wealthy businessman

type noun **1** class or category **2** printed text ▷ verb **3** to write (something) with a typewriter or word processor > **typing** noun work or activity of producing something on a typewriter or word processor

typewriter noun machine that prints a character when the appropriate key is pressed

typhoid noun (also **typhoid fever**) acute infectious feverish disease

typhoon noun violent tropical storm

typhus noun infectious feverish disease

typical adjective true to type; characteristic > **typically** adverb

typify typifies, typifying, typified verb to be typical of (a situation or thing)

typist noun person who types with a typewriter or word processor

typography noun [D&T] typography is the planning, choosing, and setting of type for printing

tyrannosaurus [tir-ran-oh-**saw**-russ] noun very large meat-eating dinosaur that walked upright on its hind legs

tyranny noun tyrannical rule

tyrant noun person who treats the people he or she has authority over cruelly and unjustly

tyre noun rubber ring, usually inflated, over the rim of a vehicle's wheel to grip the road

a b c d e f g h i j k l m n o p q r s **t** u v w x y z

u

ubiquitous [yew-**bik**-wit-uss] *adjective* being or seeming to be everywhere at once

udder *noun* the baglike organ that hangs below a cow's body and produces milk

UFO *abbreviation* unidentified flying object

Ugandan [yoo-**gan**-dan] *adjective* **1** belonging or relating to Uganda ▷ *noun* **2** someone from Uganda

ugly uglier, ugliest *adjective* of unpleasant appearance > **ugliness** *noun*

UK *abbreviation* United Kingdom

ulcer *noun* **1** open sore on the surface of the skin which takes a long time to heal **2** something similar inside the body > **ulcerous** *adjective* of, like or characterized by ulcers

ulterior *adjective* (of a motive, aim, etc) apart from or beyond what is obvious

ultimate *adjective* **1** final in a series or process **2** highest or supreme ▷ *noun* **3** best or most advanced example of something: *the ultimate in luxury* > **ultimately** *adverb*: *Ultimately, the film is more concerned with making money than reflecting reality*

ultimatum [ult-im-**may**-tum] *noun* final warning stating that action will be taken unless certain conditions are met

ultra- *prefix* **1** used to form adjectives describing extreme degrees of a quality; extremely: *ultramodern* **2** also used to describe qualities that go beyond a specified extent, range or limit *ultrasonic*; *ultraviolet*

ultramarine *adjective* vivid, deep blue

ultrasonic *adjective* of or producing sound waves with a higher frequency than the human ear can hear

ultrasound *noun* sound which cannot be heard by the human ear because its frequency is too high

ultraviolet *adjective* **1** (of light) beyond the violet end of the spectrum and invisible to the human eye. It is a form of radiation that causes your skin to darken after being exposed to the sun ▷ *noun* **2** light like this

umbilical cord *noun* long flexible tube of blood vessels that connects an unborn baby with its mother and through which the baby receives nutrients and oxygen

umbrella *noun* device used for protection against rain, consisting of a folding frame covered in material attached to a central rod

umpire *noun* **1** (Cricket, Tennis) official who makes sure that the game is played according to the rules and who makes a decision if there is a dispute ▷ *verb* **2** to act as umpire in (a game)

umpteen *adjective* (informal) very many > **umpteenth** *adjective*: *He* *checked his watch for the umpteenth time*

un- *prefix* **1** not: *unidentified* **2** denoting reversal of an action: *untie* **3** denoting removal from: *unthrone*

unabashed *adjective* not embarrassed or discouraged by something

unabated *adjective, adverb* without any reduction in intensity or amount

unable *adjective* **unable to** lacking the necessary power, ability or authority to (do something)

unacceptable *adjective* **1** not satisfactory **2** intolerable

unaccompanied *adjective* alone

unaccustomed *adjective* not used (to something)

unaffected *adjective* **1** not changed in any way by a particular thing **2** genuinely natural; unpretentious

unaided *adverb, adjective* without help

unambiguous *adjective* having only one possible meaning; clear

unanimous [yew-**nan**-im-uss] *adjective* **1** in complete agreement **2** agreed by all > **unanimity** *noun* > **unanimously** *adverb*

unannounced *adjective* happening unexpectedly and without warning

unarmed *adjective* without weapons

unassuming *adjective* modest or unpretentious

unattached *adjective* neither married nor in a steady relationship

unattended *adjective* left alone or not being cared for

unauthorized or **unauthorised** *adjective* done without official permission

unavoidable *adjective* unable to be prevented or avoided

unaware *adjective* not aware or conscious

unawares *adverb* **1** by surprise: *caught unawares* **2** without knowing

unbalanced *adjective* **1** biased, one-sided or not organized in such a way that each part receives the right amount of emphasis **2** mentally disturbed **3** unequal

unbearable *adjective* not able to be endured > **unbearably** *adverb*

unbeatable *adjective* unable to be beaten

unbelievable *adjective* **1** hard to believe or imagine **2** very great or surprising > **unbelievably** *adverb*

unborn *adjective* not yet born

unbroken *adjective* continuous or complete

uncanny *adjective* strange and difficult to explain > **uncannily** *adverb*

uncertain *adjective* **1** not knowing what to do **2** doubtful or not known > **uncertainty** *noun*

unchallenged *adjective* accepted without any questions being asked

uncharacteristic *adjective* not typical or usual

uncivilized or **uncivilised** *adjective* unacceptable, for example by being very cruel or rude

uncle *noun* **1** brother of your father or mother **2** husband of your aunt

unclear *adjective* confusing and not obvious

a b c d e f g h i j k l m n o p q r s t **u** v w x y z

uncomfortable *adjective* **1** not physically relaxed **2** anxious or uneasy >**uncomfortably** *adverb*

uncommon *adjective* **1** not happening or seen often **2** unusually great >**uncommonly** *adverb*

uncompromising *adjective* not prepared to compromise >**uncompromisingly** *adverb*

unconcerned *adjective* lacking in concern or involvement

unconditional *adjective* without conditions or limitations >**unconditionally** *adverb*

unconscious *adjective* **1** not conscious, as a result of shock, accident or injury **2** unaware **3** (of feeling, attitude) not understood by or in the conscious awareness of the person who has it > *noun* **4** part of the mind containing instincts and ideas that exist without your awareness >**unconsciously** *adverb*

uncontrollable *adjective* not able to be controlled or stopped >**uncontrollably** *adverb*

unconventional *adjective* not behaving in the same way as most other people

unconvinced *adjective* not at all certain that something is true or right

uncouth *adjective* lacking in good manners and refinement

uncover *verb* **1** to find out (something secret or hidden) **2** to remove the cover, top or lid from (something)

undaunted *adjective* not put off or discouraged

undecided *adjective* **1** not having made up your mind **2** (of an issue

or problem) not agreed or decided upon

undemanding *adjective* not difficult to do or deal with

undeniable *adjective* unquestionably true >**undeniably** *adverb*

under *preposition* **1** below or beneath **2** subject to or affected by **3** supervised by **4** less than **5** **under way** being carried out; in process

under- *prefix* **1** below: *underground* **2** insufficient or insufficiently: *underrate*

underarm *adjective* **1** (*Sport*) denoting a style of throwing, bowling or serving in which the hand is swung below shoulder level > *adverb* **2** (*Sport*) in an underarm style

undercarriage *noun* **1** the part of an aircraft, including the wheels, that supports it when it is on the ground **2** framework supporting the body of a vehicle

underclass *noun* social group consisting of those who are poorest and whose situation is unlikely to improve

underclothes *plural noun* clothes that you wear under your other clothes and next to your skin

undercover *adjective* done or acting in secret

undercurrent *noun* underlying opinion or emotion that may become stronger

undercut undercuts, undercutting, undercut *verb* to charge less than (a competitor) to obtain trade

underdeveloped *adjective* (of country) without modern

industries and having a low standard of living

underdog *noun* person or team in a weak or underprivileged position

underestimate *verb* to fail to realize how large, great or capable something or someone is

underfoot *adverb* under the feet

undergo undergoes, undergoing, underwent *verb* to experience or have (something)

underground *adjective* **1** below the surface of the ground **2** secret, unofficial and usually illegal ▷ *noun* **3** railway system in which trains travel in tunnels below ground **4** movement dedicated to overthrowing a government or forces of occupation

undergrowth *noun* small trees and bushes growing beneath taller trees in a wood or forest

underhand *adjective* sly, deceitful and secretive

underlie underlies, underlying, underlay, underlain *verb* to be the foundation, cause or basis of ▷ **underlying** *adjective* fundamental or basic

underline *verb* **1** to draw a line under **2** to emphasize

underling *noun* person of lesser rank; subordinate

undermine *verb* to weaken (something or someone) gradually

underneath *preposition, adverb* **1** below or beneath ▷ *adjective* **2** lower ▷ *noun* **3** lower part or surface

underpants *plural noun* piece of clothing worn by men and boys under their trousers; briefs

underpass *noun* section of a road that passes under another road or a railway line

underpin underpins, underpinning, underpinned *verb* to give strength or support to

underprivileged *adjective* lacking the rights and advantages of other members of society

underrate *verb* not to recognize the full value or worth of (someone or something) ▷ **underrated** *adjective*

understand understands, understanding, understood *verb* **1** to know or grasp the meaning or nature of (something or someone) **2** to interpret (something or someone) correctly **3** to assume, gather or believe

understandable *adjective* able to be understood; comprehensible ▷ **understandably** *adverb*

understanding *noun* **1** ability to learn, judge or make decisions **2** personal interpretation of a subject **3** mutual agreement, usually an informal or private one ▷ *adjective* **4** kind and sympathetic

understatement *noun* a statement that does not say fully how true something is

understudy understudies *noun* **1** actor who studies a part in order to be able to replace the usual actor if necessary ▷ *verb* **2** to act as an understudy for (someone with an important part)

undertake undertakes, undertaking, undertook, undertaken *verb* to agree to (something) or to do (something)

a b c d e f g h i j k l m n o p q r s t u v w x y z

undertaker noun person whose job is to prepare bodies for burial or cremation and arrange funerals

undertaking noun 1 task or enterprise 2 agreement to do something

undertone noun 1 quiet tone of voice 2 underlying quality or feeling

undervalue undervalues, undervaluing, undervalued verb to rate (something) as less important or valuable than it really is

underwater adverb, adjective 1 beneath the surface of the sea, a river or a lake ▷ adjective 2 designed to work in water: an underwater camera

underwear noun clothing that you wear under your other clothes and next to your skin

underwent past tense of **undergo**

undesirable adjective not desirable or pleasant; objectionable

undid past tense of **undo**

undisputed adjective definite and without any doubt: the undisputed champion

undivided adjective (of attention) complete

undo undoes, undoing, undid, undone verb 1 to open, unwrap or untie 2 to reverse the effects of

undoing noun cause of someone's downfall

undoubted adjective certain or indisputable ▷ **undoubtedly** adverb

undress verb to take off your clothes

undue adjective greater than is reasonable; excessive ▷ **unduly** adverb

undulating adjective (formal) moving gently up and down

undying adjective never ending; eternal

unearth verb to reveal or discover (something) by searching

unearthly adjective 1 strange and unnatural 2 (of time, hour) ridiculous or unreasonable

uneasy adjective (of a person) worried, anxious or apprehensive ▷ **unease** noun 1 feeling of anxiety 2 state of dissatisfaction ▷ **uneasily** adverb ▷ **uneasiness** noun

unemployed adjective 1 out of work ▷ plural noun 2 people without a job

unemployment noun state of being without a job

unending adjective having lasted for a long time and seeming as if it will never stop

unenviable adjective not to be envied

unequal adjective 1 (of society) not offering the same opportunities and privileges to all people 2 different in size, strength or ability

uneven adjective 1 (of surface) not level or smooth 2 not the same or consistent ▷ **unevenly** adverb

uneventful adjective (of period of time) without any interesting happenings

unexpected adjective surprising; not expected ▷ **unexpectedly** adverb

unfailing adjective continuous or reliable ▷ **unfailingly** adverb

unfair *adjective* not right, fair or just > **unfairly** *adverb* > **unfairness** *noun*

unfaithful *adjective* having sex with someone other than one's regular partner > **unfaithfulness** *noun*

unfamiliar *adjective* 1 (often followed by *to*) not known (to) 2 (followed by *with*) not acquainted (with)

unfashionable *adjective* not popular or no longer used by many people

unfavourable *adjective* not encouraging or promising, or not providing any advantage

unfit *adjective* 1 in poor physical condition 2 unsuitable

unfold *verb* 1 to open or spread (something) out from a folded state 2 (of a situation) to develop and become known

unforeseen *adjective* happening unexpectedly

unforgettable *adjective* impossible to forget; memorable > **unforgettably** *adverb*

unforgivable *adjective* bad or cruel to such an extent that it can never be forgiven or justified > **unforgivably** *adverb*

unfortunate *adjective* 1 unlucky, unsuccessful or unhappy 2 regrettable or unsuitable > **unfortunately** *adverb*

unfounded *adjective* without any truth; groundless

unfriendly *adjective* cold and unpleasant or unwelcoming

ungainly *adjective* moving in an awkward or clumsy way

ungrateful *adjective* not grateful or thankful

unhappy unhappier, unhappiest *adjective* 1 sad and depressed 2 not pleased or satisfied 3 unfortunate or wretched > **unhappily** *adverb* > **unhappiness** *noun*

unhealthy *adjective* 1 likely to cause illness 2 not fit or well

unheard-of *adjective* never having happened before and therefore surprising or shocking

unhinged *adjective* mentally ill

unhurried *adjective* slow and relaxed

unicorn *noun* imaginary animal that looks like a white horse with a straight horn growing from its forehead

unidentified *adjective* of which the name or nature is not known

uniform *noun* 1 special set of clothes worn by people at work or school ▷ *adjective* 2 regular and even throughout; unvarying 3 alike or like > **uniformity** *noun* > **uniformly** *adverb*

unify unifies, unifying, unified *verb* to make (something) one or to become one by joining together different elements > **unification** *noun*: *the unification of Italy*

unilateral *adjective* (of decision, action) made or done by only one person or group > **unilaterally** *adverb*

unimaginable *adjective* impossible to imagine or understand properly

unimportant *adjective* having very little significance or importance

uninhabited *adjective* without anyone living there

a b c d e f g h i j k l m n o p q r s t u v w x y z

uninhibited *adjective* behaving freely and naturally, showing your feelings

unintelligible *adjective* (*formal*) impossible to understand

uninterested *adjective* having or showing no interest in someone or something

uninterrupted *adjective* continuing without breaks or interruptions

union *noun* **1** organization of workers that aims to improve the working conditions, pay and benefits of its members **2** uniting or being united

unique [yoo-**neek**] *adjective* **1** being the only one of a particular type **2** without equal or like **3** unique to belonging or relating only to (a particular person or thing) > **uniquely** *adverb* > **uniqueness** *noun*

unisex *adjective* designed for use by both sexes

unison *noun* **in unison 1** doing the same thing together at the same time **2** in complete agreement

unit *noun* **1** single complete thing **2** group or individual regarded as a basic element of a larger whole **3** fixed quantity etc, used as a standard of measurement **4** piece of furniture designed to be fitted with other similar pieces

unite *verb* **1** to join together to act as a group **2** to cause (people or things) to enter into an association or alliance

United Kingdom *noun* Great Britain together with Northern Ireland

United Nations *noun* international organization

that tries to encourage peace, cooperation and friendship between countries

unity *noun* **1** state of being one **2** mutual agreement

universal *adjective* **1** concerning or relating to everyone in the world or every part of the universe **2** existing everywhere > **universally** *adverb*

universe *noun* the whole of space, including all the stars and planets

university universities *noun* place where students study for degrees

unjust *adjective* not fair or reasonable > **unjustly** *adverb*

unjustified *adjective* (of belief or action) without reason or basis

unkempt *adjective* untidy and not looked after properly

unkind *adjective* unpleasant and rather cruel > **unkindly** *adverb* > **unkindness** *noun*

unknown *adjective* **1** not known **2** not famous ▷ *noun* **3** unknown person, quantity or thing

unlawful *adjective* not legal

unleaded *adjective* (of petrol) containing less lead, in order to reduce environmental pollution

unleash *verb* to release (a powerful or violent force)

unless *conjunction* except under the circumstances that

unlike *adjective* **1** dissimilar or different ▷ *preposition* **2** not like or typical of

unlikely *adjective* improbable

unlimited *adjective* (of supply) not limited or restricted

unload *verb* to remove (cargo) from (a ship, truck or plane)

unlock *verb* to turn the key in (a door or container) so that it can be opened

unlucky *adjective* having or causing bad luck > **unluckily** *adverb*

unmarked *adjective* **1** with no marks of damage or injury **2** with no signs or marks of identification

unmistakable or **unmistakeable** *adjective* not ambiguous; clear > **unmistakably** or **unmistakeably** *adverb*

unmitigated *adjective* **1** not reduced or lessened in severity etc **2** total and complete

unmoved *adjective* not affected by emotion; indifferent

unnatural *adjective* **1** strange and frightening and not usual **2** artificial and not typical > **unnaturally** *adverb*

unnecessary *adjective* not necessary or required > **unnecessarily** *adverb*

unnerve *verb* to cause (someone) to lose courage, confidence or self-control > **unnerving** *adjective*

unobtrusive *adjective* not very noticeable

unoccupied *adjective* without anybody living there

unofficial *adjective* without the approval or permission of a person in authority > **unofficially** *adverb*

unorthodox *adjective* unconventional and not generally accepted

unpack *verb* **1** to remove the contents of (a suitcase, trunk, etc) **2** to take (something) out of a packed container

unpaid *adjective* **1** without pay **2** not yet paid

unpalatable *adjective* very unpleasant and hard to eat or accept

unparalleled *adjective* not equalled; supreme

unpleasant *adjective* not pleasant or agreeable > **unpleasantly** *adverb* > **unpleasantness** *noun*

unpopular *adjective* disliked by most people

unprecedented [un-**press**-id-en-tid] *adjective* (*formal*) that has never happened before or is the best of its kind so far

unpredictable *adjective* having behaviour that is impossible to predict

unprepared *adjective* not ready

unproductive *adjective* not producing anything useful

unqualified *adjective* **1** lacking the necessary qualifications **2** total or complete

unquestionable *adjective* so obviously true or real that nobody can doubt it > **unquestionably** *adverb*

unravel unravels, unravelling, unravelled *verb* **1** to unwind, disentangle or undo (something) **2** to become unravelled **3** to explain or solve (a mystery)

unreal *adjective* so strange that you find it difficult to believe

unrealistic *adjective* **1** not facing up to reality or the practicalities of a situation **2** not true to life

unreasonable *adjective* unfair and difficult to deal with or justify > **unreasonably** *adverb*

unrelated adjective not connected

unrelenting adjective continuing in a determined way without caring about any hurt that is caused

unreliable adjective that cannot be relied upon

unremitting adjective continuing without stopping

unrest noun anger and dissatisfaction in the people

unrivalled adjective better than anything else of its kind

unroll verb 1 to open out or unwind (something rolled or coiled) 2 (of something rolled or coiled) to become opened out or unwound

unruly unrulier, unruliest adjective difficult to control or organize

unsatisfactory adjective not good enough

unsaturated adjective (of oil, fat) made mainly from vegetable fats and considered healthier than saturated

unscathed adjective not harmed or injured

unscrew verb to remove (something) by turning it or by removing the screws holding it

unscrupulous adjective prepared to act dishonestly; unprincipled

unseemly adjective (of behaviour) not suitable for a particular situation and showing a lack of control and good manners

unseen adjective not seen

unsettle verb to make (someone) restless or worried

unshakable or **unshakeable** adjective (of belief, faith, etc) so strong that it cannot be destroyed

unsightly adjective unpleasant to look at

unskilled adjective (of work) not requiring any special training

unsolicited adjective given or happening without being asked for

unsound adjective 1 not based on truth or fact 2 unstable

unspeakable adjective very unpleasant

unspecified adjective not stated specifically

unspoilt or **unspoiled** adjective unchanged and still as at a previous time

unspoken adjective not talked about

unstable adjective 1 likely to change suddenly and create difficulty or danger 2 not firm or fixed properly and likely to wobble or fall

unsteady adjective 1 having difficulty in controlling the movement of your legs or hands 2 not held or fixed securely and likely to fall over > **unsteadily** adverb

unstuck adjective come unstuck to become separated from something

unsuccessful adjective not having success at something > **unsuccessfully** adverb

unsuitable adjective not right or appropriate for a particular purpose > **unsuitably** adverb

unsuited adjective not appropriate for a particular task or situation

unsung adjective not appreciated or praised enough

unsure adjective uncertain or doubtful

unsuspecting *adjective* having no idea of what is happening or going to happen

untangle *verb* to undo, removing any twists or knots

untenable *adjective* (formal) (of theory, argument or position) that cannot be successfully defended

unthinkable *adjective* out of the question; inconceivable

untidy untidier, untidiest *adjective* messy and disordered > **untidily** *adverb* > **untidiness** *noun*

untie unties, untying, untied *verb* to open or free (something that is tied)

until *conjunction* **1** up to the time that ▷ *preposition* **2** in or throughout the period before **3** **not until** not before (a time or event)

untimely *adjective* occurring before the expected or normal time

unto *preposition* (old-fashioned) to

untold *adjective* incalculably great in number or quantity

untouched *adjective* **1** not changed, moved or damaged **2** not eaten

untoward *adjective* unexpected and causing difficulties

untrue *adjective* **1** not true, incorrect or false **2** disloyal or unfaithful

unused *adjective* **1** not yet used **2 unused to** not accustomed to

unusual *adjective* uncommon or extraordinary > **unusually** *adverb*

unveil *verb* to reveal (a statue or painting) officially, by drawing back a curtain

unwanted *adjective* not wanted or desired

unwarranted *adjective* (formal) not justified or not deserved

unwelcome *adjective* not welcome or wanted

unwell *adjective* not well; ill

unwieldy *adjective* too heavy, large or awkward to be easily handled

unwilling *adjective* not willing or prepared (to do something) > **unwillingly** *adverb*

unwind unwinds, unwinding, unwound *verb* **1** to relax after a busy or tense time **2** to undo or unravel (something)

unwise *adjective* foolish or not sensible

unwitting *adjective* **1** not intentional **2** not knowing or conscious > **unwittingly** *adverb*

unworthy *adjective* (formal) not deserving or worthy

unwrap unwraps, unwrapping, unwrapped *verb* to remove the wrapping from

unwritten *adjective* **1** not printed or in writing **2** operating only through custom

up *adverb, preposition* **1** indicating movement to or position at a higher place ▷ *preposition* **2** along (a road or river) ▷ *adverb* **3** towards or being in the north: *I'm flying up to Darwin* **4** **go up** to increase ▷ *adjective* **5** of a high or higher position **6** out of bed

up-and-coming *adjective* likely to be successful

upbringing *noun* education of a person during the formative years

update *verb* to bring (something or someone) up to date

upgrade verb 1 to improve (equipment) 2 to promote (a person or job) to a higher rank

upheaval noun big change that causes a lot of trouble

uphill adjective 1 sloping or leading upwards 2 requiring a great deal of effort ▷ adverb 3 up a slope

uphold upholds, upholding, upheld verb to support and maintain (a law or decision) >**upholder** noun

upholstery noun soft covering on a chair or sofa

upkeep noun act, process or cost of keeping something in good repair

upland adjective (of area) high or relatively high >**uplands** plural noun area of high or relatively high ground

uplifting adjective making you feel happy

upload verb to transfer a computer file or program from your computer into the memory of another computer

up-market adjective sophisticated and expensive

upon preposition 1 on 2 up and on 3 in the course of or immediately after

upper adjective 1 higher in physical position, wealth, rank or status ▷ noun 2 part of a shoe above the sole

upper class noun highest social class >**upper-class** adjective

uppermost adjective 1 highest in position, power or importance ▷ adverb 2 in or into the highest place or position

upright adjective 1 vertical or erect 2 honest or just ▷ adverb 3 vertically or in an erect position ▷ noun 4 vertical support, such as a post

uprising noun rebellion or revolt

uproar noun disturbance characterized by loud noise and confusion

uproot verb 1 to displace (a person or people) from their native or usual surroundings 2 to pull (a tree or plant) out of the ground together with its roots

upset upsets, upsetting, upset adjective 1 unhappy or distressed ▷ verb 2 to sadden, distress or worry (someone) 3 to disturb the normal state or stability of (something) 4 to tip over or spill (something) 5 to make (someone) physically ill ▷ noun 6 stomach upset slight stomach illness caused by an infection or by something you have eaten >**upsetting** adjective

upshot noun final result or conclusion

upside down adjective, adverb the wrong way up

upstage verb (informal) to draw attention away from (someone) by being more attractive or interesting

upstairs adverb 1 to or on an upper floor of a building ▷ noun 2 upper floor ▷ adjective 3 situated on an upper floor

upstart noun person who has risen suddenly to a position of power and behaves arrogantly

upstream adverb, adjective in or towards the higher part of a stream

upsurge noun rapid rise or swell

uptake *noun* **quick, slow on the uptake** (*informal*) quick or slow to understand or learn

uptight *adjective* (*informal*) nervously tense, irritable or angry

up-to-date *adjective* **1** modern or fashionable **2** having the latest information

up-to-the-minute *adjective* latest and newest possible

upturn *noun* improvement

upturned *adjective* **1** facing upwards **2** upside down

upward *adjective* **1** towards a higher place, level or condition ▷ *adverb* **2** from a lower to a higher place, level or condition

uranium *noun* radioactive silvery-white metallic element, used to produce nuclear energy and weapons

Uranus *noun* seventh planet from the sun in the solar system

urban *adjective* relating to a town or city

urbane *adjective* well-mannered and comfortable in social situations

Urdu [oor-doo] *noun* official language of Pakistan; also spoken by many people in India

urge *noun* **1** strong impulse, inner drive or wish ▷ *verb* **2** to press or try to persuade (someone to do something)

urgent *adjective* requiring speedy action or attention ▷ **urgency** *noun* ▷ **urgently** *adverb*

urinal *noun* a bowl or trough fixed to the wall in a men's public toilet for men to urinate in

urinate [yoor-rin-ate] *verb* to get rid of urine from your body

urine *noun* pale yellow fluid excreted by the kidneys to the bladder and passed as waste from the body ▷ **urinary** *adjective*

URL uniform resource locator: a standardized address of a location on the internet

urn *noun* **1** vase used as a container for the ashes of the dead **2** large metal container with a tap, used for making and holding tea or coffee

us *pronoun* used by a speaker or writer to refer to himself or herself and at least one other person; used as the object of a verb or preposition

US or **USA** *abbreviation* United States (of America)

usage *noun* **1** way in which a word is used in a language **2** the degree to which something is used, or the way in which it is used

USB *abbreviation* Universal Serial Bus: standard for connecting sockets on computers

USB drive *noun* (*Computers*) small data storage device that plugs into a computer

use *verb* **1** to do something with (something) in order to do a job or achieve a purpose **2** to take advantage of (someone); exploit **3** to consume or expend (energy, resources, etc) **4 used to do something** previously did or previously had the habit of doing something: *I used to live there; He used not to like milk; He didn't use to like milk* ▷ *noun* **5** act of using something or being used **6** ability or permission to use something **7** usefulness or advantage **8** purpose for which something is used > **usable** *adjective* able to be used > **user** *noun*

used *adjective* **1** second-hand **2 used to something** accustomed to something

useful *adjective* helpful > **usefully** *adverb* > **usefulness** *noun*

useless *adjective* **1** of no use or help **2** in vain **3** (*informal*) very poor or bad at something; hopeless > **uselessly** *adverb* > **uselessness** *noun*

username *noun* (*Computers*) name entered into a computer for identification purposes

usher *noun* **1** official who shows people to their seats, as in a church ▷ *verb* **2** to conduct or escort (someone somewhere)

USSR *abbreviation* Union of Soviet Socialist Republics, a country which was made up of a lot of smaller countries including Russia, but which is now broken up

usual *adjective* happening, done or used most often > **usually** *adverb* most often, in most cases

usurp [yewz-**zurp**] *verb* to seize (a position or power) without authority > **usurper** *noun*

ute [**yoot**] *noun* (*Aust, NZ informal*) utility truck

utensil *noun* tool for practical use: *cooking utensils*

uterus [**yew**-ter-russ] *noun* womb

utility utilities *noun* **1** usefulness **2** public service, such as electricity

utility truck *noun* (*Aust, NZ*) small truck with an open body and low sides

utilize or **utilise** *verb* (*formal*) to make practical use of > **utilization** *noun*

utmost *adjective* extreme or greatest

utter *verb* **1** to express (something) in sounds or words ▷ *adjective* **2** total or absolute > **utterly** *adverb*

utterance *noun* something said or uttered

V

v. *abbreviation* **1** versus **2** very

vacant *adjective* **1** (of a toilet, room, position, etc) unoccupied **2** (of expression, look) without interest or understanding > **vacantly** *adverb*

vacate *verb* (*formal*) **1** to leave (a room) **2** to give up (a job or position)

vacation *noun* **1** time when universities and law courts are closed **2** (*Chiefly US*) holiday

vaccinate *verb* to inject (a person or animal) with a vaccine > **vaccination** *noun*

vaccine *noun* substance designed to cause a mild form of a disease to make a person immune to the disease itself

vacuum *noun* **1** space containing no air, gases or other matter ▷ *verb* **2** to clean (a room, carpet, etc) with a vacuum cleaner

vacuum cleaner *noun* electrical appliance which sucks up dust and dirt from carpets and upholstery

vagina [vaj-**jine**-a] *noun* (in female mammals) passage from the womb to the external genitals

vagrant [**vaig**-rant] *noun* person with no settled home; tramp > **vagrancy** *noun*: You'll get arrested for vagrancy

vague *adjective* **1** not clearly explained **2** unable to be seen or heard clearly **3** absent-minded > **vaguely** *adverb* > **vagueness** *noun*

vain *adjective* **1** excessively proud, especially of your appearance **2** bound to fail; futile ▷ *noun* **3 in vain** unsuccessfully > **vainly** *adverb*

vale *noun* (*literary*) valley

valentine *noun* **1** person to whom you send a romantic card on Saint Valentine's Day, 14th February **2** a card sent on Saint Valentine's Day

valet *noun* man's personal male servant

valiant *adjective* brave or courageous > **valiantly** *adverb*

valid *adjective* **1** soundly reasoned **2** officially accepted > **validity** *noun*

validate *verb* to prove (something) to be true > **validation** *noun*

valley *noun* low area between hills, often with a river running through it

valour *noun* (*literary*) bravery

valuable *adjective* having great value or worth

valuation *noun* assessment of how much something is worth

value *noun* **1** importance, usefulness **2** monetary worth **3 values** moral principles ▷ *verb* **4** to think (something) is important; appreciate **5** to assess the value of > **valued** *adjective* > **valuer** *noun*

valve *noun* **1** device to control the movement of gas or liquid through a pipe **2** small flap in your heart or in a vein which controls the flow and direction of blood

vampire noun (in folklore) corpse that rises at night to drink the blood of the living

van noun **1** motor vehicle larger than a car but smaller than a lorry, used for carrying goods **2** railway carriage for goods, luggage or mail

vandal noun person who deliberately damages property > **vandalize** or **vandalise** verb > **vandalism** noun

vane noun flat blade on a rotary device such as a weathercock or propeller

vanguard noun most advanced group or position in a movement or activity

vanilla noun seed pod of a tropical plant, used for flavouring

vanish verb **1** to disappear suddenly or mysteriously **2** to cease to exist

vanity noun feeling of excessive pride about your looks or abilities

vanquish verb (literary) to defeat (someone) completely

vapour noun **1** moisture suspended in air as steam or mist **2** gaseous form of something that is liquid or solid at room temperature

variable adjective **1** not always the same; changeable > noun **2** something that can change **3** (Maths) symbol such as x which can represent any value or any one of a set of values > **variability** noun

variance noun **at variance** at odds or not in agreement (with)

variant noun **1** something that differs from a standard or type > adjective **2** differing from a standard or type

variation noun **1** change from the normal or usual pattern **2** difference in level, amount or quantity

varicose veins plural noun knotted and swollen veins, especially in the legs

varied adjective of different types, quantities or sizes: Eat a healthy and varied diet

variety noun **varieties 1** state of being diverse or various **2** different things of the same kind; assortment **3** particular type **4** light entertainment composed of unrelated acts

various adjective **1** several **2** of several kinds > **variously** adverb

varnish noun **1** liquid which when painted onto a surface gives it a hard clear shiny finish > verb **2** to apply varnish to

vary verb varies, varying, varied **1** to change **2** to make changes in

vascular adjective (Biology) relating to tubes or ducts that carry fluids within animals or plants

vase noun ornamental jar, especially for flowers

vasectomy noun vasectomies operation to sterilize a man by cutting the tube that carries the sperm

Vaseline ® noun thick oily cream made from petroleum, used in skin care

vast adjective extremely large > **vastly** adverb > **vastness** noun

vat noun large container for liquids

VAT abbreviation (in Britain) value-added tax, a tax which is added to the costs of making or providing goods and services

vault noun 1 secure room for storing valuables 2 underground burial chamber 3 an arched roof, often found in churches > verb 4 to jump over (something) by resting your hand(s) on it > **vaulted** adjective having an arched roof

VCD abbreviation video compact disc: an optical disc used to store computer, audio or video data

VCR abbreviation video cassette recorder

VDU abbreviation visual display unit: monitor screen attached to a computer or word processor

veal noun calf meat

Veda [**vay**-da] noun ancient Hindu sacred text; also these texts as a collection > **Vedic** adjective

veer verb to change direction suddenly

vegan [**vee**-gan] noun person who eats no meat, fish, eggs or dairy products

vegetable noun 1 edible roots or leaves such as carrots or cabbage ▷ adjective 2 relating to plants or vegetables

vegetarian noun 1 person who does not eat meat, poultry or fish ▷ adjective 2 suitable for a vegetarian > **vegetarianism** noun

vegetation noun plant life in a particular area

vehement adjective expressing strong feelings > **vehemence** noun > **vehemently** adverb

vehicle noun 1 machine, especially with an engine and wheels, for carrying people or objects 2 something used to achieve a particular purpose or as a means of expression > **vehicular** adjective

veil noun piece of thin cloth covering the head or face > **veiled** adjective

vein noun 1 tube that takes blood to the heart 2 line on a leaf or an insect's wing 3 layer of ore or mineral in rock 4 streak in marble, wood or cheese 5 feature of someone's writing or speech: a vein of humour 6 mood or style: in a lighter vein > **veined** adjective

veld or **veldt** noun high grassland in southern Africa

veldskoen or **velskoen** noun (S Afr) tough ankle-length boot

velocity noun (technical) speed at which something is moving in a particular direction

velvet noun fabric with a thick soft pile > **velvety** adjective soft and smooth

vendetta noun long-lasting bitter quarrel which results in people trying to harm each other

vending machine noun machine that dispenses goods such as sweets or drinks when you put money in it

vendor noun person who sells something

veneer noun 1 superficial appearance: a veneer of sophistication 2 thin layer of wood etc covering a cheaper material

venerable adjective worthy of great respect

venerate verb (formal) to feel great respect for > **veneration** noun

vengeance noun 1 act of harming someone because they have harmed you; revenge 2 with a **vengeance** very forcefully or strongly

venison noun deer meat

venom noun 1 poison produced by snakes, scorpions and spiders, etc 2 malice or spite ▷ **venomous** adjective

vent noun 1 outlet, hole, or slit through which fumes or fluid can escape and fresh air can enter 2 **give vent to** to release (a strong feeling) in an outburst ▷ verb 3 to express (a strong feeling) in an outburst

ventilate verb 1 to let fresh air into (a room or building) 2 to discuss (ideas or feelings) openly ▷ **ventilated** adjective ▷ **ventilation** noun

ventilator noun machine that helps people breathe when they cannot breathe naturally, for example if they are very ill

ventriloquist noun entertainer who can speak without moving his or her lips, so that the words appear to come from a dummy ▷ **ventriloquism** noun

venture noun 1 risky undertaking, especially in business ▷ verb 2 to go on an unknown and possibly risky place 3 to dare to express (an opinion) 4 to dare (to do something)

venue noun place where an event is held

Venus noun second planet from the sun in the solar system

veranda or **verandah** noun platform with a roof that is attached to an outside wall of a house at ground level

verb noun word that expresses the idea of action, happening or being: run; take; become; to be

verbal adjective 1 spoken 2 relating to verbs ▷ **verbally** adverb

verdict noun 1 decision that states whether a prisoner is guilty or not guilty 2 opinion formed after examining the facts

verge noun 1 grass border along a road 2 **on the verge of** having almost reached (a point or condition) ▷ **verge on** verb to be near to (a condition)

verify verifies, verifying, verified verb to check the truth or accuracy of ▷ **verifiable** adjective ▷ **verification** noun: The winning card will be subject to verification

veritable adjective rightly called; without exaggeration: a veritable feast ▷ **veritably** adverb

vermin plural noun animals, especially insects and rodents, that spread disease or cause damage

vernacular [ver-**nak**-yew-lar] noun most widely spoken language of a particular people or place

verruca [ver-**roo**-ka] noun wart, usually on the foot

versatile adjective having many skills or uses ▷ **versatility** noun

verse noun 1 poetry 2 one part of a song, poem or chapter of the Bible

versed adjective **versed in** knowledgeable about

version noun 1 form of something, such as a piece of writing, with some differences from other forms 2 account of an event from a particular person's point of view

versus preposition 1 in opposition to or in contrast with 2 (Sport, Law) against

vertebra vertebrae noun one of the bones that form the spine

vertebrate noun any animal that has a spine

vertex vertexes or vertices noun highest point of a triangle or pyramid

vertical adjective straight up and down > **vertically** adverb

vertigo noun dizziness, usually when looking down from a high place

verve noun enthusiasm or liveliness

very adverb **1** more than usually, extremely ▷ adjective **2** absolute or exact: the very top; the very man

vessel noun **1** ship or large boat **2** (literary) container, especially for liquids **3** (Biology) thin tube along which liquids such as blood or sap move in animals and plants

vest noun **1** piece of underwear worn for warmth on the top half of the body **2** (US) waistcoat

vestige [**vest**-ij] noun (formal) small amount or trace

vestry vestries noun part of the church building where a priest or minister changes into their official clothes

vet vets, vetting, vetted noun **1** medical specialist who treats sick animals; veterinary surgeon **2** (US, Aust, NZ) military veteran ▷ verb **3** to check the suitability of

veteran noun **1** someone who has served in the armed forces, particularly during a war **2** someone who has been involved in a particular activity for a long time

veterinary adjective concerning animal health

veterinary surgeon noun medical specialist who treats sick animals

veto vetoes, vetoing, vetoed verb **1** (of person in authority) to say no to ▷ noun **2** right of someone in authority to say no to something

vexed adjective annoyed, worried or puzzled

VHF abbreviation very high frequency: a range of high radio frequencies

via preposition by way of

viable adjective **1** able to be put into practice **2** (Biology) able to live and grow independently > **viability** noun

viaduct noun long high bridge that carries a road or railway across a valley

vibrant [**vibe**-rant] adjective **1** full of life, energy and enthusiasm **2** (of a colour) strong and bright > **vibrancy** noun > **vibrantly** adverb

vibrate verb to move back and forth rapidly by a tiny amount > **vibration** noun

vicar noun priest in the Church of England

vicarage noun house where a vicar lives

vice noun **1** serious moral fault in someone's character, such as greed, or a weakness, such as smoking **2** criminal activities connected with prostitution and pornography **3** tool with a pair of jaws for holding an object while working on it

vice- prefix deputy or assistant to: vice-president

viceregal adjective **1** of or concerning a viceroy **2** (in Australia and New Zealand) viceregal means of or concerning a governor or governor-general

a
b
c
d
e
f
g
h
i
j
k
l
m
n
o
p
q
r
s
t
u
v
w
x
y
z

viceroy noun governor of a colony who represents the monarch

vice versa [vie-see [ver]-sa] adverb the other way round: *Wives criticize their husbands, and vice versa*

vicinity [viss-**in**-it-ee] noun surrounding area

vicious adjective cruel and violent >**viciously** adverb >**viciousness** noun

victim noun someone who has been harmed or injured by someone or something

victor noun person who has defeated an opponent, especially in war or sport; winner

Victorian adjective **1** of or in the reign of Queen Victoria (1837–1901) **2** of or relating to the Australian state of Victoria

victory victories noun winning of a battle or contest >**victorious** adjective

video videos, videoing, videoed noun **1** short for **video cassette, video cassette recorder, video tape** ▷ verb **2** to record (a TV programme, film or event) on video ▷ adjective **3** relating to or used in producing sound and pictures

video cassette noun cassette containing video tape

video recorder or **video cassette recorder** noun tape recorder for recording and playing back TV programmes and films

vie vies, vying, vied verb to compete (with someone)

Vietnamese [vyet-nam-**meez**] adjective **1** belonging or relating to Vietnam ▷ noun **2** someone from Vietnam **3** main language spoken in Vietnam

view noun **1** opinion or belief **2** everything that can be seen from a given place **3** picture of this **4** in view of taking into consideration **5** on view available to be seen by the public; on show ▷ verb **6** to think of (something) in a particular way

viewer noun person who watches television

viewpoint noun **1** opinion or way of thinking about something **2** place from which you get a good view of an area or event

vigil [**vij**-ill] noun night-time period of staying awake to look after a sick person, pray, make a protest etc

vigilant adjective watchful in case of danger

vigilante [vij-ill-**ant**-ee] noun person, especially one of an unofficial group, who takes it upon himself or herself to protect the community and catch and punish criminals

vigorous adjective energetic or enthusiastic >**vigorously** adverb >**vigour** noun physical or mental energy

Viking noun (History) seafaring raider and settler from Scandinavia from the 8th to the 11th centuries

vile adjective very unpleasant or disgusting

villa noun **1** large house with gardens **2** holiday home, usually in the Mediterranean

village noun **1** small group of houses and other buildings in a country area **2** rural community >**villager** noun

villain noun **1** someone who harms others or breaks the law

2 main wicked character in a play > **villainous** adjective > **villainy** noun

vindicate verb to prove (someone) right or to prove (their actions or ideas) to have been justified > **vindication** noun

vindictive adjective maliciously seeking revenge > **vindictiveness** noun

vine noun trailing or climbing plant, especially one producing grapes

vinegar noun sharp-tasting liquid made from sour wine, beer or cider > **vinegary** adjective

vineyard [vinn-yard] noun area of land where grapes are grown

vintage adjective **1** (of wine) of a good quality and stored for a number of years to improve **2** best and most typical ▷ noun **3** wine from a particular harvest of grapes

vinyl [vine-ill] noun type of plastic, used to make things such as floor coverings and furniture

viola noun [vee-oh-la] stringed instrument lower in pitch than a violin [vie-ol-la]

violate verb **1** to break (a law or agreement) **2** to disturb (someone's peace or privacy) **3** to treat (a sacred place) disrespectfully > **violation** noun

violence noun **1** use of physical force, usually intended to cause injury or destruction **2** great force or strength in action, feeling or expression

violent adjective **1** (of person) making use of physical force or weapons in a way that may cause injury or death **2** (of event)

happening unexpectedly and with great force **3** (of act, feeling, pain etc) very forceful > **violently** adverb

violet noun **1** plant with bluish-purple flowers ▷ adjective, noun **2** bluish-purple

violin noun four-stringed musical instrument played with a bow. > **violinist** noun

VIP abbreviation very important person

viper noun type of poisonous snake

virgin noun **1** person, especially a woman, who has not had sexual intercourse ▷ adjective **2** not yet used or explored; fresh > **virginity** noun

virginal adjective **1** looking young and innocent **2** looking fresh, clean and unused ▷ noun **3** keyboard instrument popular in the 16th and 17th centuries

Virgo noun sixth sign of the zodiac, represented by a girl

virile adjective having the traditional male characteristics of physical strength and a high sex drive > **virility** noun

virtual adjective **1** having the characteristics of something without being formally recognized as being that thing **2** of or relating to virtual reality > **virtually** adverb practically, almost

virtual reality noun computer-generated environment that seems real to the user

virtue noun **1** moral goodness **2** positive moral quality **3** advantage, merit **4** by virtue of (formal) by reason of > **virtuously** adverb

a
b
c
d
e
f
g
h
i
j
k
l
m
n
o
p
q
r
s
t
u
v
w
x
y
z

virtuoso virtuosos or virtuosi *noun* person with impressive skill at something, especially music > **virtuosity** *noun*

virtuous *adjective* morally good

virus viruses *noun*
1 microorganism that can cause disease 2 (*Computers*) program that alters or damages the information stored in a computer system

visa *noun* permission to enter a country, granted by its government and shown by a stamp on your passport

viscount [**vie**-count] *noun* British nobleman ranking between an earl and a baron

Vishnu *noun* Vishnu is a Hindu god and is one of the Trimurti

visibility *noun* range or clarity of vision

visible *adjective* 1 able to be seen 2 noticeable or evident > **visibly** *adverb*

vision *noun* 1 ability to see 2 mental image of something 3 foresight 4 unusual experience, in which you see things not seen by others, as a result of a mental disorder, divine inspiration or taking drugs > **visionary** *adjective* 1 showing foresight 2 idealistic but impractical ▷ *noun* 3 visionary person

visit *verb* 1 to go or come to see (someone or something) ▷ *noun* 2 instance of visiting > **visitor** *noun*

visor [**vize**-or] *noun* transparent part of a helmet that you pull down to protect your eyes or face

visual *adjective* 1 relating to sight 2 designed to be looked at

visualize or **visualise** *verb* to form a mental image of

vital *adjective* 1 essential or very important 2 energetic, exciting and full of life 3 necessary to maintain life > **vitality** *noun* physical or mental energy > **vitally** *adverb*

vitamin *noun* one of a group of substances that you need to stay healthy. They occur naturally in food

vivacious *adjective* full of energy and enthusiasm > **vivacity** *noun*

vivid *adjective* very bright in colour or clear in detail > **vividly** *adverb* > **vividness** *noun*

vivisection *noun* the act of cutting open and experimenting on living animals for medical research > **vivisectionist** *noun*

vixen *noun* female fox

v-mail *noun* video message sent by e-mail

vocabulary vocabularies *noun*
1 all the words that a person knows in a particular language 2 all the words in a language 3 specialist terms used in a given subject 4 list of words in another language used for translation

vocal *adjective* 1 relating to the voice 2 outspoken > **vocally** *adverb*

vocation *noun* 1 strong wish to do a particular job, especially one which involves serving other people 2 occupation that someone feels called to; calling 3 profession or trade

vocational *adjective* (of skills, training) directed towards a particular profession or trade

vociferous adjective (formal) outspoken or strident
> **vociferously** adverb

VOD abbreviation video on demand: TV system allowing users to watch programmes at a time of their own choosing

vodka noun spirit distilled from potatoes or grain

vogue noun fashion

voice noun sounds produced by your vocal cords as when speaking, shouting or singing, or the ability to make such sounds ▷ verb to express (an opinion or emotion)

void noun empty space or feeling

volatile adjective 1 liable to sudden change, especially in behaviour 2 evaporating quickly > **volatility** noun

volcanic adjective (of region) having many volcanoes or created by volcanoes

volcano volcanoes noun mountain with an opening through which lava, gas and ash are ejected

vole noun small mouse-like rodent

volition noun (formal) **of your own volition** out of choice rather than because persuaded to do something

volley noun 1 simultaneous firing of a lot of shots 2 burst of questions or critical comments 3 (Sport) stroke or kick at a moving ball before it hits the ground

volleyball noun team game where a ball is hit with the hands over a high net

volt noun unit used to measure the force of an electric current

voltage noun force of an electric current measured in volts

volume noun 1 amount of space occupied or contained by something 2 amount 3 loudness of sound 4 book or one of a series of books

voluminous adjective 1 (of clothes) large and roomy 2 (of writings) extensive

voluntary adjective 1 done by choice 2 done without payment > **voluntarily** adverb

volunteer noun 1 person who offers voluntarily to do something 2 person who voluntarily undertakes military service ▷ verb 3 to offer (to do something) 4 to give (information) willingly

voluptuous adjective 1 (of a woman) having a plump and sexually exciting figure 2 sensually pleasurable > **voluptuously** adverb > **voluptuousness** noun

vomit verb 1 to be sick or to bring up (the contents of your stomach) ▷ noun 2 partly digested food and drink that has come back up from someone's stomach

voodoo noun form of magic practised in the Caribbean, especially in Haiti

vote noun 1 expression of choice made in an election or at a meeting where decisions are taken 2 right to make this choice 3 total number of votes cast 4 collective voting power of a given group: the Black vote ▷ verb 5 to indicate your choice by writing on a piece of paper or by raising your hand 6 to propose

a
b
c
d
e
f
g
h
i
j
k
l
m
n
o
p
q
r
s
t
u
v
w
x
y
z

(that something should happen)
> **voter** noun

vouch verb **vouch for** **1** to provide evidence for **2** to give your personal assurance about the good behaviour or support of (someone)

voucher noun ticket used instead of money to buy specified goods

vow verb **1** to promise (something) solemnly ▷ noun **2** solemn and binding promise **3** **vows** formal promises made when marrying or entering a religious order

vowel noun sound made without your tongue touching the roof of your mouth or your teeth, or one of the letters a, e, i, o, u, which represent such sounds

voyage noun long journey by sea or in space > **voyager** noun

vulgar adjective **1** socially unacceptable or offensive: *vulgar language* **2** showing a lack of good taste or refinement > **vulgarity** noun > **vulgarly** adverb

vulnerable adjective liable to be physically or emotionally hurt > **vulnerability** noun > **vulnerably** adverb

vulture noun large bird that lives in hot countries and feeds on the flesh of dead animals

vying verb present participle of **vie**

wacky wackier, wackiest adjective (*informal*) eccentric or funny

wad noun **1** small mass of soft material **2** roll or bundle, especially of banknotes

waddle verb **1** to walk with short swaying steps ▷ noun **2** swaying walk

waddy waddies noun (*Aust*) heavy wooden club used by Australian Aborigines

wade verb **1** to walk with difficulty through water or mud **2** to proceed with difficulty

wader noun **1** long-legged water bird **2** **waders** angler's long waterproof boots

wafer noun **1** thin crisp biscuit **2** thin disc of special bread used at Communion

waffle noun **1** (*informal*) to speak or write in a vague wordy way ▷ noun **2** (*informal*) vague wordy talk or writing **3** square crisp pancake with a gridlike pattern

waft [**wahft**] verb to drift or carry gently through the air

wag wags, wagging, wagged verb **1** to move rapidly from side to side ▷ noun **2** wagging movement **3** (*old-fashioned*) humorous witty person

wage noun **1** (often plural) payment for work done, especially when paid weekly ▷ verb **2** to engage in (war)

wager noun **1** bet on the outcome of something ▷ verb **2** to bet (money) on the outcome of something

wagon or **waggon** noun **1** four-wheeled vehicle for heavy loads **2** railway freight truck

waif [**wayf**] noun young person who is, or seems, homeless or neglected

wail verb **1** to cry out in pain or misery ▷ noun **2** long unhappy cry

waist noun part of the body between the ribs and hips

waistcoat noun sleeveless garment that buttons up the front, usually worn over a shirt and under a jacket

wait verb **1** to do little or nothing until something happens **2** to be ready (for something) **3** to be delayed **4** to serve food and drink in a restaurant ▷ noun **5** act or period of waiting

waiter noun man who serves food and drink in a restaurant

waiting list noun list of people waiting for medical treatment, etc

waitress noun woman who serves food and drink in a restaurant

waive verb not to enforce (a law, right, etc)

wake wakes, waking, woke, woken verb **1** to rouse (someone) from sleep ▷ noun **2** gathering to mourn someone's death **3** track left by a moving ship **4 in the wake of** following, often as a result > **wake up** verb to stop being asleep or to rouse

(someone) from sleep > **wake up to** verb to become aware of

waken verb to wake (someone)

walk verb **1** to move on foot with at least one foot always on the ground **2** to pass through or over (a distance) on foot **3** to accompany (someone) on foot ▷ noun **4** act or instance of walking **5** distance walked **6** manner of walking **7** place or route for walking > **walker** noun person who walks > **walk into** to get into (a difficult situation) unexpectedly

walkabout noun **1** informal walk among the public by royalty or other famous people **2** period when an Australian Aborigine goes off to live and wander in the bush

walking stick noun wooden stick for leaning on while walking

Walkman ® noun small portable cassette player with headphones

walk of life noun social position or profession

walkover noun easy victory in a competition or contest

walkway noun often raised passage or path for walking along

wall noun **1** structure of brick, stone, etc used to enclose, divide or support **2** something having the function or effect of a wall ▷ verb **3** to enclose (someone or something) with a wall or walls

wallaby wallabies noun animal like a small kangaroo

wallaroo wallaroos noun large, stocky kangaroo that lives in rocky or mountainous regions of Australia

wallet noun small folding case for paper money, credit cards, etc

wallop (informal) verb 1 to hit (someone) hard ▷ noun 2 hard blow

wallow verb 1 (followed by in) to take pleasure (in an unpleasant emotion) 2 to roll (in liquid or mud) ▷ noun 3 act or instance of wallowing

wallpaper noun thick coloured or patterned paper covering the walls of rooms

walnut noun 1 edible nut with a wrinkled shell 2 tree it grows on 3 its wood, used for making furniture

walrus walruses noun large sea animal with long tusks

waltz noun 1 ballroom dance 2 music for this ▷ verb 3 to dance a waltz 4 (informal) to move in a relaxed confident way

wan wanner, wannest [rhymes with **swan**] adjective pale and sickly-looking

wand noun thin rod, especially one used in performing magic tricks

wander verb 1 to walk about without a definite destination or aim 2 to go astray ▷ noun 3 act or instance of wandering > **wanderer** noun person who wanders

wane verb 1 to decrease gradually in size or strength 2 (of the moon) to decrease in size ▷ noun 3 **on the wane** decreasing in size, strength or power

wangle verb (informal) to get (something) by crafty methods

want verb 1 to need or long for 2 to desire or wish (to do something) ▷ noun 3 act or instance of

wanting 4 lack or absence (of something) > **wanted** adjective searched for by the police

wanting adjective lacking or not good enough: The department was found wanting

wanton adjective without justification: wanton destruction

WAP abbreviation wireless application protocol: a system that allows you to access the internet through a mobile phone

war wars, warring, warred noun 1 fighting between nations 2 contest or campaign ▷ adjective 3 of, like or caused by war ▷ verb 4 to fight a war > **warring** adjective: warring husbands and wives

waratah [wor-ra-**tah**] noun (Aust) Australian shrub with crimson flowers

warble verb to sing in a high voice

ward noun 1 room in a hospital for patients needing a similar kind of care 2 political division of a town 3 child under the care of a guardian or court > **ward off** verb to prevent (something) from harming you

-ward or **-wards** suffix -ward and -wards form adverbs or adjectives that show the way something is moving or facing: homeward; westwards

warden noun 1 person in charge of a prison or youth hostel 2 official responsible for the enforcement of laws: a traffic warden

warder noun prison officer

wardrobe noun 1 cupboard for hanging clothes in 2 person's collection of clothes 3 costumes of a theatre company

ware noun **1** articles of a specified type or material: *silverware* **2** wares goods for sale

warehouse noun large building for storing goods before they are sold or distributed

warfare noun activity of fighting a war

warhead noun explosive front part of a bomb or missile

warlock noun man who practises black magic

warm adjective **1** moderately hot **2** providing warmth **3** (of a colour) mainly made up of yellow or red **4** affectionate ▷ verb **5** to make (someone or something) warm > **warmly** adverb: *warmly dressed* > **warm up** verb **1** to become warmer or make (something) warmer **2** to do gentle stretching exercises before more strenuous exercise **3** to become more lively or make (someone or something) more lively

warmth noun **1** mild heat **2** friendliness

warn verb **1** to make (someone) aware of possible danger or harm **2** to advise (someone) not to do something > **warning** noun something said or written to warn people of a problem or danger > **warn off** verb to advise (someone) not to become involved

warp verb **1** to twist (something) out of shape **2** to damage (someone's mind) ▷ noun **3** state of being warped **4** lengthwise threads on a loom

warrant noun **1** document giving official authorization to do something ▷ verb **2** to make (an action) necessary

warranty warranties noun (document giving) a guarantee

warren noun **1** series of burrows in which rabbits live **2** overcrowded building or part of a town

warrigal [**wor**-rih-gl] (Aust) noun **1** dingo ▷ adjective **2** wild

warrior noun person who fights in a war

warship noun ship designed and equipped for fighting in wars

wart noun small hard growth on the skin

wartime noun period of time during which a country is at war

wary warier, wariest [**ware**-ree] adjective watchful or cautious > **warily** adverb > **wariness** noun state of being wary

was verb first and third person singular past tense of **be**

wash verb **1** to clean (oneself, clothes, etc) with water and usually soap **2** to be washable **3** to flow gently **4** (informal) to be believable or acceptable: *That excuse won't wash* ▷ noun **5** act or process of washing **6** clothes washed at one time **7** thin coat of paint **8** disturbance in the water after a ship has passed by > **washable** adjective able to be washed without being damaged > **wash away** verb to carry (something) away by moving water > **wash up** verb to wash dishes and cutlery after a meal

washbasin noun a deep bowl, usually fixed to a wall, with taps for hot and cold water

washer noun ring put under a nut or bolt or in a tap as a seal

washing noun clothes and bedding to be washed

a b c d e f g h i j k l m n o p q r s t u v w x y z

washing machine *noun* machine for washing clothes in

washing-up *noun* washing of dishes and cutlery after a meal

wasp *noun* stinging insect with a slender black-and-yellow striped body

wastage *noun* **1** loss by wear or waste **2** reduction in size of a workforce by not replacing people who have left

waste *verb* **1** to use (time, money, etc) carelessly or thoughtlessly **2** to fail to take advantage of (an opportunity) ▷ *noun* **3** act of wasting or state of being wasted; misuse **4** anything wasted **5** rubbish **6 wastes** desert ▷ *adjective* **7** rejected as worthless or unwanted > **waste away** *verb* to become weak and ill > **waster** or **wastrel** *noun* layabout

wasted *adjective* unnecessary: *a wasted journey*

wasteful *adjective* extravagant

wasteland *noun* land that is not being used, e.g. because it is infertile

wasting *adjective* (of disease) causing gradual and relentless weight loss and loss of strength and vitality

watch *verb* **1** to look at (someone or something) closely **2** to guard or supervise (someone or something) ▷ *noun* **3** small clock for the wrist or pocket **4** period of guarding or supervising **5** sailor's spell of duty > **watch for** *verb* to keep alert for (something) > **watch out** *verb* **1** to be very careful **2 watch out for** to keep alert for (something)

watchdog *noun* **1** dog kept to guard property **2** person or group guarding against inefficient or illegal conduct in companies

watchful *adjective* careful to notice everything that is happening

watchman *noun* man employed to guard a building or property

water *noun* **1** clear colourless tasteless liquid that falls as rain and forms rivers etc **2** body of water, such as a sea or lake **3** level of the tide **4** urine: *to pass water* ▷ *verb* **5** to put water on or into **6** (of the eyes) to fill with tears **7** (of the mouth) to fill with saliva > **water down** *verb* **1** to dilute (a drink) **2** to make (something) weaker

watercolour *noun* **1** paint thinned with water **2** painting done in watercolours

watercress *noun* edible plant growing in clear ponds and streams, whose leaves are eaten in salads

waterfall *noun* place where the waters of a river drop vertically

waterfront *noun* street or piece of land next to an area of water

watering can *noun* container with a handle and a long spout, which you use to water plants

waterlogged *adjective* (of land) soaked through, with water on the surface

watermelon *noun* large melon with green skin and red flesh

waterproof *adjective* **1** not letting water through ▷ *noun* **2** waterproof garment ▷ *verb* **3** to make (a garment) waterproof

watershed noun important period or event that marks a turning point

watersider noun (NZ) person employed to load and unload ships

water-skiing noun sport of riding over water on skis towed by a speedboat

water table noun the water table is the level below the surface of the ground at which water can be found

watertight adjective 1 not letting water through 2 having no loopholes or weak points

waterway noun a canal, river, etc that ships or boats can sail along

waterworks noun building where the public water supply is stored and cleaned, and from where it is distributed

watery adjective (of food or drink) thin like water

watt [wott] noun unit of electrical power

wattle [wott-tl] noun Australian acacia tree with spikes of brightly coloured flowers

wave verb 1 to move (the hand) from side to side as a greeting or signal 2 to move or flap (something) from side to side ▷ noun 3 moving ridge of water on the surface of the sea 4 curve in the hair 5 prolonged spell of something: the crime wave 6 gesture of waving 7 vibration carrying energy through a substance

wavelength noun distance between the same points of two successive waves of energy

waver verb 1 to hesitate or be undecided 2 to be unsteady

wavy wavier, waviest adjective having waves or regular curves

wax noun 1 solid shiny fatty or oily substance used for sealing, making candles, etc 2 sticky yellow substance in the ear ▷ verb 3 to coat or polish (something) with wax 4 to increase in size or strength 5 (of the moon) to get gradually larger

way noun 1 manner or method 2 characteristic manner 3 route or direction 4 track or path 5 distance 6 room for movement or activity: You're in the way 7 passage or journey

wayside noun side of a road

wayward adjective difficult to control ▷ **waywardness** noun quality of being wayward

WC abbreviation water closet: toilet

we pronoun (used as the subject of a verb) 1 the speaker or writer and one or more others 2 people in general 3 formal word for I used by editors and monarchs

weak adjective 1 lacking strength; feeble 2 likely to break 3 unconvincing 4 lacking flavour ▷ **weaken** verb to become weak or make (someone or something) weak ▷ **weakly** adverb feebly

weakling noun feeble person

weakness noun 1 lack of moral or physical strength 2 great liking (for something)

wealth noun 1 state of being rich 2 large amount of money and valuables 3 great amount or number

wealthy wealthier, wealthiest *adjective* having a large amount of money and valuables

wean *verb* 1 to accustom (a baby or young mammal) to food other than mother's milk 2 to coax (someone) to give up former habits

weapon *noun* 1 object used in fighting 2 anything used to get the better of an opponent > **weaponry** *noun* weapons collectively

wear wears, wearing, wore, worn *verb* 1 to have (clothes or jewellery) on the body 2 to show (a particular expression) on your face 3 to deteriorate by constant use or action 4 to endure constant use (well or badly) ▷ *noun* 5 clothes suitable for a particular time or purpose: *beach wear* 6 damage caused by use > **wear down** *verb* 1 to make (something) flatter and smoother as a result of repeated rubbing 2 to cause (someone) to stop resisting and to fall in with your wishes by repeatedly doing something or asking them to do something > **wearer** *noun*: *contact lens wearers* > **wearing** *adjective* very tiring > **wear off** *verb* to gradually become less intense > **wear on** *verb* (of time) to pass slowly > **wear out** *verb* to become or make (something) worn, weak, damaged and unusable through frequent use

wear and tear *noun* damage caused to something by normal use

weary *adjective* wearier, weariest; wearies, wearying, wearied 1 tired or exhausted 2 tiring ▷ *verb* 3 (followed by *of*) to become weary (of something) > **wearily** *adverb* in a weary manner > **weariness** *noun* state of being weary

weasel *noun* small animal with a long body and short legs

weather *noun* 1 day-to-day condition of the atmosphere of a place 2 **under the weather** (*informal*) slightly ill ▷ *verb* 3 to be affected by the weather 4 to come safely through (a difficult time)

weather vane *noun* device on a roof that revolves to show the direction of the wind

weave *verb* weaves, weaving, wove, woven 1 to make (fabric) by crossing threads on a loom 2 to make up (a story) 3 to move from side to side while going forwards > **weaver** *noun* person who weaves cloth

web *noun* 1 net spun by a spider 2 anything intricate or complex: *web of deceit* 3 skin between the toes of a duck, frog, etc 4 **the Web** short for **World Wide Web** > **webbed** *adjective* (of feet) having skin between the toes

weblog *noun* same as **blog**

website *noun* group of connected pages on the World Wide Web

wed *verb* weds, wedding, wedded or wed 1 to marry 2 to unite (things) closely

wedding *noun* act or ceremony of marriage

wedge *noun* 1 piece of something such as wood, metal or rubber with one thin end and one thick end that can be used to wedge something in place ▷ *verb* **2** to fix (something) in place with a wedge **3** to squeeze (something) into a narrow space

wedlock *noun* marriage

Wednesday *noun* day between Tuesday and Thursday

wee *adjective* (*Brit, Aust, NZ informal*) small or short

weed *noun* **1** wild plant growing where undesired **2** (*informal*) thin feeble person ▷ *verb* **3** to clear (a garden) of weeds ▷ **weed out** *verb* to remove or eliminate (what is unwanted)

week *noun* **1** period of seven days, especially one beginning on a Sunday **2** hours or days of work in a week

weekday *noun* any day of the week except Saturday or Sunday

weekend *noun* Saturday and Sunday

weekly weeklies *adjective, adverb* **1** happening, done, etc once a week ▷ *noun* **2** newspaper or magazine published once a week

weep weeps, weeping, wept **1** to shed tears **2** to ooze liquid

weevil *noun* small beetle that eats grain etc

weft *noun* cross threads in weaving

weigh *verb* **1** to have (a specified weight) **2** to measure the weight of **3** to consider (something) carefully **weigh anchor** to raise a ship's anchor or (of a ship) have its anchor raised ▷ **weigh down** *verb* to stop (someone) moving easily because of added weight ▷ **weigh up** *verb* to assess

weight *noun* **1** heaviness of an object **2** unit of measurement of weight **3** object of known mass

used for weighing **4** heavy object **5** importance or influence ▷ *verb* **6** to add weight to (something)

weighted *adjective* a system that is weighted in favour of a particular person or group is organized in such a way that this person or group will have an advantage

weightlifting *noun* exercise or competitive sport in which participants lift heavy weights ▷ **weightlifter** *noun*

weighty weightier, weightiest *adjective* **1** important or serious **2** very heavy

weir [rhymes with **near**] *noun* river dam

weird *adjective* **1** strange or bizarre **2** unearthly or eerie

weirdo weirdos [**weer**-doe] *noun* (*informal*) peculiar person

welcome *verb* **1** to greet (a guest) with pleasure **2** to receive (something) gladly ▷ *noun* **3** friendly greeting ▷ *adjective* **4** received gladly **5** freely permitted ▷ **welcoming** *adjective*

weld *verb* **1** to join (pieces of metal or plastic) by softening with heat ▷ *noun* **2** welded joint ▷ **welder** *noun* person who welds pieces of metal or plastic

welfare *noun* **1** wellbeing **2** help given to people in need

welfare state *noun* system in which the government takes responsibility for the wellbeing of its citizens

well better, best; wells, welling, welled *adverb* **1** satisfactorily **2** skilfully **3** completely **4** intimately **5** considerably **6** very likely ▷ *adjective* **7** in good health

▷ *interjection* **8** exclamation of surprise, anger, etc ▷ *noun* **9** hole drilled into the earth to reach water, oil or gas ▷ *verb* **10** to flow upwards or outwards

well-advised *adjective* sensible or wise

well-balanced *adjective* sensible and without serious emotional problems

wellbeing *noun* state of being well and happy

well-earned *adjective* thoroughly deserved

well-heeled *adjective* (*informal*) wealthy

wellies *plural noun* (*Brit, Aust informal*) wellingtons

well-informed *adjective* knowing a lot about a subject or subjects

wellingtons *plural noun* (*Brit, Aust*) high waterproof rubber boots

well-meaning *adjective* having good intentions

well-off *adjective* (*informal*) quite wealthy

well-to-do *adjective* quite wealthy

well-worn *adjective* **1** (of a word or phrase) boring from overuse **2** so much used as to be shabby

Welsh *adjective* **1** of Wales ▷ *noun* **2** language of Wales

Welshman *Welshmen noun* a man from Wales

welt *noun* raised mark on the skin caused by a blow

welter *noun* jumbled mass

wench *noun* (*facetious*) young woman

wept *verb* past of **weep**

were *verb* form of the past tense of *be* used after {*we, you, they,*} or a plural noun

werewolf *werewolves noun* (in folklore) person who can turn into a wolf

Wesak [**wess**-suck] *noun* Buddhist festival celebrating the Buddha, held in May

west *noun* **1** (direction towards) the part of the horizon where the sun sets **2** region lying in this direction **3 the West** western Europe and the US ▷ *adjective* **4** to or in the west **5** (of a wind) from the west ▷ *adverb* **6** in, to or towards the west ▷ **westerly** *adjective* to or towards the left

western *adjective* **1** of or in the west ▷ *noun* **2** film or story about cowboys in the western US

West Indian *noun* person from the West Indies

westward *adjective* **1** towards the west **2** lying in the west ▷ *adverb* **3** towards the west ▷ **westwards** *adverb* towards the west

wet *adjective* wetter, wettest; wets, wetting, wet or wetted **1** covered or soaked with water or another liquid **2** not yet dry **3** rainy **4** (*Brit informal*) (of a person) feeble or foolish ▷ *noun* **5** moisture or rain **6** (*Brit informal*) feeble or foolish person ▷ *verb* **7** to make (someone or something) wet ▷ **wetness** *noun*

wet suit *noun* close-fitting rubber suit worn by divers etc

whack *verb* **1** to strike (someone or something) with a hard blow ▷ *noun* **2** such a blow **3** (*informal*) share **4** (*informal*) attempt

whale *noun* **1** large fish-shaped sea mammal **2 have a whale of a time** (*informal*) to enjoy yourself very much

whaling noun hunting of whales for food and oil ▷ **whaler** noun person who hunts whales

wharf wharves or wharfs [**worf**] noun platform at a harbour for loading and unloading ships

what pronoun **1** which thing **2** that which **3** request for a statement to be repeated **4 what for?** why? ▷ interjection **5** exclamation of anger, surprise, etc ▷ adverb **6** in which way, how much: *what do you care?*

whatever pronoun **1** everything or anything that **2** no matter what

whatsoever adverb at all

wheat noun **1** grain used in making flour, bread and pasta **2** plant producing this

wheel noun **1** disc that revolves on an axle, usually fixed under a vehicle to make it move ▷ verb **2** to push or pull (something with wheels) **3** to turn round suddenly

wheelbarrow noun shallow cart for carrying loads, with a wheel at the front and two handles

wheelchair noun chair with wheels for use by people who cannot walk

wheeze verb **1** to breathe with a hoarse whistling noise ▷ noun **2** wheezing sound **3** (*informal*) trick or plan ▷ **wheezy** adjective making a hoarse whistling noise

whelk noun edible snail-like shellfish

when adverb **1** at what time? ▷ conjunction **2** at the time that **3** although **4** considering the fact that ▷ pronoun **5** at which time

whence adverb, conjunction (*obsolete*) from what place or source

WORD TIP

You should not write *from whence* because *whence* already means 'from where'

whenever adverb, conjunction at whatever time

where adverb **1** in, at or to what place? ▷ pronoun **2** in, at or to which place ▷ conjunction **3** in the place at which

whereabouts noun **1** present position ▷ adverb **2** at what place

whereas conjunction but on the other hand

whereby pronoun by which

whereupon conjunction at which point

wherever conjunction, adverb at whatever place

wherewithal noun necessary funds, resources, etc

whet whets, whetting, whetted verb **1** to sharpen (a tool) ▷ **2 whet someone's appetite** to increase someone's desire

whether conjunction used to introduce an indirect question or a clause expressing doubt or choice

whey [**way**] noun watery liquid that is separated from the curds in sour milk when cheese is made

which adjective, pronoun **1** used to request or refer to a choice from different possibilities ▷ pronoun **2** used to refer to a thing already mentioned

whichever adjective, pronoun **1** any out of several **2** no matter which

whiff noun **1** slight smell **2** trace or hint

while conjunction **1** at the same time that **2** but ▷ noun **3** period of time ▷ **while away** verb to pass (time) idly but pleasantly

whilst conjunction while

whim noun sudden desire; impulse

whimper verb 1 to cry in a soft whining way ▷ noun 2 soft unhappy cry

whimsical adjective unusual and playful

whine noun 1 high-pitched unhappy cry 2 annoying complaint ▷ verb 3 to make such a sound > **whining** verb, adjective making a whining sound

whinge whinges, whinging or whingeing, whinged (Brit, Aust, NZ informal) verb 1 to complain ▷ noun 2 complaint

whinny whinnies, whinnying, whinnied verb 1 to neigh softly ▷ noun 2 soft neigh

whip whips, whipping, whipped noun 1 cord attached to a handle, used for beating animals or people 2 dessert made from beaten cream or egg whites ▷ verb 3 to strike (an animal or a person) with a whip, strap or cane 4 (informal) to pull, remove or move (something) quickly 5 to beat (especially eggs or cream) to a froth 6 to rouse (people) into a particular condition 7 (informal) to steal (something) > **whip up** verb to cause and encourage (an emotion) in people: people who try to whip up hatred against minorities

whip bird noun Australian bird whose cry ends with a sound like the crack of a whip

whiplash injury noun neck injury caused by a sudden jerk to the head, as in a car crash

whippet noun racing dog like a small greyhound

whirl verb 1 to spin or revolve 2 to be dizzy or confused ▷ noun 3 whirling movement 4 intense activity 5 confusion or dizziness

whirlpool noun strong circular current of water

whirlwind noun 1 column of air that spins round and round very fast ▷ adjective 2 much quicker than normal

whirr noun 1 continuous soft buzz ▷ verb 2 to make a whirr

whisk verb 1 to move or remove quickly 2 to beat (especially eggs or cream) to a froth ▷ noun 3 egg-beating tool

whisker noun 1 any of the long stiff hairs on the face of a cat or other mammal 2 **by a whisker** (informal) only just 3 **whiskers** hair growing on a man's face

whisky whiskies noun strong alcoholic drink made from grain such as barley

whisper verb 1 to speak softly, using the breath but not the throat 2 to rustle ▷ noun 3 soft voice 4 (informal) rumour 5 rustling sound

whist noun card game in which one pair of players tries to win more tricks than another pair

whistle verb 1 to produce a shrill sound by forcing the breath through pursed lips 2 to signal (something) by a whistle ▷ noun 3 whistling sound 4 instrument blown to make a whistling sound: the whistling of the wind

whit noun **not a whit** not the slightest amount

white *adjective* **1** of the colour of snow **2** pale **3** light in colour **4** (of coffee) containing milk or cream ▷ *noun* **5** colour of snow **6** clear fluid round the yolk of an egg **7** white part, especially of the eyeball ▷ **whiteness** *noun*

white-collar *adjective* (of a worker) working in an office rather than doing manual work

white lie *noun* harmless lie, told to prevent someone's feelings from being hurt

whitewash *noun* **1** mixture of lime and water used for painting walls white ▷ *verb* **2** to cover (something) with whitewash **3** to conceal or gloss over (unpleasant facts)

whither *adverb* (*obsolete*) to what place

whiting *noun* edible sea fish

whittle *verb* to cut or carve (wood) with a knife ▷ **whittle down, away** *verb* to reduce (something) or wear (it) away gradually

whizz or **whiz** whizzes, whizzing, whizzed *verb* **1** to make a loud buzzing sound **2** (*informal*) to move quickly ▷ *noun* **3** loud buzzing sound **4** (*informal*) person who is skilful at something

who *pronoun* **1** which person **2** used to refer to a person or people already mentioned

whoa [woh] *interjection* command to slow down or stop a horse

whoever *pronoun* **1** any person who **2** no matter who

whole *adjective* **1** containing all the elements or parts **2** uninjured or undamaged ▷ *noun* **3** complete thing or system **4 on the whole** in general ▷ **wholeness** *noun*

▷ **wholly** [hoe-lee] *adverb* completely

wholehearted *adjective* enthusiastic and sincere
▷ **wholeheartedly** *adverb*

wholemeal *adjective* **1** (of flour) made from the whole wheat grain **2** made from wholemeal flour

wholesale *adjective, adverb* **1** buying goods cheaply in large quantities and selling them to shopkeepers **2** on a large scale ▷ **wholesaler** *noun* person who works in the wholesale trade

wholesome *adjective* good for the health or wellbeing

whom *pronoun* objective form of **who**

whoop *verb* **1** to shout or cry in excitement ▷ *noun* **2** shout or cry of excitement

whooping cough [hoop-ing] *noun* infectious disease marked by violent coughing and noisy breathing

whore [hore] *noun* (*offensive*) a prostitute, or a woman believed to act like a prostitute

whose *pronoun* of whom or of which

WORD TIP

Many people are confused about the difference between *whose* and *who's*. *Whose* is used to show possession in a question or when something is being described: *whose bag is this? the person whose car is blocking the exit. Who's*, with the apostrophe, is a short form of *who is* or *who has: who's that girl? who's got my ruler?*

why *adverb* **1** for what reason ▷ *pronoun* **2** because of which

wick *noun* cord through a lamp or candle which carries fuel to the flame

wicked *adjective* **1** morally bad; evil **2** mischievous >**wickedly** *adverb* in a wicked manner >**wickedness** *noun* state of being wicked

wicker *adjective* made of woven cane

wicket *noun* **1** set of three cricket stumps and two bails **2** ground between the two wickets on a cricket pitch

wide *adjective* **1** large from side to side; broad **2** having a specified width **3** spacious or extensive **4** far from the target **5** opened fully ▷ *adverb* **6** to the full extent **7** over a wide area **8** far from the target >**widely** *adverb* >**widen** *verb* to make (something) wider or to become wider

wide-awake *adjective* completely awake

wide-ranging *adjective* covering a variety of different things or a large area

widespread *adjective* affecting a wide area or a large number of people; common

widow *noun* woman whose husband is dead and who has not remarried

widowed *adjective* whose husband or wife has died

widower *noun* man whose wife is dead and who has not remarried

width *noun* **1** distance from side to side **2** quality of being wide

wield [weeld] *verb* **1** to hold and use (a weapon) **2** to have and use (power)

wife wives *noun* woman to whom a man is married

Wi-Fi *noun* system of accessing the internet from machines such as laptop computers that aren't physically connected to a network

wig *noun* artificial head of hair

wiggle *verb* **1** to move jerkily from side to side ▷ *noun* **2** wiggling movement

wigwam *noun* Native American's tent

wiki *noun* website (or page within one) that can be edited by anyone who looks it up on the internet

wild *adjective* **1** (of an animal) not tamed or domesticated **2** (of a plant) not cultivated **3** excited and uncontrolled **4** violent or stormy **5** (*informal*) furious **6** random ▷ *noun* **7 the wilds** desolate or uninhabited place >**wildly** *adverb* extremely or intensely

wilderness *noun* uninhabited uncultivated region

wildfire *noun* **spread like wildfire** to spread quickly and uncontrollably

wild-goose chase *noun* search that has little chance of success

wildlife *noun* wild animals and plants collectively

Wild West *noun* western part of the USA when first settled by Europeans

wiles *plural noun* crafty tricks

wilful *adjective* **1** headstrong or obstinate **2** intentional >**wilfully** *adverb* in a wilful manner

will¹ *verb* (often shortened to 'll) used as an auxiliary verb to form the future tense, to indicate intention or expectation, and to express invitations and requests: *Tom and I will go shopping later; I will not let you down; Robin will be annoyed; Will you have something to drink?; Will you do me a favour?*

will² *noun* **1** strong determination **2** desire or wish **3** instructions written for disposal of your property after death ▷ *verb* **4** to use your will in an attempt to do (something) **5** to wish or desire (something): *if God wills it* **6** to leave (property) to someone in a will: *The farm was willed to her*

willing *adjective* **1** ready or inclined (to do something) **2** keen and obliging ▷ **willingly** *adverb* voluntarily ▷ **willingness** *noun* state of being willing

willow *noun* **1** tree with long thin branches **2** its wood, used for making cricket bats

wilt *verb* to become limp or lose strength

wily wilier, wiliest [**wie**-lee] *adjective* crafty or sly

wimp *noun* (*informal*) feeble timid person

win wins, winning, won *verb* **1** to come first in (a competition, fight, etc) **2** to gain (a prize) in a competition **3** to get (something) by effort ▷ *noun* **4** victory, especially in a game ▷ **win over** *verb* to gain the support or consent of (someone)

wince *verb* **1** to draw back, as if in pain ▷ *noun* **2** act of wincing

winch *noun* **1** machine for lifting or hauling using a cable or chain wound round a drum ▷ *verb* **2** to lift or haul (something) using a winch

wind¹ [rhymes with **tinned**] *noun* **1** current of air **2** hint or suggestion **3** ability to breathe easily **4** gas produced in the stomach, causing discomfort ▷ *verb* **5** to render (someone) short of breath

wind² winds, winding, wound [rhymes with **mind**] *verb* **1** to coil or wrap (something) round something else **2** to tighten the spring of a (clock or watch) **3** to move in a twisting course ▷ **wind up** *verb* **1** to reach an end or bring (something) to an end **2** to tighten the spring of a clock or watch) **3** (*informal*) to annoy or tease (someone)

windfall *noun* sum of money received unexpectedly

wind instrument *noun* musical instrument played by blowing

windmill *noun* machine for grinding grain or pumping water, driven by sails turned by the wind

window *noun* **1** opening in a wall, usually with a glass pane or panes, to let in light or air **2** display area behind the window of a shop **3** area on a computer screen that can be manipulated separately from the rest of the display area **4** period of unbooked time in a diary or schedule

window box *noun* a long, narrow container on a windowsill in which plants are grown

windowsill *noun* ledge along the bottom of a window

windpipe *noun* tube linking the throat and the lungs

windscreen *noun* front window of a motor vehicle

a b c d e f g h i j k l m n o p q r s t u v w x y z

windsurfing noun sport of riding on water using a surfboard propelled and steered by a sail

windswept adjective (of a place) exposed to strong winds

windy windier, windiest adjective involving a lot of wind: *It was windy and cold*

wine noun **1** alcoholic drink made from fermented grapes **2** similar drink made from other fruits ▷ verb **3** wine and dine to entertain (someone) with fine food and drink

wing noun **1** one of the limbs or organs of a bird, insect or bat that are used for flying **2** one of the winglike supporting parts of an aircraft **3** side part of a building that sticks out **4** group within a political party **5** part of a car body surrounding the wheels **6** (Sport) (player on) either side of the pitch **7** wings sides of a stage ▷ verb **8** to fly **9** to wound (a bird) slightly in the wing or (a person) slightly in the arm ▷ winged adjective having wings

wink verb **1** to close and open (an eye) quickly as a signal **2** (of a light) to twinkle ▷ noun **3** winking **4** smallest amount of sleep

winkle noun shellfish with a spiral shell ▷ winkle out verb (informal) to get (information) from someone

winner noun person who wins a prize, race or competition

winning adjective **1** gaining victory **2** charming

winter noun **1** coldest season ▷ verb **2** to spend the winter

wintry adjective **1** of or like winter **2** cold or unfriendly

wipe verb **1** to clean or dry (something) by rubbing **2** to erase (a tape) ▷ noun **3** wiping ▷ wipe out verb to destroy (people or a place) completely

wire noun **1** thin flexible strand of metal **2** length of this used to carry electric current ▷ verb **3** to equip (a place) with wires

wireless noun (old-fashioned) same as **radio**

wireless application protocol noun see **WAP**

wiring noun system of wires

wiry wirier, wiriest adjective **1** lean but strong **2** (of hair) stiff and rough

wisdom noun **1** good sense and judgment **2** knowledge collected over time

wisdom tooth noun any of the four large molar teeth that come through usually after the age of twenty

wise adjective having wisdom; sensible ▷ wisely adverb

wisecrack (informal) noun clever, sometimes unkind, remark

wish verb **1** to want or desire (something) **2** to feel or express a hope about someone's wellbeing, success, etc ▷ noun **3** expression of a desire **4** thing desired

wishbone noun V-shaped bone above the breastbone of most birds

wishful thinking noun hope or wish that is unlikely to come true

wishy-washy adjective (informal) not firm or clear

wisp noun **1** light delicate streak **2** twisted bundle or tuft ▷ wispy adjective (of hair) thin and untidy

wistful *adjective* sadly longing
> **wistfully** *adverb* sadly and
longingly

wit *noun* **1** ability to use words
or ideas in a clever and amusing
way **2** person with this ability
3 (sometimes plural) practical
intelligence

witch *noun* **1** person, usually
female, who practises (black)
magic **2** ugly or wicked woman

witchcraft *noun* use of magic

witch doctor *noun* (in certain
societies) a man appearing to
cure or cause injury or disease
by magic

witchetty grub *noun* (Aust) large
Australian caterpillar, eaten by
Aborigines

with *preposition* indicating
presence alongside, possession,
means of performance,
characteristic manner, etc:
*walking with his dog; a man with
two cars; hit with a hammer; playing
with skill*

withdraw withdraws,
withdrawing, withdrew,
withdrawn *verb* to take
(something) out or away or to
move out or away

withdrawal *noun* **1** taking
something away **2** changing or
denying a statement **3** taking
money from a bank account

withdrawal symptoms *noun*
unpleasant effects suffered by an
addict who has suddenly stopped
taking a drug

withdrawn *adjective* unusually
shy or quiet

wither *verb* to wilt or dry up

withering *adjective* (of a look or
remark) scornful

withhold withholds, withholding,
withheld *verb* not to give
(something)

within *preposition, adverb* in or
inside

without *preposition* not
accompanied by, using or having

withstand withstands,
withstanding, withstood *verb*
to oppose or resist (something)
successfully

witness *noun* **1** person who has
seen something happen **2** person
giving evidence in court ▷ *verb*
3 to see (an incident) at first hand
4 to sign (a document) to confirm
that it is genuine

witticism [**wit**-tiss-izm] *noun*
witty remark

witty wittier, wittiest *adjective*
clever and amusing > **wittily**
adverb in a clever and amusing
manner

wives *noun* plural of **wife**

wizard *noun* **1** magician **2** person
with outstanding skill in a
particular field > **wizardry** *noun*
something that is very cleverly
done

wizened [**wiz**-zend] *adjective*
wrinkled

wobbegong [**wob**-bi-gong]
noun (Aust) Australian shark with
brown-and-white skin

wobble *verb* **1** to move unsteadily
2 to tremble or shake ▷ *noun*
3 wobbling movement or sound

wobbly *adjective* unsteady

woe *noun* grief

wok *noun* bowl-shaped Chinese
cooking pan, used for stir-frying

woke *verb* past tense of **wake**¹

woken *verb* past participle of
wake¹

a
b
c
d
e
f
g
h
i
j
k
l
m
n
o
p
q
r
s
t
u
v
w
x
y
z

wolf wolves; wolfs, wolfing, wolfed noun **1** wild hunting animal related to the dog **2** cry **wolf** to raise a false alarm ▷ verb **3** to eat (food) quickly and greedily

woman women noun **1** adult human female **2** women collectively

womanhood noun state of being a woman

womb [woom] noun hollow organ in female mammals where unborn babies grow

wombat [wom-bat] noun (Aust) small heavily-built burrowing Australian animal

wonder verb **1** to be curious (about something) **2** to be amazed (at something) ▷ noun **3** wonderful thing; marvel **4** emotion caused by an amazing or unusual thing ▷ adjective **5** spectacularly successful: a wonder drug

wonderful adjective **1** very fine **2** magnificent or remarkable > **wonderfully** adverb

wondrous adjective (old-fashioned) wonderful

wont [rhymes with **don't**] adjective **1** accustomed or inclined (to do something) ▷ noun **2** custom

woo verb **1** to try to persuade (someone) **2** (old-fashioned) to try to gain the love of (a woman)

wood noun **1** substance trees are made of, used in carpentry and as fuel **2** area where trees grow

wooded adjective covered with trees

wooden adjective **1** made of wood **2** stiff and without expression

woodland noun forest

woodpecker noun bird that drills holes into trees with its beak to find insects

woodwind adjective, noun (of) a type of wind instrument made of wood, played by being blown into

woodwork noun **1** parts of a house that are made of wood, e.g. doors and window frames **2** making things out of wood

woodworms woodworms noun insect larva that bores into wood

woody woodier, woodiest adjective **1** (of a plant) having a hard tough stem **2** (of an area) covered with trees

woof noun **1** barking noise made by a dog **2** cross threads in weaving

wool noun **1** soft hair of sheep, goats, etc **2** yarn spun from this

woollen adjective made from wool > **woollens** plural noun clothes made from wool

woolly woollies; woollier, woolliest adjective **1** of or like wool **2** vague or muddled ▷ noun **3** knitted woollen garment

woolshed noun (Aust, NZ) large building in which sheep are sheared

woomera noun (Aust) notched stick used by Australian Aborigines when throwing a spear

word noun **1** single unit of speech or writing **2** brief remark, chat or discussion **3** message **4** promise **5** command ▷ verb **6** to express (something) in words

wording noun choice and arrangement of words

word processor noun machine with a keyboard, microprocessor and VDU for electronic organization and storage of text

work noun **1** physical or mental effort directed to making or doing something **2** paid employment **3** duty or task **4** something made or done **5 works a** factory **b** total of a writer's or artist's achievements **c** activities relating to building and construction **d** mechanism of a machine ▷ adjective **6** of or for work ▷ verb **7** to do work **8** to be employed **9** to operate (something) **10** (of a plan etc) to be successful **11** to cultivate (land) **12** to manipulate, shape or process **13** to cause (someone) to reach a specified condition > **work out** verb **1** to find (the solution to a problem) by using your reasoning **2** to happen or progress > **work up** verb **1** to make (yourself) very upset or angry about something **2** to develop **3** work up to to progress towards (something) gradually > **worked up** adjective

workable adjective able to operate successfully; practical

workaholic noun person obsessed with work

worker noun a person employed in a particular industry or business

workforce noun people who work in a particular place

workhouse noun (in England, formerly) building where poor people were given food and lodgings in return for work

working class noun social class consisting of manual workers > **working-class** adjective: a working-class background

workload noun amount of work to be done

workman workmen noun a man whose job involves physical skills

workmanship noun skill with which an object is made

workmate noun fellow worker

workout noun session of physical exercise

workshop noun room or building with equipment for making or repairing things

world noun **1** planet earth **2** people in general **3** society of a particular area or period **4** a person's life and experiences ▷ adjective **5** of the whole world

worldly worldlier, worldliest adjective **1** not spiritual **2** wise in the ways of the world

world war noun war that involves countries all over the world

worldwide adjective throughout the world

World Wide Web noun worldwide communication system which people use through computers; the internet

worm noun **1** small thin animal with no bones or legs **2** (Computers) type of virus **3 worms** illness caused by parasites in the intestines ▷ verb **4** to rid (an animal) of worms > **worm out** verb to extract (information) from someone craftily

worn verb past participle of **wear**

worn-out adjective **1** used until too thin or too damaged to be of further use **2** extremely tired

worried adjective unhappy and anxious; troubled

worry worries, worrying, worried *verb* **1** to be anxious or uneasy or to cause (someone) to be anxious or uneasy **2** to annoy or bother (someone) **3** (of a dog) to chase and try to bite (sheep etc) ▷ *noun* **4** (cause of) anxiety or concern ▷ **worrying** *adjective: a worrying report about smoking*

worse *adjective, adverb* comparative of **bad, badly**

worsen *verb* to grow worse or make (something) worse

worse off *adjective* having less money or being in a more unpleasant situation than before

worship worships, worshipping, worshipped *verb* **1** to show religious devotion to (a god) **2** to love and admire (someone) ▷ *noun* **3** act or instance of worshipping **4 Worship** title for a mayor or magistrate ▷ **worshipper** *noun* person who worships

worst *adjective, adverb* **1** superlative of **bad, badly** *noun* **2** worst thing

worth *preposition* **1** having a value of **2** deserving or justifying ▷ *noun* **3** value or price **4** excellence **5** amount to be had for a given sum

worthless *adjective* having no real value or use

worthwhile *adjective* worth the time or effort involved

worthy worthier, worthiest; worthies *adjective* **1** deserving admiration or respect ▷ *noun* **2** (*informal*) notable person

would *verb* (often shortened to *'d*) used as an auxiliary verb to express invitations and requests,

to talk about hypothetical situations, to describe habitual past actions and to replace *will* in reported speech: *Would you like some tea?; We'd like two tickets, please; I'd write to him if I were you; I wouldn't have come if I'd known; She would always watch the late news; He said he would call back*

would-be *adjective* wanting to be or claiming to be: *a would-be pop singer*

wound[1] *noun* **1** physical injury, especially a cut **2** injury to the feelings ▷ *verb* **3** to cause a wound to (someone) ▷ **wounded** *adjective*

wound[2] *verb* past of **wind**[2]

wow *interjection* **1** exclamation of astonishment ▷ *noun* **2** (*informal*) astonishing person or thing

WPC *abbreviation* woman police constable

wrangle *verb* **1** to argue noisily ▷ *noun* **2** noisy argument

wrap wraps, wrapping, wrapped *verb* **1** to fold (something) round (a person or thing) so as to cover ▷ *noun* **2** garment wrapped round the shoulders **3** sandwich made by wrapping a filling in a tortilla ▷ **wrap up** *verb* **1** to fold paper round **2** to put warm clothes on **3** (*informal*) to finish or settle (a matter)

wrapped up *adjective* (*informal*) (followed by *in*) giving all your attention (to someone or something)

wrapper *noun* cover for a product

wrapping *noun* material used to wrap

wrath [roth] *noun* intense anger

wreak [reek] *verb* **wreak havoc** to cause chaos

wreath [reeth] *noun* twisted ring or band of flowers or leaves used as a memorial or tribute

wreck *verb* **1** to destroy ▷ *noun* **2** remains of something that has been destroyed or badly damaged, especially a vehicle **3** person in very poor condition > **wrecked** *adjective*

wreckage *noun* wrecked remains

wren *noun* small brown songbird

wrench *verb* **1** to twist or pull (something) violently **2** to sprain (a joint) ▷ *noun* **3** violent twist or pull **4** sprain **5** difficult or painful parting **6** adjustable spanner

wrest [rest] *verb* to take (something) by force

wrestle *verb* **1** to fight, especially as a sport, by struggling with and trying to throw down (an opponent) **2** to struggle hard (with a problem) > **wrestler** *noun* person who wrestles

wrestling *noun* sport of struggling with and trying to throw down an opponent

wretch *noun* wicked or unfortunate person

wretched [retch-id] *adjective* **1** unhappy or unfortunate **2** worthless > **wretchedly** *adverb* in a wretched manner > **wretchedness** *noun* state of being wretched

wriggle *verb* **1** to move (the body) with a twisting action ▷ *noun* **2** wriggling movement > **wriggle out of** *verb* to manage to avoid (doing something) > **wriggly** *adjective*

wring wrings, wringing, wrung *verb* **1** to twist, especially to squeeze liquid out of (a wet cloth) **2** to clasp and twist (the hands)

wrinkle *noun* **1** slight crease, especially one in the skin due to age ▷ *verb* **2** to become slightly creased or make (something) slightly creased > **wrinkled** *adjective* > **wrinkly** *adjective*: wrinkly stockings

wrist *noun* joint between the hand and the arm

writ *noun* legal document that orders a person to do something

write writes, writing, wrote, written *verb* **1** to mark paper etc with (letters, words or numbers) **2** to set (something) down in words **3** to communicate with someone by (letter) **4** to create (a book, piece of music, etc) > **write down** *verb* to record (something) on a piece of paper > **write up** *verb* to write a full account of (something), often from notes

writer *noun* **1** author **2** person who has written something specified

writhe [rieth] *verb* to twist or squirm in or as if in pain

writing *noun* **1** something that has been written **2** person's style of writing **3** piece of written work

written *verb* past participle of **write**

wrong *adjective* **1** incorrect or mistaken **2** immoral or bad **3** not intended or suitable **4** not working properly ▷ *adverb* **5** in a wrong manner ▷ *noun* **6** something immoral or unjust ▷ *verb* **7** to treat (someone)

a b c d e f g h i j k l m n o p q r s t u v **w** x y z

unfairly or unjustly > **wrongly**
adverb in a wrong manner
wrongful *adjective* illegal, unfair or
immoral > **wrongfully** *adverb*
wrought iron *noun* pure form
of iron formed into decorative
shapes
wry *adjective* 1 drily humorous
2 (of a facial expression) twisted
> **wryly** *adverb* in a wry manner

X or **x** *noun* 1 indicating an error, a
choice, or a kiss 2 indicating an
unknown, unspecified, or variable
factor, number, person, or thing
xenophobia [zen-oh-**fobe**-ee-a]
noun fear or hatred of people from
other countries > **xenophobic**
adjective: xenophobic attitudes
Xerox ® [**zeer**-ox] *noun* 1 machine
for copying printed material
2 copy made by a Xerox machine
▷ *verb* 3 to copy (a document)
using such a machine
Xmas [**eks**-mass] *noun* (*informal*)
Christmas
XML *abbreviation* extensible
markup language: a computer
language used in text formatting
X-ray or **x-ray** *noun* 1 stream of
radiation that can pass through
some solid materials 2 picture
made by sending X-rays through
someone's body to examine the
inside of it ▷ *verb* 3 to photograph
or examine (someone or
something) using X-rays
xylem [**zy**-lem] *noun* (*technical*)
plant tissue that conducts water
and minerals from the roots to all
other parts. It forms the wood in
trees and shrubs
xylophone [**zile**-oh-fone] *noun*
musical instrument made of a
row of wooden bars of different
lengths played with hammers

y

-y *suffix* used to form nouns: *anarchy*

yabby yabbies *noun* small edible Australian crayfish

yacht [**yott**] *noun* boat with sails or an engine, used for racing or for pleasure trips

yachting *noun* sport or activity of sailing a yacht

yachtsman yachtsmen *noun* man who sails a yacht > **yachtswoman** *noun*

yak *noun* Tibetan ox with long shaggy hair

yakka or **yacker** *noun* (*Aust, NZ informal*) work

yam *noun* tropical root vegetable

yank *verb* **1** to pull or jerk (something) suddenly ▷ *noun* **2** sudden pull or jerk

Yankee or **Yank** *noun* (*informal*) person from the United States

yap yaps, yapping, yapped *verb* to bark with a high-pitched sound

yard *noun* **1** unit of length equal to 36 inches or about 91.4 centimetres **2** enclosed area, usually next to a building and often used for a particular purpose: *builder's yard*

yardstick *noun* standard against which to judge other people or things

yarn *noun* **1** thread used for knitting or making cloth **2** (*informal*) long

involved story, often with invented details to make it more interesting or exciting

yashmak *noun* veil worn by some Muslim women over their faces when they are in public

yawn *verb* **1** to open your mouth wide and take in more air than usual, often when tired or bored ▷ *noun* **2** act of yawning

yawning *adjective* (of gap or opening) very wide

ye [**yee**] *pronoun* **1** (*archaic or dialect*) you **2** (in language intended to appear old) the

yeah *interjection* (*informal*) yes

year *noun* **1** period of twelve months or 365 days (366 days in a leap year), which is the time taken for the earth to travel once around the sun **2** period of twelve consecutive months, not always January to December, on which administration or organization is based: *the current financial year*

yearling *noun* animal between one and two years old

yearn *verb* to long (for something or to do something) very much > **yearning** *noun*

yeast *noun* fungus used to make bread rise and to ferment alcoholic drinks

yell *verb* **1** to shout or scream loudly ▷ *noun* **2** loud shout or cry of pain, anger or fear

yellow *noun, adjective* **1** the colour of buttercups, egg yolks or lemons ▷ *adjective* **2** (*informal*) cowardly ▷ *verb* **3** to become or make (something) yellow, often with age > **yellowish** *adjective*

yellow box *noun* a large Australian eucalyptus tree

yellow fever noun serious infectious tropical disease

yelp verb **1** to give a sudden, short cry ▷ noun **2** sudden, short cry

yen noun **1** monetary unit of Japan **2** (informal) longing or desire

> **WORD TIP**
> The plural of *yen* in sense 1 is *yen*

yes interjection expresses agreement, acceptance or approval or acknowledges facts

yesterday adverb **1** on the day before today **2** in the recent past ▷ noun **3** the day before today **4** the recent past

yet adverb **1** up until then or now **2** now or until later **3** still **4** used for emphasis: *She's changed her mind yet again* ▷ conjunction **5** nevertheless or still

yeti noun same as **abominable snowman**

yew noun evergreen tree with needle-like leaves and red berries

Yiddish noun language of German origin spoken by many Jewish people of European origin

yield verb **1** to give in **2** to give up control of or surrender (something) **3** to break or give way **4** to produce or bear (a crop or profit) ▷ noun **5** amount of food, money or profit produced from a given area of land or from an investment

yippee interjection exclamation of happiness or excitement

yob noun (informal) bad-mannered or aggressive youth

yodel yodels, yodelling, yodelled verb to sing normal notes with high quick notes in between

yoga noun Hindu method of exercise and discipline aiming

at spiritual, mental and physical wellbeing

yogurt or **yoghurt** noun slightly sour thick liquid food made from milk that has had bacteria added to it, often sweetened and flavoured with fruit

yoke noun **1** wooden bar put across the necks of two animals to hold them together, and to which a plough or other tool may be attached **2** (literary) oppressive force: *the yoke of the tyrant* **3** fitted part of a garment to which a fuller part is attached

yokel noun person who lives in the country and is regarded as being rather stupid and old-fashioned

yolk noun yellow part of an egg

Yom Kippur noun annual Jewish religious holiday; Day of Atonement

yonder adjective, adverb (old-fashioned or dialect) (situated) over there

yore noun **of yore** (literary) a long time ago

Yorkshire pudding noun baked batter made from flour, milk and eggs and usually eaten with roast beef

you pronoun (refers to) **1** the person or people addressed **2** people in general

young adjective **1** in an early stage of life or growth ▷ plural noun **2** young people in general **3** babies or offspring, especially referring to young animals

youngster noun young person

your adjective **1** of, belonging to or associated with you **2** of, belonging to or associated with people in general

yours *pronoun* something belonging to you

yourself yourselves *pronoun* **1** used as the object of a verb or pronoun when the person being spoken to is both doing an action and also being directly affected by it: *Have you hurt yourself?*; *Keep a copy for yourself* **2** used to emphasize you: *You yourself will understand*

youth *noun* **1** time of being young **2** boy or young man **3** young people as a group > **youthful** *adjective*: *youthful enthusiasm* > **youthfulness** *noun*

youth hostel *noun* place where young people can stay cheaply when they are on holiday

yo-yo yo-yos *noun* toy consisting of a spool attached to a string. You play by making the yo-yo rise and fall on the string

Yugoslav [**yoo**-goe-slahv] *adjective* **1** belonging or relating to the country that used to be known as Yugoslavia ▷ *noun* **2** someone who came from the country that used to be known as Yugoslavia

Yule *noun* (old-fashioned) Christmas (season)

yuppie *noun* young highly-paid professional person, especially one who has a materialistic way of life

Z

Zambian [**zam**-bee-an] *adjective* **1** belonging or relating to Zambia ▷ *noun* **2** someone from Zambia

zany zanier, zaniest [**zane**-ee] *adjective* comical in an endearing way

zap zaps, zapping, zapped *verb* **1** (informal) to kill or destroy **2** to change (TV channels) rapidly by remote control

zeal *noun* great enthusiasm or eagerness > **zealous** [**zel**-luss] *adjective* extremely eager or enthusiastic > **zealously** *adverb*

zealot [**zel**-lot] *noun* fanatic or extreme enthusiast

zebra *noun* black-and-white striped African animal of the horse family

zebra crossing *noun* pedestrian crossing marked by black and white stripes on the road

Zen or **Zen Buddhism** *noun* Japanese form of Buddhism that concentrates on learning through meditation and intuition

zenith *noun* (literary) highest point of success or power

zero zeros or zeroes, zeroing, zeroed *noun* **1** the number 0 **2** point on a scale of measurement from which the graduations commence **3** lowest point **4** nothing, nil ▷ *adjective* **5** having no measurable quantity or size ▷ **zero in on** verb to aim at (a target)

zest noun **1** enjoyment or excitement **2** interest, flavour or charm **3** peel of an orange or lemon, used for flavouring

zigzag zigzags, zigzagging, zigzagged noun **1 a** line or course that has a series of sharp turns to the right and left ▷ verb **2** to move in a zigzag

Zimbabwean [zim-**bahb**-wee-an] adjective **1** belonging or relating to Zimbabwe ▷ noun **2** someone from Zimbabwe

zinc noun bluish-white metal used in alloys and to coat other metals to stop them rusting

zip zips, zipping, zipped noun **1** fastener with two rows of teeth that are closed or opened by a small clip pulled between them ▷ verb **2** to fasten (something) with a zip

zipper noun the same as a **zip**

zodiac noun imaginary strip in the sky which contains the planets and stars which astrologers think are important influences on people. It is divided into 12 sections, each with a special name and symbol

zombie zombies noun **1** (informal) person who appears to be lifeless, apathetic or totally lacking in independent judgment **2** (in voodoo) corpse brought back to life by witchcraft

zone noun area with particular features or properties

zoo zoos noun place where live animals are kept so that people can look at them

zoology noun study of animals ▷ **zoological** adjective ▷ **zoologist** noun

zoom verb to move or rise very rapidly ▷ **zoom in** verb (often followed by on) to give a close up picture (of)

zucchini zucchini or zucchinis [zoo-**keen**-ee] noun (US, Aust) courgette

Zulu Zulus noun **1** member of a group of Black people of southern Africa **2** language of this people

Guide to Punctuation, Spelling and Grammar

Contents

Guide to Punctuation

Punctuation marks are essential parts of written language. They help the reader understand what the writer wants to convey, and how something should be read.

APOSTROPHE (') 1: used to show possession 's is added to the end of singular words:

a child's cry • Hannah's book

's is added to the end of plural words not ending in s:

children's games • women's clothes

' An apostrophe alone is added to plural words ending in s:

workers' rights • ladies' fashion

's is added to the end of names and singular words ending in s:

James's car • the octopus's tentacles

But if the word is a classical Greek name, an apostrophe alone is preferred:

Socrates' Athens

> **Tip:** To test whether an apostrophe is in the right place, think about who the owner is, since the apostrophe always follows the noun or name referring to the owner:
>
> the **boy's** books [= the books belonging to the **boy**]
> the **boys'** books [= the books belonging to the **boys**]

> **Note:** An apostrophe is not used to form possessive pronouns, possessive adjectives, or plurals:
>
> Is it yours? • Its cover is torn. • 2 kilos of potatoes

APOSTROPHE (') 2: used in shortened forms of words where letters have been missed out:

It's [= It is] a lovely day • He'll [= He will] be pleased

BRACKETS ( ): used to enclose a word or words which can be left out and still leave a meaningful sentence:

The area planted with conifers (see map below) is approximately 4000 hectares.

COLON (:): used to introduce a list, a quotation, or an explanation:

I used three colours: green, blue, and pink • He received a telegram which read: "Return home immediately" • They didn't like the room: it was small and dingy

COMMA (,): marks a short pause between different elements in a sentence:

➤ **separating subsidiary parts of the sentence from the main part:**

If we get another goal before full-time, we'll have won the league. • He'll be there, come what may • When you're ready, give me a call

➤ **before and after words like *however*, *therefore*, and *moreover*:**

The forecasters got it wrong. There was no warning, therefore, of the heavy rain and flooding that hit the south.

➤ **separating off extra, non-essential information starting with *who*, *which*, or *that* from the main part of the sentence:**

A new model, which will be made in Spain, is to be introduced in the spring.

> **Tip:** Don't include a comma if the part starting with *who*, *which*, or *that* is essential in order to understand who or what is being talked about:
>
> *The boy who's just come in is my brother.*

➤ **separating the name of the person or people being addressed from the rest of the sentence:**

And now, ladies and gentlemen, please raise your glasses in a toast.

➤ **separating items in a list or series:**

bread, butter, and jam • Winners of a Highly-Commended

Prize: Alice Howard, Ayesha Singh, Thomas McAdam.

➤ **separating words in quotation marks from the rest of the sentence, when there is no question mark or exclamation mark at the end of the quotation:**

"I don't understand this question," said Peter.

> **Tip:** Note that the comma comes before the closing quotation mark in such cases.

➤ **after reporting verbs such as** *say*, *ask*, **and** *exclaim*, **when they are followed by a quotation:**

Tom said, "Dream on!"

DASH (–): marks an abrupt change in the flow of a sentence, either showing a sudden change of subject, or marking off extra information:

Now children – Kenneth, stop that immediately! – open your books at page 20 • Boots and shoes – all shapes, sizes, and colours – tumbled out of the cupboard

EXCLAMATION MARK (!): used after exclamations and emphatic expressions:

I can't believe it! • Oh, no! Look at this mess!

> **Tip:** The exclamation mark can lose its effect if overused. Use a full stop instead after a sentence expressing only mild excitement or humour:
> *It was such a beautiful day.*

FULL STOP (.): used to mark the end of any sentence that is not a question or an exclamation:

Harry loves football.

➤ Full stops are also sometimes used after initials or abbreviations, especially if the last letter of the abbreviation isn't the last letter of the word it's standing in for:

C. Bell • etc. • Rev. Adams • misc.

➤ A full stop is used after an indirect question or instructions phrased as polite requests:

He asked if the London train had arrived. • May I see the menu.

HYPHEN (-): separates different parts of words. It is used when there would otherwise be an awkward combination of letters, or confusion with another word:

re-elect • re-covering furniture • a no-nonsense approach

INVERTED COMMAS or QUOTATION MARKS (" " or ' '): mark the beginning and end of *direct speech* (a speaker's words written down exactly as they were said):

"I didn't understand," said Peter. • Mr Evans declared abruptly, "We're leaving."

➤ Inverted commas are not used for *indirect* or *reported* speech (an account of what someone has said rather than their exact words):

Peter said that he didn't understand the question • Mr Evans declared abruptly that they were leaving

➤ Inverted commas are used to indicate the title of a

book, poem, piece of music, film, or work of art:

Have you read "The Lord of the Rings"? • music from "Swan Lake"

➤ Inverted commas are also used to show that a word is being used in an unusual way, or that the word itself is being discussed:

Braille allows a blind person to "see" with the fingers • What is the French for "egg"?

QUESTION MARK (?): marks the end of a question:

When will we get there? • Do you like hockey?

➤ A full stop, rather than a question mark, is used after an indirect question or a polite request:

George asked when we would get there. • Will you please return the completed forms to me.

SEMICOLON (;): marks a stronger break than a comma, but a weaker one than a full stop. It is used to mark a break between two main clauses when there is a balance or contrast between the clauses, and to separate clauses or items in a long list:

I'm not that interested in jazz; I prefer classical music.
• The holiday was a disaster: the flight was four hours late; the hotel was overbooked; and it rained for the whole fortnight

SLASH (/): separates letters, words, or numbers. It is used to indicate alternatives and ratios and ranges:

he/she/it • you and/or your partner • 200 km/hr
• the 2009/10 accounting year

Spelling rules

English has a small number of rules that underpin
how words and certain types of word ought to be spelt.
If you can learn these rules, you will be on your way to
becoming a better and more confident speller. Don't
be put off if the rule sounds complicated – look at the
examples and you will begin to see spelling patterns
emerging.

Although these rules do not cover every word in the
language, they can often help you make a good attempt
at guessing how an unfamiliar word ought to be spelt.

Q is always followed by U

One of the simplest and most consistent rules is that
the letter **Q** is always followed by **U**.

*qu*ick   *qu*ack   *qu*iet

> The only exceptions are a few unusual words
> that have been borrowed from other languages,
> especially Arabic: bur*q*a, Ira*q*i.

J and V are followed by a vowel

These letters are rarely followed by a consonant and
do not usually come at the ends of words.

If you come across a sound you think might be a **J** at the end of a word or syllable, it is likely to be spelt using the letters **GE** or **DGE**.

*pa**ge*** *ed**ge*** *fora**ge***

If a word ends with the sound represented by **V**, there is likely to be a silent **E** after the **V**.

*recei**ve*** *gi**ve*** *lo**ve***

Double consonants don't occur at the start of a word

If a word begins with a consonant, you can be confident that it is a single letter.

> The only exceptions are a few unusual words that have been borrowed from other languages, such as *llama*.

H, J, K, Q, V, W, and X are not doubled

The consonants **B, C, D, F, G, L, M, N, P, R, S, T,** and **Z** are commonly doubled in the middle and at the end of words, but **H, J, K, Q, V, W, X** and **Y** are not, so you can be confident about them being single.

rejoice *awake* *level*

10

There are occasional exceptions in compound words (such as *withhold* and *bookkeeping*), words borrowed from other languages (such as *tikka*), and informal words (such as *savvy* and *bovver*).

A, I, and U don't come at the end of words

In general, English avoids ending words with **A**, **I**, and **U** and adds an extra letter to stop this happening.

say   *tie*   *due*

However, there are quite a lot of exceptions to this rule, most of which are words that have been borrowed from other languages.

banana   *ravioli*   *coypu*

The three-letter rule

'Content words' (words that name and describe things and actions) have at least three letters.

Words that do not name or describe things but exist to provide grammatical structure (prepositions, conjunctions and determiners) do not need to have as many letters as this.

This rule accounts for the fact that some content words have extra or doubled letters.

buy   *bee*   *inn*

Note that these extra letters are not found in non-content words with similar sounds.

by   *be*   *in*

> Two important exceptions to this rule are the verbs *do* and *go*.

I before E, except after C

When the letters **I** and **E** are combined to make the '**EE**' sound, the **I** comes before the **E**.

brief   *chief*   *field*
niece   *siege*   *thief*

When they follow the letter **C** in a word, the **E** comes before the **I**.

ceiling   *deceit*   *receive*

There are a few exceptions to this rule.

caffeine   *protein*   *seize weird*

The rule does not hold true when the letters **I** and **E** combine to make a different sound from '**EE**'.

foreign   *surfeit*   *their*

Adding a silent E makes a short vowel become long

As noted on page 5, the vowels **A, E, I, O**, and **U** each have a 'short' sound when they appear on their own in short words.

cat	*rat*	*hat*
men	*pen*	*ten*
bit	*hit*	*sit*
dot	*lot*	*got*
but	*nut*	*hut*

Each of the vowels also has a characteristic 'long' sound, which is created by adding an **E** to the consonant after the vowel. The **E** is not sounded in these words.

date	*rate*	*hate*
scene	*swede*	*theme*
bite	*mite*	*like*
note	*lone*	*mole*
flute	*rule*	*brute*

If there is more than one consonant after a short vowel, adding a silent **E** does not make the vowel become long.

lapse	*cassette*	*gaffe*

C and G are soft before I and E but hard before A, O, and U

The letters **C** and **G** both have two sounds: one 'soft' and one 'hard'.

These letters always have a hard sound when they come before **A**, **O**, and **U**.

card	**c**ot	re**c**ur
gang	**g**one	**g**um

> Note that the word *margarine* is an exception to this rule.

In general these letters have a 'soft' sound before **I** and **E** (and also **Y**).

cent	**c**ircle	**c**ycle
gentle	**g**iraffe	**g**yrate

The rule is very strong for **C**, but there are a lot of exceptions for **G**.

gibbon	**g**irl	**g**et

> Note that some words add a silent **U** after the **G** to keep the sound hard.

guess	**gu**ide	**gu**illotine
guilty	**gu**itar	fati**gu**e

Adding endings to words ending in E

Many English words end with a silent **E**. When you add a suffix that begins with a vowel onto one of these words, you drop the **E**.

> *abbreviate* + ion = abbreviation
> *appreciate* + ive = appreciative
> *desire* + able = desirable
> *fortune* + ate = fortunate
> *guide* + ance = guidance
> *hope* + ing = hoping
> *response* + ible = responsible
> *ventilate* + ed = ventilated

Words that end in **CE** and **GE** are an exception to this rule. They keep the final **E** before adding a suffix that begins with **A**, **O** or **U** in order to preserve the 'soft' sound.

> *change* + able = changeable
> *notice* + able = noticeable
> *advantage* + ous = advantageous

However you do drop the **E** in these words before adding a suffix that begins with **E**, **I** or **Y**.

> *stage* + ed = staged
> *notice* + ing = noticing
> *chance* + y = chancy

Adding the ending LY to words ending in LE

When you make an adverb by adding the suffix **LY** to an adjective that ends with **LE**, you drop the **LE** from the adjective.

> gent**le** + ly = gently
> id**le** + ly = idly
> subt**le** + ly = subtly

Adding endings to words ending in Y

When you add a suffix to a word that ends with a consonant followed by **Y**, you change the **Y** to **I**.

> appl**y** + ance = appliance
> beaut**y** + ful = beautiful
> craz**y** + ly = crazily
> happ**y** + ness = happiness
> smell**y** + er = smellier
> wooll**y** + est = woolliest

However, in certain short adjectives that end with a consonant followed by **Y**, you keep the **Y** when you add the ending **LY** to make an adverb.

> sh**y** + ly = shyly
> spr**y** + ly = spryly
> wr**y** + ly = wryly

Adding endings to words ending in C

You add a **K** to words that end in **C** before adding a suffix that begins with **I**, **E**, or **Y** in order to preserve the 'hard' sound.

> *mimic + ing = mimicking*
> *frolic + ed = frolicked*
> *panic + y = panicky*

The word *arc* is an exception to this rule.

> *arc + ing = arcing*
> *arc + ed = arced*

When you make an adverb by adding the suffix **LY** to an adjective that ends with **IC**, you add **AL** after the **IC**.

> *basic + ly = basically*
> *genetic + ly = genetically*
> *chronic + ly = chronically*

The word *public* is an exception to this rule.

> *public + ly = publicly*

Adding endings to words ending in a single consonant

In **words of one syllable** ending in a short vowel plus a consonant, you double the final consonant when you add a suffix that begins with a vowel.

> *run* + *ing* = *running*
> *pot* + *ed* = *potted*
> *thin* + *est* = *thinnest*
> *swim* + *er* = *swimmer*

This does not apply to words ending in the consonants **H, J, K, Q, V, W, X** and **Y**, which are never doubled (see page 10).

> *slow* + *est* = *slowest*
> *box* + *er* = *boxer*

In **words of more than one syllable** ending in a single vowel plus a consonant, if the word is pronounced with the stress at the end, you double the final consonant when you add a suffix that begins with a vowel.

> *admit* + *ance* = *admittance*
> *begin* + *ing* = *beginning*
> *commit* + *ed* = *committed*
> *occur* + *ence* = *occurrence*

If the word does not have the stress at the end, the rule is that you don't double the final consonant when you add a suffix that begins with a vowel.

> target + ed = targeted
> darken + ing = darkening

However, when you add a suffix that begins with a vowel to a word that ends in a single vowel plus **L** or **P**, you always double the **L** or **P** regardless of the stress.

> appal + ing = appalling
> cancel + ation = cancellation
> dial + er = dialler
> fulfil + ed = fulfilled
> handicap + ed = handicapped
> kidnap + er = kidnapper
> slip + age = slippage
> wrap + ing = wrapping

The word *parallel* is an exception to this rule.

> parallel + ed = paralleled

Words that are Often Spelled Incorrectly

To make them easier to remember, the following words have been grouped alongside words that share certain letter clusters:

-sion and -tion		
aggression	concentration	pronunciation
conclusion	participation	proportion
extension	creation	proposition
obsession	evaluation	reaction
occasion	explanation	recommendation
possession	preparation	

-ance and -ence		
performance	consequence	sequence
extravagance	evidence	existence
relevance	reference	occurrence
audience		

-ate and -ite		
definite	accommodate	desperate
chocolate	commemorate	resuscitate
unfortunately	commiserate	separate

-our and -ous		
glamour	continuous	nervous
humour	jealous	glamorous
resources	miscellaneous	humorous

cc, dd, ee

accelerator	occur	committee
broccoli	success	foresee
moccasin	address	

ff, gg, ll

graffiti	actually	galloping
paraffin	parallel	millionaire
aggravating	appalling	usually

-mm, nn, pp

commit	mayonnaise	opportunity
commitment	questionnaire	disappear
recommend	unnecessary	disappointment
beginning	appal	happened
cinnamon	apparent	supplement

rr, ss, tt

curriculum	marriage	harassment
diarrhoea	tomorrow	necessary
embarrass	assessment	obsess
embarrassed	business	pattern
haemorrhage	issue	boycott
interrupt	process	omelette

Commonly Confused Words

We all have blindspots when it comes to certain words, especially words that have similar pronunciations. Use this quick guide if you're unsure of what spelling to use.

accept *verb*: Please accept this gift
except *preposition*: every day except Friday

advice *noun*: He always gives good advice
advise *verb*: I wouldn't advise doing that

affect *verb*: Tiredness affects concentration
effect *noun*: the beneficial effects of eating fruit

a lot *noun*: A lot of people were at the concert
allot *verb*: Space was allotted for visitors' cars

bought *verb*: He bought a newspaper at the kiosk
brought *verb*: She brought the book with her yesterday

braking *verb*: The train has an automatic braking system
breaking *verb*: breaking the world record

choose *verb*: Please choose your favourite
chose *verb*: She chose a silver MP3 player

compliment *noun, verb*: My compliments to the chef
• He complimented her on her taste
complement *noun, verb*: our full complement of staff
• wine to complement your meal

conscience *noun*: He seems to have a guilty conscience
conscious *adjective*: She's conscious of the fact

dependent *adjective*: We're dependent on food aid

dependant *noun*: Have you any children or other dependants?

desert *noun, verb*: the Gobi desert • He had deserted his post
dessert *noun*: What's for dessert?

draft *noun, verb*: my first draft • He's drafting his reply
draught *noun*: a cold draught

its *adjective*: Her cat had hurt its paw
it's *short form*: It's a lovely day • It's been fun

licence *noun*: a driving licence
license *verb*: licensed to drive heavy goods vehicles

miner *noun*: a coal miner
minor *adjective, noun*: a minor problem • a 14-year-old minor

practice *noun*: a common practice
practise *verb*: You should practise more

precede *verb*: as summer preceded autumn
proceed *verb*: Let's proceed with the meeting

principal *noun, adjective*: the school principal • the principal reason
principle *noun*: It's against my principles

quiet *adjective*: Please be quiet!
quite *adverb*: He said their new album was quite good

threw *verb*: He threw the ball as hard as he could
through *preposition, adjective*: They managed to crawl through the tunnel • I'm through with this

to *preposition*: She gave a bunch of flowers to her mum
too *adverb*: The food was too spicy for him
two *adjective, noun*: I'd like two coffees, please • Two is a prime number

Guide to Parts of Speech

ADJECTIVE: a *describing word* that tells you more about a noun or pronoun:

a **good** man • They're **French** • two **fluffy white** clouds • a **southern** accent • I'm **better** now • the **worst** holiday we've had

➤ comparative adjectives are adjectives ending in *-er* (or preceded by *more* or *less*) that show that the thing described has more or less of a particular quality than the thing with which it is being compared:

He's **taller** than me • the **more ambitious** twin • the **less studious** brother

➤ superlative adjectives are adjectives ending in *-est* (or preceded by *most* or *least*) that show that the thing described has more or less of a particular quality than *all* of the other things with which it is being compared:

the **fastest** runner • the **most successful** businesswoman • the **least effective** method

. . . .

ADVERB: a word that is usually used with verbs, adjectives or other adverbs and gives more information about *how*, *where*, *when*, or *in what circumstances* something happens or *to what degree* something is true. Many adverbs are formed by adding **-ly** to a related adjective:

Mark laughed **loudly** • She fell **awkwardly** • The children behaved **badly** • a **horribly** violent film • Work **hard**

• He ran **faster** than me • Try getting here **earlier**
• He played **well** • The river runs **south** • Children travel
free • Do it **now** • It should arrive **soon** • She's very
pretty • I **almost** slipped

....

ARTICLE: *a, an* (indefinite articles) or *the* (definite article)

➤ Use a rather than an before nouns that begin with, or sound as if they begin with, a consonant:

a man • **a** country • **a** union • **a** European

➤ Remember to use an before a noun that begins with, or sounds as if it begins with, a vowel:

an elephant • **an** honour

....

CONJUNCTION: a *joining* word or expression that joins two words or two parts of a sentence together:

salt **and** pepper • tea **or** coffee • strange **but** true
• It's faded **because** it's been washed so often

➤ Sometimes conjunctions are made up of more than one word or are used in pairs:

She covered her face **so that** I wouldn't see her tears
• He smiled **even though** he felt like hitting her
• She speaks **both** French **and** Spanish • Use **either**
butter **or** margarine • That's **neither** here **nor** there

....

INTERJECTION or **EXCLAMATION:** a word or short phrase that expresses a feeling or emotion:

Ouch! • Good gracious! • Whew! • Mmm! • Hooray! • Tut, tut! • See you! • Hi! • Congratulations! • Thanks!

➤ Interjections often stand alone, but if an interjection is used within a sentence, it is usually separated by commas or dashes:

I turned the key and, **hey presto**, the engine started.

....

NOUN: a *naming word* that refers to a person, thing or idea

➤ common nouns, which start with small letters, are the words used to talk about any of the members of a particular category:

mountain • horse • book • tree • man • girl

➤ proper nouns, which start with capital letters, give the name of a particular person, place or object:

Harry Potter • New Zealand • Great Expectations

➤ concrete nouns are common nouns that name things you can touch:

a chair • water • her hand

➤ abstract nouns are common nouns that name things you cannot touch:

hatred • beauty • ambition • popularity

➤ collective nouns are words used to indicate groups or collections of things:

flock • team • family

....

PREPOSITION: a word that is used before a noun, pronoun or a word ending in *-ing* to relate it to other words. Prepositions may tell you the place of something in relation to another thing, or indicate movement or time:

a bird **in** a tree • The marble rolled **under** the bed • Put the cart **before** the horse • He burst **through** the doors • They're only here **for** the day • We'll arrive **on** Monday • It's used **for** cleaning brass

....

PRONOUN: a word used in place of a noun or instead of naming a person or thing:

The cat likes fish. **It** likes cream too • **She** rings every week

➤ **personal pronouns** (*I, me, we, us, you, he, him, she, her, they, them, it*) replace the subject or object of a sentence:

He phoned **me**

> **Tip:** If you're not sure whether to use *and me* or *and I* in a sentence, try using me or I on their own in the same position. If it sounds correct, you've made the right choice:
>
> *(My brother and)* **I** *love football* not *(My brother and) me love football* • *Pat is always arguing with (Mum and)* **me** not *Pat is always arguing with (Mum and) I*

27

Note: you may have to change *are* to *am* when doing this test:

My cousin and I are going shopping
- *I am going shopping*

➤ reflexive pronouns (*myself, yourself, himself, herself, ourselves, yourselves, themselves*) replace the object of a sentence when the object is the same person or thing as the subject:

Kathy burnt **herself**

➤ possessive pronouns are the words *mine, ours, yours, his, hers* and *theirs*.

➤ indefinite pronouns replace a subject or object and are used to refer to a broad or vague range of people or things:

Somebody must know the answer • Can you see **anything**?

➤ demonstrative pronouns (*this, that, these, those*) replace the subject or object of a sentence:

That is a novel • **Those** are dictionaries • Have you seen **this**?

➤ interrogative pronouns are the words *what, which, who, whose,* and *whom* used to ask questions:

What is this? • **Who** did it?

➤ relative pronouns (*which, who, whom, that*) are used to link two different parts of a sentence and always refer back to a word in the earlier part of the sentence:

We ate at the local café, **which** serves very good snacks • They have friends **who** live in the country • He is a man in **whom** you can put your trust • a girl **that** I know

....

VERB: a *doing word* that expresses an action or state of being:

He **hates** beans • We **saw** Jack at the concert

➤ present simple tense usually consists of the base form of a verb, with the addition of -*s* when it is used with *he*, *she*, *it*, or a noun. You use the present simple to talk about habits and things that happen regularly, senses and feelings, opinions and beliefs, or facts and permanent states:

I **hate** tea • She never **drives** to work • I **smell** coffee • I **think** he's a very good teacher • Birds **fly** south in the winter • We **live** in India

➤ present continuous tense is made of a present form of *be* plus the present participle (the -*ing* form) of a main verb. You use the present continuous to talk about things that are happening now, a temporary activity or situation, or things that happen often and are annoying:

What **are** you **doing**? – I **am finishing** my essay • I **am studying** accountancy at college • Kirn **is working** as a waitress at the moment • She **is** always **complaining** about work

➤ past simple tense is usually made of the base form of a verb plus -*ed* (or -*d* when the base form ends in -*e*).

You use the past simple to talk about a single action in the past or habitual actions in the past (often with adverbs of time and frequency):

He **locked** the door and **left** the house • When I lived in Cambridge, I **cycled** to work every day

➤ past continuous tense is made of a past form of *be* plus the present participle (the *-ing* form) of a main verb. You use the present continuous to talk about actions that happened before a particular point in time and ended after it, or an interrupted action:

What **were** you **doing** at eight o'clock last night? – I **was standing** at the bus stop • We **were leaving** the house when the phone rang

➤ present perfect tense is made of a present form of *have* plus the past participle (the *-ed* or *-d* form) of a main verb. You use the present perfect to talk about events that happened in the past but are relevant to the present, or periods of time:

Her daughter **has had** an accident • I **have** just **handed** in my essay • I **have** never **met** him • **Have** you ever **been** to Europe? • How long **have** you **lived** in Delhi? – I **have lived** in Delhi for fifteen years. • James **has worked** here since 2008.

➤ past perfect tense is made of *had* plus the past participle of a main verb. You use the past perfect to talk about an action that happened in the past before something else happened:

She **had** just **made** dinner when I arrived • Ashraf **had** already **known** my brother for two years when I met him

➤ the future tense does not exist in English. To talk about the future, you can use the present simple for definite plans, or the present continuous with a time expression:

The train **leaves** at 10.40 a.m. and **arrives** at 3.30 p.m • The English class **starts** at nine o'clock • I **am flying** to New York next week • **Are** you **going** to the concert on Friday? • Ravi **is coming** home tomorrow

Other ways of talking about the future are:

➤ will (or -'ll) plus the base form of a main verb to talk about future facts, to make promises, with negatives (sometimes shortened to won't), to express refusal, or with verbs like *think* and *believe*, to express opinions about future events:

I'll be on the plane this time tomorrow • We **will call** you next week • I **won't go** there again. The service was dreadful • Do you think he **will pass** the exam?

➤ be going to: a present form of *be* plus *going to* plus the base form of a main verb. You use *be going to* to talk about definite plans for the future or to make a prediction about something that will happen soon, based on something that is happening now:

I **am going to visit** Amir tonight • Sally never does any work; she **is going to fail** her exams

➤ be about to: a present form of *be* plus *about to* plus the base form of a main verb. You use *be about to* to talk about events in the very near future:

Turn off the gas – the soup **is about to** boil over
• Come on! We**'re about to** leave!

➤ auxiliary verbs are verbs used in combination with other verbs to form tenses or express requests, suggestions, intentions, politeness, likelihood, or obligation:

He **is** living abroad • They **were** laughing • She **has** decided to stay • We **had** already left • I **didn't** want to disturb you • **Do** you know where I can find him? • **Shall** I open a window? • I **won't** hurt you • **Can** you dance? • **Could** you pass me the salt? • I **might** go shopping later • It **may** be possible to go another day • He **would** like an ice cream • She **must** finish her essay by Monday